Recent Essays on Truth
and the Liar Paradox

Recent Essays on Truth and the Liar Paradox

EDITED BY

ROBERT L. MARTIN

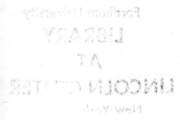

CLARENDON PRESS · OXFORD
OXFORD UNIVERSITY PRESS · NEW YORK
1984

Oxford University Press, Walton Street, Oxford OX2 6DP

London Glasgow New York Toronto
Delhi Bombay Calcutta Madras Karachi
Kuala Lumpur Singapore Hong Kong Tokyo
Nairobi Dar es Salaam Cape Town
Melbourne Auckland

and associated companies in
Beirut Berlin Ibadan Mexico City Nicosia

Oxford is a trade mark of Oxford University Press

Published in the United States
by Oxford University Press, New York

British Library Cataloguing in Publication Data
Recent essays on truth and the liar paradox
1. Liar paradox
I. Martin, Robert L.
165   BC199.P2
ISBN 0-19-824713-3
ISBN 0-19-824712-5 Pbk

Library of Congress Cataloging in Publication Data
Main entry under title:

Recent essays on truth and the liar paradox.
Includes index.
1. Truth—Addresses, essays, lectures. 2. Truthfulness and falsehood—
Addresses, essays, lectures.
3. Liar paradox—Addresses, essays, lectures. I. Martin, Robert L., 1940-   .

BC171.R38 1984   165   83-23241
ISBN O-19-824713-3
ISBN 0-19-824712-5 (pbk.)

Typeset by Eta Services (Typesetters) Ltd, Beccles, Suffolk
Printed in Great Britain at the University Press, Oxford

Contents

List of Contributors

TYLER BURGE, University of California, Los Angeles

ALONZO CHURCH, University of California, Los Angeles

SOLOMON FEFERMAN, Stanford University

ANIL GUPTA, University of Illinois, Chicago

HANS G. HERZBERGER, University of Toronto

SAUL KRIPKE, Princeton University

ROBERT L. MARTIN, California Institute of the Arts

CHARLES PARSONS, Columbia University

BRIAN SKYRMS, University of California, Irvine

PETER W. WOODRUFF, University of California, Irvine

Introduction

Robert L. Martin

The Liar paradox has intrigued and frustrated philosophers since the fourth century BC.[1] The problem is this: there are good reasons to accept as true the following two claims, *and* their incompatibility! The first claim is:

(S)   There is a sentence that says of itself only that it is not true.

This could also be put in other ways—for example: 'One can say, of what one is saying, only that it is not true', or 'There is a proposition to the sole effect that it is not true', or 'There is a sentence and a context such that the sentence evaluated at the context expresses a proposition to the sole effect that the proposition so expressed is not true'.

It is hard to reject (S) in the face of a sentence such as 'This very sentence is not true', or 'What I'm saying now is not true'. There is no claim that such a sentence has a truth-value, or is non-deviant in any particular way—just that it has the reading it seems to have, or seems to be able to have. Even those who claim that such sentences are nonsense understand them well enough to see the need to make some such claim.

The second claim is:

(T)   Any sentence is true if, and only if, what it says is the case.

This too can be formulated in various ways to match up with the various possible formulations of (S)—for example, 'One speaks truly if and only if what one says is the case'. (T) is also hard to reject—it seems simply to articulate one aspect of the concept of truth.

[1] The early history of the Liar is charmingly recounted in Alan Ross Anderson's 'St. Paul's Epistle to Titus', in R. L. Martin, ed., *The Paradox of the Liar*, second edition, with bibliographical supplement (Ridgeview Pub. Co, 1978). See also Benson Mates, *Skeptical Essays* (Chicago and London, 1981), pp. 15–17.

The incompatibility of (S) and (T) is argued as follows:

Suppose (S) is true, and let *s* be any such sentence. Then *s* cannot be true, for, since *s* says that it is not true, if it were true it would not be true (by (T)). But since *s* is not true, and since that, and only that,[2] is what *s* says, then (by (T)) *s* is true.

Before looking at possible diagnoses, let us note that the formulation of the complaint in terms of non-truth rather than falsity poses what has become known as the Strengthened Liar. This version, according to Bas van Fraassen, 'was designed especially for those enlightened philosophers who are not taken in by bivalence'.[3] (The principle of bivalence states that every sentence is true or false.) If our sentence said that it was *false*, then the second part of the incompatibility argument would fail. We could show the sentence not true, but that is not what the revised sentence says of itself. If we assumed bivalence, then from the non-truth of the Liar sentence we would infer its falsity, and then, by (T), its truth.

Since this way of distinguishing between the ordinary Liar and the Strengthened Liar has become fairly standard, it is interesting to note that the ordinary Liar is actually just as independent of the principle of bivalence as its big brother.[4] In particular we can show, without any use of the principle of bivalence, that the supposedly weaker version of (S):

(S$_0$)   There is a sentence that says of itself only that it is false,

is also incompatible with (T). The argument is of course different from the one we have given, and it does rely on some other semantic principles, besides (T); but no appeal is made to the principle of bivalence. Here is the argument:

Let s$_0$ be the ordinary Liar. First, we show that s$_0$ is not false, as follows: suppose s$_0$ is false; then, since that is what it says, it is true, and hence not false. (Principle: no sentence is both true and

---

[2] Here we make use of the stipulation that *s* says only that it is not true. If *s* said that and more besides, then the fact that *s* is shown to be not true would not suffice to make what it says the case. At least one writer in modern times has seized upon this as an escape route. See James Cargile, *Paradoxes: A Study in Form and Predication* (Cambridge, 1979).

[3] 'Presupposition, Implication, and Self-reference', *Journal of Philosophy* 65 (1968), p. 147.

[4] This was pointed out to me by Nathan Salmon. See also Burge's essay, note 8.

false.) Therefore, s_o is not false. But now we can see that s_o *is* false, since s_o says something, the negation of which (s_o is not false) is true. (Principle: a sentence is false if its negation is true.) Thus a contradiction.

For the rest of our discussion we shall return to the first formulation of the problem: the apparent incompatibility of the apparently correct claims, (S) and (T).

Here are a number of possible diagnoses.

Diagnosis 1
Both (S) and (T) seem correct because they are genuine consequences of our intuitive semantic concepts—truth, reference, etc. The incompatibility argument is certainly correct, and shows that these concepts are jointly inconsistent.[5] *Treatment* should consist in the 'rational reconstruction' of some of these concepts, so that variants (S') and (T') are obtained which are demonstrably consistent.

Diagnosis 2
The argument for the incompatibility of (S) and (T) is mistaken. If 'true' or other relevant semantic terms are understood as systematically ambiguous, then the incompatibility argument fails. Having shown that *s* is not true, we cannot go on to apply (T) to show that *s* is true after all; this is because the meaning of 'true' according to which we showed *s* not true is not the same as the meaning of 'true' as it occurs in (T). A different compatibilist approach would hold that the truth predicate is indexical, changing extension at various levels without changing meaning.

Diagnosis 3
Claim (T) is incorrect, because it ignores the fact that 'true' is a partial predicate. Applications of 'true' to sentences that lack truth-value are themselves without truth-value—further truth-value gaps are produced. This means that (T) is a universally quantified sentence some of whose instances lack truth-value. All instances of (T) which do have truth-value have the value *true* (which accounts for the intuitive strength of (T)), but since not all instances of (T) are true, (T) itself lacks truth-value.

---

[5] See Charles Chihara's, 'The Semantic Paradoxes: A Diagnostic Investigation', *The Philosophical Review* 88 (1979), pp. 590–618.

This 'truth-gap' diagnosis itself generates what we may call the *revenge problem*. On this diagnosis our Liar sentence *s* is clearly without truth-value, since if it had truth-value, (T) would apply to it. But then it seems clearly to follow that *s* is not true, which is precisely what *s* says. Even though we have restricted (T), it is counterintuitive to hold that what *s* says is the case without going on to assert that *s* is therefore true after all. Every 'gap' solution needs to deal in some way or other with the revenge problem.

Diagnosis 4
Claim (S) is incorrect—it overlooks the fact that natural languages simply do not have the concept of truth. The only languages that do have concepts of truth are those which are limited in such a way as to allow attributions of truth only to sentences not belonging to that language. *Treatment* consists in restricting one's discourse to suitable languages.

I believe this is Tarski's diagnosis of the problem, but the matter requires further comment. In at least three places[6] Tarski argues essentially as follows:

> Every language meeting certain conditions (he speaks earlier of *universality*, later of *semantic closure*), and in which the normal laws of logic hold, is inconsistent.

Although Tarski acknowledges difficulties in making precise sense in saying so, it is fairly clear that he thinks that colloquial English meets the conditions in question, and is in fact inconsistent. This argument has made many philosophers, including, perhaps, Tarski himself, quite uncomfortable.[7] It is not clear even what it means to say that a natural language is inconsistent; nor is one quite comfortable arguing in the natural language to such a conclusion about natural language.

I want to suggest that Tarski could have avoided these difficulties and given a better argument for the conclusion he wanted to

---

[6] 'The Concept of Truth in Formalized Languages', in J. H. Woodger, trans., *Logic, Semantics, Metamathematics: Papers from 1923 to 1938* (Oxford, 1956), p. 164; 'The Semantic Conception of Truth', *Philosophy and Phenomenological Research* 4 (1944), p. 59; 'Truth and Proof', *Scientific American* 220 (1969), p. 67.

[7] See Hans Herzberger, 'The Truth-conditional Consistency of Natural Language', *Journal of Philosophy* 64 (1967), pp.. 29–35.

establish: that the concept of truth is simply not expressible in natural language.[8] He should have argued as follows:

(1) To qualify as expressing the concept of truth for a language L, the predicate 'true' must be such that every T-sentence for L[9] is a true sentence.

(2) Natural language is universal. This certainly entails that for any concept expressible in a natural language, there is a sentence that denies application of the concept to that sentence. It also entails that every T-sentence for a natural language is translatable into that language.

It follows from (1) and (2), by elementary logic, that the concept of truth is not expressible in natural language. The argument is essentially the same as our incompatibility argument, given above.

Tarski's comment on the problem as I have formulated it would be, as suggested above, that (S) is false, simply because there *is* no concept of truth available for attribution.

Notice that the notion of an inconsistent language plays no role at all in the argument. According to Tarski, as I understand him, the point is simply that anyone who thinks that truth is expressed or is expressible in natural language is committed thereby to a contradiction, and so is proved wrong.

The conclusion, put this way, is of course extremely hard to swallow. But Tarski apparently saw no room for compromise as to the nature of truth (the T-sentences) or as to the universality of natural languages. He was, however, prepared to allow, probably because of his positivistic philosophical outlook, that talk of truth in natural language was nonsense.[10]

Most modern-day philosophers are more than ready to give up the claim of universality[11]—this way lies the 'levels of language' view often described as Tarskian. On this view there is a hierarchy of

---

[8] 'The Concept of Truth in Formalized Languages', p. 153, and 'Truth and Proof', p. 65.

[9] The T-sentences for L are constructed by substituting for 'x' and 'p' in the following schema T: x is a true sentence of L if, and only if, p. To form a T-sentence for L, replace 'x' by the name of a sentence of L, and replace 'p' by that sentence if it is in English, or a translation of that sentence into English.

[10] Cf. Hartry Field, 'Tarski's Theory of Truth', in *Journal of Philosophy* 69 (1972), pp. 374 ff.

[11] For discussion of this point see H. G. Herzberger, 'Paradoxes of Grounding in Semantics', in *Journal of Philosophy* 67 (1970), pp. 145–67; and R. L. Martin 'Are Natural Languages Universal?', in *Synthese* 32 (1976), pp. 271–91.

truth-predicates for a natural language, each applying to the levels below the level to which it belongs. (S) still comes out false, though not because there is no truth-concept for English; it is rather a consequence of the stratification. (Something very much like this view is Tarski's view with respect to *formalized languages*, and is called by Kripke, among others, the 'orthodox view'.) Other philosophers have been willing to consider somewhat weakened characterizations of truth. This has led many in the truth-gap direction.

There are other possible diagnoses, including many which combine elements of those already considered. Practically all that has been agreed upon is that the problem is genuine, and fascinating.

It has been thirteen years since the publication of a collection of papers on truth and the liar paradox.[12] In contrast to much of the work collected there, Charles Parsons's 1974 paper, 'The Liar Paradox', signalled a return to a form of Tarskianism—classical semantics retained by means of a hierarchy of language levels. Parsons notes that: 'the hierarchical approach ... has seemed implausible in application to natural language because there seemed to be no division of natural language into a hierarchy of "languages" such that the higher ones contain the "semantics" of the lower ones'. But Parsons responds: 'What the objection fails to appreciate is just how far the variation in the truth-conditions of sentences of a natural language with the occasion of utterance can go, and in particular how this can arise for expressions that are crucially relevant to the semantic paradoxes: perhaps not "true", but at all events quantifiers, "say", "mean", and other expressions that involve indirect speech'. As I read him, Parsons favors our Diagnosis 2: he accepts (T) and a hierarchical version of (S), based on the alleged ambiguity of 'says', and denies the incompatibility of (T) with his version of (S).

Tyler Burge's 1979 paper, 'Semantical Paradox', develops the idea that the extension of the truth-predicate itself varies with the context of utterance—an idea mentioned in the remark of Parsons above. Burge accepts claim (S) and his own hierarchical version of (T), with the truth-predicate indexed according to context, and rejects the

---

[12] *The Paradox of the Liar*, first published in 1970, Yale University Press. See note 1.

incompatibility argument. The Liar sentence, p, understood as denying truth$_i$ of itself, is *not* true$_i$ (as shown in the usual way); but the application of (T) to p yields only that p is true$_{i+1}$, due to a shift in context when we come to evaluate p. By this last move, Burge is able to account also for the intuition which is part of what I called the revenge problem, namely that the Liar sentence seems to be true after all. Burge supplies formal renderings for three variants of his account, and discusses the pragmatics of the application of the truth-predicate.

In 1975, two papers, Martin and Woodruff's 'On Representing "True-in-L" in L' and Saul Kripke's 'Outline of a Theory of Truth' extended the truth-value gap approach. The authors had arrived independently at similar inductive constructions of the truth-predicate. The part of the idea that is common to both papers can be put roughly as follows. At the beginning of the construction, the extension and counterextension of the truth-predicate are considered empty, so that all attributions or denials of truth are without truth-value. Those sentences that do not contain the truth-predicate can still be evaluated intuitively, some as true, some as false. These constitute the extension and counterextension, respectively, of the truth-predicate at the next level, from which it follows that more sentences are evaluated as true (false) at this level. The process thus begun is continued into the transfinite. The resulting extensions (counterextensions) are swept together into a 'fixed point'—a point at which all sentences that will belong to the extension (counter-extension) of 'true' already do.

In the concise Martin and Woodruff paper, the logical techniques used to prove the main result are different from those employed by Kripke, especially in the use of Zorn's lemma. In Kripke's more extended discussion, the solution he advocates is contrasted with the orthodox, Tarskian solution, and is developed in a very general logical setting.

Although Hans Herzberger's and Anil Gupta's papers in this volume make important use of variants of the inductive construction just described, philosophically they are more classical in spirit. Herzberger's 'Notes on Naive Semantics' proposes a 'semi-inductive' characterization of the truth-predicate to replace the inductive characterization. The change is required by Herzberger's decision to study the behavior of the paradoxes within exclusively classical, two-valued models. Gupta's investigation rejects the inductive construction of the truth-predicate also, and suggests instead the application of a 'revision' rule of truth, which builds up successively better approximations to represent truth. The first part of Gupta's paper consists of a study of the *desiderata* for an account of truth, and of the limits of truth-representation within orthodox (Tarskian) semantics.

Brian Skyrms's new paper, 'Intensional Aspects of Semantical Self-Reference', which continues the study of the ideas he proposed in *The Paradox of the Liar*, is also influenced by the Martin/Woodruff, and Kripke inductive constructions of truth. Skyrms devises what he calls 'intensional fixed points' for his account of truth, by modifying the inductive construction; Skyrms allows for the possibility of a true sentence, and a truth-valueless sentence, differing only in coextensive terms. Skyrms's work is best seen as addressing the *revenge* problem I discussed earlier. He accepts a truth-value gap solution, and then proposes a way of accepting the intuition that the gappy Liar sentence is indeed not true, without thereby reinstating contradiction.

In Solomon Feferman's new paper, 'Toward Useful Type-Free Theories, I', set-theoretic and semantical paradoxes are approached in parallel. Feferman presents an elegant general framework for type-free theories of partial predicates; this framework encompasses all truth-value gap work developed so far. But Feferman criticizes the truth-value gap approach, and presents ways of formulating theories of partial predicates within classical logic.

In the background of all these papers is the work of Russell and Tarski on the paradoxes. Therefore I have included Alonzo Church's 1976 paper, 'Comparison of Russell's Resolution of the Semantical Antinomies with that of Tarski'. The analytic tools devised by Church for the comparison are also important in themselves.

Robert L. Martin
July 1983

The Liar Paradox*

Charles Parsons

Why is it that today, more than sixty years after *Principia Mathematica* and nearly forty years after the first publication of Tarski's *Wahrheitsbegriff*, the Liar paradox is still discussed as if it were an open problem? What is the difference between semantical paradoxes and the paradoxes of set theory that accounts for the fact that the paradoxes of set theory are nowadays treated as solved? The general outline of an answer to this question seems to me obvious. The problem of the paradoxes of set theory has been seen as a problem of constructing a way of talking about sets that is adequate for certain *theories*, in particular those parts of mathematics which have come to be formulated in set-theoretical terms and rely on set-theoretical methods. The Liar paradox tends to be seen as much more a problem of analyzing a *given* conceptual scheme, embodied in one way or another in natural languages. But the use of the word 'true' and its translations into other languages seems to embody just the features that are responsible for the paradox, in particular the impredicativity that the paradox most immediately turns on: statements involving the word 'true' are among those that are said to be true or false. For this reason the hierarchical approach that underlies accepted set theories and which was applied to the

Charles Parsons, 'The Liar Paradox', reprinted from the *Journal of Philosophical Logic* 3 (1974), 381–412. Copyright © 1974 by D. Reidel Publishing Company, Dordrecht, Holland.

* I am indebted to Hao Wang and The Rockefeller University for a visiting appointment which provided the freedom to do much of the work on this paper. I presented an early version in January 1972 to John Wallace's seminar at Rockefeller and a version closer to the present one in lectures in March 1973 at the University of California, Berkeley and Los Angeles, and Stanford University. Among those from whose comments or discussion the paper has benefited are Rogers Albritton, Tyler Burge, Donald Davidson, Gilbert Harman, James Higginbotham, David Kaplan, George Myro, Thomas Nagel, and John Wallace. I owe much to the writings of Hans Herzberger. I am grateful to Bas van Fraassen and the referee for pointing out misunderstandings and questionable interpretations of van Fraassen's work.

semantical paradoxes by Russell, Ramsey, and Tarski, has been rejected in much recent literature on the semantical paradoxes.

I want to argue, on the contrary, that the semantical paradoxes should be treated in a way that stresses their analogies with the paradoxes of set theory. What is needed for such a treatment is to make plausible an interpretation of natural language in terms of some hierarchy such as Tarski's language levels. Part of the key to this, in my view, is to look much more critically than is usually done at the interpretation of *quantifiers* in natural languages and at their interaction with semantical expressions, and at indirect-discourse expressions such as 'say' and 'mean'. When this is done, the analogy of natural languages and the 'semantically closed languages' shown inconsistent by Tarski's methods is much less persuasive. The morals I shall draw about the treatment of quantifiers in natural languages have a wider application than just to the paradoxes.

I.

An assumption that leads naturally to the conclusion that natural languages are semantically closed in Tarski's sense is that there is a quite definite concept of truth for a natural language that is expressed by a word of that language that we can translate as 'true'. Then it seems that natural languages can express their own concepts of truth. At any rate, this latter principle seems to underlie a considerable recent literature on the Liar paradox where either some form of non-standard semantics and logic is applied, or some weakening is made of the relation supposed by Tarski between '"p" is true' and 'p', or both. Before I present my own views I should like to discuss critically some of the ideas in this literature.

The most developed and intuitively appealing theory of this kind is that of Bas van Fraassen (1968, 1970a, 1970b). I shall discuss this in some detail and then remark briefly on another due to Brian Skyrms (1970a, 1970b). However, the most subtle and interesting of these approaches is probably that of Hans Herzberger (1967, 1970a, 1970b), but his views are not yet available in a form complete enough for detailed discussion.

An idea that arises very naturally about the semantical paradoxes is that the sentences involved are semantically deficient, or at least become so in the contexts in which they are used. But since this deficiency comes to light by *arguments* in which they occur, it does not seem that we meet the difficulty by declaring them outrightly meaningless and banishing them from the language. It seems natural to regard a statement that says of itself that it is false as neither true nor false. Van Fraassen gives a formal semantics in which this possibility arises, and from certain assumptions about paradoxical sentences it *follows* that they are neither true nor false.

He considers languages based on the usual propositional and predicate logic, where the semantics allows truth-value gaps but in which the notions of logical validity and implication are the usual classical notions. The actual manner in which this is achieved need not concern us (van Fraassen, 1968, pp. 140–2), but the essence of it is that a sentence will be true or false if it is such under *all* of a certain class of interpretations in the usual classical sense. Evidently the valid formulae of classical logic will then come out true.

The typical situation in which the Liar paradox can arise in formal semantics is as follows: Sentences $A, B, \ldots$ of a certain object language have in the object language *standard names*, say $a, b, \ldots$ and can also be denoted by other expressions, say $\alpha, \beta, \ldots$. Suppose 'T' is a predicate of the object language that purports to express truth in that language. Then α may denote the sentence $\sim T\alpha$.[1] Let that sentence be A and let a be its standard name. Then the Tarski biconditional

(1) $Ta \equiv \sim T\alpha$

should be true, and since $a = \alpha$ is true we obtain the contradiction $T\alpha \equiv \sim T\alpha$ or $Ta \equiv \sim Ta$.

However, it seems that if $\sim T\alpha$ can be neither true nor false then (1) need not be always true. In the situation we have sketched it will be *false* in van Fraassen's semantics since its negation is derivable from the truth $a = \alpha$. This raises a question what relation we can suppose between a sentence A and Ta, given that 'T' is to express

---

[1] In the case of formalisms containing number theory, the standard names will be numerals for Gödel numbers of the expressions involved. The other terms $\alpha, \beta, \ldots$ can in principle be any closed primitive recursive terms, but in actual paradoxical cases they will be terms constructed by substitution functions. $a = \alpha$ will then be a provable numerical formula.

Another frequently discussed type of case is that in which the standard names are quotations, and $\alpha, \beta, \ldots$ are definite descriptions such as 'the sentence written on the blackboard in . . .'. The relevant proposition $a = \alpha$ can be verified by observation.

Note that in this section I assume that the primary truth-vehicles are *sentences*; otherwise 'T' should be read as 'expresses a true proposition'.

truth in the language. Van Fraassen's answer is that this relation is
co-necessitation: if A is true, Ta is true, and vice versa.

It would be natural to say that if A is not true then Ta is *false*: Ta
says of A that it is true, and it isn't. But in our example this does not
work: if Ta is false, $\sim Ta$ is true, but then so is $\sim T\alpha$. But that is A, so
if A is not true, it is true. But if $\sim T\alpha$ is true, Ta is true by the above,
and $\sim Ta$ is true by substitutivity of identity. So we have a
contradiction. In this case (which turns out to be an instance of what
van Fraassen calls the Strengthened Liar) we have a case of a
sentence A which is not true, but the sentence that says it is true is
not false, but rather neither true nor false.

One might find in this result the failure of 'T' to express the
concept of truth as it is used in the metalanguage. However, it is in
the first instance a matter not of expressing truth but of expressing
negation. $\sim Tx$ is true of x if Tx is false of x, and false of x if Tx is
true of x, but if Tx is neither true nor false of x, $\sim Tx$ may also be
neither true nor false of x. In order to express 'not true' as we mean it
in the *metalanguage*, it seems we need a connective (say '$\neg$') such
that $\neg A$ would be *true* whenever A is neither true nor false. But
putting this connective plus van Fraassen's assumptions about truth
into the object language produces inconsistency.

This limitation on the means of expression of van Fraassen's
language has been offered as a criticism.[2] From the point of view of
the presumed motivation of the approach it seems serious: it reveals
a divergence in sense between the predicate '$\sim T$' of the object
language and the phrase 'not true' of the metalanguage. We have a
sentence A such that (it is true to say in the metalanguage that) it is
not true, but Ta, the sentence that is supposed to say in the object
language that A is true, is not false, and $\sim Ta$ is not true. We were
supposing that it was just to prevent such divergences that the
approach was put forward in the first place: the idea was that for a
natural language there is no difference between what one can say *in*
the language and what one can say *about* the language "from
outside". But the divergence can so far be blamed on negation rather
than on 'T' and 'true'.

A sharper divergence between 'T' and 'true' does occur if we put
into the *object language* a simple principle about truth that van
Fraassen accepts. He regards the schema

[2] Herzberger (1970b), pp. 29–30.

(2) $Ta \supset A$

as harmless (1970a, p. 15 n.). In our liar situation (A is $\sim T\alpha$ and $a = \alpha$ holds) we have

$$Ta \supset \sim T\alpha$$

which, with $a = \alpha$, implies $\sim T\alpha$ and $\sim Ta$, both of which are not true.

Perhaps this just shows that (2) is not so harmless after all, as is clear from the literature on reflection principles.[3] Van Fraassen's endorsement of (2) is a passing remark, and it is not central to his approach. Other premisses concerning the expression of the theory of truth in the object language lead to a similar result.[4] But it seems that van Fraassen can escape the proof of untrue sentences by admitting a further incompleteness of expression closely related to that concerning negation, but also more elementary than he admits (in 1970a).

Thus it seems clear that van Fraassen's approach provides no escape from the problem left by Tarski's work on the paradoxes, of making sense for natural languages of the limitations of the means of expression of formalized theories. Van Fraassen's original paper (1968) attempts to deal with the liar in complete abstraction from this.[5] But (in 1970b) he writes, 'The language has, at any stage of its

---

[3] Formalisms containing number theory have a formula Bx which expresses 'x is the Gödel number of a provable formula'. The simple reflection schema $Ba \supset A$ expresses in the object language the soundness of the formalism. If α denotes $\sim B\alpha$ then $\sim B\alpha$ is Gödel's undecidable formula. The above argument with 'T' replaced by 'B' shows that if $Ba \supset \sim B\alpha$ is provable, then $\sim B\alpha$ is provable, contrary to Gödel's theorem if the formalism is consistent. Hence there is an instance of the reflection schema that is not provable.

[4] In an earlier version of this paper I showed that $\sim T\alpha$ could be deduced from a set of premisses, all of which were, I believe, unexceptionable for van Fraassen except

(i) $Ta \supset T(Ta)$

which was to express the fact that A necessitates Ta. In a letter of October 16, 1973, van Fraassen repudiated (i) and remarked that it is not justified by the semantics of (1970a), pp. 20–1. It seems that if the necessitation relation N_0 is expressed in the object language then

(ii) $aN_0b \cdot Ta \cdot \supset Tb$

should hold, as should $aN_0(Ta)$. But then (i) follows. It seems that either N_0 does not go into the object language, or '$\supset$' fails at some point to express the conditional.

[5] However, in the letter mentioned in note 4 van Fraassen suggests the contrary. Perhaps he thought of the truth-value gaps as themselves such as incompleteness.

I should remark that none of the incompletenesses that arise in recent literature is compatible with the idea that natural language is 'universal' if this is to be close to semantic closure in Tarski's sense. Cf. Martin (1976).

evolution, a certain incompleteness of means of expression, any given aspect of which may be remedied in its further evolution' (1970b, p. 61). It seems to me that once one makes this admission, one might as well admit at the outset that a natural language does not at a given 'stage of its evolution' express its own concept of truth. Then the way is open for a treatment of the paradoxes by semantical methods that are simpler and more standard than van Fraassen's, as we will show below.

Skyrms's proposal is that we restrict the substitutivity of identity so that if $F\alpha$ is neither true nor false, $F\alpha \cdot \alpha = \beta \cdot \supset F\beta$ need not be true. In our paradoxical case, this enables him to reject the inference from $T\alpha$ and $\alpha = a$ to Ta and thus to affirm $\sim Ta$ ($\sim T\alpha$ is not true) and yet reject $\sim T\alpha$ itself. He is able on this basis to construct a formal system in which a truth-predicate can be applied to sentences containing it, and the restriction on the substitutivity of identity insures consistency.

The claim motivating the restriction is that Ta may be semantically all right while $T\alpha$ is defective, in that $\sim T\alpha$ is self-referential, and indeed viciously so, while neither Ta nor $\sim Ta$ is. This seems to me to attribute too much importance to self-reference: $\sim Ta$ and $\sim T\alpha$ deny the same predicate of the same object, and in neither is there anything problematic about the manner in which the object (namely the sentence $\sim T\alpha$) is referred to, nor is there any difficulty in identifying the denotation of α (see note 1).

Evidently the proposed restriction has the effect that 'T' is no longer functioning precisely as a predicate. (There is no question of anything turning on the denotation of a or α either changing or being different 'in some other possible world'.) On Skyrms's hypothesis, the truth-value of Ta does not depend just on the denotation of a and the meaning of 'T'.[6]

II.

In order to explain my own approach to the Liar, I want now to consider two closely related Liar sentences which can arise in a language in which we can talk of a sentence *expressing a proposition*, of a proposition's being *true*, and in which we can name sentences. Nothing turns on the particular manner in which a sentence might

[6] Cf. Fitch (1970).

come to contain a singular term denoting *itself*, except that to speak of a sentence expressing a proposition, without reference to a context, implies that it does not contain demonstratives, so that devices such as 'this sentence' are excluded. But we can use Gödel numbering or other context-invariant forms of reference.

In the general case where indexical expressions are admitted, the predicate 'expresses' clearly needs to have an additional argument place or places for the features of the context that determine what proposition is expressed in that context. In my view we do not have an adequate account for a whole natural language of what these argument places are. The most complete account I know of is Lewis (1971).

Consider for example:

(1) The sentence written in the upper left-hand corner of the blackboard in Room 913-D South Laboratory, The Rockefeller University, at 3:15 p.m. on December 16, 1971 expresses a false proposition.

(2) The sentence written in the upper right-hand corner of the blackboard in Room 913-D South Laboratory, The Rockefeller University, at 3:15 p.m. on December 16, 1971 does not express a true proposition.

Let us suppose that at the time mentioned the blackboard mentioned contained exactly two sentences: (1) in the upper left-hand corner and (2) in the upper right-hand corner. Moreover let 'A' abbreviate the quotation of (1) and 'B' that of (2). Then we have

(3) $A =$ the sentence written in the upper left-hand corner of the blackboard in Room 913-D South Laboratory, The Rockefeller University, at 3:15 p.m. on December 16, 1971.

(4) $B =$ the sentence written in the upper right-hand corner of the blackboard in Room 913-D South Laboratory, The Rockefeller University, at 3:15 p.m. on December 16, 1971.

Now just what should we assume about truth? One possibility would be to assume instances of the schema '"p" expresses a true proposition $\equiv p$', and perhaps '"p" expresses a false proposition $\equiv \sim p$'. But then if we have ordinary propositional logic, we can infer

'p' expresses a true proposition $\vee$ 'p' expresses a false proposition, and therefore

'*p*' expresses a proposition.

But we want to allow for the possibility that some sentences do not express propositions. A more suitable schema might be the following

(5) $(x)(x$ is a proposition $\cdot$ '*p*' expresses x.
       $\supset \cdot x$ is true $\equiv p$).

We shall assume that propositions are bivalent; hence we can render 'false' as 'not true', and (5) implies

(6) $(x)(x$ is a proposition $\cdot$ '*p*' expresses x.
       $\supset \cdot x$ is false $\equiv \sim p$).

Suppose now x is a proposition and A expresses x. By (5)

x is true $\equiv$ the sentence written in the upper left-hand corner of the blackboard in Room 913-D South Laboratory, The Rockefeller University, at 3:15 p.m. on December 16, 1971, expresses a false proposition.

and then by (3)

(7) x is true $\equiv A$ expresses a false proposition.

Suppose x is not true. Then by existential generalization:

$(\exists x)(x$ is a proposition $\cdot \sim(x$ is true$) \cdot A$ expresses $x)$,

i.e. A expresses a false proposition. By (7), x is true. Since x is arbitrary,

(8) $(x)(x$ is a proposition $\cdot A$ expresses $x \cdot \supset x$ is true)

and hence

(9) $\sim(\exists x)(x$ is a proposition $\cdot \sim(x$ is true$) \cdot A$ expresses $x)$.

Now suppose y is a proposition and A expresses y. By (8), y is true. But (7) with y for x follows. But by (9), this is a contradiction. Hence there is no proposition y expressed by A. Hence (1) does not express a proposition.

Similarly, (2) does not express a proposition. But a contradiction is avoided because in such cases the condition for the Tarski biconditional in (5) is always false.

We might imagine that in our object language we can form descriptions of the form 'the proposition that p'. It would then be plausible to assume all sentences of the form

(10) 'p' expresses the proposition that p.

This would lead us into contradiction, at least if we use a logic according to which 'the proposition that p' must denote something. But to suppose it does is to suppose that 'p' expresses a proposition, which we do not want always to suppose. It is a matter of indifference whether we assume (10) with 'the proposition that p' a possibly nondesignating singular term, or admit (10) only where 'p' does express a proposition.

In this connection it should be observed that

(11) the proposition that p is true $\equiv p$

follows from (5), (10), and '$(\exists x)('p'$ expresses $x)$'. But there is no reason to accept (11) if 'p' does not express a proposition.

A difficulty that arises immediately is the following: (1) says of a certain sentence which turns out to be (1) itself, that it expresses a false proposition. We have shown that (1) expresses no proposition. But then (1) seems to say something false. Are we not forced to say that (1) expresses a false proposition after all?

Similarly, (2) says of itself that it does not express a true proposition; since it does not express any proposition, in particular it does not express a true one. Hence it seems to say something true. Must we then say that (2) expresses a true proposition?

In either case we shall be landed in a contradiction. A simple observation that would avoid this is as follows: The quantifiers in our object language could be interpreted as ranging over a certain universe of discourse U. Then a sentence such as

$(\exists x)$ (x is a proposition $\cdot$ A expresses x)

is true just in case U contains a proposition expressed by A, i.e., by (1). But what reason do we have to conclude from the fact that we have made sense of (1) and even determined its truth-value that it expresses a proposition which lies *in the universe U*?

We can motivate more directly the exclusion from U of propositions expressed by (1) or (2) by observing that they contain quantifiers ranging over propositions, and hence if (1) or (2) is to express a proposition in U, it must be defined impredicatively, i.e., in terms of a totality of which it is itself a member. But although objections to impredicative characterizations of propositions come readily to hand, it is not obvious that the case against them is decisive. We might suppose that propositions are extra-mental entities whose existence does not depend on the possibility of their being expressed by sentences. In the context of analysis and set theory, such realism has been taken to license some impredicative definitions.

The above version of the Liar paradox is stronger than an argument based on impredicativity. It shows that (5), a highly plausible assumption about the concepts of expression and truth, implies the existence of well-formed sentences that do not express propositions in the range of the bound variables. (5) is apparently quite compatible with realism about propositions.

In the language we are discussing, we can define a Tarskian truth-predicate for sentences: $T(y)$, say, is defined as

(12) $(\exists x)(x$ is a proposition $\cdot$ y expresses $x \cdot x$ is true$)$

and then (5) implies

(13) $(\exists x)(x$ is a proposition $\cdot$ 'p' expresses $x)$
       $\supset \cdot T($'p'$) \equiv p$

for any sentence 'p'. But on pain of contradiction, we will not always be able to prove the consequent of (13). Then our language will not be 'semantically closed' in Tarski's sense, and the Tarskian truth-predicate covers only a part of the language.

Interpreting (1) and (2) in terms of the usual semantics for predicate logic, in which the quantifiers range over a certain set U, makes it possible to understand them and to determine truth-values for them: (1) is false and (2) is true. We can even talk of the propositions they express. But these are not in U.

Taking (1) and (2) as statements in English, it is tempting to step outside this semantics and to say that the quantifiers do not range over some definite set U but over *absolutely everything*. But then our argument shows that they do not express propositions *at all*. Yet they seem to make perfectly good sense; we still have an argument for the falsity of (1) and the truth of (2). Can we accept the idea of a perfectly reasonable sentence that does not express a proposition? And what can we then be saying when we say that such a sentence is *true*, if not that it expresses a true proposition?

What I want to say about this is that there is a close analogy between this situation and the paradoxes of set theory. That a is the extension of a predicate 'Fx' is usually taken to mean that the condition

(14) $\quad (x)(x \in a \equiv Fx)$

holds. Analogously to (5) we might have

(15) $\quad (y)(y$ is extension of 'Fx' $\supset (x)(x \in y \equiv Fx))$.

Taking 'Fx' as '$x \notin x$' we can deduce

$$\sim (\exists y)(x)(x \in y \equiv x \notin x)$$

and hence

(16) $\quad \sim (\exists y)(y$ is extension of '$x \notin x$').

The same alternatives for the interpretation of the quantifiers in (14)–(16) present themselves as in the case of the Liar sentences. If the variables range over a universe U, (16) must be interpreted to mean that '$x \notin x$', taken relative to U, lacks an extension *in* U. But in our metalanguage we can probably show the existence of the relevant set (e.g. by Zermelo's *Aussonderungsaxiom*) and therefore prove that it is not in U.

This has the consequence that U falls short of containing 'all' sets. Although such an interpretation of set theory is often used in foundational studies, when one considers models of set theory, both set theorists and laymen entertain the idea of set theory as a theory about all sets in an absolute sense. This is (for the usual set theories) incompatible with interpreting the quantifiers of set-theoretic statements as ranging over a set.

If we take this interpretation seriously then we must say that the set of *all* things that are not members of themselves does not exist at all.[7] However, this does not detract in any way from the meaningfulness of the *predicate* '$x \notin x$'.

---

[7] Set theorists usually consider the set of all *sets* that are not members of themselves. But then the answer is available that although the predicate 'x is a set. $\sim (x \in x)$' indeed has some entity as its extension, this extension is not a set but a 'proper' or 'ultimate' class. The point is that if a is this object, '$x \in a \equiv x \notin x$' needs to hold only for sets, and hence it is of no moment that if fails for a. A 'set' for this purpose can be any entity capable of belonging to classes.

This way out is not available when one considers whether there can be a class or set of absolutely all objects that are not members of themselves.

The analogy I wish to draw should now be clear: A language may contain perfectly meaningful predicates such that, in a given theory formulated in that language, they cannot be said to have extensions. One would readily concede that the same must be said about the correlation of intensions to such predicates: from within, they do not have attributes as their intensions. What the Liar shows in the first instance is that the same situation arises for *sentences*: A theory expressed in a given language cannot always correlate to a sentence a proposition as its intension, even though the sentence is well-formed and may even be provable.[8] The same should be said about their 'extensions': their truth-values.

That some Liar sentences are not semantically deficient in the sense that assertive utterance of them must fail to come off, or in the sense that they cannot figure in proofs, or in the sense that it is impossible to make sense of them 'from outside', is obscured by the fact that the most typical such sentences, such as 'What I am now saying is false' are naturally interpreted so as to contain a non-denoting singular term, as 'the proposition expressed by this utterance is false'. But this semantic deficiency (whether or not it debars the statement from having a truth-value) is non-essential. (1) and (2) do not suffer from it.

The view about the Liar paradox here presented has to meet two objections: first, that it presupposes the dubious notion of sentences as expressing propositions, and of propositions as the primary bearers of truth or falsity; second and more important, it seems that in a natural language one can utter, say, (2), intending its quantifiers to be absolutely unrestricted. But then on the proposed account we should be debarred from saying, after having deduced (2) from (5), that (2) is true, or that it expresses a true proposition. But there is no indication that the conventions of English prohibit such an inference, or that a semantical theory about English would not say that (2) *entails* something like 'What (2) says is true'. But then we should be landed in contradiction. Is our proposal just another proposal for linguistic reform?

---

[8] That a sentence such as (1) or (2) might express a proposition 'from outside' that is not in the range of its own quantifiers might be suggested by the following remark of Kneale (1972, p. 243): 'The lesson to be learnt from the Liar paradox is nothing specially concerned with truth or falsity, but rather that ability to *express* a proposition can never depend on ability to *designate* it'. However, Kneale seems to think the paradox disposed of by the observation that these sentences do not express propositions.

We shall postpone considering the latter objection to Section V. In answer to the first, I would plead that it is a plausible interpretation of talk of truth and falsity in natural languages that they are predicates of intensional entities that can be construed as propositions.[9] But I would not insist on this, since the approach can also be formulated in the situation where truth-values are attributed to sentences as I shall do in the next section.

III.

I want now to consider the situation where truth is considered as a predicate of sentences. Where indexical and other context-dependent expressions are present, of course the truth-value of what is said depends not just on the sentence but on features of the context of utterance. Here the truth-predicate, like the expression predicate of the last section, would require additional argument places. But I want to continue to exclude this complication, so that 'true' will be treated as a one-place predicate of sentences.

We can construct examples like (2.1)[10] and (2.2), using 'is false' instead of 'expresses a false proposition' and 'is true' instead of 'expresses a true proposition'. Then we can have singular terms α and β such that, as a matter of fact, α denotes the sentence

(1) α is false,

and β denotes the sentence

(2) β is not true.

However, what principle is to play the role of (2.5)? Of course we obtain a contradiction if we replace (2.5) by the usual Tarski schema. I propose to replace (2.5) by

(3) 'p' is true $\vee$ 'p' is false $\cdot \supset \cdot$ 'p' is true $\equiv p$.

[9] A persuasive case for this is made in Cartwright (1962). As Davidson (1968) makes clear, logical analysis of indirect discourse in terms of propositions does not require that *we* have a substantive criterion of propositional identity. However, as Tyler Burge and James Higginbotham have made me aware, the logical coherence of ordinary discourse so construed requires that the relevant relations of 'saying the same thing' be reflexive, symmetric, and transitive. Transitivity in particular cannot be taken for granted in view of the clearly vague character of such relations. Higginbotham (1973, ch. 7) raises other difficulties, which however may not be relevant to the most ordinary discourse.

[10] (2.1) is formula (1) of Section II. This is a paradigm for our references to numbered formulae outside the section where they occur.

If we define 'x is false' as 'the negation of x is true', then (3) implies

(4)   'p' is true $\vee$ 'p' is false $\cdot \supset \cdot$ 'p' is false $\equiv \sim p$.

Taking (3) as the analogue of (2.5) amounts to taking *being either true or false* as the analogue of *expressing a proposition*. I shall defend this analogy in the course of this section. (3) follows logically from (2.5) if 'true' is defined by (2.12) and falsity is defined as truth of the negation.

However, whether or not (3) is a proper analogue of (2.5), it seems to be a plausible axiom. I know of no good reason for rejecting it. Another consideration in its favor is the following: Consider a formalized theory that contains (perhaps by Gödel numbering) its own syntax, and which also contains a truth-predicate (satisfying the Tarski schema) for a *part* of the language of the theory. If the truth-predicate is so defined that it is false of any object other than (the number of) a sentence of the relevant part, then (3) holds for *all* sentences.

An argument parallel to that showing that (2.1) and (2.2) do not express propositions shows that (1) and (2) are neither true nor false. Since α denotes (1) and β denotes (2), we can then infer

(5) $\sim(\alpha$ is true $\vee$ α is false)
(6) $\sim(\beta$ is true $\vee$ β is false)

and hence by propositional logic, (2) and the negation of (1) follow. Thus we have the same temptation to say that (1) is after all false, while (2) is after all true.

We must acknowledge a difference in sense between 'true' in the object language and 'true' in the metalanguage, because in the latter sense (2) is true and (1) false, while in the former sense, by (5) and (6), both are neither true nor false.[11]

In the last section, when we supposed the quantifiers in (2.1) and (2.2) to range over a definite universe U, we obtained such a divergence in the sense of 'expresses a true proposition': (2.1) and (2.2) expressed no proposition in the object-language sense (i.e., in U), but perhaps with a larger universe, (2.1) interpreted over U expresses a false proposition and (2.2) a true one.

---

[11] Harman (1972, p. 52) sketches a theory according to which Liar sentences are neither true nor false in an object-language sense of 'true' and yet there is a metalanguage sense of 'true' that allows no truth-value gaps, so that these sentences obtain truth-values. As with us, (3.1) is false and (3.2) true in the metalanguage sense.

But so long as we used quantifiers with the same range as in (2.1) and (2.2) themselves, we had to say that (2.1) and (2.2) express no propositions. But this was not a matter of their being syntactically or semantically ill-formed but was rather to be viewed in the same light as a predicate's failure to have an extension. Can we give a parallel explanation of the failure of (1) and (2) to be either true or false? A way of doing so is provided by following Frege and thinking of the truth-value of a sentence as an instance of the general notion of reference. We argued that just as a theory cannot correlate intensions (attributes) to all its predicates, so it cannot correlate propositions as intensions to all its sentences. Likewise, a theory cannot correlate extensions (classes) to all its predicates, and equally it cannot correlate extensions or references (truth-values) to all its sentences. The same will be true for singular terms if certain term-forming operators, such as abstraction, are present in the language.

There is a difference between the standard case of classes, on the one hand, and the present case of truth-values on the other that points up an ambiguity in our talk above of a theory failing to *correlate* intensions or extensions to its expressions. The case of classes seems to reflect an unavoidable ontological lack in a theory: the universe of an interpretation of it will just fail to contain sets or classes satisfying certain conditions. But for classical theories there are only two truth-values: any non-trivial theory can hardly be unable to name two distinct objects to represent them. The difference does not disappear if we find the identity of abstract entities such as sets arbitrary: Any attempt to identify sets of members of a universe with members of that universe must break down at some point, since there can be no one-to-one correspondence of the members of a class and all its subclasses.

The difficulty arises with respect to the *function* that assigns to each sentence its truth-value, or perhaps to each open sentence and sequence of objects its satisfaction-value. This function cannot be built up from within a theory by assigning to each singular term, predicate, and sentence an extension or reference, because the universe of the theory cannot contain an extension for every predicate, and in some cases it will not be able to contain a reference for every singular term.

I want now to develop this point in a more technical direction. The assignment of extensions to the expressions of a language re-quires a certain amount of set theory or some functional equivalent, and, for the usual set theories, presupposes that the universe of discourse exists as a set or class. It is instructive to consider the case of a theory which contains the usual first-order set theory and where the interpretation proceeds simply by assigning as universe of discourse a certain set W and otherwise sticking as close to the 'homophonic translation' as possible, by assigning to each primitive predicate $Fx_1 \ldots x_n$ the set

$$\{\langle x_1, \ldots, x_n \rangle : x_1 \ldots x_n \in W \cdot Fx_1 \ldots x_n\}.$$

We assume W is large enough to contain the denotations of all the primitive singular terms of the language. In such a language we can define a two-place predicate $T(w, x)$ which can be read to mean

x is the Gödel number of a formula which is true when its quantifiers are interpreted to range over the set w.

Let A be a closed formula and let $A^*(w)$ be the result of restricting the quantifiers of A to w. Then if n is the Gödel number of A, the formula

(9) $T(w, \bar{n}) \equiv A^*(w)$

will be provable in a rather weak set theory.

$T(W, x)$ will be the truth-predicate for the interpretation above sketched. Assuming the theory consistent, it will not yield the full Tarski biconditionals for all formulae of the language. If t denotes the number of $\sim T(W, t)$, then if n is this number we can in the usual way prove

(10) $\sim [T(W, \bar{n}) \equiv \sim T(W, t)]$

but by (9) we have

$$T(W, \bar{n}) \equiv (\sim T(W, t))^*(W)$$

and (10) then yields

$$\sim [T(W, t) \equiv T(W, t)^*(W)].$$

Thus the truth-predicate $T(W, x)$ is provably not equivalent to its own relativization to W. In other words, the interpretation proposed for taking $T(W, x)$ as a truth-predicate, and for the truth of instances of (9), is not the same as the one $T(W, x)$ itself formulates. This should not surprise us, since the latter interpretation takes W as the universe, while the 'intended interpretation' underlying the construction of the truth predicates requires W to be a set *in* the universe.

$T(W, x)$ does yield a truth-predicate for the full language, not of course satisfying Tarski's schema, but satisfying (3). (9) does yield the Tarski biconditional for the formulae provably equivalent to their relativization to W (i.e., provably absolute for W), given a concept of provability for our theory. Then (3) holds if we define 'x is true' as

x is the number of a closed formula A such that $A \equiv A^*(W)$ is provable, and $T(W, x)$.

Falsity is, as before, truth of the negation. This has the effect that formulae that are not provably absolute for W are neither true nor false.

To conclude this section, I must make a correction of the discussion of the last section. There we tried to assume as little as possible about the concept of proposition. In fact, on some accounts the failure of (2.1) to express a proposition cannot be accounted for by the absence of an appropriate proposition from its universe. Rather, the concept of expression behaves like the concept of satisfaction in the above account.

For example, suppose propositions are construed as functions from possible worlds to truth-values. Suppose further (unrealistically in my view) that there is a definite set P of possible worlds, which is constant for all the interpretations we consider. But then if the truth-values are identified with 1 and 0, 2^P is the set of *all* propositions, and the universe can be taken as a set containing 2^P and hence containing all propositions. Then just as in the extensional case, the failure of a sentence to express a proposition cannot be due to the fact that the proposition it expresses is not in the universe.

Consider an interpretation of this sort for which (2.5) is necessarily true. Consider a sentence C like (2.2) except that the definite description which is its subject and which denotes it is a rigid designator. Then 'C expresses no proposition' will be true in all possible worlds. But from outside, C expresses the necessary proposition, and if the universe U contains 2^P, this proposition (identified with the constant function 1 on P) belongs to U. But the pair $\langle$C, the necessary proposition$\rangle$ is not in the extension of 'expresses' for any possible world. Thus the difficulty arises not because the universe does not contain enough propositions but because the interpretation does not capture its own relation of expression. It should be remarked that the notion of expression here does the lion's share of the work of the Tarskian truth-predicate. The truth-predicate for propositions is essentially just functional application.

We can describe the situation in a way close to the way we described the extensional situation. An interpretation can here be construed as an assignment to certain linguistic expressions of *intensions*. Thus it is a generalized expression-relation. Of course the universe cannot contain an intension for every predicate. Thus there is the same difficulty in building up the relation of expression as there was in building up satisfaction and truth.

It should be remarked that even on the possible-worlds construal of propositions, the universe can contain all propositions only when the number of possible worlds is small compared to the number of individuals. Perhaps this is not very realistic. But an analogous situation can arise for higher-order languages.[12]

---

[12] For example, the system of Montague (1970). There propositions are of a different type from individuals. The system has a formation rule to the effect that if T is a propositional term, $T[\ \ ]$ is a formula, which might be read 'T is true'. 'The proposition that p' can be rendered as '$(\imath F)\ \square\ (F[\ \ ] \equiv p)$'. Then its existence is provable for all 'p', and moreover so is (2.11).

Consider now a theory formulated with this logic that can express its own syntax and formulate self-referential sentences. Suppose it contains a predicate for the relation of *expressing* between a sentence and a proposition. Then if α denotes the sentence 'p', we should expect

the proposition that $p = (\imath F)\ (\alpha$ expresses $F)$
that is

    (i) α expresses the proposition that p
    (ii) $(F)\ (\alpha$ expresses $F \supset F =$ the proposition that p).

But then the Liar paradox can be obtained in the usual way, say if α denotes the sentence

    (iii) $(\exists F)\ (\alpha$ expresses $F \cdot \sim F[\ \ ])$.

Thus in any model of our language, for any two-place predicate of the requisite type (in Montague's terminology $\langle -1,\ 0\rangle$), either (i) or (ii) must fail. However, in a standard second-order model, where the propositional variables range over 2^p, we cannot attribute the failure to the absence of a proposition expressed by (iii) in the range of these variables; if $(\exists F)\ (\alpha$ expresses $F)$ is necessarily false, then the identically 0 function will be such a proposition. Rather, we must suppose that the extension of 'expresses' falls short of the expressing relation 'from outside'.

If we add to the language a truth-predicate 'T_1' such that for any sentence 'p' with standard name a the formula

We can summarize the position of this section as follows: the use of 'true' as a predicate of sentences presupposes an interpretation. Such an interpretation can be an *object* of discourse only if it involves something like an assignment of extensions to the parts of the sentences of the language. But then the universe of discourse of the interpretation must also be an object. But then the interpretation can no longer cover the discourse in which it is itself formulated. In this setting, a version of the distinction of object language and metalanguage imposes itself.

This point of view cannot be the last word, because it is also possible to define truth-predicates for formalized languages that do not proceed by assignment of extensions and that, in particular, do not treat the universe as a set. The relevance of this possibility will be taken up in the next section.

IV.

So far our primary emphasis has been on interpretations in which the quantifiers range over some *set*, with the consequence that in the metalanguage we acknowledge entities not in the universe of the object language. I did consider one reason why that might not be the most relevant interpretation of the language of set theory. Moreover, a user of a language being interpreted in this way might always protest that by 'everything' he means *everything*; his quantifiers are not restricted unless such a restriction is made explicit or is clearly required by the context of an utterance. The interpretations of the type we have chiefly considered require the rejection of such claims to quantify over absolutely everything, or at least their reinterpretation in such a way that their absoluteness is lost. (The italicized

---

(iv) $\Box (T_1(a) \equiv p)$

is provable, then we can *define* 'x expresses F' as

x is a sentence $\cdot \Box (F[\ ] \equiv T_1(x))$.

Then (i) with a as α follows immediately from (iv). (ii) also follows if '$F = G$' is defined as $\Box (F[\ ] \equiv G[\ ])$.

Note that if arithmetic is necessary and the numbers are the same for all possible worlds then arithmetized syntax will be rigid: all syntactical truths will be necessary. From (iv) and these definitions it will follow that the expression relation is also rigid, that is

$(x) (F) (x$ expresses $F \supset \Box (x$ expresses $F))$.

'everything' in the protest is taken to range over a sufficiently large set, so that the protest becomes true.[13])

The idea of discourse about absolutely everything or even about absolutely all sets or propositions, poses problems that themselves could be the subject of a paper.[14] But apart from the possibility that the intended meaning of quantifiers might be thus 'absolute', an interpretation or a truth-predicate need not involve treating the universe as a set or require the metalanguage to acknowledge entities not in the universe of the object language.

The relevance to natural languages of the object-language meta-language distinction is one of the issues at stake in the discussion of the Liar. But we can certainly distinguish between a discourse of a metalinguistic character, in which for example truth and falsity is predicated of what someone *says*, and the discourse that it is about, even if it is not a priori excluded that they are sometimes identical. But it is hardly evident that in such a case the metadiscourse presupposes a richer ontology than the object discourse, at least not in the most straightforward sense.

In fact, the relation of ontological enrichment and semantic ascent is complex and subtle, as some examples I have discussed elsewhere should indicate (Parsons, 1971, 1974a). However, the situation where a theory is so interpreted that its universe is a set can be viewed as just one model for the situation where a sentence lacks a truth-value on a less comprehensive scheme of interpretation but obtains one on a more comprehensive scheme. The latter situation is more general. Consider for example a first-order language with finitely many primitive predicates which is then enlarged by adding a satisfaction predicate with the usual inductive definition. For any sentence of the original language the Tarski biconditional becomes

---

[13] George Myro pointed out that one might interpret the quantifiers of this entire paper as ranging over some sufficiently large set and thus produce a discourse to which the analysis of the Liar paradox here given would not apply. The same remark could be made about general set-theoretic discourses, including discourses about all models of set theory. In each case the 'proponent' could come back and extend his discourse so that it would cover the newly envisaged case.

Leaving aside the possibility of an 'absolute' interpretation, the generality which such a discourse as this paper has which transcends any particular set as range of its quantifiers must lie in a sort of systematic ambiguity, in that indefinitely many such sets will do. But one cannot express wherein the systematic ambiguity lies except in language that is subject to a similar systematic ambiguity. This is an illustration of the priority of the use of language to semantic reflection on it. It is also congenial to Quine's thesis (1969) of the indeterminacy of ontology.

[14] Cf. Parsons (1974a, last section) and (1974b).

derivable. If we construe the satisfaction predicate as false for formulae of the enlarged language not in the original language, then, as we indicated above, we obtain a 'truth-predicate' satisfying (3.3) in the enlarged language, in which the formulae that get truth-values are those of the original language, i.e., those not containing the satisfaction predicate. The sentence that 'says of itself that it is false' has of course no truth value, but on the intended interpretation of the enlarged language it is false; its negation should be derivable. Thus it behaves just like (3.1).

The general point I wish to make is that the *use* of language does not require that one already have a thematized *interpretation* that assigns a truth-value to everything one says. Of course one might talk of an 'intended interpretation' and of certain statements as true under it, where one has an idea of how the interpretation would go, or simply where some things one has already asserted are constraints on any interpretation. Thus those interpretations that have been formulated so that 'true' has a definite meaning with respect to a certain class of sentences cannot be expected to cover the discourse in which the interpretation itself is formulated.

There is a consideration that even in this more general setting supports the analogy of having a truth-value with having an extension and of the Liar paradox with Russell's paradox. This is that the addition to a first-order language of a satisfaction-predicate, so that every sentence of the original language gets a truth-value, is essentially equivalent to the addition to the language of predicative class variables, so that every predicate of the original language gets an extension.

A first-order theory with finitely many primitive predicates can be extended either by a satisfaction predicate with the usual inductive definition, or by class variables with predicative class existence axioms like those of Gödel (1940), Group B, p. 5). Then for each formula A of the original language we can prove in the satisfaction theory the Tarski biconditional

(1) $Sat (\langle v_0 \ldots v_{k-1} \rangle, \bar{n}) \equiv A,$ [15]

---

[15] Cf. Quine (1970, pp. 35–43). $\bar{n}$ is the formal numeral for the Gödel number n of A. $v_0 \ldots v_{k-1}$ are the first k variables in a fixed enumeration and include all those free in A.

If the given theory does not contain number theory and a theory of finite sequences of its objects, these must be added before the satisfaction and class theories are constructed. It is sufficient to add the theory of finite sets.

and in the class theory the comprehension principle

(2) $(\exists Y)(x)(x \in Y \equiv A)$.

In the class theory, by the usual reduction of inductive to explicit definitions we can define a satisfaction predicate and prove the inductive conditions.[16] We can translate the class theory into the satisfaction theory by construing a class as a pair of a one-place predicate with parameters and a sequence assigning values to the parameters. Then we can prove the translations of the class existence axioms.[17]

Thus if we go beyond mere truth and think of each sentence of a language as having a satisfaction-value with respect to any substitution for its free variables, this is equivalent to taking any predicate of the language as having, for any substitution for its free variables, a class as its extension. Talk of satisfaction (truth *of*) and talk of classes are ways of generalizing with respect to predicate positions in a language; in this sense they are equivalent ways.

V.

Up to now our discussion has been almost entirely an exercise in abstract semantics. We have not undertaken to make our ideas plausible in application to natural languages, and we have hardly taken account of any difference that might exist between a natural language and a first-order formalism.

There is one respect in which we already face a difficulty in applying to natural languages the *formulations* of the Liar paradox that we have discussed. Namely we have used either Tarskian predicates of truth of sentences under a given interpretation or the notion of expressing a proposition. Neither of these concepts is part of 'ordinary' language; they are part of the technical language of semantics. Suppose the worst case: that an irresolvable antinomy

---

[16] But not *laws* about satisfaction and truth whose proofs would need mathematical induction on formulae containing these predicates. If we begin with *ZF*, we do not have such induction in *NB*, which is stronger than the 'class theory' as we have defined it but which is still a conservative extension of *ZF*. We need the theory *NB*$^+$ of Parsons (1974a, note 15), which allows *Aussonderung* and replacement for formulae containing class variables. The corresponding extension of the satisfaction theory is obtained by allowing *Aussonderung* and replacement for formulae containing *Sat*.

[17] For a little more detail see Parsons (1974b).

arose from sentences of the sort we have been considering. Then it seems that it might be possible to attribute the contradiction to the technical semantic concepts and to avoid the claim that ordinary speakers of English are saddled with an incoherent conceptual apparatus.

In connection with the intensional formulations I want to emphasize that the concepts of expression and proposition are causing the difficulty, not the concept of truth. In any language in which sentences express propositions, there is no difficulty in having a predicate 'is true' such that, for any singular term 'α' and sentence 'p' if 'α' *denotes* the proposition that 'p' expresses, then

(1) α is true $\equiv p$

is true (in the metalinguistic sense). The intuition of some theorists of truth that (1) is tautological is supported by our analysis. We see no help to the solution to the paradoxes in restricting the validity of (1), although we might deny that there always *is* a singular term, even 'the proposition that p', which denotes a proposition expressed by 'p'.

On the other hand, we found that the realtion of *expression* between a sentence and a proposition could differ in extension between the object language and the metalanguage, even if the propositions involved were already available in the universe of the object language.

As I said earlier, I believe that the intensional point of view is more directly applicable to natural languages than the purely extensional. In English, what is said to be true or false is what is said, meant, believed, supposed, conjectured, claimed, asserted, and the like. It is certainly regimentation to identify each of these with a *proposition*, particularly in view of the implication of a uniform criterion of identity, say for two utterances to express the *same* proposition. But the lack of uniformity claimed by many writers can exist within a single "propositional attitude", so that it is not taken care of by merely splitting the notion of proposition into that of saying, meaning, belief, etc.

Are there English words that express something like the technical notion of expression? The words 'say' and 'mean' are certainly related, in that they can relate persons, or sentences, or utterances, or occasions of utterance to statements in indirect discourse of *what is said* or meant, and to truth or falsity. Saying figures essentially in the most 'ordinary' forms of the Liar paradox, such as 'What I am now saying is false'.

It seems that we would obtain a contradiction by assuming that in English the inference from 'p' uttered by a person S on an occasion O, to 'what S said on occasion O is true' is valid in both directions. For S could on occasion O say, 'S is on occasion O saying nothing that is true'.

Here we meet the question what could be meant by the charge on these grounds that English is "inconsistent", or, on the other hand, what a "solution" of the paradox is supposed to accomplish in application to English. What is meant by saying, as a descriptive remark about English, that a certain inference is *valid* between English sentences uttered on specific occasions? One thing we might be claiming is that facts about the truth-conditions of the sentences *determine* that they are valid. But an assignment of truth-conditions to sentences of English would have to satisfy some conditions of coherence, since it is not just an account of the beliefs of English speakers but an account of the conditions under which what they say is *in fact* true. But then it is hard to see how such an account could make English inconsistent: Herzberger (1967) describes plausible assumptions about an assignment of truth-conditions to sentences of a natural language from which it follows that the outcome of inconsistency is impossible, although it could still be that no such account can be given that can be squared with the data.

Alternatively, we may be trying to describe an aspect of the language by describing inferences that the speakers of the language characteristically make or would accept if others made them. But then the charge of inconsistency just comes to the claim that speakers of English have inconsistent beliefs, which, in general, no doubt they do.

In the specific case of the Liar paradox, the claim would be that speakers are disposed to accept all inferences of the form: from 'p' said by S on occasion O, to 'what S said on occasion O is true', and vice versa. That such a general disposition exists is highly likely. However, the empirical evidence (impressionistic to be sure, mostly based on the behavior of philosophers and their students) hardly bears out the idea that this amounts to a commitment to be honored come hell or high water. Confronted with the Liar paradox argument, almost anyone will recognize that something is fishy.

Most would doubt that they fully understand what is being said and suspect nonsense. The difficulty there is in agreeing on a "solution" can be interpreted to mean that speakers do accept these inferences as general principles and do not know what to believe when they see the difficulties that arise in this particular case, unless either indoctrination or their own theoretical reflection prompts them in one particular direction.

This view of the situation gives some scope for theory in dealing with the paradox. It may be that if we treat *all* the dispositions to accept statements and inferences involving 'say', 'mean', 'true', and 'false' as on the same level, the only conclusion we can arrive is at that it is impossible to attribute to all these words at once a coherent meaning. But a theory might be quite coherent and honor *most* of these dispositions, particularly those that come to light in ordinary situations. Then the others can be attributed to confusion, difficulty of understanding expressions used in very abstract contexts, and the like.

Suppose *A* says 'I am now saying something false'. Then, parallel to the argument for the claim that (2.1) does not express a proposition, I can prove using only 'ordinary' language, that *A* said nothing. Shall I go on to argue that since *A* said nothing, he did not say something false? And since he said that he *was* saying something false, he did after all say something false? Then I would be landed in a contradiction. The possibilities of escaping are manifold; there is perhaps even more than one in the spirit of our general discussion above.

'Say' in this discourse seems clearly to be ambiguous: the claim that *A* said nothing squares ill with the later inference from 'he said that he was saying something false' to 'he was saying something false'. To begin with, 'say' seems flexible with respect to the amount of sense required for someone to say something. Thus *A* may have said that he was saying something false, according to a lax standard, while saying nothing according to a stricter standard, needed for truth or falsity. Then the final, paradoxical inference is from '*A* said$_l$, that he was saying something false' and '*A* did not say$_s$ anything false' to '*A* said$_s$ something false'. But '*A* said that p' and '$\sim p$' imply '*A* said something false' only if the first premiss is true with the stricter standard.

This observation is only a first approximation to meeting a difficulty we met in the formal situation. *We* say of *A* that he did not say something false, after having shown that A said nothing. But then we express our conclusion by a sentence that is (modulo some changes of indexicals to accommodate the changed context) the negation of A's original remark. How can we have said something true or false if A did not? And how can we say of either ourselves or A that he did or did not without using such a phrase as 'says nothing' involving two of the essential elements, saying and quantification, of A's remark? And I do not see any grounds for proposing that 'A said nothing' is perfectly meaningful while 'A said nothing *false*' is not.

Must we admit that we say nothing when we say of A that *he* says nothing? The only possible rescue here must come from general considerations. These, however, reveal a further ambiguity or indexical variation in words such as 'say' that is relevant to the Liar paradox discourse.

It would seem that to attribute to A a definite general sense of 'say' is to attribute to him a general scheme for interpreting his own words and those of others. In real life, this scheme will be rather vaguely defined and shifting. For example, as regards the range of his own quantifiers, a speaker would generally have no more than certain commitments which put a lower limit on his universe. Most quantifiers in ordinary discourse are restricted and thus would give the interpreter great latitude in choosing a universe. No doubt in many situations where no restriction is explicitly stated, some is nonetheless intended, and a man interpreting himself will take this into account. But in many situations one will translate quantifiers homophonically.

Thus it seems clear that different occasions of use of a word such as 'say' can presuppose different schemes of interpretation. Moreover, it seems clear that the universe for the quantifiers does not have to be taken as constant for an entire language and even throughout a single discourse, so that this is one dimension with respect to which the schemes of interpretation presupposed in uses of words such as 'say' can differ. (Moreover, a general scheme for the semantics of a natural language would allow that the universe for quantifiers can vary with context.[18])

If all this is so, we can avoid imputing a contradiction to the Liar paradox discourse and yet allow a final inference to 'A after all said

---

[18] This seems clearly to be provided for in Herzberger's notion of 'type 3 conceptual framework' (1970a, p. 160).

something false' if we assume that the latter remark presupposes a more comprehensive scheme of interpretation than the discourse up to that point, which assigns sense or truth-values to utterances not covered by less comprehensive schemes. One way this might be is if the last remark presupposes a larger universe. The discourse up to that point vindicates the sense of *A*'s original remark by, in effect, refuting it. The last remark involves a semantical reflection that could be viewed as involving taking into one's ontology a proposition that had not been admitted before, perhaps because admitting it involves taking the universe of my own and *A*'s previous discourse as an object.

This way of interpreting the discourse attributes to the speakers an implicit theory according to which what is referred to when one talks of 'what is said' belongs to some kind of potential totality which is not exhausted by any set. This is, however, not crucial to distinguishing the interpretation presupposed in *A*'s original utterance and that presupposed in saying that he said something false.

A must presuppose a certain self-interpretation, however vaguely defined. It seems that an equivocation arises at the outset unless, in commenting on what *A* says, we presuppose the same interpretation as *A*'s. But both for us and for *A*, there is a strong temptation not to do this. For since *A* talks about what he is *saying* and we talk about what *A* said, *A*'s interpretation becomes part of what we are talking about.[19] Thus our interpretation is likely to involve reflection on *A*'s and thus be more comprehensive.

If this temptation is resisted, the above argument for the conclusion that *A* said nothing goes through. But then without passing to a more comprehensive scheme of interpretation, which changes the truth-conditions of statements involving 'say', we

---

[19] However, if we apply this remark literally in all cases of iteration of indirect-discourse operators, we shall arrive at a somewhat counterintuitive theory of them, which would assign to all occurrences of such operators subscripts such that in a context such as '*A* says that *B* says that . . .' the outer operator would have to have a higher subscript than the inner one: the sense of 'say' for *A* would have to be more comprehensive than that for *B*.

I do not have a precise theory that avoids this consequence, but it seems to me it must be possible to construct one, just as it is possible to construct predicative set theories that are not ramified (see Feferman, 1964, 1966). The passage to a more comprehensive scheme is forced on us in the Liar paradox because of the quantification over 'what is said' that cannot be cashed in terms of a particular utterance whose sense is given.

cannot go on to the paradoxical conclusion that A after all said something false.

If 'said$_1$' presupposes A's scheme of interpretation, and 'said$_2$' presupposes a scheme of ours that gives a sense of A's remark, then we can conclude that A said$_1$ nothing, it is not the case that A said$_1$ something false, and therefore, since A said$_2$ that he was saying$_1$ something false, A said$_2$ something false. But that is not what A said (1 or 2).

On the other hand, suppose that at the outset, when we inquire what A said, we presuppose the more comprehensive scheme. Then we ask whether A said$_2$ something true, but if so we can only conclude

(2) A said$_1$ something false.

From the fact that our scheme is more comprehensive, we might infer

(3) A said$_2$ something false

from which the negation of (2), and thus a contradiction, follow. Thus we can refute the hypothesis that A said$_2$ something true.

But if we now suppose A said$_2$ something false, we do not obtain a contradiction. We can infer the negation of (2), but to make the negation of (3) follow we need some such assumption as that A said$_1$ something true or false, which would yield a contradiction by the analogue of (3.3). Rejecting this assumption, we end up with the 'straightforward' conclusion that A did not say$_1$ anything true or false and thus said$_2$ something false. But again, this is not what A said.

In the discourse we have considered, there is a natural relation of the scheme of interpretation at the beginning and that at the end: the latter is more comprehensive. A more ambiguous case is the two-utterance Liar paradox, for example where A says

> B is saying something false

while B says

> A is saying something true.

Each might be thought of as purporting to have a scheme of interpretation that takes in the other's use of 'say' and is thus more comprehensive than the other's. But of course they cannot be simultaneously interpreted in this way. If we attribute to them the *same* scheme, then in those terms neither says anything. However, the sort of reasoning that shows that the typical Liar sentence says nothing will not show that *both* utterances say nothing: only that at least one does.[20] This only shows that formal principles such as (2.5) and (3.3) do not force on us the hierarchical point of view we have adopted.

If we attribute to B a more comprehensive scheme (saying$_B$) and to A a less comprehensive one (saying$_A$), then we can show that both A and B say$_A$ nothing while A says$_B$ something false. So what B says is false, at least in terms of a more comprehensive schem. If we assume A's scheme comprehends B's, it follows that A and B say$_B$ nothing, B says$_A$ something false, so that from outside what A says is true.

However vaguely defined the schemes of interpretation of the ordinary (and also not so ordinary) use of language may be, they arrange themselves naturally into a hierarchy, though clearly not a linearly ordered one. A scheme of interpretation that is 'more comprehensive' than another or involves 'reflection' on another will involve either a larger universe of discourse, or assignments of extensions or intensions to a broader body of discourse, or commitments as to the translation of more possible utterances. A less comprehensive interpretation can be appealed to in a discourse

---

[20] The relevance to my discussion of this sort of example was brought to my attention by Thomas Nagel.

Suppose α denotes the sentence

  β expresses a false proposition

and β denotes the sentence

  α expresses a true proposition.

Then it is consistent with (2.5) to suppose that neither expresses a proposition (and hence that both are 'from outside' false), or that α expresses a false proposition and β expresses none (and hence is 'from outside' false), or that β expresses a false proposition and α expresses none (and hence is 'from outside' true).

Similar latitude can arise for some single self-referential sentences. If γ denotes the sentence

  γ expresses a true proposition

(2.5) allows that γ expresses no proposition (and is false from outside) or expresses either a true or a false proposition. Since the truth condition for (2.1) is contradictory, that condition implies that (2.1) can express no proposition. The truth-condition for γ is tautological and hence imposes no constraints. But any account of (2.1) and γ is likely to treat them the same way.

for which a discourse using the more comprehensive interpretation is a metadiscourse.

To many the hierarchical approach to the semantical paradoxes has seemed implausible in application to natural languages because there seemed to be no division of a natural language into a hierarchy of 'languages' such that the higher ones contain the 'semantics' of the lower ones. Indeed, there is no such neat division of any language as a whole. What the objection fails to appreciate is just how far the variation in the truth-conditions of sentences of a natural language with the occasion of utterance can go, and in particular how this can arise for expressions that are crucially relevant to the semantic paradoxes: perhaps not 'true', but at all events quantifiers, 'say', 'mean', and other expressions that involve indirect speech.[21]

However, it would be naive to suppose that the type of account of indexical variation that is now standard in formal semantics can be fully adequate to the context-dependence of these expressions, which I have rather called 'systematic ambiguity' (note 13), which might be related to the 'typical ambiguity' of Whitehead and Russell. Herzberger (1970a) already shows the unavoidability of some such ambiguity. In a simple case such as that of the word 'I', we can describe a function that gives it a reference depending on some feature of the context of utterance (the speaker). We could treat the 'scheme of interpretation' in this way as argument to a function, but that of course is to treat it as an object, for example a set. But a discourse quantifying over *all* schemes of interpretation would, if not interpreted so that it did not really capture *all*, like talk of all sets interpreted over a set, have to have its quantifiers taken more absolutely, in which case it would not be covered by any scheme of

---

[21] It is interesting to compare the view of this paper with those of Charles Peirce. Emily Michael has discovered (1975) that Peirce early on realized one of the main difficulties that we have concentrated on: that a statement 'asserting' its own falsity or lack of truth may be assigned a truth-value by virtue of its not expressing a proposition. However, his final conclusion (*Collected Papers* 5.340) is that a sentence such as (2.2) is in a way self-contradictory: what it explicitly states is true (since it does *not* express a true proposition), but it tacitly implies something contradictory to what it states, since any statement tacitly implies its own truth (that it expresses a true proposition).

Such a contradiction would have to lie in the concepts of proposition and truth.

On our view (2.2) could only 'tacitly imply' its own truth on an interpretation more comprehensive than the one it talks about.

interpretation in the sense in question.[22] We could produce a 'superliar' paradox: a sentence that says of itself that it is not true under any scheme of interpretation. We would either have to prohibit semantic reflection on this discourse or extend the notion of scheme of interpretation to cover it. The most that can be claimed for the self-applicability of our discussion is that if it is given a precise sense by one scheme of interpretation, then there is *another* scheme of interpretation of our discourse which applies the discourse to itself under the *first* interpretation. But of course this remark applies to the concept 'scheme of interpretation' itself. Of it one must say what Herzberger says about truth (1970a, p. 150): in it 'there is something schematic . . . which requires filling in'.

Postscript, 1982*

Since the publication of this paper in 1974, a great deal of new work has been done on the semantic paradoxes. From the point of view of technical formal semantics, the picture as it had presented itself to me has been transformed. The first and largest step in this transformation was the work in 1975 of Saul Kripke.[23] Where the *philosophical* picture stands after this work is not obvious. In what follows I shall make some brief remarks about this.

---

[22] It seems to me that the best way to view the sort of truth-definition envisaged by Davidson (1967) is as involving such a fixing of the concept of scheme of interpretation. Once the definition itself is translated back into the language, it will of course no longer be complete.

Davidson's remarks (in 1967, pp. 314–15) suggest that he does not aim at completeness in this sense.

However, he writes, 'But it is not really clear how unfair to Urdu or Hindi it would be to view the range of their quantifiers as insufficient to yield an explicit definition of "true-in-Urdu" or "true-in-Hindi"'. What is to prevent a speaker of Urdu from learning enough set theory or semantics and contriving to express it in his language to give the lie to such limitation? Obviously Davidson must say that this would change the language (semantically at least). The definition of 'true-in-Urdu' could express a given stage of the development of Urdu and perhaps a hypothesis as to its future development.

[23] 'Outline of a Theory of Truth', reprinted in this volume. An idea similar to Kripke's was discovered independently, but not developed to the same extent, by Martin and Woodruff, 'On Representing "True-in-*L*" in *L*', also reprinted in this volume.

* This Postscript is a condensed version of material that appears in my book *Mathematics in Philosophy: Selected Essays*, copyright © 1983 by Cornell University Press. It is used here by permission of the publisher.

The writers discussed in section I above advanced "truth-value gap" approaches to the paradoxes as an *alternative* to a hierarchical approach in the spirit of Tarski or Russell.[24] My criticisms took them in this way. Kripke used truth-value gaps to construct a hierarchy that was in many ways more natural and satisfactory than the Tarskian hierarchy in its original form. By this the original opposition is in considerable measure *aufgehoben*. In a way, truth-value gaps arise even in my own more Tarskian treatment, since if one assumes the truth schema (3.3) one can prove that liar sentences are neither true nor false (p. 22 above). This suggests developing a theory with truth-value gaps in the framework of *classical* logic; see below.

Kripke reproaches earlier writers on the subject with not really having a theory; in practice this seems to mean a developed formal model, on the basis of which questions of truth, falsity, or truth-valuelessness can be given objective answers. As directed against me, the reproach is justified: though in some of my discussion I was running up against inherent limitations of such formal models, the general idea that a hierarchical account of truth in natural languages could be given by taking due account of the possibilities of contextual variation certainly called for working out in such terms. The analyses of section V offered only a very sketchy beginning. I have not carried the matter further since, but constructions largely in the spirit of my ideas have been carried out by Tyler Burge.[25]

My discussion makes two demands on a theory that seem to pull in different directions. On the one hand, I wanted to avoid too much shifting of the interpretation of indexical elements such as the range of quantifiers over propositions, indirect-discourse terms such as 'say', and 'true' when applied to sentences or utterances. That sentences should "seek their own levels", in Kripke's phrase, was a *desideratum* I hinted at vaguely, without in any way showing how to achieve it. But such shifts were *forced* by discourses involving paradoxical statements of the sort considered in sections II and III of the paper, in which one reasons by way of the paradox to the conclusion that a sentence *a* does not express a proposition, or is neither true nor false, and then deduces *a* itself, or its negation, from

---

[24] At the time of writing the paper, I did not sufficiently appreciate the affinity of my point of view and Russell's.

[25] 'Semantical Paradox', reprinted in this volume.

the statement of the deficiency inferred from the paradox. Only with a shift of what I called "scheme of interpretation" can one draw the natural conclusion that *a* is true (or false) without reinstating the contradiction. Following Burge,[26] I shall call such discourses Strengthened Liar discourses.

Kripke's theory enables us to avoid such shifts in many other situations, but not in these. So long as we are dealing with sentences that are grounded by Kripke's definition or another in the same spirit, Kripke's theory obviously provides a more flexible instrument than the more strictly Tarskian paradigm I followed most of the time. A Kripkean fixed-point model could be taken as a model for a "scheme of interpretation" of a certain kind of maximal comprehensiveness. In this way one can minimize the attribution of shifts of scheme. But Kripke's theory changes nothing essential in the interpretation of Strengthened Liar situations. Suppose, for example, that α denotes $\sim T\alpha$; since it is paradoxical in Kripke's sense, it is undefined at any fixed point model. Since it is undefined, it is not true, but just for this reason it does not express what we mean when we say that. The intuitive argument that since α is undefined it is certainly not true, which would lead to the conclusion $\sim T\alpha$, does not go through, however one solves a problem Kripke does not address, of formulating the principles of reasoning for a language with truth-value gaps,[27] since one cannot derive an undefined conclusion from true premises. Within Kripke's general framework, we could obtain the conclusion $\sim T\alpha$ by a shift in the extension of T by what he calls "closing off" (this volume, p. 80).

Modifications of Kripke's constructions are possible in which we hold to classical two-valued logic but build up the extensions of two predicates T and F of truth and falsity. Monotonicity is preserved by considering only sentences equivalent to those in which T and F occur positively.[28] If again α denotes $\sim T\alpha$, we can now derive $\sim T\alpha$ and $\sim F\alpha$, but without a shift of scheme we cannot conclude that α, which says it is not true, is true after all. Even at a fixed point, the inference is blocked because T occurs non-positively in $\sim T\alpha$.

---

[26] *Ibid.*, p. 87 of this volume. As the editor has pointed out to me, Burge's use of this term does not quite agree with earlier usage. The difficulty is what Martin, in his Introduction above, calls the 'revenge problem'.

[27] See Solomon Feferman, 'Toward Useful Type-Free Theories, I', reprinted in this volume, §10.

[28] Here I follow Feferman, op. cit., §13.

The most thorough investigation of the problem of interpreting Strengthened Liar discourses is that of Tyler Burge (see note 25). Agreeing with me both in discerning contextual shifts in the interpretation of key terms at crucial points and in the preference for classical logic, he has offered both formal models and a very instructive system of pragmatic principles for determining the manner in which the interpretation of semantically relevant terms is fixed by the context. In the formal models, numerical subscripts are attached to semantical predicates, which in our terms represent different schemes of interpretation. We obtain something close to his Construction C3 (this volume, p. 104) in the following way, using the above-discussed classical-logic variant of Kripke's construction. For each natural number n we have predicates T_n and F_n of truth and falsity of level n. Then we can define by induction a sequence M_0, $M_1, \ldots$ of models such that for each n, T_i, F_i for $i < n$ are treated in M_n as if they belonged to the base language and interpreted as in M_i, while for $i \geqslant n$ all the T_i, F_i are treated on the same plane as truth/falsity predicates, and M_n is the minimal fixed point *extending* M_{n-1} (simply the minimal fixed point if $n = 0$). A final model M_ω is obtained by giving to each T_n, F_n their extensions in M_n. M_ω leads to the same interpretations as C3 of the various paradoxical discourses Burge considers. The use of fixed point models means that a shift to a higher level is required only in cases of ungroundedness.

I agree with Burge and probably disagree with Kripke in thinking that some Strengthened Liar discourses belong to a part of the language that is ordinary enough so that any semantic theory should offer an account of them.[29] They are more ordinary than grounded sentences of even moderately high level (say $\geqslant \omega^\omega$). However, in general I do not believe there is a sharp line between ordinary language and what goes beyond it, in particular with respect to complexity of semantic reflection.

Burge's use in his formal constructions of numerical subscripts suggests the thesis that arbitrary finite levels would be sufficient for

---

[29] Burge, 'Semantical Paradox', esp. note 9 (p. 88 of this volume). Kripke remarks that the models he presents 'are plausible as models of natural language at a stage before we reflect on the generating process associated with the concept of truth, the stage which continues in the daily life of nonphilosophical speakers' ('Outline', note 34 (p. 80 of this volume)). If by the 'generating process' he means the recursion leading to a fixed point, it should be pointed out that reflection on it does not enter into simple Strengthened Liar situations themselves and does not play an essential role in the type of interpretation Burge and I advocate.

describing the indexicality of 'true', even in the face of paradoxes. A possible reason would be that since the levels do not appear as *arguments*, there is no way of referring to an infinity of levels at once and thus forcing an ascent into the transfinite.[30] I doubt this. My main reason is that the notion of truth *under an interpretation* is also expressed naturally using the word 'true' and was so before the word 'interpretation' was given a technical sense in model-theoretic semantics. But then the practical effect of having the levels as arguments can be achieved by using the language of truth under an interpretation, or of understanding sentences so that what they say is true. One may perhaps shunt the indexicality of 'true' onto something else (as is done in the propositional approaches of my paper) and thus save the letter of the finite-levels thesis, but then transfinite levels will just turn up elsewhere.[31]

The interpretations of Strengthened Liar situations arising from my own and Burge's approach will seem to some to be rationalizations introduced merely because of an a priori methodological preference for finding consistency in the use of language. The style of interpretation would exhibit what Charles Chihara aptly calls "the consistency view of truth", as I understand it, the view that there is a consistent set of rules fitting the known facts, which will serve as the set of rules implicitly followed by English speakers in using the word 'true'.[32] My remarks on this issue in the paper (pp. 31–5) endorse this view with important qualifications. But whether there is such a set of rules that can be squared with the facts of usage is in the end an empirical question, even granted that interpretation is to some degree rationalization. Though I think that the appeal to indexicality in interpreting the Strengthened Liar is an important step toward describing such a set of rules, even after the advances in Burge's work a more systematic theory would be desirable, one that would deal with the relations of truth, indirect discourse, proposition-like concepts, and the ranges of quantifiers. Indirect discourse and propositions offer other notorious difficulties.

---

[30] 'Semantical Paradox', p. 108 of this volume. However, Burge has informed me that he had ceased to hold the finite-levels thesis before completing the paper. No statement in the paper explicitly commits him to it.

[31] A more direct counterexample to the finite-levels thesis can be constructed if one allows infinite discourses, as in Burge (1982).

[32] Chihara (1979), p. 607. Chihara's actual formulation seems to me not to capture his intended meaning.

To say that we can attribute to speakers a *consistent* set of rules in their use of 'true' and related locutions is not to say that we can describe a *complete* set or that we should expect it to be unique. Clearly in this domain as in related ones in logic, incompleteness is the price of consistency. This shows itself in the inescapable "systematic ambiguities" discussed in the paper. One reason for preferring the verdict of incompleteness over inconsistency in our description of natural language is that we know that no rational reconstruction or linguistic reform will avoid the same fate.[33]

References

Burge, Tyler: 1982, 'The Liar Paradox: Tangles and Chains', *Philosophical Studies* 41, 353–66.

Cartwright, Richard L.: 1962, 'Propositions', in R. J. Butler (ed.), *Analytical Philosophy*, Blackwell, Oxford, pp. 81–103.

Chihara, Charles: 1979, 'The Semantic Paradoxes: A Diagnostic Investigation', *Philosophical Review* 88, 590–618.

Davidson, Donald: 1967, 'Truth and Meaning', *Synthese* 17, 304–23.

Davidson, Donald: 1968, 'On Saying That', *Synthese* 19, 130–46; also in D. Davidson and J. Hintikka (eds.), *Words and Objections*, Reidel, Dordrecht (1969), pp. 158–74.

Davidson, Donald and Harman, Gilbert (eds.): 1972, *Semantics of Natural Language*, Reidel, Dordrecht.

Feferman, Solomon: 1964, 'Systems of Predicative Analysis', *The Journal of Symbolic Logic* 29, 1–30.

Feferman, Solomon: 1966, 'Predicative Provability in Set Theory', *Bulletin of the American Mathematical Society* 72, 486–9.

Fitch, Frederic B.: 1970, 'Comments and a Suggestion', in Martin (1970), pp. 75–8.

Gödel, Kurt: 1940, *The Consistency of the Continuum Hypothesis*, Princeton University Press.

Harman, Gilbert: 1972, 'Logical Form', *Foundations of Language* 9, 38–65.

Herzberger, Hans G.: 1967, 'The Truth-Conditional Consistency of Natural Languages', *The Journal of Philosophy* 64, 29–35.

Herzberger, Hans G.: 1970a, 'Paradoxes of Grounding in Semantics', *The Journal of Philosophy* 67, 145–67.

Herzberger, Hans G.: 1970b, 'Truth and Modality in Semantically Closed Languages', in Martin (1970), pp. 25–46.

---

[33] To this issue as to others discussed in this Postscript, the Naive Semantics of Hans Herzberger and the closely related Rule of Revision theory of Anil Gupta are highly relevant. Space has not permitted including these important developments in my comments. But see the longer version of this Postscript in *Mathematics in Philosophy* (see above).

Higginbotham, James: 1972, Review of Martin (1970), *The Journal of Philosophy* 69, 398–401.

Higginbotham, James: 1973, 'Some Problems in Semantics and Radical Translation', Thesis, Columbia University.

Kneale, William: 1972, 'Propositions and Truth in Natural Languages', *Mind* (N.S.) 81, 225–43.

Lewis, David: 1971, 'General Semantics', *Synthese* 22, 18–67; also in Davidson and Harman (1972), pp. 169–218.

Martin, Robert L. (ed.): 1970, *The Paradox of the Liar*, Yale University Press, New Haven.

Martin, Robert L.: 1976, 'Are Natural Languages Universal?', *Synthese* 32, 271–91.

Michael, Emily: 1975, 'Peirce's Paradoxical Solution of the Liar's Paradox', *Notre Dame Journal of Formal Logic* 16, 369–74.

Montague, Richard: 1970, 'Pragmatics and Intensional Logic', *Dialectica* 24, 277–302; also *Synthese* 22, 69–94; also in Davidson and Harman (1972), pp. 142–68.

Parsons, Charles: 1971, 'Ontology and Mathematics', *Philosophical Review* 80, 151–76.

Parsons, Charles: 1974a, 'Informal Axiomatization, Formalization, and the Concept of Truth', *Synthese* 27, 27–47.

Parsons, Charles: 1974b, 'Sets and Classes', *Noûs* 8, 1–12.

Quine, W. V.: 1963, *Set Theory and its Logic*, Harvard University Press, Cambridge, Mass. Also 2nd ed. (1969).

Quine, W. V.: 1969, *Ontological Relativity and Other Essays*, Columbia University Press, New York.

Quine, W. V.: 1970, *Philosophy of Logic*, Prentice-Hall, Englewood Cliffs, N.J.

Skyrms, Brian: 1970a, 'Return of the Liar: Three-Valued Logic and the Concept of Truth', *American Philosophical Quarterly* 7, 153–61.

Skyrms, Brian: 1970b, 'Notes on Quantification and Self-Reference', in Martin (1970), pp. 67–74.

van Fraassen, Bas C.: 1968, 'Presumption, Implication, and Self-Reference', *The Journal of Philosophy* 65, 136–52.

van Fraassen, Bas C.: 1970a, 'Truth and Paradoxical Consequences', in Martin (1970), pp. 13–23.

van Fraassen, Bas C.: 1970b, 'Rejoinder: On a Kantian Conception of Language', in Martin (1970), pp. 59–66.

van Fraassen, Bas C.: 1970c, 'Inference and Self-reference', *Synthese* 21, 425–38; also in Davidson and Harman (1972), pp. 695–708.

On Representing 'True-in-*L*' in *L*

Robert L. Martin and Peter W. Woodruff

Given Tarski's familiar treatment of the semantic paradoxes, no formal language can adequately represent its own truth-concept.[1] But natural languages do, apparently, express their own truth-concepts and this fact alone has been enough to motivate some to seek alternative treatments of the paradoxes. In this paper we demonstrate that a language construed according to the 'category' approach,[2] modified in certain respects, can indeed express its own truth-concept.

Section I specifies the language to be studied; Section II contains the proof of the truth-representation theorem for the language. It will be seen that the possibility of truth-representation of the kind under consideration depends only on the satisfaction of rather simple conditions—conditions which clearly may be met in ways other than given here.

I.

L is a usual first-order quantificational language, including a one-place predicate constant '*T*' (to be interpreted as the truth-predicate for *L*), and with conjunction, negation, and the universal quantifier taken as primitive. There is one difference: the individual variables come in a finite number of sorts (associated with the variables is a function *s* from the positive integers into the *k* integers $1, 2, \ldots, k$, where, for positive integer i, $s(i)$ is the *sort* of the variable x_i). The sorting of variables plays no role in the definition of wff. We identify *L* with the set of its wffs.

Robert L. Martin and Peter W. Woodruff 'On Representing "True-in-*L*" in *L*', reprinted from *Philosophia* 5 (1975) 213–217. Reprinted by permission of D. Reidel Publishing Company.

First published 1975 in *Philosophia*. Reprinted in A. Kasher (ed.), *Language in Focus*. Copyright © 1976 by D. Reidel Publishing Company, Dordrecht, Holland.

[1] Tarski (1956).

[2] See Martin (1967), (1968), (1970).

For the truth-functional connectives we use Kleene's weak three-valued truth-tables,[3] labeled by $\wedge$ and $-$; shown in Table (A).

B

$A \wedge B$	$t \quad u \quad f$	$\bar{A}$
t	$t \quad u \quad f$	f
(A) A u	$u \quad u \quad u$	u
f	$f \quad u \quad f$	t

We use the quantifier $\forall$ so that for any $X \subseteq \{t, u, f\}$, $\forall X = t$ iff $X = \{t\}$, $\forall X = u$ iff $u \in X$, $\forall X = f$ otherwise.

As ranges for the sorted variables we provide a sortally segmented domain. A function v is a *valuation* on a domain $D = U_1 \cup U_2 \cup \ldots \cup U_k$ iff

(1)   for every i, $1 \leqslant i \leqslant k$, U_i is a non-empty set
(2) v assigns to each individual constant an element of D
(3) v assigns to each n-ary predicate an element of $\{t, u, f\}^{D^n}$.

A *value assignment* α is an assignment to each individual variable x_i of an element of $U_{s(i)}$. Then we may define a unique value $v\alpha$ for each term and wff as follows (where α_d^x is like α except that $\alpha_d^x x = d$):

$v\alpha x = \alpha x$ for individual variable x
$v\alpha a = va$ for individual constant a
$v\alpha F t_1 \ldots t_n = vF(v\alpha t_1, v\alpha t_2, \ldots, v\alpha t_n)$
$v\alpha \sim A = v\alpha A$ *for wff* A
$v\alpha(A \mathbin{\&} B) = v\alpha A \wedge v\alpha B$
$V\alpha(x_i)A = \forall\{v\alpha_d^{x_i} A : d \in U_{s(i)}\}$[4]

---

[3] Kleene (1950, p. 334). The use of the weak tables is not necessary for the proof of our theorem. An argument for their use, based upon category considerations and independent of the paradoxes, is given in Martin (1974). Our argument in the present paper may be adapted to any set of truth-functions ϕ which include t and f in their field and have the following properties (enunciated in Fine (1974)):

Stability: If ϕ has the value t for given truth-values as arguments, it retains that value when any argument not in $\{t, f\}$ is replaced by one of the latter.

Fidelity: Whenever all arguments are in $\{t, f\}$, ϕ behaves classically (e.g. in the present case we have $t \wedge t = t$, $t \wedge f = f \wedge t = f \wedge f = f$).

[4] We wish to preserve the usual relationship between universal quantification and conjunction. This, along with the adoption of Kleene's weak truth-tables, accounts for the requirement that $\forall X = u$ whenever $u \in X$. If the domain were not divided into sortal segments, each containing the values of one sort of variable, the above requirement would lead to excessively counter-intuitive consequences. For example, if

We note that the usual local determination lemma holds:

Lemma 0: If v and v', α and α' coincide on the constants, predicates and free variables of A, then $v\alpha A = v'\alpha' A$.

An immediate corollary is that for sentences (closed wffs) A, $v\alpha A$ is independent of α, and we may write simply vA.

II.

For each predicate F we define the truth and falsity ranges (on a valuation v) as follows:

$$vF^+ = \{\langle d_1,\ldots,d_n\rangle : vF(d_1,\ldots,d_n) = t\}$$
$$vF^- = \{\langle d_1,\ldots,d_n\rangle : vF(d_1,\ldots,d_n) = f\}$$

If v and v' are valuations in the same domain D, we say that v' is a *T-extension* of v if they coincide except that $vT^+ \subseteq V'T^+$ and $vT^- \subseteq v'T^-$. 'T', it will be recalled, is to be our truth-predicate. We designate this relation by '$<$'; it is clearly a partial ordering.

Lemma 1. If $v < v'$, then for every α in D, and wff A, $v\alpha A = t \Rightarrow v'\alpha A = t$ *and* $v\alpha A = f \Rightarrow v'\alpha A = f$.

Proof: By induction on A.

Let V be a $<$-chain of valuations in D. By $\bar{V}$ we mean the valuation which coincides with the elements of V except at T, and such that $\bar{V}T^+ = \bigcup_{v \in V} vT^+$ and $\bar{V}T^- = \bigcup_{v \in V} vT^-$. It is clear that $\bar{V}$ is an upper bound of V; i.e., for each $v \in V$, $v < \bar{V}$.

Let v be a valuation in a domain $D = U_1 \cup U_2 \cup \ldots \cup U_k$ such that, for some, j, $1 \leqslant j \leqslant k$, $L = U_j$. Thus the wffs of L are made to constitute one of the sortal segments of the domain of v. We say that v *partially represents truth* (by 'T') for L iff both $vT(A) = t \Rightarrow vA = t$ and $vT(A) = f \Rightarrow vA = f$ for each sentence $A \in L$. Let PR be the set of all v satisfying this condition. (If both implications are biconditionals, the qualification 'partially' may be dropped.)

We wish to show *not* merely that L has truth-representing interpretations, for this holds even where the semantics of L is

the domain consisted of abstract and concrete objects, and the sortal range of the predicate F ('is yellow') were restricted to concrete objects, then even if the domain contained a yellow object, the sentence '$(\exists x) Fx$' would be without truth-value. With the segmented domain, and the variable x ranging over the segment containing the concrete objects, '$(\exists x) Fx$' would be true.

classical (as long as certain conditions are met; for example, that there is no individual constant a of L such that $va = \sim Ta$). We wish to show that L has truth-representing interpretations even where there are no restrictions against self-reference.

Lemma 2. Let V be an $<$-chain of valuations in D. If $V \subseteq PR$, then $\bar{V} \in PR$.

Proof. Suppose $\bar{V}T(A) = t$. Then $A \in \bar{V}T^+$, so for some $v \in V$, $A \in vT^+$; hence, $vT(A) = t$, and since $v \in PR$, we have $vA = t$, so (since $v < \bar{V}$) $\bar{V}A = t$ (by Lemma 1). The argument is similar if $\bar{V}T(A) = f$.

By Zorn's lemma it follows from Lemma 2:

Lemma 3. Every partially representing valuation has a maximal partially representing T-extension.

Our final lemma shows that maximal elements of PR have the right property:

Lemma 4. If v is maximal in PR, then v represents truth (by T).

Proof. Suppose $vA = t$ and v' coincides with v except that $v'T(A) = t$. Then $v < v'$ by construction: we show that $v' \in PR$. Indeed, if $v'T(B) = t$, and $B = A$, then $vB = t$ by hypothesis; if $B \neq A$, $vT(B) = v'T(B) = t$, so since $v \in PR$, $vB = t$. In either case, by Lemma 1, $v'B = t$. The argument is similar if $v'T(B) = f$; hence $v' \in PR$. Since v is maximal in PR, we must have.$v = v'$, so $vT(A) = t$. A symmetrical argument shows that if $vA = f$, $vT(A) = f$.

We may now state our theorem:

Theorem: Let v be any valuation in domain $D = U_1 \cup U_2 \cup \ldots \cup U_k$ such that, for some j, $1 \leqslant j \leqslant k$, $L = U_j$. Then there is a valuation v' which coincides with v on all sentences not containing 'T', and which represents truth (by 'T'). (v may be a classical valuation: i.e., for every predicate F we may have only t and f in the range of vF.)

Proof. Let v'' be like v except that $v''T^+ = v''T^- = \Lambda$. Then v'' coincides with v on non-T sentences (by Lemma 0) and the same will be true of every T-extension of v_v. Furthermore, v'' is trivially in PR. But by the preceding lemmata there is a T-extension v' of v'' which represents truth by 'T' (and coincides with v'', and hence with v, except on 'T').

We close with a couple of brief applications.

(1) Let L contain an individual constant a, and let v_0 be a valuation of the T- and a-free fragment of L. Let v_1 and v_2 be like v_0 except that $v_1 a = v_2 a = T a$, $v_1 T^+ = \{Ta\}$, $v_1 T^- = \Lambda$, $v_2 T^+ = \Lambda$, and $v_2 T^- = \{Ta\}$. Then it is easy to see that both v_1 and v_2 partially represent truth by T, and hence have truth-representing extensions. This is a reflection of the observation that 'This sentence is true' is true if true and false if false.

(2) Let v be truth-representing and let $va = \neg Ta$. Then $v\neg Ta = t$ iff $vTa = f$ iff $va \in vT^-$ iff $\neg Ta \in vT^-$ iff (since v is truth-representing) $v\neg Ta = f$. Hence $v\neg Ta = u$ on any such valuation; the Liar is neither true nor false.

References

Fine, K., 1974, 'Vagueness, Truth and Logic', *Synthese* 30, 265–300.

Kleene, S. C., 1950, *Introduction to Metamathematics*, Van Nostrand, New York.

Martin, R. L., 1967, 'Toward a Solution to the Liar Paradox', *The Philosophical Review* 76, 279–311.

Martin, R. L., 1968, 'On Grelling's Paradox', *The Philosophical Review* 77, 321–31.

Martin, R. L., 1970, 'A Category Solution to the Liar', in R. L. Martin (ed.), *The Paradox of the Liar*, Yale Univ. Press, London and New Haven, pp. 91–112.

Martin, R. L., 1974, 'Sortal Ranges for Complex Predicates', *The Journal of Philosophical Logic* 3, 159–67.

Tarski, Alfred, 1956, 'The Concept of Truth in Formalized Languages', in *Logic, Semantics, Metamathematics*, Oxford Univ. Press, pp. 152–278.

Outline of a Theory of Truth*

Saul Kripke

I. The Problem

Ever since Pilate asked, "What is truth?" (John xviii, 38), the subsequent search for a correct answer has been inhibited by another problem, which, as is well known, also arises in a New Testament context. If, as the author of the Epistle to Titus supposes (Titus I, 12), a Cretan prophet, "even a prophet of their own", asserted that "the Cretans are always liars", and if "this testimony is true" of all other Cretan utterances, then it seems that the Cretan prophet's words are true if and only if they are false. And any treatment of the concept of truth must somehow circumvent this paradox.

The Cretan example illustrates one way of achieving self-reference. Let $P(x)$ and $Q(x)$ be predicates of sentences. Then in some cases empirical evidence establishes that the sentence '$(x)(P(x) \supset Q(x))$' [or '$(\exists x)(P(x) \wedge Q(x))$', or the like] itself satisfies the predicate $P(x)$; sometimes the empirical evidence shows that it is the *only* object

Saul Kripke, "Outline of a Theory of Truth", reprinted from *The Journal of Philosophy* 72 (1975), 690–716. Copyright © 1975 *The Journal of Philosophy*. Reprinted by permission of the Editor of *The Journal of Philosophy* and the author.

* Presented in an American Philosophical Association symposium on Truth, December 28, 1975.

Originally it was understood that I would present this paper orally without submitting a prepared text. At a relatively late date, the editors of *The Journal of Philosophy* requested that I submit at least an "outline" of my paper. I agreed that this would be useful. I received the request while already committed to something else, and had to prepare the present version in tremendous haste, without even the opportunity to revise the first draft. Had I had the opportunity to revise, I might have expanded the presentation of the basic model in sec. III so as to make it clearer. The text shows that a great deal of the formal and philosophical material, and the proofs of results, had to be omitted.

Abstracts of the present work were presented by title at the Spring, 1975, meeting of the Association for Symbolic Logic held in Chicago. A longer version was presented as three lectures at Princeton University, June, 1975. I hope to publish another more detailed version elsewhere. Such a longer version should contain technical claims made here without proof, and much technical and philosophical material unmentioned or condensed in this outline.

satisfying $P(x)$. In this latter case, the sentence in question "says of itself" that it satisfies $Q(x)$. If $Q(x)$ is the predicate[1] 'is false', the Liar paradox results. As an example, let $P(x)$ abbreviate the predicate 'has tokens printed in copies of the *Journal of Philosophy*, November 6, 1975, p. 691, line 5'. Then the sentence:

$$(x)(P(x) \supset Q(x))$$

leads to paradox if $Q(x)$ is interpreted as falsehood.

The versions of the Liar paradox which use empirical predicates already point up one major aspect of the problem: *many, probably most, of our ordinary assertions about truth and falsity are liable, if the empirical facts are extremely unfavorable, to exhibit paradoxical features.* Consider the ordinary statement, made by Jones:

(1)   Most (i.e., a majority) of Nixon's assertions about Watergate are false.

Clearly, nothing is intrinsically wrong with (1), nor is it ill-formed. Ordinarily the truth value of (1) will be ascertainable through an enumeration of Nixon's Watergate-related assertions, and an assessment of each for truth or falsity. Suppose, however, that Nixon's

---

[1] I follow the usual convention of the "semantic" theory of truth in taking truth and falsity to be predicates true of sentences. If truth and falsity primarily apply to propositions or other nonlinguistic entities, read the predicate of sentences as "expresses a truth".

I have chosen to take sentences as the primary truth vehicles *not* because I think that the objection that truth is primarily a property of propositions (or "statements") is irrelevant to serious work on truth or to the semantic paradoxes. On the contrary, I think that ultimately a careful treatment of the problem may well need to separate the "expresses" aspect (relating sentences to propositions) from the "truth" aspect (putatively applying to propositions). I have not investigated whether the semantic paradoxes present problems when directly applied to propositions. The main reason I apply the truth predicate directly to linguistic objects is that for such objects a mathematical theory of self-reference has been developed. (See also footnote 32.)

Further, a more developed version of the theory would allow languages with demonstratives and ambiguities and would speak of utterances, sentences under a reading, and the like, as having truth value. In the informal exposition this paper does not attempt to be precise about such matters. Sentences are the official truth vehicles, but informally we occasionally talk about utterances, statements, assertions, and so on. Occasionally we may speak as if every utterance of a sentence in the language makes a statement, although below we suggest that a sentence may fail to make a statement if it is paradoxical or ungrounded. We are precise about such issues only when we think that imprecision may create confusion or misunderstanding. Like remarks apply to conventions about quotation.

assertions about Watergate are evenly balanced between the true and the false, except for one problematic case,

(2)   Everything Jones says about Watergate is true.

Suppose, in addition, that (1) is Jones's sole assertion about Watergate, or alternatively, that all his Watergate-related assertions except perhaps (1) are true. Then it requires little expertise to show that (1) and (2) are both paradoxical: they are true if and only if they are false.

The example of (1) points up an important lesson: it would be fruitless to look for an *intrinsic* criterion that will enable us to sieve out—as meaningless, or ill-formed—those sentences which lead to paradox. (1) is, indeed, the paradigm of an ordinary assertion involving the notion of falsity; just such assertions were characteristic of our recent political debate. Yet no syntactic or semantic feature of (1) guarantees that it is unparadoxical. Under the assumptions of the previous paragraph, (1) leads to paradox.[2] Whether such assumptions hold depends on the empirical facts about Nixon's (and other) utterances, not on anything intrinsic to the syntax and semantics of (1). (Even the subtlest experts may not be able to avoid utterances leading to paradox. It is said that Russell once asked Moore whether he always told the truth, and that he regarded Moore's negative reply as the sole falsehood Moore had ever produced. Surely no one had a keener nose for paradox than Russell. Yet he apparently failed to realize that if, as he thought, all Moore's *other* utterances were true, Moore's negative reply was not simply false but paradoxical.[3]) The moral: an adequate theory must allow our statements involving the notion of truth to be *risky*: they risk being paradoxical if the empirical facts are extremely (and unexpectedly) unfavorable. There can be no syntactic or semantic "sieve" that will winnow out the "bad" cases while preserving the "good" ones.

I have concentrated above on versions of the paradox using empirical properties of sentences, such as being uttered by particular people. Gödel showed essentially that such empirical properties are

---

[2] Both Nixon and Jones may have made their respective utterances without being aware that the empirical facts make them paradoxical.

[3] On an ordinary understanding (as opposed to the conventions of those who state Liar paradoxes), the question lay in the sincerity, not the truth, of Moore's utterances. Paradoxes could probably be derived on this interpretation also.

dispensable in favor of purely syntactic properties: he showed that, for each predicate $Q(x)$, a syntactic predicate $P(x)$ can be produced such that the sentence $(x)(P(x) \supset Q(x))$ is demonstrably the only object satisfying $P(x)$. Thus, in a sense, $(x)(P(x) \supset Q(x))$ "says of itself" that it satisfies $Q(x)$. He also showed that elementary syntax can be interpreted in number theory. In this way, Gödel put the issue of the legitimacy of self-referential sentences beyond doubt; he showed that they are as incontestably legitimate as arithmetic itself. But the examples using empirical predicates retain their importance: they point up the moral about riskiness.

A simpler, and more direct, form of self-reference uses demonstratives or proper names: Let 'Jack' be a name of the sentence 'Jack is short', and we have a sentence that says of itself that it is short. I can see nothing wrong with "direct" self-reference of this type. If 'Jack' is not already a name in the language,[4] why can we not introduce it as a name of any entity we please? In particular, why can it not be a name of the (uninterpreted) finite sequence of marks 'Jack is short'? (Would it be permissible to call this sequence of marks "Harry", but not "Jack"? Surely prohibitions on naming are arbitrary here.) There is no vicious circle in our procedure, since we need not *interpret* the sequence of marks 'Jack is short' before we name it. Yet if we name it "Jack", it at once becomes meaningful and true. (Note that I am speaking of self-referential sentences, not self-referential propositions.[5])

In a longer version, I would buttress the conclusion of the preceding paragraph not only by a more detailed philosophical exposition, but also by a mathematical demonstration that the simple kind of self-reference exemplified by the "Jack is short" example could actually be used to prove the Gödel incompleteness theorem itself (and also, the Gödel–Tarski theorem on the undefinability of truth). Such a presentation of the proof of the Gödel theorem might be more perspicuous to the beginner than is the usual one. It also dispels the impression that Gödel was forced to replace direct self-reference by a more circumlocutory device. The argument must be omitted from this outline.[6]

[4] We assume that 'is short' *is* already in the language.

[5] It is *not* obviously possible to apply this technique to obtain "directly" self-referential *propositions*.

[6] There are several ways of doing it, using either a nonstandard Gödel numbering where statements can contain numerals designating their own Gödel numbers, or a standard Gödel numbering, plus added constants of the type of 'Jack'.

It has long been recognized that some of the intuitive trouble with Liar sentences is shared with such sentences as

(3) (3) is true.

which, though not paradoxical, yield no determinate truth conditions. More complicated examples include a pair of sentences each one of which says that the other is true, and an infinite sequence of sentences $\{P_i\}$, where P_i says that P_{i+1} is true. In general, if a sentence such as (1) asserts that (all, some, most, etc.) of the sentences of a certain class C are true, its truth value can be ascertained if the truth values of the sentences in the class C are ascertained. If some of these sentences themselves involve the notion of truth, their truth value in turn must be ascertained by looking at *other* sentences, and so on. If ultimately this process terminates in sentences not mentioning the concept of truth, so that the truth value of the original statement can be ascertained, we call the original sentence *grounded*; otherwise, ungrounded.[7] As the example of (1) indicates, whether a sentence is grounded is not in general an intrinsic (syntactic or semantic) property of a sentence, but usually depends on the empirical facts. We make utterances which we hope will turn out to be grounded. Sentences such as (3), though not paradoxical, are ungrounded. The preceding is a rough sketch of the usual notion of groundedness and is not meant to provide a formal definition: the fact that a formal definition can be provided will be a principal virtue of the formal theory suggested below.[8]

II. Previous Proposals

Thus far the only approach to the semantic paradoxes that has been worked out in any detail is what I will call the "orthodox approach",

---

[7] If a sentence asserts, e.g., that all sentences in class C are true, we allow it to be false and grounded if one sentence in C is false, irrespective of the groundedness of the other sentences in C.

[8] Under that name, groundedness seems to have been first explicitly introduced into the literature in Hans Herzberger, "Paradoxes of Grounding in Semantics", *The Journal of Philosophy*, XVII, 6 (March 26, 1970): 145–67. Herzberger's paper is based on unpublished work on a "groundedness" approach to the semantic paradoxes undertaken jointly with Jerrold J. Katz. The intuitive notion of groundedness in semantics surely was part of the folklore of the subject much earlier. As far as I know, the present work gives the first rigorous definition.

which leads to the celebrated hierarchy of languages of Tarski.[9] Let L_0 be a formal language, built up by the usual operations of the first-order predicate calculus from a stock of (completely defined) primitive predicates, and adequate to discuss its own syntax (perhaps using arithmetization). (I omit an exact characterization.) Such a language cannot contain its own truth predicate, so a metalanguage L_1 contains a truth (really satisfaction) predicate $T_1(x)$ for L_0. (Indeed, Tarski shows how to define such a predicate in a higher-order language.) The process can be iterated, leading to a sequence $\{L_0, L_1, L_2, L_3, \ldots\}$ of languages, each with a truth predicate for the preceding.

Philosophers have been suspicious of the orthodox approach as an analysis of our intuitions. Surely our language contains just one word 'true', not a sequence of distinct phrases $\ulcorner\text{true}_n\urcorner$, applying to sentences of higher and higher levels. As against this objection, a defender of the orthodox view (if he does not dismiss natural language altogether, as Tarski inclined to do) may reply that the ordinary notion of truth is systematically ambiguous: "level" in a particular occurrence is determined by the context of the utterance and the intentions of the speaker. The notion of differing truth predicates, each with its own level, seems to correspond to the following intuitive idea, implicit in the discussion of "groundedness" above. First, we make various utterances, such as 'snow is white', which do not involve the notion of truth. We then attribute truth values to these, using a predicate 'true$_1$'. ('True$_1$' means—roughly— "is a true statement not itself involving truth or allied notions.") We can then form a predicate 'true$_2$' applying to sentences involving 'true$_1$', and so on. We may assume that, on each occasion of

---

[9] By an "orthodox approach", I mean any approach that works within classical quantification theory and requires all predicates to be totally defined on the range of the variables. Various writers speak as if the "hierarchy of languages" or Tarskian approach *prohibited* one from forming, for example, languages with certain kinds of self-reference, or languages containing their own truth predicates. On my interpretation, there are no *prohibitions*; there are only *theorems* on what can and cannot be done within the framework of ordinary classical quantification theory. Thus Gödel *showed* that a classical language can talk about its own syntax; using restricted truth definitions and other devices, such a language can say a great deal about its own semantics. On the other hand, Tarski *proved* that a classical language cannot contain its own truth predicate, and that a higher-order language can define a truth predicate for a language of lower order. None of this came from any a priori restrictions on self-reference other than those deriving from the restriction to a classical language, all of whose predicates are totally defined.

utterance, when a given speaker uses the word 'true', he attaches an implicit subscript to it, which increases as, by further and further reflection, he goes higher and higher in his own Tarski hierarchy.[10]

Unfortunately this picture seems unfaithful to the facts. If someone makes such an utterance as (1), he does *not* attach a subscript, explicit or implicit, to his utterance of 'false', which determines the "level of language" on which he speaks. An implicit subscript would cause no trouble if we were sure of the "level" of *Nixon's* utterances; we could then cover them all, in the utterance of (1) or even of the stronger

(4)   All of Nixon's utterances about Watergate are false.

simply by choosing a subscript higher than the levels of any involved in Nixon's Watergate-related utterances. Ordinarily, however, a speaker *has no way of knowing the "levels" of Nixon's relevant utterances*. Thus Nixon may have said, "Dean is a liar", or "Haldeman told the truth when he said that Dean lied", etc., and the "levels" of these may yet depend on the levels of Dean's utterances, and so on. If the speaker is forced to assign a "level" to (4) in advance [or to the word 'false' in (4)], he may be unsure how high a level to choose; if, in ignorance of the "level" of Nixon's utterances, he chooses too low, his utterance (4) will fail of its purpose. The idea that a statement such as (4) should, in its normal uses, have a "level" is intuitively convincing. It is, however, equally intuitively obvious that the "level" of (4) should not depend on the form of (4) alone (as would be the case if 'false'—or, perhaps, 'utterances'—were assigned explicit subscripts), nor should it be assigned in advance by the

---

[10] Charles Parsons, "The Liar Paradox", reprinted in this volume, may perhaps be taken as giving an argument like the one sketched in this paragraph. Much of his paper, however, may be regarded as confirmed rather than refuted by the present approach. See in particular his fn 19, which hopes for a theory that avoids explicit subscripts. The minimal fixed point (see sec. III below) avoids explicit subscripts but nevertheless has a notion of level; in this respect it can be compared with standard set theory as opposed to the theory of types. The fact that the levels are not intrinsic to the sentences is peculiar to the present theory and is additional to the absence of explicit subscripting.

The orthodox assignment of intrinsic levels guarantees freedom from "riskiness" in the sense explained in sec. I above. For (4) and (5) below, the very assignment of intrinsic levels which would eliminate their riskiness would also prevent them from "seeking their own levels" (see pp. 59–60). *If we wish to allow sentences to seek their own levels apparently we must also allow risky sentences.* Then we must regard sentences as *attempting* to express propositions, and allow truth-value gaps. See sec. III below.

speaker, but rather its level should depend on the empirical facts about what Nixon has uttered. The higher the "levels" of Nixon's utterances happen to be, the higher the "level" of (4). This means that in some sense a statement should be allowed to seek its own level, high enough to say what it intends to say. It should not have an intrinsic level fixed in advance, as in the Tarski hierarchy.

Another situation is even harder to accommodate within the confines of the orthodox approach. Suppose Dean asserts (4), while Nixon in turn asserts

(5) Everything Dean says about Watergate is false.

Dean, in asserting the sweeping (4), wishes to include Nixon's assertion (5) within its scope (as one of the Nixonian assertions about Watergate which is said to be false); and Nixon, in asserting (5), wishes to do the same with Dean's (4). Now on any theory that assigns intrinsic "levels" to such statements, so that a statement of a given level can speak only of the truth or falsity of statements of lower levels, it is plainly impossible for both to succeed: if the two statements are on the same level, neither can talk about the truth or falsity of the other, while otherwise the higher can talk about the lower, but not conversely. Yet intuitively, we can often assign unambiguous truth values to (4) and (5). Suppose Dean has made at least one true statement about Watergate [other than (4)]. Then, independently of any assessment of (4), we can decide that Nixon's (5) is false. If all Nixon's other assertions about Watergate are false as well, Dean's (4) is true; if one of them is true, (4) is false. Note that in the latter case, we could have judged (4) to be false without assessing (5), but in the former case the assessment of (4) as true depended on a *prior* assessment of (5) as false. Under a different set of empirical assumptions about the veracity of Nixon and Dean, (5) would be true [and its assessment as true would depend on a prior assessment of (4) as false]. It seems difficult to accommodate these intuitions within the confines of the orthodox approach.

Other defects of the orthodox approach are more difficult to explain within a brief outline, though they have formed a substantial part of my research. One problem is that of transfinite levels. It is easy, within the confines of the orthodox, to assert

(6) Snow is white.

to assert that (6) is true, that '(6) is true' is true, that '"(6) is true" is true' is true, etc.; the various occurrences of 'is true' in the sequence are assigned increasing subscripts. It is much more difficult to assert that all the statements in the sequence just described are true. To do this, we need a metalanguage of transfinite level, above all the languages of finite level. To my surprise, I have found that the problem of defining the languages of transfinite level presents substantial technical difficulties which have never seriously been investigated.[11] (Hilary Putnam and his students essentially investigated—under the guise of a superficially completely different description and mathematical motivation—the problem for the special case where we start at the lowest level with the language of elementary number theory.) I have obtained various positive results on the problem, and there are also various negative results; they cannot be detailed here. But in the present state of the literature, it should be said that if the "theory of language levels" is meant to include an account of transfinite levels, then one of the principal defects of the theory is simply the *nonexistence* of the theory. The existing literature can be said to define "Tarski's hierarchy of languages" only for *finite* levels, which is hardly adequate. My own work includes an extension of the orthodox theory to transfinite levels, but it is as yet incomplete. Lack of space not only prevents me from describing the work; it prevents me from mentioning the mathematical difficulties that make the problem highly nontrivial.

Other problems can only be mentioned. One surprise to me was the fact that the orthodox approach by no means obviously guarantees groundedness in the intuitive sense mentioned above. The concept of truth for Σ_1 arithmetical statements is itself Σ_1, and this fact can be used to construct statements of the form of (3). Even if unrestricted truth definitions are in question, standard theorems easily allow us to construct a *descending* chain of first-order languages $L_0, L_1, L_2, \ldots$, such that L_i contains a truth predicate for L_{i+1}. I don't know whether such a chain can engender ungrounded sentences, or even quite how to state the problem here; some substantial technical questions in this area are yet to be solved.

Almost all the extensive recent literature seeking alternatives to the orthodox approach—I would mention especially the writings of Bas

---

[11] The problem of transfinite levels is perhaps not too difficult to solve in a canonical way at level ω, but it becomes increasingly acute at higher ordinal levels.

van Fraassen and Robert L. Martin[12]—agrees on a single basic idea: there is to be only one truth predicate, applicable to sentences containing the predicate itself; but paradox is to be avoided by allowing truth-value gaps and by declaring that paradoxical sentences in particular suffer from such a gap. These writings seem to me to suffer sometimes from a minor defect and almost always from a major defect. The minor defect is that some of these writings criticize a strawmannish version of the orthodox approach, not the genuine article.[13] The major defect is that these writings almost invariably are mere suggestions, not genuine theories. Almost never is there any precise semantical formulation of a language, at least rich enough to speak of its own elementary syntax (either directly or via arithmetization) and containing its own truth predicate. Only if such a language were set up with formal precision could it be said that a theory of the semantic paradoxes has been presented. Ideally, a theory should show that the technique can be applied to arbitrarily rich languages, no matter what their "ordinary" predicates other than truth. And there is yet another sense in which the orthodox approach provides a theory while the alternative literature does not. Tarski shows how, for a classical first-order language whose quantifiers range over a set, he can give a *mathematical definition* of truth, using the predicates of the object language plus set theory (higher-order logic). The alternative literature abandons the attempt at a mathematical definition of truth, and is content to take it as an

---

[12] See Martin, ed., *The Paradox of the Liar* (New Haven: Yale, 1970) and the references given there.

[13] See fn 9 above. Martin, for example, in his papers "Towards a Solution to the Liar Paradox", *Philosophical Review*, LXXVI, 3 (July 1967): 279–311, and "On Grelling's Paradox", ibid., LXXVII, 3 (July 1968): 325–31, attributes to "the theory of language levels" all kinds of restrictions on self-reference which must be regarded as simply refuted, even for classical languages, by Gödel's work. Perhaps there are or have been some theorists who believed that *all* talk of an object language must take place in a distinct metalanguage. This hardly matters; the main issue is: what constructions can be carried out within a classical language, and what require truth-value gaps? Almost all the cases of self-reference Martin mentions can be carried out by orthodox Gödelian methods without any need to invoke partially defined predicates or truth-value gaps. In fn 5 of his second paper Martin takes some notice of Gödel's demonstration that sufficiently rich languages contain their own syntax, but he seems not to realize that this work makes most of his polemics against "language levels" irrelevant.

At the other extreme, some writers still seem to think that some kind of general ban on self-reference is helpful in treating the semantic paradoxes. In the case of self-referential *sentences*, such a position seems to me to be hopeless.

intuitive primitive. Only one paper in the "truth-gap" genre that I have read—a recent paper by Martin and Peter Woodruff[14]—comes close even to beginning an attempt to satisfy any of these desiderata for a theory. Nevertheless the influence of this literature on my own proposal will be obvious.[15]

III. The Present Proposal

I do not regard any proposal, including the one to be advanced here, as definitive in the sense that it gives *the* interpretation of the ordinary use of 'true', or *the* solution to the semantic paradoxes. On the contrary, I have not at the moment thought through a careful philosophical justification of the proposal, nor am I sure of the exact areas and limitations of its applicability. I do hope that the model given here has two virtues: first, that it provides an area rich in formal structure and mathematical properties; second, that to a reasonable extent these properties capture important intuitions. The model, then, is to be tested by its technical fertility. It need not capture every intuition, but it is hoped that it will capture many.

Following the literature mentioned above, we propose to investigate languages allowing truth-value gaps. Under the influence of Strawson,[16] we can regard a sentence as an attempt to make a statement, express a proposition, or the like. The meaningfullness or

---

[14] In the terminology of the present paper, the paper by Martin and Woodruff proves the existence of *maximal* fixed points (not the minimal fixed point) in the context of the weak three-valued approach. It does not develop the theory much further. I believe the paper is as yet unpublished, but is forthcoming in a volume dedicated to Yehoshua Bar-Hillel. Although it partially anticipates the present approach, it was unknown to me when I did the work.

[15] Actually I was familiar with relatively little of this literature when I began work on the approach given here. Even now I am unfamiliar with a great deal of it, so that tracing connections is difficult. Martin's work seems, in its formal consequences if not its philosophical basis, to be closest to the present approach.

There is also a considerable literature on three-valued or similar approaches to the set-theoretical paradoxes, with which I am not familiar in detail but which seems fairly closely related to the present approach. I should mention Gilmore, Fitch, Feferman.

[16] I am interpreting Strawson as holding that 'the present king of France is bald' fails to make a statement but is still meaningful, because it gives directions (conditions) for making a statement. I apply this to the paradoxical sentences, without committing myself on his original case of descriptions. It should be stated that Strawson's doctrine is somewhat ambiguous and that I have chosen a preferred interpretation, which I think Strawson also prefers today.

well-formedness of the sentence lies in the fact that there are specifiable circumstances under which it has determinate truth conditions (expresses a proposition), not that it always does express a proposition. A sentence such as (1) is always *meaningful*, but under various circumstances it may not "make a statement" or "express a proposition". (I am not attempting to be philosophically completely precise here.)

To carry out these ideas, we need a semantical scheme to handle predicates that may be only partially defined. Given a nonempty domain D, a monadic predicate $P(x)$ is interpreted by a pair (S_1, S_2) of disjoint subsets of D. S_1 is the *extension* of $P(x)$ and S_2 is its *anti-extension*. $P(x)$ is to be true of the objects in S_1, false of those in S_2, undefined otherwise. The generalization to n-place predicates is obvious.

One appropriate scheme for handing connectives is Kleene's strong three-valued logic. Let us suppose that $\sim P$ is true (false) if P is false (true), and undefined if P is undefined. A disjunction is true if at least one disjunct is true regardless of whether the other disjunct is true, false, or undefined[17]; it is false if both disjuncts are false; undefined, otherwise. The other truth functions can be defined in terms of disjunction and negation in the usual way. (In particular, then, a conjunction will be true if both conjuncts are true, false if at least one conjunct is false, and undefined otherwise.) $(\exists x)A(x)$ is true if $A(x)$ is true for some assignment of an element of D to x; false if $A(x)$ is false for all assignments to x, and undefined otherwise. $(x)A(x)$ can be defined as $\sim(\exists x)\sim A(x)$. It therefore is true if $A(x)$ is true for all assignments to x, false if $A(x)$ is false for at least one such assignment, and undefined otherwise. We could convert the preceding into a more precise formal definition of satisfaction, but we won't bother.[18]

---

[17] Thus the disjunction of 'snow is white' with a Liar sentence will be true. If we had regarded a Liar sentence as *meaningless*, presumably we would have had to regard any compound containing it as meaningless also. Since we don't regard such a sentence as meaningless, we can adopt the approach taken in the text.

[18] The valuation rules are those of S. C. Kleene, *Introduction to Metamathematics* (New York: Van Nostrand, 1952), sec. 64, pp. 332–40. Kleene's notion of regular tables is equivalent (for the class of valuations he considers) to our requirement of the monotonicity of ϕ below.

I have been amazed to hear my use of the Kleene valuation compared occasionally to the proposals of those who favor abandoning standard logic "for quantum mechanics", or positing extra truth values beyond truth and falsity, etc. Such a

We wish to capture an intuition of somewhat the following kind. Suppose we are explaining the word 'true' to someone who does not yet understand it. We may say that we are entitled to assert (or deny) of any sentence that it is true precisely under the circumstances when we can assert (or deny) the sentence itself. Our interlocutor then can understand what it means, say, to attribute truth to (6) ('snow is white') but he will still be puzzled about attributions of truth to sentences containing the word 'true' itself. Since he did not understand these sentences initially, it will be equally nonexplanatory, initially, to explain to him that to call such a sentence "true" ("false") is tantamount to asserting (denying) the sentence itself.

Nevertheless, with more thought the notion of truth as applied even to various sentences themselves containing the word 'true' can gradually become clear. Suppose we consider the sentence,

(7)   Some sentence printed in the *New York Daily News*, October 7, 1971, is true.

(7) is a typical example of a sentence involving the concept of truth itself. So if (7) is unclear, so still is

(8)   (7) is true.

However, our subject, if he is willing to assert 'snow is white', will according to the rules be willing to assert '(6) is true'. But suppose that among the assertions printed in the *New York Daily News*, October 7, 1971, is (6) itself. Since our subject is willing to assert '(6) is true', and also to assert '(6) is printed in the *New York Daily News*, October 7, 1971', he will deduce (7) by existential generalization.

reaction surprised me as much as it would presumably surprise Kleene, who intended (as I do here) to write a work of standard mathematical results, provable in conventional mathematics. "Undefined" is not an *extra* truth value, any more than— in Kleene's book—u is an extra *number* in sec. 63. Nor should it be said that "classical logic" does not generally hold, any more than (in Kleene) the use of partially defined functions invalidates the commutative law of addition. *If* certain sentences express propositions, any tautological truth function of them expresses a true proposition. Of course formulas, even with the forms of tautologies, which have components that do not express propositions may have truth functions that do not express propositions either. (This happens under the Kleene valuation, but not under the van Fraassen.) Mere conventions for handling terms that do not designate numbers should not be called changes in arithmetic; conventions for handling sentences that do not express propositions are not in any philosophically significant sense "changes in logic". The term 'three-valued logic', occasionally used here, should not mislead. All our considerations can be formalized in a classical metalanguage.

Once he is willing to assert (7), he will also be willing to assert (8). In this manner, the subject will eventually be able to attribute truth to more and more statements involving the notion of truth itself. There is no reason to suppose that *all* statements involving 'true' will become decided in this way, but most will. Indeed, our suggestion is that the "grounded" sentences can be characterized as those which eventually get a truth value in this process.

A typically ungrounded sentence such as (3) will, of course, receive no truth value in the process just sketched. In particular, it will never be called "true". But the subject cannot express this fact by saying, "(3) is not true". Such an assertion would conflict directly with the stipulation that he should deny that a sentence is true precisely under the circumstances under which he would deny the sentence itself. In imposing this stipulation, we have made a deliberate choice (see below).

Let us see how we can give these ideas formal expression. Let L be an interpreted first-order language of the classical type, with a finite (or even denumerable) list of primitive predicates. It is assumed that the variables range over some nonempty domain D, and that the primtive n-ary predicates are interpreted by (totally defined) n-ary relations on D. The interpretation of the predicates of L is kept fixed throughout the following discussion. Let us also assume that the language L is rich enough so that the syntax of L (say, via arithmetization) can be expressed in L, and that some coding scheme codes finite sequences of elements of D into elements of D. We do not attempt to make these ideas rigorous; Y. N. Moschovakis's notion of an "acceptable" structure would do so.[19] I should emphasize that a great deal of what we do below goes through under much weaker hypotheses on L.[20]

Suppose we extend L to a language $\mathscr{L}$ by adding a monadic predicate $T(x)$ whose interpretation need only be partially defined. An interpretation of $T(x)$ is given by a "partial set" (S_1, S_2), where S_1, as we said above, is the *extension* of $T(x)$, S_2 is the *antiextension* of $T(x)$, and $T(x)$ is undefined for entities outside $S_1 \cup S_2$. Let

---

[19] *Elementary Induction on Abstract Structures* (Amsterdam: North-Holland, 1974). The notion of an acceptable structure is developed in chap. 5.

[20] It is unnecessary to suppose, as we have for simplicity, that all the predicates in L are totally defined. The hypothesis that L contain a device for coding finite sequences is needed only if we are adding satisfaction rather than truth to L. Other hypotheses can be made much weaker for most of the work.

$\mathscr{L}(S_1, S_2)$ be the interpretation of $\mathscr{L}$ which results from interpreting $T(x)$ by the pair (S_1, S_2), the interpretation of the other predicates of L remaining as before.[21] Let S_1' be the set of (codes of)[22] true sentences of $\mathscr{L}(S_1, S_2)$, and let S_2' be the set of all elements of D which either are not (codes of) sentences of $\mathscr{L}(S_1, S_2)$ or are (codes of) false sentences of $\mathscr{L}(S_1, S_2)$. S_1' and S_2' are uniquely determined by the choice of (S_1, S_2). Clearly, if $T(x)$ is to be interpreted as truth for the very language L containing $T(x)$ itself, we must have $S_1 = S_1'$ and $S_2 = S_2'$. [This means that if A is any sentence, A satisfies (falsifies) $T(x)$ iff A is true (false) by the evaluation rules.]

A pair (S_1, S_2) that satisfies this condition is called a *fixed point*. For a given choice of (S_1, S_2) to interpret $T(x)$, set $\phi((S_1, S_2)) = (S_1', S_2')$. ϕ then is a unary function defined on all pairs (S_1, S_2) of disjoint subsets of D, and the "fixed points" (S_1, S_2) are literally the fixed points of ϕ; i.e., they are those pairs (S_1, S_2) such that $\phi((S_1, S_2)) = (S_1, S_2)$. If (S_1, S_2) is a fixed point, we sometimes call $\mathscr{L}(S_1, S_2)$ a fixed point also. Our basic task is to prove the existence of fixed points, and to investigate their properties.

Let us first construct a fixed point. We do so by considering a certain "hierarchy of languages". We start by defining the interpreted language $\mathscr{L}_0$ as $\mathscr{L}(\Lambda, \Lambda)$, where Λ is the empty set; i.e., $\mathscr{L}_0$ is the language where $T(x)$ is completely undefined. (It is never a fixed point.) For any integer α, suppose we have defined $\mathscr{L}_\alpha = \mathscr{L}(S_1, S_2)$. Then set $\mathscr{L}_{\alpha+1} = \mathscr{L}(S_1', S_2')$, where as before S_1' is the set of (codes of) true sentences of $\mathscr{L}_\alpha$, and S_2' is the set of all elements of D which either are not (codes of) sentences of $\mathscr{L}_\alpha$ or are (codes of) false sentences of $\mathscr{L}_\alpha$.

The hierarchy of languages just given is analogous to the Tarski hierarchy for the orthodox approach. $T(x)$ is interpreted in $\mathscr{L}_{\alpha+1}$ as the truth predicate for $\mathscr{L}_\alpha$. But an interesting phenomenon, detailed in the following paragraphs, arises on the present approach.

Let us say that $(S_1^\dagger, S_2^\dagger)$ *extends* (S_1, S_2) [symbolically, $(S_1^\dagger, S_2^\dagger) \geqslant (S_1, S_2)$ or $(S_1, S_2) \leqslant (S_1^\dagger, S_2^\dagger)$] iff $S_1 \subseteq S_1^\dagger$, $S_2 \subseteq S_2^\dagger$. Intuitively

---

[21] $\mathscr{L}$ is thus a language with all predicates but the single predicate $T(x)$ interpreted, but $T(x)$ is uninterpreted. The languages $\mathscr{L}(S_1, S_2)$ and the languages $\mathscr{L}_\alpha$ defined below are languages obtained from $\mathscr{L}$ by specifying an interpretation of $T(x)$.

[22] I parenthetically write "codes of" or "Gödel numbers of" in various places to remind the reader that syntax may be represented in L by Gödel numbering or some other coding device. Sometimes I lazily drop the parenthetical qualification, identifying expressions with their codes.

this means that if $T(x)$ is interpreted as $(S_1{}^\dagger, S_2{}^\dagger)$, the interpretation agrees with the interpretation by (S_1, S_2), in all cases where the latter is defined; the only difference is that an interpretation by $(S_1{}^\dagger, S_2{}^\dagger)$ may lead $T(x)$ to be defined for some cases where it was undefined when interpreted by (S_1, S_2). Now a basic property of our valuation rules is the following: ϕ is a monotone (order-preserving) operation on $\leqslant$: that is, if $(S_1, S_2) \leqslant (S_1{}^\dagger, S_2{}^\dagger)$, $\phi((S_1, S_2)) \leqslant \phi((S_1{}^\dagger, S_2{}^\dagger))$. In other words, *if* $(S_1, S_2) \leqslant (S_1{}^\dagger, S_2{}^\dagger)$, *then any sentence that is true (or false) in* $\mathscr{L}(S_1, S_2)$ *retains its truth value in* $\mathscr{L}(S_1{}^\dagger, S_2{}^\dagger)$. What this means is that *if the interpretation of* $T(x)$ *is extended by giving it a definite truth value for cases that were previously undefined, no truth value previously established changes or becomes undefined;* at most, certain previously undefined truth values become defined. This property—technically, the monotonicity of ϕ—is crucial for all our constructions.

Given the monotonicity of ϕ, we can deduce that for each α, *the interpretation of* $T(x)$ *in* $\mathscr{L}_{\alpha+1}$ *extends the interpretation of* $T(x)$ *in* $\mathscr{L}_\alpha$. The fact is obvious for $\alpha = 0$: since, in $\mathscr{L}_0$, $T(x)$ is undefined for all x, any interpretation of $T(x)$ automatically extends it. If the assertion holds for $\mathscr{L}_\beta$—that is, if the interpretation of $T(x)$ in $\mathscr{L}_{\beta+1}$ extends that of $T(x)$ in $\mathscr{L}_\beta$—then any sentence true or false in $\mathscr{L}_\beta$ remains true or false in $\mathscr{L}_{\beta+1}$. If we look at the definitions, *this says that the interpretation of* $T(x)$ *in* $\mathscr{L}_{\beta+2}$ *extends the interpretation of* $T(x)$ *in* $\mathscr{L}_{\beta+1}$. *We have thus proved by induction that the interpretation of* $T(x)$ *in* $\mathscr{L}_{\alpha+1}$ *always extends the interpretation of* $T(x)$ *in* $\mathscr{L}_\alpha$ *for all finite* α. *It follows that the predicate* $T(x)$ *increases, in both its extension and its antiextension, as* α *increases. More and more sentences get declared true or false as* α *increases; but once a sentence is declared true or false, it retains its truth value at all higher levels.*

So far, we have defined only *finite* levels of our hierarchy. For finite α, let $(S_{1,\alpha}, S_{2,\alpha})$ be the interpretation of $T(x)$ in $\mathscr{L}_\alpha$. Both $S_{1,\alpha}$ and $S_{2,\alpha}$ increase (as sets) as α increases. Then there is an obvious way of defining the first "transfinite" level—call it "$\mathscr{L}_\omega$". Simply define $\mathscr{L}_\omega = \mathscr{L}(S_{1,\omega}, S_{2,\omega})$, where $S_{1,\omega}$ is the union of all $S_{1,\alpha}$ for finite α, and $S_{2,\omega}$ is similarly the union of $S_{2,\alpha}$ for finite α. Given $\mathscr{L}_\omega$, we can then define $\mathscr{L}_{\omega+1}, \mathscr{L}_{\omega+2}, \mathscr{L}_{\omega+3}$, etc., just as we did for the finite levels. When we get again to a "limit" level, we take a union as before.

Formally, we define the languages $\mathscr{L}_\alpha$ for each ordinal α. If α is a successor ordinal ($\alpha = \beta + 1$), let $\mathscr{L}_\alpha = \mathscr{L}(S_{1,\alpha}, S_{2,\alpha})$, where $S_{1,\alpha}$ is the set of (codes of) true sentences of $\mathscr{L}_\beta$, and $S_{2,\alpha}$ is the set consisting of all elements of D which either are (codes of) false sentences of $\mathscr{L}_\beta$ or are not (codes of) sentences of $\mathscr{L}_\beta$. If λ is a limit ordinal, $\mathscr{L}_\lambda = \mathscr{L}(S_{1,\lambda}, S_{2,\lambda})$, where $S_{1,\lambda} = \bigcup_{\beta < \lambda} S_{1,\beta}$, $S_{2,\lambda} = \bigcup_{\beta < \lambda} S_{2,\beta}$. So at "successor" levels we take the truth predicate over the previous level, and, at limit (transfinite) levels, we take the union of all sentences declared true or false at previous levels. *Even with the transfinite levels included, it remains true that the extension and the antiextension of $T(x)$ increase with increasing α.*

It should be noted that 'increase' does not mean "strictly increase"; we have asserted that $S_{i,\alpha} \subseteq S_{i,\alpha+1}$ $(i = 1, 2)$, which allows equality. Does the process go on forever with more and more statements being declared true or false, or does it eventually stop? That is to say, is there an ordinal level σ for which $S_{1,\sigma} = S_{1,\sigma+1}$ and $S_{2,\sigma} = S_{2,\sigma+1}$, so that no "new" statements are declared true or false at the next level? The answer must be affirmative. The sentences of $\mathscr{L}$ form a set. If new sentences of $\mathscr{L}$ were being decided at each level, we would eventually exhaust $\mathscr{L}$ at some level and be unable to decide any more. This can easily be converted to a formal proof (the technique is elementary and is well known to logicians) that there is an ordinal level σ such that $(S_{1,2}, S_{2,\sigma}) = (S_{1,\sigma+1}, S_{2,\sigma+1})$. But since $(S_{1,\sigma+1}, S_{2,\sigma+1}) = \phi((S_{1,\sigma}, S_{2,\sigma}))$, *this means that $(S_{1,\sigma}, S_{2,\sigma})$ is a fixed point.* It can also be proved that it is a "minimal" or "smallest" fixed point: *any* fixed point extends $(S_{1,\sigma}, S_{2,\sigma})$. That is, if a sentence is valuated as true or false in $\mathscr{L}_\sigma$, it has the same truth value in *any* fixed point.

Let us relate the construction of a fixed point just given to our previous intuitive ideas. At the initial stage $(\mathscr{L}_0)$, $T(x)$ is completely undefined. This corresponds to the initial stage at which the subject has no understanding of the notion of truth. Given a characterization of truth by the Kleene valuation rules, the subject can easily ascend to the level of $\mathscr{L}_1$. That is, he can evaluate various statements as true or false without knowing anything about $T(x)$—in particular, he can evaluate all those sentences not containing $T(x)$. Once he has made the evaluation, he extends $T(x)$, as in $\mathscr{L}_1$. Then he can use the new interpretation of $T(x)$ to evaluate more sentences as true or false and ascend to $\mathscr{L}_2$, etc. Eventually, when the process becomes "saturated", the subject reaches the fixed point $\mathscr{L}_\sigma$. (*Being a fixed point, $\mathscr{L}_\sigma$ is a language that contains its own truth predicate.*) So the

formal definition just given directly parallels the intuitive constructions stated previously.[23]

We have been talking of a language that contains its own truth
predicate. Really, however, it would be more interesting to extend an
arbitrary language to a language containing its own *satisfaction*
predicate. If L contains a name for each object in D, and a
denotation relation is defined (if D is nondenumerable, this means
that L contains nondenumerably many constants), the notion of
satisfaction can (for most purposes) effectively be replaced by that of
truth: e.g., instead of talking of $A(x)$ being satisfied by an object a,
we can talk of $A(x)$ becoming true when the variable is replaced
by a name of a. Then the previous construction suffices. Alternatively, if L does not contain a name for each object, we can extend
L to $\mathscr{L}$ by adding a binary satisfaction predicate $Sat(s, x)$ where s
ranges over finite sequences of elements of D and x ranges over
formulas. We define a hierarchy of languages, parallel to the
previous construction with truth, eventually reaching a fixed point
—a language that contains its own satisfaction predicate. If L is
denumerable but D is not, the construction with truth alone closes
off at a countable ordinal, but the construction with satisfaction may
close off at an uncountable ordinal. Below we will continue, for
simplicity of exposition, to concentrate on the construction with
truth, but the construction with satisfaction is more basic.[24]

[23] A comparison with the Tarski hierarchy:

The Tarski hierarchy uses a new truth predicate at each level, always changing. The
limit levels of the Tarski hierarchy, which have not been defined in the literature, but
have been to some extent in my own work, are cumbersome to characterize.

The present hierarchy uses a single truth predicate, ever increasing with increasing
levels until the level of the minimal fixed point is reached. The limit levels are easily
defined. The languages in the hierarchy are not the primary object of interest, but are
better and better approximations to the minimal language with its own truth
predicate.

[24] Consider the case where L has a canonical name for every element of D. We can
then consider pairs (A,T), (A,F), where A is true, or false, respectively. The Kleene
rules correspond to closure conditions on a set of such pairs: e.g., if $(A(a),F) \in S$ for
each name of a element of D, put $((\exists x)A(x),F))$ in S; if $((A(a),T) \in S$, put $((\exists x)A(x),T)$ in
S, etc. Consider the least set of S of pairs closed under the analogues of the Kleene
rules, containing $(A,T)((A,F))$ for each true (false) atomic A of L, and closed under the
two conditions: (i) if $(A,T) \in S$, $(T(k),T) \in S$; (ii) if $(A,F) \in S$, $(T(k),F) \in S$, where 'k'
abbreviates a name of A. It is easily shown that the set S corresponds (in the obvious
sense) to the minimal fixed point [thus, it is closed under the converses of (i) and (ii)].
I used this definition to show that the set of truths in the minimal fixed point (over an
acceptable structure), is inductive in Moschovakis's sense. It is probably simpler than
the definition given in the text. The definition given in the text has, among others, the
advantages of giving a definition of 'level', facilitating a comparison with the Tarski
hierarchy, and easy generalization to valuation schemes other than Kleene's.

The construction could be generalized so as to allow more notation in L than just first-order logic. For example, we could have a quantifier meaning "for uncountably many x", a "most" quantifier, a language with infinite conjunctions, etc. There is a fairly canonical way, in the Kleene style, to extend the semantics of such quantifiers and connectives so as to allow truth-value gaps, but we will not give details.

Let us check that our model satisfies some of the desiderata mentioned in the previous sections. It is clearly a theory in the required sense: any language, including those containing number theory or syntax, can be extended to a language with its own truth predicate, and the associated concept of truth is *mathematically* defined by set-theoretic techniques. There is no problem about the languages of transfinite level in the hierarchy.

Given a sentence A of $\mathscr{L}$, let us define A to be *grounded* if it has a truth value in the smallest fixed point $\mathscr{L}_\sigma$; otherwise, *ungrounded*. What hitherto has been, as far as I know, an intuitive concept with no formal definition, becomes a precisely defined concept in the present theory. If A is grounded, define the *level* of A to be the smallest ordinal α such that A has a truth value in $\mathscr{L}_\alpha$.

There is no problem, if $\mathscr{L}$ contains number theory or syntax, of constructing Gödelian sentences that "say of themselves" that they are false (Liar sentences) or true [as in (3)]; all these are easily shown to be ungrounded in the sense of the formal definition. If the Gödelian form of the Liar paradox is used, for example, the Liar sentence can get the form

(9) $\quad (x)(P(x) \supset \sim T(x))$

where $P(x)$ is a syntactic (or arithmetical) predicate uniquely satisfied by (the Gödel number of) (9) itself. Similarly (3) gets the form

10 $\quad (x)(Q(x) \supset T(x))$

where $Q(x)$ is uniquely satisfied by (the Gödel number of) (10). It is easy to prove, under these hypotheses, by induction on α, that neither (9) nor (10) will have a truth value in any $\mathscr{L}_\alpha$, that is, that they are ungrounded. Other intuitive cases of ungroundedness come out similarly.

The feature I have stressed about ordinary statements, that there is no intrinsic guarantee of their safety (groundedness) and that their "level" depends on empirical facts, comes out clearly in the present model. Consider, for example, (9) again, except that now $P(x)$ is an empirical predicate whose extension depends on unknown empirical facts. If $P(x)$ turns out to be true only of (9) itself, (9) will be ungrounded as before. If the extension of $P(x)$ consists entirely of grounded sentences of levels, say, 2, 4, and 13, (9) will be grounded with level 14. If the extension of $P(x)$ consists of grounded sentences of arbitrary finite level, (9) will be grounded with level ω. And so on.

Now let us consider the cases of (4) and (5). We can formalize (4) by (9), interpreting $P(x)$ as "x is a sentence Nixon asserts about Watergate". [Forget for simplicity that 'about Watergate' introduces a semantic component into the interpretation of $P(x)$.] Formalize (5) as

(11) $(x)(Q(x) \supset \sim T(x))$

interpreting $Q(x)$ in the obvious way. To complete the parallel with (4) and (5), suppose that (9) is in the extension of $Q(x)$ and (11) is in the extension of $P(x)$. Now nothing guarantees that (9) and (11) will be grounded. Suppose, however, parallel to the intuitive discussion above, that some true grounded sentence satisfies $Q(x)$. If the lowest level of any such sentence is α, then (11) will be false and grounded with level $\alpha + 1$. If in addition all the sentences other than (11) satisfying $P(x)$ are false, (9) will then be grounded and true. The level of (9) will be at least $\alpha + 2$, because of the level of (11). On the other hand, if some sentence satisfying $P(x)$ is grounded and true, then (9) will be grounded and false with level $\beta + 1$, where β is the lowest level of any such sentence. It is crucial to the ability of the present model to assign levels to (4) and (5) [(9) and (11)] that the levels depend on empirical facts, rather than being assigned in advance.

We said that such statements as (3), though ungrounded, are not intuitively paradoxical either. Let us explore this in terms of the model. The smallest fixed point $\mathscr{L}_\sigma$ is not the only fixed point. Let us formalize (3) by (10), where $Q(x)$ is a *syntactic* predicate (of L) true of (10) itself alone. Suppose that, instead of starting out our hierarchy of languages with $T(x)$ completely undefined, we had started out by letting $T(x)$ be true of (10), undefined otherwise. We then can continue the hierarchy of languages just as before. It is easy to see that if (10) is true at the language of a given level, it will remain true at the next level [using the fact that $Q(x)$ is true of (10) alone, false of everything else]. From this we can show as before that the interpretation of $T(x)$ at each level extends all previous levels, and that at some level the construction closes off to yield a fixed point. The difference is that (10), which lacked truth value in the smallest fixed point, is now *true*.

This suggests the following definition: a sentence is *paradoxical* if it has no truth value in *any* fixed point. That is, a paradoxical sentence A is such that if $\phi((S_1, S_2)) = (S_1, S_2)$, *then A is neither an element of S_1 nor an element of S_2.*

(3) [or its formal version (10)] is ungrounded, but not paradoxical. This means that we *could* consistently use the predicate 'true' so as to give (3) [or (10)] a truth value, though the minimal process for assigning truth values does not do so. Suppose, on the other hand, in (9), that $P(x)$ is true of (9) itself and false of everything else, so that (9) is a Liar sentence. Then the argument of the Liar paradox easily yields a proof that (9) cannot have a truth value in any fixed point. So (9) is paradoxical in our technical sense. Notice that, if it is merely an empirical fact that $P(x)$ is true of (9) and false of everything else, the fact that (9) is paradoxical will itself be empirical. (We could define notions of "intrinsically paradoxical", "intrinsically grounded", etc., but will not do so here.)

Intuitively, the situation seems to be as follows. Although the smallest fixed point is probably the most natural model for the intuitive concept of truth, and is the model *generated* by our instructions to the imaginary subject, the other fixed points never *conflict* with these instructions. We *could* consistently use the word 'true' so as to give a truth value to such a sentence as (3) without violating the idea that a sentence should be asserted to be true precisely when we would assert the sentence itself. The same does not hold for the paradoxical sentences.

Using Zorn's Lemma, we can prove that *every fixed point can be extended to a maximal fixed point*, where a maximal fixed point is a fixed point that has no proper extension that is also a fixed point. Maximal fixed points assign "as many truth values as possible"; one could not assign more consistently with the intuitive concept of truth. Sentences like (3), though ungrounded, have a truth value in every maximal fixed point. Ungrounded sentences exist, however, which have truth values in some but not all maximal fixed points.

It is as easy to construct fixed points which make (3) false as it is to construct fixed points which make it true. So the assignment of a truth value to (3) is *arbitrary*. Indeed any fixed point which assigns no truth value to (3) can be extended to fixed points which make it true and to fixed points which make it false. Grounded sentences have the same truth value in all fixed points. There are ungrounded and unparadoxical sentences, however, which have the same truth value in all the fixed points where they have a truth value. An example is:

(12)   Either (12) or its negation is true.

It is easy to show that there are fixed points which make (12) true and none which make (12) false. Yet (12) is ungrounded (has no truth value in the minimal fixed point).

Call a fixed point *intrinsic* iff it assigns no sentence a truth value conflicting with its truth value in any other fixed point. That is, a fixed point (S_1, S_2) is intrinsic iff there is no other fixed point $(S_1{}^\dagger, S_2{}^\dagger)$ and sentence A of L' such that $A \in (S_1 \cap S_2{}^\dagger) \cup (S_2 \cap S_1{}^\dagger)$. We say that a sentence has *an intrinsic truth value* iff some intrinsic fixed point gives it a truth value; i.e., A has an intrinsic truth value iff there is an intrinsic fixed point (S_1, S_2) such that $A \in S_1 \cup S_2$. (12) is a good example.

There are unparadoxical sentences which have the same truth value in all fixed points where they have truth value but which nevertheless lack an intrinsic truth value. Consider $P \vee \sim P$, where P is any ungrounded unparadoxical sentence. Then $P \vee \sim P$ is true in some fixed points (namely, those where P has a truth value) and is false in none. Suppose, however, that there are fixed points that make P true and fixed points that make P false. [For example, say, P is (3).] Then $P \vee \sim P$ cannot have a truth value in any intrinsic fixed point, since, by our valuation rules, it cannot have a truth value unless some disjunct does.[25]

There is no "largest" fixed point that extends every other; indeed, any two fixed points that give different truth values to the same formula have no common extension. However, it is not hard to show that there is a largest intrinsic fixed point (and indeed that the intrinsic fixed points form a complete lattice under $\leq$). The largest intrinsic fixed point is the unique "largest" interpretation of $T(x)$ which is consistent with our intuitive idea of truth and makes no arbitrary choices in truth assignments. It is thus an object of special theoretical interest as a model.

---

[25] If we use the supervaluation technique instead of the Kleene rules, $P \vee \sim P$ will always be grounded and true, and we must change the example. See p. 76 below.

It is interesting to compare "Tarski's hierarchy of languages" with the present model. Unfortunately, this can hardly be done in full generality without introducing the transfinite levels, a task omitted from this sketch. But we can say something about the finite levels. Intuitively, it would seem that Tarski predicates $\ulcorner$true$_n\urcorner$ are all special cases of a single truth predicate. For example, we said above that 'true$_1$' means "is a true sentence not involving truth". Let us carry this idea out formally. Let $A_1(x)$ be a syntactic (arithmetical) predicate true of exactly the formulas of $\mathscr{L}$ not involving $T(x)$, i.e., of all formulas of L. $A_1(x)$, being syntactic, is itself a formula of L, as are all other syntactic formulas below. Define '$T_1(x)$' as '$T(x) \wedge A_1(x)$'. Let $A_2(x)$ be a syntactic predicate applying to all those formulas whose atomic predicates are those of L plus '$T_1(x)$'. [More precisely the class of such formulas can be defined as the least class including all formulas of L and $T(x_i) \wedge A_1(x_i)$, for any variable x_i, and closed under truth functions and quantification.] Then define $T_2(x)$ as $T(x) \wedge A_2(x)$. In general, we can define $A_{n+1}(x)$ as a syntactic predicate applying precisely to formulas built out of the predicates of L and $T_n(x)$, and $T_{n+1}(x)$ as $T(x) \wedge A_{n+1}(x)$. Assume that $T(x)$ is interpreted by the smallest fixed point (or any other). Then it is easy to prove by induction that each predicate $T_n(x)$ is totally defined, that the extension of $T_0(x)$ consists precisely of the true formulas of L, while that of $T_{n+1}(x)$ consists of the true formulas of the language obtained by adjoining $T_n(x)$ to L. This means that *all the truth predicates of the finite Tarski hierarchy are definable within $\mathscr{L}_\sigma$, and all the languages of that hierarchy are sublanguages of $\mathscr{L}_\sigma$.*[26] This kind of result could be extended into the transfinite if we had defined the transfinite Tarski hierarchy.

There are converse results, harder to state in this sketch. It is characteristic of the sentences in the Tarski hierarchy that they are safe (intrinsically grounded) and that their level is intrinsic, given independently of the empirical facts. It is natural to conjecture that any grounded sentence with intrinsic level n is in some sense "equivalent" to a sentence of level n in the Tarski hierarchy. Given

---

[26] We suppose that the Tarski hierarchy defines $L_0 = L$, $L_{n+1} = L + T_{n+1}(x)$ (truth, or satisfaction, for L_n). Alternatively, we might prefer the inductive construction $L_0 = L$, $L_{n+1} = L_n + T_{n+1}(x)$ where the language of each new level contains all the previous truth predicates. It is easy to modify the construction in the text so as to accord with the second definition. The two alternative hierarchies are equivalent in expressive power at each level.

proper definitions of 'intrinsic level', 'equivalent', and the like, theorems of this kind can be stated and proved and even extended into the transfinite.

So far we have assumed that truth gaps are to be handled according to the methods of Kleene. It is by no means necessary to do so. Just about any scheme for handling truth-value gaps is usable, provided that the basic property of the monotonicity of ϕ is preserved; that is, provided that extending the interpretation of $T(x)$ never changes the truth value of any sentence of $\mathscr{L}$, but at most gives truth values to previously undefined cases. Given any such scheme, we can use the previous arguments to construct the minimal fixed point and other fixed points, define the levels of sentences and the notions of 'grounded', 'paradoxical', etc.

One scheme usable in this way is van Fraassen's notion of *supervaluation*.[27] For the language $\mathscr{L}$, the definition is easy. Given an interpretation (S_1, S_2) of $T(x)$ in $\mathscr{L}$, call a formula A true (false) iff it comes out true (false) by the ordinary classical valuation under every interpretation $(S_1^\dagger, S_2^\dagger)$ which extends (S_1, S_2) and is *totally defined*, i.e., is such that $S_1^\dagger \cup S_2^\dagger = D$. We can then define the hierarchy $\{\mathscr{L}_\alpha\}$ and the minimal fixed point $\mathscr{L}_\sigma$ as before. Under the supervaluation interpretation, all formulas provable in classical quantification theory become true in $\mathscr{L}_\sigma$; under the Kleene valuation, one could say only that they were true whenever they were defined. Thanks to the fact that $\mathscr{L}_\sigma$ contains its own truth predicate, we need not express this fact by a schema, or by a statement of a metalanguage. If $PQT(x)$ is a syntactic predicate true exactly of the sentences of $\mathscr{L}$ provable in quantification theory, we can assert:

(13) $(x)(PQT(x) \supset T(x))$

and (13) will be true in the minimal fixed point.

Here we have used supervaluations in which *all* total extensions of the interpretation of $T(x)$ are taken into account. It is natural to consider restrictions on the family of total extensions, motivated by intuitive properties of truth. For example, we could consider only *consistent* interpretations $(S_1^\dagger, S_2^\dagger)$, where $(S_1^\dagger, S_2^\dagger)$ is consistent iff S_1 contains no sentence together with its negation. Then we could define A to be true (false) with $T(x)$ interpreted by (S_1, S_2) iff A is

[27] See his "Singular Terms, Truth-value Gaps, and Free Logic", *The Journal of Philosophy*, LXIII, 17 (Sept. 15, 1966): 481–95.

true (false) classically when A is interpreted by any *consistent* totally defined extension of (S_1, S_2).

(14) $(x) \sim (T(x) \wedge T(\text{neg}(x)))$

will be true in the minimal fixed point. If we restricted the admissible total extensions to those defining *maximal* consistent sets of sentences, in the usual sense, not only (14) but even

$$(x)(Sent(x) \supset T(x) \vee T(\text{neg}(x)))$$

will come out true in the minimal fixed point.[28] The last-mentioned formula, however, must be interpreted with caution, since it is still not the case, even on the supervaluation interpretation in question, that there is any fixed point that makes every formula or its negation true. (The paradoxical formulas still lack truth value in all fixed points.) The phenomenon is associated with the fact that, on the supervaluation interpretation, a disjunction can be true without it following that some disjunct is true.

It is not the purpose of the present work to make any particular recommendation among the Kleene strong three-valued approach, the van Fraassen supervaluation approaches, or any other scheme (such as the Fregean weak three-valued logic, preferred by Martin and Woodruff, though I am in fact tentatively inclined to consider the latter excessively cumbersome). Nor is it even my present purpose to make any firm recommendation between the minimal fixed point of a particular valuation scheme and the various other fixed points.[29] Indeed, without the nonminimal fixed points we could not have defined the intuitive difference between 'grounded' and 'paradoxical'. My purpose is rather to provide a family of flexible instruments which can be explored simultaneously and whose fertility and consonance with intuition can be checked.

I am somewhat uncertain whether there is a definite factual question as to whether natural language handles truth-value gaps— at least those arising in connection with the semantic paradoxes—by the schemes of Frege, Kleene, van Fraassen, or perhaps some other. Nor am I even *quite* sure that there is a definite question of fact as to

---

[28] A version of the Liar paradox due to H. Friedman shows that there are limits to what can be done in this direction.

[29] Though the minimal fixed point certainly is singled out as natural in many respects.

whether natural language should be evaluated by the minimal fixed point or another, given the choice of a scheme for handling gaps.[30] We are not at the moment searching for *the* correct scheme. The present approach can be applied to languages containing modal operators. In this case, we do not merely consider truth, but we are given, in the usual style of modal model theory, a system of possible worlds, and evaluate truth and $T(x)$ in each possible world. The inductive definition of the languages $\mathcal{L}_\alpha$ approximating to the minimal fixed point must be modified accordingly. We cannot give details here.[31]

Ironically, the application of the present approach to languages with modal operators may be of some interest to those who dislike intensional operators and possible worlds and prefer to take modalities and propositional attitudes as predicates true of sentences (or sentence tokens). Montague and Kaplan have pointed out, using elementary applications of Gödelian techniques, that such approaches are likely to lead to semantic paradoxes, analogous to the Liar.[32] Though the difficulty has been known for some time, the

---

[30] I do not mean to *assert* that there are no definite questions of fact in these areas, or even that I myself may not favor some valuation schemes over others. But my personal views are less important than the variety of tools that are available, so for the purposes of this sketch I take an agnostic position. (I remark that if the viewpoint is taken that logic applies primarily to propositions, and that we are merely formulating conventions for how to handle sentences that do not express propositions, the attractiveness of the supervaluation approach over the Kleene approach is somewhat decreased. See fn 18.)

[31] Another application of the present techniques is to "impredicative" substitutional quantification, where the terms of the substitution class themselves contain substitutional quantifiers of the given type. (For example, a language containing substitutional quantifiers with arbitrary sentences of the language itself as substituends.) It is impossible in general to introduce such quantifiers into classical languages without truth-value gaps.

[32] Richard Montague, "Syntactical Treatments of Modality, with Corollaries on Reflexion Principles and Finite Axiomatizability", *Acta Philosophica Fennica, Proceedings of a Colloquium on Modal and Many Valued Logics*, 1963: 153–67; David Kaplan and Montague, "A Paradox Regained", *Notre Dame Journal of Formal Logic*, I, 3 (July 1960): 79–90.

At present the problems are *known* to arise only if modalities and attitudes are predicates applied to sentences or their tokens. The Montague–Kaplan arguments do not apply to standard formalizations taking modalities or propositional attitudes as intensional operators. Even if we wish to quantify over objects of belief, the arguments do not apply if the objects of belief are taken to be propositions and the latter are identified with sets of possible worlds.

However, if we quantify over propositions, paradoxes may arise in connection with propositional attitudes given appropriate empirical premises. [See, e.g., A. N. Prior,

extensive literature advocating such treatments has usually simply ignored the problem rather than indicating how it is to be solved (say, by a hierarchy of languages?). Now, if a necessity operator and a truth predicate are allowed, we could define a necessity predicate $Nec(x)$ applied to sentences, either by $\Box T(x)$ or $T(\text{nec}(x))$ according to taste,[33] and treat it according to the possible-world scheme sketched in the preceding paragraph. (I do think that any necessity predicate of sentences should intuitively be regarded as derivative, defined in terms of an operator and a truth predicate. I also think the same holds for propositional attitudes.) We can even "kick away the ladder" and take $Nec(x)$ as primitive, treating it in a possible-world scheme *as if* it were defined by an operator plus a truth predicate. Like remarks apply to the propositional attitudes, if we are willing to treat them, using possible worlds, like modal operators. (I myself think that such a treatment involves considerable philosophical difficulties.) It is possible that the present approach can be applied to the supposed predicates of sentences in question without using either intensional operators or possible worlds, but at present I have no idea how to do so.

It seems likely that many who have worked on the truth-gap approach to the semantic paradoxes have hoped for a universal language, one in which everything that can be stated at all can be expressed. (The proof by Gödel and Tarski that a language cannot contain its own semantics applied only to languages without truth gaps.) Now the languages of the present approach contain their own truth predicates and even their own satisfaction predicates, and thus to this extent the hope has been realized. Nevertheless the present approach certainly does not claim to give a universal language, and I doubt that such a goal can be achieved. First, the induction defining the minimal fixed point is carried out in a set-theoretic meta-language, not in the object language itself. Second, there are assertions we can make about the object language which we cannot

---

"On a Family of Paradoxes", *Notre Dame Journal of Formal Logic*, II, 1 (January 1961): 16–32.] Also, we may wish (in connection with propositional attitudes but not modalities), to individuate propositions more finely than by sets of possible worlds, and it is possible that such a "fine structure" may permit the application of Gödelian arguments of the type used by Montague and Kaplan directly to propositions.

[33] As a formalization of the concept intended by those who speak of modalities and attitudes as predicates of sentences, the second version is generally better. This is true especially for the propositional attitudes.

make in the object language. For example, Liar sentences are *not true* in the object language, in the sense that the inductive process never makes them true; but we are precluded from saying this in the object language by our interpretation of negation and the truth predicate. If we think of the minimal fixed point, say under the Kleene valuation, as giving a model of natural language, then the sense in which we can say, in natural language, that a Liar sentence is not true must be thought of as associated with some later stage in the development of natural language, one in which speakers reflect on the generation process leading to the minimal fixed point. It is not itself a part of that process. The necessity to ascend to a meta-language may be one of the weaknesses of the present theory. The ghost of the Tarski hierarchy is still with us.[34]

The approach adopted here has presupposed the following version of Tarski's "Convention T", adapted to the three-valued approach: If 'k' abbreviates a name of the sentence A, $T(k)$ is to be true, or false, respectively iff A is true, or false. This captures the intuition that $T(k)$ is to have the same truth conditions as A itself; it follows that $T(k)$ suffers a truth-value gap if A does. An alternate intuition[35] would assert that, if A is either false or undefined, then A is *not true* and $T(k)$ should be *false*, and its negation *true*. On this view, $T(x)$ will be a totally defined predicate and there are no truth-value gaps. Presumably Tarski's Convention T must be restricted in some way.

It is not difficult to modify the present approach so as to accommodate such an alternate intuition. Take any fixed point $L'(S_1, S_2)$. Modify the interpretation of $T(x)$ so as to make it false of any sentence outside S_1. [We call this "closing off" $T(x)$.] A modified

---

[34] Note that the metalanguage in which we write this paper can be regarded as containing no truth gaps. A sentence either does or does not have a truth value in a given fixed point.

Such semantical notions as "grounded", "paradoxical", etc. belong to the metalanguage. This situation seems to me to be intuitively acceptable; in contrast to the notion of truth, none of these notions is to be found in natural language in its pristine purity, before philosophers reflect on its semantics (in particular, the semantic paradoxes). If we give up the goal of a universal language, models of the type presented in this paper are plausible as models of natural language at a stage before we reflect on the generation process associated with the concept of truth, the stage which continues in the daily life of nonphilosophical speakers.

[35] I think the primacy of the first intuition can be defended philosophically, and for this reason I have emphasized the approach based on this intuition. The alternate intuition arises only after we have reflected on the process embodying the first intuition. See above.

version of Tarski's Convention T holds in the sense of the conditional $T(k) \vee T(\text{neg}(k)) . \supset . A \equiv T(k)$. In particular, if A is a paradoxical sentence, we can now assert $\sim T(k)$. Equivalently, if A had a truth value before $T(x)$ was closed off, then $A \equiv T(k)$ is true.

Since the object language obtained by closing off $T(x)$ is a classical language with every predicate totally defined, it is possible to define a truth predicate for that language in the usual Tarskian manner. This predicate will *not* coincide in extension with the predicate $T(x)$ of the object language, and it is certainly reasonable to suppose that it is really the metalanguage predicate that expresses the "genuine" concept of truth for the closed-off object language; the $T(x)$ of the closed-off language defines truth for the fixed point *before* it was closed off. So we still cannot avoid the need for a metalanguage.

On the basis of the fact that the goal of a universal language seems elusive, some have concluded that truth-gap approaches, or any approaches that attempt to come closer to natural language than does the orthodox approach, are fruitless. I hope that the fertility of the present approach, and its agreement with intuitions about natural language in a large number of instances, cast doubt upon such negative attitudes.

There are mathematical applications and purely technical problems which I have not mentioned in this sketch; they would be beyond the scope of a paper for a philosophical journal. Thus there is the question, which can be answered in considerable generality, of characterizing the ordinal σ at which the construction of the minimal fixed point closes off. If L is the language of first-order arithmetic, it turns out that σ is ω_1, the first nonrecursive ordinal. A set is the extension of a formula with one free variable in $\mathscr{L}_\sigma$ iff it is Π^1_1, and it is the extension of a totally defined formula iff it is hyperarithmetical. The languages $\mathscr{L}_\alpha$ approximating to the minimal fixed point give an interesting "notation-free" version of the hyperarithmetical hierarchy. More generally, if L is the language of an acceptable structure in the sense of Moschovakis, and the Kleene valuation is used, a set is the extension of a monadic formula in the minimal fixed point iff it is inductive in the sense of Moschovakis.[36]

---

[36] Leo Harrington informs me that he has proved the conjecture that a set is the extension of a totally defined monadic formula iff it is hyperelementary. The special case of the Π^1_1 and hyperarithmetical sets if L is number theory is independent of whether the Kleene or the van Fraassen formulation is used. Not so for the general case, where the van Fraassen formulation leads to the Π^1_1 sets rather than the inductive sets.

Semantical Paradox*

Tyler Burge

Frege remarked that the goal of all sciences is truth, but that it falls to logic to discern the laws of truth. Perceiving that the task of determining these laws went beyond Frege's conception of it, Tarski enlarged the jurisdiction of logic, establishing semantics as truth's lawyer.[1]

At the core of Tarski's theory of truth and validity was a diagnosis of the Liar paradox according to which natural language was hopelessly infected with contradiction. Tarski construed himself as treating the disease by replacing ordinary discourse with a sanitized, artificial construction. But those interested in natural language have been dissatisfied with this medication. The best ground for dissatisfaction is that the notion of a natural language's harboring contradictions is based on an illegitimate assimilation of natural language to a semantical system. According to that assimilation, part of the nature of a "language" is a set of postulates that purport to be true by virtue of their meaning or are at least partially constitutive of that "language". Tarski thought that he had identified just such postulates in natural language as spawning inconsistency. But postulates are contained in theories that are promoted by people. Natural languages *per se* do not postulate or

Tyler Burge, "Semantical Paradox", reprinted from *The Journal of Philosophy* 76 (1979), 169–98. Copyright © 1979 *The Journal of Philosophy*. Reprinted by permission of the Editor of *The Journal of Philosophy* and the author.

* I am grateful to Robert L. Martin for several helpful discussions; to Herbert Enderton for proving the consistency (relative to that of arithmetic) of an extension of Construction C3; to Charles Parsons for stimulating exchanges back in 1973 and 1974; and to the John Simon Guggenheim Foundation for its support. (Added 1982): I am also indebted to John Pollock for finding an error in the earlier formulation of axiom (0), section IV. The present formulation captures the original intent.

[1] Gottlob Frege, "The Thought", in E. D. Klemke, ed., *Essays on Frege* (Urbana: Univ. of Illinois Press, 1968). Alfred Tarski, "The Concept of Truth in Formalized Languages", in *Logic, Semantics, Metamathematics*, J. H. Woodger, trans. (New York: Oxford, 1956). Nothing that I say will depend heavily on precisely how one views the scope of logic.

assert anything.[2] What engenders paradox is a certain naive theory or conception of the natural concept of truth. It is the business of those interested in natural language to improve on it.

Another just ground for dissatisfaction with Tarski's diagnosis is that it does not deal with various intuitions associated with the natural notion of truth. A philosophically satisfying theory must administer to these intuitions. Post-Tarskian treatments of the paradoxes, with a very few exceptions, have shared this second failing in greater or lesser degree. Although the motivation for these treatments is purportedly to provide a more natural or intuitive account of truth, they tend at least implicitly to place a higher premium on technical ingenuity than on intuitive adequacy. There results a variety of emendations of classical semantics without any thoroughly developed motivation. Important intuitive aspects of the paradoxes are usually left untouched.

My objective is an account of the "laws of truth" whose application accords as far as possible with natural "pre-theoretic" semantical intuition. Under these laws I shall be prosecuting the Grelling and Liar Paradoxes. The puzzles of Berry and Richard present slightly different cases; somewhat further afield are the epistemic and modal paradoxes.[3] But, although each of these cases deserves a special hearing, the basic outlook of this paper is intended to carry over to them.

I.

Tarski's analysis of the Liar allowed three escape routes. One could deprive the language of the means to name its own sentences. One

---

[2] This point runs far deeper than these brief remarks indicate. The problem of diagnosing Tarski's mistake has been most extensively and carefully discussed by Hans Herzberger, in "The Logical Consistency of Language", in J. A. Emig, J. T. Fleming, and H. M. Popps, eds., *Language and Learning* (New York: Harcourt, Brace, & World, 1966); and "The Truth-conditional Consistency of Natural Languages", *The Journal of Philosophy*, LXIV, 2 (Feb. 2, 1967): 29–35. I do not find Herzberger's diagnoses, which attribute to Tarski a rather simple inconsistency, entirely convincing either intuitively or textually. In my view, Tarski's error is more like a category mistake than an inconsistency.

[3] Cf. my "Buridan and Epistemic Paradox", *Philosophical Studies*, XXXIV, 1 (July 1978): 21–35; David Kaplan and Richard Montague, "A Paradox Regained", *Notre Dame Journal of Formal Logic*, I, 3 (July 1960): 79–90; and Richard Montague, "Syntactical Treatments of Modality with Corollaries on Reflexion Principles and Finite Axiomatizability", *Acta Philosophica Fennica*, XVI (1963): 153–67.

could limit the practice of asserting the results of substituting, for each sentence of the language in which the antinomy is constructed, a name of the sentence for 'X' and the sentence itself for 'P' in the truth schema

$$X \text{ is true if and only if } P.$$

Or one could restrict classical rules of transformation or alter semantical assumptions underlying classical logic. The first route is not viable for anyone who wishes to account for natural language or deductive reasoning in mathematics. Tarski chose the second and rejected the third out of hand.

Roughly speaking, Tarski's approach involves attaching numerical subscripts to 'true' (yielding a hierarchy of predicate constants) and treating as ill-formed any attempt to predicate $\ulcorner true_m \urcorner$ of a sentence containing $\ulcorner true_n \urcorner$, $n \geqslant m$. Thus a truth$_m$ schema is restricted to apply only to sentences containing no predicate $\ulcorner true_n \urcorner$, $n \geqslant m$. This requirement effectively blocks the derivation of contradiction, and it has become standard among mathematical logicians. But philosophers writing on the subject, with a few exceptions, have tended to agree with Tarski in denying the applicability of the approach to natural language.

Criticisms of Tarski's construction as a resolution of the natural-language paradoxes have taken several forms. It has been held that Tarski gave little motivation for the hierarchy except as an obstruction to contradiction and provided little insight into the use of the term 'true'; that 'true' is univocal, whereas Tarski fragments the notion of truth into infinitely many predicate constants; that there are global applications of 'true'—"every proposition is either true or not"—that Tarski's theory cannot represent; that paradoxical sentences are not ungrammatical and sometimes lead to difficulty not because of anything odd about their meaning, but because of empirical facts; and finally that there are cases of perfectly normal semantical evaluation which are pronounced abnormal from Tarski's viewpoint. All these criticisms have some merit as applied to Tarski's own theory, though I think that none reach quite so deeply as their authors have supposed.

The past fifteen years or so have seen a swell of support for combining the second avenue of escape with the third. That is, restrictions on the truth schema are conjoined with alterations of classical transformations or classical semantical assumptions. Such approaches always include rejection of the principle of bivalence. The intuitive motivations for this strategy have been various, and articulated only sketchily if at all. For reasons of space, my discussion of them will be correspondingly sketchy.

One motivation is a desire to integrate a solution to the semantical paradoxes with a theory of presupposition associated with Frege and Strawson.[4] It is certainly desirable to mark the difference between presupposition failure and falsity, ordinarily so-called, in our theory of language. But it is doubtful that adequately marking such a difference requires alterations in the semantics of elementary logic.[5] More important, as will be seen below, the appeal to the alterations occasioned by the Frege–Strawson theory is insufficient to explain certain features of the paradoxes.

A second motivation for altering classical semantics is a desire to assimilate a solution of the paradoxes to a theory of category mistakes.[6] Epimenides' error matches category mistakes in blatancy, but seems to have little else to do with them. Paradoxical statements can be constructed in which the reference of the singular term seems to be the right *sort* of thing for the semantical predicate to apply to— for almost any independently motivated view as to what the right sort is. The relevance of category considerations is thus obscure.

---

[4] Bas C. van Fraassen, "Presupposition, Implication, and Self-reference", *The Journal of Philosophy*, LXV, 5 (Mar. 7, 1968): 136–52; Frege, "On Sense and Reference" in P. T. Geach and Max Black, eds., *The Philosophical Writings of Gottlob Frege* (Oxford: Blackwell, 1966); P. F. Strawson, "On Referring", *Mind*, LIX, 235 (July 1950): 320–44; and *Introduction to Logical Theory* (London: Methuen, 1952).

[5] Cf. H. P. Grice, "Logic and Conversation" in D. Davidson and G. Harman, eds., *The Logic of Grammar* (Encino, Calif.: Dickenson, 1975); Robert Stalnaker, "Presuppositions", *Journal of Philosophical Logic*, II, 4 (October 1973): 447–57, and "Pragmatic Presuppositions", in Milton Munitz and Peter Unger, eds., *Semantics and Philosophy* (New York: NYU Press, 1974); Enrique Delacruz, *Presupposition: Towards an Analysis* (dissertation, UCLA, 1974); Jay Atlas, "Frege's Polymorphous Concept of Presupposition and its Role in a Theory of Meaning", *Semantikos*, I (1975): 29–44.

[6] This approach is one of several implicit in Gilbert Ryle, "Heterologicality", *Analysis*, XI, 3 (January 1951): 61–9. It has been more subtly developed by Robert L. Martin, "Toward a Solution to the Liar Paradox", *Philosophical Review*, LXXVI, 3 (July 1967): 279–311; and "A Category Solution to the Liar" in Martin, ed., *The Paradox of the Liar* (New Haven, Conn.: Yale, 1970). Martin now rests little weight on the category idea. He sees it as subsumable under considerations of presupposition. I would apply remarks similar to those which follow to occasional suggestions that vagueness is the root difficulty. Cf. also the beginning of sec. III.

Moreover, as before, accounting for category mistakes does not clearly require alterations in classical semantics, and such alterations as have been proposed are intuitively inadequate.

A third motivation is a yearning to produce a language in which there is a single truth predicate with constant extension which applies to everything that can be said (truly) in the language.[7] I shall argue that this ideal overlooks certain simple intuitions about truth. It is also doubtful that the ideal is technically attainable without exorbitant intuitive costs. This latter point, however, reaches beyond our present treatment.

Consistent, nonbivalent logics with a univocal truth predicate are certainly constructible. But no such logic, insofar as it assumes a truth predicate with a constant extension, has given a plausible account of the semantical paradoxes. This is because of a family of problems that have become known as the "Strengthened Liar". *The Strengthened Liar* (perhaps better called "The Persistent Liar") is really the original Liar reiterated for the sake of those who seek to undercut paradox primarily by appeal to a distinction between falsehood and some other kind of truth failure. Failure to resolve the Strengthened Liar is not a difficulty of detail or a mere drawback in a solution. It is a failure to account for the basic phenomenon. Any approach that suppresses the liar-like reasoning in one guise or terminology only to have it emerge in another must be seen as not casting its net wide enough to capture the protean phenomenon of semantical paradox.

The Strengthened Liar in its simplest form is this. If we analyze

(β) (β) is not true

as being neither true nor false, then it intuitively follows that the sentence displayed is not true. But the sentence displayed is (β). So it seems to follow that (β) is not true after all. We have now apparently asserted what we earlier claimed was neither true nor false. Moreover, the assertion that (β) is not true would seem to commit us to asserting that '(β) is not true' is true, contrary to our original analysis.[8] It is important to see that this informal reasoning is entirely intuitive.

Although the problem is well known, truth-value-gap theorists— theorists who propose to handle the paradoxes primarily by denying bivalence and who espouse a semantics with "truth-value gaps"— have had little illuminating to say about it. For example, in a technically elegant and critically acute paper, Saul Kripke raises the issue almost as an afterthought.[9] He admits that the Liar sentences are not true in his gap-containing object language and that this point cannot be expressed in that language. And he goes on to suggest a further truth predicate in a bivalent metalanguage. But, since Kripke's admission is couched in natural language, the proposal in terms of truth-value gaps *a fortiori* does not cover (at least one use of) 'true' in natural language. In short, an account of truth in the metalanguage—and in natural language—is still needed. Since the

---

[8] The general problem was first articulated by A. P. Ushenko, *The Problems of Logic* (London: Allen & Unwin, 1941), pp.. 78 ff. Cf. also W. W. Rozeboom, "Is Epimenides Still Lying?", *Analysis*, XVIII, 5 (April 1958): 105–13; and van Fraassen, op. cit. The term 'Strengthened Liar' is van Fraassen's. He may apply it somewhat more narrowly than I do.

It has been suggested that there is another paradox for truth-value-gap theories, which centers on falsity. Take '(a) is false'. Suppose (a) is neither true nor false. Then (a) is not false. We have now asserted '(a) is not false'. So we are committed to its truth. '(a) is not false' is the negation of (a). So the negation of (a) is true. But if the negation of (a) is true, then (a) itself is false. (This latter is a principle that even most truth-value-gap theories have accepted.) In my view, this reasoning is indeed a problem for truth-value-gap theories. But it is slightly more complicated than the reasoning I fix upon. The theory I develop will, however, handle this version of the "Strengthened" Liar in an obvious way, regardless of whether one counts 'false' as equivalent to 'is well-formed and is not true'.

[9] "Outline of a Theory of Truth", reprinted in this volume, pp. 79–81. Kripke remarks that certain technical terms (like 'paradoxical', 'grounded') do not occur in natural language "in its pristine purity". I see no interesting or clear distinction between terms reflectively introduced into natural language for unchallenged explanatory purposes and terms that slip in by other means. But, even if there were a relevant distinction, the theoretical situation would not be altered, since 'true' causes the difficulty unaided by more technical terms. Kripke further suggests that 'true' as it appears in his metalanguage corresponds to a 'true' in natural language different from (more technical than?) the 'true' that the predicate in his gap-containing object language corresponds to. The idea is that the former use of 'true' arises at a "later stage in the development of natural language" as a result of reflection on the use of 'true' in the gap-containing language. I find this unsatisfying, since I see no intuitive or philological basis for the claim that the natural-language 'true' changes its sense or logic as a result of reflection. Kripke's suggestion is similar to the view in van Fraassen, "Truth and Paradoxical Consequences", in *The Paradox of the Liar*, op. cit.

account envisioned is apparently something like Tarski's, the explanatory value of the gaps is unclear.

There have been three types of response among those truth-value gap theorists who have discussed the Strengthened Liar in detail. One is simply to reject the remark that the sentence displayed (under any description) is not true. The rationale goes: one must take seriously one's claim that 'true' is undefined or "gappy" for some arguments; the Strengthened Liar simply seduces one into forgetting this insight.[10] Sometimes the point is made in terms of the pathological statement's being "indeterminate" in some non-epistemic sense, terms that seem unusually promising of intuitive obscurity.

Implicit in this rationale is the view that the metalanguage for the gap-containing object language must itself have the same gaps the object language has. The response manifests a courageous and admirable methodological consistency, but is hardly credible. Informally and intuitively, to say that a sentence is neither true nor false is to imply that the sentence is not true.

Claiming that in the problem sentence the truth predicate is undefined or its application indeterminate does not help matters. For one may still reason that, if a sentence's predication is undefined or indeterminate, then the sentence is not true. This reasoning may or may not involve a broadening of the domain of discourse or a sharpening of the extension of 'true'. But it is informally quite intuitive. And the response does nothing to account for it.

Even apart from these problems, the response merely encourages the paradox to assume a different terminology. This can be seen by considering versions of the Strengthened Liar adapted to fit the very words of the response:

(i)   (i) is either false or undefined
(ii) (ii) is not determinately true.

After claiming that (β) is neither true nor false (or "bad" in some other sense), the gap-theorist must still face a precisely analogous Strengthened Liar tailored to his favorite description of the gaps.

---

[10] J. L. Mackie, *Truth, Probability and Paradox* (New York: Oxford, 1973), pp. 290–5; Martin, "A Category Solution", op. cit., pp. 92, 96. The indeterminacy idea that follows is Mackie's. On this issue it is a mistake to get too wound up in purely formal issues regarding the difference between choice negation and exclusion negation. There is clearly a use of negation in English which acts enough like exclusion negation to cause the problem, and we may start the paradox with this use.

A second response is to place restrictions on substitutivity of identity to block the move from remarking that the displayed sentence is not true to asserting that (β) is not true.[11] The response is palpably *ad hoc*. And it comes to feel more so when one considers that paradoxes can be constructed without using substitutivity of identity, or even singular terms. Brian Skyrms has proposed to meet some of these problems by restricting universal instantiation and by denying the validity of relettering bound variables. There is no evident unifying conception behind these restrictions—no basis other than minimum mutilation on which to choose restrictions as difficulties arise. Even as it stands the logic is cumbersome and unintuitive.

In addition, there are intuitions that the approach does not capture. I adapt an example given by Buridan:

(A) Suppose Plato at time t_1 says, "What Aristotle says at t_1 is not true" and Aristotle at time t_1 says "What Plato says at t_1 is not true". Since the two sentences are related to one another in exactly the same way, there can be no reason for saying that one is true and the other is not. But if we assume the naive truth schema, if one sentence is true the other must not be. It follows that neither statement is true—both are pathological and will not fit the naive schema. But intuitively, a third party who goes through the appropriate reasoning could well say, "What Plato says at t_1 is not true" (as well as "What Aristotle says at t_1 is not true") without saying anything paradoxical.

The third party uses the same singular term ('what Plato says at t_1') that Aristotle did (and the term could obviously be made non-indexical). Paradoxicality does not seem to depend purely on what mode of reference is used.[12]

There is another argument that the mode of reference in the Liar sentence is not the real source of paradox:

(B) Suppose I conduct you into a room in which the open sentence type 'it is not true of itself' is written on a blackboard. Pointing at the expression, I present the following reasoning: Let us consider it as an argument for its own variable or pronoun. Suppose it is true of itself. Then since it is the negation of the self-predication of the notion of *being true of*, it is not true of itself. Now suppose it is not true of itself. Then

[11] Skyrms, "Return of the Liar", op. cit.; and "Notes on Quantification and Self-reference", in *The Paradox of the Liar*, op. cit.

[12] Jean Buridan, *Sophisms on Meaning and Truth*, Kermit Scott, trans. (New York: Meredith, 1966), pp. 200 ff. A similar point can be made if A says 'what P says is not true' and P says 'what A says is true'.

since it is the negation of the self-predication of the notion of *being true of*, it is true of itself. In response you suggest that it is undefined for itself, from which we conclude that it is not true of itself. But then, I ask, why have we not made the same predications we were just criticizing? If we have, we seem committed to its being true of itself after all.

Here we have a variant of the Grelling paradox, analogous to the Strengthened Liar. Yet we have used only one mode of reference— the pronoun 'it' whose antecedent is a demonstration. I conclude that this second response to the Strengthened Liar is misguided.

Examples (A) and (B) leave rather little room in which to maneuver. In the passage from recognizing the relevant expression as pathological to noting *in the very words of the expression* that it is not true (or not true of itself) and then counting *this* remark true (or true of itself), we have an intuitive change of evaluation. The change does not seem attributable to the relevant singular expressions. That appears to leave a shift in the extension of the truth predicate and a shift in the applications of negation as possible sources of the change in evaluation.[13]

A third response by gap theorists fixes on negation.[14] The idea is that when we say of 'it is not true of itself' that it is not true of itself, we are using a broader sense of negation than the sense used in the pathological occurrence of 'it is not true of itself'. This idea seems the most plausible of those discussed here. But it does not promise a unified account of the paradoxes. There are semantical sentences lacking negation ('This is true') which, though not paradoxical, are pathological in a way intuitively analogous to the Liar. Moreover, it

---

[13] Actually there are other possibilities. Two interesting ones are suggested by Charles Parsons, "The Liar Paradox", reprinted in this volume. Parsons develops the ideas that there may be shifts in the domain of discourse or shifts in the extension of the notion of *expressing*—a relation between sentences and propositions. A thorough discussion of these ideas would take us too far afield. Suffice it here to say that in (A) and (B), we seem to be speaking of an English expression, standardly construed, throughout the example. The domain of discourse appears to remain constant. As for shifts of expression, one needs an argument for the universal applicability of the model which relates sentences to nonlinguistic intensional entities. It seems natural to think that paradox may arise even where the truth bearers are sentences (as interpreted in a context) or tokens. Moreover, many of the points we make below will apply by analogy to an "expression" relation. On the latter of Parson's approaches we do not yet have a systematic account of how truth value is determined by the semantical or pragmatic roles of sentential components.

[14] Frederic B. Fitch, "Universal Metalanguages for Philosophy", *Review of Metaphysics*, XVII, 3, 67 (March 1964): 396–402. Fitch does not actually discuss the present problem. But his treatment of a related problem involves this approach.

is known that semantical paradoxes can be produced *without* negation, using only the truth schema, *modus ponens*, and the inference rule: from $A \supset . A \supset B$ to infer $A \supset B$.[15] These negation-less paradoxes can be cast into strengthened form by informal reasoning about the material conditional. Now one might use the restrictions on the truth schema, which all gap theorists appeal to, to treat the "ordinary" paradoxes (and pathologies like 'This is true'), and a hierarchy of negations (and material conditionals!) to deal with the strengthened versions. But such an approach, though technically feasible, promises little philosophical illumination. The semantical paradoxes are remarkable in their similarity. The Strengthened Liar does not appear to have sources fundamentally different from those of the ordinary Liar. What is wrong with the proposed account is that it gives no insight into the general phenomenon of semantical pathology and offers instead a hodge-podge of makeshift and merely technical remedies. A theory of semantical paradox should focus on semantical notions.

The Strengthened Liar indicates that whatever other virtues truth-value gaps may have, they do not themselves mitigate the force of paradox. Indeed, they do little more than mark, in a specially dramatic way, the distinction between pathological sentences and sentences that are ordinarily labeled "false".

We have always had reason to distinguish 'x is false' from 'x is not true'. Nonsentences (or even open sentences apart from a context of application) are obviously or categorically not true. But one has no inclination to call them "false". Tarski regarded 'is false' as amounting to 'is a closed sentence that is not true'. Truth-value-gap theorists have seen this identification as unnatural, since some (closed) sentences seem to go wrong in ways that are deeper or prior to falsity. I am sympathetic with this viewpoint, at least as directed toward natural-language 'false'. If for the moment we ignore (with Tarski) qualifications needed for indexical sentences, we may see 'false' as appropriately applied to a proper subset of closed sentences that are not true—a subset meeting certain further *pragmatic* conditions. Such a view is compatible with retention of a highly general interpretation of the business of semantics, as giving laws for sorting true sentences, interpreted in a context, from those which are

---

[15] Haskell B. Curry, "The Inconsistency of Certain Formal Logics", *Journal of Symbolic Logic*, VII, 3 (September 1942): 115–17; P. T. Geach, "On *Insolubilia*", *Analysis*, XV, 3 (January 1955): 71/2.

not. Tarski himself rarely used the term 'false', sticking mostly with 'true' and negation. From this viewpoint, truth is not strictly the *value* of a function, as Frege held. It is rather seen on the model of a property that the relevant truth bearers, and everything else, either have or lack. This view is efficient as well as traditional. To treat the paradoxes, there is no need to give it up. Restricting the truth schema is the essential curative.

We have seen that some gap theorists envision combining truth-value gaps with some sort of hierarchy. And I believe that a move in this direction is necessary even to begin to cope with the intuitive evidence. But such a move seems to draw in its wake all or almost all the criticisms, mentioned at the beginning of this section, that gap theorists have leveled at Tarski's hierarchy. In view of the preceding, it would seem simpler to worry less about the gaps and rethink the hierarchy.

II.

In all the variants of the Strengthened Liar so far discussed, we started with (*a*) an occurrence of the Liar-like sentence. We then reasoned that the sentence is pathological and expressed our conclusion (*b*) that it is not true, in the very words of the pathological sentence. Finally we noted that doing this seemed to commit us to saying (*c*) that the sentence is true after all. Example (A) is especially striking. We seem to pass without intuitive difficulty from the hopeless tangle that Plato and Aristotle have got themselves into to the reasoned comment of the third party. Yet the third party uses the same sentence that was used by one or both of the tangled. The first task of an account of semantical paradox is to explicate the moves from (*a*) to (*b*) and from (*b*) to (*c*).

Most recent accounts have either ignored such reasoning as the above or sought simply to block it by formal means.[16] I think a more satisfying approach is to interpret the reasoning so as to *justify* it. The intuitiveness of the informal reasoning that generally occurs in the throes of paradox has been obscured by a concentration on simple, obviously perverse examples. I think it well to review a case

---

[16] There are exceptions. See A. N. Prior, "On a Family of Paradoxes", *Notre Dame Journal of Formal Logic*, II, 1 (January 1961): 16–32. Cf. also Herzberger, "Truth and Modality in Semantically Closed Languages", in *The Paradox of the Liar*, op. cit., esp. p. 31; and Parsons, op. cit.

(derived from Prior; cf. note 16) that is formally similar but less bizarre than the preceding.

(C) Suppose a student, thinking that he is in room 10 and that the teacher in room 9 is a fraud, writes on the board at noon 8/13/76: (a) 'There is no sentence written on the board in room 9 at noon 8/13/76 which is true as standardly construed'. Unfortunately, it being Friday the 13th, the student himself is in room 9, and the sentence he writes is the only one on the board there-then. The usual reasoning shows that it cannot have truth conditions. From this, we conclude that it is not true. But this leads to the observation that (b) there *is* no sentence written on the board in room 9 at noon 8/13/76 which is true as standardly construed. But then we have just asserted the sentence in question. So we reason (c) that it is true.

Before interpreting the reasoning in detail, I shall interpret it in summary. In the moves from (a) to (b) to (c) in example (C), there seems to be no change in the grammar or linguistic meaning of the expressions involved. This suggests that the shifts in evaluation should be explained in pragmatic terms. Since there is a shift from saying that the relevant sentence is not true to saying that the same sentence *is* true [(b) to (c)]—a shift in truth value without change of meaning—there is an indexical element at work.

The indexicality is most plausibly attributed to the truth predicate. As we have seen, there may or may not be a singular term in the examples, and any such singular term may or may not be indexical. Negation is not a regular feature in semantical pathology. Thus indexicality in the semantical predicates seems to be the natural alternative. The central idea in accounting for the move from (b) to (c) will be to interpret 'true' as contextually shifting its extension. In (b) we claim that the original paradoxical sentence (at the relevant occurrence) is not true—given the context of application of the occurrence of 'true' within it. Let us mark this occurrence as 'true$_i$'. But from a broader, or subsequent application of 'true', undertaken in (c), the sentence (at the relevant occurrence) is true (true$_k$)—since, in effect, it says it is not true$_i$; and it is not.

This explanation, which is sketchy and somewhat misleading, will be developed in sections IV and V. It is worth noting now, however, that the original sentence as interpreted at the relevant occurrence is not granted truth$_i$ conditions. That is, we should not insert the sentence so interpreted into the truth schema for 'true' construed as it occurs in that sentence ('true$_i$') and assert the resulting biconditional. All the solutions agree on some such restriction. The truth schema for 'true$_k$', however, may take the original sentence [interpreted as it is in step (*b*) and containing 'true$_i$'] as instance. The sentence is *not true$_i$*—not because its truth$_i$ conditions are not fulfilled, but because it has no truth$_i$ conditions. But it does have truth$_k$ conditions and indeed is true$_k$.

What of the move from (*a*) to (*b*)? For reasons that I will give in section III, I think that it does not strictly involve an indexical element in the sentences themselves. Rather, there is a shift in certain implicatures pragmatically associated with the sentence occurrences.

The relevant implicature is that *sentences being referred to or quantified over are to be evaluated with the truth schema for the occurrence of 'true' in the evaluating sentence.* In the paradoxical occurrence (*a*) the sentence referred to or quantified over is the evaluating sentence itself [as interpreted in occurrence (*a*)]. So it is implicated that that sentence is to be evaluated with a truth$_i$ schema. The sentence is shown to be pathological by taking the implicature seriously and applying the relevant schema. The implicature is scrutinized in the reasoning that shows that the application of the truth$_i$ schema leads to absurdity. When the same sentence is reasserted in (*b*) (and this sentence occurrence also lacks truth$_i$ conditions), the implicature has been canceled. The sentence [as it occurs in both (*a*) and (*b*)] may be evaluated in a broader semantical context (that of 'true$_k$'). But the reasoning behind the assertion of the sentence in step (*b*) is precisely that the truth$_i$ schema does not apply.

A simplified summary of the interpretation of examples like (C) follows:

step (a): (I):   (I) is not true
                  Represented as: (1): (1) is not true$_i$
                  Implicature: (1) is evaluated with truth$_i$ schema.
step (b):   (I) is not true (because pathological)
                  Represented as: (1) is not true$_i$
                  The implicature of step (a) is canceled.
step (c):   (I) is true after all
                  Represented as: (1) is true$_k$
                  Implicature: (1) is evaluated with truth$_k$ schema.

I have taken (1) to be a sentence interpreted in a context. But one may just as well take it to be a token.

III.

In this section I want to discuss the reasons for interpreting the move from (*a*) to (*b*) in terms of implicature. A natural reaction to example (C) is to say that the token of the sentence that is in room 9 is pathological or fails to express a proposition, whereas tokens outside room 9 are true.[17] This reaction may be interpreted as compatible with our viewpoint. The failure to express a proposition might be taken to *consist in* failure to be assigned truth conditions by the truth schema that is implicated to be appropriate.

This way of seeing the matter provides a partial rapprochement between our view and truth-value-gap approaches. We agree that in a limited sense not every well-formed sentence interpreted as used in a context is true or false, or even has truth conditions: Certain such sentences fail to be true (given an indexical use of 'true'—call it 'true$_i$') not because their truth$_i$ conditions are not fulfilled, but because they have none. Where our view differs from the truth-value-gap approaches is in its observation that this "failure to have truth conditions" (truth$_i$ conditions) is not an absolute affair. The same sentence interpreted in a context (or, if you prefer, same token) that lacks truth$_i$ conditions may, indeed will, have truth$_k$ conditions, and can be evaluated as true$_k$ or false$_k$. The plausible intuition that a given sentence, interpreted in a context, (or sentence token in room 9) has gone "bad" in a sense prior to falsity depends on the fact that the truth$_i$ schema that is pragmatically implicated to be appropriate for evaluating the sentence is not applicable to it. (At this point, the reader need not worry about the precise significance of the subscripts on 'true'. That will be explained in sections IV and V. It is enough to see them as marking contextually different applications of 'true' which yield different extensions for the indexical predicate.)

There are two important restrictions on any intuitive claim that the sentence (or token) occurring in room 9 in example (C) does not express a proposition or statement. First, the precise sense of 'proposition' must be explicated. For, if the term is taken in certain traditional senses, the claim will be mistaken. One cannot reasonably say that all paradox-producing sentences fail to have a

[17] Ushenko, "An Addendum to the Note on the Liar Paradox", *Mind*, LXVI, 1, 261 (January 1957): 98; Keith Donnellan, "A Note on the Liar Paradox", *The Philosophical Review*, LXVI, 3 (July 1957); 394–7; C. H. Whiteley, "Let Epimenides Lie!", *Analysis*, XIX, 1 (October 1958): 23/4; Jonathan Bennett, Review, *Journal of Symbolic Logic*, XXXII, 1 (March 1967): 108–12.

meaning or sense. Such sentences can be used in informal reasoning; we can express their content via semantic ascent; and their paradoxicality sometimes results from empirical facts, rather than anything intrinsic to their meaning. Further, such sentences can seemingly express reasonable beliefs or thoughts, even on occasions where they lead to paradox. This point is subject to further discussion elsewhere.[18] But, dogmatically speaking, we could have imagined the student in example (C) thinking about thoughts rather than writing about sentences. So 'failure to express a proposition' is not plausibly taken to mean 'failure to express something that could be believed'. Further, we are in the process of arguing that 'failure to express a proposition' need not mean 'failure to express something true or false', in any absolute sense of 'failure' or 'express'. Lacking some explication of 'proposition', then, the claim will be empty. Moreover, as it stands, the claim does not appear to touch the Richard paradox or the paradoxes of grounding.

Second, the claim does not obviate the need to explain the semantic or pragmatic mechanism whereby a given sentence changes from "not expressing a proposition" to being true. What is it about the use or meaning of the sentence (or its components) that accounts for the shift?

A tempting construal is to take the move from (a) to (b) to involve a shift in extension via some sort of indexicality, presumably in the truth predicate. On this view, the problem sentence as it occurs in (a) and (b) would receive different semantical evaluations: "bad" and "true", respectively. Unfortunately, the interpretation immediately leads to problems. Suppose we make explicit the extension of 'true' as it occurs in the pathological sentence token, by marking it with a subscript: 'true$_i$'. Thus, in example (C) step (a), we have (α) 'No sentence written in room 9 . . . is true$_i$'. The comment in step (b) on (α) would then involve a shift of extension yielding (β) 'No sentence written in room 9 . . . is true$_k$'. But one wants to know whether the sentence in the context marked by (α) is *true$_i$* or not. To say we can't ask (or answer) this question is obscurantist and needlessly mysterious. To say something amounting to "neither" is to head back in the direction of truth-value gaps, which we saw merely postpone the question. I take it as obvious that we should not say that the sentence as it occurs in step (a) represented by (α) is true$_i$. This would lead immediately to contradiction.

<hr>

[18] Cf. my "Buridan and Epistemic Paradox", op. cit.

Thus we should say that the sentence as it occurs in step (a) represented by (α) is not true$_i$: not true, because it lacks truth$_i$ conditions. This is in effect what we do say in step (b). So the occurrence of the problem sentence in step (b) can be represented by (β′), 'No sentence written in room 9 . . . is true$_i$'. Step (b) is thus reasonably seen as answering the question of whether (α) in step (a) is true$_i$ or not. Now it is difficult to see how there could be a shift of truth value or semantical evaluation between (α) and (β′), since they are one and the same!

Actually, this remark (though I think it is correct) prejudices the issue slightly since we have not fully formalized the occurrences of the problem sentence in steps (a) and (b). One might think, for example, that, since the occurrence in step (a) is in some broad sense self-referential while the occurrence in (b) is not, there must be some difference in formalization. (Strictly speaking since the problem sentence is and quantifies over a type not a token, it is self-referential in both (a) and (b); but there is an implicated self-referential element, not affecting formalization, which is present in step (a) but not in step (b)—which I shall identify shortly.) One might think that such a difference would reveal a difference of semantical evaluation.

Undermining this thought takes a further argument. Here it is. We have agreed that 'true' does not shift its extension between steps (a) and (b). But the quantifier phrase [which could be simplified to a singular term, as in examples (A) and (B), section I] does not, or need not, shift its domain or extension either. We can regard ourselves as making reference to a single sentence, interpreted in a contextually determined way, in both step (a) and step (b). (We could also revise the example so that we make reference to a single sentence *token* in room 9. Compare note 13.) So whatever formalizations one gives of the occurrences of the problem sentence in steps (a) and (b) respectively (even if the formalizations are not identical as I think they should be), those formalizations have the same component referents or extensions: they are extensionally isomorphic. So either there is no genuine shift of truth value or semantical evaluation between the formalizations [and between the occurrences of the natural-language problem sentence in (a) and (b)], or 'true' taken with a contextually fixed extension ('true$_i$') is nonextensional— producing truth bearers with different truth values when applied to terms with the same extensions. But there is no independent reason to regard 'true' as nonextensional. It has usually been taken to be *paradigmatically* extensional. Since some cases do not strictly involve loss of self-reference *or even change in the manner of reference* [examples (B) and (C)], the relevant restrictions on extensionality would seem as unmotivated as those associated with Skyrms' proposal (section 1). So it is reasonable to conclude that a change in truth value or semantical evaluation is not strictly involved in the move from (*a*) to (*b*) in example (C).

The move should be explicated pragmatically—in terms of change in implicatures or background assumptions on the part of those propounding or interpreting the relevant sentences. In step (*a*) when the problem sentence is first asserted, the implicature is that the sentence quantified over (satisfying the condition on the quantifier) is to be evaluated by a truth schema containing an occurrence of 'true' with the same extension as the occurrence of 'true' ('true$_i$') in the asserted problem sentence. The sentence quantified over turns out to be the asserted problem sentence, and accepting the implicature leads to contradiction. Nothing in the semantics of the problem sentence changes in step (*b*) when it is reasserted. The difference is that the implicature of step (*a*) has been canceled. The problem sentence as it occurs in our assertion in step (*b*) is not true$_i$ [just as it was in step (*a*)]. But we no longer expect it to have truth$_i$ conditions. To this degree paradox results from false expectations.[19]

This account explains why there *seems* to be a change of truth value. The sentence at the paradoxical occurrence in (*a*) is pathologically not true (not true$_i$) under the indexical application of 'true' that is implicated to be appropriate. The sentence at its occurrence in (*b*) is true (true$_k$) under the application that is there implicated to be appropriate. Thus there is a change from our thinking of the sentence at the first occurrence (*a*) as pathologically not true$_i$ to thinking of the same sentence at its second occurrence (*b*) as true$_k$. But the sentence at both occurrences is not true$_i$, and true$_k$.

---

[19] Cf. Grice, "Logic and Conversation", op. cit. Cancelability is the primary mark of implicatures. Grice's other general mark is that they are nondetachable in a certain conditional sense. This criterion is vague. But I believe that the relevant implicatures are detachable only insofar as Grice's condition is not satisfied; the manner of expression typically is crucial to the self-reference, hence to the calculation of the implicature.

IV.

The move from (*b*) to (*c*) in our examples is a shift from taking a sentence under a contextually determined interpretation as pathologically not true in taking the same sentence under the same interpretation as true. I have proposed to explain such shifts by regarding semantical predicates as indexical. The relevant notion of indexicality must be explicated from two viewpoints, structural and material. We shall take the structural viewpoint first.

The language I espouse as a model of natural language (at least for present purposes) has as its underlying logic standard first-order quantification theory. We place no general restrictions on quantification. Within this language occurs an indexical predicate 'satisfies', which has the usual formal relation to 'true'. (I shall henceforth speak informally only of 'true', and assume for simplicity's sake that no other semantical predicates occur.) These predicates are indexical in the sense that their extensions are not fixed, but vary systematically depending on their context of use. Thus the predicates are not strictly constants, though they may be and often are treated as such for a fixed context. They are not variables either, since we do not quantify over them. Though certain higher-order logics that make special ramification provisions (e.g., ramified type theory) do not quantify into the place of these predicates, these theories do not seem to model natural language perspicuously. Thus 'true' is a schematic predicate. In a given context 'true' takes on a specific extension, and in that context we can represent 'true' with a predicate 'Tr' (or 'Sat') subscripted numerically. The use of *numerical* subscripts is a matter we shall discuss shortly. How a subscript is established in a context is the "material" side of indexicality (section v).

There is considerable agreement that the semantical and set-theoretic paradoxes depend partly on the fact that *truth* and *set* are derivative notions. A sentence like (α) "(α) is true", which is intuitively pathological in the same way that the Liar sentence is, is pathological because (one feels) nothing is stated that can be evaluated as true. Something independent of the evaluation must be established before normal evaluation is possible. Similarly, the notion of a set's containing itself as a member is (to many) pathological because sets are (often) conceived as collections of entities. To be collectible, the members must exist independently of the set. Tarski's language-levels may be regarded as a means of expressing derivativeness. Part of the intuitive meaning of our subscripts on 'true' is implicit in Tarski's construction. Actually, Tarski's own construction is formally analogous to only one of several constructions—and not the most plausible one—which I shall develop from our indexical viewpoint. But it has the advantage of familiarity; so I shall expound it (or rather its analogue) first.

The basic idea behind all the constructions is to define a notion of a pathological$_i$ sentence. (From here on, I speak of *sentences*, understanding them to be *sentences as interpreted in a context*.) Then we claim that pathological$_i$ sentences are *not true$_i$*, and assert all and only instances of the truth$_i$ schema got from substituting sentences that are not pathological$_i$.[20] A sentence that is pathological$_i$ may be nonpathological$_k$, or indeed true$_k$, $k > i$. *Pathologicality is not an intrinsic condition but a disposition to produce disease for certain semantical evaluations*—evaluations that in a context may or may not be implicated as appropriate. There is nothing wrong with deducing or asserting a pathological$_i$ sentence, as long as one's implicatures are respectable and as long as the sentence is true$_k$, for some relevant $k > i$. [Cf. step (*b*) in the examples above.] For the general case, interpretations of instances of our axioms are to be understood as carrying the next higher subscript.

On *Construction 1* (C1), the analogue of Tarski's, all and only sentences containing 'true$_k$' $k \geqslant i$, $i \geqslant 1$, are pathological$_i$. Pathological$_i$ sentences are not true$_i$. Instances of the truth$_i$ schema are asserted for all (and only) sentences that are not pathological$_i$. Construction 1 differs from Tarski's only in taking the application of 'true$_i$' to pathological$_k$, $k \geqslant i$, strings to be well-formed, and in appropriately conditionalizing the truth schema. The advantages of this difference are twofold. First, natural-language sentences that lead to paradox do not seem to be ungrammatical or in some cases even odd [cf. example (C)]. Second, the present construction allows us to give truth conditions at higher levels to predications that Tarski counts ungrammatical. This captures an intuition we want. The sentence in example (C) led to paradox when we applied the truth schema corresponding to the occurrence of 'true' in the sentence (call it 'true$_i$'), and was thus not true$_i$ (pathological$_i$). But

[20] Schemas like this are alluded to in passing by Parsons, op. cit., pp. 21, 28–29. A conceptually similar schema is mentioned by Kripke, op. cit., p. 81, although its intended interpretation is importantly different. Cf. also Buridan, op. cit., pp. 92, 192, 195.

since this is just what the sentence said, we want on reflection to call it true (true$_{i+1}$) after all.

Construction 1 agrees with Tarski's in immunizing pathological$_i$ strings from the assignment of truth$_i$ conditions via the truth$_i$ schema. Self-referentially intended strings like 'This sentence is true$_i$' are not true$_i$—not because their truth$_i$ conditions are not fulfilled (they have no truth$_i$ conditions), but because they are pathological$_i$ in not applying 'true$_i$' ('true' at the appropriate occurrence) derivatively.

Construction 1 rules pathological the sentences that are intuitively empty or lead to paradox. But to some (including myself) it seems too stringent. The intuition behind Construction 2 is that the results of logically valid$_i$ inferences from true$_i$ sentences that contain no predications of $\ulcorner$true$_k\urcorner$, $k \geqslant i$, are true$_i$. From the premise that 'All snow is white' is true$_i$, we could get that 'All snow is white or a is not true$_i$' is true$_i$ (regardless of what 'a' denotes). Complex sentences that contain predications of $\ulcorner$true$_k\urcorner$, $k \geqslant i$, but whose truth$_i$ or falsity$_i$ is fixed by other components are nonpathological$_i$ and can be given truth$_i$ conditions.[21] On C2 a semantical evaluation of a sentence is derivative (nonpathological) only if the evaluation can be determined purely by reference to components of the sentence (or instances of its quantification) which either are non-semantical or are semantical predications with lower subscripts.

In what follows, I shall be assuming standard, first-order rules for well-formedness. What counts as a sequence may be determined by reference to any standard set theory. As for special vocabulary, let 'Sat$_i$' be the satisfaction predicate; 'P$_i$' represents 'is pathological$_i$ (relative to an assignment)'; 'α' and 'α_1' range over sequences; 't' and 't_1' over terms; 'x' over variables; and 'Γ', 'β' and 'ϕ', over well-formed formulas (actually only 'ϕ' must be so construed). We shall indulge in the use of corners, understanding them to be convertible into a system of Gödel numbering or a concatenation theory.

Construction 2 (C2) is summed up in the following principles: First, the definition of 'is pathological$_i$':

(1) $P_i(\ulcorner Sat_k(t, t_1)\urcorner, \alpha)$, $P_i(\ulcorner P_j(t, t_1)\urcorner, \alpha)$ $k, j \geqslant i$

(2)   If $P_i(\Gamma, \alpha)$, then $P_i(\ulcorner \sim \Gamma\urcorner, \alpha)$

---

[21] The idea behind Construction 2 is very much like the intuition behind S. C. Kleene's strong tables for three-valued logic. Construction 1 is roughly analogous to the weak tables. See his *Introduction to Metamathematics* (Princeton, N.J.: Van Nostrand, 1952), pp. 332 ff. No doubt, other constructions are worth thinking through.

(3)   If $[P_i(\beta, \alpha) \vee P_i(\Gamma, \alpha)]$ and $[\sim \text{Sat}_i(\alpha, \ulcorner \sim \beta \urcorner) \wedge \sim \text{Sat}_i(\alpha, \Gamma)]$,
$$\text{then } P_i(\ulcorner \beta \supset \Gamma \urcorner, \alpha)$$

(4)   If $(\exists \alpha_1) P_i(\phi, \alpha_1)$ and $\sim (\exists \alpha_1)(\alpha_1 \overset{x}{\approx} \alpha \wedge \text{Sat}_i(\alpha_1, \ulcorner \sim \phi \urcorner))$,
$$\text{then } P_i(\ulcorner (x)\phi \urcorner, \alpha)$$

where '$\alpha_1 \overset{x}{\approx} \alpha$' means '$\alpha_1$ differs from α at most in its assignment to variable x'. The rules for determining pathologicality of conjunctions, disjunctions, biconditionals, and existential quantifications can easily be developed by reference to these.

(5)   An expression is pathological$_i$ relative to an assignment only if it is so by (1)–(4) or by their analogues for other logical constants.

One point worth noting about this definition is that 'P_i' is relativized to a sequence even though this relativization plays no role in the basis clause (1). 'P_i' is defined partly in terms of 'Sat$_i$', which does not enter until clause (3). What I want to allow for is that an open sentence like '(x is not a mathematical sentence $\supset$ Sat$_2(\alpha, x)$)' may be true$_2$ (or true$_1$) relative to one assignment to 'x' (e.g., "2 + 2 = 4"), but pathological$_2$ relative to another (e.g., "Dogs are mammals").

Now we connect 'P_i' and 'Sat$_i$', counting pathological$_i$ sentences untrue$_i$:

(6) $P_i(\beta, \alpha) \supset \sim \text{Sat}_i(\alpha, \beta)$

We could, if we wished, *define* 'P_i' in terms of a sentence and its negation both being untrue$_i$.

We then relativize the semantical rules for the logical constants in the light of (1)–(6), arriving at a recursive characterization of truth:

(7) $\sim P_i(\ulcorner \sim \beta \urcorner, \alpha) \supset . \text{Sat}_i(\alpha, \ulcorner \sim \beta \urcorner) \equiv \sim \text{Sat}_i(\alpha, \beta)$

(8) $\sim P_i(\ulcorner \beta \supset \Gamma \urcorner, \alpha) \supset : \text{Sat}_i(\alpha, \ulcorner \beta \supset \Gamma \urcorner) \equiv . \text{Sat}_i(\alpha, \beta)$
$$\supset \text{Sat}_i(\alpha, \Gamma)$$

(9) $\sim P_i(\ulcorner (x)\phi \urcorner, \alpha) \supset . \text{Sat}_i(\alpha, \ulcorner (x)\phi \urcorner \equiv (\alpha_1)(\alpha_1 \overset{x}{\approx} \alpha$
$$\supset \text{Sat}_i(\alpha_1, \phi))$$

Similarly, for the other standard logical constants. We also note this principle, which has an analogue for 'P_j':

(10) $\sim P_i(\ulcorner \text{Sat}_j(t, t_1) \urcorner, \alpha) \supset . \text{Sat}_i(\alpha, \ulcorner \text{Sat}_j(t, t_1) \urcorner)$
$$\equiv \text{Sat}_j(\alpha(t), \alpha(t_1))$$

where '$\alpha(t)$' means 'the assignment of α to t'.

The restricted truth schemas are

(T) $\sim P_i(S, \alpha) \supset . \operatorname{Sat}_i(\alpha, S) \equiv P$

where 'S' stands for the name of any well-formed sentence and 'P' stands for the sentence itself.

On both C1 and C2, truth is cumulative: a sentence that is true$_i$ is true$_k$, $k > i$:

(11) $\operatorname{Sat}_i(\alpha, \Gamma) \supset \operatorname{Sat}_k(\alpha, \Gamma)$ $k > i$

From (11) it follows that a sentence not true$_k$, is not true$_{k-1}$, $k \geqslant 2$. As noted earlier, however, it is crucial that there be sentences not true$_i$, but true$_{i+1}$.

Iteration (on both C1 and C2) is appropriately expressed by ascending subscripts:

(12) $\operatorname{Sat}_i(\alpha, \Gamma) \supset \operatorname{Sat}_k(\alpha_1, \ulcorner\operatorname{Sat}_i(t, t_1)\urcorner), k > i; \alpha_1(t) = \alpha;$
$$\alpha_1(t_1) = \Gamma$$

A construction still more liberal in its certifications of non-pathologicality is possible. The intuition behind *Construction 3* (C3) is that if a sentence is true$_i$, then not only logically valid$_i$ inferences from it, but claims that it is true$_i$ are true$_i$.[22]

Thus we take all nonsemantical true$_1$ sentences, add sentences logically derivable from them; add all sentences that say that these sentences are true$_1$ (and that their negations are not true$_1$); then add sentences logically derivable from them; add all sentences that say these are true$_1$ (and that their negations are not true$_1$); and so on. Then do the same for true$_2$, beginning with all true$_2$ sentences that either are nonsemantical *or contain only 'true$_1$'*. And so on. C3 differs from C2 in that it does not force all iteration to ascend a level. On C2 '"Snow is white" is true$_i$' is pathological$_i$ though true$_{i+1}$. On C3 the same sentence is true$_i$ as well as true$_{i+1}$.

The guiding idea of C3 is close to the view that sound semantical evaluation should be grounded.[23] The important difference is that C3 does not require that nonpathological semantical evaluations be grounded in nonsemantical soil; they may be *rooted* either in

---

[22] Substantially this idea was discovered independently by John Ruttenberg in my seminar on the paradoxes.

[23] For discussions of the notion of grounding, see Herzberger, "Paradoxes of Grounding in Semantics", *The Journal of Philosophy*, LXVII, 6 (Mar. 26, 1970): 145–67; and Kripke, op. cit.

nonsemantical statements or in lower levels of semantical evaluations. This departure is needed to account for intuitions about the move from (*b*) to (*c*) in our examples of section II.

C3 differs in its axioms from C2 essentially in that it weakens (1) and strengthens (12). But C3 is more perspicuously expressed in terms of a formula's being *rooted*, understanding pathologicality to consist in rootlessness. Letting 'R_i' mean 'is rooted$_i$ (relative to an assignment)', C3 is stated as follows:

(0) $R_i(\Gamma, \alpha)$, where the largest subscript in $\Gamma < i$.
(We understand that if there are no subscripts in Γ, 'the largest subscript in Γ' will denote 0.)

(1') If $R_i(\Gamma, \alpha)$, then $R_i(\ulcorner Sat_i(t, t_1)\urcorner, \alpha_1)$ and
$R_i(\ulcorner R_i(t, t_1)\urcorner, \alpha_1)$, where $\alpha_1(t) = \alpha$ and $\alpha_1(t_1) = \Gamma$

(2') If $R_i(\Gamma, \alpha)$, then $R_i(\ulcorner \sim \Gamma \urcorner, \alpha)$

(3') If $[R_i(\beta, \alpha) \wedge R_i(\Gamma, \alpha)] \vee [Sat_i(\alpha, \ulcorner \sim \beta \urcorner) \vee Sat_i(\alpha, \Gamma)]$,
then $R_i(\ulcorner \beta \supset \Gamma \urcorner, \alpha)$

(4') If $(\alpha_1)R_i(\phi, \alpha_1) \vee (\exists \alpha_1)(\alpha_1 \overset{x}{\approx} \alpha \wedge Sat_i(\alpha_1, \ulcorner \sim \phi \urcorner))$,
then $R_i(\ulcorner (x)\phi \urcorner, \alpha)$.

Rules for other logical constants are analogous.

(5') An expression is rooted$_i$ relative to an assignment only if it is so by (0')–(4') or their analogues.

(6') $\sim R_i(\Gamma, \alpha) \supset \sim Sat_i(\alpha, \Gamma)$

$\ulcorner P_i \urcorner$ is defined as $\ulcorner \sim R_i \urcorner$, and (12) is strengthened to

(12') $Sat_i(a, \Gamma) \supset Sat_k(\alpha_1, \ulcorner Sat_i(t, t_i)\urcorner)$
$k \geqslant i; \alpha_1(t) = \alpha; \alpha_1(t_1) = \Gamma$

Otherwise, the axioms of C2 carry over to C3, with the understanding that $\ulcorner P_i \urcorner$ changes its meaning according to the new definition.

It is possible to liberalize (1') still further by changing the subscripts on 'Sat' and 'R' as they occur within the corners to *j* and *k* respectively, $j, k \geqslant i$. This allows as rooted$_i$ "loops" like

$$\text{'}Tr_i(\text{``}Tr_{i+3}(\text{'}2 + 2 = 4\text{'})\text{''})\text{'}$$

C3 is probably closest to intuition. But the key to the choice between C2 and C3 is iteration. If one could motivate the hierarchy better than I now know how to for *normal* cases of iteration ("'2 + 2 = 4' is true" is true), then C2 would become more attractive. And its ruling that "'2 + 2 = 4' is true$_i$" is pathologically not true$_i$

(though true$_{i+1}$) would take on appeal. I shall discuss differences among the constructions more concretely in section v.

On all three constructions, the law of excluded middle $\ulcorner P \vee \sim P \urcorner$ is valid (where validity attributions are subscripted in a manner suitable to the substitutions for '*P*'). And all closed sentences are (indeed, everything is) true$_i$ or not true$_i$ for any *i*. We do relinquish the idea that every closed (or maximally interpreted) sentence or its negation is true$_i$. But we have direct intuitive evidence for this. Neither (α), "It is not the case that (α) is true$_i$," nor its negation should be counted true$_i$. Either (α) or its negation [namely, (α)] is, however, true$_k$, $k > i$.

What is the justification for making the relation between indexical uses linear, and the subscripts numerical? Having gone through the reasoning that leads to counting a pathological$_i$ sentence true$_k$, we can get ourselves into hot water again by adding, perversely, "But this very sentence isn't". We may regard ourselves as having intentionally and anaphorically taken over the context of use for 'true$_k$'. To evaluate our perverse afterthought, we need a new context. So there is no limit on the number of different contextual applications of 'true' that might be required. Self-referential circles, like that in example (A) require that the relationship among markers of the contexts be transitive and asymmetric. Since sentences that do not contain semantical predicates (or other predicates of propositions, like 'knows', 'believes', or 'is necessary'—cf. note 3) do not produce paradoxes, it is natural to think of semantical predicate occurrences that apply to these sentences as having the lowest subscript.

To establish a linear relation, there remains only the requirement of comparability—that, for any two contexts of use for 'true', either the occurrences of 'true' have the same extension, or one of the occurrences is capable of evaluating or rationalizing the other. There is no compelling reason for this requirement in interpreting actual usage: does 'true' in example (B) have a higher or lower subscript than 'true' in example (C)? (One *could* relativize the hierarchy to a context, broadly conceived.) A natural consideration, however, leads to accepting the requirement. Any occurrence of a predicate can be assigned the lowest subscript compatible with the principles of material interpretation that we shall set out in section v. Assuming that the requirement is compatible with usage, I shall accept it as a means of rendering the formal model simpler.

What of the univocality criticism of Tarski? (Cf. section I.) Unlike Tarski, we do not interpret our systems as involving constant truth predicates.

In natural language there is a single indexical predicate. We represent this predicate by the schematic predicate expression $\ulcorner true_i \urcorner$. This expression may in particular contexts be filled out by any of an unlimited number of numerical subscripts. Any one of the resulting predicates (formally, there are infinitely many) may represent a particular occurrence of 'true' in a context in which its application is fixed. Thus numerals substituted for 'i' mark not new predicate constants, but contextual applications of the indexical 'true'. We have a general method for using this predicate. The existence of this method, which is represented in the formal principles given above and the material principles discussed in section V, provides considerable substance to the notion that 'true' has a single meaning.[24] On the other hand, the view that 'true' has a single extension is in conflict with intuitions about the Strengthened Liar [the moves from (*b*) to (*c*) in our examples].

A point often offered in favor of appealing to a "global" truth predicate is our ability to say such things as "All sentences are either true or not" or "God is omniscient". Such statements might be taken as asserted within a particular context (governed by a particular subscript). But one feels that they have broader import. These statements should be seen in the same light as principles, (0)–(12′). They are schematic generalizations. In the formal principles, the subscripts marking contexts of use stand open, ready to be filled in as the occasions arise. Similarly with our global English statements, including many statements in this paper. The first statement above, for example, should be formalized: $(s)(Tr_i(s) \lor {\sim} Tr_i(s))$. When we judge the schematic statement itself to be true, we make an equally schematic statement with the context for our evaluation schematically fixed as that of $\ulcorner true_{i+1} \urcorner$.

---

[24] I am ignoring the flexibility of 'true' as applied to different truth vehicles. As applied to sentences, two other contextual parameters enter in. The term must be relativized to a person and time to handle its application to nonsemantical, indexical sentences. And it must be seen to have another contextual parameter (not, I think, to be handled in tems of relativization to a language) which accounts for the fact that the same sentence may have different truth evaluations in different languages. Intralinguistic ambiguity is handled by interpreting the formalization of 'true' as applying to formal representations of the ambiguous surface sentence.

The indexical-schematic character of semantical predicates cannot be formally obviated by adding an argument place—relativizing them to a language, a level, a context, or a viewpoint. For quantification into the argument place will provide an open sentence just as subject to paradox as the "naive" truth-predicate formalization.[25]

Attempts to produce a "Super Liar" parasitic on our symbolism tend to betray a misunderstanding of the point of our account. For example, one might suggest a sentence like (a), '(a) is not true at any level'. But this is not an English reading of any sentence in our formalization. Our theory is a theory of 'true', not 'true at a level'. From our viewpoint, the latter phrase represents a misguided attempt to quantify out the indexical character of 'true'; it has some of the incongruity of 'here at some place'. No relativization will "deindexicalize" 'true'. Even in such English phrases as 'true at a level', the indexes occur implicitly on 'true'.

When we are given a semantical theory for nonsemantical indexical sentences, we relativize the semantical predicate to the context so as to generalize over all possible uses of the relevant indexical expressions. But insofar as we regard a semantical theory as a theory of the semantical predicate itself, there is no higher ground in which to absorb the indexical element. Theories of truth are in this sense models of or idealized directions for the use of the truth predicate. Axiom schemas like (7) are schematized directions for making statements whose component extensions are contextually fixed. The concept of truth cannot be defined or adequately represented in non-indexical terms. The indexical character of the language must be represented schematically.

V

The chief question about the application of the formal structure is how the subscripts are established in context. In our discussion of the linear structure of the hierarchy we suggested that the relevant subscript be the lowest subscript compatible with certain material

[25] Cf. Bertrand Russell, "Mathematical Logic as Based on the Theory of Types", in *Logic and Knowledge*, Robert C. Marsh, ed. (New York: Capricorn, 1971), pp. 64–9. See also Parsons, op. cit., note 13.

principles of interpretation. To begin with, natural-language statements are to be attributed no more pathologicality than other relevant considerations (specified below) dictate. More generally, subscripts on 'true' are assigned *ceteris paribus* so as to maximize the interpreter's ability to give a sentence truth conditions by way of a truth schema. We shall call this the *Principle of Verity*.

This principle is analogous to Quine's Principle of Charity in that it forms a general constraint on linguistic interpretation. But whereas Charity is motivated by an attempt to maximize the speaker's rationality, Verity applies in cases where the speaker's rationality is not at issue. If paradox is to be avoided, the subscript on a truth predicate in a quantified sentence of the form $\ulcorner(x)(Ax \supset$ $\sim Tr_i x)\urcorner$ must sometimes be higher than the subscript on truth predicates in sentences that satisfy A. For example, if someone said, "Everything Descartes said that does not concern mechanics was true", the subscript on 'true' would be high enough to interpret satisfactorily or give truth conditions to everything Descartes said that did not concern mechanics. The speaker and interpreter may not know what these subscripts are (even supposing they attached subscripts quite self-consciously) or be any less rational for their ignorance. The subscript (even if it remains schematic) is fixed by the context as the lowest that fits the interpreter's interpretative purpose.

The pragmatic justification for *Verity* should be pretty obvious. It excuses us in ordinary discourse from worrying about paradox, or semantical pathology generally, unless there is pressing reason to do so. Thus the extension of 'true' is a product not merely of the intentions of the speaker or hearer, but also of facts about the context of use and general conventions about the language. In this, it is roughly similar to the indexicality involved in a sign reading '(you) slow down'.

In the usual case, Verity will ensure healthy semantical statements. For example, if Construction 2 is preferred, normal iteration in surface English will be appropriately represented with ascending subscripts. How then does paradox arise? Sometimes the conditions laid down in a quantification or definite description (A in $\ulcorner(x)(Ax \supset$ $\sim Tr_i x)\urcorner$) will be clearly satisfied by the statement itself. If there is nothing in the subject's intentions, or in the context, that would warrant restricting the quantifier or descriptions, the statement is vulnerable to trouble. The student in example (C) unwittingly lands himself in difficulty. Occasionally, the subject's own intentions force the issue—sometimes perversely, as with the original Epimenides form of the Liar, sometimes constructively, as in the argument for Tarski's theorem. The Principle of Verity then is prevented from sanitizing all discourse by standard conventions in interpreting the rest of a subject's expressions.

A less important principle is that of *Justice*. One should not give one statement truth conditions instead of another without some reason. In (A), for example, there is no evident reason for treating Plato's statement any differently from Aristotle's. Although we are logically forced only to deny that both statements can be true, we should *ceteris paribus* assign both predicates the same subscript (1) and count both pathological.

Let us see how these principles operate to solve a problem that has been raised against Tarski's treatment. Suppose Dean says:

(i)   All Nixon's utterances about Watergate are untrue

and Nixon asserts

(ii)   Everything Dean utters about Watergate is untrue.

Each wishes to include the other's assertion within the scope of his own assertion. To ensure Justice, each person's truth predicate should be assigned the same subscript, i. To ensure Verity, we assume i is high enough to interpret any statement by Dean or Nixon other than (i) or (ii). I shall discuss the example on Constructions 2 and 3, which handle it deftly. On C2, in evaluating (i) and (ii) *we* use 'true$_{i+1}$', since on this approach sound semantical evaluation will be forced to a higher level. On C3 we must use 'true$_i$'. I shall place C3's reasoning in parentheses.

Suppose Dean has uttered at least one truth$_i$ about Watergate. It follows from the semantical rules for the quantifier [cf. (4), (5), (4'), (12'), (9)] that Nixon's assertion (ii) is nonpathological$_{i+1}$ and not true$_{i+1}$ (also nonpathological$_i$ and not true$_i$ on C3). If none of Nixon's other Watergate utterances besides (ii) are true$_i$, then since (ii) itself is not true$_i$ [since it is pathological$_i$ by (1)–(6) on C2; since its truth$_i$ conditions are not fulfilled on C3], Dean's (i) is true$_{i+1}$ (also true$_i$ on C3). On the other hand, if Nixon eked out at least one true$_i$ statement, then Dean's (i) is not true$_{i+1}$ (also not true$_i$ on C3). By erasing the subscripts and ignoring the parenthetical remarks in the previous four sentences, we have a piece of reasoning that is intuitive. Our theory accounts for the reasoning.[26]

The difference between C2 and C3 can be further elucidated by the following example.[27] Suppose Nixon says

(iii)   Mitchell is innocent and (iv) is not true

and Dean says

(iv)   (iii) is not true.

Let the occurrences of 'true' in (iii) and (iv) be marked by 'true$_i$'. Since (iii)'s first conjunct is not true$_i$, (iii) has truth$_i$ conditions and is not true$_i$ on both C2 and C3; so (iv) is true$_{i+1}$ (true$_i$ and true$_{i+1}$ for C3). Now there is a tendency for us to reason

(v)   Since (iv) is true and the second conjunct of (iii) says it's not, the second conjunct cannot be true.

The two constructions handle the case differently. C2 can accept (v) only if it is understood to involve a potential equivocation. (iv), by the preceding reasoning, is true$_{i+1}$. The second conjunct of (iii), interpreted not as it is in the context of Nixon's statement but as a denial of ours ['(iv) is not true$_{i+1}$'], is not true—not true$_{i+2}$. By contrast, the second conjunct of (iii) as it is interpreted in *Nixon's* statement ('(iv) is not true$_i$') is in no position to evaluate Dean's (iv) (according to C2) since it is not appropriately derivative. Dean's (iv) is trivially not true$_i$ since it lacks truth$_i$ conditions. So the second conjunct of (iii) interpreted as it is in Nixon's own statement is trivially true$_{i+1}$—not because Dean's (iv) is false$_i$ as Nixon would like us to imagine, but because it lacks truth$_i$ conditions. C2 suspends Nixon's right to evaluate Dean's (iv) because of the mutually reflexive situation. But it accounts for our ability to adjudicate the situation. Interpreted as a judgment from our point of view, (v) is justified.

Construction C3 treats the matter in a more straightforward and, I think, more natural way. Since (iv) is true$_i$ and rooted$_i$, and (iii)'s second conjunct says it's not true$_i$, that second conjunct is rooted$_i$ and not true$_i$. No fundamental distinction is drawn between our

---

[26] Kripke, op. cit., pp. 59–60, uses the example to show that Tarski's method of fixing the levels (applied literally to natural language) would counter-intuitively pronounce at least one of the statements ill-formed or nonsensical.

[27] I owe the example to Nathan Salmon, who had a different purpose in mind.

evaluation and Nixon's. Our intuitions about what the protagonists in such semantical entanglements can or cannot do are perhaps not clear-cut. Still, in the absence of reasons to the contrary, C3 is probably to be preferred.

VI

Let us survey the dividends of our account. We make no change in classical logic, no general restriction on quantification, no unintuitive postulations of ungrammaticality or meaninglessness. Our restrictions on the applications of 'true' are directly motivated by intuitive considerations. The theory provides a basis for explicating the univocality of 'true'. It gives weight to intuitions both about the "global" character of some uses of 'true' and about the context-dependent character of others. And it accounts for rather than merely obstructs paradoxical reasoning.

A bonus is that the account places no unnatural restrictions on translation of semantical discourse between natural languages. One of Tarski's characterizations of universality of a natural language is that any word in another language can be translated. Some writers seeking to apply Tarski's theory have argued that natural languages are not universal in this sense, holding for example that our predicate 'true in Urdu' cannot be translated into Urdu.[28]

The reasoning seems to go somewhat as follows. If Tarski's theory is to be applied to natural language, one must take a semantical system like his (including semantical postulates) as standing for or representing a natural language. A truth predicate in a natural language (e.g., 'true in English' or 'true in Urdu') should be represented by a predicate constant, with a fixed extension (e.g., all the true sentences of English) determined by the predicate's form and meaning. If Tarski's theory is to be applied, this constant must be governed by the usual semantical postulates. But, by Tarski's theorem, any such predicate for evaluating all the sentences of a

---

[28] Tarski, op. cit., 164; Herzberger, "Paradoxes of Grounding", op. cit., p. 167; Donald Davidson, "Truth and Meaning", *Synthese*, XVII, 3 (September 1967): 304–23, pp. 313/14. I have no desire to get into the somewhat vague question of whether artificial languages with non-indexical semantical predicates could always be translated into English. Of course, I think natural languages are not universal or closed, under Tarski's more precise characterization in terms of the capacity for self-reference and an unrestrictedly applicable truth schema with a truth predicate with constant extension. Cf. note 2, above.

semantical system cannot be introduced and used in the semantical system (with the usual semantical postulates) on pain of contradiction. So if Tarski's theory is to be applied, a truth predicate like 'true in English' cannot be allowed or cannot occur in English itself. Roughly this argument has played a role in criticisms (e.g., Tarski's criticism) as well as defenses of applying Tarski's theory to natural language, the difference in opinion focusing on whether the conclusion is a *reductio* of the initial if-clause.

Our account rejects the two initial assumptions of the argument. First, as noted at the outset, natural languages are not the sort of thing that can be inconsistent. One cannot assume that Tarski's "object language", "metalanguage" terminology can be cashed out in ordinary "language" language. So consistency restrictions on formal definability or formal introduction in a theory have little to do with conditions on translatability between natural languages. In the second place, Tarski's results bear on the definability or introducibility of predicate constants with an intuitively fixed extension. But the predicate 'true' (or 'true in Urdu') is not fixed apart from contexts of use. Tarski's results do bear on what extensions the predicate can have in given contexts. But they cannot prevent the occurrence or use of such a predicate even within consistent (context-dependent) formal systems, much less in natural languages.

On our view, 'true in Urdu' ('true$_i$ in Urdu') translates into Urdu without difficulty. The context-dependence and "implicit" subscripts are no less present when the predicate is used in English than when its analogue is used in Urdu. And this feature should be preserved under translation. The principles for establishing the level of a subscript on 'true' are not motivated purely by a desire to avoid contradiction. They are designed to capture the derivative feature of semantical evaluation in natural discourse.

Our reflections have suggested two general aspects of the use of indexical semantical predicates like 'true'. One is that their application is *derivative*. Their correct application is to statements which can be formulated and which have sense and reference, independently of the application. As a consequence, no statement can sit in semantical judgment on itself. Russell's vicious-circle principle and Tarski's appeal to a metalanguage were attempts to elucidate this important aspect of semantical notions. Truth-value gaps articulate it in their own way. Redundancy theories (e.g., Ramsey's and Strawson's) represent an extreme emphasis on it. A second aspect of our use of 'true' is that its applications are *evaluative*. In using the term we scrutinize sentences or statements to determine whether they are factually satisfactory, or, more loosely, whether things are as they are represented. Tarski's target biconditionals and his accompanying semantical analysis constituted a brilliant illumination of the structure of this evaluative use. Aristotle's well-worn dictum and traditional correspondence theories (e.g., the early Wittgenstein's and Austin's), for better or worse, were inspired by it.

The approaches to the paradoxes that we have criticized treat the derivative feature of semantical predicates as a fixed or absolute limitation on their evaluative use. Such approaches do not work because reflection on the proposed solution (in the Strengthened Liar) produces a new evaluation which cannot be expressed in terms of the solution or which is incompatible with it. The intuitive staying power of the evaluative use of the semantical predicates has been seriously underestimated in most post-Tarskian discussions: we have evaluative intuitions even in pathological cases. Semantical paradox issues from counterclaims between the derivative and evaluative aspects of semantical predicates. Our theory describes laws that resolve the conflict, while attempting to do justice to both claimants.

Postscript to "Semantical Paradox", 1982

"Semantical Paradox" is guided by two ideals. One is that it is possible to accommodate specific judgments about truth that arise in the course of reasoning that leads to paradox. Specific judgments are to be distinguished from those that attach to generalizations, principles, or schemas about truth. The distinction has, of course, a fuzzy borderline and should not be relied upon heavily; but I think it useful. The other ideal is that it is possible to identify in a semantical and pragmatic theory actual aspects of language or thought whose neglect yields the paradoxes. There are many ways to "block" the paradoxes. Any number of devices, provisions, or systems can be invoked to do so. A few of these have independent mathematical interest. Yet most ignore specific, widely shared judgments or propose theories whose distinctions are *ad hoc*, at least considered as accounts of actual usage, and which do not cohere well with the rest of linguistic theory. Our aim is to dissolve the paradoxes by accounting for specific judgments by means of a theory of language that does not require us to make implausible claims about the linguistic or pragmatic properties of the discourse, and that is motivated as directly as possible by those judgments.

These ideals are vague. And it is certainly not clear that they will determine a unique theory. Nevertheless, they have seemed to me to have considerable restrictive force, when applied seriously.

Except for the alteration of principle (0) (noted above), the basic theory is not much changed since its original publication. One refinement is a canonical ordering governing application of the pragmatic principles. The proper ordering seems to be: *Justice, Verity, Minimalization* (perhaps better labeled '*Beauty*'). This point and several special applications are discussed in "The Liar Paradox: Tangles and Chains", *Philosophical Studies* (1981).

Other possible refinements through application concern the variety of other notions that (arguably) are paradox-producing and that are not strictly semantical: class membership, necessity, knowledge, belief, acceptance, fearing, wanting, saying, promising, ordering, and so forth. I intend to use the theory to compare and contrast semantical notions and cognitive notions like belief and occurrent acceptance.

There is, of course, considerable room for technical refinement and development. Making explicit provisions for extending the constructions into the transfinite is of particular technical importance. The lack of such provisions in 'Semantical Paradox', together with some remarks that were intended as merely illustrative, have misled some into thinking that I intended to restrict the subscripts on semantical predicates to finite levels. In fact, there are no such restrictions on the subscripts in our statement of the formal principles. I believed and still believe that no such restrictions are appropriate. I was persuaded of this by Bill Hart in the course of writing the paper, and my views have since been enriched by work of Charles Parsons. Provisions must be made for the subscripts to range over transfinite ordinals and for the associated limit levels. I did not confront this issue in 'Semantical Paradox' because I realized that it raised substantial mathematical and conceptual difficulties and because I believed (and believe) that their solution would not profoundly affect the basic approach that I proposed in the article. I should, however, have made my view on this more explicit.

A further sort of refinement I envision concerns the philosophical interpretation of the theory. The theory is committed to there being two uses of 'true' in natural language: indexical uses and schematic uses. A predicate is *indexical* on an occasion of use if and only if it has a definite, fixed extension (or extensional application) on that occasion that depends not only on the contextually appropriate conventional meaning of the predicate, but further on the immediate context of its use. A predicate is *schematic* on an occasion of use if and only if it lacks a definite extension on that occasion, but through its conventional use on that occasion provides general systematic constraints on the extension(s) of the same predicate (or importantly related ones) on other occasions of use. The specific examples discussed in "Semantical Paradox" largely concern indexical uses. (There is no claim, incidentally, that the theory itself uses indexicals.) The formal principles are stated, as they must be, schematically. But these formal principles, and the pragmatic ones, apply to both indexical uses and schematic uses. This remark should forestall the confused criticism, which I have heard twice, that the basic formal principles are, according to the theory, neither true nor false. Such principles are true. In saying so we are using 'true' schematically.

Use of schematic principles in mathematical logic is common and well-established. I believe that it is primitive and not in general eliminable. We can express the "generality" intended by the subscript quantificationally. But in so doing, we invoke a meta-linguistic formula and a further semantical predicate. This predicate will itself be schematic. Thus we can say schematically: $\ulcorner \phi$ is true$_i \urcorner$ (suppose 'ϕ' is a name of a formula). We can express the intended "generality" in the form of a quantification:

For any ordinal number i $\ulcorner \phi$ is true$_i \urcorner$ is true.

But this latter occurrence of 'true' will also be schematic. There is no deschematizing the schema.

In view of its mathematical entrenchment and usefulness, schematic usage can hardly be seen as mysterious in the sense of 'suspect'. On the other hand, there is considerable room for improved philosophical understanding of it. The distinction between indexical and schematic uses connects with some of the most profound and difficult questions in interpreting foundational theories in mathematics, both type theories and set theories. One avenue that promises to deepen understanding is the comparison between schematic uses of 'true' and discourse about classes (as distinguished from sets) in set theory. There are several formal and intuitive parallels between indexical (extension-fixing) uses of 'true' and talk about sets, on one hand, and between schematic uses and talk about classes, on the other.

The circle of related notions may be wider. I think that the attempts by Reinhardt and Parsons to say something about the class–set distinction by reference to modal principles may be useful in illumining the indexical–schematic distinction as applied to 'true of'. (W. N. Reinhardt, "Remarks on Reflection Principles, Large Cardinals, and Elementary Embeddings", in *Axiomatic Set Theory* (*Proceedings of Symposia in Pure Mathematics*, vol. 13, 1974), part II, pp. 189–206; Charles Parsons, "What is the Iterative Conception of Set?" in *Logic, Foundations of Mathematics, and Computability Theory* (D. Reidel, Dordrecht, 1977).)

On the other hand, as Parsons notes, the analogy between modal notions and class-like notions is limited by the fact that the set–class distinction infects the interpretation of the modal language itself. Moreover, if (as I believe) the fundamental notions of necessity are expressed via predicates of sentential or propositional entities, rather than as intensional operators, the modal notions themselves will be expressed in indexical–schematic language. For, as is well-known, modal paradoxes analogous to the Liar emerge in a language in which modality is expressed as predication of sentences (or propositions with something like sentential structure). I believe that there is no transcending the indexical–schematic distinction—or reducing it to other terms, such as modal terms. But understanding it can benefit from structural and intuitive analogies to other conceptual systems.

Intensional Aspects of Semantical Self-Reference*

Brian Skyrms

I. *Prima Facie* Intensional Aspects of the Semantical Paradoxes

What would be required of a theory, for that theory to give the result that the Liar sentence is neither true nor false, and that we can say so truly and without equivocation? Let the Liar sentence in question be:

(1)   (1) is not true

and consider:

(2)   '(1) is not true' is not true.

Intuitively, we want (1) to be neither true nor false, and (2) to be true. Since one can move between (1) and (2) by substitution of coreferential singular terms, such a theory must be *intensional*. Notice that although (1) and (2) refer to the same sentence, (1) is *self-referential* whereas (2) is not. This simplest example suggests that an adequate treatment of the semantical paradoxes will turn on intensional aspects of semantical self-reference.[1]

The intuitions mobilized by the foregoing example extend to slightly more complex cases. Consider:

(3)   Socrates: "The next utterance of Plato will not be true".
(4)   Plato: "Socrates speaks truly".
(5)   Chrysippus: "Neither of the foregoing utterances is true or false. They are more like the cries of animals".

Brian Skyrms "Intensional Aspects of Semantical Self-Reference". Copyright © 1982 by Brian Skyrms.

* I would like to thank Bob Martin, Terry Parsons, and especially Peter Woodruff for valuable discussions on the topic of this paper.

[1] See Skyrms (1970). Kripke takes notice of the problem in Kripke (1975), 80, when he considers the "closing off" of the truth predicate, but this stratagem is not adequate for the concerns expressed here.

Intuitively, the situation can be characterized by diagram (A), where the arrow represents a relation of reference. I emphasize that this is simply a preliminary intuitive picture, since no theory of this relation has been given.

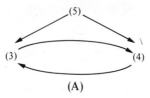

(A)

Although neither (3) nor (4) is, strictly speaking, self-referential, they are nevertheless involved in a vicious circle. The Chrysippian intuition is that they lack a truth value for this reason. (5), on the other hand, stands above the fray, and thus can comment truly on it.

We usually speak of the truth of sentences, but in certain cases we are forced to move (at least) to the level of tokens. Consider the following example due to Buridan:

(6)   Plato at t_1: What Aristotle says at t_1 is not true.
(7)   Aristotle at t_1: What Plato says at t_1 is not true.
(8)   Chrysippus at t_2: What Plato says at t_1 is not true.

Intuitively (6) and (7) are untrue, while (8) is true, but Chrysippus used the very same *sentence* as Aristotle. So to satisfy our intuitions, we have to attribute truth to *sentence tokens* (or sentence-context pairs). Plato's and Aristotle's tokens refer to each other. Chrysippus' token stands above the circle of reference and comments truly on it. Here, the failure of extensionality occurs at the level of tokens.[2]

Given the connections of the other semantical paradoxes with the paradoxes concerning truth, one would expect them to yield *prima facie* counterexamples to extensionality as well. Consider the following form of the Grelling:

(9)   'does not yield a truth when appended to its own quotation' does not yield a truth when appended to its own quotation.

Let us suppose that (9) is neither true nor false, and we can truly say so. In particular, suppose that:

(10)   (9) is not true

---

[2] Compare the treatment of this example in Burge (1979), 90–91.

is true. But (9) is scarcely different from:

(9') The result of appending 'does not yield a truth when appended to its own quotation' to its own quotation is not true.

But (9') differs from (10) only in that it contains a different name for (9). Assuming that (9') lacks a truth value if (9) does, we have another *prima facie* counterexample to extensionality.

II. Intensionality in the Arithmetization of Metamathematics

The area where self-reference is best understood results from Gödel's arithmetization of syntax. Here we have a rich array of results rather than a mere assortment of puzzles. It is tempting to try to extend the insights there gained to a more general treatment of the semantical paradoxes. Gödel himself ventured some thoughts along these lines:

Tarski has stressed in his lecture (and I think justly) the great importance of the concept of general recursiveness (or Turing's computability). It seems to me that this importance is largely due to the fact that with this concept one has for the first time succeeded in giving an absolute definition of an interesting epistemological notion, i.e., one not depending on the formalism chosen. In all other cases treated previously, such as demonstrability or definability, one has been able to define them only relative to a given language, and for each individual language it is clear that the one thus obtained is not the one looked for. For the concept of computability however, although it is merely a special kind of demonstrability or decidability the situation is different. By a kind of miracle it is not necessary to distinguish orders, and the diagonal procedure does not lead outside the defined notion. This, I think, should encourage one to expect the same thing to be possible also in other cases.[3]

What is responsible for the miracle? For partial recursive functions, the diagonal procedure does not lead outside the category, the reason being that the functions are *undefined* in the crucial place. Why not model a theory of truth which admits self-reference along these lines? I think that it is fair to say that the idea is already really there in Gödel (1944) and (1946). It has come to fruition in contemporary truth-value-gap treatments of self-reference, especially in the work of Kripke.

Gödel's investigations led not only to "gaps", but also to a kind of intensionality. This enters at the level of his second undecidability

---

[3] Gödel (1946).

theorem, "If arithmetic is consistent, then it cannot prove its own consistency". This statement holds for the canonical proof predicate of arithmetic, but as Mostowski (1966), Feferman (1960), and others have pointed out, the canonical proof predicate is only one of several formulas strongly representing "x is a proof of y", and for some of those formulas, the second incompleteness theorem fails.

Let k be the Gödel number of the formula $0 \neq 0$, and $\bar{k}$ be the numeral of that number. Let F be the formula that Gödel constructs which strongly represents the "proof of" relation in the formal theory in question. Then the consistency claim *Wid* is the formula $(x)[-F(x, \bar{k})]$. But if F strongly represents the "proof of" relation, then so does F', where $F'(x, y)$ is $F(x, y) \& -F(x, \bar{k})$, providing that the theory is consistent. Let *Wid'* be the formula $(x)[-F'(x, \bar{k})]$; that is, $(x) - [F(x, \bar{k}) \& -F(x, \bar{k})]$. *Wid'* is certainly provable, so if the theory is consistent, it can prove its own consistency in the sense of *Wid'* but not in the sense of *Wid*.[4]

Here we have perhaps the beginnings of an analogy with the treatment that I suggest for the Liar paradox. There are, however, also pressing disanalogies. The most obvious is that intensionality here enters at the level of the second incompleteness theorem rather than the first, but it is in the first incompleteness theorem that we find the closest analogy to the Liar sentence. Why does intensionality not enter at the level of the sentence that "says": "I am not provable"? The answer is that it has been regimented away by a device familiar enough in intensional logic; the device of standard names. The standard name for a Gödel number (and by extension for the expression that it is a number of) is its numeral. If we confine ourselves to such standard names, it is not surprising that we find no counterexamples to the substitutivity of identity. Suppose, however, that we augment our theory with definite descriptions as primitive designators. Then we find intensionality at the level of the first incompleteness theorem as well.

Let $B'y$ abbreviate the formula $(\exists x)[F'(x, y)]$. Let a be the Gödel number of the sentence $-B'\bar{a}$ (which "says of itself that it is not provable"). Let d abbreviate the description $(\imath x)[(-B'\bar{a} \supset x = \bar{a}) \& (B'\bar{a} \supset x = \bar{k})]$. Assuming that the theory of arithmetic in question is consistent, the description d and the numeral $\bar{a}$ both designate the number a (and in the appropriate sense, the sentence of

---

[4] See Mostowski (1966), 23–4.

which it is a Gödel number, $-B'\bar{a}$). But even though the sentence $-B'\bar{a}$ is not provable, the sentence $-B'd$ is, and the second comes from the first by substitution of a true identity. (The truth of the identity is, of course, not provable in the theory in question, but only in stronger theories.) I do not wish to claim that the analogy is more than an analogy. Provability is not truth.[5] The occurrence here of intensionality like the occurrence of partial functions, suggests rather than establishes the desirability of similar features in a theory of semantical self-reference.

III. Intensional Fixed Points in a Theory of Truth

I wish to consider a construction which is a variation on that discussed by Kripke in "Outline of a Theory of Truth". The difference[6] is in the function f, which maps the set of partial valuations of the language into itself. (By a partial valuation I mean a pair (S_1, S_2) consisting of an extension, S_1, and an antiextension, S_2, for the truth predicate. I do not require as part of the definition of a partial valuation that S_1 and S_2 be disjoint.) Let f be the function which maps a partial valuation (S_1, S_2) onto the partial valuation (S_1^+, S_2^+) such that:

(A) If x in S_1 then x in S_1^+. If x in S_2 then x in S_2^+.

(B) If the interpretation of the language based on (S_1, S_2) makes x true, then x is in S_1^+; if the interpretation of the language based on (S_1, S_2) makes x false, or if x is a non-sentence, then x is in S_2^+.

(In (B) the interpretation is extended to the whole language by means of the Kleene strong three-valued truth tables extended to

---

[5] And the notions of strong and weak representability in arithmetic are intensional on their face, due to the way in which they involve provability. But I think that intensionality at the level of the first incompleteness theorem of the kind I have just pointed out also has a deeper source. That is a theme which runs through all the paradoxes; the difference between what can be established inside and outside a given system. In the case just discussed, the crucial coextensiveness of designators can only be established from outside; can only be proved from the external perspective of a stronger system. Here we can say that the external and internal perspectives have to do with different senses of *proof*. But if we are trying to maintain one grand overarching sense of *truth*, the analogous move is not an option.

[6] I presuppose familiarity with Kripke (1975), 66–70, here.

quantification as in Kripke.[7]) The difference from Kripke's presentation is that his function ϕ is defined without clause (A) and with Iffs in clause (B). However, for the orbits leading to his fixed points, Kripke shows that (A) holds. So every fixed point of Kripke's function ϕ is a fixed point of our function f.

The treatment of paradoxical sentences is somewhat different. On Kripke's treatment, if the Liar sentence is in S_1 in partial valuation V, it moves to S_2 in $\phi(V)$, and back to S_1 in $\phi(\phi(V))$, etc. Assigning a paradoxical sentence a truth value sets up oscillations at the finite stages of the construction. On my variant construction, if the Liar sentence is in S_1 in V, or if it is in S_2 in V, it is in both S_1 and S_2 in $f(V)$, $f(f(V))$, and thereafter. Let us say that a valuation is *paradoxical* iff in it the intersection of S_1 and S_2 is non-empty. A *sentence* is paradoxical iff every partial valuation which gives it a truth value leads (by the action of iterations of f) to a paradoxical valuation. A *set of sentences* is paradoxical iff every partial valuation which gives all members of the set a truth value leads to a paradoxical partial valuation.

An *intensional* partial valuation will be one which assigns two sentences which differ only by substitution of coreferential designators, to different categories (the categories being: in S_1 but not S_2, S_2 but not S_1, both, neither). There are *intensional non-paradoxical fixed points*. Let $a = $ 'a is not true', $b = $ 'a is not true', $c = $ 'b is not true'. Let us move from the minimal fixed point to another partial valuation, V, by moving c into S_1, but leaving a in neither S_1 nor S_2.[8] Now go along the orbit of V (by iterating f) until you reach a fixed point. This will lead to a non-paradoxical intensional fixed point. We won't get in trouble because our

---

[7] How is the function f defined for paradoxical partial valuations? Just the same as before, except that we have to use the Kleene strong three-valued truth tables more than once. For example, if p is both true and false and q is neither true nor false, their disjunction is true. It receives no truth value on the Kleene tables by virtue of p being false and q neither, but attains the value true by p being true and q neither. Likewise, if p is both true and false, then its negation is also; false by virtue of the truth of p and true by virtue of the falsity of p. Peter Woodruff has pointed out to me that this procedure is equivalent to using the Dunn–Belnap four-valued truth tables (where the values are: both true and false; true but not both; false but not both; neither). See Dunn (1969), (1976); and Belnap (1976). Paradoxical partial valuations lead to paradoxical fixed points. My concern here is with non-paradoxical fixed points. Paradoxical fixed points will be investigated in a forthcoming paper by Peter Woodruff.

[8] We would move to a more satisfying partial valuation of 'T' by putting the negation of c in S_2, etc. We will see later how to get this without fiddling.

construction never looks back. Once a sentence gets in S, no further questions are asked. From the standpoint of the path from V to the fixed point, sentence c might as well have been "grass is green". On the other hand, the fixed point will make sentence a neither true nor false, since the only way f will give it a truth value is if it had one at an earlier stage. Thus we have an intensional non-paradoxical fixed point.

So although sentences a and c differ only in that they contain coextensive singular terms, they behave quite differently with respect to f. Sentence a is paradoxical. Making it true or false leads to a paradoxical point. Sentence c is not. It is true in some non-paradoxical fixed point. *This is a realization of the intuition that sentence a is viciously self-referential, whereas sentence c is not self-referential.*

It is, however, true that although sentence c is in the extension of the truth predicate in the non-extensional fixed point described, it is not assigned the value *true* by the interpretation corresponding to that valuation. This is because we are using *extensional* interpretations. Since a and c refer to the same sentence, i.e., a, extensional interpretations must treat them alike. It is worth noticing that we can get this much intensionality even with extensional interpretations, but we can move to a more adequate theory by introducing intensional interpretations.

If 'T' is our truth predicate, then the truth value of a sentence consisting of 'T' concatenated with a singular term should not be a function of the extension of the singular term, but also of other factors, including the term itself. Thus, in our theory of truth, we need to replace the extension and anti-extension of 'T' with sets whose members specify enough things to determine truth. I'll call these new sets the *D-tension*, D_1, and *anti-D-tension*, D_2, of 'T'. The members of these sets will be ordered n-tuples, whose first member is an object, and whose second member is the name of an object. (The relevant pairs for D_1 will be pairs consisting of sentences and names of sentences respectively. Such pairs and others as well will get into D_2). Other places in the n-tuple can be used to handle indexicality. I will abstract from this problem here, so in the following the members of D_1 and D_2 will be ordered pairs. The union of the D-tension and anti-D-tension of 'T' will be called its *range of significance* (in the interpretation). The set of first members of ordered pairs in the D-tension of 'T' is the *extension* of 'T'; similarly for the *anti-extension*.

Intensional interpretations work as follows: The truth value of atomic truth-ascription sentences—sentences of the form 'T' concatenated with a singular term—are now just read off the D-tension and anti-D-tension. If a singular term denotes a sentence, and the pair consisting of the sentence and the singular term denoting it are in D_2, then the interpretation assigns the sentence consisting of 'T' concatenated with that singular term the value 1 (i.e., "true"). Likewise for the anti-D-tension and the value 0 (i.e., false). The assignment of truth values is extended to the truth functions by using the Kleene strong truth tables, and to quantifiers taking them substitutionally and using the Kleene strong truth tables. [We assume that our language has at least one name for every sentence in the domain. We assume for convenience that it also has a name for every object in the domain. The second assumption could be dispensed with at the cost of a small complication of the treatment of quantifiers, since the only intensional aspect of the language has to do with the truth of sentences.]

Now let g be the function which maps (D_1, D_2) onto (D_1^+, D_2^+) such that:

(A) If x is in D_1 then x is in D_1^+. If x is in D_2, then x is in D_2^+.
(B) If the interpretation of the language based on (D_1, D_2) makes x true and y is any name of x, then (x, y) is in D_1^+. If the interpretation of the language based on (D_1, D_2) makes x false or x is a non-sentence, and y is any name of x, then (x, y) is in D_2^+.

Once an interpretation assigns the value *true* to a sentence, it's safe to say it's true by any name. Likewise with *false*. The function g doesn't introduce any intensionality, but it respects intensionality that's already there. If we look at what g does to the first members of the ordered pairs (x, y), we see the function f which we previously considered. The extensional theory with which we began this section can be embedded in this theory. A point in the old theory consisting of an extension and anti-extension (S_1, S_2) corresponds to a point in the new theory consisting of a D-tension and anti-D-tension (D_1, D_2) such that if x is in S_1 and y is a name of x, (x, y) is in D_1. Likewise for S_2 and D_2.

Now, let us reconsider the example we have been discussing; $a = b =$ 'a is not true', $c =$ 'b is not true'. We start at the minimal fixed point. This is the same as Kripke's minimal fixed point (embedded in the new theory in the way just discussed). At this point, neither $(a, `a')$ nor $(b, `b')$ is in $D_1 \cup D_2$. Now we move to another point by putting $(a, `b')$ in D_2. Now, we move along the orbit of this point to a fixed point. For example, after one application of g, we move to a point where c by any name is in D_1, negation of c by any name is in D_2, etc.[9] Eventually we get to an intensional, non-paradoxical fixed point, as before. However, at this point, we no longer have a disagreement between the partial valuation of the truth-predicate 'T', described by (D_1, D_2) and the truth values assigned by the interpretation based on that partial valuation. This is because this fixed point is now intensional in a full-blown sense of the word; both on the side of (D_1, D_2) and on the side on the interpretation of the language.

IV. Propositions

There is a great temptation to say that, in some sense of proposition, the Liar sentence and its ilk simply do not express a proposition. If one is willing to talk about propositions in this way, one can maintain that propositions are much better behaved than sentences (or sentence tokens). Suppose that one believes that truth and falsity apply primarily to propositions and only secondarily to sentences or sentence tokens which express them. One can then, both adopt a truth-value gap approach to the paradoxes at the level of sentences and save the principle of *bivalence* at the level of propositions. Truth-value gaps at the level of notation will be held to occur just when there is no proposition to correspond to the notation. Several writers have found such a line attractive. It should therefore not go unnoticed that this strategy also allows one to adopt an intensional treatment of semantical self-reference at the level of notation, while maintaining a version of *extensionality* at the level of propositions. On the approach I am suggesting, substitution of coextensive designators never takes one from a true sentence to a false one, although it may take one from either to one with no truth value and conversely. Then the story that we can tell to save bivalence at the level of propositions also saves the following principle of extensionality: If two sentences of the theory are extensionally equivalent and if they both express propositions, then they both have the same

[9] This discharges the promise of footnote 8.

truth value. (We are assuming here that the base language with which we start is extensional.)

The foregoing may take on more interest if we have a *theory of propositions*. What are the sorts of propositions that the Liar sentence fails to express, but that sentences which differ from it only by the substitution of coreferential terms can express? Taking a cue from the verifiability theory of meaning, we could say that *the proposition expressed by a sentence consists of the set of all orbits leading to a non-paradoxical fixed point which makes it true*. Or, giving falsifiability its due, we could take the ordered pair whose first member is the set just described, and whose second member is the set of all orbits leading to a non-paradoxical fixed point which assigns it to the anti-extension of true. The degenerate case, $\langle \Lambda, \Lambda \rangle$, is no proposition. (Really we mean an ordered pair of mereological sums, or something of the kind, rather than of sets).

Then paradoxical sentences express no proposition (or if you prefer no non-degenerate proposition). Furthermore, substitution of coextensive designators can take one from a sentence which expresses a proposition to one which doesn't; e.g. in the last section c expresses a proposition while a doesn't.

V. Extensionally Equivalent Truth Predicates

We have defined the extension of a truth predicate as the set of sentences of which it is true by some name; that is, as the set of first members of ordered pairs in its *D*-tension; likewise for the anti-extension. It is conceivable that two truth predicates could be extensionally equivalent, in that they share the same extension and anti-extension, and yet have different ranges of significance (because of the non-extensional nature of *D*-tension and anti-*D*-tension).

Consider a language with two truth predicates, 'T' and 'T^*'. Suppose that $b = a = $ '$-Ta$' and $c = d = $ '$-T^*c$'. Now, according to the approach being developed here, it is plausible to move from the minimal fixed point to one which puts $(a, \text{`}b\text{'})$ but not $(a, \text{`}a\text{'})$ in D_2 of 'T', leading to an interpretation which makes '$-Tb$' true while assigning no truth value to '$-Ta$'. By parity of reasoning, one would, on this approach, put $(c, \text{`}d\text{'})$ but not $(c, \text{`}c\text{'})$ in D_2 of 'T^*' leading to an interpretation which makes '$-T^*d$' true while leaving '$-T^*c$' without a truth value.

But it should be noticed, that we can concatenate the predicate 'T^*' with names 'a' and 'b' with as little danger of paradoxical self-reference as concatenating 'T' with 'b'. [Likewise with the predicate 'T' and the names, 'c' and 'd'.] Thus, we could also put $(a, 'a')$ and $(a, 'b')$ in the D_2 of 'T^*' and $(c, 'c')$, and $(c, 'd')$ in the D_2 of 'T'. This would lead to an interpretation, salient features of which are collected in the following table:

'$-Ta$'	no value
'$-Tb$'	true
'$-Tc$'	true
'$-Td$'	true
'$-T^*a$'	true
'$-T^*b$'	true
'$-T^*c$'	no value
'$-T^*d$'	true

for the intuitive reasons summarized in diagram (B).

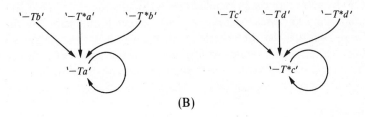

(B)

So it is possible to have two predicates, 'T' and 'T^*', extensionally equivalent, and have the substitution of one for the other lead from a true sentence to one which has no truth value.

VI. Conclusion

In commenting on Russell's resolution of the paradoxes, Gödel (1944) makes a provocative suggestion:

It should be noted that the theory of types brings in a new idea for the solution of the paradoxes, especially suited to their intensional form. It consists in blaming the paradoxes not on the axiom that every propositional function defines a concept or class, but on the assumption that every concept gives a meaningful proposition, if asserted of an arbitrary object or objects as arguments. The obvious objection that every concept can be extended to all arguments by defining another one which gives a false proposition whenever the original one was meaningless, can easily be dealt with by pointing out that the concept "meaningfully applicable" need not itself always be meaningfully applicable.

The theory of simple types (in its realistic interpretation) can be considered as a carrying through of this scheme, based, however, on the following assumption concerning meaningfulness: "Whenever an object x can replace another object y in one meaningful proposition, it can do so in every meaningful proposition." . . . What makes the above principle particularly suspect, however, is that its very assumption makes its formulation as a meaningful proposition impossible. . . .

It is not impossible that the idea of limited ranges of significance could be carried out without the above restrictive principle. It might even turn out that it is possible to assume every concept to be significant everywhere except for certain "singular points" or "limiting points" so that the paradoxes would appear as something analogous to dividing by zero. Such a system would be more satisfactory in the following respect: our logical intuitions would then remain correct up to certain minor corrections, i.e., they could be considered to give an essentially correct, only somewhat "blurred" picture of the real state of affairs.[10]

The restrictions on ranges of significance can be loosened even more by giving up the principle of extensionality implicit in Gödel's initial remarks. Meaningfulness might depend not only on the objects, but also on the notation—on the way bits of language are put together in an attempt to formulate a claim about the objects. The intensional solutions which then become possible allow us to approach more closely the state envisioned in his closing sentences.

References

Burge, T. (1979), "Semantical Paradox", reprinted in this volume.

Belnap, N. D., Jr. (1976), "A Useful 4-valued Logic", in *Modern Uses of Multiple-Valued Logic*, ed. Epstein and Dunn (Reidel: Dordrecht, 1976).

Dunn, J. M. (1969), "Natural Language vs. Formal Language", presented to the joint APA–ASL symposium, N.Y. Dec. 27, 1969 (mimeo).

Dunn, J. M. (1976), "Intuitive Semantics for First-Degree Entailments and 'Coupled Trees'", *Philosophical Studies* 29, 149–68.

Feferman, S. (1960), "Arithmetization of Metamathematics in a General Setting", *Fundamenta Mathematica*, 35–92.

Gödel, K. (1944), "On Russell's Mathematical Logic" in *The Philosophy of Bertrand Russell*, ed. P. A. Schilpp (Tudor: New York), reprinted in *Philosophy of Mathematics, Selected Readings*, ed. P. Benacerraf and H. Putnam (Prentice-Hall: N.Y. 1964), 211–32.

[10] Gödel (1944), 228–9.

Gödel, K. (1946), "Remarks before the Princeton Bicentennial Conference on Problems in Mathematics—1946", in *The Undecidable*, ed. Davis (Raven Press: Hewlett, N.Y., 1965).

Kripke, S. (1975). "Outline of a Theory of Truth", reprinted in this volume.

Mostowski, A. (1966), *Thirty Years of Foundational Studies* (Barnes and Noble: New York).

Skyrms, B. (1970), "Return of the Liar; Three-Valued Logic and the Nature of Truth", *American Philosophical Quarterly*, 7, 153–61.

Notes on Naive Semantics*

Hans G. Herzberger

I. Introduction

These notes sketch a modification of Kripke's theory of truth, within which it seems possible to reconstruct so-called "naive semantics" in an unexpectedly systematic way. This is something which does not seem to have been undertaken before, and perhaps could not have been undertaken without the guidance of Kripke [9].

Various authors have used the term "naive semantics" to refer to some primordial beliefs about the concept of truth, which are held responsible for the semantic paradoxes. The term invokes some analogy with "naive set theory", but there is a prominent disanalogy: whereas naive set theory was a highly developed mathematical discipline, its counterpart in semantics has never been systematically worked out. In fact there is a widespread opinion, expressed in the writings of Tarski and others, that naive semantics

Hans G. Herzberger, "Notes on Naive Semantics", reprinted from the *Journal of Philosophical Logic* 11 (1982), 61–102. Copyright © 1982 by D. Reidel Publishing Company, Dordrecht, Holland.

* These notes are intended as a working report on material that is still in a very provisional formulation. Work on this material was supported in 1979–80 by a Leave Fellowship from the Social Sciences and Humanities Research Council of Canada, and in 1980–1 by a Visiting Fellowship from All Souls College, Oxford. Previous versions of these notes have been circulating since mid-1980 and were the basis for talks given at Oxford and Keele Universities in 1980–1. Subsequently, Dana Scott and Alasdair Urquhart put me on the track of the completely independent work which Anil Gupta had been pursuing during the same period. There is considerable overlap between "naive semantics" and Gupta's approach, both of which spring from a common concern: to modify Kripke's theory of truth so as to admit the classical valuation scheme. I am indebted to Steve Yablo for many discussions on topics covered in these notes, especially for helping me to sharpen the distinction between grounding and stability; and to Saul Kripke for generous criticism and some telling counterexamples. I have benefited very much from discussions with many people, including George Boolos, Michael Dummett, Bill Hart, Hans Kamp, David Lewis, John Mackie, Charles Parsons, Christopher Peacocke, Hilary Putnam, Dana Scott, Neil Tennant, and David Wiggins. I also owe a special debt to the recent work of Tyler Burge [3], which played a catalytic role in the early stages of these investigations.

could not be systematically worked out because it is a fundamentally incoherent, or inconsistent, or otherwise logically defective body of beliefs (see [18], p. 267).

Much recent work on the semantic paradoxes involves some form of nonstandard logic or model theory, and for this reason cannot illuminate naive semantics in any fully satisfactory way.[1] Two approaches of this kind may be mentioned. On one approach, paradoxical statements have been treated as neither true nor false; this leads in the direction of many-valued or supervaluational semantics.[2] On the other approach, paradoxical statements have been treated as somehow both true and false; this leads in the direction of so-called antinomic or dialectical logic.[3]

The present reconstruction is different in spirit from either of the two approaches just mentioned. Unlike many previous treatments of the paradoxes, this one uses only ordinary models and classical two-valued valuations. This seems appropriate, inasmuch as it is reasoning in accordance with classical logic which in the first instance gives rise to the semantic paradoxes. On the present reconstruction, paradoxical statements will not be treated as both true and false, nor will they be treated as neither true nor false. They will be treated as statements which are systematically unstable in their semantic valuation. Within this reconstruction, a paradoxical statement is one which is evaluated as true on one level, false on some higher level, true again on some still higher level, and so on. Because the semantics is hierarchical or at least semi-hierarchical, it can accommodate this kind of semantic instability without contradiction or incoherence. It makes available a novel reconstruction of what some people have felt to be the "inconsistency" of natural languages.

What is perhaps unexpected in this reconstruction is the highly systematic character of the semantic instability of paradoxical statements. Far from being incoherent or in any way unmanageable,

---

[1] An important exception to this trend is the recent work of Feferman and others, which manages to use classical two-valued semantics by resorting to inductions based on partial jump operations. These "selective" inductive constructions relate closely to the languages that result from closing off Kripke's fixed-point models. See Feferman [5] and references therein to the work of Fitch, Gilmore, Scott, and others.

[2] An early treatment of this sort is Bochvar [2]. Later work in this direction by Martin, Skyrms, van Fraassen, and others is reported in Martin [12]; *v.* also Kripke [9].

[3] See Rescher and Brandom [17] for discussion and references; and also Priest [13].

naive semantics turns out to be no less systematic than Kripke's inductive semantics, and also in some respects stronger than anything accessible within the inductive framework. Consequently, it may afford a sharper characterization of the nature of semantic paradoxes. It certainly does provide an instrument for studying those paradoxes and a new accommodation to them. Rather than attempting to resolve the paradoxes by rendering critical statements truth-valueless or otherwise neutralizing them, naive semantics undertakes to exhibit and characterize their specific patterns and degrees of instability. This is to some extent in the spirit of Charles Chihara's recent efforts [4] to "diagnose" the semantic paradoxes.

Technically what makes it possible to reconstruct naive semantics in this systematic way, is a modification of Kripke's theory of truth to admit the classical valuation-scheme. Whereas Kripke's construction is "monotonic" and inductive, the present construction will be non-monotonic and "semi-inductive" in a sense that will be explained.

II. A Thought Experiment

What would happen on Kripke's construction if one started out from some classical model with an initial truth-predicate whose "anti-extension" complemented its extension? Because classical models have no "gaps" the construction might never reach a fixed-point. But nevertheless it may be of some interest to consider what it would be like.

Finite levels would at first appear to be somewhat chaotic, with valuations inconsistent from one level to the next. The simplest Liar statements like 'I am false' would be declared true at one stage, false at the next, then true again and so on. Now this accords rather closely with naive intuition, for the Liar statement does seem to have just this kind of semantic instability under continued efforts to evaluate it. Other well-known paradoxical statements might have slightly more complicated patterns of instability: some might be true only at every n-th stage, and so on. By way of contrast, ordinary "grounded" statements of finite rank would sooner or later obtain fixed and stable values. Some of them might alternate initially, but they would eventually settle down.

It would be highly interesting if this construction were able just to sort itself out completely in this way, so that on sufficiently high levels all grounded statements would have stabilized, leaving only pockets of instability around paradoxical statements. But this idea cannot be carried through on Kripke's theory as it stands, because one would not be able to reach sufficiently high levels. That theory is closely tailored to "monotonic" constructions, and will not continue the present sort of construction even to the first infinite stage. The reason is that Kripke's construction forms unions of all previous stages at each limit stage, so that at stage ω it would put the Liar statement in the extension of T and it would also put that same statement in the anti-extension of T. But then the Liar statement would get evaluated as both true and false at stage ω (see [9], p. 64), which is absurd. Or, to put the matter another way, the various valuation-schemes admissible within Kripke's theory, all presuppose and require the extension for any predicate to be disjoint from its anti-extension; they are not equipped to accommodate predicates with overlapping extension and anti-extension. Since this situation might arise at limit stages if one started out from some classical model, it seems right to say that Kripke's construction could not carry through the present experiment beyond the finite stages.

Now it is not difficult to modify Kripke's construction by changing the "union rule" which specifies limit stages. This can be done in a rather natural way, but it requires a fairly thorough rethinking of the whole problem, inasmuch as the "union rule" is deeply embedded in the theory of inductive definitions and even has its origins in Cantor's construction of the transfinite ordinal numbers. The problem then, as conceived in these notes, is a problem not specific to semantics, nor to elementary logic, nor even to the spirit of Kripke's theory of truth; but it lies at a more basic level, in the theory of inductive definitions which forms the infrastructure for Kripke's theory. And the solution proposed here is fairly simple, but rather far-reaching in its consequences and potential applications.

III. Kripke's Inductive Construction

This section recapitulates Kripke's inductive definitions of truth. Assume a first-order syntax with a distinguished monadic predicate T, and with "partial models" assigning partial truth-functions to predicates. The T-predicate is to be interpreted through an inductive process. Suppose some *primary model* to be given, subject to the constraint that T has an empty extension and anti-extension under the primary model. Although it is not essential to Kripke's approach it will simplify some of the discussion to follow if we assume that T is the only partially-interpreted predicate and that all other primitives have totally defined interpretations.[4]

The models we want to consider are all "T-expansions" of the primary model; they differ from the primary model at most on the interpretation of T. Sentences are to be evaluated through some "valuation-scheme" which is a function V that maps partial models m into partial valuations Vm, subject to the *monotonicity condition* that as the model expands, so does the valuation (if $m \leqslant n$ then $Vm \leqslant Vn$).[5] Additional constraints on the valuation scheme will be discussed in Section X.

For any expansion m of the primary model, let Tm be the function that m assigns to the distinguished predicate T; this represents the statements that are *declared* true or false in m. The function Vm represents the statements that *are* true or false under m; and the construction arises from an interplay between these two functions. It is based on the idea that the set of statements that are true (false) at any given stage of the construction, are to be declared true (false) at the next stage. This idea is incorporated in Kripke's "jump" operation, which assigns to any partial model another partial model:

Relative to a valuation scheme V the *Kripke jump* of any partial model m for our syntax is that T-variant of m whose T-predicate is interpreted by the partial function Vm.

Implicit in the construction is the requirement that at any stage the model should be *semantically sound* in the sense that everything declared true (false) at that stage actually be true (false) at that stage.

---

[4] To simplify many formulations, it will be assumed throughout that all statements of the language in question (including those in which the predicate T occurs) belong to the domain of the primary model.

[5] We can think of the expansion relation $\leqslant$ as defined in the first instance between partial functions regarded as sets of ordered n-tuples, where it means set-inclusion. This relation applies directly to valuations when they are regarded as partial functions from the syntax into $\{\top, \bot\}$. It extends in a natural way to partial models when they are regarded as interpreting predicates by partial functions: let $m \leqslant n$ mean that for each predicate p of the syntax, $m(p) \leqslant n(p)$, and that m and n are otherwise identical. Since we are assuming that T is the only partially interpreted predicate, $m \leqslant n$ in the present discussion holds iff m and n differ at most in that Tn expands Tm.

Relative to a valuation scheme V any partial model m for our syntax will be called *semantically sound* iff the interpretation it assigns to T is compatible with the valuation it generates under V, in the sense that $Tm \leqslant Vm$.

This will of course be fulfilled if the starting point is the primary model, which assigns the empty interpretation to T. It tends to be violated for total models, as in Section 2. Soundness characterizes what might be thought of as "good starting points" for the inductive construction. If the starting point is sound, so will be its Kripke jump, and so on. It follows, by the monotonicity property, that any sound starting point will generate a monotonically increasing sequence of models; and any such sequence can be continued into the transfinite inductively.[6] Let $m = (m, 0)$ be our starting model, $(m, 1)$ its Kripke jump, and so on. Then for any ordinal α and any positive limit ordinal λ:

K1. *Successor Rule*: $T(m, \alpha + 1)$ is the Kripke jump of $T(m, \alpha)$
K2. *Limit Rule*: $T(m, \lambda)$ is the Union $(\alpha < \lambda)$ of $T(m, \alpha)$.

Because the Kripke jump operation is monotonic, the sequence must reach a fixed point—a model which coincides with its own Kripke jump—at which stage the process becomes stationary. More specifically, the interpretation of T will increase strictly up to some critical stage γ and remain constant thereafter. This has a conceptual interpretation which gives it significance for the theory of truth. As already remarked, so long as the starting point is sound the T-predicate will be sound at every stage, in the sense that everything declared true at that stage is true at that stage: $T(m, \alpha) \leqslant V(m, \alpha)$. Upon reaching stage γ, the language becomes "equalized" in the sense that exactly those things declared true (false) at that stage are true (false) at that stage, and for all subsequent stages. It is this property which gives a special import to the fixed-point stages of the construction.

Relative to a valuation scheme V any partial model m for our syntax will be called *semantically equalized* iff the interpretation it assigns to T exactly coincides with the valuation it generates under V, in the sense that $Tm = Vm$.

This is the kind of "semantic closure" enjoyed by Kripke's fixed-point languages. It is in a way a semantic analogue to Tarski's

---

[6] Assuming that the valuation scheme has a sufficiently extensive domain; see §X.

Convention *T*, and more precisely to the "co-necessitation principle" [T(A) ⊣⊢ A] of van Fraassen [19].

Continuing to assume a sound starting point, the construction inductively builds up an equalized model, which declares true exactly those things which are true under that model, and which declares false exactly those things which are false under that model. The primary model generates a fixed point that is smallest among all fixed points generated by expansions of that primary model. A statement is *Kripke-grounded* (relative to a valuation-scheme) iff it has a truth-value in the smallest fixed point. It follows that grounded statements are those that are everywhere bivalent, that is have a truth-value in every one of the fixed-point models. A statement is *Kripke-paradoxical* (relative to a valuation-scheme) iff it has a truth-value in none of the fixed-point models. A statement is *uniform* iff it is everywhere nonfalse or everywhere nontrue under fixed-point models. Let a fixed-point model be called *intrinsic* iff it assigns truth-values to uniform statements only. Finally, let a statement be called *intrinsically true* iff it is true in at least one intrinsic fixed-point and *intrinsically false* iff it is false in at least one intrinsic fixed-point.

At some places in our discussion we will need to make reference to some particular valuation-scheme in order to fix the extension of these and other concepts. For this purpose we shall use the "Strong Kleene" (*SK*) valuation-scheme which Kripke used to illustrate his theory. The *SK* scheme can most simply be described by ordering the three values True > Undefined > False. The *SK* value for any conjunction then is the minimum of the *SK* values for its parts, and the *SK* value for any universally quantified statement is the minimum of the *SK* values for its instances. Disjunctions and existentially quantified statements are evaluated dually, with 'minimum' replaced by 'maximum' in these prescriptions. Any negated sentence ∼ *A* is true iff *A* is false, and is false iff *A* is true. By *SK*-grounding we will now understand grounding relative to the Strong Kleene valuation scheme, and so on for other concepts like paradoxicality.

Relative to this valuation-scheme we can give some examples of various types of statement within Kripke's classification:

[E]   'I am false' is *SK*-paradoxical, as are [*TE* ≡ *E*], [*TE*], [*TE* ∨ *T* ∼ *E*], and even [*E* ≡ *E*].

[B]   'I am true or false' is *SK*-ungrounded but intrinsically true.

[N] 'I am neither true nor false' is SK-ungrounded but intrinsically false, as is 'I am both true and false' [C].

[W] 'I am true' is SK-ungrounded, but neither SK-intrinsic nor SK-paradoxical. It can be true in some fixed points and false in others.

[S] 'Snow is white' is SK-grounded, as are ' "Snow is white" is true' [TS], and also [TTS], ..., [TS ≡ S], [S ∨ W], and even [S ∨ E].

Certain compound statements have an intermediate status. They are not quite intrinsic but nevertheless have a uniform truth-value in all fixed points under which they have any truth-value at all. Examples are [W ≡ W], [TW ∨ W] and [W ∨ E] which are uniformly true insofar as they have any truth-values. They are not SK-intrinsic, since none of them receives any SK truth-values unless W does, but W is true at some SK fixed points and false at others.

IV. A Semi-Inductive Construction

Following Cantor, the union, or least upper bound, for a sequence of sets can reasonably be called the limit of that sequence in case the sequence is monotonically increasing. This amounts to saying that an element belongs to the limit if it belongs to any set in the sequence. But clearly this is not a general limit concept for sequences of sets. For example, the union of a monotonically decreasing sequence of sets (like $2n$, $2n > 2$, $2n > 4$, ... where $2n > i$ is the set of all even integers greater than i) is certainly not a limit which that sequence approaches; rather it seems to approach the intersection or greatest lower bound of the sequence, as a limit. And for arbitrary nonmonotonic sequences which may oscillate in various complicated ways, the union cannot be identified with the limit.

For present purposes it is not quite the pure limit concept which we want, but something more closely connected with what is called *Lim Inf* (inferior, or lower limit) in function theory (see, for example [11], Ch. 4, §2). The idea is to form a limit set pointwise by collecting together all those elements which belong to all sufficiently far-out sets in the sequence. Under some fairly general conditions, these are the elements which belong to "almost all" sets in the sequence (for example this holds for all sequences of length ω^α for any ordinal α). For countable sequences these are the elements which belong to all but a finite number of sets in the sequence; and for ordinal sequences more generally they are the elements which are common to all but some initial segment of the sequence. For any ordinal sequence $f(\alpha)$ and any ordinal number κ within the domain of this sequence, the *lower limit* of the sequence $f(\alpha)$ up to κ, is the set:

$$Lower\ Limit\ (\alpha < \kappa) f(\alpha) = \{x: (\exists \delta < \kappa)(\forall \gamma: \delta \leqslant \gamma < \kappa) x \in f(\gamma)\}$$

I propose this as an alternative "limit rule" which is better suited to the present project and which reduces to the inductive limit rule, in the case of monotonically increasing sequences. So the new rule will be a generalization of the old one. And the "semi-inductive" process to be described in terms of the new rule, will be a generalization of the familiar process of inductive definition. (For a previous use of something like the lower limit rule, see Putnam [14].)[7]

The new construction differs from Kripke's precisely in the rule specifying limit stages. Once again we have a first order syntax with a distinguished monadic predicate T, whose interpretation is to be built up through a transfinite ordinal process, this time a semi-induction. The construction begins with the primary model or some T-variant of it, and uses any desired valuation-scheme, for example the classical two-valued scheme. A transfinite ordinal sequence of T-variants of the starting model is generated by the following two rules. Let α be any ordinal number and λ be any positive limit ordinal:

S1. Successor Rule: $T(m, \alpha + 1)$ is the Kripke jump of $T(m, \alpha)$
S2. Limit Rule: $T(m, \lambda)$ is the Lower Limit $(\alpha < \lambda)$ of $T(m, \alpha)$

It is not essential to the semi-inductive construction that the classical valuation scheme be used; but this is the implementation of immediate interest in connection with naive semantics. For other applications, intuitionistic semantics or any other scheme would be usable; see §XIV. For naive semantics we will provisionally fix on the classical valuation scheme.

---

[7] I am indebted to Hans Kamp for the suggestion that semi-inductive processes are a very special case of some much more general "quasi-inductive" processes defined by alternative limit rules; and for the observation that the periodicity theorem 7.1 could be extended over some very substantial range of alternative processes. Many of these alternative processes however will not generate perfectly stabilized sets. For such processes there will be no counterparts to the theorems 8.1 and 8.2 which in semantic applications support the introduction of stability predicates in the object language.

As before, a Liar statement may be true under $(m, 1)$, false under $(m, 2)$ and so on. Then it will be declared true under $(m, 2)$, declared false under $(m, 3)$, declared true under $(m, 4)$ and so on. By the Lower Limit rule, it will not belong to $T(m, \omega)$ at the first transfinite stage. At stage ω, what will belong to the extension of T will be exactly those statements which have settled down at some finite stage i in the sense that they belong to $T(m, j)$ for every finite stage $j \geq i$. More generally, at any transfinite limit stage what will be declared true will be exactly those statements which have been declared true at all sufficiently advanced previous stages. Consequently, what will be declared true at any limit stage will be exactly those statements which are true at all sufficiently advanced previous stages. Caution: this will *not* always coincide with what *is* true at the limit stage.

Assuming that there is at least one Liar statement, the naive construction will never reach a fixed point. The initial question for the theory of naive semantics then is what kind of stability properties it can provide to play the role which fixed points play within Kripke's construction. This question will be approached by stages. The first step will be to sketch a qualitative comparison between grounding in the inductive construction, and stability in the semi-inductive construction.

V. Semantic Stability

In the next sections the stability properties of sentences will be studied and compared with correlative notions from Kripke's theory. Then the qualitative concept of stability will be replaced by a measure of degrees of stability so that various kinds of instability can be classified and systematically examined.

We have supposed a certain primary model to be given, so that throughout these sections 'starting points' may be understood as $(\leqslant)$-expansions of that primary model.

For any expansion m of the primary model and any ordinal number α, the two rules S1 and S2 determine a definite model (m, α), called the α*th semi-inductive descendant of* m. Let a statement A be called *stable at* m in case $Tm(A) = Tn(A)$ for every semi-inductive descendant n of the model m. Let A be called *stable from* m in case it is stable at some semi-inductive descendant of m: that is, in case it is destined to become stabilized as the construction is carried sufficiently far. This is just our lower-limit concept, applied to the sequence of declared values for a given statement; and it implies constancy of actual truth-values as well.

5.1 Statements which are stable at a given model have a constant truth-value at all of its semi-inductive descendants.

Proof: Assume that A is stable at m; let n be any semi-inductive descendant of m; let m' and n' be their respective Kripke jumps. By hypothesis $Tm(A) = Tm'(A) = Tn(A) = Tn'(A)$. But $Vm = Tm'$ and $Vn = Tn'$; so $Vm(A) = Vn(A)$.

In terms of these local stability concepts various more global concepts can be defined. A statement will be called *naively stable* in case it is stable from every expansion of the primary model, and *naively unstable* in case it is unstable from every expansion of the primary model.

In §I a qualitative notion of paradoxicality was ascribed to naive semantics: a statement was called paradoxical in case it was evaluated as true on one level, false on some higher level, true again on some still higher level, and so on. When this is understood to hold for all starting points relative to a given primary model, it is (by 5.1) coextensive with the notion of naive instability.

In several—but not all—respects, the stable statements of naive semantics resemble the bivalent statements of the inductive construction. Some subtle and highly consequential differences will also emerge as their properties are developed.

To begin with one structural analogy, the bivalent statements at any stage of the inductive construction have two properties. As the construction proceeds, the set of bivalent statements:

i. increases monotonically in magnitude; and
ii. its members remain fixed in truth-value.

On the semi-inductive construction, the set of all statements with property (ii) has property (i). The statements which are stable at any given stage of the construction are exactly those which have property (ii) at that stage. But the set of all those statements has property (i): statements which are stable at some model are also stable at any descendant of that model. Therefore the set of stabilized statements increases monotonically under the semi-inductive construction.

Although naive semantics does not satisfy Kripke's monotonicity condition—it does not generate a monotonically increasing sequence of models or valuations—it does have a monotonicity property of its own, a sort of "interior monotonicity" in connection with the stable statements.

As already remarked, naive semantics cannot be expected to generate fixed-point models. Nevertheless there is an analogue to the fixed-point theorem, concerning stable statements. Let a model be called *fully stabilized* in case every statement which is stable *from* that model is already stable *at* that model. Then:

> 5.2   Any starting point generates a fully stabilized descendant.

Proof: If A is stable from m there is a least ordinal γ such that A is stable at (m, γ). The set of all such "stabilization ordinals" for m has some least upper bound σ. Every statement that is stable from (m, σ) is stable from $(m, 0)$; every statement that is stable from $(m, 0)$ is stable at (m, σ); therefore (m, σ) is fully stabilized.

The bounding ordinal σ of 5.2 is the stabilization ordinal for the naive construction generated by m. Assuming a countable set of statements in the syntax, it will be some countable ordinal. In terms of power it is generally comparable with the closure ordinal of the inductive construction.[8] And it is worth remarking that there is no restriction here to "good" starting points. Although the construction may begin with, and pass through, models which are unsound we shall find (8.2 below) that it ultimately generates a sound model.

Once the stabilization stage has been reached, the naive construction has a kind of interior constancy: all subsequent variations will involve unstable statements only. Subsequent to the stabilization stage, the T-predicate is always equalized in a restricted sense:

> 5.3   At any fully stabilized model, the predicate T is semantically equalized over all locally stable statements.

Proof: Let m be any fully stabilized model and let n be any semi-inductive descendant of m. For any statement A that is stable from m, the argument of 5.1 establishes that $Tm(A) = Tn(A) = Vm(A) = Vn(A)$; so $Tn(A) = Vn(A)$.

This is only the first step in the analysis of the construction. Nothing so far precludes the possibility that T might be unsound at

---

[8] This comparison in terms of power leaves room for very considerable differences of magnitude between stabilization and closure ordinals, and Saul Kripke has informed me that in some cases the stabilization ordinal may be much greater in magnitude than the corresponding inductive closure ordinal.

fully stablized models; it might for example include in its extension some unstable nontruths. Therefore we will be on the lookout for what may be called *perfectly stabilized models*, which are fully stabilized and also have T confined to stable statements. Under perfectly stabilized models the extension of T is exactly the set of stable truths. Their existence will be proved in Section VIII.

VI. Degrees of Instability

So far we have dealt with a dichotomy of statements into those which are stable and those which are unstable, from a given starting model; and with a trichotomy of statements into those which are everywhere stable, nowhere stable, and all the rest. This pattern follows that found by Kripke in connection with the notion of bivalence from a model. Now we shall find that the semi-inductive construction permits a richer articulation, within which qualitative notions can be replaced by quantitative ones, so that ultimately every statement may be assigned some ordinal index of its degree of instability.

We will begin with some qualitative observations about the known paradoxes. All the well-known semantic paradoxes are not only unstable, but are highly regular in their instability. This remarkable fact does not seem to have been given much attention in the previous literature. One of the immediate dividends of naive semantics is that it permits this question to be studied in a systematic way, and thereby may provide a somewhat deeper insight into the nature of semantic paradoxes than has been available on previous approaches.

The simplest version of the Liar paradox, the 'I am false' statement E, reverses its value at every stage: it cycles with a periodicity of two stages. It is always out of phase with its "truth-statement" TE, and in such a way that its Tarski biconditional $[TE \equiv E]$ is stably false.

Well-known variations on the Liar paradox cycle in value with various larger finite periodicities. Suppose that Socrates says "Plato speaks falsely" and he says nothing else; and that Plato says "Socrates speaks truly" and he says nothing else. Then each of their statements will reverse its value at every other stage, and so will cycle in value with periodicity four. Table (A) shows two of the simplest instability patterns.

	E	TE	$TE \equiv E$	S	P	$TS \equiv S$
$V(m, 0)$	1	0	0	1	0	0
$V(m, 1)$	0	1	0	1	1	1
$V(m, 2)$	1	0	0	0	1	0
$V(m, 3)$	0	1	0	0	0	1
$V(m, 4)$	1	0	0	1	0	0

(A)

Paradoxical statements of periodicity four, as in the example of Socrates and Plato, can have true Tarski biconditionals. Thus $[TS \equiv S]$ is true at $(m, 1)$ and again at $(m, 3)$ in the example. But when this happens the paradoxical statement always turns "nontarskian" at some descendant of the given model. In this case $[TS \equiv S]$ is false at $(m, 2)$ and again at $(m, 4)$. What distinguishes the stable statements then is not their tarskian character at a model, but rather the stability of their tarskian character. For paradoxical statements of higher degree than one, it is more relevant to consider "higher order Tarski biconditionals"; thus the "second order Tarski biconditional" for S is $[TTS \equiv S]$, and this is stably false.

More generally, for any finite degree i there are paradoxical statements A whose "i-th order Tarski biconditionals" will be stably false. Examples of paradoxical statements can be constructed by continuing the pattern illustrated in the scholastic "insolubles". Imagine a sequence of speakers: Socrates, Plato, Aristotle, Alexander, and so on, where each is the teacher of the next. Suppose that each of Plato, Aristotle, Alexander, and so on says: "My teacher speaks truly" and he says nothing else; and that Socrates picks a generation, say the third, and says: "My third generation student (Alexander) speaks falsely" and he says nothing else. Then Socrates' statement, which denies its own "third order T-statement" is paradoxical with degree 3 and it cycles with periodicity 6. Its third order Tarski biconditional $[T^3S \equiv S]$ is stably false.

Paradoxical statements exhibiting these simplest instability patterns $(1 + 1, 2 + 2,$ and generally $n + n)$ have been discussed in the literature since the fourteenth century. It is certainly possible to construct paradoxical statements which exhibit more complicated instability patterns, just by forming truth-functional combinations of these simplest paradoxical statements. For example, the conjunction

[$S \& P$] of the simply paradoxical statements S and P, would be a paradoxical statement with periodicity 4 and instability pattern $1 + 3$. For another pattern, in the third degree Socrates–Alexander example, consider the conjunction of the statements of Plato and Aristotle. This compound statement has periodicity 6 and instability pattern $2 + 4$, that is it cycles over the sextuple of values (110000). From these examples one sees that for any finite periodicity there is a way of constructing some paradoxical statement having that periodicity and any combinatorially possible pattern within it. What may be called the paradoxes of finite degree then have a comprehensible and highly regular valuational structure.

It is also possible to construct paradoxical statements of transfinite degree. First we may look at one case of special interest, and then schematize a more general case. For any statement A we are supposing that our language has the means of formulating a "T-statement" TA, which in Kripke's terminology "declares" A to be true. Let E be an 'I am false' statement, and let BE be the disjunction $[TE \lor T \sim E]$ which declares E to be either true or false. To have a short label one can call BE a "bivalence statement" for E; but some caution must be exercised to avoid being misled by this label. At certain (limit) stages BE will be false; but this doesn't mean that E is "nonbivalent" at those stages. What it means is that BE doesn't quite succeed in expressing the appropriate instance of the law of bivalence. Now if the starting point for the naive construction is the primary model, with T empty, BE will be false at stage 0 and then will be true at every subsequent finite stage. By the semi-inductive limit rule, BE will again be false at the first transfinite stage ω, and it will again be true at every finite descendant $\omega + i$ of that stage. It has periodicity ω and the instability pattern $(0111\ldots)$. Apart from providing an example of a transfinite paradox, BE-statements have an intrinsic interest for the theory of truth. On the semi-inductive construction they are true everywhere except for limit stages.

To generalize still further on the scholastic insolubilia, any statement A can be taken to generate an ordinal sequence of "higher order T-statements", where:

$$T^0 A = A$$
$$T^{\alpha+1} A = \text{'My predecessor is true' } [TT^\alpha A]$$
$$T^\lambda A = \text{'All my predecessors are true' } [(\forall \alpha < \lambda)(TT^\alpha A)]$$

as high up into the ordinals α and limit ordinals λ as the means of expression of the language can reach. Now for different choices of ordinal number κ one obtains a paradoxical statement of degree κ by forming such a sequence whose initial member A is the statement: 'My κ-th order T-statement is not true'. And so we have paradoxical statements of higher and higher transfinite degree, and this raises the question of whether there is or is not any upper bound to degrees of instability.

It is possible to prove that there must be an upper bound to degrees of instability, and to estimate its magnitude. Therefore every sentence of the language can be assigned a definite degree of instability, relative to a given starting point. The method of proof maps out in a general way the bounds and limits of the instability patterns that may arise. This method determines abstractly an upper bound on the instability of the whole construction.

VII. Periodicity

The large-scale regularities of naive semantics result from its underlying semi-inductive framework, and can be most readily determined in an abstract study of semi-inductive processes. The main result in this area is that all such processes are "almost periodic". This not only establishes an upper bound for degrees of instability, but also maps out the patterns of instability that may in principle arise. The whole construction will always have something analogous to a stabilization point. Until this stage is reached, it may have an apparently irregular and almost chaotic character. Beyond this stage it becomes periodic: a fixed pattern of stages crystallizes and then repeats endlessly.

A rigorous treatment of these matters involves a number of technicalities connected with ordinal arithmetic. Not the least of these is the problem of extending the concept of periodicity to transfinite sequences. Details are given separately in [7]. I will proceed here with an informal description of the periodicity theorem, based on the intuitive notion of a periodic process as one that endlessly repeats a fixed pattern.

There are two ways that a process can be almost periodic, and to avoid misunderstandings they must be distinguished. The process can be everywhere approximately periodic, or it can be nearly-everywhere exactly periodic. Examples of the first kind are the trigonometric polynomials called *fastperiodisch*, as in [1]. The second kind is the one which is important for present concerns; and here some very familiar examples are the recurrent decimals.

The recurrent decimals provide us with a fairly reliable picture of the structure of semi-inductive processes, once allowances are made for the special features of transfinite sequences. The decimal expansion for any rational number m/n in general has two parts. It can be represented in the form:

$$[p_1 \ldots p_k](q_1 \ldots q_r)^*$$

with an initial nonrecurring segment up to the k-th place, followed by a recurrent segment of length r. The (*) indicates that the sequence continues by repetition of the recurrent segment. The system of all decimal expansions of this form is complete relative to the rational numbers: every decimal of this form is the expansion of some rational number m/n; and there is a standard algorithm for producing that rational number, given its decimal expansion. While there is no finite upper bound to the characteristic numbers k and r over all rational numbers m/n, they are in each particular case bounded as a function of m and n. For example, the fundamental periodicity r for the decimal expansion of m/n, is always less than n, assuming m/n to be in reduced form.

All semi-inductive processes follow an analogous two-part pattern, although their characteristic indices are ordinal numbers κ, ρ which may be transfinite. For the special case of inductive processes, $\rho = 1$ by the fixed point theorem.

By a *semi-inductive process* let us now understand more definitely any transfinite ordinal sequence $f(\alpha)$ which is generated in a prescribed way from a "jump" operation J on a fixed family of sets B called the "base set". We will call $f(\alpha)$ semi-inductive iff for any ordinal number α and any positive limit ordinal λ:

0. $f(\alpha) \in B$
1. $f(\alpha + 1) = J(f(\alpha))$
2. $f(\lambda) = Lim(\alpha < \lambda)f(\alpha)$.

Clause 0, restricting the range of f to the base set, plays a crucial role in forcing the process to settle into a periodic pattern. For the ordinal numbers will always outrun the possible sequences of members of *B* which conform to clauses 1 and 2:

7.1.   *Saturation Lemma*: For any semi-inductive process there is a saturation point: an ordinal μ such that for every x in the range of f, there is an ordinal $\alpha < \mu$ such that $f(\alpha) = x$.

This holds without any restrictions on the jump operation, which is not required to be monotonic. For the proof see (6.1) of [7].

Once a saturation point has been reached, every subsequent stage repeats some earlier stage and the process becomes cyclic. On account of its transfinite character, the first cycle it enters is not necessarily the last one; but there will always be a last one. What will happen is that the process will "uncoil" through a cascade of cycles of increasing length, until a certain stage is reached where a "grand loop" is formed. The process thereafter cycles endlessly through this loop. The analysis of this phase of the process, which involves at most a finite number of rounds after the saturation point, shows why a grand loop must be formed and why the sequence never leaves that loop once it has entered it. For details see §6 of [7]. To summarize this part of the discussion:

7.2   *Periodicity Theorem*: Every semi-inductive process is almost-everywhere periodic.

For any semi-inductive process there are ordinals κ (its enclosure ordinal) and ρ (its fundamental periodicity) such that the process enters its "grand loop" $[\kappa, \kappa + \rho)$ by the enclosure stage, and thereafter cycles permanently through the stages in that loop.

VIII. The Grand Loop

Having described the formation of the grand loop, it may be instructive now to develop some consequences of the periodic structure for naive semantics. In particular we shall find that the grand loop always contains at least one model which is perfectly stabilized in the sense of Section V.

The main facts are most readily developed in the abstract setting. Naive semantics as conceived in these notes, derives its main structure from the abstract properties of semi-inductive processes. Similarly, Kripke's theory of truth inherits its main structure from the abstract properties of inductive processes. And the main differences between naive semantics and Kripke's theory of truth seem to be derivable from abstract differences between the inductive and the semi-inductive frameworks.

Now consider any semi-inductive process f over a base set B, with grand loop L. For some purposes the order of elements in the grand loop may be significant, but for present purposes the main interest lies in the unordered set of sets which belong to L (its range) and in the set CL of basic elements common to all these sets.

Like the base set B, the range of L is a family of sets of things which we may call basic elements. For semantic applications the basic elements might be sentences, in applications which build up truth predicates. In semantic applications which build up satisfaction predicates the basic elements would be ordered pairs of some sort.

Basic elements can be classified in various ways, relative to the given semi-inductive process. As before the principal dichotomy divides the basic elements into those which are stable and those which are unstable under the whole construction; and the stable elements will be either positively or negatively stable:

$$x \text{ is} \begin{cases} \text{positively stable iff } x \in f(\alpha) \text{ for all sufficiently large } \alpha \\ \text{negatively stable iff } x \notin f(\alpha) \text{ for all sufficiently large } \alpha \\ \text{unstable otherwise.} \end{cases}$$

For semantic applications in which $f(\alpha)$ is the set of sentences declared true at stage α, the positively stable elements would be the stable truths and the negatively stable elements would be the stable falsehoods. Where the classical valuation scheme is being used, the stable falsehoods will always be exactly those statements whose negations are stable truths.

The grand loop induces another division of basic elements, into those which are "variable" and those which are "constant" under L. Let a basic element be called positively constant under L iff it belongs to all sets in the range of L; negatively constant under L iff it belongs to no sets in the range of L; and variable within L iff it belongs to some but not all sets in the range of L.

This trichotomy coincides with the earlier one. The unstable elements are exactly those which are variable within the grand loop: anything variable within L is clearly unstable in the process; and conversely any basic element which is constant under L will have stabilized as soon as the process enters L, so anything which is unstable in the process must be variable within L. Our principal interest lies in the way in which CL coincides with the positively stable elements of the process:

8.1 Any semi-inductive process generates a set (at the enclosure point and periodically thereafter) which consists of precisely the positively stable elements under that process.

Proof: Let f be any semi-inductive process with enclosure point κ, periodicity ρ, and grand loop L. After the enclosure point the process cycles permanently through its grand loop, and in this cycling passes periodically through the set CL; for details see [7]. In particular this set occurs at the enclosure point—the initial stage of the grand loop—and thereafter recurs with periodicity ρ. That is, $f(\kappa) = CL$, $f(\rho + \kappa) = CL$, etc. But CL is precisely the set of elements which are positively constant under L. Clearly these are all positively stable under the process f. Conversely, any basis element which is positively stable under f must belong to CL, since nothing but the members of L occur at stages beyond the enclosure point.

The stabilization theorem (5.2) obviously carries over to the abstract setting, and we can be confident that stabilization occurs no later than the enclosure stage, inasmuch as all positively stable elements must belong to $f(\kappa) = CL$. Therefore the initial stretch of the process, up to its enclosure stage, can be viewed as a gradual (monotonic) building up of positively stable elements, together with a haphazard but ultimately complete filtering out of unstable elements. Subsequently, as the grand loop forms and periodically thereafter, the ongoing construction waxes and wanes. Periodically all unstable elements re-enter the construction, and periodically they are filtered out again. As one follows this from "close up", stage by stage, it may present itself as rather haphazard; but from a longer-range viewpoint, encompassing the whole grand loop and its periodic recurrence, a fixed and orderly pattern emerges.

A corollary of (8.1) is the "perfect stabilization" theorem promised in Section V:

8.2 Any construction of naive semantics generates a perfectly stabilized model at the enclosure stage. Under this model exactly the stable truths are declared true.

At the enclosure point and periodically thereafter, T will be everywhere sound as well as being equalized over all stable statements. This guarantees the construction of a sound and relatively equalized model, even though the starting point and many of the intermediate stages are not sound. In this sense the process of naive semantics is "self-correcting". At the enclosure point and periodically thereafter, a restricted version of Tarski's Schema *T* will be valid. To formulate this scheme, let us define a *stability predicate*: let '*Sx*' mean '*Tx* ∨ *T*(*neg x*)'. At the enclosure point the extension of *S* will be exactly the set of stable statements. At this point *T* conforms to a restricted schema *T*: [*TA* ≡ *A*&*SA*]. This is valid for any primary model, any starting point and any statement *A*. The unrestricted form of Schema *T*: [*TA* ≡ *A*] is valid for any primary model, any starting point, and any stable statement *A*.

IX. The Tangled Hierarchy

We now have a picture of semi-inductive processes as having two major phases. The initial phase will be a possibly haphazard nonrecurrent interval $[0, \kappa)$ which is followed by a recurrent interval whose length is the fundamental periodicity ρ of the process.

This same picture carries over to individual basic elements, as follows. In the context of a given ordinal process f, each basic element z can be described by a characteristic function whose value for any ordinal number α tells us whether or not z belongs to the set $f(\alpha)$ which occurs at stage α of the process:

$$f_z(\alpha) = \begin{cases} 1 \text{ iff } z \in f(\alpha) \\ 0 \text{ otherwise} \end{cases}$$

For each basic element, the ordinal process induces a separate two-valued characteristic function. Now various concepts which have been introduced in connection with ordinal processes can be carried over to the individual characteristic functions which those processes induce. And these will help us to consolidate and systematize various parts of the previous discussion.

In the first place, it now seems natural to regard stability and instability as special cases of the periodic structure: to think of the stable elements as those with fundamental periodicity 1. On this construal stabilization would be a special case of enclosure: it would be enclosure for stable elements.

Each basic element z will now have two characteristic ordinal numbers: a rank $\kappa(z)$ and a fundamental periodicity $\rho(z)$. These two numbers will in every case be bounded from above by the corresponding ordinals κ, ρ of the underlying process.

In semantic applications, we now have a hierarchy of levels of some sort, over all statements. It is perhaps a "tangled hierarchy" in the sense of [8]. But it shows how the notion of ranks (or levels) of statements, which is restricted to grounded statements within an inductive framework like Kripke's, can be extended over all statements within the semi-inductive framework of naive semantics.

On Kripke's theory, the level of a statement is the first stage at which it assumes its ultimate truth-value; and this notion is of necessity restricted to statements which have an ultimate truth-value. Within naive semantics, the rank of a statement is the first stage at which it assumes its ultimate pattern of valuation; and this applies to all statements—for by the periodicity theorem every statement, whether stable or not, ultimately assumes a definite cyclic pattern of valuation.

To strengthen our grasp of the concept of stability we shall want to draw out some comparisons and contrasts with Kripke's concept of grounding. A few steps in this direction will be taken in Sections XI and XII, after some preliminary discussion of the notion of a valuation scheme.

X. Standard Valuation Schemes

Several examples of valuation schemes are presented and discussed in Kripke [9] and [10], although the general notion is not defined. Abstractly one might regard as a valuation scheme any partial mapping from partial models into partial valuations. This concept would be broad enough to include all the various examples that have so far been discussed. But in several respects it bears tightening up.

The only admissibility condition mentioned in Kripke [9] is monotonicity (that $m \leqslant n$ implies $Vm \leqslant Vn$). Monotonicity plays a role in the fixed point theorem, and it secures relative soundness of the construction: if valuations are monotonic, then constructions generated by sound starting models will consist of sound models at every stage.

There is a broad spectrum of monotonic schemes, and a correspondingly broad spectrum of grounding concepts relative to those schemes. Indeed, any constant valuation scheme (such that $Vm = Vn$ for every m and n) is monotonic. Each constant scheme generates exactly one fixed point. Therefore, any arbitrarily chosen set of statements is "grounded" relative to at least one monotonic scheme. The "empty" scheme $(Vm = \emptyset)$ renders all statements "paradoxical" and none "grounded"; the "full" scheme $(Vm(A) = T$ for every $A)$ renders all statements "grounded" and none "paradoxical".

The constant schemes are trivial, and these two examples are limiting cases: the first is excessively weak and the second excessively strong. Between these two extremes there lies a spectrum of monotonic schemes, some of which are wild in more complicated ways: for example, excessively weak in some respects and excessively strong in others. Some turn every partial model into a fixed point; there might be others with no fixed points at all. To bring this variety under some control, I propose to focus on valuation-schemes that are comparatively well-behaved, in order to facilitate comparisons with naive semantics. I believe this can be done in such a way as to render the problems of comparison manageable without ruling out of bounds all interesting schemes. I shall propose three conditions jointly defining what I will call "standard" valuation schemes.

There was no suggestion in [9] that all conceivable monotonic schemes would be equally admissible, nor even that strictly all of them would be admissible. What Kripke there wrote was:

Just about any scheme for handling truth-value gaps is usable, provided that the basic property of the monotonicity of ϕ is preserved. (p. 76.)

The stated purpose of [9] was to sketch in broad outlines "an area rich in formal structures and mathematical properties" and "to provide a family of flexible instruments which can be explored simultaneously and whose fertility and consonance with intuition can be checked" ([9], p. 63 and p. 77). The search for additional constraints on monotonic schemes seems to be broadly in accordance with that spirit.

Six valuation schemes were described and discussed in Kripke [9] and [10]: two of them are "truth-functional" and four are "super-valuational" schemes.

[WK] Weak Kleene Valuations: WKm interprets all operators classically for all totally defined arguments, and as undefined whenever any of their arguments are undefined.

[SK] Strong Kleene Valuations: SKm is as described in Section III above.

[*SV*] Ordinary Supervaluations: *SVm* is the supervaluation generated by the class of all *T*-completions of *m*.

Next are three restricted supervaluational schemes based on alternative ways of restricting the generating class of *T*-completions. Let a *T*-completion of *m* be called *consistent* in case it assigns to *T* an extension that contains no statement together with its negation; *maximal consistent* in case it assigns to *T* a maxiset of statements for its extension; and *inconsistent* in case it assigns to *T* an extension that contains at least one statement together with its negation.

[*CSV*] Consistency-Restricted Supervaluations: *CSVm* is the supervaluation generated by the class of all consistent *T*-completions of *m*.

[*MSV*] Maxiset-Restricted Supervaluations: *MSVm* is the supervaluation generated by the class of all maximal consistent *T*-completions of *m*.

[*NSV*] Inconsistency-Restricted Supervaluations: *NSVm* is the supervaluation generated by the class of all inconsistent *T*-completions of *m*.

Additional variations result from other choices of restrictions on the generating class of *T*-completions: that the extension of *T* be a theory, that it be a consistent theory, that it be a classically satisfiable set, that it be a set which is satisfied by some *T*-completion of *m*, and so on. These are all monotonic schemes, but not all of them are equally reasonable. Two of them (*MSV* and *NSV*) were introduced in [9] and [10] in the course of emphasizing the somewhat excessive flexibility of restricted supervaluational schemes. They bring out potentially anomalous effects of increasingly narrow and arbitrary restrictions on the generating class of *T*-completions. For example, *MSV* evaluates as true at all fixed points:

(i) $(\forall x)[\text{Sent}(x) \supset .T(x) \vee T(\text{neg}(x))]$

even though what this seems to say (that every sentence is either true or has a true negation) doesn't hold for the fixed-point languages in question. And the valuation scheme *NSV* shows what happens when completely arbitrary restrictions are countenanced, restrictions which are in no way "motivated by intuitive properties of truth" ([9], p. 76). *NSV* evaluates as true at all fixed points:

(ii) $(\exists x)[T(x) \& T(\text{neg}(x))]$

even though what this seems to say (that some truths have true negations) even more egregiously fails to hold for the fixed-point languages generated by that valuation scheme. Neither of these schemes is "meta-sound": each of them evaluates as true some statements whose translation into the metalanguage would be false. In this respect they seem to be excessively strong.

These examples already suggest one direction in which to look for additional constraints on admissibility. One might try to draw a defensible boundary somewhere between *CSV*, which appears to be meta-sound, and schemes like *MSV* and *NSV* which appear to be meta-unsound.

Instead of trying to explicate the intuitive notion of meta-soundness, I will offer a simple "upper bound" condition that sorts out at least the known cases in the desired way. It has the merit at least of ruling out of bounds problematic schemes like *MSV* and *NSV* while admitting within bounds the four central valuation schemes singled out above (*WK, SK, SV, CSV*). This upper bound uses an idea initially due to Frege ("amalgamation of horizontals") and subsequently developed by Bochvar; it may be called the "Strong Frege" scheme.[9] For any partial model m, let hm be that total model which results from m by expanding anti-extensions while preserving all extensions intact. This process is called "closing off" the model in [9], p. 80; it amounts to filling in truth-value gaps with falsity everywhere. Strong Frege valuations over partial models now are defined as precisely the classical valuations over their correlated completions:

[*SF*]   Strong Frege Valuations: *SFm* is the classical valuation over the model *hm*.

Whereas all the central valuation schemes are uniformly weaker than *SF*, this is not true for the "meta-unsound" schemes *MSV* and *NSV*. For example, consider any primary model—one which assigns the empty interpretation to *T*. Under *MSV* the statement (i) is true at the primary model; under *NSV* the statement (ii) is true at the primary model; under *SF* neither of these statements is true at the primary model. Moreover, neither is true at the primary model under any of the central valuation schemes. So I propose an upper bound in strength to "standard" valuation schemes:

Upper Bound Condition: $Vm \leqslant SFm$ for every partial model m within the domain of applicability of the valuation scheme V.

[9] See Frege [6], §§5, 6, and 8: and Bochvar [2].

I think this condition draws an upper boundary which has at least some initial plausibility.

Examples like the empty scheme suggest that there may also be a boundary to be drawn somewhere "below" the central schemes. One way of doing this is to use the Weak Kleene scheme as a standard:

> *Lower Bound Condition*: $WKm \leqslant Vm$ for every partial model m within the domain of applicability of the valuation scheme V.

This is a sort of generalized condition of "normality" in the sense of Rescher [16]; it is intended to guarantee that logical operators will behave classically over classical arguments. The scheme WK, like SF, has roots in Frege's semantics; [9] calls WK "the Fregean weak three-valued" scheme (p. 77).

The Lower Bound condition secures the paradoxicality of familiar "Liar" statements, whenever they arise within the domain of V. At the same time it secures the groundedness of many statements, such as those that are T-free. And it draws a lower boundary which is far enough down to admit all the central monotonic schemes.

Some attention finally needs to be paid to closure conditions on the domains of valuation schemes. Without some controls on the domain of applicability there might be no smallest fixed point; indeed there might be no fixed points at all. One way this could happen would be if constructions broke down before closure ordinals could be reached. To make sure that constructions can be carried far enough into the transfinite, something in addition to monotonicity and the bounding conditions is required. Let a partial model be called an *inductive generator* for a valuation scheme iff it generates an unbounded ordinal sequence of descendants under the inductive rules $K1$ and $K2$ of Section III. This notion, which concerns the length of constructions, is quite independent of soundness, which concerns their monotonicity. The inductive generators for a valuation scheme form a subset of its domain of applicability, distinguished by the fact that constructions proceeding from them can always be carried indefinitely far into the transfinite.

To secure the existence of sufficiently many generators and sufficiently many fixed points, we now want to define some sort of "coherence" condition on partial models. The idea is that the extension of T ought to incorporate some minimal "intuitive properties of truth". Relative to a coherence condition, standard valuation schemes could be restricted to those whose inductive generators include at least all semantically coherent partial models. The more stringent the coherence condition, the more liberal the resulting domain condition will be: there is an inverse correlation between the two. The weakest coherence condition that comes to mind is that the extension of T be a noncontradictory set of statements. Stronger conditions might require it to be satisfiable on suitable expansions of the given model. For present purposes a rather stringent condition can be imposed, adapting the notion of soundness from Section III. Let any partial model m be called *classically sound* iff all statements declared true at m are true in the Strong Frege valuation over m: $(Tm \leqslant SFm)$.

Domain Condition: The inductive generators for V include at least all classically sound partial models.

This condition is satisfied by all of Kripke's examples, and it should suffice to guarantee the existence of sufficiently many indefinitely extendible constructions and sufficiently many fixed points.

Let a *standard valuation scheme* be any monotonic scheme that satisfies this Domain condition as well as the Upper and Lower bound conditions. We have now marked out a broad class of well-behaved valuation schemes for which comparisons between inductive and naive semantics are fairly straightforward. I am not prepared to defend these conditions as *sine qua non* for inductive constructions; but I think that the study of nonstandard valuation schemes may reasonably be deferred while we focus on those that are standard.

XI. Stability and Grounding: Comparisons

We are now ready to draw out some comparisons and contrasts between Kripke's inductive approach and naive semantics. In the remaining sections of these notes, it will always be assumed that some standard valuation scheme is being used for the inductive approach.

Returning to the analogy between bivalence and stability (Section V) one might look for correlations between the statements that are grounded on standard inductive constructions and those that are stable within naive semantics. To begin with, one positive result can be easily established:

11.1 All grounded statements are naively stable.

A plausibility argument for this proposition might be based on the lower bound condition, which secures that the valuation scheme used in the inductive construction will agree with the classical valuation scheme over all bivalent statements. Consequently, one might argue that unstable statements could not be bivalent at fixed-point models—eventually they would be bound to alternate in value between truth and falsehood. We can firm up this plausibility argument and show that there is even a correlation in detail between ranks in naive semantics and Kripke levels—so far as grounded statements are concerned. Grounded statements are not only everywhere stable, they also stabilize in naive semantics at almost exactly the same stages where they first become bivalent on the inductive construction. This is an interesting result of high generality; but as the next section will show, it by no means establishes anything close to coextensiveness between grounding and stability-everywhere. We now want to establish on general principles that:

11.2   *First Comparison Theorem*: The semi-inductive rank for any statement is less than or equal to its inductive level on any comparable standard inductive construction.

where an inductive construction is considered comparable to any semi-inductive construction which expands it and which begins from the same starting point. The simplest way to establish 11.2 is to derive it from an abstract comparison theorem for semi-inductive constructions. This can be done because inductive constructions are a special case of semi-inductive constructions, based on monotonic jump operations.

In what follows, semi-inductive constructions will be represented by their jump operations (G, J) and starting points (X, Y). Particular stages in those constructions will be indexed by ordinals; thus $G\alpha X$ represents the αth semi-inductive descendant of the set X under the generating operation G.

11.3   *Comparison Lemma*: $G\alpha X \subseteq J\alpha X$, for any monotonic jump operation G, any expansion J of G, any ordinal number α and any starting point X.

Proof: Assume that G is any monotonic operation on subsets of some base set $(X \subseteq Y \rightarrow GX \subseteq GY)$ and J is any expansion of G $(GX \subseteq JX)$; it is not assumed that J is monotonic. The proof is now by induction on stages for $G\alpha X \subseteq J\alpha X$. The case $\alpha = 0$ holds by the hypothesis that J expands G. Assume now that $G\alpha X \subseteq J\alpha X$ for all

$\alpha < \eta$. If η is a successor ordinal $\eta = v + 1$, then $GvX \subseteq JvX$ by the induction hypothesis. $G\eta X = G(GvX)$ and $J\eta X = J(JvX)$. By monotonicity of G, $G(GvX) \subseteq G(JvX)$ and by the expansion property $G(JvX) \subseteq J(JvX)$; so $G(GvX) \subseteq J(JvX)$ and thereby $G\eta X \subseteq J\eta X$. If η is a limit ordinal, then $G\eta X = Lower\ Limit(\alpha < \eta)G\alpha X$ and $J\eta X = Lower\ Limit(\alpha < \eta)J\alpha X$. Since for each $\alpha < \eta$, $G\alpha X \subseteq J\alpha X$ it follows that $G\eta X \subseteq J\eta X$. This completes the induction.

Now 11.2 follows as a corollary of this Lemma, for all standard inductive constructions. The idea is to construe certain models of the semi-inductive construction as partial models in the sense of [9]. This can be done because under any standard valuation scheme the true statements determine the false ones: as exactly those having true negations. Therefore without loss of generality the extension of T can be taken as determining its anti-extension in the same way: as exactly those statements having negations in the extension. This holds in any case with the possible exception of initial stages. In this way partial models can be represented within classical models: by those which are semantically consistent. The expansion relation between partial models will be represented by $\leqslant$ over semantically consistent models. Under this construal, any semantically consistent model which is an inductive generator for the partial valuation scheme, can be taken as common starting point for both inductive and semi-inductive constructions. The set X of the Comparison Lemma represents the extension of T at the initial stage. G represents the jump operation determined by some given standard valuation scheme and fixed primary model; and J represents the naive jump operation determined by the given primary model. Let X be any set which represents an inductive generator for G; then for any ordinal α, $G\alpha X$ represents the extension of T at the αth inductive descendant of X, and $J\alpha X$ represents the extension of T at the αth semi-inductive descendant of X. Now let A be any inductively grounded true statement having Kripke level κ. Since $A \in G\kappa\emptyset$ and $\emptyset \subseteq X$, monotonicity of G secures that $A \in G\alpha X$ for any $\alpha \geqslant \kappa$. By the Comparison Lemma then $A \in J\alpha X$ for any $\alpha \geqslant \kappa$, that is A is positively stable from X with rank $\leqslant \kappa$. By a parallel argument, any false grounded statement is negatively stable from X with rank $\leqslant \kappa$. So all grounded statements are naively stable from X; and by the Domain condition, all grounded statements are naively stable from all SF-sound starting points. Finally, we observe that every construction of naive semantics passes through at least one classically sound model, at the enclosure stage (see 8.1). If m is the model at that stage, Tm is exactly the set of statements that are positively stable from m; so $Tm \leqslant SFm$ holds. Therefore any statement which is stable from all classically sound starting points is naively stable; and 11.2 is proved, along with 11.1.

XII. Stability and Grounding: Contrasts

One should not expect stability and grounding to coincide, for the classical valuation scheme is stronger than any standard scheme. This follows from the Upper Bound condition, and the fact that the Strong Frege scheme (which agrees with the classical scheme) is not monotonic and so lies outside the class of standard schemes. Therefore the grounded statements relative to any standard inductive construction will form a proper subset of the everywhere-stable statements of naive semantics.

Some very familiar types of intuitively ungrounded statements are indeed everywhere stable. However, any attempt to prove this and other "negative" results in this area is liable to encounter a difficulty of principle in connection with the relativity of Kripke's concept of grounding. Statements which are ungrounded relative to one valuation scheme may well turn out to be grounded relative to some alternative scheme, and so it is somewhat difficult to establish boundaries for the concept of grounding. The problem of relativity is large enough to warrant a separate treatment, which will be deferred until the next section. For now it seems advisable to keep the discussion at a more concrete level by provisionally adopting a particular valuation scheme for Kripke's construction; this will be the Strong Kleene scheme described in Section III.

In the first place, as expected:

12.1 There can be naively unstable statements that are SK-ungrounded.

One type of example is an 'I am true' statement (W). Because it coincides with its own T-statement, W is self-stabilizing. If it is declared true at any stage it will be stably true at that stage, and otherwise it will be stably false. Several other types of example could be adduced to confirm 11.1. Examination of each case will show why statements of that type are semantically stable in spite of being intuitively ungrounded. Before leaving this first case of the self-stabilizing statement, it is worth reflecting on a structural difference it brings out between stability and grounding. Statements which are Kripke-grounded will always have the same truth value from all starting points and indeed will have intrinsic truth values. But W, which is everywhere-stable, is stably true from some starting points and stably false from others.

So we might interpose an intermediate class between the grounded and the stable statements. In Section III a statement was called uniform in the inductive framework iff it was everywhere nonfalse or everywhere nontrue under fixed-point models. The guiding idea was that different fixed-point models never assign it conflicting values. This notion can be extended to the semi-inductive framework by calling a statement *uniform* in case it is true-wherever-stable or else false-wherever-stable. A slightly stronger notion is that of a *uniformly stable* statement, which is one that is both everywhere stable and also has a constant truth-value from all starting points. This is a much more restrictive notion than that of stability everywhere. Nevertheless:

  12.2 There can be uniformly stable statements that are SK-ungrounded.

Some examples are $[W \equiv W]$, $[TW \equiv W]$ and $[B]$ which are stably true, and $[N]$ and $[C]$ which are stably false, although none of them is SK-grounded. (See Section III for the statements these schemata encode.)

There are several different kinds of uniformly stable statements, depending on the aspect of their semantic structure which renders them uniformly stable. One simple kind consists of statements having the form of tautologies or contradictions, and more generally of logically valid or contravalid statements. Thus $[S \equiv S]$, $[W \equiv W]$, and even $[E \equiv E]$ are all uniformly stably true in naive semantics, and their negations are uniformly stably false.

Another kind of uniformly stable statement arises from interlocking instabilities. For example, if E is an 'I am false' statement with periodicity 2, its "T-statement" TE will also be unstable with periodicity 2 but will be one step out of phase with E, and consequently the biconditional $[TE \equiv E]$ will be stably false. This is one of the simplest examples of a very general and systematic phenomenon whereby compounds of unstable statements can be stable due to interlocking of the instabilities.

We now have at least the structure in diagram (A) to contend with. Many of Kripke's "intrinsic" statements fall between the uniformly

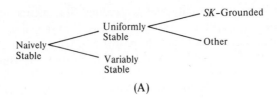

(A)

stable and the SK-grounded statements, to drive the wedge a little more deeply between stability and grounding.

In the inductive framework there is a smallest fixed point; this is generated by the primary model ($T = \emptyset$) and it contains exactly the grounded statements. In naive semantics the situation is a bit more complicated. The primary model does not always generate exactly the everywhere-stable statements:

> 12.3 There can be statements which are stable from the primary model but unstable from other starting points.

Consider a sequence of statements $A_1, A_2, A_3, \ldots$ where each is a statement to the effect that its successor in the sequence is true. Each of these statements A_i will be stably false from the primary model. Now let n be that T-expansion of the primary model which declares true exactly the odd-numbered members of this sequence; then each A_i is unstable from n.

It follows from this example that the primary model does not always generate a smallest enclosure point; for in this example there were statements that were stably true from the primary model but not stably true from other starting points. Finally we can show that under certain conditions no smallest enclosure point exists:

> 12.4 If there is at least one variably stable statement then there is no smallest enclosure point.

Proof: Assume a primary model under which at least one variable but everywhere-stable statement Z is expressible, and let m be any T-expansion of the primary model. Z is either stably true from m or it is stably false from m. If Z is stably true from m then by hypothesis there is at least one expansion n of the primary model ($n \neq m$) from which Z is stably false and so not stably true; consequently m does not generate a smallest enclosure point. If on the other hand Z is stably false from m then by a parallel argument its negation $\sim Z$ will be stably true from m

but not stably true from at least one expansion of *m*; and so in this case also *m* does not generate a smallest enclosure point.

XIII. Relativity and the Concept of Paradox

The development so far indicates that naive semantics may be or become something more than just an unwary approach to semantic problems. It can apparently be developed into a systematic theory which could undertake to illuminate some of the structures of natural language. This section will re-examine the phenomenon of paradox from the standpoint of naive semantics, and compare this with Kripke's relativistic account of the matter. In this matter the standpoint of naive semantics is that classical logic is what informs our intuitions of paradox. Kripke's theory admits various alternative valuation schemes, each with its own class of paradoxical statements. All standard schemes are weaker than the classical valuation scheme, and consequently no one of them seems to be altogether free from intuitive wrinkles.

For example, consider the Strong Kleene scheme which Kripke uses to illustrate his theory in [9]. There are some undeniably attractive features to this scheme, but one feature that seems a bit counterintuitive is that some everywhere-stably-true statements get classified as "paradoxical" under the *SK* scheme. For an illustration of this, tautological compounds of *SK*-paradoxical statements, like $[E \equiv E]$, will be *SK*-paradoxical. And yet those compounds are classically valid and so everywhere-stably true. Other compounds like $[E \& \sim E]$ are classically contravalid and so everywhere-stably-false. And yet all of them are *SK*-paradoxical. There is something to be said on both sides of this issue, and I will not try to resolve it here. But it clearly raises the question of justifying the *SK* scheme, inasmuch as the same statements may be nonparadoxical relative to alternative valuation schemes.

As already remarked, a critical feature of Kripke's definitions for the concepts of grounding, paradoxicality, and so forth, is their relativity to the valuation scheme. Either one must fix upon a particular valuation scheme, or else search for invariants. In a sense this is no less true for such concepts as stability and periodicity in the semi-inductive framework; but whereas there is a naturally favoured valuation scheme for naive semantics (the classical valuation scheme), it seems to be much more difficult to single out any uniquely "natural" valuation scheme for the inductive construction. This may very well be a simple consequence of the fact that the classical valuation scheme is not monotonic and so not admissible within the inductive framework.

A number of standard valuation schemes were presented in Section X, and discussed and contrasted with some nonstandard schemes. Even under the conditions defining standard schemes there will be a vast array of different ones, including restricted supervaluation schemes generated by many different conditions on T-completions. Beyond the restriction to consistent sets, there could be restrictions to classically satisfiable sets, to theories, to consistent theories and so on. Some of these standard schemes could be arranged in order of increasing strength; others will be strictly incomparable in their strength and thereby in their concepts of grounding and paradox. Even though all will have some common domain of applicability (the classically sound partial models) their domains in general may overlap in complicated ways that render comparisons of strength partly indeterminate.

While Kripke expresses some personal preference for the Strong Kleene scheme, he suggests that each of several schemes has its advocates, each may have some advantages and disadvantages, and that there may not even be any objective basis for choosing among them.[10]

I am somewhat uncertain whether there is a definite factual question as to whether natural language handles truth-value gaps—at least those arising in connection with the semantic paradoxes—by the schemes of Frege, Kleene, van Fraassen, or perhaps some other. ([9], p. 77.)

Perhaps each standard scheme embodies a "compromise" of some sort, some retrenchment from the classical valuation scheme.[11] The classical (Strong Frege) scheme stands above all standard schemes as an external bound constraining them while not itself being a standard

---

[10] The qualifying footnote which accompanies this passage should not be overlooked:

"I do not mean to *assert* that there are no definite questions of fact in these areas, or even that I myself may not favor some valuation schemes over others. But my personal views are less important than the variety of tools that are available, so for the purposes of this sketch I take an agnostic position." ([9], p. 78, n. 30.)

[11] As with set theory according to Quine: "Each proposed scheme is unnatural, because the natural scheme is the unrestricted one that the antinomies discredit." ([15], p. 18.) But I think we might reconsider—in semantics at any rate—whether the antinomies really do discredit "the natural scheme". Similar questions might be raised in set theory by applying semi-inductive methods to the construction of the membership relation.

scheme. Now if there were no basis for choosing among standard schemes, if all were equally "correct", then Kripke's classification of statements into grounded, paradoxical, and so forth, would to that extent be ineliminably vague.

We could nonetheless search for invariants. Let a statement be called *absolutely grounded* iff it is grounded relative to every standard valuation scheme. There is a weakest standard scheme, which is that restriction of WK whose inductive generators are precisely the classically sound partial models. Call this the Restricted Weak Kleene (RWK) scheme; clearly it generates exactly the absolutely grounded statements. So here is something that can be pinned down independently of the problem of choice among standard valuation schemes. And it may be remarked that the RWK-grounded statements exactly coincide with the WK-grounded statements; so WK could also be used to generate the absolutely grounded statements. This can be seen from the fact that any WK fixed point model is classically sound ($Tm = Vm$ and $Vm \leqslant SFM$, so $Tm \leqslant SFm$).

In connection with grounding it does seem defensible to regard absolute grounding as the "core" of our intuitive notion. Statements that are grounded only in the relative sense (on schemes stronger than WK) do seem to be correspondingly less firm from an intuitive standpoint. Even intuitions about the "Nixon-Dean" statements of [9] (which are SK-grounded but not WK-grounded) might be accommodated in some other way—for example by reflecting that those statements are naively stable. Once the notion of stability is available, some of our intuitions about the "goodness" or "acceptability" of statements might be restructured around it. It could supplement the notion of (absolute) grounding in perhaps interesting ways.

So the notion of absolute grounding might have some import in an explanatory theory of our semantic intuitions. It would however leave some intuitions unexplained. We seem to have fairly firm intuitions of "ungrounding", that is it seems intuitively clear that certain statements are definitely ungrounded; the 'I am true' statements would be one sort of example. And yet are these absolutely ungrounded, that is ungrounded on all standard valuation schemes? That seems doubtful, in view of the great flexibility of the restricted supervaluational method. So the straightforward invariance approach to the concept of grounding, while initially promising, does seem to leave us with residual problems, and it is not immediately clear how one would carry it further.

Matters are more complicated in connection with the concept of paradoxicality. Once again the notion is relative to the choice of valuation-scheme, and here no standard offers itself, not even in connection with invariants. Let a statement be called *absolutely paradoxical* iff it is paradoxical relative to every standard valuation scheme. It seems very doubtful that any standard valuation scheme generates exactly the absolutely paradoxical statements. Certainly the Weak Kleene scheme is a non-starter, having far too extensive a class of relatively paradoxical statements. If any standard scheme could capture the absolute notion of paradoxicality it would be far removed from *WK*. The best one could hope for along these lines would be a pair of schemes, one for grounding and the other for paradoxicality. And once again an additional problem would arise in connection with intuitions of nonparadoxicality.

Assuming that there is no maximally strong standard scheme, one might nevertheless consider the possibility that the Strong Frege scheme, even though it is nonstandard, might somehow serve as an external bench mark for the absolute notion of paradoxicality. For example, this situation might be realized in case the absolutely paradoxical statements happened to coincide with the everywhere-unstable statements of naive semantics. In this connection I have only been able to obtain a partial result so far:

13.1   *Second Comparison Theorem*: All naively unstable state-
        ments are absolutely Kripke-paradoxical.

Proof: Consider any statement A which is Kripke-nonparadoxical under some standard valuation scheme V. Assume first that A is true under V at some fixed point model m. In the terms introduced for the abstract Comparison Lemma 11.3, this means that for some set X of statements and some ordinal number κ, $A \in G\kappa X$. By 11.3 then $A \in J\alpha X$ for all $\alpha \geqslant \kappa$, so A would be positively stable from the *SF*-jump hm of the partial model m. By a parallel argument if A were false at m it would be negatively stable from hm. Either way, if A is nonparadoxical under V it must be naively stable from at least one starting model. By contraposition there can be no standard valuation scheme under which any naively unstable statement is not Kripke-paradoxical.

The converse of 13.1 is an attractive proposition which I have not so far been able to prove or refute. It could be proved if the conditions defining standard valuation schemes were relaxed a bit. But the only way I know of doing this is to relax the monotonicity condition, and to do that would pretty clearly take one beyond the scope of the theory of truth outlined in [9].

XIV. Towards a Unified Theory

Our efforts to compare standard inductive semantics with naive semantics have so far been only partly successful. What they have suggested is that certain correlative concepts—like grounding and stability—may not be rival explications for a unitary set of underlying intuitions. They might instead be supplementary concepts, each contributing something distinctive to the explications of complex semantic intuitions. The situation is more uncertain at the other end of the scale, where Kripke paradoxicality and naive instability so far still look like rival explications for the same set of intuitions. To obtain a richer understanding of the inductive and naive approaches, the next step would be to aim for a unified theory capable of encompassing both. The framework for such a theory is already in place, within the general conception of semi-inductive constructions. So far we have tried to compare semi-inductive semantics for classical languages with inductive semantics for partially interpreted languages. Various strands can be woven together by forming the "cross-point" of these two approaches: a semi-inductive semantics for partially interpreted languages. Its jump operation will be based on some standard valuation scheme as on the inductive approach; its limit rule will be the semi-inductive lower limit function. Within such a framework all the concepts of standard inductive semantics could be represented alongside all the concepts of naive semantics, in addition to quite a number of bridging concepts. In this section I will sketch very briefly a few of the most elementary of these concepts.

Semi-inductions as so far presented build up sets; as a special case they can be used to build up partial functions construed as sets of ordered pairs. For the simplest semantic applications these will be partial truth-functions; their members will be ordered pairs $\langle A, v \rangle$ each consisting of a statement A and a truth-value $v \in \{\top, \bot\}$. Partial truth-functions can be used to represent partial valuations, and they can also be used to represent partial semantic interpretations for the predicate T.

Basic elements will now be ordered pairs $\langle A, v \rangle$ and these could be classified as before in terms of stability properties. But the main semantic interest is not in these pairs but in the statements that make up their first members; and here we will find that some new possibilities for classification have been opened up. Before proceeding to these classifications, I want to show how both inductive and naive semantic constructions can be represented in the extended theory.

For what follows, let any primary partial model and any standard valuation scheme V be fixed. To simplify the formulations let us provisionally assume that V has an unlimited domain of applicability, so that it defines a valuation for every expansion of the primary model. Now we can single out two special classes of semi-inductive constructions that proceed from two distinct (usually disjoint) classes of starting models.

An expansion m of the primary model will be called *semantically sound* iff it is sound relative to the valuation scheme ($Tm \leqslant Vm$). Since V is monotonic, the semi-inductive construction from any semantically sound starting model leads to a fixed point model and exactly recapitulates an inductive construction from that starting model. In the extended theory, constructions generated by semantically sound starting points will be called *inductive constructions*.

An expansion m of the primary model will be called *semantically complete* iff it is maximally expanded under $\leqslant$, so that Tm is a total function (and $m = hm$). Since V is bounded from below by WK and from above by SF, the semi-inductive construction from any semantically complete starting model exactly recapitulates a naive semantic construction from that starting model. This follows from the fact that $WKm = SFm$ for any semantically complete model m. Since Vm is sandwiched between WK and SF, completeness of m secures that Vm and SFm exactly coincide. In the extended theory, constructions generated by semantically complete starting points will be called *naive constructions*.

We now have an enriched semantic space within which two special classes of constructions have been singled out; and these constructions, along with others, can be used to obtain a very much enriched semantic classification of statements. One of the main innovations of the extended theory will be that it takes into account the behaviour of statements within a much wider class of constructions, including those that are neither inductive nor classically naive.

We have assumed a fixed primary model and standard valuation scheme that is defined over all partial models. For the following series of definitions, let A be any statement and m be any T-expansion of the primary model. For any ordinal number α, let *V*α*m* be the αth semi-inductive descendant of *m* under the jump operation determined by *V* and the Kripke jump rule.

A is
$\begin{cases}\end{cases}$

positively stable from m iff for any sufficiently large ordinal number α, ⟨*A*, ⊤⟩ belongs to *V*α*m*.

negatively stable from m iff for any sufficiently large ordinal number α, ⟨*A*, ⊥⟩ belongs to *V*α*m*.

neutralized from m iff for any sufficiently large ordinal number α, neither ⟨*A*, ⊤⟩ nor ⟨*A*, ⊥⟩ belongs to *V*α*m*.

unstable from m otherwise.

Because the valuation scheme is monotonic, the only sort of instability that could arise will be some pattern of variation between truth and falsity. There will be no statements that alternate indefinitely between truth and "gap", for example, nor any that alternate indefinitely between falsity and "gap", for another example. Neutralization is a new category, which somehow lies between stability and instability as previously encountered. From a purely formal standpoint it would be possible to construe it as some kind of doubly negative stability; but our intended interpretation strongly suggests treating it together with instability. In what follows, neutralization and instability will be regarded as two different types of some more general sort of "rejection" from the truth-function under construction. There is a curious complementarity between them: there is no instability from semantically sound starting points, nor any neutralization from semantically complete starting points. It is only by taking in the whole range of possible starting points that we can study their interaction.

A is
$\begin{cases}\end{cases}$

inductively stable iff *A* is stable from all semantically sound starting points.

inductively neutralized iff *A* is neutralized from all semantically sound starting points.

These definitions reconstruct the notions of Kripke-grounding and Kripke-paradoxicality within the extended theory. As a simple consequence of the monotonicity of *V*, inductive stability is always uniformly positive or uniformly negative; there are no inductively variably-stable statements.

A is $\begin{cases} classically\ stable \text{ iff } A \text{ is stable from all semantically complete starting points.} \\ classically\ unstable \text{ iff } A \text{ is unstable from all semantically complete starting points.} \end{cases}$

These definitions reconstruct within the extended theory the naive notions of stability and instability "everywhere". Within the extended theory they no longer have reference to all starting points, but rather to a quite special class of selected starting points. We shall also want to introduce some extended notions that have reference to *all* starting points within the domain of V.

A is $\begin{cases} everywhere\ stable \text{ iff } A \text{ is uniformly stable from every starting point.} \\ everywhere\ rejected \text{ iff from every starting point, } A \text{ is either unstable or neutralized.} \end{cases}$

These categories are by no means exhaustive; they define two extreme cases of special semantic interest.

14.1   *Stability Lemma*: Any statement that is stable from a model m is stable in the same sense from any expansion of m.

Proof: This follows from a more general monotonicity property. For any ordinal α, and any partial models m and n: $m \leqslant n$ implies that $V\alpha m \leqslant V\alpha n$, which can be proved by induction on α. So if A is positively stable from m, it is also positively stable from any $n \geqslant m$; if A is negatively stable from m, it is also negatively stable from any $n \geqslant m$, and its stabilization ordinal from n is less than or equal to its stabilization ordinal from m.

14.2   All inductively stable statements are everywhere stable.

Proof: Immediate from 14.1 and the fact that every possible starting point is an expansion of the primary model. Any inductively stable statement is stable from the primary model, and so is stable in the same sense from any starting point.

14.3   Classically unstable statements are everywhere rejected.

Proof: Consider any starting model m and any statement A that is not rejected from m. Being neither unstable nor neutralized from m, A must be stable from m. By 14.1, A is stable from hm, the Fregean completion of m; so A is not classically unstable. By contraposition, 14.3 is secured.

Because of the previously mentioned complementarity, there will be no statements that are everywhere unstable. From sound starting points, standard valuation-schemes automatically neutralize classically unstable statements. For this reason some rough correlation between classical instability and inductive neutralization is inevitable. For a wide range of primary models the relation seems to be one of proper inclusion: classically unstable statements will be inductively neutralized, and other statements will be inductively neutralized as well. There is even a tendency to neutralize statements from the other end of the spectrum, statements that are classically stable and in some cases even classically valid. This tendency relates in some way to the combination of monotonicity together with the upper bound condition—every standard valuation scheme is strictly weaker than the classical scheme. It underlies the impression that standard schemes embody some retrenchment or compromises by comparison with the classical scheme. For a wide range of primary models, some statements will be inductively neutralized on account of their instability properties, and other statements will be inductively neutralized on account of particular weaknesses in the valuation scheme.

References

[1] Besicovitch, A. F., *Almost-Periodic Functions* (Cambridge, 1932).
[2] Bochvar, D. A., "On a Three-Valued Calculus and Its Application in the Analysis of the Paradoxes of the Extended Functional Calculus", *Matematicheskii Sbornik*, N.S. 4, 46 (1938), 287–308.
[3] Burge, Tyler, "Semantical Paradox", this volume.
[4] Chihara, Charles, "The Semantic Paradoxes: A Diagnostic Investigation", *The Philosophical Review*, 88 (October 1979), 590–618.
[5] Feferman, S., "Comparison of Some Type-Free Theories of Partial Operations and Classifications", typescript 1976. Revised version in this volume and *The Journal of Symbolic Logic*.
[6] Frege, G., *The Basic Laws of Arithmetic*, translated and edited, with an introduction, by Montgomery Furth (University of California, 1967).
[7] Herzberger, H. G., "Notes on Periodicity", typescript May 1980.
[8] Hofstadter, D., *Gödel, Escher, Bach: An Eternal Golden Braid* (Basic Books, 1979).
[9] Kripke, S., "Outline of a Theory of Truth", this volume.
[10] Kripke, S., Lectures on Truth, three lectures delivered at Princeton University in 1975.
[11] Kuratowski, K. and Mostowski, A., *Set Theory*, 2nd Edition (North-Holland, 1976).

[12] Martin, R. L., editor, *The Paradox of the Liar*, 2nd Edition with supplementary bibliography (Ridgeview, 1978).

[13] Priest, G., "The Logic of Paradox", *Journal of Philosophical Logic* 8 (May 1979), 219–41.

[14] Putnam, H., "Trial and Error Predicates and the Solution to a Problem of Mostowski", *Journal of Symbolic Logic* 30 (March 1965), 49–57.

[15] Quine, W. V. O., "The Ways of Paradox", in his *The Ways of Paradox and Other Essays* (Random House, 1966), 3–20.

[16] Rescher, N., *Many-Valued Logic* (McGraw-Hill, 1969).

[17] Rescher, N. and Brandom, R., *The Logic of Inconsistency* (Rowman and Littlefield, 1980).

[18] Tarski, A., "The Concept of Truth in Formalized Languages", in his *Logic, Semantics, Metamathematics* (Oxford, 1956), 152–278.

[19] van Fraassen, B., "Presupposition, Implication, and Self-Reference", *The Journal of Philosophy* 65 (1968), 136–52.

Truth and Paradox*

Anil Gupta

I

The Liar paradox raises two distinct though related problems about the concept of truth. The first is the *descriptive* problem of explaining our use of the word 'true', and, in particular, of giving the meaning of sentences containing 'true'. It is a fact that although we do not have clear intuitions about the meaning of some sentences containing 'true', e.g., the paradoxical sentences, yet we do manage to use successfully various other sentences that contain the word 'true' and we do have fairly clear intuitions about what these sentences mean.

Anil Gupta, "Truth and Paradox", reprinted from the *Journal of Philosophical Logic* 11 (1982), 1–60. Copyright © 1982 by Anil Gupta.

* The results reported in this essay were obtained for the most part in February and March 1980 during my stay at the University of Pittsburgh. I discussed these results in informal talks given at the University of Pittsburgh in March and April 1980, and in my seminar on logic given in the Fall of 1980 at McGill University. More recently, talks based on this paper were given at Syracuse University (November 1981) and at the Eastern Division meetings of the American Philosophical Association (December 1981).

In preparing this essay I have incurred a number of debts. My first and foremost is to my teacher and friend Professor Nuel Belnap. During my stay in Pittsburgh in the Winter semester of the academic year 1979–80, he willingly and generously spent many hours working with me on the ideas reported here. He helped me to find my way out of numerous blind alleys, and he made numerous positive suggestions that have greatly benefitted my work. The proof of the main lemma given in Section II, in particular, would have been much more inelegant were it not for his suggestions. It would be difficult now to detail his contributions exactly. Let me just say that they are very great indeed. At Pittsburgh, I also benefitted from discussions with Professor Richmond Thomason. He raised the question of how non-vicious reference should be defined. My answer to his question is given in the definition of the Thomason model (Section IV). To Professor Allen Hazen I am indebted for correspondence on the problem of the paradoxes and for useful comments on the first draft. Professor John Macnamara also read the first draft and made numerous suggestions for improvement. With my student Mr. John Hawthorn, who has written his doctoral dissertation on the Liar paradox, I have had fruitful discussions for over three years. I have discussed this subject with many other people as well. I would like to mention

However, the division between these two classes of sentences is not a straightforward one. It cannot be said, for example, that the first class consists of all and only those sentences that involve one form of self-reference or another. For there are many sentences that involve self-reference that are not in any obvious way problematic. One example among many is the law: 'No sentence is both true and false'. Most naturally understood, this says of every sentence, including itself, that it is not both true and false. Intuitively, the sentence is meaningful and indeed true. And an account which says that it is not is unacceptable unless strong reasons are given to controvert our intuition. Similarly there is no straightforward and simple account of what the sentences belonging to the second class, the trouble-free sentences, mean. For example, no simple redundancy theory of truth manages to explain the meaning of those trouble-free sentences that contain self-reference. For any attempt at the elimination of the concept of truth in these sentences results in an unending cycle. So we have the following situation: we have no difficulty in using the word 'true' in many sentences but we have no systematic understanding of what distinguishes these trouble-free sentences from the troublesome ones, and we have no systematic understanding of what these trouble-free sentences mean. The task of providing such a systematic understanding falls under the first problem.

The second problem that the Liar paradox raises about the concept of truth is the *normative* one of discovering the changes (if any) that the paradox dictates in our conception and use of 'true'. The reasoning in the derivation of the paradox shows that some of our usual assumptions go awry in the case of the liar sentence. But it

especially David Conter, Steven Davis, François Dongier, Vishwas Govitrikar, Dorothy Grover, Lily Knezevich, Storrs McCall, and Michel Paquette.

As the present essay was nearing completion, I received three recent papers from Professor Hans Herzberger: his "Notes on Naive Semantics", "Notes on Periodicity", and "Naive Semantics and the Liar Paradox". These papers develop a theory which is, in many respects, similar to the one presented in this essay. Professor Herzberger has studied the notions of stability, paradoxicality, etc., in the context of Definition 2. The main areas of overlap in the results we have obtained appear to be facts 4 to 11. The main area that he has studied that I have not is the cycling of the revision process. I hope to take account of his important work on cycling in a later essay.

I have not attempted to deal with all the approaches to the paradoxes that are found in the literature. I have discussed only those that give (or attempt to give) a systematic solution to the first problem of Section I. The bibliography lists the most important recent papers on the Liar paradox known to me.

is not at all clear what conclusions about our concept of truth we should draw from this fact. Should we say that the paradox shows that our concept is incoherent? But isn't it equally plausible to say that the concept—as it is reflected in use—is quite coherent but that in the Liar reasoning the appearance of paradox is due to some highly plausible but nonetheless false assumption concerning our concept of truth? Even if the concept is incoherent, we should ask whether it is incoherent in ways that interfere with its utility. For it might be that the concept is incoherent in cases that are of little importance so far as the point and the utility of the concept are concerned. Finally, if the concept is incoherent in ways that demand reform we need to decide what paradox-free concept or concepts should replace it. These are the questions that the second problem sets us. In their present formulation they are not entirely clear and free from ambiguity, but it *is* clear that they can be adequately answered only when we have arrived at a systematic understanding of our concept of truth, i.e., only when we have gone some way towards solving the first problem. It is only when we know the role of truth in our conceptual scheme that we can evaluate the damage that the paradox does, and the reforms (if any) that it necessitates.

The aim of this essay is to work towards a solution of the first problem within a limited and idealized context and to see what this work suggests for the solution of the second problem. The limitations and idealizations are forced upon us by the complexity and enormity of the task before us. In order to give the meaning of *all* paradox-free sentences containing 'true', we would need not only to arrive at a general understanding of what meaning is and what form a theory purporting to give the meaning of sentences should take (something that is much disputed in present-day philosophy), but we would also need to give an account of a great many perplexing linguistic phenomena such as indexicals, vagueness, modality, etc. If we are even to begin to work towards a description of our concept of truth we need to set aside some of these problems or, at least, make a tentative decision about their solution. For this purpose I propose to make the following four assumptions. (I should emphasize that I am not suggesting that these assumptions are true of natural languages. I do not believe that they are. Even so I believe that the assumptions do not make our results irrelevant to natural languages. The analogy with idealization in the natural sciences is useful here. Many assumptions true of the idealized model are not true of its real-life counterpart, but this does not interfere with the applicability of the idealization. In any case, a theorist unwilling to make the assumptions I suggest below will find much in this essay that is translatable into his own favorite scheme under his own favorite assumptions.)

(i) I assume that the language (or the language fragment; henceforth I assume that the context supplies this additional qualification) under study has, aside from the concept of truth, none of the other complicating factors: indexicals, vagueness, ambiguity, intensional constructions, truth-value gaps, etc. Thus I assume that apart from the concept of truth the language can be viewed as a classical first-order quantificational language. This assumption is satisfied only by very limited fragments of natural languages, but I believe that it removes little that is of immediate interest to us in our study of the interaction of truth and self-reference.

(ii) I assume that the theory of meaning of a class of sentences gives the assertibility conditions of sentences belonging to that class. It tells us for each sentence of the class the conditions under which the sentence is correctly assertible and the conditions under which it is not correctly assertible. By making this assumption I do not mean to judge the realist/anti-realist dispute in semantics. My aim is rather to prevent a certain misunderstanding. If I had said that the theory of meaning gives the truth-conditions of sentences, it could easily have been supposed that the theory gives the extension of truth under various conditions. And this is something that I do not wish to suggest. The theory of meaning on the present assumption gives the sentences that are assertible under various conditions. The point will become clear later in this essay. For present purposes it is sufficient to note that I do not mean to decide the important issues between realists and anti-realists. If necessary we can bypass these issues by making an additional assumption to the effect that all sentences of the language under consideration are decidable (perhaps by some idealized knower).

The next two assumptions are more specific than the foregoing. They concern the *logic* of truth. Assumption (iii) rules on the logical category to which the concept of truth belongs, and assumption (iv) on the "objects" of truth.

(iii) I assume that truth is (expressed by) a predicate. Under any other assumption concerning the logical category of truth—such as that it is (expressed by) a singular term or a sentence operator or a prosentence[1]—we would need to countenance propositional quantifiers and intensional constructions in the logic of the language. For there are many meaningful sentences containing 'true' whose contents are expressible (under the assumptions in question) only if we allow propositional quantifiers and intensional constructions. An example is provided by the sentence 'everything Jones believes is true'. If truth is not treated as a predicate, this example must be viewed as containing in its analysis the open sentence 'Jones believe that p', where 'Jones believes that' is an intensional sentential operator and 'p' is a propositional variable. So, for example, on the sentence-operator theory, this sentence will be analysed thus:

$(\forall p)$ (If Jones believes that p then it is true that p).

Now I do not wish to argue that there is something wrong with intensional operators or with propositional quantifiers. However, since in accordance with assumption (i) I wish to avoid the complications arising from intensionality, I prefer to work under the assumption that truth is a predicate. Note that the theory of truth that we give below can be used to interpret propositional quantifiers (on a substitutional reading). Indeed the problems of interpreting propositional quantifiers and the truth predicate are exactly parallel. They suffer from the same sort of impredicativity.

(iv) I assume that the objects of truth are sentences. A more nominalistic construal of truth bearers, such as their identification with sentence-tokens, is not plausible because of the obvious difficulty that there are unexpressed truths, just as there are many unnamed objects. And a more intensional proposal, such as that the objects of truth are statements or propositions, is not acceptable to us because of our desire to avoid the problems of intensionality. In any case a theorist who insists that it is the latter that are the objects of truth may take us to be giving a theory not of truth but rather of the concept "being a sentence that expresses a true statement (proposition)".

In view of these assumptions we can formulate the task set by the first problem quite precisely. It is to give for a first-order language L equipped with a truth predicate T an account of those sentences that

[1] See Grover, Camp, and Belnap (1975) for an account of the prosentential theory of truth; Tarski (1969) attributes the sentence-operator theory to Tadeusz Kotarbiński; and perhaps Frege can be viewed as holding the singular-term theory.

are paradoxical and those that are not, and for the latter sentences we have to give an account of the conditions under which they are assertible and the conditions under which they are not assertible. Now as all constants of L, except perhaps T, are behaving in a classical way, we can give a precise account of the notion of *condition*. We can identify conditions with the classical models of the T-free fragment of L. The idea here is that a speaker of L who knew the extensions of all the nonlogical constants (T is counted, like identity, a *logical* constant) would also know what sentences of L can be asserted and what cannot be asserted. Classical models of the T-free fragment of L give the extensions of all the nonlogical constants of L. They can be viewed as representing possible ways things might have been. So the task of giving an account of the conditions under which a sentence is assertible can be construed as that of defining the models in which the sentence is assertible. There is just one respect in which our models must differ from the classical models of the T-free fragment of L, due to the fact that the presence of T in L means that L talks about its own sentences. So we must ensure that the models of L contain in their domains sentences of L.

Definition 1.   A *model* M *for* L is an ordered pair $\langle D, I \rangle$ consisting of a domain D and an interpretation function I such that

  (i)   the set of sentences of L (henceforth, S) $\subseteq$ D,
  (ii) I assigns to each name in L a member of D; to each n-place nonlogical predicate in L a subset of D^n; to each n-place function symbol in L a member of D^{D^n}.

(Ideally we should allow the possibility that the object-language conception of sentence may not coincide with the metalanguage conception. For example, in the object language, sentences may be identified with certain natural numbers but in the metalanguage they may be identified with certain strings of symbols. To allow for this possibility we should weaken clause (i) of Definition 1 to require that the *representatives* of sentences of L belong to D, and make the definition of model relative to a 1–1 mapping of S onto a subset of D. But the generality thus introduced gains us nothing except terminological complications, and it could also be confusing. I stick to the simpler definition given above.)

Kripke has emphasized that sentences that are unproblematic in one context become paradoxical if some of the facts had been otherwise. This is already clear in the classical version of the Liar paradox in which a Cretan says that all Cretans are liars. As things stand this sentence is not paradoxical. (I am assuming that the phrase 'are liars' applies to those persons who haven't uttered and never will utter a single truth, and I am also assuming that some Cretans have uttered or will utter, perhaps unintentionally, some truths.) However it is easy to imagine circumstances in which the Cretan's pronouncement would be paradoxical: we need only imagine a situation in which all Cretan utterances, aside from the one under consideration, are false. This shows that the demarcation between the paradoxical/non-paradoxical sentences is itself relative to how things are. So our theory of truth must give for the language L an account of what sentences are paradoxical (or in other ways problematic) *in a model* M and what sentences are assertible in M. The theory is to be tested by how well it captures our intuitions about what is paradoxical and what is assertible in a given situation.

I turn to the general task of constructing a theory of truth in the last section of this essay. First I study (in Sections II and III) the concept of truth in certain limited classes of models. This study will lead to a better understanding of some of the desiderata that the general theory must satisfy.

II

It is a fundamental intuition about truth that from any sentence A the inference to another sentence that asserts that A is true is warranted. And conversely: from the latter sentence the inference to A is also warranted. It is this intuition that in enshrined in Tarski's famous Convention T. Tarski requires, as a material adequacy condition, that a definition of truth for a language L imply all sentences of the form

(T)   x is true iff p,

where 'p' is replaced by an object language sentence (or its translation, if the definition is not homophonic) and 'x' is replaced by a standard name of the sentence. (Sentences of the form (T) will sometimes be called "Tarski biconditionals", sometimes "T-biconditionals", and sometimes, when the context ensures that no confusion will result, simply "biconditionals".) Now the Liar paradox shows that if the instances of (T) are asserted in the language L itself, *and* the usual laws of classical logic hold, *and* certain kinds of self-referential sentences are allowed in L then a contradiction follows. For suppose that L has some device for forming standard names of all its sentences, say by quotation, and suppose there is a name '*b*' in L that denotes the sentence '*b* is not true'. Then one of the instances of the (T) scheme for L will be,

'*b* is not true' is true iff *b* is not true.

And this implies a contradiction if we allow the classically valid law of substitutivity of identicals. Tarski is led by this argument to require that the concept of truth for a language L be contained in a metalanguage ML and not in L itself.

The Liar paradox shows, then, that in the case of a classical language that has its own truth predicate the fundamental intuition cannot be preserved under *all* conditions (i.e., all models). This leads to the question whether there are any conditions under which the intuition can be preserved? Intuitively it would seem that there are. It would seem that when the language does not contain the sort of self-referential devices that generate the paradox the Tarski biconditionals can be consistently held. The reasoning of the Liar paradox, it seems, cannot be reenacted within such a language. There are many logicians and philosophers, however, who view such a possibility with great scepticism. They see the Liar paradox arising even in circumstances where there does not seem to be any self-reference at all. And this leads many to believe that any classical language that possesses its own concept of truth is bound to be inconsistent. Some it leads to even stronger conclusions. For example, Wallace (1972) says:[2]

A language cannot contain its own truth predicate; that is, "true-in-myself" is not a concept of any language. This point is an effect of the semantic paradoxes (p. 222).

A similar point is made by Prior (1967).

Further, Tarski argues, a sentence asserting that some sentence *S* is a true sentence of some language *L* cannot itself be a sentence of the language *L*, but must belong to a metalanguage in which the sentences of *L* are not used, but are mentioned and discussed. He is led to this view by the paradox of the "liar" (Vol. 2, p. 230).

---

[2] Wallace attributes the point to Tarski. I have not, however, been able to find such a sweeping claim in Tarski's work.

These opinions[3] may have their source in Tarski's paper "The Semantic Conception of Truth". After a discussion of an empirical version of the Liar paradox in which a contradiction is deduced from an obviously true empirical premiss with the aid of the T-biconditionals, Tarski writes:

If we now analyze the assumptions which lead to the antinomy of the liar, we notice the following:

(I) We have implicitly assumed that the language in which the antinomy is constructed contains, in addition to its expressions, also the names of these expressions, as well as semantic terms such as the term *"true"* referring to sentences of this language; we have also assumed that all sentences which determine the adequate usage of this term can be asserted in the language. A language with these properties will be called *"semantically closed"*.

(II) We have assumed that in this language the ordinary laws of logic hold.

(III) We have assumed that we can formulate and assert in our language an empirical premise [of the sort that] has occurred in our argument.

It turns out that the assumption (III) is not essential, for it is possible to reconstruct the antinomy of the liar without its help. But the assumptions (I) and (II) prove essential. Since every language which satisfies both of these assumptions is inconsistent, we must reject at least one of them.

It would be superfluous to stress here the consequences of rejecting the assumption (II), that is, of changing our logic (supposing this were possible) even in its more elementary and fundamental parts. We thus consider only the possibility of rejecting the assumption (I). Accordingly, we decide *not to use any language which is semantically closed* in the sense given (Linsky (1952), pp. 20–1).

Tarski claims in this passage that semantically closed languages for which the laws of classical logic hold are inconsistent. This is a surprising result because the syntactic resources necessary for a language to qualify as semantically closed are minimal. The only requirement is that it have names for its own expressions. It is not at all obvious that such names allow us to construct the sort of self-reference that is responsible for the Liar paradox. In a footnote Tarski gives an argument that may be thought to provide a proof of his claim. The footnote is appended to his statement that the paradox of the Liar can be derived without the aid of an empirical premiss.

[3] For other expressions of similar opinions see Russell (1940), p. 59, Popper (1965), p. 310, and Mackie (1973), p. 31.

This can roughly be done in the following way. Let S be any sentence beginning with the words "*Every sentence*". We correlate with S a new sentence S^* by subjecting S to the following two modifications: we replace in S the first word, "*Every*", by "*The*"; and we insert after the second word, "*sentence*", the whole sentence S enclosed in quotation marks. Let us agree to call the sentence S "(self-)applicable" or "non-(self-)applicable" dependent on whether the correlated sentence S^* is true or false. Now consider the following sentence:

> *Every sentence is non-applicable.*

It can easily be shown that the sentence just stated must be both applicable and non-applicable; hence a contradiction (Linsky (1952), p. 43, fn. 11).

Now this note certainly establishes that an empirical premiss is not essential in the derivation of the paradox. It does not, however, show that all classical semantically closed languages are inconsistent. The argument applies to only those languages that have enough resources to express the syntactic function *, and it has not been shown that the function is expressible in all semantically closed languages. Still, we cannot claim to have shown that semantically closed languages are sometimes consistent. Lack of obviousness is no argument that Tarski's claim is false. We know from Gödel's proof of the incompleteness of arithmetic that self-reference may be present even in languages that have the most innocuous-looking syntactic notions. So let us show formally that semantically closed languages (in which classical logic holds!) can be consistent. (Readers unwilling to work through the proof should at least read up to Definition 2 below before skipping to the part entitled "Remarks".)

Let L be a classical first-order language that contains besides various predicates, function symbols and names, a special one-place logical predicate T and quotation marks $\ulcorner\urcorner$ and $\ulcorner\urcorner$. We allow in L quotation names for closed formulas (sentences) only. Thus, if $\ulcorner(\forall x)(Fx \supset Tx)\urcorner$ is a sentence of L then $\ulcorner(\forall x)(Fx \supset Tx)'\urcorner$ is a name in L.[4] (We *could* have allowed quotation names for all expressions of

---

[4] A note concerning the symbolic conventions employed in this essay. I use italicised symbols as metalinguistic variables ranging over various categories of expressions of the object language L. In particular, the variables 'A', 'B', 'C', etc., range over formulas; 'a', 'b', 'c', etc., over individual constants; 'x', 'y', 'z', etc., over variables; 's', 't', 't_1', etc., over terms; 'f', 'g', 'h', etc., over function symbols; 'F', 'G', 'H', etc., over predicates. I use corner quotes in the manner of Quine. Ordinary single quotes have two uses. Within corner quotes they are used autonymously: they name quotes in the object language. Elsewhere they are used in the usual way: as a device that forms names of expressions.

L, well-formed or not; that is, we could have allowed names such as $\ulcorner (\forall x) \supset F \urcorner$. But this results in a little bit of complication. For we now need a way of disambiguating formulas such as $\ulcorner (F(`a`) \& G(`b`) \& H(`c`)) \urcorner$. Does this assert of the strings $\ulcorner a`) \& G(`b \urcorner$ and $\ulcorner c \urcorner$ that they are F and H respectively? Or, does it assert of the strings $\ulcorner a \urcorner$ and $\ulcorner b`) \& H(`c \urcorner$ that they are F and G respectively? By allowing quotation names only for sentences we bypass this problem and lose nothing that is important for our present aims.)

We now proceed to construct a classical model of L in which all the Tarski biconditionals are true. The construction establishes that a language can consistently meet Tarski's requirements (I) and (II) in the passage quoted above.[5]

We begin with some definitions. Let M $(= \langle D, I \rangle)$ be a model for L. (See Definition 1.) Then, an ordered pair $\mathcal{M}$ $(= \langle D', I' \rangle)$ is a *standard extension* of M iff $D = D'$ and I' is just like I except that I' assigns to T a subset of D. We will say that $\mathcal{M}$ is *the standard extension generated by* M *and* $I'(T)$. (Symbolically, $\mathcal{M} = M + I'(T)$.) A *standard model* is an ordered pair that is a standard extension of some model of L. Tarski's theory of truth defines the notion "is a true sentence of L in the standard model $\mathcal{M}$". We use this notion in the construction below.

Let M $(= \langle D, I \rangle)$ be a model of L that meets the following condition.

Condition 1.
   (i)   I assigns to a quotation name $\ulcorner `A` \urcorner$ the sentence A.
   (ii) If a is not a quotation name than $I(a) \notin S$ (the set of sentences of L).
   (iii) If F is an n-place predicate and $d_i \in S$ $(1 \leqslant i \leqslant n)$ then $\langle d_1, \ldots, d_j, \ldots, d_n \rangle \in I(F)$ iff for all $d_i' \in S$, $\langle d_1, \ldots, d_i', \ldots, d_n \rangle \in I(F)$.
   (iv) If f is an n-place function symbol then the range of $I(f)$ does not contain any sentences. Further if $d_i, d_i' \in S$ $(1 \leqslant i \leqslant n)$ then, $I(f)(d_1, \ldots, d_i, \ldots, d_n) = I(f)(d_1, \ldots, d_i', \ldots, d_n)$.

If clause (ii) ((iii), (iv)) is satisfied we say that the names (predicates, function symbols) of L are S-*neutral* in M. Models that meet

---

[5] Strictly speaking, to meet Tarski's requirement (I) we have to ensure that L has names for *all* expressions, including ones that are not sentences. But clearly this is not a problem. If we suppose that there are non-quotational names for all the nonsentences, our construction obviously goes through.

Condition 1 will be called S-*acceptable*. Intuitively, the above condition ensures that aside from quotation names and the truth predicate, L does not have any other concepts that distinguish among the sentences of L in the model M. We show below that, under this condition, M can be extended to a standard model $\mathcal{M}$ in which all the T-biconditionals hold. As the existence of M is beyond doubt, it follows that L is a consistent semantically-closed language in which the laws of classical logic are valid.

We remark that the construction below goes through with much weaker conditions on M than the one imposed above. We shall explore some of these weakenings later.

Our construction of the standard model utilizes the notion "the truth set of L at ordinal level α for the set U" (abbreviated to "$\text{Tr}(\alpha, U)$") which we define by transfinite recursion as follows:

Definition 2. Let $U \subseteq D$. Then,

(i) If $\alpha = 0$ then $\text{Tr}(\alpha, U) = U$.

(ii) If $\alpha = \beta + 1$ then $\text{Tr}(\alpha, U) =$ the set of sentences true in the standard model $M + \text{Tr}(\beta, U)$.

(iii) If α is a limit ordinal then

$$\text{Tr}(\alpha, U) = \left\{ d : \exists \beta < \alpha \left(d \in \bigcap_{\beta \leqslant \gamma < \alpha} \text{Tr}(\gamma, U) \right) \right\}.$$

For $U \subseteq D$, we claim that $M + \text{Tr}(\omega, U)$ is a standard model of L in which all the Tarski biconditionals are true. The proof of this claim rests on the Main Lemma, which we state after a preliminary definition.

Definition 3.

(i) The degree of a name that is not quotational, and of a variable, is 0.

(ii) If A is a closed sentence of degree n then the degree of $\ulcorner `A` \urcorner$ is $n + 1$.

(iii) If F is an n-place predicate and $t_1, \ldots, t_n$ are terms of degree $i_1, \ldots, i_n$ respectively then the degree of $F(t_1, \ldots, t_n)$ is $\max\{i_1, \ldots, i_n\}$. Similarly for function symbols.

(iv) If a wff A has degree n then the degree of $\ulcorner (\forall x)A \urcorner$ and $\ulcorner \sim A \urcorner$ is also n.

(v) If A and B have degrees m and n respectively then the degree of $(A \supset B)$ is $\max\{m, n\}$.

Intuitively, the degree of a term or a formula gives the extent of the embedding of quotations within quotations in it.

Main Lemma. For all natural numbers n and all ordinals $\alpha > n + 1$ and all sentences A of degree n and all $U, V \subseteq D$,

$$A \in Tr(n + 2, U) \quad \text{iff} \quad A \in Tr(\alpha, V).$$

Proof. By induction on n. We suppose, as our hypothesis of induction, that for all natural numbers $m < n$ and all ordinals $\alpha > m + 1$ and all sentences A of degree m and all $U, V \subseteq D$,

$$A \in Tr(m + 2, U) \quad \text{iff} \quad A \in Tr(\alpha, V). \tag{1}$$

We need to show that the claim holds for sentences of degree n. We establish this by induction over α. Our second hypothesis of induction is that for all ordinals β such that $n + 1 < \beta < \alpha$ and all sentences A of degree n and all $U, V \subseteq D$,

$$A \in Tr(n + 2, U) \quad \text{iff} \quad A \in Tr(\beta, V). \tag{2}$$

Now α is either zero or a limit ordinal or a successor ordinal. The first two cases are trivial. The first obviously; and the second by hypothesis (2) and the definition of Tr. The interesting case is when α is a successor ordinal. Let $\alpha = \delta + 1$.

We observe that:

(a) On sentence of degree $< n$, $Tr(n + 1, U)$ and $Tr(\delta, V)$ coincide. By induction hypothesis (1).

(b) Of sentences of degree $\geqslant n$ there are denumerably many that fall under $Tr(n + 1, U)$ and denumerably many that do not. This is so because $Tr(n + 1, U)$ is the set of sentences true in $M + Tr(n, U)$. Hence all tautologies belong to $Tr(n + 1, U)$ and no contradiction belongs to it. But there are denumerable many of each of these that are of degree $\geqslant n$.

(c) A similar claim holds for $Tr(\delta, V)$, and for similar reasons. Note that the case when δ is limit is also covered by a simple extension of the above argument.

Let ϕ be a 1–1 function that maps the set of sentences of degree $\geqslant n$ onto itself and that meets the conditions that

$$A \in Tr(n + 1, U) \quad \text{iff} \quad \phi(A) \in Tr(\delta, V).$$

Our observations (b) and (c) ensure that there is such a function. Let ψ be the identity function from the rest of the domain D onto itself. And let $\chi = \phi \cup \psi$. The construction of χ is represented geometrically in diagram (A).

It can be shown that χ is a restricted isomorphism of $M + \mathrm{Tr}(n + 1, U)$ onto $M + \mathrm{Tr}(\delta, V)$. More precisely, χ preserves the interpretation in these standard models of all names of degree $\leqslant n$ and of all predicates and function symbols. It is easy to verify the following facts that ensure that χ is a restricted isomorphism in the intended sense.

(a) χ is 1–1 from D onto D.

(b)   For all $d \in D$, $d \in \mathrm{Tr}(n + 1, U)$ iff $\chi(d) \in \mathrm{Tr}(\delta, V)$. That is, χ preserves the interpretation of T. It is obvious in view of the definition of χ.

(c)   For all n-place predicates F other than T and all $d_1, \ldots,$ $d_n \in D$, $\langle d_1, \ldots d_n \rangle \in I(F)$ iff $\langle \chi(d_1), \ldots, \chi(d_n) \rangle \in I(F)$. That is, χ also preserves the interpretation of all other predicates. This claim is a direct consequence of clause (iii) of Condition 1 imposed on M.

(d)   Similarly the interpretation of the function symbols is preserved. By clause (iv) of Condition 1 we have that for all $d_1, \ldots, d_n \in D$ and all n-place function symbols f,

$$\chi(I(f)(d_1, \ldots, d_n)) = I(f)(\chi(d_1), \ldots, \chi(d_n)).$$

(e)   Finally, if a name t has degree $\leqslant n$ then

$$\chi(I(t)) = I(t).$$

That is, the interpretation of all names of degree $\leqslant n$ is preserved. Given clause (ii) of the condition on M the claim is obvious if t is not quotational. If t is quotational then it denotes a sentence of degree $< n$. But for these sentences χ is an identify function. So the denotation of these names is preserved as well.

Since $M + \mathrm{Tr}(n + 1, U)$ and $M + \mathrm{Tr}(\delta, V)$ are isomorphic with respect to a fragment of L (the fragment consisting of names of degree $\leqslant n$ and the constants of the other logical categories) we conclude that if the degree of a formula A is $\leqslant n$ then A is true in one

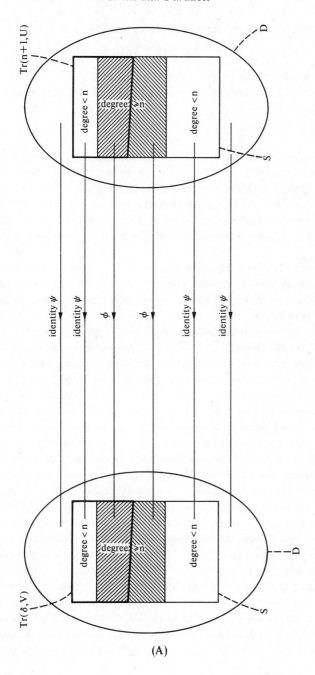

(A)

model iff it is true in the other. Hence we have that

$A \in \text{Tr}(n + 2, U)$ iff $A \in \text{Tr}(\delta + 1, V)$.

This completes the proof of the Main Lemma.

Now it is an immediate consequence of this lemma that for all sentences A

$A \in \text{Tr}(\omega, U)$ iff $A \in \text{Tr}(\omega + 1, U)$.

And this implies that the Tarski biconditional $\ulcorner T('A') \equiv A \urcorner$ is true in $M + \text{Tr}(\omega, U)$. For A must be either true or not true in $M + \text{Tr}(\omega, U)$. If it is true then $A \in \text{Tr}(\omega + 1, U)$ and hence $A \in \text{Tr}(\omega, U)$. So $\ulcorner T('A') \urcorner$ is also true in $M + \text{Tr}(\omega, U)$. The argument for the other case is parallel. So a language can consistently meet Tarski's requirements (I) and (II) in the passage quoted above.

Remarks. (1) The above argument with minimal modifications goes through when the requirements on the model M are weakened to allow L to distinguish among sentences that do not contain the truth predicate.

This means that a classical language L can consistently contain the concept "true-in-L" and yet have enough resources to be adequate not only for arithmetic, geology, physics, and the other sciences that do not concern themselves with language but for the *logic* and *semantics* of these sciences as well. Speakers of such a language would be able to prove not only theorems belonging to these special sciences but also metatheorems *about* these sciences. Thus, for example, they would have enough resources to prove Tarski's theorem of the inexpressibility of arithmetical truth within arithmetic. To carry out Tarski's proof syntactic concepts that apply to the *whole* of language are not necessary. Only syntactic concepts for the language of arithmetic are needed and these are allowed by our weakened condition on M. It is sometimes said that Tarski has shown that a language containing arithmetic cannot contain its own truth concept. This is at best a very misleading claim. Taken literally it is false. For as just observed, not only can a language L that contains arithmetic have the concept "true-in-L" but it can have enough resources for Tarski's theorem to be provable in L. Perhaps the point of Tarski's theorem can be made clear this way. The Liar paradox teaches us this basic lesson: the combination classical logic + the truth concept + sufficiently rich syntax leads to inconsistency; when all three ingredients are present, the T-biconditionals imply a contradiction. Now Tarski is able to represent sufficiently rich syntactic concepts in arithmetic by using Gödel's ingenious method of arithmetization of syntax. So it is natural to expect (and it can be shown formally) that the concept of truth cannot be represented in arithmetic in a consistent manner. However, if the syntactic resources are weak, as they are for L in so far as the fragment containing the truth predicate is concerned, then there is no contradiction even if the language contains its own truth concept. So there is no difficulty in L's having the concept "true-in-L". Speakers of L can employ this concept to arrive at Tarski's insight. Moreover to do this they do not need to ascend the Tarskian hierarchy.

(2) We can also allow the concepts of L to distinguish among certain sorts of sentences that contains the predicate T without endangering our construction. The idea is that certain kinds of interactions of truth and self-reference (unlike the sort of interaction that generates the paradox) do not create any difficulty for the fundamental intuition. An elementary example: let the name b denote the sentence $\ulcorner Tb \vee \sim Tb \urcorner$. Now there is self-reference in this sentence and the truth predicate is employed also, but this creates no problem for our conception of truth. The biconditional $\ulcorner T('Tb \vee \sim Tb') \equiv Tb \vee \sim Tb \urcorner$ can be consistently asserted, and indeed yields that the sentence $\ulcorner Tb \vee \sim Tb \urcorner$ is true. Another elementary illustration: let c denote the sentence $\ulcorner Gc \& \sim Tc \urcorner$. Again this sentence talks about itself and says, among other things, that it itself is false. Still it generates no paradox if $\ulcorner Gc \urcorner$ is false. The Tarski biconditional can be consistently held.

Now, what sorts of self-reference can we allow in L? What kinds of distinctions among the sentences containing the truth predicate can we make without violating the fundamental intuition? I do not know how best to answer these questions. However, it may be worth observing that there is no difficulty if the constants of L distinguish among sentences that are grounded in M (in the sense of "grounded" defined in Kripke (1975)). Very roughly, grounded sentences are those whose truth-value gets decided in a certain process. When we evaluate the truth or falsity of a sentence containing 'true' we are sometimes led to evaluate the truth or falsity of other sentences. These sentences may themselves contain 'true' and thus lead us to yet other sentences. Sometimes this process yields a truth-value for the initial sentence, as in our second illustration above. Sometimes the truth-value of a sentence is left undecided by the process. Grounded sentences are those whose truth-value gets decided in this process. Formally the notion is defined thus. Let M ($= \langle D, I \rangle$) be a model of L. Let M + (U, V) (for U, V $\subseteq$ D, U $\cap$ V = Λ) be the three-valued model of L that assigns to T the interpretation $\langle U, V \rangle$. All other constants are totally defined in the model. Following Kripke, define the function κ_M thus: Let $\kappa_M(\langle U, V \rangle) = \langle U', V' \rangle$ where U' is the set of sentences true in the model M + (U, V) according to the Strong Kleene valuation rules, and V' is the set of sentences false in the model by the same rules. It can be shown that κ_M has a minimal fixed point: there are sets U*, V* such that $\kappa_M(\langle U^*, V^* \rangle) = \langle U^*, V^* \rangle$ and for all fixed points $\langle U, V \rangle$ of κ_M, U* $\subseteq$ U and V* $\subseteq$ V. Members of U* $\cup$ V* are the grounded sentences. (See Section IV for further elaboration of this definition.) Let K_M be the set of sentences that are *not* grounded in the model M, the ungrounded sentences of M. We say that a model M is K-acceptable if the names, predicates, and function symbols of L are K_M-neutral in M. (See Condition 1 and the definition following it.) It can be shown that K-acceptable models can be extended to standard models in which the Tarski biconditionals are true.

(*Outline of the proof*: We can show that if the level of a grounded sentence A is α (see Kripke (1975) for definition of this notion) then for all $\beta > \alpha$

$$A \in \mathrm{Tr}(\alpha, U) \quad \text{iff} \quad A \in \mathrm{Tr}(\beta, V).$$

That is, if a sentence becomes decided at level α then it becomes stable after α in our construction. The sentence does not flip-flop after α. So if α_0 is the least ordinal at which the minimal fixed point is reached then in our construction all grounded sentences become stable by α_0. Now we can adapt the proof given above to show an analogue of our Main Lemma.

Lemma. For all natural numbers n and all ordinals $\alpha > \alpha_0(n + 1)$ and all sentences A of degree *n* and all U, V $\subseteq$ D,

$$A \in \mathrm{Tr}(\alpha_0 + (n + 2), U) \quad \text{iff} \quad A \in \mathrm{Tr}(\alpha, V).$$

This yields immediately that K-acceptable models can be extended to standard models in which the Tarski biconditionals are true.)

Instead of using Strong Kleene valuation rules in the definition of the function κ_M above we could have employed van Fraassen's supervaluations. We could then have defined as above the notions of a V-grounded sentence and of a V-acceptable model. Our construction could then be used to show that V-acceptable models are extendible to standard models in which the Tarski biconditionals are true. So we can allow the language to distinguish among V-grounded sentences and yet preserve the fundamental intuition in all its instances.

(3) We can also add to L some concepts that distinguish between ungrounded sentences without any damage to our construction. For example, we can add to L predicates (*Neg, Conj*) that express the syntactical notions of negation and conjunction. It is clear that any model in which these terms receive their intended interpretations will violate the requirements of K-acceptability (also of V-acceptability). For the negation of an ungrounded sentence is not the negation of every ungrounded sentence. (Let A, B be distinct ungrounded sentences. Then $\langle \ulcorner \sim A \urcorner, A \rangle$ belongs, but $\langle \ulcorner \sim A \urcorner, B \rangle$ does not belong to the interpretation of *Neg*. This violates the condition of K_M-neutrality.) Nonetheless such a model permits our argument to go through if the interpretations of the other constants in the model meet the condition of K_M-neutrality. We can still prove a version of our Main Lemma. (Note that in this case the function χ used in our proof has to be constructed with greater care.)

So a language L may have some syntactical concepts that apply to the *whole* of the language, and still it can consistently contain the concept "true-in-L" that meets the Tarskian standard.

(4) When we add to the language further syntactic resources of the kind mentioned in remark (3), the difficulties of carrying through our argument increase considerably. We known from the proof of Tarski's theorem that not *all* syntactic notions can be added to the langauge without making the T-biconditionals inconsistent. Thus, for example, we cannot add to L the function $\ulcorner sub(x, y) \urcorner$ (read: the result of replacing all occurrences of the singular term a in x by the quotation name of y). For now the sentence

$$sub('\sim \mathsf{T}(sub(a, a))', '\sim \mathsf{T}(sub(a, a))')$$

$$= '\sim \mathsf{T}(sub('\sim \mathsf{T}(sub(a, a))', '\sim \mathsf{T}(sub(a, a))'))'$$

will be true in those models where *sub* gets its intended interpretation. Hence in no such model can the Tarski biconditional

$$T(`\sim T(sub(`\sim T(sub(a, a))', `\sim T(sub(a, a))')))'$$

$$\equiv \sim T(sub(`\sim T(sub(a, a))', `\sim T(sub(a, a))'))$$

be true.

The question that now arises is: How much syntax can a language have without falling prey to the Gödel–Tarski argument? Can the language contain, for instance, enough syntax to do its own semantics? We know from remark (3) that a language can have enough resources to give the recursion clauses for its propositional connectives. Can it have resources enough to give the clause for the quantifier? Now we need to add to the language "satisfaction" instead of "truth". Further we need ancillary devices such as "sequence", "number", "nth value of a sequence", etc., and syntactic notions such as "formula", "nth variable", "quantification on the nth variable". Can a language L have all these resources and yet have "satisfaction-in-L"? If it cannot, an argument of the kind given above should be constructed using only the limited syntactic resources of L. If it can then something like our Main Lemma has to be proven. [Added: A. Visser has given a negative answer to the question.]

(*Problem*: Can a language L that contains the truth predicate, quotation names, *Neg*, and *Conj* also contain *Inst* (read: "—— is an instance of the quantified sentence ——". We understand this relation to hold between pairs of closed formulas of the following kind: $\ulcorner(\forall x)Fx\urcorner$, $\ulcorner Fa\urcorner$; $\ulcorner(\forall x)(Fx \supset Gx)\urcorner$, $\ulcorner(Fb \supset Gb)\urcorner$) without making the T-biconditionals inconsistent?)

We conclude, then, that in a variety of circumstances we can consistently maintain the fundamental intuition. I suggest that it is a reasonable adequacy condition on any theory that purports to explain the meaning of 'true' that under such circumstances it preserve the fundamental intuition—or at least the intuition should be preserved if it does not come into conflict with some other intuitions that are of equal or greater importance. So we require that a theory that purports to explain for a first-order language L what sentences are assertible in a model M should meet the following adequacy condition. For models M belonging to a certain class—a class that we have not formally defined but which in intuitive terms contains models that permit only benign kinds of self-reference—the theory should entail that all Tarski biconditionals are assertible in the model M. We will see that many accounts of truth fail to meet this adequacy condition.

III

Tarski biconditionals represent one important feature that we believe, perhaps uncritically, to belong to the concept of truth. Let us call this feature, following Putnam (1978), the "disquotation" feature. It encodes the fact that from a sentence of the form $\ulcorner T(`A')\urcorner$ we allow the inference to the sentence that results by the deletion of the truth predicate and the quotation marks; and conversely. That is, we treat sentences $\ulcorner T(`A')\urcorner$ and A as equivalent. There is another way of characterizing this feature for first-order languages that is independent of quotation names. Supposing that L is a first-order language with a truth predicate. Let M $(=\langle D, I \rangle)$ be a model for L (note well: a model, *not* a standard model). Further, let $\tau_M(U)$, where $U \subseteq D$, be the set of sentences of L true in the standard model M + U. The disquotation feature requires that τ_M has *fixed points*: that there is a set $V \subseteq D$ such that $\tau_M(V) = V$. We have seen in Section II that the concept of truth has the disquotation property in certain models but not in others. Let us call models in which truth is disquotational *normal* models—that is we shall call a model M normal if and only if τ_M has fixed points.

Disquotation is one important and well-known feature that we ascribe to the concept of truth. There are also other features that we ascribe to the concept of truth but which have not received as much attention. I would like to remark on two such features. They seem to me to be as much a part of our concept of truth as disquotation, and as in the case of disquotation they are violated when certain kinds of self-reference are present in the language.

Whereas disquotation views the T-biconditionals as analytic of the concept of truth, the first of the two concepts I wish to remark on goes further and views the T-biconditionals as *exhausting* the concept of truth, as defining (in a loose sense of "defining") the concept of truth. In intuitive and rough terms the point is that Tarski biconditionals provide a *complete* explanation of the concept of truth. If we had to explain the word 'true' to someone who had at his command the rest of our language, we could do not better than to teach him the T-biconditionals. We think, perhaps erroneously, that our explanation will provide the learner with a complete guide for the use of the word 'true'.

The first feature, disquotationality, implies that the addition of the T-biconditionals to the stock of the knowledge of the learner will not generate inconsistency. The second feature, which I will call *Tarskian reducibility* for reasons that will become clear, implies that the biconditionals fix the assertion conditions for all the sentences in the extended language provided, of course, the assertion conditions of the sentences without any occurrences of 'true' in them are fixed. If the speaker's stock of knowledge constituted a complete theory initially, then the addition of the biconditionals would result in a theory that is complete also. Formally this means that if M is a model for a language with the truth predicate then there is only one way of extending it to a standard model in which all the biconditionals are true. If there were two such ways, M + U and M + V, there would be a sentence *A* that belonged to U but not to V. And the biconditionals would not determine completely the use of *A*. The theory that results by adding the biconditionals to the sentences true in M would leave *A* undecided. Thus Tarskian reducibility may be expressed by saying that τ_M has at most one fixed point. Models where this condition is satisfied we shall call *proper* models. Models that are both normal and proper will be called *Tarskian*.

Even when the two features mentioned so far obtain, even when the Tarski biconditionals can be held consistently and they determine entirely the extension of truth, it cannot always be said that all our preconceptions about the notion of truth are satisfied. A further feature, which I shall call *local determination*, may be violated. This feature is easy to explain but difficult to define precisely. The intuitive idea is this. When we determine the truth or falsity of a sentence we are not necessarily required to determine the extensions of *all* the names, predicates, and function symbols in the language. We need only determine the extensions of a limited number of these nonlogical constants. Thus if we wish to determine .the truth of the sentence 'Jones is a good philosopher' we need only discover the extensions of 'Jones' and 'is a good philosopher'. The extensions of such constants as 'is on display in', 'the Museum of Modern Art', are entirely irrelevant. Thus there are a certain limited number of nonlogical constants that we think are relevant to determining the truth of a sentence. These nonlogical constants I shall say constitute the *dependency range* of the sentence. The difficulty in stating the local determination property precisely arises in the definition of the dependency range. The dependency range of a sentence that does not contain the truth predicate is easy to define: it just consists of all the nonlogical constants that occur in the sentence. Further the dependency range of certain sentences containing 'true' is also easily specified. Thus the dependency range of the sentence ' "Jones is a good philosopher" is true' is the same as the dependency range of 'Jones is a good philosopher' and consists of 'Jones' and 'is a good philosopher'. The problem arises when we come to quantified sentences such as 'every sentence in this book is true'. Intuitively, the dependency range of this sentence is a function of what sentences are found in "this book". Thus assuming that the book is very short and contains only one sentence, 'Jones is a good philosopher', the dependency range of 'every sentence in this book is true' consists of 'is a sentence in', 'this book', 'Jones', and 'is a good philosopher'. It is not at all clear how to frame a definition that would give the intuitively right results in this and other similar cases.

Fortunately for our immediate purpose of showing that the first two features of truth do not guarantee the third, we can afford to work with a rather coarse definition of dependency range. Let us say that the sentence A *immediately depends on* the sentence B in a model M ($= \langle D, I \rangle$) iff (i) $A = B$, or (ii) there is a constant c such that $B = I(c)$ and $\ulcorner T(c) \urcorner$ is a subformula of A, or (iii) there is a variable x such that $\ulcorner T(x) \urcorner$ is a subformula of A. The sentence A *depends on* B iff A immediately depends on B or A immediately depends on some sentence that itself immediately depends on B or . . . . (We can make this precise via Frege's definition of the ancestral of a relation.) A nonlogical constant *falls in the dependency range of A* iff it occurs in some sentence on which A depends. Finally, we say that models M ($= \langle D, I \rangle$) and M' ($= \langle D', I' \rangle$) are *A-equivalent* iff (i) $D = D'$, and (ii) A has the same dependency range in M and M', and (iii) I and I' agree on the interpretation of all the nonlogical constants in the dependency range of A in these models. The local determination property requires that if M and M' are A-equivalent then A should belong to the extension of truth in M iff A belongs to the extension of truth in M'.

It should be observed that by our definition the dependency ranges of some sentences are wider than what we would intuitively expect them to be. (For example, by our definition the dependency ranges of quantified sentences that have $\ulcorner T(x) \urcorner$ as a subformula contain all the nonlogical constants.) Still, this does not detract from the usefulness of the definition for our immediate purpose. If we can show that under certain conditions the truth value of a sentence depends upon constants that lie *outside* its dependency range as defined above, we shall have shown that under these conditions local determination is violated. We now show that this indeed is the case if the extension of truth is determined whenever possible in accordance with the T-biconditionals. That is, we show that in some models disquotation and Tarskian reducibility conflict with local determination.

Let M $(=\langle D, I \rangle)$ be a model in which the interpretations of all the constants except b and c are well behaved (their interpretations are, say, K_M-neutral). Let the interpretations of b and c be as follows:

$I(b) = \ulcorner Tb \urcorner$

$I(c) = \ulcorner Tb \vee \sim Tc \urcorner.$

Suppose that M′ $(=\langle D', I' \rangle)$ is a model just like M except that

$I'(c) = \ulcorner \sim Tb \vee \sim Tc \urcorner.$

It can be shown that τ_M and $\tau_{M'}$ have unique fixed points; the Tarski biconditionals determine a unique extension of truth in these models. Let U be the unique fixed point of τ_M. Clearly the biconditional

$Tc \equiv Tb \vee \sim Tc$

is true in the standard model M + U. Hence $\ulcorner Tb \urcorner$ and $\ulcorner Tc \urcorner$ are also true in M + U. Since U is a fixed point of τ_M it follows that $\ulcorner Tb \urcorner$ and $\ulcorner Tc \urcorner$ belong to U. So by the Tarskian standard we should rule that $\ulcorner Tb \urcorner$ and $\ulcorner Tc \urcorner$ belong to the extension of truth in M. By a parallel argument it is easily shown that $\ulcorner \sim Tb \urcorner$ and $\ulcorner Tc \urcorner$ belong to the extension of truth in M′. However, models M and M′ are $\ulcorner Tb \urcorner$-equivalent, and we expect that $\ulcorner Tb \urcorner$ either belongs to the extension of truth in both models or in neither. However if the extension of truth is determined according to the T-biconditionals this expectation is not fulfilled. M and M′ are Tarskian models, but if truth obeys the Tarskian standard then local determination is violated.

When M is a Tarskian model let τ_M^u be the unique fixed point of τ_M. We say that a Tarskian model M is *regular* iff for all sentences A and all Tarskian models M′ that are A-equivalent to M, $A \in \tau_M^u$ iff

$A \in \tau^{\mathrm{u}}_{\mathrm{M}'}$. A Tarskian model that is not regular we call *irregular*. Irregular Tarskian models are those where local determination fails if truth is evaluated by the Tarskian ideal. We cannot, however, say the converse: that local determination holds in regular models. For the definition of dependency range given above is much too coarse. It allows models to qualify as regular in which local determination is violated. It would be worthwhile to try to formulate a finer definition of dependency range and regularity but we shall not attempt to do so here.

How central is local determinability to our conception of truth? If we allow it to be violated then some very curious, if not absurd, consequences follow. It can then happen that the truth value of a sentence such as ⌜Tb⌝ depends upon what other naming ceremonies are performed in the language, even though this sentence says nothing about these ceremonies. Thus if the naming ceremonies are performed in accordance with the model M above, i.e., c is made a name of the sentence ⌜$Tb \vee \sim Tc$⌝ then ⌜Tb⌝ will turn out true; if it is performed in accordance with M', i.e., c is made a name of ⌜$\sim Tb \vee \sim Tc$⌝, then ⌜Tb⌝ will turn out false. This is curious given that ⌜Tb⌝ says nothing about these naming ceremonies. Another illustration may help to make the point clearer. Suppose a man truthful like Moore but less modest says "I always tell the truth". Given that all the other utterances of this man are true, the Tarski biconditionals do not force a particular truth value on this sentence. However, if we take the biconditionals as the standard for truth, and allow local determinability to be violated, *I* have the power to make what the man says true or false even though the man may not have said anything about my doings or about things that I can bring about. By merely asserting "Either that man tells the truth or this very assertion is false", I ensure that his utterance is true. Had I made the different assertion "Either that man does not tell the truth or this very assertion is false", I would similarly have made his utterance false. And had I made both assertions, presumably I would have made his assertion paradoxical. This is extremely curious and, I think, unacceptable. We do not allow the truth value of a statement to depend upon factors so unconnected with the statement.

There is another reason for taking local determinability seriously. In our wide variety of uses of 'true' there are some uses that are paradoxical and incoherent but many others that are not. There are fragments of our language in which the use of 'true' does not create any difficulties. Here all our various intuitions are sustained. This happens, for example, when K-acceptable models characterize the fragment of the language and its interpretation. Now local determination ensures that well-behaved fragments are not polluted by the fragments containing pathological features. It ensures that the status of a sentence (truth, falsity, paradoxicality, etc.) depends only on the interpretation of a certain limited number of non-logical constants. The interpretation of the other constants is irrelevant. So if in a fragment of a language the interpretation of certain constants is such as to make the uses of sentences that depend upon them unproblematic then we can be sure that the presence of paradoxical and problematic elements elsewhere does not vitiate the use of these sentences. Local determination serves to insulate the good cases from the bad. The Tarskian standard, if allowed to operate wherever possible, makes truth holistic in an unacceptable way.

These considerations, I suggest, make plausible the following requirements on the theory of truth.

(1) A theory of truth need not entail that all the T-biconditionals are assertible in *all* the Tarskian models. However it should entail that the biconditionals are assertible in a certain subclass of regular Tarskian models. (I am forced to employ the vague locution "a certain subclass of regular Tarskian models" because as already observed our definition of regularity is not entirely satisfactory. It allows models that do not meet the intuitive condition of local determinability to be regular.) Roughly, the present requirement is that when there are no bad kinds of self-reference in the language (sorts of self-reference that violate the three properties explained above), then the theory of truth should entail that all the biconditionals are assertible. In particular this requirement implies that in S-acceptable (also K-acceptable, V-acceptable) models the theory of truth should entail the assertibility of the biconditionals. However, we do not expect the theory to imply this in *all* Tarskian models.

(2) The status of a sentence A (whether A is true or false or paradoxical or something else) should be the same in all A-equivalent models. (Note that this requirement could be strengthened by weakening the conditions on A-equivalency.)

We observe that requirement (1) is a revised version of Tarski's convention T, and that requirement (2) is dictated by the local determinability of truth.

Sometimes the biconditionals fail to determine the extension of truth not because they violate local determinability but because no unique extension of truth satisfies them. There are models M for which τ_M has more than one fixed point. That is, there are improper models. An example is provided by a model M in which all constants except b are well behaved and in which b denotes the sentence $\ulcorner Tb \urcorner$. It can be shown that τ_M has exactly two fixed points. $\ulcorner Tb \urcorner$ belongs to one fixed point but not to the other. So truth is not Tarski-reducible in all models. Tarski biconditionals do not determine the use of 'true' in all contexts.

There is a sense however in which truth is reducible, though not Tarski-reducible. This sense may be expressed roughly by saying that there are no semantical facts. The question of the truth or falsity of a sentence containing 'true' *reduces* to the question of the truth or falsity of sentences not containing 'true'. Thus, if someone says 'what Joe wrote on the blackboard is true' and if all that Joe wrote was 'snow is white' then the question of the truth or falsity of the original ·utterance reduces to the question of the truth or falsity of the sentences 'the only thing that Joe wrote on the blackboard was "snow is white"' and 'snow is white'. Similarly, in the example above where a truth teller says 'I always tell the truth', the question of the truth or falsity of his assertion reduces to the truth or falsity of his other assertions. I do not want to make the idea of reducibility employed here precise; nonetheless it is clear that when we set about to determine the truth or falsity of a sentence containing 'true' we have in the end to determine how things are, we have to determine whether such and such objects have such and such properties. And truth is *not* one of these properties. This fact is reflected in our definition of model. A model of L, so to speak, gives all the facts that are relevant for determining the truth or falsity of a sentence. But our models do *not* give any extension for truth.

In suggesting that truth is reducible I am advocating a much weakened version of the redundancy theory of truth. The redundancy theory implies the reducibility of truth. For if all occurrences of 'true' were eliminable entirely then any sentence containing 'true' would be equivalent to some sentence that did not contain any occurrence of 'true'. And clearly the truth or falsity of the latter sentence would depend only on the names, predicates, and function symbols occurring in it. The reducibility of truth, however, does not imply the redundancy theory. According to reducibility, the truth or falsity of any sentence rests ultimately on nonsemantical facts. This does not mean that the statements containing 'true' are logically equivalent to statements not containing 'true'. In our earlier example the truth or falsity of 'what Joe wrote on the blackboard is true' reduces to the truth or falsity of 'the only thing Joe wrote on the blackboard was "snow is white" and snow is white'. However, it is not implied that the one is logically equivalent to the other, It is easy to conceive of situations in which one is true but the other is false. Only in this weakened version does the redundancy theory seem to me plausible.

Truth, then, is reducible. The extension of truth (in L) in a model is determined entirely by the information provided by the model. And Tarski biconditionals yield the extension of truth in some models (e.g., K-acceptable models). However, they do not do so in *all* models. So truth is not in general *Tarski*-reducible.

IV

Let us now turn to the first of the two problems mentioned in Section I. The problem is to separate the problematic sentences from the unproblematic ones and to give the meaning of these latter sentences. Given the assumptions we made in Section I, this reduces to the problem of separating those sentences of a first-order language (with a truth predicate) that are assertible in a model from those that are not assertible and from those that are problematic. That is, suppose that we know all the relevant nonsemantical facts. How do we go about determining which sentences are to be asserted, which denied, etc.?

It is clear that this separation of sentences is to be achieved by some sort of stage-by-stage or level-by-level process. Reflection on the nonsemantical facts leads us to say of such sentences as 'snow is white' that they are true. This is stage one. Reflection on the nonsemantical facts and the results of stage one leads us to say of such sentences as ' "snow is white" is true' and 'some sentences are true' that they are true. This is stage two. And we can see roughly how the later stages will repeat the procedure of the earlier stages. The central problem for a theory of truth is to give a more definite content to this stage-by-stage picture. I will first examine two ways of elaborating this picture that are found in the literature and then I will propose another way which seems to me to be in some respects superior.

The first way of elaborating the stage-by-stage picture utilizes Tarski's idea of a hierarchy of languages or of truth predicates. Tarski himself viewed his idea not so much as providing a description of our use of the word 'true' but rather as providing a device for ridding our language of the antinomies that confound it. That is, Tarski viewed his idea as a solution to the second problem mentioned in Section I. But his idea has some promise so far as our first problem is concerned and we should examine how it might be deployed here. Following Tarski we view the stage-by-stage process as defining a series of truth predicates. At stage one we define the predicate 'true at stage one' (abbreviated to 'true$_1$'). It applies to sentences such as 'snow is white' that are ruled true at stage one. Sentences that contain the truth predicate are not yet ruled true and so do not belong to the extension of 'true$_1$'. At stage two we define the predicate 'true$_2$'. This applies to a wider class of sentences: the sentences may now contain the predicate 'true$_1$'. Sentences such as ' "snow is white" is true$_1$' belong to the extension of 'true$_2$', but sentences such as ' "snow is white" is true$_2$' fall outside the extension of 'true$_2$'. We proceed similarly at the later stages. We get by this process an infinity of predicates that tell us what sentences are true at what levels. So far we have followed Tarski. The next element in this conception is due to Kripke and to Burge (1979). Kripke has noted that the Tarskian levels of ordinary language sentences must not be made intrinsic to the sentences themselves but must be allowed to depend upon the facts. Thus the level that should be assigned to 'true' in the sentence 'everything John says is true' depends upon the things that John has, as a matter of fact, said. If he has not employed the words 'true' and 'false' in his utterances (and has not in any other way spoken about the truth or falsity of sentences) then the level can be quite low. If, on the other hand, he has uttered sentences with multiple embeddings of 'true' within 'true' then the level must be higher. (This means that in order to assign levels to T in the sentences of our first-order language L we must take account of the model. The notion of level must be relativized to that of a model.) Burge has used this fact to defend the claim that truth is an indexical notion. When we use the word 'true' in a sentence it acquires a level, and the level that it acquires depends on the context of use, on how things are. Burge has proposed pragmatic rules which should guide us in assigning levels to the various uses of 'true', but like all pragmatic rules they are (and, I suppose, Burge would argue that they have to be) sloppily stated and do not constitute a theory of levels. Presumably on Burge's account a theory of levels is to a theory of truth as a theory of the present is to a theory of tenses. The levels of the uses of 'true' must be specified *before* anything can be said about the assertibility of sentences containing 'true', just as the present moment must be specified before anything can be said about the assertibility of sentences containing tenses. In formal terms the suggestion seems to be this: the assertibility of the sentences of a language L in a model M should be relativized to an assignment of levels to the various occurrences of the truth predicate. And the assignment of levels is a pragmatic matter not in the domain of the semantics of 'true'.

It seems to me, *pace* Burge, that if we follow the Tarskian route then the theory of levels constitutes the heart of a theory of truth. It does not belong in the garbage dump of informal pragmatics. Given a model M for a language L we know *all* that we need to know for the evaluation of the unproblematic sentences. We do not need to know anything else. The case is quite unlike that of the regular indexicals such as tenses and demonstratives. To interpret and evaluate sentences containing these we *do* need to be told what the present moment is and what the denotations of the demonstratives are. We do not similarly need to know the levels of the various occurrences of T in order to evaluate the sentences of L in a model M. If a theory of truth follows the Tarskian idea of a hierarchy of truth predicates then it must give an account (and not just presuppose it or leave it to pragmatics) of the levels of the various occurrences of T in the sentences of L (relative to a model M). Burge's remarks fail to constitute a theory of truth because they do not yield a theory of levels.

Can a theory of levels that complements the Tarskian hierarchy be provided? John Hawthorn has worked on this problem and his investigations lead me to believe that the task is not an easy one. It *looks* easy because of the narrow range of cases that are used to motivate the Tarskian hierarchy—sentences such as 'snow is white', ' "snow is white" is true', ' " 'snow is white' is true" is true' and so on. But once we get away from these simple examples it is not at all clear what the levels of the various occurrences of 'true' should be (what, for example, is the level of 'true' in sentences such as 'nothing is both true and untrue', 'every truth in X's works is already to be found in Y's works') and, more important, it is not at all clear what *principles* should be used for the assignment of levels. Relative to an assignment of levels and relative to an account of the hierarchy of truth predicates we know what sentences are assertible and what are not assertible. But not all assignments are reasonable. On the basis of what principles do we choose among the multifarious possibilities here? What reason have we for thinking that they will yield a unique assignment of levels? One point deserves emphasis: we cannot in general assign levels on a sentence-by-sentence basis. When assigning levels in some favourable cases we may only have to consider small groups of sentences. The general case, however, demands that we proceed not even with groups of sentences but wholesale: that we choose among possible assignments to *all* the occurrences of 'true'. But how do we do this? And what makes us believe that the notion of *the* level will be well defined? A final point: the Tarskian account seems to conflate two things that ought to be kept distinct. First there is the stage or level at which we can say that a sentence is true or assertible—thus we can say that the sentence ' " 'snow is white' is true" is true' is true and assertible at stage three. Second there is the interpretation of the truth predicate that occurs in the sentence so decided. Thus in our example one is led to say that the second occurrence of 'true' means "true at stage two". However the fact that a sentence is decided to be true at stage n does not mean that occurrences of 'true' in the sentence are to be interpreted to mean "true at stage m" (m < n). A logical law such as "no sentence is both true and untrue" can be known to be true at the first level but this is no reason for reading the word 'true' in it to mean "true at level zero". The present point is that the level or stage at which a sentence gets decided is one thing and the interpretation of the truth predicates in it is another. These should not be conflated.

The Tarskian approach to truth divides the problem into two parts: first the problem of giving a theory of "truth at level n" and second the problem of giving a theory of levels. The difficulties encountered in solving the second part suggest that this division of the problem may not be good strategy. Let us see if we can elaborate the stage-by-stage picture without interpreting truth to mean "truth at level n". A most interesting way of doing this is given by Kripke in his paper "Outline of a Theory of Truth" (1975). (Some of Kripke's technical results are anticipated by Martin and Woodruff in their elegant paper "On Representing 'True-in-L' in L" (1975). The intuitive conception outlined below, however, is due to Kripke. For information on the relationship between Kripke's and Martin and Woodruff's work see footnote 14 in Kripke's essay.) The central idea in Kripke's theory is to view the stage-by-stage process as deciding the truth values of increasing numbers of sentences. Initially, at stage zero, we assume nothing about the truth or falsity of any sentence. The truth value of every sentence is undecided. *Relative to stage zero* the extension of the truth predicate is the null set. And similarly *relative to stage zero* the antiextension of the truth predicate is also the null set. Now despite the fact that the interpretation of the truth predicate is so meager, we can evaluate *some* sentences for truth and falsity. For example, the poverty of the interpretation of the truth predicate at stage zero does not at all hinder the evaluation of 'snow is white'. The denotation of 'snow' and the extension of 'is white' will allow us to give a definite truth value to that sentence. The case is different with a sentence such as ' "snow is white" is true'. To evaluate it we need to consult the interpretation of the truth predicate. Since 'snow is white' belongs neither to the extension nor to the antiextension of the truth predicate, the status of ' "snow is white" is true' is left undecided at stage zero. So, given the interpretation of the truth predicate at stage zero certain sentences can be deemed true and certain others deemed false, and the remaining sentences left undecided. The first sort of sentences we put in the extension and the second sort in the antiextension of the truth predicate at stage one. Thus, the interpretation of the truth predicate at stage one is richer. Now relative to this new interpretation of the truth predicate we can again evaluate sentences for truth and falsity. Obviously the sentences that were deemed true (false) at stage zero will again be deemed so at stage one. But some of the sentences that were undecided at stage zero will become decided now. Thus, since the sentence 'snow is white' belongs either to the extension or to the antiextension of truth at stage one, we will now be able to decide the truth value of the sentence ' "snow is white" is true', which was undecided at stage zero. Evaluation of sentences relative to the interpretation of truth at stage one yields a richer interpretation for truth at stage two. By repeating the process over and over again we get fatter and fatter extensions and antiextensions for the truth predicate. Kripke has shown that after sufficiently many repetitions the process saturates: it adds no new elements to the extension and antiextension of truth. The interpretation reached by this process, Kripke has suggested, provides a natural model for our concept of truth.

It may be helpful to contrast Kripke's approach with the Tarskian one. In the Tarskian approach different predicates are defined at different stages, and each is *totally* defined over the whole domain. In Kripke's approach we stick with just one truth predicate but it gets a wider interpretation at higher stages. The process of evaluation defines the truth predicate for more and more sentences.

Let us present Kripke's ideas a little more formally. Let $M(=\langle D, I \rangle)$ be a model for a first order language L. Let $M + (U, V)$ (where $U, V \subseteq D$ and $U \cap V = \Lambda$) be as before the three-valued model for L such that all the constants of L except T are totally defined (in accordance with M) and the interpretation of T is $\langle U, V \rangle$. Let ψ represent the scheme used to evaluate sentences in a model $M + (U, V)$. Let $\psi_M(\langle U, V \rangle) = \langle U', V' \rangle$ where U' (V') is the set of sentences true (false) in the model $M + (U, V)$ according to the scheme ψ. Finally, let $\langle U, V \rangle \leqslant \langle U', V' \rangle$ iff $U \subseteq U'$ and $V \subseteq V'$, and let us say that ψ is *monotonic* iff $\psi_M(\langle U, V \rangle) \leqslant \psi_M(\langle U', V' \rangle)$ if $\langle U, V \rangle \leqslant \langle U', V' \rangle$. It can be shown that a number of familiar three-valued schemes meet the condition of monotonicity. For later use we note that this is so for the following: the Weak Kleene scheme adopted by Martin and Woodruff (represented by μ); the Strong Kleene scheme (κ) used by Kripke (though he mentions the other schemes also); van Fraassen's supervaluations (σ); the first refinement of van Fraassen's technique (σ_1) in which when evaluating sentences in the model $M + (U, V)$ [$U \subseteq S$] we do not consider all total interpretations that extend $\langle U, V \rangle$ but only these interpretations $\langle U', V' \rangle \geqslant \langle U, V \rangle$ in which U' is consistent (U' contains no sentence together with its negation (Kripke (1975), p. 76)); the second refinement of van Fraassen's supervaluations (σ_2) in which we consider only maximally consistent extensions of $\langle U, V \rangle$ (that is, we consider only those extensions $\langle U', V' \rangle$ in which U' is maximally consistent).

In Kripke's account of the stage-by-stage process we begin with the interpretation of truth as $\langle \Lambda, \Lambda \rangle$. Now we can decide for some sentences whether they are true or false. Suppose that things are in accordance with the model M and we are using the scheme κ for the evaluation of sentences. (Strong Kleene, as already noted, is the scheme that Kripke uses in his discussion. He points out that we could have used any of the other schemes $\mu, \sigma, \sigma_1, \sigma_2$, in its place.) The process of evaluation will yield a set U of sentences that are true in the model $M + (\Lambda, \Lambda)$ and a set V of sentences (and other things; Kripke includes the nonsentences in V also) that are false in

M + (Λ, Λ). At stage one the interpretation of the truth predicate is $\langle$U, V$\rangle$ and we now evaluate sentences in M + (U, V). The point to observe is that $\langle$U, V$\rangle$ = $\kappa_M(\langle\Lambda, \Lambda\rangle)$. Application of the κ_M function to the interpretation of truth at a given level yields the interpretation of truth at the next level. So, for example, the interpretation of the truth predicate at stage two is $\kappa_M(\kappa_M(\langle\Lambda, \Lambda\rangle))$. Since κ_M is monotonic the later interpretations of T are always larger than the earlier interpretations (or at least they are never smaller). The process of evaluation at the later stages never yields a different judgment on a sentence decided earlier. It at most assigns a truth value to some sentences that were left undecided at the earlier stages. Kripke has shown that the evaluation procedure κ_M, if it is applied sufficiently many times—indeed transfinitely many times—yields the minimal fixed point of κ_M. The process yields a fixed point $\langle$U, V$\rangle$ such that if $\langle$U', V'$\rangle$ is any fixed point of κ_M then $\langle$U, V$\rangle \leqslant \langle$U', V'$\rangle$. Kripke has proposed that the minimal fixed point is a natural interpretation of truth. (Martin and Woodruff have established that μ_M has a fixed point. Kripke has shown that κ_M has a variety of fixed points, and that the minimal fixed point is reached by the natural stage-by-stage process described above.) A sentence B *has a truth value in a fixed point* $\langle$U, V$\rangle$ iff B $\in$ U $\cup$ V. Kripke calls a sentence *grounded in a model* M iff it has a truth value in the minimal fixed point of κ_M. A sentence, according to Kripke, is *paradoxical in* M iff it has no truth value in any fixed point of κ_M. (When we wish to distinguish between the various notions of groundedness, paradoxicality, etc., that result from different schemes, we will talk about κ-groundedness, μ-paradoxicality, etc. Unless the notions are so qualified the scheme should be understood to be Strong Kleene.)

Kripke's (and Martin and Woodruff's) work is truly insightful, but I think that the intuitive picture of the stage-by-stage process that is sketched by Kripke is unacceptable. It does not, I want to argue, adequately describe our ordinary concept of truth. I will focus my criticisms on the version of Kripke's theory in which a Strong Kleene valuation scheme is used but I should note that Kripke has not committed himself to the use of this scheme. He says:

It is not the purpose of the present work to make any particular recommendation among the Kleene strong three-valued approach, the van Fraassen supervaluation approaches, or any other scheme . . . . Nor is it even my present purpose to make any firm recommendation between the minimal fixed point of a particular valuation scheme and the various other fixed points.*

* Though the minimal fixed point certainly is singled out as natural in many respects (Kripke (1975), p. 77 and footnote 29).

So when I speak of "Kripke's theory" below I should be understood to be speaking about a theory that Kripke has outlined but not necessarily one that he is committed to. I will briefly consider the use of other valuation schemes and the use of other fixed points also. None, it seems to me, can save the intuitive picture of the concept of truth that underlies Kripke's theory. Criticisms:

(1) By Kripke's definition various logical laws are sometimes paradoxical. For example, his definition entails that the law $\ulcorner (\forall x)$ $\sim (Tx \,\&\, \sim Tx) \urcorner$ is paradoxical when there is a liar-type sentence in the language—for now the law does not have a truth value in any of the Kripkean fixed points. [Suppose that $\ulcorner (\forall x) \sim (Tx \,\&\, \sim Tx) \urcorner$ has a truth value in the fixed point $\langle U, V \rangle$. Then all the instances of this sentences must also have a truth value in $\langle U, V \rangle$. Let A be a paradoxical sentence and let t be a name of it. It follows that $\ulcorner \sim (Tt \,\&\, \sim Tt) \urcorner$ has a truth value in $\langle U, V \rangle$. This can occur in the Strong Kleene scheme only if $\ulcorner Tt \urcorner$ has a truth value in the fixed point. But this contradicts the paradoxicality of A.] Intuitively the law does not seem to be paradoxical. In fact even in the presence of paradoxical sentences, far from finding the law paradoxical, we are inclined to believe it.

(2) A related criticism is that according to Kripke's theory the law $\ulcorner (\forall x) \sim (Tx \,\&\, \sim Tx) \urcorner$ is not grounded but pathological even when there isn't any self-reference of the sort that generates the paradoxes. The sentence $\ulcorner (\forall x) \sim (Tx \,\&\, \sim Tx) \urcorner$ is never true in the Kripkean minimal fixed point. The reason for this is that in Kripke's construction sentences have a truth value in the minimal fixed point only if they get decided in the stage-by-stage process outlined above. And under the Strong Kleene scheme it is a feature of this process that a sentence $\ulcorner (\forall x) A \urcorner$ cannot get decided until either A is already false of some value of x or A is decided and true of all values of x. So in this process $\ulcorner (\forall x) \sim (Tx \,\&\, \sim Tx) \urcorner$ cannot become decided until either $\ulcorner \sim (Tx \,\&\, \sim Tx) \urcorner$ becomes false of some value of x or is decided and true of all values of x. The first possibility cannot arise. Hence the sentence can only become decided when $\ulcorner \sim (Tx \,\&\, \sim Tx) \urcorner$ is decided for all values of x. This cannot happen until the truth of $\ulcorner (\forall x) \sim (Tx \,\&\, \sim Tx) \urcorner$ is already decided because it itself is one of the

values of x. Result: $\ulcorner(\forall x) \sim (Tx \,\&\, \sim Tx)\urcorner$ is not grounded in any model—even in models in which there is no vicious self-reference of any sort. It is counterintuitive to say that in such models the logical laws should not be asserted to be true. But this is what we would have to say if the minimal fixed point is taken as the model for truth.

(3) There are types of reasoning that we allow in everyday discourse that are invalidated by Kripke's account. Suppose for example that we have a situation in which speakers A and B make the assertions displayed below.

A says:

(a1) Two plus two is three. (false)
(a2) Snow is always black. (false)
(a3) Everything B says is true. (——)
(a4) Ten is a prime number. (false)
(a5) Something B says is not true. (——)

B says:

(b1) One plus one is two. (true)
(b2) My name is B. (true)
(b3) Snow is sometimes white. (true)
(b4) At most one thing A says is true. (——)

Now we do not find it problematic to argue as follows:

A contradicts himself by asserting both (a3) and (a5). Hence (a3) and (a5) cannot both be true. Since all the other assertions of A are false, it follows that at most one thing that he says is true. So B's assertion (b4) is true. Hence (a3) is true and (a5) is false.

If we accept Kripke's theory and treat the minimal fixed point as our model for truth then we must reject such pieces of reasoning. Sentences (a1), (a2), (a4), (b1), (b2) and (b3) all get decided, in Kripke's account, at the first level. But sentences (a3) and (a5) will be left undecided pending decision on (b4), and (b4) will be left undecided pending decision on (a3) and (a5). These three sentences never get decided in the Kripkean construction. They are ungrounded. If the minimal fixed point modelled our notion of truth, we would neither assert nor deny any of them. [We observe that if we "close off" the minimal fixed point interpretation (see Kripke (1975), p. 80) then (a3), (a5), and (b4) fall in the antiextension of truth, and in exact opposition to our intuition we are led to assert (a5) and deny (a3). (The sentence (b4) is, as before, assertible.)]

(4) Kripke's account does not satisfy the first desideratum for the theory of truth posited in Section III. We require that a theory of truth should make all Tarski biconditionals true under those conditions in which there is no vicious self-reference. In particular we require that all the Tarski biconditionals should come out true in a model M that meets Condition 1 of Section II. Called a fixed point $\langle U, V \rangle$ *classical* iff $U \cup V = D$. Then this requirement implies that truth must be modelled in M by a classical fixed point. However the minimal fixed point is never classical (under the scheme κ). Hence under no conditions are all the Tarski biconditionals true on Kripke's theory. This criticism may be put a little more intuitively thus: we showed in Sections II and III that there are special conditions under which all our intuitions about truth are coherent, and we expect that under such conditions the theory of truth would preserve all our intuitions. But this expectation is not fulfilled by Kripke's theory.

Concerning the use of other schemes: Obviously all these objections apply if the Weak Kleene scheme is used in place of the Strong Kleene in Kripke's theory. If, however, the supervaluation schemes are used objections (1) and (2) no longer apply. And if the scheme σ_2 is used then objection (3) does not apply as stated. But a variant of objection (3) can still be urged against the theory. Finally, objection (4)—and it is this objection that I put the greatest weight on—applies to all the supervaluation schemes σ, σ_1, and σ_2. There are cases in which there is no vicious self-reference but the minimal fixed point obtained using these schemes is not classical.

Concerning the other fixed points: It seems to me that the most promising candidate here is the largest intrinsic fixed point.[6] It is the fixed point that gives truth values to as many sentences as possible without giving an arbitrary truth value to any sentence. Kripke calls a fixed point $\langle U, V \rangle$ *intrinsic* iff there is no fixed point $\langle U', V' \rangle$ and no sentence A such that $A \in (U \cap V') \cup (V \cap U')$. A sentence *has an intrinsic truth value* iff it has a truth value in some intrinsic fixed point. It can be shown that there is a largest intrinsic fixed point: there is an intrinsic fixed point $\langle U, V \rangle$ such that $\langle U', V' \rangle \leqslant \langle U, V \rangle$

---

[6] Allen Hazen has urged on me the virtues of the largest intrinsic fixed point as an interpretation of truth.

for all intrinsic fixed points $\langle U', V' \rangle$. Obviously it follows that there is something that is *the* largest intrinsic fixed point. Now if this fixed point is used to model truth then our main objection—objection (4)—does not apply. But a modified version of (3) does apply. If (a3) and (a5) in the example are replaced by

(a3†)   (a3†) is true.

and

(a5†)   '(a3†) is not true' is true.

respectively, we get a case in which (b4) does not have a truth value in the largest intrinsic fixed point of μ, κ, σ, σ_1. (This is so because if (a3†) and (a5†) do not have a truth value in a fixed point then (b4) cannot have a truth value in that fixed point. And clearly (a3†) and (a5†) do not have an intrinsic truth value.) Intuitively, though, we can argue that (b4) is true. A second, and more important, objection is this. It is not at all clear how the largest intrinsic fixed point fits in with the intuitive picture of truth that we get from Kripke. By what sort of stage-by-stage process do we reach this fixed point? If the process is of the cumulative sort that is described by Kripke then it is not at all clear how it can saturate at the largest intrinsic fixed point.

I suggest that we look for another way of characterizing the concept of truth than the cumulative procedure given by Kripke. I propose as an alternative that we view the concept of truth as characterized by a *revision* procedure. I suggest that truth, unlike ordinary concepts such as red, blue, and sum, does not in general have an *application* procedure associated with it. Idealizing somewhat, we can say that underlying our use of words such as 'red' is an application procedure that divides objects into two classes: those objects to which the word applies and those to which it does not apply. The same holds for words such as 'sum'. Underlying them there is also an application procedure, though a logically more complex one: the procedure is recursive. In contrast, I am suggesting that underlying our use of 'true' there is not an application procedure but a revision procedure instead. When we learn the meaning of 'true' what we learn is a rule that enables us to *improve* on a proposed candidate for the extension of truth. It is the existence of such a rule, I wish to argue, that explains the characteristic features of the concept of truth.

The revision rule associated with truth is very simple: it is essentially the rule that was formalized by Tarski in his definition of "truth-in-a-model". Given a language and given the denotations, extensions, etc., of *all* its constants we know intuitively how to determine which sentences of the language are true and which sentences are false. Tarski formalized this intuitive procedure to give us a definition of truth for a language that does not contain its own truth concept. It is clear, however, that neither our intuitive procedure nor Tarski's formal definition yields the extension of truth in those cases where the language does contain its own truth concept. In order to apply the procedure in such cases we would *already* need to know the extension of truth. An attempt might be made (as it was made by Kripke) to turn this procedure into a cumulative one of the sort described above. However, the difficulties that we encounter here suggest that we approach the subject somewhat differently.

We begin by observing that although our intuitive procedure does not yield the extension of truth because of the circularity just noted, nevertheless it can still be applied under the fictitious supposition that the extension of truth is given by some arbitrary set U. Now it would yield a set V of sentences that come out true under this fiction. *The important point is that V is a better candidate for the extension of truth than U (or at least it is as good a candidate as U).* Suppose, for example, that facts are such that the sentence $\ulcorner Ga \urcorner$ is true. Now while U may nor may not contain $\ulcorner Ga \urcorner$, V is bound to contain it. More generally, U may or may not be right on sentences that do not contain the truth predicate, but V is bound to be right. Further, if U gets these first-level sentences right then V will get the second-level sentences right also whether U gets them right or not. And so on up the Tarskian levels. Our observation may be put formally as follows: Let L be a language with the truth predicate and let M be a model for it. (See Definition 1.) Further, let U be a candidate for the extension of truth. Then the set $\tau_M(U)$ of sentences true in the standard model M + U is at least as good a candidate for the extension of truth as U. We may view τ_M as a rule that improves (or at least does not worsen: henceforth I take this qualification for granted) a candidate for the extension of truth. More generally τ_M represents a rule that we learn in learning the meaning of 'true'. This rule does not in all cases define the extension of truth. (It does so only in limited contexts.) What the rule does is enable us to improve a given candidate for the extension of truth. The rule is a rule of revision.

An application of the rule for truth to an arbitrary set U results in an improved candidate V, which may itself be in need of improvement. Illustration: let the language L contain just two constants G and a. (We suppose as usual that it has quotation names.) Let $M(=\langle D, I\rangle)$ be a model for L such that $D = S \cup \{1\}$ (where S is the set of sentences of L) and $I(G) = \{1\}$ and $I(a) = 1$. Let the set $U = \Lambda$. Now the set $\tau_M(\Lambda)$ is a much better candidate for the extension of truth than Λ. For we have:

$$\ulcorner Ga \urcorner, \ulcorner Ga \vee \sim Ga \urcorner, \ulcorner (\exists x)Gx \urcorner, \ldots \in \tau_M(\Lambda)$$

and

$$\ulcorner \sim Ga \urcorner, \ulcorner Ga \& \sim Ga \urcorner, \ulcorner (\forall x) \sim Gx \urcorner, \ldots \notin \tau_M(\Lambda).$$

But this new candidate is not perfect because of the following oddities:

$$\ulcorner \sim T(`Ga\text{'})\urcorner, \ulcorner (\forall x) \sim Tx \urcorner, \ulcorner (\forall x)(Tx \supset Gx)\urcorner, \ldots \in \tau_M(\Lambda)$$

and

$$\ulcorner T(`Ga\text{'})\urcorner, \ulcorner T(`(\exists x)Gx\text{'})\urcorner, \ulcorner (\exists x)Tx \urcorner, \ldots \notin \tau_M(\Lambda).$$

By applying the function τ_M to $\tau_M(\Lambda)$ we gain a further improvement. We now have:

$$\ulcorner T(`Ga\text{'})\urcorner, \ulcorner T(`(\exists x)Gx\text{'})\urcorner, \ldots \in \tau_M(\tau_M(\Lambda))$$

and

$$\ulcorner \sim T(`Ga\text{'})\urcorner, \ulcorner (\forall x) \sim Tx \urcorner, \ldots \notin \tau_M(\tau_M(\Lambda)).$$

However, $\tau_M(\tau_M(\Lambda))$ needs improvement as well. It gets the second-level sentences right but it is not right on the third-level sentences such as $\ulcorner T(`T(`Ga\text{'})\text{'})\urcorner$. Still this and similar problems could be removed with more and more applications of the function τ_M. Repeated applications of τ_M yield better and better candidates for the extension of truth. It is clear, however, that any finite number of applications of the procedure will result in a set that itself is in need of improvement. Hence we need to apply the procedure transfinitely many times. But now we face the problem of determining how exactly this is to be done. Intuitively what is wanted is a way of summing up the improvements that are brought about by each successive application of τ_M. That is, we want a way of going from the improvements that are severally brought about by the various applications of τ_M to the improvements that are collectively brought about by those applications. But how exactly are we to make this transition?

I suggest that to achieve this we rely on the *stability* property of improvements. A genuine improvement brought about by the τ_M function is preserved by the later applications of τ_M. Thus in the example above $\ulcorner Ga \urcorner$ belongs to sets that result from all applications of τ_M. A sentence such as $\ulcorner T('T('Ga')') \urcorner$ fluctuates a little in the early stages—it belongs to $\tau_M(\tau_M(\tau_M(\Lambda)))$ but does not belong to $\tau_M(\tau_M(\Lambda))$—still, after the third application of τ_M it belongs to all later improvements. This suggests that to sum up the effects of all the finite applications of τ_M to an initial set U, we separate out sentences that eventually belong to all successive improvements and the sentences that eventually belong to no successive improvement. And to obtain the effect of all the improvements on U we add to it the first sort of sentences and subtract from it the second sort. Let us make this idea more precise. Let us define by transfinite recursion the notion "the result of α applications of τ_M to U" (abbreviated $\tau_M^\alpha(U)$).

Definition 4.

   (i)   If $\alpha = 0$ then $\tau_M^\alpha(U) = U$.

  (ii)   If $\alpha = \beta + 1$ then $\tau_M^\alpha(U) =$ the set of sentences true in the standard model $M + \tau_M^\beta(U)$.

 (iii)   If α is a limit ordinal then $\tau_M^\alpha(U) = X \cup ((S \sim Y) \cap U)$ where

$$X = \{A : \exists \beta < \alpha (A \in \bigcap_{\beta \leqslant \gamma < \alpha} \tau_M^\gamma(U))\}$$

and

$$Y = \{A : \exists \beta < \alpha (A \notin \bigcup_{\beta \leqslant \gamma < \alpha} \tau_M^\gamma(U))\}.$$

If A belongs to X(Y) we say that A is *locally stably true* (*false*) at α, and if A belongs to $X \cup Y$ we say that A is *locally stable* at α.

Clause (iii) of the above definition implies that to sum up the effects of all the finite applications of τ_M to U, we subtract from (U $\cap$ S) the sentences that are locally stably false at ω and add to it the sentences that are locally stably true at ω. Geometrically we can represent the construction as in diagram (B).

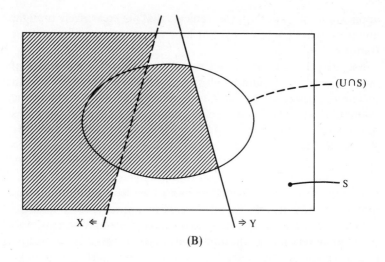

(B)

In this diagram the region to the left of the straight broken line represents the sentences that are locally stably true at ω; the region to the right of the straight solid line represents the sentences that are locally stably false at ω; and the shaded area represents $\tau_M^\omega(U)$.

Having obtained the results of ω improvements on U, we begin the process of revision over again. And after an infinity of revisions of $\tau_M^\omega(U)$ we sum up as before the effects of all these revisions. In summary, then, at successor stages we improve on the previous candidates by an application of the function τ_M, and at limit stages we sum up the effects of all the earlier improvements. Let us note to avoid possible misunderstanding that sentences that are locally stable at a limit ordinal α may not be locally stable at higher limit ordinals. So we should understand the process at limit levels as summing up "seeming improvements". These "seeming improvements" may turn out to be illusory in light of later revisions.

Our rule of revision, then, yields better and better candidates for the extension of truth. It can be shown that the rule has the extremely desirable property that in favorable conditions successive applications of it eventually yield a set that needs no improvement. The revisions yield a set V such that $\tau_M(V) = V$. The revisions stabilize at a fixed point. And, furthermore, *no matter what initial set we begin with the process stabilizes at the same fixed point* V! It is a general fact that the applications of the revision rule to a set U yield sets that are increasingly independent of U. The character of $\tau_M^\alpha(U)$

depends less and less on U as α increases. Let us illustrate this in terms of the model M given a few paragraphs ago. Whether the sentence $\ulcorner T(`Ga')\urcorner$ belongs to $\tau^1_M(U)$ is clearly dependent on U. If $\ulcorner Ga\urcorner$ belongs to U then $\ulcorner T(`Ga')\urcorner$ belongs to $\tau^1_M(U)$; otherwise not. But whether $\ulcorner T(`Ga')\urcorner$ belongs to $\tau^2_M(U)$ is entirely independent of U. No matter what the character of U may be, $\ulcorner T(`Ga')\urcorner$ belongs to $\tau^2_M(U)$. In general, for many sentences A, whether A belongs to $\tau^\alpha_M(U)$ does not depend upon U when α is sufficiently large. In favorable conditions this is true of *all* the sentences. The revision rule wipes away entirely the arbitrary character of the initial starting set.

This phenomenon occurs, for example, when the model M meets Condition 1 of Section II. We can easily adapt the proof of the Main Lemma given in Section II to show that if the degree of a formula A is n then for all ordinals $\alpha > n + 1$ and all initial starting sets, U, V,

$$A \in \tau^{n+2}_M(U) \quad \text{iff} \quad A \in \tau^\alpha_M(V).$$

That is, after the n + 2nd application of the τ_M rule it is fixed whether A belongs to the resultant revisions quite irrespective of the starting set. Thus in this case the arbitrary character of the starting set is entirely wiped away after ω revisions. In some models the rule of revision has the stability property (revisions applied to any initial set result in a fixed point) and the convergence property (no matter where we start the process we get the same fixed point), but the arbitrary character of the initial set is not so quickly removed. It takes many more applications of the revision rule. In K-acceptable models, for example, we have both stability and convergence but it can take up to $\alpha_0 + \omega$ (α_0 = the ordinal level at which Kripke's minimal fixed point is reached) applications of the τ_M rule to ensure that all the arbitrariness is removed from the initial set. A similar claim holds for V-acceptable models.

It is useful to distinguish models in which the rule of revision has these extremely desirable properties of stability and convergence.

Definition 5. A model M ($= \langle D, I \rangle$) is a *Thomason model* iff there is a set $V \subseteq D$ such that for all $U \subseteq D$ there is an ordinal α which meets the condition that

$$\tau_M(V) = V \quad \text{and} \quad \tau^\alpha_M(U) = V.$$

In Thomason models the process of revision has an intrinsic stability. It leads to the same result from all starting points, and therefore it fixes completely the extension of truth. So in a Thomason model M, τ_M has exactly one fixed point. It is obvious that τ_M has at least one fixed point. Suppose, for reductio, that τ_M has distinct fixed points V and V'. Then by definition there is a fixed point V* such that

$$\tau_M^\alpha(V) = V^* \quad \text{and} \quad \tau_M^\beta(V') = V^*.$$

But since $\tau_M(V) = V$ and $\tau_M(V') = V'$, it follows that

$$\tau_M^\alpha(V) = V \quad \text{and} \quad \tau_M^\beta(V') = V'.$$

So we have V = V', contradicting our assumption that V and V' are distinct fixed points. We conclude that:

Fact 1: All Thomason models are Tarskian.

And in the light of our earlier observations we may conclude that:

Fact 2: S-, K-, V-acceptable models are Thomasonian.

We have not defined the notion of "vicious self-reference" so we cannot prove the following intuitively plausible claim that is suggested by fact 2: all and only models in which there isn't any vicious sort of self-reference are Thomasonian. I propose, however, that we accept this claim as a working hypothesis. [Perhaps we should prove this hypothesis by getting an independent definition of "vicious self-reference"; or perhaps we should accept the hypothesis as defining the notion of "vicious self-reference".[7] (In the latter case

---

[7] A remark concerning the notion of vicious self-reference. It is well known that vicious self-reference may be present in the language even though there is no *self*-reference in the strict sense. Pairs of sentences such as

(a)   b is true.
(b)   a is true.

exemplify vicious self-reference, even though neither, strictly speaking, refers to itself. In this example the process of determining the truth or falsity of each sentence does loop back to the original sentence, and hence if may be maintained that we have here an indirect sort of self-reference. But even such indirect self-reference may be absent as is shown by the following infinitely descending sequence:

(c_0) c_1 is true.
(c_1) c_2 is true.
(c_2) c_3 is true.
              .
              .
              .

In summary, the 'self-' part in 'vicious self-reference' is not to be taken too seriously. Perhaps a less misleading locution would be 'vicious reference'.

the definition is to be tested by its fruitfulness.) I leave the status of the hypothesis ambiguous.] We conclude that when only benign forms of self-reference are present, the process of revision is at its best. It is stable. It converges to a single set from all starting points. It fixes the extension of truth. In sum, it preserves all our intuitions about truth.

Rules of revision are not always as well behaved as the rule for truth is in Thomason models. Rules of revision can exhibit various degrees of instability in various applications. Our rule for truth is not exempt from this. In the presence of certain kinds of self-reference the revision rule for truth manifests instability. Thus there are conditions under which the revision procedure applied to an initial set U stabilizes at a fixed point V, and furthermore, the procedure has a weakened version of the convergence property also: applied to another set U' it stabilizes at the same fixed point V if it stabilizes at all. However, the procedure does not stabilize at all initial starting points. This phenomenon occurs in irregular Tarskian models. Suppose that in the model $M(=\langle D, I \rangle)$ all constants except b and c are well-behaved. Suppose that $I(b) = \ulcorner Tb \urcorner$ and $I(c) = \ulcorner Tb \vee {\sim} Tc \urcorner$. It is easily shown that all starting sets U that contain $\ulcorner Tb \urcorner$ reach a fixed point (and the same fixed point) through revision. But starting points that do not contain $\ulcorner Tb \urcorner$ do not yield fixed points. The process of revision never settles down. Model M is Tarskian but not Thomasonian.

Fact 3: Not all Tarskian models are Thomasonian.

A second kind of instability that the rule for truth manifests is this. Under certain conditions the revision rule results in a fixed point when it is applied to any starting set U, but the rule does not yield the same fixed point from all starting sets. In these conditions our rule of revision results in stability in each application but it does not converge. The revisions induced do not bring all starting points closer and closer to just one set. This phenomenon occurs in improper models in which local determination holds. Suppose that in a model $M' (=\langle D', I' \rangle)$ the interpretation of all constants except d is well behaved. Let $I'(d) = \ulcorner Td \urcorner$. It can be shown without much difficulty that the revisions brought about by $\tau_{M'}$ on any set U always results in a fixed point. [More precisely: for all U there is an α such that $\tau_{M'}^{\alpha}(U) = \tau_{M'}(\tau_{M'}^{\alpha}(U))$.] However the process of revision does not converge. Sets that contain $\ulcorner Td \urcorner$ stabilize at a different fixed point than sets that do not contain $\ulcorner Td \urcorner$.

Obviously by combining the sorts of self-reference exemplified in M and M' we obtain a deeper grade of instability. Now the revision procedure does not stabilize from all initial points. And when it does stabilize it does not converge on one fixed point.

The final and deepest grade of instability occurs when no initial point settles down to a fixed point.[8] Here the procedure of revision ceaselessly revises the results of revision. This happens when the sort of self-reference that occurs in the Liar paradox is exemplified in the model. (In such cases the model is non-normal.) Let M'' ($= \langle D'', I'' \rangle$) be a model in which all constants are well behaved except for e. Let $I''(e) = \ulcorner \sim Te \urcorner$. Obviously $\tau_{M''}$ has no fixed points. Hence for no set U and no ordinal α do we have

$$\tau_{M''}^{\alpha}(U) = \tau_{M''}^{\alpha+1}(U).$$

Thus the result of a revision is always revised further by our rule.

The revision rule for truth may fruitfully be viewed as generating a preference ordering on the power set of D ($= \mathscr{P}D$). The ordering determines what members of $\mathscr{P}D$ are better candidates for the extension of truth than others. In Thomason models, in which there is only benign self-reference, the preference ordering induced has an upper bound. There is something that is *the most preferable*

---

[8] A comparison with the three-valued approaches. The three-valued approaches yield fixed points where the two-valued one does not. Let ψ be any monotonic three-valued approach. Then, ψ_M has fixed points for all models M, but τ_M has fixed points only when paradoxical-type self-reference is not present in M. The abundance of fixed points in the three-valued languages is to be explained by the expressive incompleteness (the fact that not all three-valued functions are expressible) and the semantical incompleteness (the fact that not all the semantical concepts are present) in these languages. Thus, for example, the Strong Kleene scheme κ behaves much like τ if we add to the language not only the truth predicate T but also the predicate N (standing for "neither true nor false"). Now we do not get fixed points in all models but only in those that do not contain paradoxical self-reference. Formally the point is this. Let $M + (U, V) + (U_1, V_1)$ be the three-valued model in which T is assigned $\langle U, V \rangle$ and N is assigned $\langle U_1, V_1 \rangle$. Define the function κ'_M so that $\kappa'_M(\langle \langle U, V \rangle, \langle U_1, V_1 \rangle \rangle)$ $= \langle \langle U', V' \rangle, \langle U'_1, V'_1 \rangle \rangle$ where U' (V'; U'$_1$; V'$_1$) is the set of sentences true (false; neither true nor false; either true or false) in the model $M + (U, V) + (U_1, V_1)$ by the scheme κ. Now κ' does not have fixed points in all M. We observe that we can gain fixed points here also by deepening expressive incompleteness. For example, a Weak Kleene scheme yields fixed points in all models even when the language has both T and N: the function μ'_M has fixed points for all M. (Professor Robert L. Martin has independently established this fact.) Upshot: the paucity of fixed points of τ_M is to be explained by the expressive completeness of two-valued languages.

candidate for the extension of truth. Here our revision rule does fix the extension of truth. In non-Thomason models, however, the preference ordering does not have an upper bound. The preference ordering yields a number of sets that are equally good candidates for the extension of truth.

Definition 6.   V *is one of the best candidates for the extension of truth in a model* M *relative to* U (abbreviated to V $\in \mathscr{C}_M(U)$) iff for all ordinals α there is an ordinal $\beta > \alpha$ such that $\tau_M^\beta(U) = V$.

Clearly the values of $\tau_M^\alpha(U)$ for varying α's cannot all be distinct. If they were then the fact that $\tau_M^\alpha(U)$ is always a member of $\mathscr{P}D$ would imply that there is a set of all the ordinals (by the axiom schema of replacement). Hence for all U there are distinct α, β such that $\tau_M^\alpha(U) = \tau_M^\beta(U)$. In fact something stronger can easily be established, viz.:

Fact 4: $\mathscr{C}_M(U)$ is never an empty set.

(For suppose, for reductio, that $\mathscr{C}_M(U)$ is empty. Then for all V $\in \mathscr{P}S$ it follows that there is a least ordinal α such that for all ordinals $\beta > \alpha, \tau_M^\beta(U) \neq V$. By replacement we can deduce that there is a set of all such least ordinals α. Letting γ be the least ordinal greater than these, we get the absurdity that $\tau_M^\gamma(U) \notin \mathscr{P}S$.) So all initial starting points U yield at least one set that is one of the best candidates for the extension of truth relative to U. When the revision procedure achieves stability the set of best candidates, $\mathscr{C}_M(U)$, is a unit set. This is not, however, always the case. For example, if there is a Liar-type sentence in the language then $\mathscr{C}_M(U)$ will not be a unit set. For if V belongs to $\mathscr{C}_M(U)$ then $\tau_M(V)$ ($\neq V$) also belongs to $\mathscr{C}_M(U)$. This is so because we can establish by transfinite induction that

If $\tau_M^\alpha(U) = \tau_M^\beta(U)$ then for all ordinals γ, $\tau_M^{\alpha+\gamma}(U) = \tau_M^{\beta+\gamma}(U)$.

And this yields the following general fact.

Fact 5:   If V $\in \mathscr{C}_M(U)$ and there are ordinals α, β such that $\beta > \alpha$ and V $= \tau_M^\alpha(U)$ and V$' = \tau_M^\beta(U)$ then V$' \in \mathscr{C}_M(U)$.

This means that once one of the best candidates is reached in the revision procedure, the sets given by revision are repeated over and over again. In fact it can be shown that after sufficiently many applications, the revision procedure cycles: the *same* pattern of revisions is repeated over and over again.[9] The sets occurring in this pattern are the best candidates for the extension of truth so far as the initial set is concerned. If we treat all initial starting sets equally, we may define "V is one of the best candidates for the extension of truth in a model M" (abbreviated to $V \in \mathscr{B}_M$) as follows:

Definition 7. $V \in \mathscr{B}_M$ iff there is a set $U \subseteq D$ such that $V \in \mathscr{C}_M(U)$.

In a Thomason model M, $\mathscr{B}_M$ is a unit set. When vicious sorts of self-reference are present this is not so. Our rule of revision does not yield *the* extension of truth in such cases.

Even though in non-Thomason models the extension of truth is not fixed, this does not mean that the rule of revision leaves the truth or falsity of *all* sentences indeterminate. In fact quite the contrary is true. The status of most sentences is decided by the revision procedure; only the status of some of the sentences is left undecided. The revision rule for truth yields the same core sentences from all initial starting points. Only on the periphery does it unrelentingly force revisions. Let us say that a sentence A is *stably true in* M iff $A \in \cap \mathscr{B}_M$. A is *stably false in* M iff $A \notin \cup \mathscr{B}_M$. Finally, A is *stable in* M iff A is either stably true or stably false in M. Sentences that are not stable in M will be called *unstable* in M. We define in a parallel manner a relativized notion of stability. A is *stably true* (*stably false; stable*) *in* M *relative to* U iff $A \in \cap \mathscr{C}_M(U)$ ($A \notin \cup \mathscr{C}_M(U)$; $A \in \cap \mathscr{C}_M(U)$ or $A \notin \cup \mathscr{C}_M(U)$). A *is unstable in* M *relative to* U iff A is not stable in M relative to U. In view of fact 5 we have the following:

Fact 6: A is stably true in M relative to U iff there is an ordinal α such that for all ordinals $\beta \geqslant \alpha$, $A \in \tau_M^\beta(U)$.

Fact 7: A is stably false in M relative to U iff there is an ordinal α such that for all ordinals $\beta \geqslant \alpha$, $A \notin \tau_M^\beta(U)$.

Fact 8: A is stably true in M iff A is stably true in M relative to all U.

Fact 9: A is stably false in M iff A is stably false in M relative to all U.

---

[9] The cyclicity of the revision process was first established by Professor Hans Herzberger. I am grateful to him for correcting an error in my earlier formulation.

The revision procedure, then, decides the truth and falsity of stable sentences in all models, Thomasonian or not. Only on unstable sentences is it equivocal.

On ordinary unproblematic sentences the revision procedure yields a definite verdict. These, I claim, are stable. This is obviously so for sentences that do not have any occurrences of the truth predicate. About the other sentences my claim is that they are stable if they do not involve vicious self-reference. Evidence for this is that all μ-, κ-, σ-grounded sentences are stable. Indeed something quite general can be established here. Let ψ be a monotonic scheme used to evaluate sentences in the three-valued model $M + (U, V)$. (We are only interested in these restricted types of three-valued models for the present.) Let ψ meet the following condition:

Condition 2. For every model $M + (U, V)$ and all sets U^* if $U \subseteq U^*$ and $V \subseteq D \sim U^*$ and if $\psi_M(\langle U, V \rangle) = \langle U', V' \rangle$ then $U' \subseteq \tau_M(U^*)$ and $V' \subseteq D \sim \tau_M(U^*)$.

(This says essentially that the truth value given to a sentence in a model $M + (U, V)$ by the scheme ψ does not conflict with the truth value that would be given to it by the classical scheme in any of the classical extensions of $M + (U, V)$.) We can show that:

Fact 10:   All ψ-grounded sentences are stable.

I omit the detailed proof of this fact but give an outline of it. Let $\langle \psi_M^\alpha +, \psi_M^\alpha - \rangle$ be the interpretation given to the truth predicate at ordinal level α in Kripke's cumulative procedure. Now fact 10 is a consequence of the following:

Fact 11: $\psi_M^\alpha + \subseteq \tau_M^\alpha(U)$ and $\psi_M^\alpha - \subseteq D \sim \tau_M^\alpha(U)$,   for all
$U \subseteq D$

This fact is easily established by transfinite induction. The base clause is trivial because the Kripkean construction assigns to the truth predicate the ordered pair $\langle \Lambda, \Lambda \rangle$ at level zero. The successor clause follows in view of Condition 2 on ψ. The limit clause holds in virtue of the fact that the Kripkean construction is cumulative. Now if the Kripkean minimal fixed point is reached at ordinal α_0 then fact 11 implies that the true grounded sentences, $\psi_M^{\alpha_0} +$, are included in $\tau_M^\beta(U)$ and that the false grounded sentences, $\psi_M^{\alpha_0} -$, are included in $D \sim \tau_M^\beta(U)$ at all ordinals $\beta \geqslant \alpha_0$ and all sets $U \subseteq D$. It follows (using facts 6–9) that all ψ-grounded sentences are stable. We observe that all the three schemes considered above (μ, κ, σ) meet Condition 2.[10]

There are stable sentences that are not κ-grounded. For example, logical laws are stable but, as observed earlier, they are not κ-grounded. Examples can be given to show that not all stable sentences are σ-grounded. It follows that stable sentences include as a proper part sentences that are grounded by any of the three schemes we have considered. Whether this is so for all monotonic schemes that meet Condition 2 is as yet an open question.

Logical laws are stably true. So also are their cousins, the semantical laws, provided they are restricted to stable sentences. Suppose that the language L has the syntactic resources of negation, conjunction, and instantiation ($\ulcorner Neg(x, y) \urcorner$, $\ulcorner Conj(x, y, z) \urcorner$ and $\ulcorner Inst(x, y) \urcorner$: read respectively as "$x$ is the negation of the sentence y", "x is the conjunction of the sentences y and z", "x is an instance of the universally quantified sentence y"). Then the following sentences of L are stably true provided that t and t' denote stable sentences.

(SL1)　$(\forall x)[Neg(x, t) \supset (T(x) \equiv \sim T(t))]$

(SL2)　$(\forall x)[Conj(x, t, t') \supset (T(x) \equiv (T(t) \& T(t')))]$

(SL3)　$(\forall x)[Inst(x, t) \supset (T(t) \supset T(x))]$.

If we had employed the substitutional interpretation of quantifiers a stronger version of (SL3) would have been stably true.

When no vicious self-reference is present in the language all the sentences are stable. As observed earlier, in such cases the rule for truth fixes completely the extension of truth, and *all* our intuitions

---

[10] Schemes σ_1 and σ_2 do not meet Condition 2, and fact 10 does not hold for them. There are σ_1-grounded sentences that are not stable. An example (given to me by Professor Saul Kripke) that shows this is $\ulcorner (\forall x) \sim (T(x) \& T(neg(x))) \urcorner$ (where *neg* is a function symbol that expresses the notion "the negation of" in the object language). This sentence is not stable in models that contain Liar-type sentences. It is unstable relative to those starting sets that contain a Liar-type sentence and its negation. One way of establishing a connection between stability and groundedness for these schemes is to employ Belnap's idea of a "bootstrapping policy". A bootstrapping policy Γ yields for each limit ordinal α a set Γ_α that is used to decide the locally unstable sentences at α. We keep the same definition of revision as before (definition 4) except that we relativize it to Γ also and replace U by Γ_α in the limit-ordinal case. Call a bootstrapping policy *acceptable* iff at each limit ordinal α, Γ_α is consistent and contains all the sentences that are locally stable at α. Now if a sentence is σ_1-grounded then it is stable relative to all acceptable Γ. A similar maneuver works for the σ_2 scheme. Note that there are sentences stable by the new definition (and by the old also) that are neither σ_1- nor σ_2-grounded.

about the concept of truth are preserved. Thus our account is not subject to objection (4) given above against Kripke. It is worth noting that our account meets the other three objections as well. In particular, it yields the correct judgments on the case given under objection (3): sentences (a3) and (b4) are stably true and (a5) is stably false. We also get the right judgment in the variant of objection (3) discussed above.

Stable sentences, then, constitute a large class, and it is reasonable to believe that they include all the unproblematic sentences. Now the concept of truth is well behaved over stable sentences. If A is stably true then so is $\ulcorner T(`A')\urcorner$. If $A$ is stably false then so is $\ulcorner T(`A')\urcorner$. Furthermore, converses of these conditionals are true as well. The fundamental intuition about truth holds for all stable sentences: if A is a stable sentence then $\ulcorner T(`A') \equiv A\urcorner$ (and more generally, $\ulcorner T(t) \equiv A\urcorner$, where t denotes A) is stably true. The use of the Tarski biconditionals in connection with stable sentences is entirely legitimate. Furthermore, if stably true sentences logically imply a sentence A then A is stably true as well. Hence the use of classical reasoning is legitimate also. We conclude, then, that our theory accounts for the use of unproblematic sentences: it accords with, and explains, the fact that with such sentences we allow the free use of the biconditionals and classical reasoning.

The problematic sentences—such as the Liar and the truth teller ("This very sentence is true")—are, by our account, unstable. On these the rule for truth does not yield a definite verdict. It is equivocal. These sentences belong to some, but not all, of the sets that count as the best candidates for the extension of truth. It is this, I suggest, that explains our attitude towards the problematic sentences that we cannot with any reason say that they are true or that they are not true. Either claim seems equally arbitrary and counter to what we intuit about truth. We feel that these sentences are problematic because we think that there must be something that is *the* extension of truth. But there is no such thing when vicious self-reference is present in the language.

Liar-type sentences are to be distinguished from the other unstable sentences in that they exhibit the deepest grade of instability. No matter what set we begin the process of revision with, these sentences never become stable. This is clear with the simple Liar sentence. Consider the model M″ given above in which I″(e) = $\ulcorner \sim Te\urcorner$. In this model the sentence $\ulcorner \sim Te\urcorner$ is not stable relative to any starting set U. If it belongs to $\tau^\alpha_{M''}(U)$ then at the next stage it is thrown out by the revision rule: $\ulcorner \sim Te \urcorner \notin \tau^{\alpha+1}_{M''}(U)$. But a stage later we have $\ulcorner \sim Te \urcorner \in \tau^{a+2}_{M''}(U)$. Paradoxical sentences fluctuate in and out of the revisions of all starting sets.

Definition 8. *A* is *paradoxical in* M iff *A* is neither stably true nor stably false relative to any set $U \subseteq D$.

Truth-teller-type sentences do not exhibit this oscillation. They are stable relative to all starting sets. However, relative to some they are stably true and relative to the others they are stably false. Let us call such sentences "weakly unstable".

Definition 9. *A* is *weakly unstable in* M iff *A* is stable in M relative to all $U \subseteq D$ but *A* is not stable in M.

Observe that there are unstable sentences that are neither paradoxical nor weakly unstable. Three sorts of such sentences can be distinguished as displayed in diagram (C).

Let us illustrate these distinctions. Let L be a language that has, aside from the truth predicate and the quotational names, a one

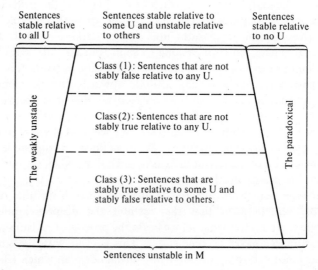

(C)

place predicate G and names a through h. Let M^* ($= \langle D^*, I^* \rangle$) be a model for L in which $D^* = S \cup \{1, 2\}$ and $I^*(G) = \{1\}$; $I^*(a) = 1$; $I^*(b) = 2$; $I^*(c) = \ulcorner Tc \urcorner$; $I^*(d) = \ulcorner \sim Td \urcorner$; $I^*(e) = \ulcorner Tc \vee \sim Te \urcorner$; $I^*(f) = \ulcorner Tc \& \sim Tf \urcorner$; $I^*(g) = \ulcorner Tg \urcorner$; and $I^*(h) = \ulcorner Tg \& (Tc \vee \sim Th) \urcorner$. The following facts are easily verified:

Fact 12: (i) Sentences $\ulcorner Ga \urcorner$, $\ulcorner (\exists x)Gx \urcorner$, $\ulcorner (\forall x)(Tx \vee \sim Tx) \urcorner$, $\ulcorner Gb \urcorner$, and $\ulcorner (\forall x)(Tx \& \sim Tx) \urcorner$ are stable in M^*. The first three are stably true in M^* and the last two are stably false in M^*.

        (ii) Sentences $\ulcorner T(`Ga') \urcorner$, $\ulcorner T(`T(`Ga')') \urcorner$, and $\ulcorner T(`Ga') \equiv Ga \urcorner$ are also stably true in M^*.

        (iii) Sentences $\ulcorner Tc \urcorner$, $\ulcorner Tg \urcorner$, $\ulcorner \sim Tc \urcorner$, $\ulcorner Tc \vee Gb \urcorner$, $\ulcorner (\forall x)(Gx \supset Tc) \urcorner$ are weakly unstable in M^*. The biconditional $\ulcorner T(`Tc') \equiv Tc \urcorner$ is, however, stably true in M^*.

        (iv) Sentences $\ulcorner Td \urcorner$, $\ulcorner \sim Td \urcorner$, $\ulcorner Ga \& Td \urcorner$ are paradoxical in M^*.

        (v) Sentences $\ulcorner Tc \vee \sim Te \urcorner$, $\ulcorner Tc \& \sim Tf \urcorner$, $\ulcorner Tg \& (Tc \vee \sim Th) \urcorner$ belong respectively to the classes (1), (2), and (3) (as defined in the diagram above).

Concerning fact 12(v) we note that if the starting set U does not contain $\ulcorner Tg \urcorner$ then the sentence $\ulcorner Tg \& (Tc \vee \sim Th) \urcorner$ is stably false relative to U; if U does contain $\ulcorner Tg \urcorner$ and also contains $\ulcorner Tc \urcorner$ then $\ulcorner Tg \& (Tc \vee \sim Th) \urcorner$ is stably true relative to U; and finally if U contains $\ulcorner Tg \urcorner$ but does not contain $\ulcorner Tc \urcorner$ then $\ulcorner Tg \& (Tc \vee \sim Th) \urcorner$ is unstable relative to U.

Unstable sentences share the feature that they belong to some of the best candidates for the extension of truth, but not to others. This, I have suggested, explains the fact that on the problematic sentences we find it equally arbitrary to assign either truth value. Now there are important differences between different sorts of problematic sentences and I want to argue that our account explains these differences also.

The weakly unstable sentences—and the truth-teller-type sentences belong here—are the least problematic of all. Since they are stable relative to all starting sets, their T-biconditionals are stably true, and the usual semantic laws (e.g., (SL1)–(SL3)) hold for them. These sentences do not result in anything that conflicts with our presumptions about truth. In fact if only the kind of self-reference that is found in such sentences were exemplified in the language, we could easily define *the* extension of truth. We simply have to restrict the starting sets we allow when generating the best candidates for the extension of truth. And now all our intuitions about truth are preserved. This is reflected in the fact that once we assign truth-teller-type sentences a definite truth value nothing problematic remains.

When we consider sentences that belong to any of the classes (1), (2), and (3), tensions with our presumptions about truth begin to arise. Now the Tarski biconditionals and the semantical laws are no longer stably true. Still we do not find these sentences as problematic as the paradoxical ones. These sentences do become stable relative to some starting sets. So relative to these starting sets the Tarski biconditionals and the semantical laws are stably true. Hence, the biconditionals and the semantical laws can be consistently maintained: they do not yield a contradiction even when combined with our other beliefs. The cost is that we may violate the local determinability of truth: the truth value of some sentences may become dependent upon factors that are intuitively irrelevant to those sentences.[11] For example, in the model M* given above the

---

[11] I do not say that this occurs in all cases because of the infinite descending sequences such as:

(a_0)	a_1 is true.
(a_1)	a_2 is true.
(a_2)	a_3 is true.

.
.
.

Curiously there are starting sets relative to which the sentences in the above sequence are unstable. An example is provided by a set that contains only the odd-numbered members of the sequence. There are obviously sets relative to which the sentences are stably true and sets relative to which they are stably false. Hence these sentences belong to class (3). It is not clear, however, that local determinability is violated if we restrict ourselves to those starting sets that result in stability for these sentences.

Observe that if we had used Definition 2 in place of Definition 4 then the sentences in the above sequence would have turned out to be weakly unstable. However, this would not be so for sentences in a sequence such as the following:

(b_0)	b_1 is true.
(b_1)	b_2 is not true.
(b_2)	b_3 is true.

.
.
.

cost of maintaining the biconditional for the class (1) sentence $\ulcorner Tc \vee \sim Te \urcorner$ is that we violate the local determinability of $\ulcorner Tc \urcorner$, and the cost of maintaining the biconditional for the class (3) sentence $\ulcorner Tg \& (Tc \vee \sim Th) \urcorner$ is that we violate the local determinability of $\ulcorner Tg \& \sim Tc \urcorner$.

The paradoxical sentences show up our presumptions for what they are, hasty generalizations of the laws that hold only for the stable sentence. We cannot any longer maintain the Tarski biconditionals or the semantical laws even at the expense of local determinability. We cannot any longer eliminate the multiplicity of candidates for the extension of truth even if we allow only one starting set. The revision rule itself multiplies the candidates for the extension of truth. This is reflected in the fact that any judgment about the truth of a Liar-type sentence has an unstable character. Our understanding of the concept of truth leads us to revise our judgment to its opposite. And the revision procedure does not rest there either. It revises the result to give us our previous judgment back again. The cyclical pattern that emerges in ordinary arguments involving the Liar is explained by our theory.

When paradoxical-type sentences are present in the language the rule for truth does not fix *the* extension of truth. It yields a number of different sets that have an equal claim to be the extension of truth, and none of these sets preserves all the biconditionals. Does this show that out concept of truth is incoherent or, at least, imperfect? That it needs to be revised? The concept of truth is imperfect *if* it is an absolute standard for concepts that the notion of *the* extension of the concept be well defined. But what is the source of this standard? Is a concept more useful if the standard is met? More easily grasped? More simple to use? More "logical"? I cannot discuss these questions in any thorough way, but I remark that the account of truth given above lends plausibility to the idea that the concept of truth does not need revision for ordinary uses, and indeed that it is beautifully tailored to serve the functions that it is supposed to serve. Underlying it is a simple rule working in a simple way. Yet on all the unproblematic sentences—and it is these that really count from the viewpoint of ordinary uses—the rule works in the right way. Only on the problematic ones is the rule equivocal. But from the ordinary viewpoint these are the "don't care" cases anyway. Furthermore if we consider ways of improving the concept we find the cure worse than the disease. Clearly the most plausible way of "improving" the concept would be to equip it with a rule that would pick one of the best candidates that are generated by the revision rule and let it be the extension of truth. Now not only do we make the concept of truth more complex but we also lose the connection between truth and assertion.[12] Suppose that the extension of truth in a model M is, according to the proposed rule, U. Logic demands that if U is the extension of truth we assert the sentences $\tau_M(U)$. But when paradoxical sentences are present $\tau_M(U) \neq U$. So there is a sentence A such that either $A \in \tau_M(U)$ and $A \notin U$ or $A \notin \tau_M(U)$ and $A \in U$. This means that in the first case we would assert A but deny $\ulcorner T(`A`) \urcorner$ and in the second case we would deny A but assert $\ulcorner T(`A`) \urcorner$. In contrast with such a supposed improvement, our ordinary concept preserves the connection—and it does so without the use of any artificial devices. (For, A is stably true (false) iff $\ulcorner T(`A`) \urcorner$ is stably true (false).) The demand that the notion of *the* extension of a concept be well defined is not an absolute but a relative one. It has its source in the fact that a certain degree of simplicity is gained if it is met. Our concept of truth violates the demand because by doing so it is able to achieve a greater gain in simplicity elsewhere.

I should emphasize that I have claimed only that the concept of truth does not need revision so far as *ordinary uses* are concerned. It may be that the uses to which the concept is put in some special sciences, e.g., semantics, do require that the concept be revised. I cannot discuss the question concerning the special sciences here. It requires much too extended a treatment.

There are several other topics—mainly technical—that I cannot discuss, though they should be discussed in a more complete account and defence of the theory. I will mention a few. *First*, there are many interesting notions that can be defined in the theory given above, and their properties explored. For example, the theory suggests a notion of *level* that applies to all sentences, stable and unstable. We can define the notion roughly as follows. We define first the level of a sentence relative to a starting set as the least ordinal after which the truth value exhibits a regular pattern (possibly a constant pattern, possibly some other). Now we understand the level of a sentence as the least ordinal α greater than

---

[12] Another way of fixing the extension of truth is to let it be the set of all the stably true sentences. This way too, however, results in a loss of connection between truth and assertion.

all ordinals that give the level of the sentence relative to the starting sets. The level of a sentence gives the ordinal level by which the character of the sentence is fixed irrespective of the starting point. It would be worthwhile to examine the levels of various sorts of sentences and their connections. *Second*, there are interesting relationships between the notions that we have defined that require investigation. For example, it would be fruitful to investigate the relationship between sentences that have an intrinsic truth value and sentences that are stable. *Third*, there are alternative technical developments of the idea that the rule for truth is a rule of revision which should be explored. It may be that these are in some respects superior to the way I have developed the idea above. (Professors Nuel Belnap and Richmond Thomason have made interesting suggestions in this connection.) I did consider one alternative fairly seriously but chose not to follow it. In that alternative we define the revision function τ_M^α in the way we defined the function Tr in Section II (Definition 2). We keep the same clauses for zero and the successor ordinals but treat the limit-ordinal case differently. At limit ordinal α we let $\tau_M^\alpha(U)$ be the set of sentences that are locally stably true at α. The resulting definition is simpler. But I did not adopt it because, first, it does not fit as neatly with the idea of revision and, second, it yields somewhat odd results. Suppose $\ulcorner \sim Ta \urcorner$ and $\ulcorner \sim Tb \urcorner$ are two paradoxical sentences; suppose a designates $\ulcorner \sim Ta \urcorner$ and that b designates $\ulcorner \sim Tb \urcorner$. The proposed definition implies that $\ulcorner \sim Ta \vee \sim Tb \urcorner$ and $\ulcorner Ta \vee Tb \urcorner$ are paradoxical but that $\ulcorner Ta \vee \sim Tb \urcorner$ and $\ulcorner \sim Ta \vee Tb \urcorner$ are stably true. But there is no reason to so distinguish the first two sentences from the second two.

In intuitive terms the conception I have tried to defend is this. When we learn the meaning of 'true' we learn a rule that enables us to determine the extension of truth *provided* that we know the denotations and extensions of all the names, predicates, and function symbols in the language. This rule, which I have called the rule for truth, cannot be used to determine the extension of truth if the language itself contains the truth predicate—for to apply the rule we already need to know the extension of truth. I have tried to argue that if we view this intuitive rule as a rule of revision then a variety of phenomena concerning truth fall into place: all are seen to result from the way the revision rule works in various contexts. In some contexts the rule functions in an ideal way. It has the stability property. No matter where we begin the process, the revisions stabilize; after a time no more revisions are necessary. And it has the convergence property. No matter where we begin we end up with the same result. When the rule has these properties, it fixes the extension of truth. All our intuitions, and all our uses of truth, are preserved. Everything works the way it is supposed to. These are the contexts in which no vicious self-reference is present in the language. In other contexts the revision rule fails to be stable or if it is stable it fails to converge. In such cases the rule of revision does not yield *the* extension of truth. It yields only a number of sets that, from the viewpoint of the rule, are equal contenders for the extension of truth. The rule for truth behaves in this way when vicious self-reference is present in the language. But even here the rule fixes the truth and falsity of the unproblematic sentences in the right way. The best candidates for the extension of truth agree among themselves on the unproblematic sentences. They differ from each other only on the problematic cases. Viewing the rule for truth as a rule of revision explains the fact that with the problematic sentences we find it arbitrary and counterintuitive to say that they are true or that they are not true. The idea explains also the differences between various sorts of problematic sentences. With the truth-teller type it yields that the Tarski biconditionals and the semantical laws hold. There is an arbitrariness in assigning a definite truth value to these sentences, but, at least, they do not go counter to many of our generalizations about truth and semantics. They do not jar our intuitions. They seem harmless. The paradoxical sentences exhibit a deeper grade of instability. For them our theory predicts that the biconditionals and the semantical laws do not hold. Hence these sentences go counter to commonly held beliefs about truth and semantics. They stand as evidence against our overhasty generalizations about truth and semantics. For this reason we find them much more problematic than the truth-teller-type sentences. All our intuitions about truth that are controverted by the paradoxical sentences seem to have their source in our erroneous belief that the rule for truth fixes *the* extension of truth. Underlying these intuitions, I am suggesting, is a more fundamental one, namely that which is embodied in the rule for truth. And it is this deeper intuition working as a rule of revision that accounts for the limited validity (and invalidity) of our more superficial intuitions—the T-biconditionals, the semantical laws, etc. We get a clearer view of our concept of truth, and of our uses of 'true', if we see them as characterized by a simple rule of revision.

I should stress, to save misunderstanding, that I am not saying that we *use* the rule for truth as a rule of revision—that we consciously apply the rule in this manner. That would be an absurd piece of sociology. I am saying that our diverse uses of 'true' fall into a simple coherent pattern if we view the rule for truth as a rule of revision. We arrive at our judgments about truth in a variety of ways, but we do not have any systematic understanding of these ways. I am proposing that these ways can be understood and explained if we view the rule for truth as a rule of revision.

Finally, it is a perennial problem with theories of truth that while they apparently resolve one paradox, they allow the generation of another more vicious. It may be objected that our account is not exempt from this. For a sentence such as 'This very sentence is not stably true' presents us with a difficulty. If it is not stably true then it does not belong to the extension of 'stably true'. Hence it will fall in the extension of truth from all starting points and so be stably true. On the other hand, if it is stably true then it belongs to the extension of 'stably true'. Hence it does not fall in the extension of truth from any starting point and so is not stably true. In response to this I observe that the notion of "stable truth" may be viewed in three ways. First, as belonging to the metalanguage. This is the way we have used it above. We have used it in the metalanguage to give an account of the concept of truth in the object language L. This, it seems to me, does not in any way vitiate our account of the concept of truth. Further, when the notion is viewed this way the paradox does not arise. Second, the notion may be viewed as belonging to L itself but under the condition that L has sufficiently weak syntax as far as the predicate that expresses the notion of stable truth is concerned. (Compare with the case of truth discussed in Section II.) Under such conditions we can envisage formulating the entire theory of truth given above in the language L itself. (Of course we will need other notions as well, and the technical details will be messy, if not overwhelming.) The paradox still does not arise. Third, the notion may be viewed as belonging to L when L does not meet the condition of sufficiently weak syntax. Now the paradox is present for the concept "stably true in L". But we must ask how is the concept "stably true in L" added to L? It must be added, it would appear, via a rule of revision. But then can we not give an account of the new paradox parallel to that we gave of the old?

Postscript to "Truth and Paradox", 1983

(i) I am no longer satisfied with the treatment of the limit stages in Definition 4. Nuel Belnap's idea of a "bootstrapping policy" (implemented somewhat along the lines of footnote 10 above) provides, it seems to me, a more general and better treatment. (ii) The most important changes in the present reprinting of the paper concern the variants of objection (3) to Kripke on page 36 of the *JPL* version. The starred variant has been dropped because it is inadequate; the dagger variant has been modified and the claim following it has been weakened.

References

Burge, Tyler, 1979, "Semantical Paradox", reprinted in this volume.

Chihara, Charles, 1979, "The Semantic Paradoxes: A Diagnostic Investigation", *The Philosophical Review* 88, pp. 590–618.

Davidson, Donald and Harman, Gilbert (eds.), 1972, *Semantics of Natural Language*, Dordrecht and Boston: D. Reidel Publishing Company.

Grover, Dorothy L., 1977, "Inheritors and Paradox", *The Journal of Philosophy* 74, pp. 590–604.

Grover, Dorothy L., Camp, Joseph L. and Belnap, Nuel D., 1975, "A Prosentential Theory of Truth", *Philosophical Studies* 27, pp. 73–125.

Hawthorn, John, 1983, "The Liar and Theories of Truth", doctoral dissertation, McGill University.

Herzberger, Hans G., 1967, "The Truth-Conditional Consistency of Natural Languages", *The Journal of Philosophy* 64, pp. 29–35.

Herzberger, Hans G., 1970a, "Paradoxes of Grounding in Semantics", *The Journal of Philosophy* 67, pp. 145–67.

Herzberger, Hans G., 1970b, "Truth and Modality in Semantically Closed Languages", in Martin (1970), pp. 25–46.

Kasher, Asa (ed.), 1976, *Language in Focus*, Dordrecht and Boston: D. Reidel Publishing Company.

Kripke, Saul A., 1975, "Outline of a Theory of Truth", reprinted in this volume.

Linsky, Leonard, 1952, *Semantics and the Philosophy of Language*, Urbana, Chicago, and London: University of Illinois Press.

Mackie, John L., 1973, *Truth, Probability, and Paradox*, Oxford: Oxford University Press.

Martin, Robert L., 1967, "Toward a Solution to the Liar Paradox", *The Philosophical Review* 76, pp. 279–311.

Martin, Robert L., 1968, "On Grelling's Paradox", *The Philosophical Review* 77, pp. 321–31.

Martin, Robert L. (ed.), 1970, *The Paradox of the Liar*, New Haven and London: Yale University Press. 2nd edition with supplementary bibliography (Ridgeview, 1978).

Martin, Robert L., 1970a, "A Category Solution to the Liar", in Martin (1970), pp. 91–112.

Martin, Robert L. and Woodruff, Peter W., 1975, "On Representing 'True-in-*L*' in *L*", reprinted in this volume.

Parsons, Charles, 1974, "The Liar Paradox", reprinted in this volume.

Popper, Karl R., 1965, *Conjectures and Refutations*, New York: Harper Torchbooks.

Prior, Arthur N., 1961, "On a Family of Paradoxes", *Notre Dame Journal of Formal Logic* 2, pp. 16–32.

Prior, Arthur N., 1967, "Correspondence Theory of Truth", in Paul Edwards (ed.), *The Encyclopedia of Philosophy*, vol. 2, pp. 223–32.

Putnam, Hilary, 1978, *Meaning and the Moral Sciences*, London, Henley, and Boston: Routledge & Kegan Paul.

Russell, Bertrand, 1940, *An Inquiry into Meaning and Truth*, London: George Allen & Unwin (Pelican edition, 1962).

Skyrms, Brian, 1970a, "Return of the Liar: Three-Valued Logic and the Concept of Truth", *American Philosophical Quarterly* 7, pp. 153–61.

Skyrms, Brian, 1970b, "Notes on Quantification and Self-Reference", in Martin (1970), pp. 67–74.

Tarski, Alfred, 1944, "The Semantic Conception of Truth", *Philosophy and Phenomenological Research* 4, pp. 341–76, reprinted in Linsky (1952), pp. 13–47.

Tarski, Alfred, 1956, "The Concept of Truth in Formalized Languages", in *Logic, Semantics, Metamathematics*, pp. 152–278, Oxford: Clarendon Press.

Tarski, Alfred, 1969, "Truth and Proof", *Scientific American* 220, pp. 63–77.

van Fraassen, Bas C., 1968, "Presupposition, Implication, and Self-Reference", *The Journal of Philosophy* 65, pp. 136–52.

van Fraassen, Bas C., 1970a, "Truth and Paradoxical Consequences", in Martin (1970), pp. 13–23.

van Fraassen, Bas C., 1970b, "Rejoinder: On a Kantian Conception of Language", in Martin (1970), pp. 59–66.

Wallace, John, 1972, "On the Frame of Reference", in Davidson and Harman (1972), pp. 219–52.

Toward Useful Type-Free Theories, I*

Solomon Feferman

Contents of Parts I and II

A. Issues for Semantics and Mathematics

1. *The paradoxes: a continuing challenge.* There is a distinction between *semantical paradoxes* on the one hand and *logical* or *mathematical paradoxes* on the other, going back to Ramsey 1925. Those falling under the first heading have to do with such notions as *truth, assertion* (or *proposition*), *definition,* etc. while those falling under the second have to do with *membership, class, relation, function* (and derivative notions such as *cardinal* and *ordinal number*), etc. There are a number of compelling reasons for maintaining this separation but, as we shall see, there are also many close parallels from the logical point of view.

The initial solutions to the paradoxes on each side—namely Russell's theory of types for mathematics and Tarski's hierarchy of

Solomon Feferman, 'Toward Useful Type-Free Theories, I', also published in the *Journal of Symbolic Logic.* Copyright © 1982 by the *Association for Symbolic Logic.*

* Research for this paper has been supported by grants from the National Science Foundation. Part I (reproduced here) is based on my notes Feferman 1976, which I was much encouraged to bring to published form by Dagfinn Føllesdal and Robert L. Martin. More recently, the material of both Parts I and II was presented in a course at Stanford University in Autumn 1981. I have benefited from a number of comments of those attending, particularly Hans Kamp. I wish also to thank Martin W. Bunder, Frederick Fitch, Dagfinn Føllesdal, Allen Hazen, and the referee for a number of useful comments and for catching various minor errors.

language levels for semantics—were early recognized to be excessively restrictive. The first really workable solution to the mathematical paradoxes was provided by Zermelo's theory of sets, subsequently improved by Fraenkel. The informal argument that the paradoxes are blocked in ZF is that its axioms are true in the _cumulative hierarchy of sets_ where (i) unlike the theory of types, a set may have members of various (ordinal) levels,[1] but (ii) as in the theory of types, the level of a set is greater than that of each of its members. Thus in ZF there is no set of all sets, nor any Russell set $\{x \mid x \notin x\}$ (which would be universal since $\forall x(x \notin x)$ holds in ZF). Nor is there a set of all ordinal numbers (and so the Burali–Forti paradox is blocked).

The step to the theory BG of sets and classes developed by Bernays and improved by Gödel is intuitively modeled in the cumulative hierarchy extended to one further top level at which we find the _proper classes_; classes of lower levels are identified with sets. In BG one proves the existence of the class V of all sets, but not of all classes; further we have a class ON of all sets which are ordinal numbers. V and ON are proper classes and $V \notin V$, $ON \notin ON$.

The theories ZF and BG (when augmented by AC, the Axiom of Choice, also intuitively true in the cumulative hierarchy) provide a framework in which practically all of current mathematics can be systematically represented in an unforced manner. The exceptions are marginal; one which will be at the center of attention here is the informal general theory of _mathematical structures_, particularly the _theory of categories_.[2] It is natural in certain situations to consider all structures of a given kind as forming a new structure, of which they are the elements. For example, the class B consisting of all structures $(A, \circ, =_A)$ with a commutative and associative binary operation $\circ$ itself forms such a structure under Cartesian product $\times$; that is, $(B, \times, \cong)$ is naturally considered as a member of B. Category theory deals with structures of a more sophisticated kind which are useful in extensive parts of algebra and topology. It is mathematically natural to impose a category structure $(CAT, \ldots)$ on the class CAT of all categories and thus to consider the former as a member of the latter.

---

[1] These levels are usually called _ranks_ in current set theory.

[2] Another exception is Brouwer's theory of choice sequences. In that case, the formal reduction of theories with choice sequences to theories without, accomplished by Kleene/Vesley 1965 and Kreisel/Troelstra 1970, ends with systems interpretable in ZF.

However, the logical problem of dealing with such is already present in simpler structures such as $(B, \ldots)$ above (or even with the class of all classes). We are blocked from forming B in ZF or BG, though in the latter we can form the class B' of all (commutative and associative) structures $(a, \circ, =_a)$ where $a \in V$. This is the basis for a distinction between "small" and "large" structures whose domains are sets, respectively classes (cf. MacLane 1977, sec. I.7 for its employment in category theory, e.g. with the category of all small groups, the category of all small categories, etc.). The systematic use of this distinction serves all practical ends in category theory, though it is not without awkward turns. We shall return to its troublesome aspects in Part II-C below.

ZF and BG are both *untyped* formalisms, i.e. the levels which we have in mind in their informal interpretations do not appear explicitly in the syntax.[3] Thus we can form expressions $x \in y$ without restriction, in particular the expression $x \in x$. On the other hand, one usually refers to a formal framework (a theory or structure) as being *type-free* if it admits significant instances of *self-application*. Evidently a direct account of the informal theory of categories would be type-free in this sense. There has been extensive experience in mathematical logic with type-free structures from work in *recursion theory* and with the λ-*calculus*.[4] While the structures met there have meager mathematical content, this experience among others lends hope to the pursuit of richer type-free models and theories.

There has indeed been considerable work on type-free mathematical theories, i.e. theories of classes and/or theories of functions.[5] The motivations have been various, ranging from the *ideological* (as in Frege's and Curry's programs) to specifically *useful* (as emphasized here). For some workers the challenge has simply been "logical": to find a simple, consistent but mathematically expressive type-free theory. There have been no notable successes, at least none which speak for themselves. But there is an interesting variety of "solutions" which have a corresponding variety of merits. How to

[3] There have been axiomatizations of set theory in which the ranks (fn. 1) appear explicitly, though of course as variables; cf. Scott 1960.

[4] Self-application occurs naturally elsewhere in mathematics, e.g. whenever a set of actions (such as a group of operators) is taken to be acting on itself.

[5] The bibliography to this paper will give the reader a first quick direction toward such; cf. also the historical notes in §14 below and the bibliography to Feferman 1975c.

assess these and where to look for further progress seems to me to require a more explicit analysis of the problem or problems to be solved than has been provided thus far. One of the main purposes of this paper is to advance such an analysis.

On the semantical side there has been an (equally) extensive pursuit of type-free frameworks, especially by workers in philosophical logic.[6] This is partly motivated by the fact that natural language abounds with directly or indirectly self-referential yet apparently harmless expressions—all of which are excluded from the Tarskian framework. Fretting about the severe restrictions placed by that solution, philosophers have sought to liberalize semantic theory so as to accommodate such expressions while still blocking the paradoxes. Another purpose of the present paper is to show how a logical analysis of problems and solutions on the semantical side closely parallels that on the mathematical side—at least to a point. But when one indulges in this kind of comparison, several striking points of difference emerge: (i) There has been no success for semantics comparable to that achieved by ZF (or even Z) for mathematics.[7] (ii) Unlike mathematics, the need for a type-free account is immediately apparent. (iii) Solutions to the semantic paradoxes have been *local* rather than taking their place within *global* (i.e. overall) semantical frameworks; thus relatively few constraints have been considered. In my view, (iii) points to the need for more extensive criteria to be met by type-free semantical solutions.

2. *Plan of the present paper (I and II)*. Most of the body of the paper consists of a review of work by the author over the last seven years and of related work by others—particularly Peter Aczel—aimed at constructing useful type-free theories. The main new material will be found in Part II-D. In the remainder of this part A, I take up an analysis of both the Liar paradox and Russell's paradox, emphasizing the parallel features which lead to a contradiction. The possible solution routes are also paralleled. These consist in restrictions of

---

[6] Some of this can be found in the bibliography here and in §14; the bibliography to Martin 1970 and in its 2nd edition (1978) is a much better source.

[7] There is no problem with the idea of a cumulative hierarchy of languages L_n (or even transfinite hierarchy L_α); indeed as ordinarily construed one has $L_n \subseteq L_{n+1}$ in the Tarski hierarchy and the truth predicate T_n for L_n makes sense when applied to statements in all earlier languages (cf. §4 below). But there is (to my knowledge) no natural theory for such in which the level distinctions make no explicit appearance.

(1°) language, (2°) logic, or (3°) basic principles. The solutions of Tarski and Russell fall under (1°); in the remainder of the paper only the routes (2°) and (3°) are considered. A common move in (2°) is to pass to some sort of 3-valued logic, while in (3°) one has to deal with restrictions of the *truth scheme* (TA) resp. *comprehension scheme* (CA) in a type-free language with ordinary logic. The following points are immediately observed: (i) Only the *constructive* part of ordinary reasoning is required in deriving the contradictions, and the paradoxes pose as much of a problem for the constructivist as for the classical logician; (ii) the *extensionality principle*, which is frequently considered to be fundamental for mathematical theories of classes, plays no role in Russell's paradox.[8] Particular attention will be paid in the following to *non-extensional theories* which may be considered equally well within classical or intuitionistic logic. For simplicity, though, we take ordinary logic to be represented in CPC, the 1st order classical predicate calculus with equality, unless otherwise specifically indicated.

A common suggestion to get around the paradoxes is that one is somehow dealing with undefined propositions, i.e. statements which are neither true nor false in the ordinary sense. Different logics which are *restrictions* of CPC have been proposed to express this idea formally. They are here considered within the single framework of logics for structures with *partial predicates*, which is the subject of part B. Special attention is given to different interpretations of the biconditional, since that is the critical operator in both (TA) and (CA). Arguments are presented against 3-valued and other restrictive logics due to their debilitating effects on ordinary reasoning. Theories of partial predicates formulated within ordinary logic are promoted instead. It turns out that such may be treated most elegantly within an *extension* of CPC by use of a new biconditional $\equiv$ which was introduced in the paper Aczel/Feferman 1980. The main result there yields consistency of the truth and comprehension schemes in the form

$$(\text{TA})_{\equiv} \quad \phi \equiv \text{Tr}(\ulcorner \phi \urcorner)$$

and

$$(\text{CA})_{\equiv} \quad \forall y[y \in \{x \mid \phi(x)\} \equiv \phi(y)],$$

---

[8] The first of these points is not novel. The second is so obvious it hardly seems worth mentioning, except as a corrective to the widespread and uncritical assumption of extensionality.

242   *Truth and the Liar Paradox*

without restriction on ϕ. In the logic of $\equiv$, a partial predicate $P(x)$ is treated as a pair of predicates $(P(x) \equiv t)$, $(P(x) \equiv f)$ where t, f are identically true and false statements, resp. The consistency result is established by an inductive fixed-point argument; this has been used frequently in the construction of models for partial-predicate versions of (TA) and (CA) but it is here given a new twist (due to Aczel). The new approach described here absorbs the previous treatments of partial classes in the papers Feferman 1975b, 1977.

It is seen from the description just given that part B is presented in a form equally applicable to semantical and mathematical theories. However, on the mathematical side its content is shown to be rather meager. In Part II-C we take up specifically mathematical criteria for a richer useful type-free theory. Such a theory is to account not only for the notions and structures of ordinary mathematical experience but also for such objects as the category of all groups, the category of all categories, and the category of all functors between two given categories. Here a certain asymmetry is brought out between the roles of functions and classes, so that the former appear in a way conceptually prior to the latter (just as in certain constructive theories). Furthermore, while functions are treated naturally as partial objects in ordinary mathematical discourse, classes do not have that character. A final topic of Part II-C is how to get along without extensionality as a matter of course.

All of the preceding motivates the passage in Part II-D to nonextensional type-free theories of partial operations and total classes. Such theories had been formulated previously for constructive purposes in Feferman 1975a, 1979. (We interpolate their connection with another approach to a semantical theory due to Aczel 1980, for what he calls *Frege structures*.) In Part II-D we shall now study the possible utility of these systems (both in their original formulation and with special modifications) as a formal framework for the general theory of mathematical structures, particularly category theory.

The paper (II) concludes with a discussion which retraces some of the choices made here, raises questions about alternative approaches, and looks to directions where further progress may be possible.

3. *Analysis of the Liar paradox.* We here essentially follow Tarski 1956 p. 165 (from the translation of his 1935 paper on the concept of

truth). (While there is nothing novel here, the details are put down for purposes of further discussion and comparison with Russell's paradox.) The contradiction results from a combination of the following features of ordinary language usage: construction of statement names and in particular of self-referential statements, acceptance of ordinary reasoning, and acceptance of the passage from the truth of a statement to the statement itself and vice versa.[9]

These features are analyzed here formally in terms of a logical system S specified by a syntax, underlying logic, and basic postulates. We use 'ϕ', 'ψ', ... to range over the statements of L (the language of S); these are assumed to be closed under the usual propositional operators here symbolized by $\neg$, $\wedge$, $\vee$, $\rightarrow$, $\leftrightarrow$. Formulas ϕ with at most one free variable x are indicated by $\phi(x)$; then for t an individual term, $\phi(t)$ denotes the result of substituting t for x in ϕ.

1°. *Syntax*

   (i) (*Naming*). Each statement ϕ of L has a name in the language, i.e. there is an associated closed term $\ulcorner\phi\urcorner$ of L.

   (ii) (*Self-reference*). For each formula $\psi(x)$ we can construct a statement ϕ which is equivalent in S to $\psi(\ulcorner\phi\urcorner)$.

2°. *Logic*. The axioms and rules of ordinary propositional calculus are accepted.

3°. *Basic principles*. The following axioms are accepted for a predicate $T(x)$ which is interpreted as expressing that x is true:

(TA) $T(\ulcorner\phi\urcorner) \leftrightarrow \phi$,

for each statement ϕ of L_S.

For the derivation of a contradiction in S we take ϕ with $\phi \leftrightarrow \neg T(\ulcorner\phi\urcorner)$ (in S). Using (TA) and transitivity of equivalence we obtain $T(\ulcorner\phi\urcorner) \leftrightarrow \neg T(\ulcorner\phi\urcorner)$ in S. Let $\theta = T(\ulcorner\phi\urcorner)$. Thus both $(\theta \rightarrow \neg\theta)$ and $(\neg\theta \rightarrow \theta)$ are provable. It is a result of ordinary logic that $(\theta \rightarrow \neg\theta) \rightarrow \neg\theta$, hence $\neg\theta$ follows by *modus ponens*.

---

[9] Burge 1979 argues that the contradiction does not lie in natural language itself but in theories "promoted by people" about their language: "Natural languages *per se* do not postulate or assert anything. What engenders paradox is a certain naive theory or conception of the natural concept of truth. It is the business of those interested in natural language to improve on it." (loc. cit., pp. 83–4).

But then θ follows from the second implication. Then S is inconsistent.

Discussion

Ad 1° (i) The process of statement naming in natural language is accomplished uniformly by quotation. However, there are other non-uniform means which are frequently applied, e.g. numbering of statements in a text or use of such locutions as 'the statement you just made', etc. In formal languages statement naming may be accomplished by an enumeration ϕ_n ($n = 0, 1, 2, \ldots$) of all the well-formed statements and an assignment to ϕ_n of a term denoting n (e.g. the numeral $\bar{n}$).

Ad 1° (ii) Natural language is rife with implicit self-reference, e.g. in such statements as 'You're not listening to me', or 'I never tell a lie', or 'English is easy to teach foreigners', and of course by explicit fabrication, e.g. 'This statement has less than ten words'. The possibility of self-reference for formal systems was realized by Gödel 1931. From this one can show in a fragment of elementary number theory that with each formula $\psi(x)$ is associated ϕ such that $\phi \leftrightarrow \psi(\ulcorner \phi \urcorner)$ is provable.

By the analysis of Jeroslow 1973, one actually has a term τ in number theory such that ϕ is identical with $\psi(\tau)$ and for which $\ulcorner \phi \urcorner = \tau$ is provable. In natural language we have the stronger possibility of *literal self-reference*, i.e. construction of ϕ identical with $\psi(\ulcorner \phi \urcorner)$. But this can also be accomplished in any language containing at least one closed term τ, by the *ad hoc* baptismal process which takes $\ulcorner \phi \urcorner$ to be τ for the statement $\psi(\tau)$ as ϕ. The conclusion from all this is that the hypothesis 1° (ii) is not by itself pernicious.

Ad 2°. It can be argued that the laws of logic implicit in ordinary reasoning are just those of the *classical 2-valued propositional* (and predicate) *calculus*. However inspection of the argument to contradiction above shows that the law of excluded middle is not used, so the argument is already one in *intuitionistic logic*. It is usual in the latter to identify $\neg\theta$ with $\theta \to f$ where f is an identically false statement. Then the principle $(\theta \to \neg\theta) \to (\neg\theta)$ translates into $(\theta \to (\theta \to f)) \to (\theta \to f)$ which is a special case of $(\theta \to (\theta \to \chi)) \to (\theta \to \chi)$. All the other laws of $\to$ and $\leftrightarrow$ applied in the derivation of the contradiction are clearly valid intuitionistically.[10] {In fact the argument already takes place in what is called *minimal logic* (cf. Prawitz 1965), where we have the usual axioms and rules for →. The conclusion of the argument is a specific contradiction θ and $\neg \theta$, i.e. θ and $(\theta \rightarrow f)$, hence f; intuitionistically we can go on to infer any statement, but not in minimal logic. However, we could replace f by an arbitrary χ to begin with, if one wants to derive full inconsistency using only minimal logic.}

Ad 3°. Truth in natural language is used both as a *predicate* and as an *operator*. An example of the former is 'What you just said is true', and of the latter is 'It is true that inflation has not abated'. Treated formally, truth as an operator would assign to each statement ϕ a new statement $T^*\phi$ where T^* corresponds to the phrase 'It is true that'. Self-reference provides no way to construct ϕ with $\phi \leftrightarrow \neg T^*\phi$. The basic axioms for T^* would be:

(T*A) $\phi \leftrightarrow T^*\phi$

for each statement ϕ. No contradiction results from taking these axioms in place of (TA) since we can interpret T^* as the identity operator.

4. *Solution routes for the Liar paradox.* By a "solution" to the paradox is meant the production of a *consistent system S* which has more or less the properties 1°–3° of §3. Since the 'more or less' is vague there cannot be a unique definite solution to the problem posed by the paradox. Usually further criteria are brought to bear (implicitly or explicitly) to test proposed solutions. The most demanding would be to situate the solution within a coherent global (overall) semantics for natural language. We shall return to the question of such criteria in Part II-C. Here the matter is considered only locally; the following is just a preliminary survey of possible solution routes.

---

[10] As already mentioned, this observation is not novel, though hardly emphasized in the literature. It was first brought to my attention some years ago by Harvey Friedman. Several readers of the MS of this paper have pointed out that this observation is already contained in Curry's derivation of a contradiction in certain logics based on combinatory systems ("Curry's paradox"); cf. Curry 1942 or Curry 1980, pp. 94–5. The difference is that in Curry's ("illative") systems, the combinatory and logical aspects are intertwined. In deriving the paradox, the former is used to construct a "paradoxical" combinator Y which then leads to a variety of forms of self-reference. Still it is fair to say that when the logical part of the argument is disengaged, it can be seen to proceed entirely within intuitionistic (indeed, minimal) logic.

To obtain some generality we assume that a consistent theory S_0 with language $L_0 = L(S_0)$ is given whose syntax and semantics are regarded as unproblematic, and that S is to be found as an extension of S_0 (with $L = L(S)$ an extension of L_0). S_0 might correspond to a fragment of natural language or it could be an axiomatic system for a part of science or mathematics.

Corresponding to 1°–3°, there are three kinds of restrictions which might be made.

1*. *Restriction of syntax.*
2*. *Restriction of logic.*
3*. *Restriction of basic principles.*

The escape route 1* is that taken in a Tarskian approach. A truth predicate T for L_0 is available only in a secondary ('higher' or 'meta') language L. Statement-naming $\ulcorner \phi \urcorner$ is provided only for ϕ in L_0; thus $T(\ulcorner \phi \urcorner)$ is a sentence of L only for ϕ in L_0. This restriction blocks full self-reference, i.e. there is no ϕ of L for which $\phi \leftrightarrow \neg T(\ulcorner \phi \urcorner)$ holds. We may use full classical logic in L and all available instances of (TA), i.e. $T(\ulcorner \phi \urcorner) \leftrightarrow \phi$ just for ϕ in L_0 (in that sense the solution is also a restriction of 3°). Tarski's set-theoretical definition of truth for L_0 provides a consistency-proof of this system S. Evidently, the solution can be iterated to give a hierarchy of languages $L_0, L_1, L_2, L_3, \ldots$ for each of which the truth predicate is available only in the following language.[11]

For the reasons given in §1, only solution routes 2* and/or 3* will be pursued in the present paper. Actually, the Tarskian solution for L_0 can be recast alternatively as falling under 3*. Simply take a system S in which one meets the conditions 1°(i) and (ii) and 2° without restriction, but where (TA) is restricted to: $T(\ulcorner \phi \urcorner) \leftrightarrow \phi$, for ϕ a sentence of L_0. This is shown consistent by incorporating enough arithmetic in S to carry out Gödel numbering of $L(S)$ within S and thence all of 1° followed by Tarski's consistency proof in which

---

[11] In his 1935 paper, Tarski stated: "In my opinion the considerations of §1 prove emphatically that the concept of truth (as well as other semantical concepts) when applied to colloquial language in conjunction with the normal laws of logic leads inevitably to confusions and contradictions." He saw the only possible way out in the "reform" of this language which would amount to a split "into a series of languages . . . each of which stands in the same relation to the next in which a formalized language stands to its metalanguage". But Tarski doubted that such could be done while preserving the naturalness of everyday language. Cf. the translation in Tarski 1956, p. 267.

T is interpreted as the truth predicate for L_0. However, this solution is rather weak: though we have sentences $T(\ulcorner\phi\urcorner)$ in L for all ϕ in L, and in particular for ϕ such that $\phi \leftrightarrow \neg T(\ulcorner\phi\urcorner)$, nothing interesting can be said about these statements. Further, there is no evident means of iterating this procedure, i.e. to find acceptable instances of $T(\ulcorner\phi\urcorner) \leftrightarrow \phi$ for ϕ not in L_0.

Remarks

(i) It is common in the literature on the semantical paradoxes to present a *model* $\mathfrak{M}$ for a solution S without explicitly describing S. (Actually, the model itself is often not even described precisely; rather, an account is given which would lead to a model.) Obviously, once $\mathfrak{M}$ is constructed, one can take S to be the set of statements true in $\mathfrak{M}$. We have formulated the search for solutions as the construction of suitable consistent S for several reasons. Firstly, there may be means other than provision of a model to establish consistency of such S, e.g. the use of proof-theoretic methods. Secondly, a criterion which might be applied is that the passage of S_0 to S is only to be a *matter of convenience* in the sense that S is supposed to be a *conservative extension of* S_0, i.e. for ϕ in L_0 we are to have $S \vdash \phi$ only if $S_0 \vdash \phi$.[12] Finally, I believe that mere presentation of a model $\mathfrak{M}$ does not give full appreciation of the merits or faults of a proposed solution when it is not said for what system S this is a model.

(ii) Solutions sometimes involve several kinds of restrictions simultaneously, e.g. as Tarski's restriction of 1° automatically required a restriction of 3°. But there is another possibility to consider: one may make an *extension* of ordinary logic provided there is a compensating restriction elsewhere. This is the approach taken in part B, §§11–12.

5. *Analysis of Russell's paradox.* This analysis parallels that of the Liar in many, but not all respects. Classes are regarded as being somehow the objectification of properties, and a theory S of classes counts such among the objects of its universe of discourse. However, there is no presumption that all objects are classes. In the formal

---

[12] It is true that there is a necessary and sufficient model-theoretic condition for S to be a conservative extension of S_0 when these are theories formulated in 1st order CPC, namely: for every model $\mathfrak{M}_0$ of S_0 there exists an expansion of $\mathfrak{M}_0$ (by additional relations, etc.) to a model $\mathfrak{M}$ of S. However, this does not necessarily carry over to theories in other logics.

framework of S, properties are expressed by formulas ϕ with a distinguished free variable, say (x). We write $\phi(x)$ for such, or $\phi(x, \ldots)$ when we want to stress that ϕ may contain other free variables ("parameters"). For a term τ, $\phi(\tau)$ denotes the result of substituting τ for x at all its free occurrences in ϕ (assuming τ is free for x in ϕ, i.e. there are no collisions of variables).

The following is assumed of S and L $(= L(S))$.

1°. *Syntax* (*class-naming*). With each formula $\phi(x)$ of L is associated a term $\{x \,|\, \phi(x)\}$ (in which 'x' is bound).

2°. *Logic*. The axioms and rules of ordinary propositional and predicate calculus are accepted in S.

3°. *Basic principles*. There is a binary relation $y \in z$ in L which is taken to express that y is a member of the class z. The following comprehension axiom scheme is accepted in S for each $\phi(x)$ in L:

(CA) $\forall y[y \in \{x \,|\, \phi(x)\} \leftrightarrow \phi(y)]$

The possibility of 'self-reference' arises in L by consideration of formulas of the form $t \in t$. Take $r = \{x \,|\, \neg(x \in x)\}$ so that $\forall y[y \in r \leftrightarrow \neg(y \in y)]$ holds by (CA). Then by the rules of the predicate calculus, we have $[r \in r \leftrightarrow \neg(r \in r)]$ in S. Thus for $\theta = (r \in r)$ we have $S \vdash (\theta \leftrightarrow \neg\theta)$, so the inconsistency of S follows just as in §3.

It is common to incorporate Frege's idea of *classes as extensions of concepts* in a theory of classes, by assumption of an *axiom of extensionality*. The following is its direct expression in the present framework:

(Ext) $\{x \,|\, \phi(x)\} = \{x \,|\, \psi(x)\} \leftrightarrow \forall x[\phi(x) \leftrightarrow \psi(x)]$.

Note that the inconsistency of S depends in no way on this further assumption. Thus S can be considered equally well as a theory of properties (conceived of as objects), in which $\{x \,|\, \phi(x)\}$ is read as 'the property of x, that $\phi(x)$' and $y \in z$ is taken to express that y has the property z. Since the terminology of class and membership is established in mathematics, and it is the mathematical uses of such a theory that interest us, we shall not follow this reading in terms of properties. In other words, *we countenance non-extensional theories of classes*.

Discussion

(i) *Ad* 1°. The hypothesis that classes may be named in the language, by the formation of abstracts $\{x \mid \phi(x)\}$ as terms, is inessential if we replace 3° by $\exists z \forall y [y \in z \leftrightarrow \phi(y)]$.

(ii) *Ad* 2°. On the other hand, using 1° as it stands, we do not need the full predicate calculus to derive the contradiction—its quantifier-free part ('free-variable logic') suffices if we drop the quantifier '$\forall y$' in 3°. Note in any case, just as for the Liar paradox, that the inconsistency is established using only intuitionistic logic (in fact, minimal logic).

(iii) Under the given assumptions on S, we can't define which objects in the universe are classes. It will prove convenient later to consider theories with an additional predicate $Cl(z)$ expressing that z is a class. In this case (CA) is written as $Cl(\{x \mid \phi(x)\}) \wedge \forall y [y \in \{x \mid \phi(x)\} \leftrightarrow \phi(y)]$, or as

$$\exists z([\{x \mid \phi(x)\} = z \wedge Cl(z)] \wedge \forall y [y \in z \leftrightarrow \phi(y)]),$$

then (Ext) would be strengthened to

$$Cl(a) \wedge Cl(b) \wedge \forall x [x \in a \leftrightarrow x \in b] \to a = b.$$

(iv) Such a predicate Cl is clearly unnecessary when the universe is conceived as consisting entirely of classes. In that case, extensionality is simply formulated as $\forall x [x \in a \leftrightarrow x \in b] \to a = b$.

6. *Solution routes for Russell's paradox.* Here we parallel §4, assuming to begin with an initial consistent S_0 in a language $L_0 = L(S_0)$. The problem is to find a consistent extension S satisfying more or less the conditions 1°–3° of §5. As before, there are three kinds of restrictions one can make.

1*. *Restriction of syntax.*
2*. *Restriction of logic.*
3*. *Restriction of basic principles.*

The escape route 1* is that taken in Russell's theory of types, as simplified by Ramsey 1925 (i.e. the "simple" or "unramified" theory of types). Instead of variables ranging unrestrictedly over a single universe of discourse, one has for each n, variables $x^{(n)}, y^{(n)}, \ldots$ of type n. The variables of the initial language L_0 are now taken to be of type 0. Each term τ will also be of a definite type and $(\sigma \in \tau)$ is a formula only for σ of type n and τ of type $(n + 1)$ for some n. Then formulas are built up by the operations of the predicate calculus, and if $\phi(x^{(n)})$ is a formula, $\{x^{(n)} \mid \phi(x^{(n)})\}$ is a term of type $(n + 1)$. Then (CA) is necessarily restricted to

$$\forall y^{(n)}[y^{(n)} \in \{x^{(n)} \mid \phi(x^{(n)})\} \leftrightarrow \phi(y^{(n)})].$$

If extensionality is also to be included, one adds for each n,

$$\forall x^{(n)}[x^{(n)} \in a^{(n+1)} \leftrightarrow x^{(n)} \in b^{(n+1)}] \rightarrow a^{(n+1)} = b^{(n+1)},$$

since the objects of each type $n + 1$ are conceived to be classes. A set-theoretical model of the resulting system is obtained by starting with a model $\mathfrak{M}_0 = (M_0, \ldots)$ of S_0 and interpreting the variables of type n as ranging over M_n where for each n, M_{n+1} is taken to be the set of all subsets of M_n.

In the following we shall only pursue solutions based on restrictions of type 2* or 3*. The theory of Zermelo (or ZF) with (possible) urelements gives a solution based on a type 3* restriction. This has just one sort of variable and the relation $\sigma \in \tau$ is formed without restriction. There is a predicate $Cl(x)$, read here as 'x is a set'. The urelements are those x such that $\neg Cl(x)$, and the axioms S_0 are taken relativized to the urelements. Instead of $\{x \mid \phi(x)\}$ in general one has only special cases, corresponding to *separation*, *pairing*, *union*, *power set*, etc. But the *axiom of foundation* prevents any instance of self-membership $x \in x$.

In Part II-C we shall discuss mathematical criteria for a type-free theory of classes, in which there are significant instances of self-membership (and of self-application in a broader sense).

B. Type-free Theories of Partial Predicates
(Truth and Membership)

7. *Partial predicates and structures.* At the outset we consider the route of restricting logic without restricting language. Though this direction will eventually be abandoned, it turns out that useful results can be garnered from its pursuit. It is a common move to try to pin the difficulty in the paradoxes on reasoning with *meaningless statements*, indeed with meaningless instances of basic predicates such as $T(x)$ or $(x \in y)$, (often called *truth-gaps* in the literature on the semantic paradoxes). If these are not to be banned syntactically then the logic must somehow be altered to handle reasoning with potentially meaningless statements. Various logics have been de-

vised for this purpose; some of them will be examined in §§8–10. The notion of *partial predicates* and the associated *partial structures* provide a common framework for their comparison.

We write t, f for the two truth-values "true" and "false". Let M be an arbitrary set. By a *partial k-ary predicate* $\tilde{R}$ on M $(1 \leqslant k < \omega)$ is meant a partial function $\tilde{R}$ from M^k to $\{t, f\}$. Introducing the symbol 'u' for "undefined", where $u \neq t$, $u \neq f$, every such predicate can be identified with a function $\tilde{R}: M^k \to \{t, f, u\}$.[13] Alternatively, we may identify $\tilde{R}$ with a *disjoint pair* $(R, \bar{R})$ of ordinary k-ary relations in M, i.e. where $R \subseteq M^k$, $\bar{R} \subseteq M^k$ and $R \cap \bar{R} = \varnothing$. In the following we shall move according to convenience from one form to another of regarding partial predicates. $\tilde{R}$ is said to be *total* if it is a total function from M^k to $\{t, f\}$, i.e. if u is not in the range of $\tilde{R}$ as a map into $\{t, f, u\}$. Viewed as a disjoint pair $(R, \bar{R})$, the predicate is total if $R \cup \bar{R} = M^k$; then $\bar{R}$ is just the complement $M^k - R$.

The set of truth-values $\{t, f, u\}$ is partially ordered by $u \leqslant t, u \leqslant f$ in addition to $u \leqslant u$, $t \leqslant t, f \leqslant f$; diagramatically:

Given two k-ary partial predicates $\tilde{R}, \tilde{R}'$ we put $\tilde{R} \leqslant \tilde{R}'$ if for all $m_1, \ldots, m_k \in M$, $\tilde{R}(m_1, \ldots, m_k) \leqslant \tilde{R}'(m_1, \ldots, m_k)$. This means that in their guise as partial functions from M^k to $\{t, f\}$, $\tilde{R}$ is a sub-function of $\tilde{R}'$. Equivalently, in their guise as disjoint pairs $(R, \bar{R})$ and $(R', \bar{R}')$, the relation holds when $R \subseteq R'$ and $\bar{R} \subseteq \bar{R}'$. Note that if $\tilde{R} \leqslant \tilde{R}'$ and $\tilde{R}' \leqslant \tilde{R}$ then $\tilde{R} = \tilde{R}'$.

In the following we shall consider *partial structures* $\mathfrak{M} = (\mathfrak{M}_0, \tilde{R}_1, \ldots, \tilde{R}_n, \ldots)$ constituted from some fixed structure $\mathfrak{M}_0 = (M, \ldots)$ in the ordinary ("total") sense of the word for a language L_0, together with one or more partial predicates $\tilde{R}_n$ on M. For simplicity, much of our work with such will be illustrated by $\mathfrak{M} = (\mathfrak{M}_0, \tilde{R})$ where $\tilde{R}$ is binary. For example, given such $\mathfrak{M}$ and $\mathfrak{M}' = (\mathfrak{M}_0, \tilde{R}')$ we put $\mathfrak{M} \leqslant \mathfrak{M}'$ if $\tilde{R} \leqslant \tilde{R}'$.

---

[13] This is just a special case of a general notion of Ω-*valued predicate* $R: M^k \to \Omega$ (and thence of Ω-valued structures) where Ω is any set of "truth-values". Only the special cases $\Omega = \{t, f, u\}$ and $\Omega = \{t, f\}$ are used here.

Inductive constructions of partial structures are ubiquitous in the present subject. They may be subsumed under the following general approach. Let $\mathcal{K}$ be the class of structures $\mathfrak{M} = (\mathfrak{M}_0, \tilde{R})$, with fixed $\mathfrak{M}_0$ ordered by $\leqslant$. An operator Γ on $\mathcal{K}$ associates with each $\mathfrak{M}$ a new structure $\Gamma(\mathfrak{M}) = (\mathfrak{M}_0, \tilde{R}')$; we also write $\Gamma(\tilde{R})$ for $\tilde{R}'$. Γ is called a *monotonic operator* if $\mathfrak{M} \leqslant \mathfrak{M}' \Rightarrow \Gamma(\mathfrak{M}) \leqslant \Gamma(\mathfrak{M}')$.

FIXED-POINT THEOREM. *For any monotonic operator* Γ *and any* $\mathfrak{M} \leqslant \Gamma(\mathfrak{M})$ *there is a least* $\mathfrak{M}^*$ *with* $\mathfrak{M} \leqslant \mathfrak{M}^*$ *and* $\Gamma(\mathfrak{M}^*) = \mathfrak{M}^*$.

Proof. By the usual inductive fixed-point argument. We here treat the $\tilde{R}$ as partial functions. Given $\mathfrak{M} = (\mathfrak{M}_0, \tilde{R})$ define $\tilde{R}^{(\alpha)}$ for ordinals α by $\tilde{R}^{(0)} = \tilde{R}$, $\tilde{R}^{(\alpha+1)} = \Gamma(\tilde{R}^{(\alpha)})$ and $\tilde{R}^{(\lambda)} = \bigcup_{\alpha < \lambda} \tilde{R}^{(\alpha)}$ for limit λ. It is proved by induction on α that $\tilde{R}^{(\alpha)} \leqslant \tilde{R}^{(\alpha+1)}$. This holds for $\alpha = 0$ by hypothesis; if true for α it is true for $\alpha + 1$ by monotonicity. Finally, $\tilde{R}^{(\lambda+1)} = \Gamma(\bigcup_{\alpha < \lambda} \tilde{R}^{(\alpha)}) \geqslant \bigcup_{\alpha < \lambda} \Gamma(\tilde{R}^{(\alpha)}) = \bigcup_{\alpha < \lambda} \tilde{R}^{(\alpha)} = \tilde{R}^{(\lambda)}$, so we have passage to the limits. It follows that $\alpha < \beta \Rightarrow \tilde{R}^{(\alpha)} \leqslant \tilde{R}^{(\beta)}$, hence each $\tilde{R}^{(\alpha)}$ is indeed a partial function. Finally, there exists a least v with $\tilde{R}^{(v)} = \tilde{R}^{(v+1)} = \Gamma(\tilde{R}^{(v)})$. Take this to be $\tilde{R}^*$. Suppose $\tilde{R} \leqslant \tilde{R}' = \Gamma(\tilde{R}')$ then it is proved by induction on α that $\tilde{R}^{(\alpha)} \leqslant \tilde{R}'$; hence $\tilde{R}^* \leqslant \tilde{R}'$, i.e. $\tilde{R}^*$ is the least fixed-point of Γ extending $\tilde{R}$.

The hypothesis of this theorem is of course met if we start with $\mathfrak{M} = (\mathfrak{M}_0, \tilde{U})$ where $\tilde{U}$ is the completely undefined function.

Whatever the plausibility of the role of partial predicates in connection with the paradoxes (which is to be examined below) they appear naturally in other contexts. For example, let $M = \omega$ and identify t, f with $1, 0$ respectively. In this case, partial k-ary predicates are partial functions from ω^k into $\{0, 1\}$. They arise naturally in recursion theory, where each partial recursive function into $\{t, f\}$, with index e say, determines a *partial recursive predicate* $(R, \tilde{R})$ by:

$$(x_1, \ldots, x_k) \in R \Leftrightarrow \{e\}(x_1, \ldots, x_k) \simeq t,$$
$$(x_1, \ldots, x_k) \in \bar{R} \Leftrightarrow \{e\}(x_1, \ldots, x_k) \simeq f,$$

or simply: $\tilde{R}(x_1, \ldots, x_k) \simeq \{e\}(x_1, \ldots, x_k)$. Of course, every partial function is extendible to a total function, say by taking $F_e(x_1, \ldots, x_k) = t$, if $\{e\}(x_1, \ldots, x_k) \simeq t$, otherwise f, but in general there is no such recursive extension. Thus u is to be read here as *undefined* relative to the specified computation procedures, and not as something inherently undefinable.

A related interpretation of partial predicates $\tilde{R}$ is as: what is *known* by a given stage σ in a computation process for a $\{t, f\}$ valued function. If by stage σ we have evaluated $\{e\}(x_1, \ldots, x_k)$ and found $\{e\}(x_1, \ldots, x_k) = t$ then $(x_1, \ldots, x_k)$ is known to be in R, while if $\{e\}(x_1, \ldots, x_n) = f$ then $(x_1, \ldots, x_k)$ is known definitely not to be in R, i.e. $(x_1, \ldots, x_k) \in \bar{R}$. But if neither is yet known, we ascribe the value u to $\tilde{R}$, with the meaning *unknown thus far* (at stage σ). This interpretation gives natural significance to the relation $\tilde{R} \leqslant \tilde{R}'$, which holds when $\tilde{R}'$ corresponds to what is known at a later stage σ' in the computational process.

More generally, consider an *investigation* by specified means to determine which elements of a set M have a certain property. This investigation is assumed to proceed in stages. The state of knowledge at any given stage is represented by a partial predicate $\tilde{R}$ on M, and the predicate $\tilde{R}'$ for what is known at a later stage is an extension of $\tilde{R}$. An investigation is said to be *systematic* if we have a prescribed procedure Γ for moving from any given stage to a succeeding stage. It is reasonable to prescribe that Γ is a monotone operator. Suppose we start the investigation with certain information $\tilde{R}$ handed to us, and which will not be altered by Γ. Then the least Γ-fixed point $\tilde{R}^*$ extending $\tilde{R}$ represents *all possible information that may be garnered by the given means of investigation* Γ. Of course, $\tilde{R}^*$ need not be total (unless Γ is the kind of investigation which leaves no stone unturned).

8. *Three-valued partial truth operations and semantics.* Let I be an index set; an *I-ary 3-valued propositional operation* F is a map $F: \{t, f, u\}^I \rightarrow \{t, f, u\}$. We write $F(\langle p_i \rangle_{i \in I})$ in general and $F(p)$ or $F(p, q)$ when F is unary, resp. binary (with $p, q, p_i \in \{t, f, u\}$). F is said to be *monotonic* if whenever $p_i \leqslant q_i$ for each $i \in I$ then $F(\langle p_i \rangle_{i \in I}) \leqslant F(\langle q_i \rangle_{i \in I})$.

Various extensions of the familiar 2-valued operations to 3-values have been considered. We recall those proposed by Łukasiewicz (cf. papers 1–3 in McCall 1967) and Kleene 1952, §64. These agree for negation ($\neg$), conjunction ($\wedge$), and disjunction ($\vee$), but not for the conditional and biconditional. We symbolize Łukasiewicz's operations for the latter by $\supset$ and $\equiv$, and Kleene's by $\rightarrow$ and $\leftrightarrow$, resp. The tables in Table (A) tell how these operations are computed (reading down for p arguments and across for q arguments).

	$\neg p$
t	f
f	t
u	u

$p \wedge q$	t	f	u
t	t	f	u
f	f	f	f
u	u	f	u

$p \vee q$	t	f	u
t	t	t	t
f	t	f	u
u	t	u	u

$(p \rightarrow q)$	t	f	u
t	t	f	u
f	t	t	t
u	t	u	u

$(p \leftrightarrow q)$	t	f	u
t	t	f	u
f	f	t	u
u	u	u	u

$(p \supset q)$	t	f	u
t	t	f	u
f	t	t	t
u	t	u	t

$(p \equiv q)$	t	f	u
t	t	f	u
f	f	t	u
u	u	u	t

(A)

Note that the tables for $(p \rightarrow q)$ and $(p \supset q)$ differ only in the values $(u \rightarrow u) = u$, $(u \supset u) = t$; similarly $(u \leftrightarrow u) = u$ while $(u \equiv u) = t$. We have further: $(p \wedge q) = \neg(\neg p \wedge \neg q)$, $(p \rightarrow q) = (\neg p \vee q)$, $(p \leftrightarrow q) = (p \rightarrow q) \wedge (q \rightarrow p)$, and $(p \equiv q) = (p \supset q) \wedge (q \supset p)$.

Kleene's operations are monotonic (or *regular*, in his terminology) while those of Łukasiewicz for $\supset$ and $\equiv$ are not. Kleene also introduced *weak* extensions of the 2-valued operations, obtained simply by assigning u as value if any of the arguments is u. All such are trivially monotonic. The above operations are called *strong* by Kleene; only these will be considered here.

Kleene's operations are the appropriate ones to consider for the recursion-theoretic (or more general investigative) interpretations of partial predicates discussed in the preceding section. As emphasized by Kleene (and subsequently by others), u is not to be thought of in this respect as a definite truth-value on a par with t, f (contrary to Łukasiewicz's approach), but rather as a lack of such. Each of the operations with the tables above can be composed with partial predicates $\tilde{R}, \tilde{S}$ considered as operations on M^k to $\{t, f, u\}$. We use the same symbols for these compositions, e.g. $\neg \tilde{R}$, $\tilde{R} \vee \tilde{S}$, $\tilde{R} \wedge \tilde{S}$, etc. It is easily seen that if $\tilde{R}, \tilde{S}$ are partial recursive then so are their combinations by any of Kleene's (weak or) strong propositional operations. (For this, it is best to think of the computation procedures for $\tilde{R}$ and $\tilde{S}$ as operating in *parallel* so as to permit an answer to be provided even when one of these is undefined. The weak operations are appropriate for combinations of predicates to be computed *sequentially*.) On the other hand, we do *not* have closure of the partial recursive predicates under the operations $\supset$ and $\equiv$.

There is a direct extension of $\wedge$, $\vee$ to infinitary conjunctions and disjunctions defined by:

$$\bigwedge_{i \in I} p_i = \begin{cases} t & \text{if each } p_i = t \\ f & \text{if some } p_i = f \\ u & \text{otherwise} \end{cases}$$

$\bigvee_{i \in I} p_i$ is defined dually or as $\neg \bigwedge_{i \in I} \neg p_i$. Thus both $\bigwedge_{i \in I}$ and $\bigvee_{i \in I}$ are monotonic I-ary operations.

We now pass to a first-order language L for partial structures. For simplicity, this is described just for $\mathfrak{M} = (\mathfrak{M}_0, \tilde{R})$ where $\tilde{R}$ is binary. The symbols of L are those of L_0 together with a single binary relation symbol R. We also consider an expanded language $L^{(M)}$ in which a constant symbol $\bar{m}$ is adjoined for each $m \in M$. The atomic formulas of L are those of L_0 together with all formulas of the form $R(\tau_1, \tau_2)$ where τ_1, τ_2 are terms of L_0. The formulas $\phi, \psi, \ldots$ of L are generated by closing under the following operations: $\neg \phi$, $\phi \wedge \psi$, and $\forall x \phi$. Then $\phi \vee \psi$, $\phi \rightarrow \psi$, $\phi \leftrightarrow \psi$, and $\exists x \phi$ are defined from these as usual. We write $\phi(x_1, \ldots, x_n)$ for a formula with at most $x_1, \ldots, x_n$ free.

For each sentence (closed formula) ϕ of $L^{(M)}$ we define $\|\phi\|_{\mathfrak{M}}$ recursively as follows (where the subscript '$\mathfrak{M}$' is omitted for simplicity):

(i) If ϕ is an atomic sentence of $L_0^{(M)}$ then

$$\|\phi\| = \begin{cases} t & \text{if } \mathfrak{M}_0 \models \phi \\ f & \text{otherwise.} \end{cases}$$

(ii) For $\phi = R(\tau_1, \tau_2)$ with τ_1, τ_2 closed terms of $L_0^{(M)}$,

$$\|\phi\| = \tilde{R}(\mathrm{Val}(\tau_1), \mathrm{Val}(\tau_2)).$$

(iii) $\|\neg \phi\| = \neg \|\phi\|$

(iv) $\|(\phi \wedge \psi)\| = (\|\phi\| \wedge \|\psi\|)$
(v) $\|\forall x\, \phi(x)\| = \bigwedge_{m \in M} \|\phi(\bar{m})\|.$

In (ii), $\mathrm{Val}(\tau)$ denotes the value in M of a closed $L_0^{(M)}$-term τ; this is completely determined by $\mathfrak{M}_0$. The following is immediate.

LEMMA 1. *For each sentence ϕ of $L_0^{(M)}$ we have $\|\phi\|_{\mathfrak{M}} = t$ or f, and $\|\phi\|_{\mathfrak{M}} = t \Leftrightarrow \mathfrak{M}_0 \vDash \phi$.*

We shall also consider extensions of the language L obtained by closing under the operation $\phi \equiv \psi$ as well as by just closing under the operation $\phi \supset \psi$. The resulting languages are denoted $L(\supset)$, $L(\equiv)$ resp., and when all constants $\bar{m}(m \in M)$ are included, by $L^{(M)}(\supset)$, $L^{(M)}(\equiv)$ resp. $L(\equiv)$ may be treated as a sublanguage of $L(\supset)$ (and similarly for $L^{(M)}(\equiv)$). The semantics for these languages is obtained by extending (i)–(v) in the obvious way:

(vi) $\|\phi \supset \psi\| = (\|\phi\| \supset \|\psi\|)$
(vii) $\|\phi \equiv \psi\| = (\|\phi\| \equiv \|\psi\|).$

The following is immediate from the table for $\equiv$.

LEMMA 2. *For ϕ, ψ sentences of $L^{(M)}(\supset)$, and any $\mathfrak{M}$*

$$\|\phi \equiv \psi\|_{\mathfrak{M}} = t \Leftrightarrow \|\phi\|_{\mathfrak{M}} = \|\psi\|_{\mathfrak{M}}.$$

LEMMA 3. *L-semantics is monotonic, i.e. for each sentence ϕ of $L^{(M)}$,*

$$\mathfrak{M} \leqslant \mathfrak{M}' \Rightarrow \|\phi\|_{\mathfrak{M}} \leqslant \|\phi\|_{\mathfrak{M}'}.$$

Proof. By a straightforward induction on ϕ, using the monotonicity of the operations $\neg$, $\vee$ and $\bigwedge_{m \in M}$.

NB. Monotonicity does *not* hold for ϕ in $L^{(M)}(\supset)$ or even ϕ in $L^{(M)}(\equiv)$. For example, let $l, m \in M$, $l \neq m$. Take $\theta = R(\bar{l}, \bar{l})$, $\psi = R(\bar{m}, \bar{m}), \phi = \|\theta \equiv \psi\|$ and choose $\tilde{R} \leqslant \tilde{R}'$ with $\|\theta\|_{\tilde{R}} = \|\psi\|_{\tilde{R}} = u$ and $\|\theta\|_{\tilde{R}'} = t$, $\|\psi\|_{\tilde{R}'} = f$. Then $\|\phi\|_{\tilde{R}} = t$ while $\|\phi\|_{\tilde{R}'} = f$.

The strong Kleene operators and the infinitary $\bigwedge_{i \in I}$, $\bigvee_{i \in I}$ are by no means the only natural ones yielding a monotonic semantics for partial structures. A wide class of such are provided by *generalized quantifiers* as handled in *generalized recursion theory* (cf., e.g., Kechris/Moschovakis 1977, pp. 694–696). One defines a *quantifier Q on M* to be any collection of subsets of M satisfying

$$X \subseteq Y \subseteq M \,\&\, X \in Q \Rightarrow Y \in Q.$$

The *dual quantifier* $\check{Q}$ is defined by $\check{Q} = \{X \subseteq M : (M - X) \notin Q\}$, so $X \subseteq Y$ and $X \in \check{Q}$ implies $Y \in \check{Q}$. Then $\check{\check{Q}} = Q$.

For any quantifier Q we introduced a corresponding formal operator Qx; the formulas ϕ of $L(Q)$ are generated by closing under the additional operation $Qx\phi$. Again, $L^{(M)}(Q)$ is the same, with a constant $\bar{m}$ for each $m \in M$. The semantics is extended to closed $Qx\phi(x)$ in $L^{(M)}(Q)$ by

(viii) $\quad \|Qx\phi(x)\| = \begin{cases} t & \text{if } \{m \in M : \|\phi(\bar{m})\| = t\} \in Q \\ f & \text{if } \{m \in M : \|\phi(\bar{m})\| = f\} \in \check{Q} \\ u & \text{otherwise.} \end{cases}$

It is readily seen that $L(Q)$ *semantics is monotonic*, i.e. Lemma 3 also holds for sentences in $L^{(M)}(Q)$.

Special quantifiers to consider are the following:

$$\forall = \{M\}, \quad \exists = \{X \subseteq M : X \neq \varnothing\},$$

$$\forall_A = \{X \subseteq M : A \subseteq X\}, \quad \exists_A = \{X \subseteq M : X \cap A \neq \varnothing\}$$

$$(A \text{ any subset of } M),$$

$$\exists_{\geqslant \kappa} = \{X \subseteq M : \text{card}(X) \geqslant \kappa\} \quad (\kappa \text{ any cardinal}).$$

Then $\check{\forall} = \exists$, and the semantics of $\|\forall x\phi(x)\|$ according to (viii) is the same as by (v). Further $\check{\forall}_A = \exists_A$ and

$$\|\forall_A x\phi(x)\| = \begin{cases} t & \text{if } A \subseteq \{m \in M : \|\phi(\bar{m})\| = t\} \\ f & \text{if } A \cap \{m \in M : \|\phi(\bar{m})\| = f\} \neq \varnothing \\ u & \text{otherwise.} \end{cases}$$

Finally

$$\|\exists_{\geqslant \kappa} x\phi(x)\| = \begin{cases} t & \text{if } \text{card}\{m \in M : \|\phi(\bar{m})\| = t\} \geqslant \kappa \\ f & \text{if } \text{card}[M - \{m \in M : \|\phi(\bar{m})\| = f\}] < \kappa \\ u & \text{otherwise.} \end{cases}$$

Note that the set A is explicitly definable in $L(\forall_A)$ or equivalently $L(\exists_A)$ by the formula $\chi_A(x) = \exists y_A(x = y)$. This yields $\|\chi_A(\bar{m})\| = t$ for $m \in A$ and $\|\chi_A(\bar{m})\| = f$ for $m \notin A$.

It is also possible to consider *relativized quantifiers* Q_a which associate a quantifier in the above sense with each $a \in M$. Then we have a corresponding formal operation $Q_z x . \phi$ which only binds x

(distinct from z), and $\|Q_{\bar{a}}x.\phi(x)\|$ is defined as above for each assignment to z of $a \in M$. Again the semantics is monotonic. Finally we may obtain a monotonic semantics by extending the language by any combination of quantifiers and relativized quantifiers. We denote any such language by $L^+ = L(Q, \ldots)$. Note that Lemma 2 holds for $L^+(\supset)$.

9. *Three-valued models for type-free principles.* To formulate principles like (TA) and (CA) we need some statement-naming and/or abstraction devices. For simplicity, this is achieved here as follows. Assume that the language L_0 contains a constant symbol $\bar{O}$ (also written O), a binary operation symbol P, and two unary operation symbols P_1, P_2. We write (τ_1, τ_2) for $P(\tau_1, \tau_2)$. Assume further that the following formulas are provable in S_0 (of which $\mathfrak{M}_0$ is assumed to be a model):

   (i) $(x, y) \neq \bar{O}$
   (ii) $P_1(x, y) = x \wedge P_2(x, y) = y$.

Thus $(\cdot, \cdot)$ acts a *pairing operation* from M^2 into $M\text{-}\{0\}$, for which P_1, P_2 are the corresponding *projection operations*. The natural number structure may be represented by defining $x' = (x, \bar{O})$. Then P_1 also acts as the predecessor operation and we derive

   (iii) $x' \neq \bar{O}$
   (iv) $x' = y' \rightarrow x = y$.

from (i) and (ii). (If preferred, one can take $'$ to be an additional basic symbol satisfying the axioms (iii), (iv).) Any $\mathfrak{M}_0 = (M, \ldots)$ satisfying these axioms is infinite, and the natural numbers can be identified with the subset N of M generated from O by the $'$ operation. (Then N is definable in $L(\exists_N)$.) For $n \in N$ we write both $\bar{n}$ and n for the corresponding constant symbol in L_0.

   Tuples $(\tau_1, \ldots, \tau_k)$ are introduced recursively by: $(\tau_1) = \tau$ and $(\tau_1, \ldots, \tau_{k+1}) = ((\tau_1, \ldots, \tau_k), \tau_{k+1})$. There are corresponding projection operations P_i^k ($1 \leqslant i \leqslant k$) satisfying $P_i^k(x_1, \ldots, x_k) = x_i$ in S_0. Suppose ϕ is any formula of L, or even of any effectively specified extension language L^+ of the kind considered in §8. We then write $\ulcorner \phi \urcorner$ for the Gödel-number of ϕ or its corresponding numeral in L_0. If ϕ has free variables among $x_1, \ldots, x_k, y_1, \ldots, y_n$ then $(\ulcorner \phi \urcorner, y_1, \ldots, y_n)$ serves as an operation in L_0 which "abstracts"

$x_1, \ldots, x_k$, treating the $y_1, \ldots, y_n$ as parameters. We thus define

$$\Delta_k \quad \phi[\hat{x}_1, \ldots, \hat{x}_k, y_1, \ldots, y_n] = (\ulcorner \phi \urcorner, y_1, \ldots, y_n)$$

In particular, for $k = 1$ we write

$$\Delta_1 \quad \{x \,|\, \phi(x, y_1, \ldots, y_n)\} = \phi[\hat{x}, y_1, \ldots, y_n]$$

but for $k = 0$ we write again

$$\Delta_0 \quad \phi[y_1, \ldots, y_n] = (\ulcorner \phi \urcorner, y_1, \ldots, y_n),$$

which is identified with $\ulcorner \phi \urcorner$ when $n = 0$. In Δ_k the x_is are considered bound and may be renamed by other bound variables. (To be more precise in each case, $\ulcorner \phi \urcorner$ is to be the Gödel-number of ϕ together with a specified pair of lists of variables $(x_1, \ldots, x_k)$, $(y_1, \ldots, y_n)$ of length $k \geqslant 0$, $n \geqslant 0$, which together contain all the free variables of ϕ.)

The purpose of the denotational devices Δ_k is in connection with a common generalization of the truth-axioms and comprehension axioms (TA) and (CA). This is achieved by introducing for each k a $(k + 1)$-placed predicate symbol T_k where $T_k(x_1, \ldots, x_k, z)$ is read: $(x_1, \ldots, x_k)$ *satisfies* z. The appropriate axiom scheme is

$$(\mathrm{T}_k\mathrm{A}) \quad T_k(x_1, \ldots, x_k, \phi[\hat{u}_1, \ldots, \hat{u}_k, y_1, \ldots, y_n])$$
$$\leftrightarrow \phi(x_1, \ldots, x_k, y_1, \ldots, y_n),$$

for each formula ϕ with the indicated free variables. For $k = 0$ this reduces to

$$(\mathrm{T}_0\mathrm{A}) \quad T_0(\phi[y_1, \ldots, y_n]) \leftrightarrow \phi(y_1, \ldots, y_n),$$

and in particular for $n = 0$ to

$$T_0(\ulcorner \phi \urcorner) \leftrightarrow \phi.$$

We may thus identify T_0 with the *truth-predicate* T. For $k = 1$ the scheme appears as

$$(\mathrm{T}_1\mathrm{A}) \quad T_1(x, \{u \,|\, \phi(u, y_1, \ldots, y_n)\}) \leftrightarrow \phi(x, y_1, \ldots, y_n).$$

We may thus identify T_1 with the *membership relation* E or $\in$.

In 3-valued logic, there is an alternative formulation to consider of the axioms $(\mathrm{T}_k\mathrm{A})$, namely

$$(\mathrm{T}_k\mathrm{A})_\equiv \quad T_k(x_1, \ldots, x_k, \phi[\hat{u}_1, \ldots, \hat{u}_k, y_1, \ldots, y_n])$$
$$\equiv \phi(x_1, \ldots, x_k, y_1, \ldots, y_n).$$

We shall now show how to define a partial model $\mathfrak{M}^*$ for these axioms *provided* that the scheme is restricted to ϕ built up by monotonic operators.

FIXED-MODEL THEOREM. *Let L^+ be L or any extension $L(Q, \ldots)$ which has monotonic semantics, containing one or more of the predicate symbols T_k ($k \geqslant O$). Then for any model $\mathfrak{M}_0$ of S_0 we can find a (least) partial structure $\mathfrak{M}^* = (\mathfrak{M}_0, \ldots, \tilde{T}_k, \ldots)$ such that for each T_k in L^+ and formula $\phi(x_1, \ldots, x_k, y_1, \ldots, y_n)$ of L^+ we have:*

$$\| T_k(\bar{m}_1, \ldots, \bar{m}_k, \phi[\hat{u}_1, \ldots, \hat{u}_k, \bar{m}_{k+1}, \ldots, \bar{m}_{k+n}]) \|_{\mathfrak{M}^*}$$

$$= \| \phi(\bar{m}_1, \ldots, \bar{m}_k, \bar{m}_{k+1}, \ldots, \bar{m}_{k+n}) \|_{\mathfrak{M}^*}.$$

Proof. For simplicity we just consider the binary relation symbol T_1 for which we write E, and look at interpretations $\mathfrak{M} = (\mathfrak{M}_0, \tilde{E})$ of this language. Let Form be the subset of M consisting of all $(\ulcorner\phi\urcorner, m_1, \ldots, m_n)$ where $\phi = \phi(x, y_1, \ldots, y_n)$ is a formula of L^+ with at most $x, y_1, \ldots, y_n$ free. Then define an operator Γ on such by:

$$\Gamma(\mathfrak{M}) = (\mathfrak{M}_0, \Gamma(\tilde{E}))$$

where

$$\Gamma(\tilde{E})(m, l) = \begin{cases} \tilde{E}(m, l) & \text{for all } l \notin \text{Form} \\ \| \phi(\bar{m}, \bar{m}_1, \ldots, \bar{m}_n) \|_{\mathfrak{M}} & \text{for } l = (\ulcorner\phi\urcorner, m_1, \ldots, m_n), \\ & \qquad l \in \text{Form}. \end{cases}$$

Γ is monotonic. For if $\mathfrak{M} = (\mathfrak{M}_0, \tilde{E}) \leqslant \mathfrak{M}' = (\mathfrak{M}_0, \tilde{E}')$ and m, $l \in M$ then for $l \notin$ Form we have $\tilde{E}(m, l) \leqslant \tilde{E}'(m, l)$ while for $l = (\ulcorner\phi\urcorner, m_1, \ldots, m_n)$ we have $\| \phi(\bar{m}, \bar{m}_1, \ldots, \bar{m}_n) \|_{\mathfrak{M}} \leqslant$ $\| \phi(\bar{m}, \bar{m}_1, \ldots, \bar{m}_n) \|_{\mathfrak{M}'}$, thus $\Gamma(\tilde{E}) \leqslant \Gamma(\tilde{E}')$. Now the conclusion follows from the fixed-point theorem of §7, starting with $\mathfrak{M} = (\mathfrak{M}_0, \tilde{U})$ where $\tilde{U}$ is completely undefined.[14] The same argument works with any number of basic symbols T_k.

---

[14] Observe that when starting with $\tilde{U}$ for $\tilde{E}$ we have $\tilde{E}^{(\alpha)}(m, l) = u$ for all m and $l \notin$ Form. So in obtaining the least fixed point we may as well define $\Gamma(\tilde{E})$ $(m, (\ulcorner\phi\urcorner, m_1, \ldots, m_n)) = \| \phi(\bar{m}, \bar{m}_1, \ldots, \bar{m}_n) \|_{(\mathfrak{M}_0, \tilde{E})}$, with $\Gamma(\tilde{E})(m, l) = u$ otherwise. Translated into the language of partial predicates $\tilde{E} = (E, \check{E})$, $\Gamma(\tilde{E}) = (E', \check{E}')$ we have for $n = 0$: $(m, \ulcorner\phi\urcorner)$ is in $E' \Leftrightarrow \phi(\bar{m})$ is true in $(\mathfrak{M}_0, (E, \check{E}))$ and $(m, \ulcorner\phi\urcorner)$ is in $\check{E} \Leftrightarrow \phi(\bar{m})$ is false in $(\mathfrak{M}_0, (E, \check{E}))$. Thus at the fixed point $\mathfrak{M}^*$, $E(\bar{m}, \ulcorner\phi\urcorner)$ (or $\bar{m} \in \{x | \phi(x)\}$) is true (false) in $\mathfrak{M}^*$ iff $\phi(\bar{m})$ is true (false) in $\mathfrak{M}^*$.

As in §7 we can formulate a more general statement, obtaining a fixed-point $\mathfrak{M}^*$ for the Γ constructed in the proof extending any given $\mathfrak{M}$ which happens to satisfy $\mathfrak{M} \leqslant \Gamma(\mathfrak{M})$.

Actually one can obtain a much more general Fixed-Model Theorem (Aczel/Feferman 1980). Taking any basic symbols R_k, assume given any sequence of $L^{+(M)}$ sentences $\theta_{k,m_1,\ldots,m_k}$. Then we can construct $\mathfrak{M}^*$ satisfying

$$\|R_k(\bar{m}_1, \ldots, \bar{m}_k)\|_{\mathfrak{M}^*} = \|\theta_{k,m_1,\ldots,m_k}\|_{\mathfrak{M}^*}.$$

The theorem stated is the special case obtained by taking $R_{k+1} = T_k$ and $\theta_{k+1,m_1,\ldots,m_k,l} = \phi(\bar{m}_1,\ldots,\bar{m}_k)$ when $l = \phi[\hat{u}_1,\ldots,\hat{u}_k]$.

If we specialize the Fixed-Model Theorem to L with just the predicate $T = T_0$ applied to closed ϕ of L we obtain a least $\mathfrak{M}^*$ satisfying

$$\|T(\ulcorner\phi\urcorner)\|_{\mathfrak{M}^*} = \|\phi\|_{\mathfrak{M}^*}.$$

Recasting this as a result about models of the form $(\mathfrak{M}, \tilde{T})$ where $\tilde{T} = (T, \bar{T})$ is a disjoint pair, one obtains the model-theoretic content of Kripke 1975.[15] The proof is basically the same.[16] Actually, such construction for type-free theories of predication and classes were given much earlier by Fitch and Gilmore. The history will be picked up in the following sections and particularly in §14.

Specializing the Fixed-Model Theorem to L with just the predicate $E = T_1$, also written $\in$, we obtain a least $\mathfrak{M}^*$ such that

$$\|\forall y_1, \ldots, \forall y_n \exists a \forall x[x \in a \equiv \phi(x, y_1, \ldots, y_n)]\|_{\mathfrak{M}^*} = t$$

for each $\phi(x, y_1, \ldots, y_n)$ in L. This is a result due to Brady 1971 for consistency of a form of (CA) in Łukasiewicz 3-valued logic.[17] The proof is basically the same.

---

[15] See fn. 14 for this kind of recasting. It is also mentioned in Kripke 1975, p. 706, that his result can be extended to languages with generalized quantifiers.

[16] The inductive method is not the only way one can establish existence of fixed points. It was shown in Martin/Woodruff 1975 (independently of Kripke's work), that this can be proved by Zorn's lemma; that was also observed by Kripke. The difference is that the inductive method establishes the existence of *minimal* fixed-points while Zorn's lemma yields *maximal* ones.

[17] This improved Skolem 1960; cf. the notes in §14 below. It is stated in Brady 1971 that $\mathfrak{M}^*$ is also a model for the axiom of extensionality. However, that is so only in the weak sense that $\|\forall x(x \in m_1 \equiv x \in m_2)\|_{\mathfrak{M}^*} = t \Rightarrow \|\forall y(m_1 \in y \equiv m_2 \in y)\|_{\mathfrak{M}^*} = t.$

To conclude this section we give a *counter-example* to $\exists a \forall x[x \in a \equiv \phi(x)]$ in 3-valued models when ϕ is in $L(\equiv)$. This is based on Table (B).

p	$\neg p \wedge \neg (p \equiv \neg p)$	$p \equiv \neg p \wedge \neg (p \equiv \neg p)$
t	f	f
f	t	f
u	f	u

(B)

Then $\exists a \forall x[x \in a \equiv \neg (x \in x) \wedge \neg (x \in x \equiv \neg (x \in x))]$ cannot receive the value t in any structure $\mathfrak{M} = (\mathfrak{M}_0, \bar{E})$. For if it did, taking $p = \|a \in a\|$ gives a contradiction.

10. *Type-free formal systems with Łukasiewicz and Kleene logics.* We now turn to the formulation of type-free systems for which the semantical constructions of §§8–9 provide a model.

Consider first the language $L(\supset)$ for Łukasiewicz predicate logic with basic operators, $\neg$, $\wedge$, $\supset$, and $\forall$. A formula $\phi(x_1, \ldots, x_k)$ is said to be *Ł-valid* if for every partial structure $\mathfrak{M}$ with domain M and any $m_1, \ldots, m_k \in M$ we have $\|\phi(\bar{m}_1, \ldots, \bar{m}_k)\|_{\mathfrak{M}} = t$. A complete recursive Hilbert-style axiomatization of the Ł-valid formulas may be found in Rosser/Turquette 1952 (this will not be repeated here). It follows from the work of §9 that the scheme

$$(CA)_{\equiv} \quad \forall y_1, \ldots, \forall y_n \exists a \forall x[x \in a \equiv \phi(x, y_1, \ldots, y_n)\}$$

is Ł-consistent *provided ϕ is restricted to the language L*, i.e. ϕ only involves $\neg$, $\vee$, $\forall$ in its build-up. This is the consistency result of Brady 1971. We have similar results for the other predicates T_k, e.g. consistency of the scheme

$$(TA)_{\equiv} \quad T(\ulcorner \phi \urcorner) \equiv \phi$$

for ϕ in L. These restrictions are essential, since we saw at the end of §9 that $(CA)_{\equiv}$ is already inconsistent in the expanded language $L(\equiv)$. Assuming the means to construct self-referential statements, $(TA)_{\equiv}$ also leads to an inconsistency in $L(\equiv)$ by the same argument.[18] On the other hand, Russell's paradox itself is avoided in

---

[18] The inconsistency can be demonstrated more simply in $L(\supset)$, using $\exists a(x \in a \equiv [x \in x \supset \neg (x \in x)])$ since $((p \supset \neg p) \supset p$ is Ł valid. This applies similarly to $(TA)_{\equiv}$ in $L(\supset)$.

the Ł-system with the restricted $(CA)_=$, even though we have $\exists a \forall x[x \in a \equiv \neg(x \in x)]$. This is by the circumstance that $p \equiv \neg p$ has the value t when p has the value u.

We next turn to K-logic which is obtained simply by restricting Ł-logic to the language L. Thus a formula is said to be K-*valid* if it is in L and is Ł-valid. It follows from the complete recursive axiomatization of the Ł-valid formulas that the set of K-valid formulas is recursively enumerable. However, its explicit axiomatization is another matter. The reason is that the main rule of Ł-propositional logic is *modus ponens*, in the form ϕ, $(\phi \supset \psi)/\psi$. Since $\supset$ is not available in K-logic, we cannot use it there for the rule of modus ponens. If we take the connective $(\phi \to \psi)$ instead (where $(p \to q) = \neg(p \wedge \neg q) = (\neg p \vee q)$) we *do* have closure under the rule ϕ, $(\phi \to \psi)/\psi$ in the K-valid formulas, but we then run into trouble elsewhere; for example, the expected axioms $(\phi \to \phi)$, $\forall x \phi(x) \to \phi(\tau)$, etc. are not K-valid.

An axiomatization of K-logic was given in Wang 1961 by use of an auxiliary symbol (here denoted) $\vdash$, which is *not iterated*. Given formulas ϕ, ψ in L, we say that $\phi \vdash \psi$ is K-*valid* if for every partial structure $\mathfrak{M}$ and assignment to the free variables of ϕ, ψ in M we have $\|\phi\| = t \Rightarrow \|\psi\| = t$. Wang gave a simple natural system of axioms and rules of inference for combinations $(\phi \vdash \psi)$ which is complete for this extended notion of validity. He also axiomatized the K^*-*valid* combinations $\phi \vdash \psi$, which are defined to be those K-valid $\phi \vdash \psi$ such that for every $\mathfrak{M}$ and assignment to the free variables, also $\|\psi\| = f \Rightarrow \|\phi\| = f$.

Wang's system has the character of a Gentzen sequential calculus. More recently, Scott 1975 gave a complete Gentzen-style system for *sequents* $\phi_1, \ldots, \phi \vdash \psi_1, \ldots, \psi_m$ whose validity is defined like that of K^*-validity, namely: for each $\mathfrak{M}$ and interpretation in M of the variables, (i) $\|\phi_1\| = \ldots = \|\phi_l\| = t \Rightarrow$ some $\|\psi_j\| = f$ and (ii) $\|\psi_1\| = \ldots = \|\psi_m\| = f \Rightarrow$ some $\|\phi_i\| = f$.

The K-valid formulas are just those ϕ with $\vdash \phi$ derivable in Wang's or Scott's system. Thus one obtains a very satisfactory axiomatization of K-logic in this way. The question then is how type-free principles corresponding to (TA) and (CA) are to be formulated in such K-logics. We cannot use Kleene's $\leftrightarrow$ of §8 as the principal connective, since $p \leftrightarrow \neg p$ is never t. Scott's solution is to introduce the symbol $\vdash\!\dashv$, where $(\phi \vdash\!\dashv \psi)$ abbreviates $(\phi \vdash \psi)$ and $(\psi \vdash\!\dashv \phi)$. Of course we cannot literally form the conjunction of

($\phi \vdash \psi$) and ($\psi \vdash \phi$), but we could say that a system based on "axioms" of the form $\phi \vdash\!\dashv \psi$ is consistent if there is a model which satisfies both $\phi \vdash \psi$ and $\psi \vdash \phi$ for each assignment to the free variables. In this sense the scheme (for each ϕ in L)

$(CA)_{\vdash\!\dashv} \quad x \in \{u \mid \phi(u, y_1, \ldots, y_n)\} \vdash\!\dashv \phi(x, y_1, \ldots, y_n)$

is consistent, as is the schema

$(TA)_{\vdash\!\dashv} \quad T(\ulcorner\phi\urcorner) \vdash\!\dashv \phi$

for each ϕ in L. This is a direct consequence of the fixed-model theorem and the fact that $\|\phi \equiv \psi\| = t \Leftrightarrow \|\phi\| = \|\psi\|$. It follows by the same result that we have consistency of the schemata $(T_k A)_{\vdash\!\dashv}$ in this sense for each k. Note that the use of abstracts is essential to state these consistency results, for there is no direct sense given in the formalism to such combinations as $\exists a \forall x[x \in a \vdash\!\dashv \phi(x)]$.

Discussion. Both the type-free systems in Ł-logic and K-logic that we have just described are superficially attractive. However, to my mind they are unsatisfactory in a number of respects which I shall now detail.

    (i)   The *main defect for the scheme* $(CA)_\equiv$ as restricted above is that the basic connectives $\supset$, $\equiv$ of $L(\supset)$ may not appear in the formula to the right of the $\equiv$ sign.

    (ii)   Similarly, the *main defect for the scheme* $(CA)_{\vdash\!\dashv}$ is that the "operator" $\vdash\!\dashv$ may not be iterated.

    (iii)   The same criticism applies *mutatis mutandis* to the other schemes $(T_k A)_\equiv$ and $(T_k A)_{\vdash\!\dashv}$.

    (iv)   In each logic there are laws which we might expect to hold that don't. Of course ($\phi \vee \neg\phi$) does not hold in either logic, but also $\neg(\phi \wedge \neg\phi)$ is not derivable. We have ($\phi \supset \phi$) but not $\phi \wedge (\phi \supset \psi) \supset \psi$ in Ł-logic; nor do we derive ($\phi \supset \neg\phi$) $\supset \neg\phi$. On the other hand we don't have ($\phi \rightarrow \phi$) in K-logic. In the system of Wang 1961 (or Scott 1975) for K-logic, we don't have implication introduction (i.e. the Deduction Theorem) for the $\rightarrow$ operator. Multiplying such examples, I conclude that *nothing like sustained ordinary reasoning can be carried on in either logic*.

    (v)   It was stressed in the analyses of the Liar and Russell's Paradox in (§§3 and 5) that the contradiction in each case is carried out within intuitionistic logic. The conclusion was drawn that a solution to the paradoxes ought to accommodate itself equally well to a constructive as well as a classical setting. But in Ł-logic non-constructive statements like $(\neg\neg\phi \supset \phi)$ are valid while in K-logic there is nothing like the constructive use of implication ($\phi \to \psi$ is not constructively equivalent to $\neg\phi \lor \psi$). Finally, the dual treatment of $\land, \lor$ and $\forall, \exists$ is completely non-constructive.

Discussion, continued. The objections so far have been based on formal, logical considerations. One may ask to what extent the proposed 3-valued solutions which have been described are satisfactory from a philosophical point of view. Some of the considerations here are, briefly, as follows.

(vi) If the basic idea is that the sentences appearing in the paradoxes are meaningless, then Ł-logic is clearly not the appropriate one. For this gives the truth-value t to compounds of entirely meaningless statements, e.g. $p \supset \neg p$ when p has the value u. Łukasiewicz' own interpretation was of 'u' as *contingent*, but this has been much disputed (cf., e.g., Prior 1967). Indeed, my impression is that no really satisfactory informal interpretation of Ł-logic has ever been given.

(vii) On the other hand Kleene's logic does seem to correspond more closely to the interpretation of u as *meaningless*. However, some argue that only his *weak connectives* are appropriate for this interpretation, since the result of combining a meaningless statement with meaningful ones should still be regarded as meaningless. The *strong connectives* are appropriate instead for the interpretation in terms of what is known in the process of an investigation, with u interpreted as *unknown*.

(viii) For the latter point of view it seems that one should ascribe a definite truth-value t or f to each statement, and that u only reflects incompleteness of our knowledge. But in that case we ought to accept statements such as $(\phi \to \phi)$ and $(\phi \lor \neg\phi)$ for each ϕ. It seems that considerations like this have led van Fraassen 1968 to argue for looking at partial structures within a logical framework which he calls *supervaluations*. A statement ϕ is said to be true in van Fraassen's sense in $\mathfrak{M} = (\mathfrak{M}_0, \bar{R})$ if ϕ is true (in the usual sense) in every *total* extension $\mathfrak{M}' = (\mathfrak{M}_0, R')$ of $\mathfrak{M}$. In this picture, not all statements $R(\bar{m})$ are true or false, but all classically valid statements are automatically true.

(ix) Finally, there have been objections to "truth-gap" theories on the grounds that they too are subject to paradoxes, e.g. the

Extended Liar; cf., e.g., Burge 1979. Indeed, at an informal level this criticism is valid. Namely one looks again at a ϕ which is supposed to be the same as $\neg T(\ulcorner \phi \urcorner)$. According to the truth-gap argument, ϕ is neither true nor false. But since ϕ says of itself it is not true, it is true after all. So there is no gap, and the usual Liar paradox is then produced as before.

If we analyze the preceding argument in terms of the model-theoretic construction of $\mathfrak{M}^*$ in §9, the paradox disappears. In $\mathfrak{M}^*$ we have ϕ with $\| \phi \equiv T(\ulcorner \phi \urcorner) \| = t$ and by self-referential construction $\| \phi \equiv \neg T(\ulcorner \phi \urcorner) \| = t$. It follows that $\| \phi \| \neq t, f$. Thus ϕ is not true in $\mathfrak{M}^*$, i.e. $\| \phi \| \neq t$, so $\| T(\ulcorner \phi \urcorner) \| \neq t$. But that does not tell us that $\neg T(\ulcorner \phi \urcorner)$ is true in $\mathfrak{M}^*$. The puzzle is sorted out by the inequivalence between 'ϕ is not true' and '$\neg T(\ulcorner \phi \urcorner)$ is true'. Still, consideration of the Extended Liar does leave one with a further bit of malaise about truth-gap approaches, since the formal model-theoretic constructions don't match up with informal usage.

11. *A type-free formal system in an extension of the classical predicate calculus.* In this section we will describe results concerning a new type-free system $S(\equiv)$ presented in Aczel/Feferman 1980. $S(\equiv)$ overcomes two of the defects of 3-valued systems brought out in the preceding section, namely: (i) it is based on type-free principles like $(CA)_\equiv$ where now *any* formula of $L(\equiv)$ can stand to the right of the $\equiv$ sign, and (ii) the logic is that of full classical predicate calculus (CPC) augmented by natural laws for $\equiv$. However $S(\equiv)$ is not fully satisfactory in other respects which will be brought out in the discussion at the end of the section and in §13.

We assume S_0 satisfies the conditions of §9, and that one or more of the predicate symbols T_k is adjoined to L_0 to provide the atomic symbols of L. We also follow the abbreviations for abstracts $\Delta_n, \Delta_1, \Delta_0$ of §9. The formulas of $L(\equiv)$ are built up using $\neg, \wedge, \equiv$, and $\forall$. Write $\phi \not\equiv \psi$ for $\neg(\phi \equiv \psi)$. The operators $\vee, \rightarrow, \leftrightarrow, \exists$ are defined classically as before. Let $t = (0 = 0), f = \neg t$ and for each ϕ,

$$D(\phi) = [\phi \equiv t \vee \phi \equiv f].$$

$D(\phi)$ is read: ϕ is *determinate*. The axioms for $\equiv$, denoted $Ax(\equiv)$ are as follows (over and above the axioms of CPC):

(1) $\equiv$ is an equivalence relation
(2) $\equiv$ is preserved by $\neg, \wedge, \equiv$, and $\forall$

(3)   (i) $(\phi \equiv t) \leftrightarrow \phi$ for ϕ atomic

      (ii) $(\phi \equiv f) \leftrightarrow \neg\phi$ for ϕ atomic in L_0

(4)   (i) $(\neg\phi) \equiv t \leftrightarrow \phi \equiv f$

      (ii) $(\neg\phi) \equiv f \leftrightarrow \phi \equiv t$

(5)   (i) $(\phi \wedge \psi) \equiv t \leftrightarrow \phi \equiv t \wedge \psi \equiv t$

      (ii) $(\phi \wedge \psi) \equiv f \leftrightarrow \phi \equiv f \vee \psi \equiv f$

(6)   (i) $(\forall x\phi(x)) \equiv t \leftrightarrow \forall x[\phi(x) \equiv t]$

      (ii) $(\forall x\phi(x)) \equiv f \leftrightarrow \exists x(\phi(x) \equiv f)$

(7)   (i) $(\phi \equiv \psi) \equiv t \leftrightarrow \phi \equiv \psi$

      (ii) $(\phi \equiv \psi) \equiv f \leftrightarrow D(\phi) \wedge D(\psi) \wedge \phi \not\equiv \psi.$

The following explains (1) and (2) in more detail. (1) consists of the schemata $(\phi \equiv \phi)$. $(\phi \equiv \psi) \to (\psi \equiv \phi)$, and $(\phi \equiv \psi) \wedge (\psi \equiv \theta) \to (\phi \equiv \theta)$. For (2), let O be one of the n-ary operations $\neg, \wedge, \equiv$ (so $n = 1$ or 2). The statement that $\equiv$ is preserved by O is:

(2a) $(\phi_1 \equiv \psi_1) \wedge \ldots \wedge (\phi_n \equiv \psi_n) \to O(\phi_1, \ldots, \phi_n)$
$$\equiv O(\psi_1, \ldots, \psi_n)$$

The statement that $\equiv$ is preserved by $\forall$ is given by

(2b) $\forall x[\phi(x) \equiv \psi(x)] \to [\forall x\phi(x) \equiv \forall x\psi(x)].$[19]

We shall also consider a (seemingly) slight variant $Ax'(\equiv)$ obtained by modifying (7) to (7)', where (7)'(ii) is the same as (7)(ii) while 7(i) is replaced by

(7)'(i) $(\phi \equiv \psi) \equiv t \leftrightarrow D(\phi) \wedge D(\psi) \wedge (\phi \equiv \psi).$

LEMMA. *The following are consequences of both* $Ax(\equiv)$ *and* $Ax'(\equiv)$.

   (i) $t \not\equiv f$

   (ii) $(\neg f) \equiv t$

   (iii) D *is closed under* $\neg, \wedge, \equiv,$ *and* $\forall$, *i.e.*

$$D(\phi) \to D(\neg\phi), D(\phi) \wedge D(\psi) \to D(\phi \wedge \psi) \wedge D(\phi \equiv \psi),$$

$$\forall x D(\phi(x)) \to D(\forall x\phi(x)) \quad \text{for any } \phi, \psi.$$

   (iv) $D(\phi)$ *for each* ϕ *of* L_0.

---

[19] The axioms for $\equiv$ given in Aczel/Feferman 1980 are a little different; the operators $\wedge, \forall$ are there treated in Kleene's weak sense, so that $D(\phi \wedge \psi) \leftrightarrow D(\phi) \wedge D(\psi)$ and $D(\forall x \phi(x)) \leftrightarrow \forall x D(\phi(x))$. Here $\wedge, \forall$ are treated in Kleene's strong sense. The handling of the systems is the same, otherwise.

(v) $(\phi \equiv t) \to \phi$ and $(\phi \equiv f) \to \neg \phi$, for each ϕ.

(vi) $D(\phi) \to [(\phi \equiv t) \leftrightarrow \phi] \wedge [(\phi \equiv f) \leftrightarrow \neg \phi]$, for each ϕ.

Proof. (i) follows from Axiom (3)(ii) taking $\phi = t$, using symmetry of $\equiv$. (ii)–(iv) are immediate. The statements in (v) are proved simultaneously by induction on ϕ. Then (vi) follows directly.

The axioms of $S(\equiv)$, respectively $S'(\equiv)$, are those of S_0 plus $Ax(\equiv)$, respectively $Ax'(\equiv)$, together with all formulas of the following form for T_k a symbol of L, and ϕ any formula of $L(\equiv)$:

$(T_kA)_\equiv$ $T_k(x_1, \ldots, x_k, \phi[\hat{u}_1, \ldots, \hat{u}_k, y_1, \ldots, y_n])$

$$\equiv \phi(x_1, \ldots, x_k, y_1, \ldots, y_n).$$

THEOREM. *The systems $S(\equiv)$ and $S'(\equiv)$ are both conservative extensions of S_0.*

Proof.   The first of these is the main result of Aczel/Feferman 1979. For its proof we developed an analogue of the Church–Rosser theorem. A much simpler proof due to Aczel (in §6 of our joint paper) can be given for conservation of the system $S'(\equiv)$ over S_0. We shall follow that here; it makes use instead of the results for 3-valued models established in §9 above.[20]

The method is to expand any model $\mathfrak{M}_0$ of S_0 in L_0 to a model $\mathfrak{M} = (\mathfrak{M}_0, \ldots, T_k, \ldots)$ of $S'(\equiv)$ in $L(\equiv)$. $\mathfrak{M}$ is a 2-valued model. We shall use as an intermediary the 3-valued fixed-point model of §9. The crucial point is that $\| \phi \equiv \psi \|_{\mathfrak{M}^*}$ will be evaluated according to the rules for Kleene $\leftrightarrow$. To make the different treatments of equivalence clear, let us write $\phi^{(K)}$ for the result of replacing each operation symbol $\equiv$ in ϕ by the operation symbol $\leftrightarrow$. However we still write $\phi[\hat{u}_1, \ldots, y_n]$ for the term $\phi^{(K)}[\hat{u}_1, \ldots, y_n]$. The fixed-model theorem thus provides us with a partial structure $\mathfrak{M}^* = (\mathfrak{M}_0, \ldots, \tilde{T}_k, \ldots)$ such that

(1) $\| T_k(\bar{m}_1, \ldots, \bar{m}_k, \phi[\hat{u}_1, \ldots, \hat{u}_k, \bar{m}_{k+1}, \ldots, \bar{m}_{k+n}]) \|_{\mathfrak{M}^*}$

$$= \| \phi^{(K)}(\bar{m}_1, \ldots, \bar{m}_k, \bar{m}_{k+1}, \ldots, \bar{m}_{k+n}) \|_{\mathfrak{M}^*}$$

---

[20] The systems corresponding to $S(\equiv)$, $S'(\equiv)$ in Aczel/Feferman 1980 were theories of classes, i.e. only involved the axioms $(CA)_\equiv$ for the predicate T_1. Furthermore, the abstracts $\{x \,|\, \phi(x, y_1, \ldots, y_n)\}$ were treated as new (iterable) term-builders. This caused (what I now view as) unnecessary complications, esp. loc. cit., §4.2.

for each ϕ with the appropriate free variables. To simplify matters we shall illustrate the further work just with the membership relation (T_1) and drop the subscript '$\mathfrak{M}^*$' in evaluations. Thus

$$(2) \quad \|\bar{m} \in \{u \mid \phi(u, \bar{m}_1, \ldots, \bar{m}_n)\}\| = \|\phi^{(K)}(\bar{m}, \bar{m}_1, \ldots, \bar{m}_n)\|$$

for all $\phi(x, y_1, \ldots, y_n)$ of $L(\equiv)$. Now define satisfaction for sentences of $L^{(M)}(\equiv)$ in the 2-valued model $\mathfrak{M}$ as follows:

$$(3) \quad \text{(i)} \quad \mathfrak{M} \vDash (\bar{m} \in \bar{l}) \Leftrightarrow \|\bar{m} \in \bar{l}\| = t$$
$$\text{(ii)} \quad \mathfrak{M} \vDash \neg \phi \Leftrightarrow \mathfrak{M} \nvDash \phi$$
$$\text{(iii)} \quad \mathfrak{M} \vDash (\phi \wedge \psi) \Leftrightarrow \mathfrak{M} \vDash \phi \ \& \ \mathfrak{M} \vDash \psi$$
$$\text{(iv)} \quad \mathfrak{M} \vDash (\phi \equiv \psi) \Leftrightarrow \|\phi^{(K)}\| = \|\psi^{(K)}\|$$
$$\text{(v)} \quad \mathfrak{M} \vDash \forall x \phi(x) \Leftrightarrow \text{ for each } m \in M, \mathfrak{M} \vDash \phi(\bar{m}).$$

(In other words the relation T_k in $\mathfrak{M}$ is the positive part of $\tilde{T}_k$ considered as a disjoint pair $(T_k, \bar{T}_k)$.) To show that $\mathfrak{M}$ is a model of $S'(\equiv)$, we first verify

$$(4) \quad \mathfrak{M} \vDash [\bar{m} \in \{u \mid \phi(u, \bar{m}_1, \ldots, \bar{m}_n)\} \equiv \phi(\bar{m}, \bar{m}_1, \ldots, \bar{m}_n)]$$

for each ϕ. This is immediate from (2) and (3)(iv). It is straightforward to show that each of the axioms $Ax'(\equiv)$ is true in $\mathfrak{M}$ under the definition (3)(iv). Here we consider only the axioms $(7)'$, leaving the others for the reader to check. Let ϕ, ψ be sentences of $L^{(M)}(\equiv)$. For $(7)'$, we use $\mathfrak{M} \vDash [(\phi \equiv \psi) \equiv t] \Leftrightarrow \|\phi^{(K)} \leftrightarrow \psi^{(K)}\| = t$ and $\mathfrak{M} \vDash [(\phi \equiv \psi) \equiv f] \Leftrightarrow \|\phi^{(K)} \leftrightarrow \psi^{(K)}\| = f$. Now $\|\phi^{(K)} \leftrightarrow \psi^{(K)}\|$ receives one of the values t, f only if each of $\|\phi^{(K)}\|, \|\psi^{(K)}\|$ receives the values t, f. Further, $\mathfrak{M} \vDash D(\phi) \Leftrightarrow \mathfrak{M} \vDash (\phi \equiv t)$ or $\mathfrak{M} \vDash (\phi \equiv f)$, so $\mathfrak{M} \vDash D(\phi) \Leftrightarrow \|\phi^{(K)}\| = t$ or $\|\phi^{(K)}\| = f$. The conclusion is that

$$(5) \quad \text{(i)} \quad \mathfrak{M} \vDash [(\phi \equiv \psi) \equiv t] \Leftrightarrow$$
$$\mathfrak{M} \vDash D(\phi) \ \& \ \mathfrak{M} \vDash D(\psi) \ \& \ \mathfrak{M} \vDash (\phi \equiv \psi)$$
$$\text{(ii)} \quad \mathfrak{M} \vDash [(\phi \equiv \psi) \equiv f] \Leftrightarrow$$
$$\mathfrak{M} \vDash D(\phi) \ \& \ \mathfrak{M} \vDash D(\psi) \ \& \ \mathfrak{M} \vDash (\phi \equiv \psi).$$

Thus $(7)'$(i), (ii) of $Ax'(\equiv)$ are true in $\mathfrak{M}$. This completes the proof.

Remarks

(i) The unexpected aspect of Aczel's proof is that it uses two different interpretations of $\equiv$, namely first as Kleene's $\leftrightarrow$ in the 3-valued model $\mathfrak{M}^*$ and then as Łukasiewicz's in passing from $\mathfrak{M}^*$ to $\mathfrak{M}$ (in (3)(iv)). The first interpretation is necessary in order to be able to apply the fixed-model theorem of §9. One also sees clearly from the last part of the proof why his method fails to give a model of $(\phi \equiv \psi) \equiv t \leftrightarrow (\phi \equiv \psi)$.

(ii) Consider the system $S'(\equiv)$ with axioms for the ϵ-relation (T_1),

$$(CA)_\equiv \quad x \in \{u \mid \phi(u, y_1, \ldots, y_n)\} \equiv \phi(x, y_1, \ldots, y_n).$$

Let $r = \{u \mid u \notin u\}$, so $\psi \equiv \neg \psi$ for $\psi = (r \in r)$. It follows that $\neg D(\psi)$, for otherwise we should have $t \equiv f$. Further we can prove $\neg \psi$ in this system since we have $\psi \to (\psi \equiv t)$ (ψ being atomic) and then successively $\psi \equiv t \to (\neg \psi) \equiv t$, $(\neg \psi) \equiv t \to \psi \equiv f$, $\psi \equiv f \to (\neg \psi)$ and finally $\psi \to \neg \psi$.

(iii) By the preceding, we do *not* have closure of $S'(\equiv)$ (or $S(\equiv)$) under the rule $\phi_1, \phi_1 \equiv \phi_2/\phi_2$; otherwise the system would be inconsistent. Nor do we have closure under $\phi_1 \equiv \phi_2$, $\phi_1 \leftrightarrow \phi'_1$, $\phi_2 \leftrightarrow \phi'_2/\phi'_1 \equiv \phi'_2$. In that sense, $\equiv$ *is an intensional operator*.

(iv) What informal interpretation is to be given of $\equiv$ as it is used in the systems $S'(\equiv)$ and $S(\equiv)$? In the paper Aczel/Feferman 1980 it was proposed to read $\phi \equiv \psi$ as: ϕ *is equivalent to ψ in consequence of basic definitions*, namely the axioms $(T_k A)_\equiv$, which are taken to be definitions of application of abstracts $\phi[\hat{u}_1, \ldots, \hat{u}_k, y_1, \ldots, y_n]$, i.e. of the conditions under which they apply to elements $(x_1, \ldots, x_k)$. This is a reading for which the axioms $Ax(\equiv)$ are plausible, though our intuitions are not firm in this respect. If this interpretation is accepted, our conservation results which give eliminability of the additional axioms provide one precise realization of the ideas of Behmann 1931 for a resolution of the paradoxes.[21] What is attractive about the reading is that given definitions may be "internally self-contradictory", i.e. lead to statements $\phi \equiv \neg \phi$ yet without leading to any inconsistency. In opposition to it, the logical points of the preceding remark may be considered as disturbing to the proposed interpretation.

(v) A clear informal interpretation of $\equiv$ would decide between the axioms (7)(i) and (7)'(i) of $Ax(\equiv)$, which give some quite distinct results. Take $(CA)_\equiv$ for $\psi = (r \in r)$. With (7)(i) one has $(\psi \equiv \neg \psi) \equiv t$ while with (7)'(i) one has $(\psi \equiv \neg \psi) \not\equiv t$. The interpretation proposed in the preceding remark (iv) seems to me to favor (7)(i). But as we shall see in §12, the useful consequences of $S(\equiv)$ follow just as well from $S'(\equiv)$.

[21] Cf. also Behmann 1959 and §14 below. The connection with Behmann's work was brought to our attention both by W. Craig and G. Kreisel.

(vi)   The systems considered provide us with the advantage of full use of ordinary reasoning, if that is understood in the sense of classical logic. But the approach of this section does not meet the overall criterion (proposed earlier) that a solution of the paradoxes ought to be equally satisfactory within the setting of constructive logic.

(vii)   As a final technical point, it should be noted that there is an obvious extension of $S'(\equiv)$ to a system $S'(\supset)$ in $L(\supset)$, for which the conservation theorem still holds. In $L(\supset)$, we define $(\phi \equiv \psi)$ as $(\phi \supset \psi) \wedge (\psi \supset \phi)$. Then take for $Ax'(\supset)$ the same (1)–(6) as before (expanding (2) to preservation of $\equiv$ by $\supset$), but with (7)′ replaced by:

(7)″   (i) $(\phi \supset \psi) \equiv t \leftrightarrow D(\phi) \wedge D(\psi) \wedge (\phi \equiv f \vee \psi \equiv t)$
   (ii) $(\phi \supset \psi) \equiv f \leftrightarrow \phi \equiv t \wedge \psi \equiv f.$

Then we take $S'(\supset)$ to consist of $Ax'(\supset)$ with the $(T_kA)_=$ axioms. I don't know a corresponding extension $S(\supset)$ of $S(\equiv)$. For efforts in this direction cf. Bunder 1982.

12. *A type-free "modal" theory.* To get a good view of the consequences of $S(\equiv)$ or $S'(\equiv)$ formulated entirely in a classical language (i.e. without the connective $\equiv$), it proves useful to pass first through a language $L(\square)$ with laws of modal character. $L(\square)$ is obtained from L by adjoining the unary propositional operator $\square$, where $\neg$, $\wedge$, $\forall$ continue to be the basic operators of L.

Take $Ax(\square)$ to consist of all formulas of the following form in $L(\square)$:

(1) $\square \phi \rightarrow \phi$
(2) $\square \phi \rightarrow \square \square \phi$
(3) $\phi \rightarrow \square \phi$, for any atomic ϕ
(4) $\neg \phi \rightarrow \square \neg \phi$, for L_0 atomic ϕ
(5) $\square \neg \neg \phi \leftrightarrow \square \phi$
(6)   (i) $\square(\phi \wedge \psi) \leftrightarrow \square \phi \wedge \square \psi,$
   (ii) $\square \neg (\phi \wedge \psi) \leftrightarrow \square \neg \phi \vee \square \neg \psi$
(7)   (i) $\square(\forall x \phi) \leftrightarrow \forall x \square \phi,$
   (ii) $\square \neg \forall x \phi \leftrightarrow \exists x \square \neg \phi.$

Remark. The statement that these laws are of modal character is rather loose. Though we use the $\square$ symbol familiar from modal theory as the necessity operator, it should not be interpreted in that way here. Rather it is preferable to read $\square \phi$ as: ϕ *is established,* thinking in terms of the *investigative interpretation* discussed at the end of §7. One basic difference in the two interpretations is that $\Box(\phi \vee \neg\phi)$ is accepted in modal logic, but not here since by (5) and (6) $\Box(\phi \vee \psi) \leftrightarrow \Box\phi \vee \Box\psi$ (cf. the next lemma). There is a similar divergence w.r. to $\exists$. Finally, Barcan's formula (7)(i) is not always accepted in modal logic.

In the following we define

$$D\phi = \Box\phi \vee \Box\neg\phi$$

LEMMA. The following are consequences of $Ax(\Box)$:

(i) $\neg(\phi \wedge \Box\neg\phi)$

(ii) $\neg(\Box\phi \wedge \Box\neg\phi)$

(iii) $\Box(\phi \vee \psi) \leftrightarrow \Box\phi \vee \Box\psi$,

        $\Box\neg(\phi \vee \psi) \leftrightarrow \Box\neg\phi \wedge \Box\neg\psi$

(iv) $\Box(\phi \to \psi) \to (\Box\phi \to \Box\psi)$

(v) $\Box(\exists x\phi) \leftrightarrow \exists x \Box\phi$, $\Box\neg(\exists x\phi) \leftrightarrow \forall x \Box\neg\phi$

(vi) $D\phi \to (\phi \leftrightarrow \Box\phi)$

(vii) $D\phi$ for each formula ϕ of L_0.

The proofs are straightforward. We note only (iii). By definition, $(\phi \vee \psi) = \neg(\neg\phi \wedge \neg\psi)$, so we have the chains of equivalences $\Box(\phi \vee \psi) \leftrightarrow \Box\neg(\neg\phi \wedge \neg\psi) \leftrightarrow \Box\neg\neg\phi \vee \Box\neg\neg\psi \leftrightarrow \Box\phi \vee \Box\psi$, and $\Box\neg(\phi \vee \psi) \leftrightarrow \Box\neg\neg(\neg\phi \wedge \neg\psi) \leftrightarrow \Box(\neg\phi \wedge \neg\psi) \leftrightarrow \Box\neg\phi \wedge \Box\neg\psi$.

Now for each of the relation symbols $T_k(x_1, \ldots, x_k, z)$ of $L - L_0$ define

$$(\overline{}) \quad \bar{T}_k(x_1, \ldots, x_k, z) = \Box\neg T_k(x_1, \ldots, x_k, z).$$

It follows from (i) of the preceding lemma that $(T_k, \bar{T}_k)$ form a disjoint pair. The associated abstract axioms are here formulated as follows, for each symbol T_k of L and each formula $\phi(x_1, \ldots, x_k, y_1, \ldots, y_n)$ of $L(\Box)$.

$$(T_kA)_\Box \begin{cases} T_k(x_1, \ldots, x_k, \phi[\hat{u}_1, \ldots, \hat{u}_k, y_1, \ldots, y_n]) \\ \qquad\qquad\qquad \leftrightarrow \Box\phi(x_1, \ldots, x_k, y_1, \ldots, y_n) \\ \bar{T}_k(x_1, \ldots, x_k, \phi[\hat{u}_1, \ldots, \hat{u}_k, y_1, \ldots, y_n]) \\ \qquad\qquad\qquad \leftrightarrow \Box\neg\phi(x_1, \ldots, x_k, y_1, \ldots, y_n) \end{cases}$$

We define $S(\Box)$ to consist of S_0 plus $Ax(\Box)$ plus $(T_kA)_\Box$ for T_k in L.

THEOREM. $S(\Box)$ *is interpretable in both* $S(\equiv)$ *and* $S'(\equiv)$ *by:* $\Box\phi = (\phi \equiv t)$. *Hence* $S(\Box)$ *is a conservative extension of* S_0.

Proof. Note first that $\Box \neg \phi \leftrightarrow \phi \equiv f$ for any ϕ. Then it is a routine check to show that $Ax(\Box)$ follows from $Ax(\equiv)$; here (7)(i) is used only in the form: $D(\psi) \rightarrow [(\phi \equiv \psi) \equiv t \leftrightarrow \phi \equiv \psi]$, which follows from both forms (7)(i) and (7)'(i). Now for $(T_kA)_\Box$, let $\theta = T_k(x_1, \ldots, x_k, \phi[\hat{u}_1, \ldots, \hat{u}_k, y_1, \ldots, y_n])$, and $\bar{\theta}$ the same with $\bar{T}_k$, and write ϕ for $\phi(x_1, \ldots, x_k, y_1, \ldots, y_n)$. The axiom $(T_kA)_\equiv$ tells us that $\theta \equiv \phi$. Hence $\theta \equiv t \leftrightarrow \phi \equiv t$ so $\theta \leftrightarrow \Box\phi$, θ being atomic. Also $\theta \equiv f \leftrightarrow \phi \equiv f$; so $\Box \neg \theta \leftrightarrow \Box \neg \phi$, i.e. $\bar{\theta} \leftrightarrow \Box \neg \phi$ by the definition ($\bar{}$). Thus the axioms $(T_kA)_\Box$ are verified.

As always, the two cases of $(T_kA)_\Box$ of special interest to us are those for $k = 0, 1$:

$(\text{TA})_\Box \quad \begin{cases} T(\ulcorner\phi\urcorner) \leftrightarrow \Box\phi \\ \bar{T}(\ulcorner\phi\urcorner) \leftrightarrow \Box \neg \phi \end{cases}$

$(\text{CA})_\Box \quad \begin{cases} x \in \{u \mid \phi(u, y_1, \ldots, y_n)\} \leftrightarrow \Box\phi(x, y_1, \ldots, y_n) \\ x \bar{\in} \{u \mid \phi(u, y_1, \ldots, y_n)\} \leftrightarrow \Box \neg \phi(x, y_1, \ldots, y_n). \end{cases}$

Consistency of a scheme $(\text{CA})_\Box$ is due to Fitch 1966.

13. *Theories in the CPC for partial predicates as disjoint pairs.* Finally we pass to a completely classical language. The price for doing this is to replace each basic relation symbol T_k of L (outside L_0) by a *pair of basic symbols* $(T_k, \bar{T}_k)$. The resulting language is denoted $L(+/-)$. It is useful here to take all of $\neg, \wedge, \vee, \forall, \exists /$ as basic operators. A formula of $L(+/-)$ is said to be *positive* over L_0 if it is equivalent to one built up without $\neg$ from atomic formulas and negations of L_0-atomic formulas. Every formula ϕ has associated with it a formula ϕ^+ which is positive over L_0 and which approximates ϕ. One way to obtain ϕ^+ is to put ϕ in prenex disjunctive normal form and replace each occurrence $\neg T_k$ or $\neg \bar{T}_k$ by $\bar{T}_k$ or T_k, resp. Let $\phi^- = (\neg\phi)^+$ be the positive approximant of the negation of ϕ. We can also define ϕ^+, ϕ^- inductively as follows:

(i) $\phi^+ = \phi$ for all atomic ϕ
(ii) If ϕ is L_0-atomic, $\phi^- = \neg\phi$; if $\phi = T_k(\ldots)$ then $\phi^- = \bar{T}_k(\ldots)$ and if $\phi = \bar{T}_k(\ldots)$ then $\phi^- = T_k(\ldots)$.
(iii) $(\neg\phi)^+ = \phi^-$ and $(\neg\phi)^- = \phi^+$

(iv) $(\phi \wedge \psi)^+ = \phi^+ \wedge \psi^+, (\phi \wedge \psi)^- = \phi^- \vee \psi^-$
(v) $(\phi \vee \psi)^+ = \phi^+ \vee \psi^+, (\phi \vee \psi)^- = \phi^- \wedge \psi^-$
(vi) $(\forall x\phi)^+ = \forall x\phi^+, (\forall x\phi)^- = \exists x\phi^-$
(vii) $(\exists x\phi)^+ = \exists x\phi^+, (\exists x\phi)^- = \forall x\phi^-.$

LEMMA 1.
(i) *For each* ϕ *both* ϕ^+ *and* ϕ^- *are positive over* L_0.
(ii) *If* ϕ *is positive over* L_0 *then* ϕ *is equivalent to* ϕ^+.

As basic axioms in $L(+/-)$ we take

$$\text{Dis}(T_k, \bar{T}_k) \quad \neg(T_k(x_1, \ldots, x_k, z) \wedge \bar{T}_k(x_1, \ldots, x_k, z))$$

which express that $(T_k, \bar{T}_k)$ form a disjoint pair. Dis is used to denote the collection of all these axioms for T_k a symbol of L.

LEMMA 2. Dis *implies* $(\phi^+ \to \phi)$ *and* $(\phi^- \to \neg\phi)$ *for each* ϕ.

Now we take $S(+/-)$ to consist of $S_0 + \text{Dis}$ plus the following for each symbol T_k of the language and each formula $\phi(x_1, \ldots, x_k, y_1, \ldots, y_n)$:

$$(T_k A)_{(+/-)} \begin{cases} T_k(x_1, \ldots, x_n, \phi[\hat{u}_1, \ldots, \hat{u}_k, y_1, \ldots, y_n]) \\ \qquad\qquad\qquad \leftrightarrow \phi^+(x_1, \ldots, x_k, y_1, \ldots, y_n) \\ \bar{T}_k(x_1, \ldots, x_n, \phi[\hat{u}_1, \ldots, \hat{u}_k, y_1, \ldots, y_n]) \\ \qquad\qquad\qquad \leftrightarrow \phi^-(x_1, \ldots, x_k, y_1, \ldots, y_n). \end{cases}$$

THEOREM. $S(+/-)$ *is interpretable in* $S(\square)$ *by the definition* ($\overline{}$) *in* §12 *of* $\bar{T}_k$ *in* $L(\square)$. *Hence* $S(+/-)$ *is conservative over* S_0.

Proof. Assume $Ax(\square)$ and define $\bar{T}_k(\ldots) = \square \neg T_k(\ldots)$ as in §12. Then one proves $\phi^+ \leftrightarrow \square\phi$ and $\phi^- \leftrightarrow \square \neg \phi$ by induction on ϕ. Note that here $\vee, \exists$ are treated as basic operators while in $S(\square)$ they were treated as defined operators. For example, to prove $(\phi \vee \psi)^+ \leftrightarrow \square(\phi \vee \psi)$ and $(\phi \vee \psi)^- \leftrightarrow \square \neg (\phi \vee \psi)$, assuming $\phi^+ \leftrightarrow \square\phi$, $\phi^- \leftrightarrow \square \neg \phi$, $\psi^+ \leftrightarrow \square\psi$, $\psi^- \leftrightarrow \square \neg \psi$, we use $(\phi \vee \psi)^+ = \phi^+ \vee \psi^+ \leftrightarrow \square\phi \vee \square\psi \leftrightarrow \square(\phi \vee \psi)$ (by the Lemma (iii) of §12) while $(\phi \vee \psi)^- = \phi^- \wedge \psi^- \leftrightarrow \square \neg \phi \wedge \square \neg \psi \leftrightarrow \square \neg (\phi \vee \psi)$ (again by Lemma (iii) of §12). $\exists$ is handled similarly.

As usual the two cases of the schemes $(T_kA)_{(+/-)}$ of special interest to us are those for $k = 0, 1$.

$$(TA)_{(+/-)} \quad \begin{cases} T(\ulcorner\phi\urcorner) \leftrightarrow \phi^+ \\ \bar{T}(\ulcorner\phi\urcorner) \leftrightarrow \phi^- \end{cases} \quad \text{for each sentence } \phi.$$

$$(CA)_{(+/-)} \quad \begin{cases} x \in \{u \mid \phi(u, y_1, \ldots, y_n)\} \leftrightarrow \phi^+(x, y_1, \ldots, y_n) \\ x \bar{\in} \{u \mid \phi(u, y_1, \ldots, y_n)\} \leftrightarrow \phi^-(x, y_1, \ldots, y_n) \end{cases}$$
$$\text{for each formula } \phi(x, y_1, \ldots, y_n).$$

The consistency of the scheme $(CA)_{(+/-)}$ is (essentially) due to Gilmore 1974.[22] Gilmore obtained a fixed-model result for structures of the form $\mathfrak{M} = (M, \in, \bar{\in})$ by an inductive argument, observing that positive formulas as preserved under $\leqslant$. Extensions of this were given in Feferman 1975b, 1977.

We now look at mathematical consequences for a theory of classes. The axioms $\mathrm{Dis}(\in, \bar{\in})$ and $(CA)_{(+/-)}$ are assumed in the following without further remark. The first problem is to see for which ϕ we have the ordinary instance of

$$(CA) \quad x \in \{u \mid \phi(u, y_1, \ldots, y_n)\} \leftrightarrow \phi(x, y_1, \ldots, y_n)$$

derivable. The second problem is to see for which ϕ we have

$$x \bar{\in} \{u \mid \phi(u, y_1, \ldots, y_n)\} \leftrightarrow x \notin \{u \mid \phi(u, y_1, \ldots, y_n)\}.$$

There are some immediate easy answers: (CA) holds for all ϕ which are positive over L_0, and the above equivalence of $\bar{\in}$ with $\notin$ holds when $\phi^- \leftrightarrow \neg\phi$, so it holds when $\neg\phi$ is positive over L_0.

DEFINITION. (i) $Cl(a) = \forall x(x \in a \lor x \bar{\in} a)$
　　　　　　 (ii) $Cl = \{a \mid Cl(a)\}$.

We are thus treating Cl both as a formula and as an object. But since the formula is positive, we have

$$a \in Cl \leftrightarrow Cl(a).$$

Note that $a \in Cl$ iff $\forall x[x \bar{\in} a \leftrightarrow x \notin a]$, and that $a \bar{\in} Cl$ is false for all a.

LEMMA 3. $Cl \notin Cl$.

Proof. Suppose $Cl \in Cl$. The Russell argument is adapted to yield a contradiction. Let $r = \{a \mid a \in Cl \land a \bar{\in} a\}$. Then $a \in r \leftrightarrow a \in Cl \land$

---

[22] Gilmore first publicized his work in 1967; cf. the notes in §14 below.

$a \,\bar{\in}\, a \leftrightarrow a \in Cl \wedge a \notin a$. Also by $(CA)_{(+/-)}$, $a \,\bar{\in}\, r \leftrightarrow (a \in Cl \wedge a \in a)^- \leftrightarrow a \,\bar{\in}\, Cl \vee a \in a$. Since $Cl \in Cl$, we have $a \,\bar{\in}\, Cl \leftrightarrow a \notin Cl$. Thus $a \,\bar{\in}\, r \leftrightarrow a \notin Cl \vee a \in a \leftrightarrow a \notin r$. Hence $r \in Cl$. It follows that $r \in r \leftrightarrow r \notin r$, which gives a contradiction.

DEFINITION. (i) $a \subseteq b \leftrightarrow \forall x(x \in a \rightarrow x \in b)$,
           (ii) $a \equiv b \leftrightarrow a \subseteq b \wedge b \subseteq a$.

Since we are not assuming Extensionality it is necessary to consider the relation $\equiv$ of extensional equality. Lemma 3 can be strengthened to: $\neg \exists c (c \equiv Cl \wedge c \in Cl)$, using the same argument.

The elements of Cl are called *total classes*, thinking of a *partial class* c as one for which we need not have $x \notin c \leftrightarrow x \,\bar{\in}\, c$, or as a pair of disjoint classes $(\{x \mid x \in c\}, \{x \mid x \,\bar{\in}\, c\})$. By Lemma 3, Cl is an example of a partial class which is not total. We shall now derive some closure conditions on Cl which allow us to construct new total classes from given ones.

Let $\phi(x, y_1, \ldots, y_n, a_1, \ldots, a_m)$ be a formula without any $\bar{\in}$ symbols. We say that ϕ is in $\in (a_1, \ldots, a_m)$-*form* if each atomic subformula $s \in t$ of ϕ is of the form $s \in a_i$ for some i. (There are no other restrictions, e.g. we might have $a_i \in a_i$ in ϕ.) Write $x_1, \ldots, x_n \in a$ for $x_1 \in a \wedge \ldots \wedge x_n \in a$.

LEMMA 4. If $\phi = \phi(x, y_1, \ldots, y_n, a_1, \ldots, a_m)$ is in $\in (a_1, \ldots, a_m)$ form, then $a_1, \ldots, a_m \in Cl \rightarrow (\phi^+ \leftrightarrow \phi) \wedge (\phi^- \leftrightarrow \neg \phi)$. Hence $a_1, \ldots, a_m \in Cl \rightarrow \{x \mid \phi(x, y_1, \ldots, y_n, a_1, \ldots, a_m)\} \in Cl$.

Proof. We can prove this by induction on ϕ in $\in (a_1, \ldots, a_m)$-form, relative to given $a_1, \ldots, a_m$ in Cl. The basis step is with ϕ of the form $(s \in a_i)$. Here $(s \in a_i)^- = (s \,\bar{\in}\, a_i) \leftrightarrow \neg (s \in a_i)$.

DEFINITION.

(i) $V = \{x \mid x = x\}$, $\Lambda = \{x \mid x \neq x\}$
(ii) $\{y_1, y_2\} = \{x \mid x = y_1 \vee x = y_2\}$
(iii) $a \cup b = \{x \mid x \in a \vee x \in b\}$, $a \cap b = \{x \mid x \in a \wedge x \in b\}$
(iv) $-a = \{x \mid x \notin a\}$
(v) $a \times b = \{x \mid x = (P_1(x), P_2(x)) \wedge P_1(x) \in a \wedge P_2(x) \in b\}$
(vi) $\mathscr{D}(a) = \{x \mid \exists y (x, y) \in a\}$
(vii) $\check{a} = \{x \mid x = (P_1(x), P_2(x)) \wedge (P_2(x), P_1(x)) \in a\}$
(viii) $\cup a = \{x \mid \exists y (y \in a \wedge x \in y)\}$

(ix) $\cap a = \{x \mid \forall y (y \in a \to x \in y)\}$

(x) $\mathscr{P}a = \{x \mid Cl(x) \land x \subseteq a\}.$

LEMMA 5.

(i) $\Lambda, V, \{y_1, y_2\} \in Cl$

(ii) $a, b \in Cl \to a \cup b, a \cap b, -a, a \times b, \mathscr{D}a, \breve{a} \in Cl$

(iii) $a \in Cl \land a \subseteq Cl \to \cup a, \cap a \in Cl.$

Proof. (i), (ii) are by Lemma 4. (iii) requires an additional argument. By $(CA)_{(+/-)}$ we have $x \in \cup a \leftrightarrow \exists y (y \in a \land x \in y)$, $x \bar{\in} \cup a \leftrightarrow \forall y (y \bar{\in} a \lor x \bar{\in} y)$. Then the hypothesis $a \in Cl \land a \subseteq Cl$ shows $x \bar{\in} \cup a \leftrightarrow x \notin \cup a$. Also $x \in \cap a \leftrightarrow \forall y (y \bar{\in} a \lor x \in y)$, $x \bar{\in} \cap a \leftrightarrow \exists y (y \in a \land x \bar{\in} y)$. Once more the hypothesis gives $x \bar{\in} \cap a \leftrightarrow x \notin \cap a$ and indeed $x \in \cap a \leftrightarrow \forall y (y \in a \to x \in y)$.

Since $\forall x (x \in V)$ we have $V \in V$ in particular. This is our first instance of *self-application*, though by itself not one of special interest.

Discussion. It appears that with Lemma 5 one is setting a course for a reasonable development of a (non-extensional) type-free theory of classes in this framework. However, the next steps usually taken run into *obstacles*, which are now taken up.

(i) First of all, $a \in Cl$ does not imply $\mathscr{P}a \in Cl$, since $\mathscr{P}V$ is extensionally equal to Cl.[23]

(ii) The usual way of defining ordered pairs set-theoretically, $\langle y_1, y_2 \rangle = \{\{y_1\}, \{y_1, y_2\}\}$, is also available to us here. However, that is unnecessary as ordered pairs (y_1, y_2) are already provided by the theory S_0. Thus in defining the notion of function from one class to another, we can take:

$$(c: a \to b) \leftrightarrow c \subseteq a \times b \land \forall x \in a \exists! y \in b[(x, y) \in c].$$

But if we then define $b^a = \{c \mid Cl(c) \land (c: a \to b)\}$ we are not able to show that $a, b \in Cl \to b^a \in Cl$. (In this case the counter-example is $\{0, 1\}^V \notin Cl$.) Since the formation of *function classes* is essential to the definition of the real number system and analysis, this is a *critical*

---

[23] One might think to define $\mathscr{P}a$ instead as $\{x \mid x \subset a\}$. Then one would have $x \in \mathscr{P}a \leftrightarrow \forall y (y \bar{\in} x \lor y \in a) \leftrightarrow (-x) \cup a \equiv V$. Take $a = V - \{Cl\}$ and $x = Cl$. Then $x \subset a$ but $(-x) \equiv \Lambda$ so $(-x) \cup a \not\equiv V$. Thus it is not the case that $x \in \mathscr{P}a \leftrightarrow x \subseteq a$ under this definition even for $a \in Cl$.

defect. (It is such even more so in view of our stated aim to deal with the analogous functor categories.)

(iii)   The *natural number system* would have to be treated prior to analysis. One way to try to introduce numbers would follow the Fregean approach through the *cardinals*. Define

$$(a \sim b) \leftrightarrow \exists c(Cl(c) \wedge c: a \rightarrow b \wedge \forall y \in b \exists ! x \in a[(x, y) \in c]).$$

Then $\sim$ is an equivalence relation on classes. The corresponding equivalence "classes" would be

$$[a] = \{b \,|\, Cl(b) \wedge a \sim b\}.$$

However, we do not have $[a] \in Cl$ when $a \in Cl$. Further, without extensionality we do not have the usual property $[a] = [b] \leftrightarrow a \sim b$, only $[a] \equiv [b] \leftrightarrow a \sim b$. Thus we cannot develop the theory of cardinals as cardinal equivalence types.

(iv)   An alternative approach would be to try to define the natural numbers as the smallest class a containing O and closed under $'$, where these are defined in S_0 by §9. Formally, this suggests taking

$$\mathbb{IN} = \{x \,|\, \forall a[Cl(a) \wedge O \in a \wedge \forall y(y \in a \rightarrow y' \in a) \rightarrow x \in a]\}.$$

While the matrix is equivalent to $\forall a[Cl(a) \rightarrow O \,\bar{\in}\, a \vee \exists y(y \,\bar{\in}\, a \vee y' \in a) \vee x \in a]$, there is still the negative subformula '$Cl(a)$' which cannot be circumvented. Thus we cannot prove that $\mathbb{IN}$ satisfies its defining condition. Even if it did, we would not obtain full induction on $\mathbb{IN}$, since not every formula defines a member of Cl.

(v)   One way around this problem is to build $\mathbb{IN}$ in from the beginning by use of the quantifiers $\forall_{\mathbb{IN}}$ and $\exists_{\mathbb{IN}}$ (§8). Since these are monotonic, the fixed-model theorem and all the results of §§9–12 can be extended to include them in the language. Then $\mathbb{IN}$ is definable as $\{x \,|\, \exists_{\mathbb{IN}} y(x = y)\}$, we have $\mathbb{IN} \in Cl$, and by the semantics of $\exists_{\mathbb{IN}}$ we have

$$(\mathbb{IN}) \begin{cases} O \in \mathbb{IN}, \forall x(x \in \mathbb{IN} \rightarrow x' \in \mathbb{IN}), \text{ and} \\ \phi(O) \wedge \forall x(\phi(x) \rightarrow \phi(x')) \rightarrow \forall x(x \in \mathbb{IN} \rightarrow \phi(x)) \text{ for each } \phi. \end{cases}$$

While this may be considered "cheating", it serves at least to show that one can obtain consistent type-free theories of classes which include the (IN) axioms for $\mathbb{IN}$ as a total class.

(vi)   Similarly the notion of *well-ordering relation* with the usual inductive properties can be handled in this framework by the incorporation of a suitable generalized quantifier, but cannot be managed directly without such. In any case, we cannot develop the theory of *ordinals* as isomorphism types of well-ordered relations, for the same reasons as in (iii).

(vii)   To conclude, the mathematical content of the type-free theory of classes finally reached in this section is rather meager. Part II of this paper is devoted to the construction of much richer type-free mathematical theories. In addition, we should want such to be a theory of *total classes* to begin with (i.e. with the sole relation ∈ of membership), since the idea of partial classes (in contrast to that of partial functions) is not felt to be a natural one, mathematically.

14. *Summary and historical notes.* In B (§§7–13) we have rung a series of changes on the theme of type-free semantical and mathematical theories of partial predicates. In doing so we made a transition from theories in 3-valued logics to theories in the classical predicate calculus (CPC), passing via extensions of CPC by the additional operators $\equiv$ and $\Box$. This has in effect constituted a transition from the solution route 2° for the paradoxes ("restriction of logic") to the solution route 3° ("restriction of basic principles"). In addition, the treatment unified the semantical and mathematical theories by means of a more general theory of predicates T_k. At each step the defects and disadvantages of a given formal solution were weighed against its attractions and advantages. Only at the end (in §13) did specifically mathematical goals make their appearance. These goals will take control in Part II in order to move toward improved solutions. The work carried out so far will help there to focus both on what is to be avoided and what is to be accomplished. In addition, the criterion that a solution should be equally satisfactory from a constructive point of view, which has not so far been met, will be dealt with there.

   The work described above has not been presented in the historical order in which it evolved and the references to other sources have been rather perfunctory. We thus conclude this part with some notes on relevant work, presented in (essentially) chronological order. Even so, what follows is far from comprehensive, especially on the semantical side. In addition, the notes only attempt to indicate what

I take to be the main direction or character of the contributions (insofar as they are connected with the present work).[24]

Behmann 1931 presented informal ideas for the avoidance of paradoxical abstraction, by analysis of reduction procedures such as that of $t \in \{x : \phi(x)\}$ to $\phi(t)$. Paradoxical abstraction leads to non-terminating reduction sequences. These ideas were spelled out more fully in Behmann 1959 but never in exact form. (The handling of the system $S(\equiv)$ in Aczel/Feferman 1980 is motivated by similar ideas.)

In 1941 and during the 1950s, Ackermann published a series of papers on type-free systems: cf., e.g., Ackermann 1950 and 1957. Some of these were simplified and extended by Schütte; cf. Schütte 1953 and 1960, Ch. VIII. A common feature of these systems is that they do not contain the full law of excluded middle, but are classical in other logical respects; in that sense they are based on a form of 3-valued logic. However, they are not keyed to any prior semantics. Some of the systems make use of an additional unary propositional operator **B** ("Beweisbar") which has a □-like character.

Fitch 1948 inaugurates a series of papers (continuing to Fitch 1980) in which the inductive method is used to set up consistent combinatory systems with strong means for representing logical and mathematical notions. I trace the use of the inductive method in this subject (for the construction of partial fixed-point models) to Fitch's work. (Readers may not find the connection so clear, since his systems involve an unusual mixing of combinatory and logical syntax and since his pursuit of extensionality complicates matters.)

Halldén 1949 is an original and ambitious essay on the philosophical side setting up a "logic of nonsense" to deal with the paradoxes and other problems. This is based on a form of (Kleene) weak 3-valued logic. Halldén also suggested modal extensions. Unfortunately, this work is not easily available. (More recent treatments of some of his systems are to be found in Segerberg 1965 and Woodruff 1973.)

The study of the comprehension scheme $(CA)_\equiv$ in Łukasiewicz 3-valued logic was initiated by Skolem 1960 (cf. also Skolem 1963 and the work of Brady below).

As explained in §10, Wang 1961 gave a complete Gentzen-style

---

[24] I believe a serious comparative study would be of value in this subject, since in many cases it is not easy to assess what is accomplished.

axiomatization of Kleene's strong 3-valued logic.[25] Apparently a successor to that paper with applications to set theory was planned, but does not appear to have been published.

Fitch 1963 is central to his approach inaugurated in 1948, described above. Somewhat differently, in an abstract Fitch 1966, he states the consistency of the scheme $\exists a \forall x[x \in a \leftrightarrow \Box \phi(x)]$ for arbitrary ϕ in an extension of ordinary predicate calculus. But in a detailed paper in the *JSL*. v. 32 (1967), 93–103, Fitch returns to a modal extension of a combinatory system closer to his system CΔ of 1963 (though weaker in other respects); cf. also Fitch's article in the *Monist* v. 51 (1967), 104–109.

In 1967 Gilmore wrote a report on his system of partial set theory where one works in the classical logic of a disjoint pair $(\in, \bar{\in})$ (as taken up in §13 above). This was reported to the 1967 Institute on Set Theory at UCLA (but not published until Gilmore 1974), and is where I first saw the use of partial predicate models and the inductive method of building fixed-point models.[26]

In the discussion (viii) of §10 we have already mentioned the interesting idea of van Fraassen 1968 to use partial models so as to avoid the semantic paradoxes but at the same time retain classical logical validity through the device of supervaluations. Though the motivation to stay within ordinary reasoning is the same as here, the solution is different. As far as I know, the logic of supervaluations has not been pursued in any detailed systematic way, though the idea has been applied further by van Fraassen and others, e.g. Skyrms 1970; cf. also the collection Martin 1970 of essays on the Liar paradox for a number of related discussions and suggestions of alternative approaches. In addition that volume contains a very good bibliography (further extended in the 1978 edition), particularly on the semantical side of the subject.

Brady 1971 much strengthened Skolem's result for consistency of forms of $(CA)_=$ in Łukasiewicz 3-valued logic, using Gilmore's

---

[25] Such systems keep being rediscovered; cf., e.g., Thomason 1969 and Scott 1975.

[26] At the time I did not pay much attention to these methods and results, and in fact my view then of work on type-free theories was rather negative. What I did not realize was the potential utility of type-free theories for fairly specific mathematical purposes. In contrast, the work I had seen was dominated (at least implicitly) by an attempt to reconstruct Frege's global program for the foundations of mathematics. It took me a while to recognize that formal work for the latter could be enlisted in the cause of the former.

inductive method. He extended this in 1972 to a system containing Bernays–Gödel set theory, but the idea of the proof is the same.

The paper Nepeĭvoda 1973 presents an infinitary system for Kleene 3-valued logic in the context of number theory. Though the stated interest there is in the subject of predicativity, in effect he builds a partial model for $(CA)_{\sqcup}$ in that system. (Nepeĭvoda had several related papers in the period 1973–74.)

Kripke 1975 appears to be the first paper on the semantical side to make use of the inductive construction of fixed-point models, in this case with Kleene strong 3-valued logic. Kripke's paper contains an interesting discussion of the problems which that construction solves and considerations of some alternatives. The construction itself was carried out independently by Kindt 1976. Also independently, Martin/Woodruff 1975 dealt with fixed-points for partial truth predicates, but instead of producing minimal fixed-points inductively, applied Zorn's lemma to obtain maximal fixed-points.

My own work on type-free theories dates to 1974, with the first publications being in 1975.[27] The first of these, 1975a, was concerned with non-extensional theories of partial functions and total classes (called operations and classifications, resp.) for the formalization of Bishop-style constructive mathematics. While this provided examples of self-membership, the framework did not appear adequate for applications to an unrestricted theory of structures and categories. Pursuit of the latter led me to theories of partial functions and partial classes wherein, like the constructive systems, functions appear prior to classes. This "two-stage" approach was a principal new feature of the work. It can be described in terms of the presentation here as the assumption that S_0 contains a suitably strong theory of partial functions (and secondarily that abstracts $\{x \mid \phi(x, y_1, \ldots, y_n)\}$ in S are functions of their parameters $y_1, \ldots, y_n$ in the sense of S_0). In this paper such an assumption will only make its explicit appearance and be motivated in Part II.

My notes 1975b presented a form of $S(\square)$ for $(CA)_\square$ over a theory S_0 of partial functions, reading $\square\phi$ as: ϕ is established in the course of a (possibly transfinite) investigation (cf. §12 above). This was followed in 1975c by a system like $S_{(+/-)}$ for $(CA)_{(+/-)}$ over such S_0. In my 1976 notes I initiated a comparative (and parallel) study of

[27] Actually my interest in the foundations of category theory goes back somewhat earlier. In Feferman 1969 I had applied the reflection principle in ZF to avoid the distinction between "small" and "large" categories.

semantical and mathematical type-free theories in various logics for partial models. The present paper grew out of those notes and incorporates most of the material from there. A Part II was planned for the paper 1975c but never published: however, much of the intended material was eventually used in Feferman 1977, which described the $\Box$-systems and also sketched applications to category theory.

The paper Scott 1975 combines features of (one stage of) my 1975c paper with the system $S_{\vdash}$ for $(CA)_{\vdash}$ in Kleene 3-valued logic, described above in §10. Cantini 1979a adapted Nepeĭvoda 1973 and Feferman 1975c to a semantical type-free theory; the approach through a modal system like $S(\Box)$ was similarly adapted in Cantini 1979b.

The axioms for $S(\equiv)$ and the idea for a conservation proof by Church–Rosser methods were first introduced in 1977 at a Symposium at Yale in honor of Professor Fitch. As a result of later improvements and additions by Aczel, particularly with the approach to $S'(\equiv)$ described in §11 above, the work appeared finally as Aczel/Feferman 1980. No special strong assumptions were made on S_0 there, though it can also be made part of a two-stage theory as indicated above. The interesting constructive semantical theory of Aczel 1980 will be described in Part II, where its relevance will become clear.

I have concentrated here on works most directly relevant to the approaches and matters taken up in this part; admittedly even that has been far from comprehensive.[28] Nothing has been said about quite different type-free approaches, e.g. via stratified theories or illative combinatory systems.[29] It is my plan to comment on those and others at the end of Part II. Finally, the issue of extensionality vs. non-extensionality—which has been largely ignored here—will be taken up there.

[28] Some further references that I have not mentioned or only barely touched on can be found in the present bibliography and in that of Feferman 1976c as well, of course, as in Martin 1970 (and 1978). For a useful bibliography of many-valued logic cf. Wolf 1977. *Added note*: the interesting paper Bochvar 1981 (translation of a 1939 paper) was brought to my attention by Albert Visser, at a point too late to mention in the historical notes of the text. This introduces a logic of 'internal' and 'external' 3-valued operators. The former corresponds to Kleene's weak operators; the latter includes truth and falsity operators, which allow one to define $\downarrow p$ ("p is meaningless, i.e. not true or false"). It appears that Bochvar anticipated Halldén 1949 in major respects.

[29] Good introductions to the work of the Curry school on illative combinatory logic are to be found in Bunder 1980 and Curry 1980.

References

Aczel, P., 1980, 'Frege structures and the notions of proposition, truth and set', in *The Kleene Symposium* (eds.. Barwise, Keisler, Kunen), North-Holland, 31–59.

Aczel, P., and Feferman, S., 1980, 'Consistency of the unrestricted abstraction principle using an intensional equivalence operator', in Seldin and Hindley 1980, 67–98.

Ackermann, W., 1950a, 'Widerspruchsfreier Aufbau der Logik. Typenfreies System ohne Tertium non datur', *Journal of Symbolic Logic* 15, 33–7.

Ackermann, W., 1950b, 'Ein typenfreies System der Logik mit ausreichender mathematischer Anwendingsfähigkeit I', *Archiv für math. Logik u. Grundlagenforschung* 4, 1–26.

Behmann, H., 1931, 'Zu den Widersprüchen der Logik und der Mengenlehre', *Jahresber. der Deutschen Math.-Vereinigung* 40, 37–48.

Behmann, H., 1959, 'Der Prädikatenkalkül mit limitierten Variablen: Grundlegung einer natürlichen exaketn Logik', *Journal of Symbolic Logic* 24, 112–40.

Bochvar, D. A., 1981, 'On a three-valued logical calculus and its application to the analysis of the paradoxes of the classical extended functional calculus, *History and Philosophy of Logic* 2, 87–112 (translation by M. Bergmann from *Mat. Sbornik* 4 (1939), 287–308.

Brady, R. T., 1971, 'The consistency of the axioms of abstraction and extensionality in three-valued logic', *Notre Dame Journal of Formal Logic* 12, 447–53.

Bunder, M. W., 1980, 'The naturalness of illative combinatory logic as a basis for mathematics', in Seldin and Hindley 1980, 55–64.

Bunder, M., 1982, 'Some results in Aczel–Feferman logic and set theory', *Zeitschrift f. math. Logik* (to appear).

Burge, T., 1979, 'Semantical paradox', reprinted in this volume.

Cantini, A., 1979a, *A note on three-valued logic and Tarski theorem on truth definitions*, Math. Inst., München, 16 pp.

Cantini, A., 1979b, *"Tarski extensions" of theories*, Math. Inst., München, 18 pp.

Curry, H. B., 1942, 'The inconsistency of certain formal logics', *Journal of Symbolic Logic* 7, 115–17.

Curry, H. B., 1980, 'Some philosophical aspects of combinatory logic', in *The Kleene Symposium* (eds. Barwise, Keisler, Kunen) North-Holland Pub. Co., 85–101.

Feferman, S., 1969, 'Set-theoretical foundations of category theory' (with an Appendix by G. Kreisel), in *Reports of the Midwest Category Seminar* III, Lecture Notes in Mathematics 106 (Springer), 201–47.

Feferman, S., 1975a, 'A language and axioms for explicit mathematics', in *Algebra and Logic*, Lecture Notes in Mathematics 450 (Springer), 87–139.

Feferman, S., 1975b, 'Investigative logic for theories of partial functions and relations', I and II, unpub. notes, Stanford, 21 pp. and 13 pp.

Feferman, S., 1975c, 'Non-extensional type-free theories of partial operations and classifications I', in *Proof Theory Symposion Kiel* 1974, Lecture Notes in Mathematics 500 (Springer), 73–118.

Feferman, S., 1976, 'Comparison of some type-free semantic and mathematical theories', unpub. notes, Stanford, 18 pp.

Feferman, S., 1977, 'Categorical foundations and foundations of category theory', in *Logic, Foundations of Mathematics and Computability Theory* (eds. Butts, Hintikka), Reidel, 149–69.

Feferman, S., 1979, 'Constructive theories of functions and classes', in *Logic Colloquium* 78 (eds. Boffa, van Dalen, McAloon), North-Holland, 159–224.

Fitch, F. B., 1948, 'An extension of basic logic', *Journal of Symbolic Logic* 13, 95–106.

Fitch, F. B., 1963, 'The system C$\triangle$ of combinatory logic', *Journal of Symbolic Logic* 28, 87–97.

Fitch, F. B., 1966, 'A consistent modal set theory' (abstract), *Journal of Symbolic Logic* 31, 701.

Fitch, F. B., 1980, 'A consistent combinatory logic with an inverse to equality', *Journal of Symbolic Logic* 45, 529–43.

Gilmore, P. C., 1974, 'The consistency of partial set theory without extensionality', *Axiomatic Set Theory*, Proc. Symposia Pure Maths. XIII, Part II, Amer. Math. Soc., 147–53.

Gilmore, P. C., 1980, 'Combining unrestricted abstraction with universal quantification', in Seldin and Hindley 1980, 99–123.

Gödel, K., 1931, 'Über formal unentscheidbare Sätze der Principia Mathematica und verwandter Systeme I', *Monatsh. f. Math. u. Physik* 38, 173–98.

Halldén, S., 1949, *The logic of nonsense*, Uppsala Universitets Årskrift 1949: 9.

Herzberger, H. G., 1970, 'Paradoxes of grounding in semantics', *Journal of Philosophy* 67, 145–67.

Jeroslow, R. G., 1973, 'Redundancies in the Hilbert–Bernays derivability conditions for Gödel's second incompleteness theorem', *Journal of Symbolic Logic* 38, 359–67.

Kechris, A., and Moschovakis, Y, 1977, 'Recursion in higher types', in *Handbook of Mathematical Logic* (ed. Barwise), North-Holland, 681–737.

Kindt, W., 1976, 'Uber Sprachen mit Wahrheitsprädikat', in *Sprachdynamik und Sprachstruktur* (eds. Habel, Kanngiesser), Tübingen.

Kleene, S. C., 1952, *Introduction to Metamathematics*, van Nostrand.

Kleene, S. C., and Vesley, R., 1965, *The Foundations of Intuitionistic Mathematics, Especially in Relation to Recursive Functions*, North-Holland.

Krasner, M., 1962, 'Le définitionnisme', in Actes du Colloques de Mathématiques, Pascal Tricentenaire, I *Ann. Fac. des Sciences*, Université de Clermont, no. 7, 55–81.

Kreisel, G., and Troelstra, A. S., 1970, 'Formal systems for some branches of intuitionistic analysis', *Ann. Math. Logic* 1, 229–387.

Kripke, S., 1975, 'Outline of a theory of truth', reprinted in this volume.

Martin, R. L. (editor), 1970, *The Paradox of the Liar*, Ridgeview Pub. Co. (2nd edn. 1978).

Martin, R. L. and Woodruff, P. W., 1975, 'On representing "True-in-*L*" in *L*', reprinted in this volume.

McCall, S. (editor), 1967, *Polish Logic 1920–1939*, Oxford University Press.

MacLane, S., 1971, *Categories for the Working Mathematician*, Springer-Verlag.

Nepeïvoda, N. N., 1973, 'A new notion of predicative truth and definability' (Eng. transl. of Russian orig.), Mathematical Notes 13 (1973), 493–5.

Parsons, C., 1974, 'The Liar paradox', reprinted in this volume.

Prawitz, D., 1965, *Natural Deduction, a Proof-Theoretical Study*, Almquist and Wiksell.

Prior, A., 1967, 'Many-valued logic', in *Encyclopedia of Philosophy* 5, MacMillan Pub. Co., 1–5.

Ramsey, F. P., 1925, 'The foundations of mathematics', *Proc. London Math. Soc.* Ser. 2, 25, 338–84, (also in *Foundations*, Humanities Press, 152–212).

Rosser, J. B., and Turquette, A. R., 1952, *Many-Valued Logics*, North-Holland Pub. Co.

Schütte, K., 1953, 'Zur Widerspruchsfreiheit einer typenfreien Logik', *Math. Annalen* 125, 394–400.

Schütte, K., 1960, *Beweistheorie*, Springer-Verlag.

Scott, D., 1960, 'The notion of rank in set-theory', in *Summaries of talks presented at the Summer Institute for Symbolic Logic, Cornell University 1957*, 2nd edn., Inst. for Defense Analyses, 267–9.

Scott, D., 1975, 'Combinators and classes', in *λ-Calculus and Computer Science Theory*, Lecture Notes in Computer Science 37 (Springer), 1–26.

Segerberg, K., 1965, 'A contribution to nonsense-logics', *Theoria* 31, 199–217.

Seldin, J. P., and Hindley, J. R. (editors), 1980, *To H. B. Curry: Essays on Combinatory Logic, Lambda Calculus and Formalism*, Academic Press.

Skolem, T., 1960, 'A set theory based on a certain three-valued logic', *Mathematica Scandinavia* 8, 127–36.

Skolem, T., 1963, 'Studies on the axiom of comprehension', *Notre Dame Journal of Formal Logic* 4, 162–70.

Skyrms, B., 1970, 'Return of the liar: three-valued logic and the concept of truth', *Amer. Phil. Quarterly* 7, 153–61.

Tarski, A., 1956, *Logic, Semantics, and Metamathematics* (papers 1923–1938, ed. and transl. by J. H. Woodger), Oxford University Press.

Thomason, R., 1969, 'A semantical study of constructive falsity', *Zeitschr. Math. Logik u. Grundlagen d. Math.* 15, 247–57.

van Fraassen, B., 1968, 'Presupposition, implication and self-reference', *Journal of Philosophy* 65, 135–52.

Wang, H., 1961, 'The calculus of partial predicates and its extension to set theory I', *Zeitschr. f. Math. Logik und Grundlagen d. Math.* 7, 283–8.

Wolf, R. G., 1977, 'A survey of many-valued logic' (1966–1974), in *Modern Uses of Multiple-Valued Logic* (eds. Dunn, Epstein), Reidel Pub. Co., 167–323.

Woodruff, P., 1969, 'Foundations of Three-valued Logic, Dissertation, Dept. of Philosophy, Pittsburgh University.

Woodruff, P., 1973, 'On constructive nonsense logic', in *Modality, Morality and other Problems of Sense and Nonsense*, CWK Gleerup Bokförlag, 192–205.

Comparison of Russell's Resolution
of the Semantical Antinomies
with that of Tarski*

Alonzo Church

1. *Ramified theory of types.* In this paper we treat the ramified type theory of Russell [6], afterwards adopted by Whitehead and Russell in *Principia mathematica* [12], so that we may compare Russell's resolution of the semantical antinomies by ramified type theory with the now widely accepted resolution of them by the method of Tarski in [7], [8], [9].

To avoid impredicativity the essential restriction is that quantification over any domain (type) must not be allowed to add new members to the domain, as it is held that adding new members changes the meaning of quantification over the domain in such a way that a vicious circle results. As Whitehead and Russell point out, there is no one particular form of the doctrine of types that is indispensable to accomplishing this restriction, and they have themselves offered two different versions of the ramified hierarchy in the first edition of *Principia* (see Preface, p. vii).[1] The version in §§58–59 of the writer's [1], which will be followed in this paper, is still slightly different.[2]

Alonzo Church, "Comparison of Russell's Resolution of the Semantical Antinomies with That of Tarski", reprinted from the *Journal of Symbolic Logic* 41 (1976), 747–60. Copyright © 1977 by the *Association for Symbolic Logic*.

* This research has been supported by the National Science Foundation, grant no. GP–43517.

[1] Russell's earlier version of the ramified type hierarchy is in [6] and in the Introduction to the first edition of [12]. The later version is in *12 and in (Russell's) Introduction to the second edition of [12].

[2] Differences among the three versions of ramified type theory are unimportant for the purpose of resolving the antinomies. The version which is here adopted from [1] is close to Russell's earlier version. But by using "levels" in addition to, and partly in place of, Russell's "orders" and by allowing levels and orders to be cumulative in a sense in which Russell's orders are not, it facilitates comparison both with the simple theory of types and with the hierarchy of languages and meta-languages that enters into Tarski's resolution of the semantical antinomies.

To distinguish Russellian types or types in the sense of the ramified hierarchy from types in the sense of the simple theory of types,[3] let us call the former *r-types*.

There is an r-type i to which the individual variables belong. If $\beta_1, \beta_2, \ldots, \beta_m$ are any given r-types, $m \geqslant 0$, there is an r-type $(\beta_1, \beta_2, \ldots, \beta_m)/n$ to which there belong m-ary functional variables of level n, $n \geqslant 1$. The r-type $(\alpha_1, \alpha_2, \ldots, \alpha_m)/k$ is said to be *directly lower* than the r-type $(\beta_1, \beta_2, \ldots, \beta_m)/n$ if $\alpha_1 = \beta_1, \alpha_2 = \beta_2, \ldots, \alpha_m = \beta_m$, $k < n$.

The intention is that the levels shall be cumulative in the sense that the range of a variable of given r-type shall include the range of every variable of directly lower r-type.

The *order* of a variable is defined recursively as follows. The order of an individual variable is 0. The order of a variable of r-type $(\beta_1, \beta_2, \ldots, \beta_m)/n$ is $N + n$, where N is the greatest of the orders that correspond to the types $\beta_1, \beta_2, \ldots, \beta_m$ (and $N = 0$ if $m = 0$). This is Russell's notion of order as modified by the cumulative feature which was just described.

The notations for r-types are abbreviated by writing the numeral m to stand for $(i, i, \ldots, i)$, m being the number of i's between the parentheses. For example ( )/n is abbreviated as $0/n$, $(i, i, i)/n$ is abbreviated as $3/n$ and $((i)/2, ( )/2)/1$ is abbreviated as $(1/2, 0/2)/1$.

There must be a separate alphabet of variables for each r-type, the r-type being indicated by a superscript on the letter. In writing well-formed formulas (wffs) we may often omit these r-type-superscripts as an abbreviation, if it is clear from the context what the superscript should be or if explained in words accompanying the formula. Or we may write the superscript on only the first occurrence of a particular letter, understanding the superscript to be the same on all later

---

[3] It is types in the sense of the simple theory that are called simply *types* in [1]. See footnote 578 on page 349.

The writer takes the opportunity to make a correction to his 'Russellian simple type theory' (*Proceedings and addresses of the American Philosophical Association*, vol. 47, pp. 21–33), the need for which was called to his attention by John M. Vickers. In line 21 on p. 26, after the words "may be empty" it is necessary to add "and the domains $\mathfrak{T}$ and $\mathfrak{F}$ must be disjoint". Instead of this it would be possible to correct by changing the words "and otherwise the value of (a)P is in $\mathfrak{F}$" in line 15 on p. 27 to "and the value of (a)P is in $\mathfrak{F}$ if the value of P is in $\mathfrak{F}$ for some value of a". This alternative correction may not be without interest on its own account. But it was not the original intention of the paper. Moreover, it is not historically accurate; i.e., it is not anything which might be supposed to have been intended by Russell, even implicitly, or even at a time when he still maintained the notion of proposition.

occurrences of the same letter—not only in a particular formula but even throughout a particular passage such as a proof.

We take the range of a variable of r-type $0/n$ as propositions of level n, counting propositions as 0-ary propositional functions.[4] And the range of a variable of r-type $(\beta_1, \beta_2, \ldots, \beta_m)/n$, where $m > 0$, is to consist of m-ary propositional functions which are of level n and for which the appropriate arguments are of r-types $\beta_1, \beta_2, \ldots, \beta_m$ respectively.

The formation rules provide that a propositional variable (i.e., a variable of one of the r-types $0/n$) shall constitute a wff when standing alone. Also a formula $\mathbf{f}(\mathbf{x}_1, \mathbf{x}_2, \ldots, \mathbf{x}_m)$ is well-formed (wf) if and only if $\mathbf{f}$ is a variable (or a primitive constant) of some r-type $(\beta_1, \beta_2, \ldots, \beta_m)/n$, where $m > 0$, and $\mathbf{x}_1$ is a variable (or a primitive constant) whose r-type is β_1 or directly lower than β_1, and $\mathbf{x}_2$ is a variable (or a primitive constant) whose r-type is β_2 or directly lower than β_2, and . . ., and $\mathbf{x}_m$ is a variable (or a primitive constant) whose r-type is β_m or directly lower than β_m.

Besides an infinite alphabet of variables in each r-type and the notation for application of a function to its arguments (already used in the preceding paragraph), the primitive symbols comprise an unspecified list of primitive constants,[5] each of definite r-type, and the usual notations for negation, disjunction, and the universal

---

[4] Thus we take propositions as values of the propositional variables, on the ground that this is what is clearly demanded by the background and purpose of Russell's logic, and in spite of what seems to be an explicit denial by Whitehead and Russell in [12], pp. 43–4.

In fact Whitehead and Russell make the claim: "that what we call a 'proposition' (in the sense in which this is distinguished from the phrase expressing it) is not a single entity at all. That is to say, the phrase which expresses a proposition is what we call an 'incomplete' symbol. . . ." This seems to mark the beginning of Russell's long search for a substitute for propositions, or other way to be rid of them. It is probably a late addition to the *Introduction* of [12], as no trace of it appears in [6] or in the main text of [12].

Many passages in [6] and [12] may be understood as saying or as having the consequence that the values of the propositional variables are sentences. But a coherent semantics of Russell's formalized language can hardly be provided on this basis (notice in particular that, since sentences are also substituted for propositional variables, it would be necessary to take sentences as names of sentences). And since the passages in question seem to involve confusions of use and mention or kindred confusions that may be merely careless, it is not certain that they are to be regarded as precise statements of a semantics.

[5] It is intended that additions to the list of primitive constants may be made from time to time, so that Russell's formalized language is an open language rather than a language of fixed vocabulary.

quantifier.[6] The remaining formation rules, not already stated, provide that $\sim \mathbf{P}$, $[\mathbf{P} \vee \mathbf{Q}]$, and $(\mathbf{a})\mathbf{P}$ are wf whenever $\mathbf{P}$ and $\mathbf{Q}$ are wf and $\mathbf{a}$ is a variable.

In abbreviating wffs we follow the conventions of [1], as adapted to the present context.[7] The signs of material implication, conjunction,[8] and material equivalence are of course introduced by the definitions *1.01, *3.01, *4.01 of [12]. And as explained in footnote 6, *10.01 is used as definition of the existential quantifier.

We do not follow the rules of inference and axioms of either [6] or [12], as these are in some respects insufficient and also involve some

---

[6] This means that we use the definition *10·01 of the existential quantifier rather than take it as primitive.

The Frege–Russell assertion sign, ⊢, should also properly be listed as one of the primitives. But we here follow [1] in taking the mere writing of a wff on a separate line or lines as a sign of assertion (unless the context shows otherwise), and in introducing the sign ⊢ in a different (syntactical) sense.

Historically, it must be confessed, this change of notation is unfortunate. For Frege is right that an asserted sentence has a different meaning from a sentence occurring, e.g., as antecedent or consequent of an implication. And the assertion *of* a wff (sentence or propositional form) is of course not the same as the assertion *about* the wff that it is a theorem, or that it is a demonstrable consequence of certain listed wffs.

[7] The use of dots as brackets follows a simplified form of the Peano–Russell conventions that is explained in [1]. Briefly a bold dot stands for an omitted pair of brackets with the scope extending from the point at which the dot appears, forward, either to the end of the innermost explicitly written pair of brackets, [ ], within which the dot appears or to the end of the formula if there is no such explicitly written pair of brackets; and if square brackets are omitted without replacement by a dot, the restoration of the brackets is to follow the convention of association to the left and the convention about categories, as these are explained on pp. 74–9, 171.

We also allow that any wf part of a wff may first be enclosed in square brackets (if not already so enclosed) and then these square brackets may be eliminated by replacing the first of the pair by a bold dot in accordance with the same conventions about scope of the omitted brackets that are used in other cases of replacement of brackets by dots. This may often increase the perspicuity of the abbreviated formula when dots are used for brackets.

The foregoing statement of the conventions about the use of dots as brackets is sufficient for our present purpose, and indeed is sufficient in most contexts in which very complicated formulas are not used. For cases of the kind represented by the displayed formulas on p. 80 of [1], the convention which is there intended requires some restatement for accuracy (as was pointed out by Philip Tartaglia in 1963); perhaps the shortest way of putting the required amendment is to provide that the convention about higher and lower categories that is introduced on page 79 shall be used only when none of the connectives (with which the affected bracket-pairs belong) is written with a bold dot after it.

[8] The conjunction of P and Q is to be written simply as [PQ], or where the brackets are omitted, as PQ. If in the expression of a conjunction a bold dot appears between P and Q, this dot represents an omitted pair of brackets in accordance with the conventions explained in footnote 7—not excluding, however, the case described in the second paragraph of footnote 7, in which the dot, by representing a fictitious pair of brackets, serves only the purpose of perspicuity.

oddities[9] (as they would now seem). But rather we suppose that a system of rules and axioms for propositional calculus and laws of quantifiers is adopted from some standard source. And to these we adjoin the two following comprehension axiom schemata:[10]

$$(\exists \mathbf{p}) . \mathbf{p} \equiv \mathbf{P}, \quad \mathbf{p} \text{ not free in } \mathbf{P},$$

where $\mathbf{p}$ is a propositional variable of r-type $0/n$, the bound (in Russell's terminology, "apparent") variables of $\mathbf{P}$ are all of order less than n, and the free (in Russell's terminology, "real") variables of $\mathbf{P}$ and the constants of $\mathbf{P}$ are all of order not greater than n;

$$(\exists \mathbf{f}) . \mathbf{f}(\mathbf{x}_1, \mathbf{x}_2, \ldots, \mathbf{x}_m) \equiv {}_{\mathbf{x}_1 \mathbf{x}_2 \ldots \mathbf{x}_m} \mathbf{P}, \quad \mathbf{f} \text{ not free in } \mathbf{P},$$

where $\mathbf{f}$ is a functional variable of r-type $(\beta_1, \beta_2, \ldots, \beta_m)/n$ and $\mathbf{x}_1, \mathbf{x}_2, \ldots, \mathbf{x}_m$ are distinct variables of r-types $\beta_1, \beta_2, \ldots, \beta_m$, and the bound variables of $\mathbf{P}$ are all of order less than the order of $\mathbf{f}$, and the free variables of $\mathbf{P}$ (among which of course some or all of $\mathbf{x}_1, \mathbf{x}_2, \ldots, \mathbf{x}_m$ may be included) and the constants occurring in $\mathbf{P}$ are all of order not greater than the order of $\mathbf{f}$.

From the comprehension axiom schemata there follow rules of substitution for propositional and functional variables[11] which are like *510 in [1], as generalized to higher types, but have the two following restrictions: (i) the wff $\mathbf{P}$ which is substituted for $\mathbf{p}$ or the wff $\mathbf{P}$ which is substituted for $\mathbf{f}(\mathbf{x}_1, \mathbf{x}_2, \ldots, \mathbf{x}_m)$ must obey the same conditions that are attached to the comprehension axiom schemata; (ii) all occurrences of the variable $\mathbf{p}$ or $\mathbf{f}$ in the wff $\mathbf{A}$ into which the substitution is made must be at extensional places.[12]

Using this reconstruction of the logic of *Principia mathematica* (with ramified type theory), as just outlined, we shall present proofs in the manner of [1]—making use in particular of the deduction theorem. The following abbreviations will be used to refer to certain primitive and derived rules of inference, as indicated:

---

[9] Some of the oddities arise from the fact that Russell does not use a different alphabet of variables for each r-type but in effect has only one alphabet, thus leaving the r-types (or rather the relative r-types) to be determined from the wff itself in which the variables appear. And this seems to be due in turn to Russell's intention (see §*II* of [6]) that, in an asserted wff, although each bound variable must be restricted to a particular r-type as its range, the free variables may have a wider range.

[10] Readers not previously familiar with ramified type theory should notice that the significance of the notion of order, which we have not yet explained, first becomes clear in the restrictions that are attached to these schemata.

[11] The proof is similar to that in Henkin [5].

[12] I.e., places at which substitutivity of material equivalence holds.

mod. pon.: The rule of *modus ponens*, from $P \supset Q$ and P to infer Q.

P: Laws of propositional calculus.

ded. thm.: The deduction theorem.

univ. inst.: The rule of universal instantiation, from $(a)P$ to infer the result of substituting b for all free occurrences of a throughout P, if a is a variable, if b is a variable or a constant and is either of the same r-type as a or of r-type directly lower than that of a, and (in case b is a variable) if there is no capture of b that results by the substitution described.

ex. gen.: The rule of existential generalization, from Q to infer $(\exists a)P$, where Q is the result of substituting b for all free occurrences of a throughout P, and where a, b, and P obey the same conditions which were just stated in connection with the rule of universal instantiation.

ex. inst.: The rule of existential instantiation,[13] if $P_1, P_2, \ldots, P_n$, $Q \vdash S$ and if the variable a is free in none of the wffs except Q, then $P_1, P_2, \ldots, P_n, (\exists a)Q \vdash S$; also if $P_1, P_2, \ldots, P_n, QR \vdash S$ and if the variable a is free in none of the wffs except Q and R, then $P_1, P_2, \ldots, P_n, (\exists a). QR \vdash S$.

2. *Grelling's antinomy.* As an example of one of the semantical antinomies we select Grelling's[14] as being perhaps the simplest to reproduce in a formalized language, although it is not one of the antinomies ("contradictions") that are discussed in [6] and [12]. Applied to one of the familiar natural languages, such as English or German, Grelling's antinomy is concerned with *adjectives* and with *properties* which the adjectives express.[15] In the formalized language which we are here treating it is propositional forms with one free variable that most nearly take the place of adjectives. But the semantics appropriate to such a *propositional form* is rather than it has a *value* for each value of its free variable, and we shall follow this in reproducing Grelling's antinomy.

---

[13] For want of a better we adopt this name from "natural inference" logic, notwithstanding its inappropriateness in the present context.

[14] This first appears in [4], where it is credited to Grelling.

[15] An adjective is called autological if it has the property which it expresses, and otherwise it is called heterological. E.g. if the language is English, the adjectives 'polysyllabic' and 'unequivocal' are autological, while the adjectives 'long' and 'unusual' are heterological. Then is the adjective 'heterological' autological or heterological?

We assume that symbols and formulas are to be counted among the individuals. This choice is convenient for our purpose and is allowable on the ground that any well-defined domain may be taken as the individuals. It is believed that a different choice will make no important difference in what follows.[16]

It will be sufficient to deal with the case of propositional forms having just one free variable and to assume that this is an individual variable, although there are evident generalizations of the antinomy which concern the case of propositional forms having more than one free variable or free variables of higher r-type or both. Therefore we introduce the infinite list of primitive constants val^2, val^3, val^4, ..., with the intention that $val^{n+1}(a^i, v^i, F^{1/n})$ shall mean that a^i is an individual variable and v^i is a wff (propositional form) having no other free variable than a^i and for every value x^i of the variable a^i the value of v^i is $F^{1/n}(x^i)$.[17]

As no reason to the contrary appears, we take the constants val^{n+1} to be of level 1 (i.e. in Russell's terminology, predicative). The r-type of val^{n+1} is therefore $(i, i, 1/n)/1$, and it may indeed be convenient to regard the notation val^{n+1} as an abbreviation for $val^{(i, i, 1/n)/1}$. The order of val^{n+1} is $n + 1$.

Based on the intended meaning the following postulates involving the constants val^{n+1} suggest themselves as evident.

First there is the principle of univocacy, which may be taken in the strong form:[15a]

$$(1) \quad val^{m+1}(a, v, F^{1/m}) \supset_{avF} . val^{n+1}(b, v, G^{1/n}) \supset_{bG} . F = G.$$

[15a] I am indebted to Angela De Paola, a student in philosophy at the University of Florence (in Italy), for pointing out an error in the proof of theorem (6) as it appeared in the original publication of this paper. In order to correct the error it has been necessary to strengthen postulate (1) and its consequence (2), but it is thought that the strengthened (1) and (2) are still informally evident.

[16] Not even a choice that puts primitive symbols and formulas into different types, or different r-types.

[17] In this sentence, those who wish to be very accurate about use–mention distinctions may enclose the constants 'val^1', 'val^2', 'val^3', and the wff 'val^n (a^i, v^i, $F^{1/n}$)' in Frege's single quotation marks to show that they are mentioned rather than used. But observe that nothing else in the sentence is to be enclosed in single quotation marks. There should be no confusion over the point that, since individual variables are included among the individuals, the individual variable 'a^i' may have an individual variable as value (which latter individual variable is then spoken of as "the variable a^i"). [*Added in proof*, 1976: The writer has just noticed that the use of quotation marks that is suggested in the first sentence of this footnote is itself inaccurate; but the footnote may nevertheless serve its purpose of clearing up a possible misunderstanding of what is said in the text.]

Since $[F = G]$ is defined as $(H) \cdot H(F) \supset H(G)$, where the type of H is $(1/k)/1$ (with k chosen as the greater of m and n), we may infer from (1):

$$(2) \quad \mathrm{val}^{m+1}(a, v, F^{1/m}) \supset_{avF} \cdot \mathrm{val}^{n+1}(b, v, G^{1/n}) \supset_{bG} \cdot F(x) \equiv_x G(x).$$

We shall need only the weak, or extensional principle of univocacy (2). Then there is the following postulate schema, which (without extending the formalized language) can be stated only in the extensional form shown, and whose truth (for each **P**) may be seen informally by taking v to be the propositional form **P** and a to be the individual variable (x):

$$(3) \quad (\exists a)(\exists v)(\exists F^{1/n}) \cdot \mathrm{val}^{n+1}(a, v, F) \cdot F(x) \equiv_x \mathbf{P},$$

where **P** is a wff in which there is no free variable other than 'x', in which all the bound variables are of order less than n, and in which all the constants are of order not greater than n. And finally there are the following postulates which express the cumulative character of the constants val^{n+1} that was implicit in our informal explanation of the meaning:

$$(4) \quad \mathrm{val}^{n+1}(a, v, F^{1/n}) \supset \mathrm{val}^m(a, v, F^{1/n}), \quad \text{where} \quad m > n + 1.$$

Corresponding to the word 'heterological' that appears in the verbal statement of Grelling's antinomy, we make the definition:[18]

$$\mathrm{het}^{n+1}(v) \to (\exists a)(\exists F^{1/n}) \cdot \mathrm{val}^{n+1}(a, v, F) \cdot \sim F(v).$$

Then we prove the following theorems:

$$(5) \quad \mathrm{het}^{n+1}(v) \supset \mathrm{het}^{m+1}(v), \quad \text{if} \quad m \geqslant n.$$

PROOF. Suppose that $m \geqslant n$.
By (4) and P, $\mathrm{val}^{n+1}(a, v, F^{1/n}) \vdash \mathrm{val}^{m+1}(a, v, F)$.
Hence by P, $\mathrm{val}^{n+1}(a, v, F) \cdot \sim F(v) \vdash \mathrm{val}^{m+1}(a, v, F) \cdot \sim F(v)$.
Hence by ex. gen.[19] $\mathrm{val}^{n+1}(a, v, F) \cdot \sim F(v) \vdash \mathrm{het}^{m+1}(v)$.
Hence by ex. inst. $\mathrm{het}^{n+1}(v) \vdash \mathrm{het}^{m+1}(v)$.
Hence (5) follows by ded. thm.

[18] For strict accuracy the letters v and a should be in bold type—i.e., syntactical variables, as in [1]. If we here follow the common informal practice of using object-language variables, it is to avoid obtruding use–mention distinctions where they are not in fact important for understanding what is being said.

[19] We here follow the strong form of the rule of existential generalization as this is stated above, taking **b** to be $F^{1/n}$ and **a** to be $F^{1/m}$.

(6) $[\mathrm{val}^{m+2}(a, v, G^{1/m+1}) \cdot G(x) \equiv_x \mathrm{het}^{m+1}(x)] \supset$
$$\sim \mathrm{het}^{n+1}(v), \quad \text{if} \quad m \geqslant n.$$

PROOF. Suppose that $m \geqslant n$.
By (2), univ. inst., and mod. pon.,

$$\mathrm{val}^{m+2}(b, v, G^{1/m+1}), \mathrm{val}^{n+1}(a, v, F^{1/n}) \vdash F(x) \equiv_x G(x).$$

Hence by univ. inst. and P,

$$\mathrm{val}^{m+2}(b, v, G), \mathrm{val}^{n+1}(a, v, F), \sim F(v) \vdash \sim G(v).$$

Hence by ex. inst., $\mathrm{val}^{m+2}(b, v, G), \mathrm{het}^{n+1}(v) \vdash \sim G(v)$.
Hence by ded. thm., $\mathrm{val}^{m+2}(b, v, G) \vdash \mathrm{het}^{n+1}(v) \supset \sim G(v)$.
Hence, by univ. inst. and P,

$$\mathrm{val}^{m+2}(b, v, G), G(x) \equiv_x \mathrm{het}^{m+1}(x) \vdash \mathrm{het}^{n+1}(v) \supset \sim \mathrm{het}^{n+1}(v).$$

Hence by (5) and P,

$$\mathrm{val}^{m+2}(b, v, G), G(x) \equiv_x \mathrm{het}^{m+1}(x) \vdash \sim \mathrm{het}^{n+1}(v).$$

Hence (6) follows by P, ded. thm., and substitution.

(7) $[\mathrm{val}^{m+2}(a, v, G^{1/m+1}) \cdot G(x) \equiv_x \mathrm{het}^{m+1}(x)]$
$$\supset \mathrm{het}^{n+1}(v), \quad \text{if} \quad m < n.$$

PROOF. Suppose that $m < n$.
By P and ex. gen., $\mathrm{val}^{m+2}(a, v, G^{1/m+1}), \sim G(v) \vdash \mathrm{het}^{m+2}(v)$.
Hence by univ. inst. and P,

$$\mathrm{val}^{m+2}(a, v, G), G(x) \equiv_x \mathrm{het}^{m+1}(x), \sim \mathrm{het}^{m+1}(v) \vdash \mathrm{het}^{m+2}(v).$$

Hence by (5) (used twice) and P,

$$\mathrm{val}^{m+2}(a, v, G), G(x) \equiv_x \mathrm{het}^{m+1}(x), \sim \mathrm{het}^{n+1}(v) \vdash \mathrm{het}^{n+1}(v).$$

Hence by ded. thm. and P,

$$\mathrm{val}^{m+2}(a, v, G), G(x) \equiv_x \mathrm{het}^{m+1}(x) \vdash \mathrm{het}^{n+1}(v).$$

Hence (7) follows by P and ded. thm.
Also as an instance of (3) we have:

(8) $(\exists a)(\exists v)(\exists G^{1/m+1}) \cdot \mathrm{val}^{m+2}(a, v, G) \cdot G(x) \equiv_x \mathrm{het}^{m+1}(x).$

If we reduce to simple type theory by dropping all level indicators, the infinitely many constants val^{n+1} coalesce into a single constant, val, whose type (in the sense of simple type theory) is $(i, i, (i))$. The informal explanation of the meaning of val^{n+1} then becomes an explanation of the meaning of val, and the postulates (1), (3) still seem to be evident from this intended meaning; moreover (2) is still a consequence of (1), and (4) becomes tautologous. The proofs of theorems (5)–(8) still hold, after dropping the level indicators, and the last three theorems then constitute a contradiction. This is Grelling's antinomy, as it arises in simple type theory.

The resolution of the antinomy by ramified type theory consists not merely in the fact that, after restoration of the level indicators, theorems (6)–(8) are no longer a contradiction, but also in that the question "Is the propositional form $\text{het}^{m+1}(x)$ autological or heterological?" can now be answered: namely it is (by (6)) autological at all levels $\leqslant m + 1$, and it is (by (7)) heterological at all levels $> m + 1$.

3. *The language L.* Now let L be the language of ramified type theory (as here formulated) with addition of all the constants

$$\text{val}^{(i, i, \ldots, i, (\beta_1, \beta_2, \ldots, \beta_m)/n)/1}$$

and appropriate postulates involving them. Here m is any non-negative integer, $\beta_1, \beta_2, \ldots, \beta_m$ are any m r-types, n is any level $\geqslant 1$, and in the superscript

$$(i, i, \ldots, i, (\beta_1, \beta_2, \ldots, \beta_m)/n)/1$$

that indicates the r-type of the constant there are to be exactly $m + 1$ i's preceding the r-type-symbol

$$(\beta_1, \beta_2, \ldots, \beta_m)/n.$$

The constants val^{n+1} that were introduced above are special cases, corresponding to $m = 1$, $\beta_i = i$. Generally, the wff

$$\text{val}^{(i, i, \ldots, i, (\beta_1, \beta_2, \ldots, \beta_m)/n)/1} (a_1, a_2, \ldots, a_m, v, F^{(\beta_1, \beta_2, \ldots, \beta_m)/n})$$

shall mean that $a_1, a_2, \ldots, a_m$ are distinct variables of types $\beta_1, \beta_2, \ldots, \beta_m$ respectively, and v is a wff having no other free variables than $a_1, a_2, \ldots, a_m$, and for every system of values

$$x_1^{\beta_1}, x_2^{\beta_2}, \ldots, x_m^{\beta_m}$$

of the variables $a_1, a_2, \ldots, a_m$ the value of v is

$$F^{(\beta_1, \beta_2, \ldots, \beta_m)/n}(x_1^{\beta_1}, x_2^{\beta_2}, \ldots, x_m^{\beta_m})$$

(Compare footnote 17).

We put down only the postulates that are generalizations of (1), (3), (4) above.[20] As an abbreviation in stating these we take the r-type of F to be always

$$(\beta_1, \beta_2, \ldots, \beta_m)/n;$$

and the r-type of G is to be

$$(\beta_1, \beta_2, \ldots, \beta_m)/k;$$

and the r-type of val is to be, at each occurrence, the lowest that is compatible with its arguments, unless the contrary is said. The postulates are

(9) $\mathrm{val}(a_1, a_2, \ldots, a_m, v, F) \supset_{a_1 a_2 \ldots a_m v F}.$
$$\mathrm{val}(a_1, a_2, \ldots, a_m, v, G) \supset_G . F = G,$$

(10) $(\exists a_1)(\exists a_2) \ldots (\exists a_m)(\exists v)(\exists F) . \mathrm{val}(a_1, a_2, \ldots, a_m, v, F) .$
$$F(x_1, x_2, \ldots, x_m) \equiv_{x_1 x_2 \ldots x_m} \mathbf{P},$$

where $\mathbf{P}$ is a wff in which there are no free variables other than 'x_1', 'x_2', ..., 'x_m' and in which all the bound variables are of order less than the order of 'F' and all the constants of order not greater than the order of 'F'.

(11) $\mathrm{val}(a_1, a_2, \ldots, a_m, v, F) \supset \mathrm{val}(a_1, a_2, \ldots, a_m, v, F),$

where the constant, val, on the right is of the lowest r-type that is compatible with the arguments it has, while that on the left is of any other r-type that is compatible with these arguments.

For $n = 1, 2, 3, \ldots$, let L_n be the sublanguage of L obtained by

---

[20] Additional postulates relating the semantical propositional functions, val, to the syntax of L can be expressed only after adding still further primitives enabling us to express the syntax of L. There are indeed some additional things holding that can be expressed without introducing new primitives, for example:

$$\mathrm{val}(a, v, F) \supset . \mathrm{val}(b, v, F) \supset . a = b \vee (x)F(x) \vee (x){\sim}F(x),$$
$$\mathrm{val}(a, b, v, F) \supset . \mathrm{val}(b, a, v, G) \supset . F(x, y) \equiv_{xy} G(y, x),$$
$$a = b \supset {\sim}\mathrm{val}(a, b, v, F).$$

But our present purpose does not make it necessary to explore the question of additional postulates which may therefore be wanted.

deleting all variables and constants of order greater than n, and allowing the variables of order n to occur only as free variables.

Then L_1 is a functional calculus of first order[21] in the presently standard sense, i.e., only individual variables occur as bound variables. None of the semantical constants, val, are in L_1, as the lowest order of these is 2. And the propositional and functional variables in L_1 are of first order, having superscripts of the form $m/1$ $(m = 0, 1, 2, \ldots)$.

In L_2 there are propositional and functional variables with superscripts $m/2$, where $m \geqslant 0$; and also propositional and functional variables with superscripts $(\beta_1, \beta_2, \ldots, \beta_m)/1$, $m \geqslant 0$, where each of $\beta_1, \beta_2, \ldots, \beta_m$ is either i or of the form $k/1$, $k \geqslant 0$. But only individual variables and propositional and functional variables of first order are used as bound variables. And the semantical constants, val, which are present in L_2 are those having the r-types $(i, i, \ldots, i, m/1)/1$, $m = 0, 1, 2, \ldots$, and thus are precisely those needed for the semantical metatheory of L_1.

We may therefore regard L_2 are a semantical meta-language of L_1. However, L_2 is stronger than L_1 not only in having the semantical predicates (semantical functional constants) that are needed for the semantics of L_1 but also in having additional free variables beyond those of L_1, namely the variables of second order, and in admitting as bound variables certain variables which appear only as free variables in L_1, namely the variables of first order.

And so we may continue through the hierarchy of languages $L_1, L_2, L_3, \ldots$, the situation being always that L_{n+1} is a semantical meta-language of L_n, containing the semantical predicates that are applicable to L_n, and containing also L_n itself plus additional r-types of free variables and additional r-types of bound variables that are not present in L_n. Moreover it is quite indifferent whether we speak of a single language L and a hierarchy of orders of variables and predicates within it or whether we speak of an infinite hierarchy of

[21] The terminology, functional calculus of first order, second order, etc., is appropriate primarily to simple type theory and represents a different meaning of the word 'order' from that which is needed in connection with ramified type theory. The hierarchy of languages $L_1, L_2, L_3, \ldots$ is in fact quite different from the hierarchy of functional calculi of first, second, third, ... orders. And except in such phrases as 'functional calculus of second order' we shall always use the word 'order' in the sense (essentially Russell's) which was defined at the beginning of this paper. (Footnote 578 of [1] overlooks that the notion of "level", though useful, cannot wholly supersede Russell's notion of "order" in treating ramified type theory.)

languages $L_1, L_2, L_3, \ldots$, as it is evident that the distinction is merely terminological.

4. *Comparison with Tarski.* It is Tarski's solution of the problem of the semantical antinomies that the semantical predicates for a particular language must be contained, not in the language itself, but always in a meta-language. Indeed the semantical predicates val are intensional, whereas Tarski at the date of [7] and [8] is concerned only with the extensional semantical notions of truth and satisfaction and perhaps would have denied corresponding intensional notions. But it is intensional semantical predicates that are primarily appropriate to the language L (or to L_1, L_2, etc.). The essential point of the resolution of the semantical antinomies by Tarski is unrelated to a distinction of intension and extension, and is simply that the semantical predicates (and propositional forms) appropriate to a language must be put into a meta-language of it.

In the light of this it seems justified to say that Russell's resolution of the semantical antinomies is not a different one than Tarski's but is a special case of it.

This conclusion may be supported by supplying in L (or in L_2, L_3, etc.) the following definitions to express the extensional semantical notions, that v is a true sentence of L_n,

$$\mathrm{tr}^{n+1}(v) \to (\exists p^{0/n}) . \mathrm{val}^{(i,\,0/n)/1}(v, p) . p,$$

and that v is a propositional form of L_{N+n} and is satisfied by the values $x_1, x_2, \ldots, x_m$ of the variables $a_1, a_2, \ldots, a_m$,

$$\mathrm{sat}^{N+n+1}(a_1, a_2, \ldots, a_m, x_1, x_2, \ldots x_m, v)$$
$$\to (\exists F) . \mathrm{val}(a_1, a_2, \ldots, a_m, v, F) . F(x_1, x_2, \ldots, x_m)$$

where in the latter definition, F is of r-type $(\beta_1, \beta_2, \ldots, \beta_m)/n$ and order $N + n$, and val is of r-type $(i, i, \ldots, i, (\beta_1, \beta_2, \ldots, \beta_m)/n)/1$, and $x_1, x_2, \ldots, x_m$ are of r-types $\beta_1, \beta_2, \ldots, \beta_m$ respectively (where $m \geqslant 1, n \geqslant 1$).

As the propositional form $\mathrm{tr}^{n+1}(v)$ contains a bound variable of order n, a constant of order $n + 1$, and as its only free variable, the individual variable 'v', it follows that $\mathrm{tr}^{n+1}(v)$ belongs to the language L_{n+1} but not to L_n. Also similarly the propositional form $\mathrm{sat}^{N+n+1}(a_1, a_2, \ldots, a_m, x_1, x_2, \ldots, x_m, v)$ belongs to the language L_{N+n+1} but not to L_{N+n}. And this is just what Tarski's resolution of the semantical antinomies requires.

It should be remarked that if we *begin* with extensional semantics, we may then naturally take as primitive a predicate or infinite list of predicates, tr, which require an individual variable as argument, and an infinite list of predicates, sat, which require $2m + 1$ arguments of r-types $i, i, \ldots, i, \beta_1, \beta_2, \ldots, \beta_m, i$. In this case the levels of the primitive predicates, tr and sat, must be assigned *ad hoc* to avoid antinomy, and the ramified theory of types may seem to play only a secondary role.

However, such priority of extensional semantics is just not appropriate to the language L—and does not accord with the way in which the resolution of the "contradictions" is informally explained in [6] and [12].[22] Moreover, as we have just seen, we are able by taking the intensional predicates val as primitive to supply definitions of $\text{tr}^{n+1}(v)$ and $\text{sat}^{N+n+1}(a_1, a_2, \ldots, a_m, x_1, x_2, \ldots, x_m, v)$. But the reverse does not hold: if the predicates tr and sat of various r-types are primitive, we are unable from them to define $\text{val}(a_1, a_2, \ldots, a_m, v, F)$ suitably, but only an extensional analogue which we may call $\text{valext}(a_1, a_2, \ldots, a_m, v, F)$. For example, if

$$\text{valext}^{n+1}(a, v, F^{1/n}) \rightarrow F(x) \equiv_x \text{sat}^{(i, i, i)/n+1}(a, x, v),$$

we have for $\text{valext}^{n+1}(a, v, F)$, unlike $\text{val}^{n+1}(a, v, F)$, that if it is satisfied by given values of the variables a, v, F then it is satisfied also by the same values of a and v and any coextensive (or formally equivalent) value of F.

By taking the intensional semantics as prior, and proceeding from it to the extensional semantical notions, ramified type theory resolves the semantical antinomies in a straightforward way, without *ad hoc* additional assumptions, and it is seen only after the event that the resolution is a subcase of Tarski's.

---

[22] For example, in his explanation regarding the Epimenides antinomy in §I of [6] or p. 62 of [12], when Russell says that the notion of "all propositions" is illegitimate and that a statement about all propositions of some order must be itself of higher order, we may take a "statement" or a "proposition" (the two words seem to be synonymous) to be "in the sense in which this is distinguished from the phrase expressing it", or we may take it to be a declarative sentence *considered together with* its meaning. But for a sentence, either as a finite sequence of sounds (or of printed or written characters) or as a class or class concept of such, organized by a particular syntax but not yet associated with a meaning, there is in the nature of the case nothing illegitimate in the totality of all sentences. And in setting up the language L we have in fact taken the symbols, sentences, and propositional forms of L as being, all of them, members of a single r-type.

5. *Axioms of reducibility.* To secure adequacy for classical mathematics it is necessary to adjoin to the language L an axiom of infinity, axioms of choice in some form, and the axioms of reducibility.[23]

As our concern is with the resolution of the semantical antinomies by ramified type theory, it is only the axioms of reducibility that need concern us here. They are:

$$(F^{(\beta_1, \beta_2, \ldots, \beta_m)/n})(\exists G^{(\beta_1, \beta_2, \ldots, \beta_m)/1}) \cdot F(x_1, x_2, \ldots, x_m)$$
$$\equiv_{x_1 x_2 \ldots x_m} G(x_1, x_2, \ldots, x_m),$$

where $m = 1, 2, 3, \ldots,$[24] and the variables $x_1, x_2, \ldots, x_m$ are of r-types $\beta_1, \beta_2, \ldots, \beta_m$ respectively.

The effect of the axioms is that the range of the functional variables is already extensionally complete at level 1, in the sense that it contains a propositional function that is extensionally (or in the terminology of [12], "formally") equivalent to any propositional function which enters as a value of the functional variables at any higher level; and that it is only in intension that we are to think of additional values of the functional variables as arising at each new level. Thus the rejection of impredicative definition is annulled in extensional but not in intensional matters.[25] And this

---

[23] We treat the system of the first edition of [12], with ramified type theory and axioms of reducibility. The modification which is suggested in Russell's Introduction to the second edition (and is based on ideas of Wittgenstein), to replace the axioms of reducibility by axioms of extensionality, one in each type, is unsatisfactory—because the resulting system is not adequate for classical mathematics (as Russell admits, see pp. xiv, xxix, xliv–xlv, and compare Weyl [10]), and because if Russell's attempt is successful, in Appendix C of the second edition of [12], to be rid of intensional contexts, he thereby abandons some of his own important contributions to logic. As regards this last, we have already seen how a strictly extensional approach prejudices the resolution of the semantical antinomies by ramified type theory; and Russell's theory of descriptions loses its point as a solution of the puzzle about King George IV and the author of Waverley if there are no intensional contexts.

[24] Only the cases $m = 1, 2$ are used in [6] and [12], but the case of greater m is referred to briefly.

[25] That the restoration of impredicative definition is confined to extensional contexts might be defended on the ground that there are antinomies which are about intensional matters but are not semantical in character. For example, Bouleus believes that he is sometimes mistaken, but (with the possible exception of some that are logically implied by this one together with his true beliefs) all his other beliefs are in fact true. Is it then true that Bouleus is sometimes mistaken?

This is implicitly a correction of the first paragraph of §59 of [1], as it is only by confining attention to extensional logic that it can be said that ramified type theory with axioms of reducibility has no interest as an intermediate position between pure ramified type theory and simple type theory.

much is enough for classical mathematics, especially mathematical analysis.

The danger may be feared that the axioms of reducibility will restore the semantical antinomies which it was intended to avoid by means of the ramified type hierarchy. But this does not appear to be realized, at least not in any obvious way.

Let us take the case of Grelling's antinomy as an illustration. By using the appropriate one of the axioms of reducibility, we may indeed prove:

$$(12) \quad (\exists H^{1/1}) \,.\, H(v) \equiv_v (\exists a)(F^{1/n}) \,.\, \mathrm{val}^{n+1}(a, v, F) \,.\, {\sim} F(v).$$

Then if we take as hypothesis

$$(13) \quad H^{1/1}(v) \equiv_v (\exists a)(\exists F^{1/n}) \,.\, \mathrm{val}^{n+1}(a, v, F) \,.\, {\sim} F(v),$$

we may repeat the proofs of (6) and (7) in modified form, treating them as proofs from the hypothesis (13). In this way we get, as proved from the hypothesis (13), both

$$[\mathrm{val}^2(a, v, G^{1/1}) \,.\, G(x) \equiv_x H(x)] \supset {\sim} H(v)$$

and

$$[\mathrm{val}^2(a, v, G^{1/1}) \,.\, G(x) \equiv_x H(x)] \supset H(v).$$

No contradiction results, as it does not appear that a similar analogue of (8) can be obtained. But from the two last formulas we get by propositional calculus

$$G(x) \equiv_x H(x) \supset {\sim} \mathrm{val}^2(a, v, G),$$

still as proved from the hypothesis (13); then deduction theorem and a substitution for the functional variable H enable us to prove the theorem:

$$(14) \quad G^{1/1}(x) \equiv_x \mathrm{het}^{n+1}(x) \supset_{avG} {\sim} \mathrm{val}^2(a, v, G).$$

Also by alphabetic changes of bound variable in (12):

$$(15) \quad (\exists G^{1/1}) \,.\, G(x) \equiv_x \mathrm{het}^{n+1}(x).$$

This is an empiric justification of the axioms of reducibility, based on the failure of the direct attempt to restore Grelling's antinomy by means of them, and on the fact that the resulting situation as expressed by (14) and (15) not only is intelligible but even is to be expected in the light of Tarski's theorem about truth.[26] If the axioms of reducibility are included in the hierarchy of languages $L_1, L_2, L_3, \ldots$, each at its appropriate place, it therefore seems that the resulting hierarchy of languages will still conform to Tarski's resolution of the semantical antinomies.[27] But this again is only an empiric justification because the actual conformity to Tarski's plan of resolution of the antinomies depends on the unprovability of certain theorems,[28] which must here remain a conjecture.

The principal significance of theorems(14) and (15) is that there must be, among the values of the variables in L_1 of r-type 1/1, propositional functions such that no coextensive function is expressible by a propositional form in L_1, but only in some language arbitrarily far along in the hierarchy $L_1, L_2, L_3, \ldots$.

---

[26] In fact consider the case that the superscript $n + 1$ in (14) and (15) is 2, and let (14') and (15') be the sentences obtained from (14) and (15) respectively by replacing 'het$^2(x)$' by 'tr$^2(x)$'. Suppose further that the languages L_1 and L_2 are consistent and that 'tr$^2(x)$', as a propositional form of L_2, is satisfied by those and only those values of 'x' which are true sentences of L_1. Then (15') must hold if the range of the singulary functional variables of L_1 is to be extensionally complete, and (14') can be taken as an expression of Tarski's theorem.

And that what holds of truth—i.e., expressibility only in a meta-language—must be expected to hold also of other semantical notions, including heterologicality, is already implicit in the description of Tarski's resolution of the semantical antinomies as we gave it above.

[27] Weyl's use [10] of Grelling's antinomy to support what is in effect ramified type theory without axioms of reducibility is therefore not in itself compelling. That is, it is not demonstrated that a system which allows impredicative definition must therefore be inconsistent. But if one agrees with Weyl [10], [11] that impredicative definition is intrinsically unsound, a *circulus vitiosus* whether or not it leads to antinomy, then indeed ramified type theory without axioms of reducibility is what results; and while first-order arithmetic can be obtained by adjoining either Peano's postulates for the natural numbers (under some appropriate choice of r-types for the variables and constants occurring in them) or an axiom of infinity strong enough to yield this, it will still be impossible to obtain more than a weakened form of the classical theory of real numbers.

[28] For example sat$^2(a, x, v)$, defined as $(\exists F^{1/1}) . \mathrm{val}^2(a, v, F) . F(x)$, is supposed to express the semantical satisfaction relation only as it applies to L_1; if theorems could be proved by which it could be regarded as expressing this relation also for L_2, the Tarski plan for avoiding antinomy would be violated. Something may depend on whether postulates (4) and (11) are assumed only in the weak form which was given to them above or whether they are strengthened by putting $\equiv$ in place of $\supset$. It is conjectured that L remains consistent after adjoining both the axioms of reducibility and the strong form of postulates (4) and (11). But this conjecture, if correct, deserves support by a relative consistency proof, relative perhaps to the consistency of the simple theory of types or of standard axiomatic set theory.

References

[1] Church, Alonzo, *Introduction to mathematical logic*, Volume 1, Princeton, 1956.

[2] Copi, Irving M., *The theory of logical types*, London, 1971.

[3] Fraenkel, Abraham A. and Bar-Hillel, Yehoshua, *Foundations of set theory*, Amsterdam, 1958; second edition 1973, by Fraenkel, Bar-Hillel, and Azriel Levy with collaboration of Dirk van Dalen.

[4] Grelling, Kurt and Nelson, Leonard, 'Bemerkungen zu den Paradoxieen von Russell und Burali-Forti', *Abhandlungen der Fries'schen Schule*, n.s. vol. 2 (1907–08), pp. 301–24.

[5] Henkin, Leon, 'Banishing the rule of substitution for functional variables', *Journal of symbolic logic*, vol. 18 (1953), pp. 201–8.

[6] Russell, Bertrand, 'Mathematical logic as based on the theory of types', *American journal of mathematics*, vol. 30 (1908), pp. 222–62.

[7] Tarski, Alfred, 'Pojęcie prawdy w językach nauk dedukcyjnych', *Travaux de la Société des Sciences et des Lettres de Varsovie, Classe III*, no. 34, Warsaw, 1933.

[8] Tarski, Alfred, 'Der Wahrheitsbegriff in den formalisierten Sprachen' (German translation of [7] with added *Nachwort*), *Studia philosophica*, vol. 1 (1936), pp. 261–405.

[9] Tarski, Alfred, 'The concept of truth in formalized languages' (English translation of [8]), *Logic, semantics, metamathematics, Papers from 1923 to 1938, by Alfred Tarski*, London, 1956, pp. 152–278.

[10] Weyl, Hermann, *Das Kontinuum, Kritische Untersuchungen über die Grundlagen der Analysis*, Leipzig, 1918.

[11] Weyl, Hermann, 'Der circulus vitiosus in der heutigen Begründung der Analysis', *Jahresbericht der Deutschen Mathematiker-Vereinigung*, vol. 28 (1919), pp. 85–92.

[12] Whitehead, A. N. and Russell, Bertrand, *Principia mathematica* (three volumes), Cambridge, 1910–13; second edition, Cambridge, 1925–27.

Index of Names

7

Travels Abroad

Car nous sommes où nous ne sommes pas.
                              Pierre-Jean Jouve

In his youth Debussy had been a great traveller. He was stimulated by new places and peoples, and in his travels as in his work he was driven on by a restless exploratory spirit. By the time he was thirty he had travelled extensively in his own country, he had been twice to Italy, Germany, and Russia, and had even made plans to go to America. We cannot be sure of all his movements in the last decade of the nineteenth century, but it seems likely that he was at any rate occasionally abroad during this period too.[1] In the latter part of his life he again became a restless traveller, but for different and rather sadder reasons. Throughout the first World War, when he was fighting a losing battle against disease, he was glad to find some peace of mind for a month or two in a country villa or hotel, and these war years were accordingly spent moving from one part of France to another. Before that he was obliged to travel abroad to earn fees conducting his works, and at any rate from 1907 onwards he was obliged to sacrifice some of his idealism to financial considerations. Commissions had to be accepted for works which otherwise would certainly not have been written. Engagements as a conductor in foreign towns had to be sought out. There was nothing harmful here, of course; Debussy was not a hothouse plant unable to withstand the rougher worldly shocks. The trouble was that all the contemporary evidence shows that he had no gifts as a conductor. There was nothing of the extrovert in his nature and he

[1] A poem of Pierre Louÿs addressed to Debussy and beginning 'Doux maître qui revient des terres étrangères' is presumed to refer to a journey to Mercin in 1898, but may be taken to refer literally to a foreign land.

consequently abhorred appearing in public. Also, from the time of his first London appearance, in January 1908, he was always likely to be ill, often seriously.

It is indeed pathetic that these foreign engagements were calculated to devour more and more of the time which remained to him. They moreover frustrated him in his creative work and caused additional physical suffering. The following list of journeys from 1902 onwards, undertaken for personal and professional reasons shows the extent of his travels. (After the death of Osiris, that is from 1908 onwards, all the journeys were made to fulfil conducting engagements.)

July	1902	London
May–June	1903	London
July	1904	London, Jersey
July–August	1905	Eastbourne
January	1907	Brussels
January	1908	London
February	1909	London
May	1909	London
November	1910	Vienna, Budapest
June	1911	Turin
December	1913	Moscow, St. Petersburg
February	1914	Rome
February–March	1914	The Hague, Amsterdam
April	1914	Brussels
July	1914	London

In assessing contemporary criticisms of Debussy's work outside his own country one is struck by the wide range of associations it evoked. In England, where a resemblance to Rossetti was observed, his work was said to reflect the æsthetic principles of Poe, Mallarmé, and Walter Pater. In Vienna, where he appeared when Schoenberg's paintings had become known, comparisons were made between his work and that of the German Art-Nouveau painter Gustav Klimt. The Italians, after giving a hostile reception to *Pelléas et Mélisande*, welcomed him like the English, as an antidote to Richard Strauss. In Russia he was held to be 'the spiritual heir of Moussorgsky and Rimsky-Korsakov'. It is clear from all this that Debussy's journeys stirred up great controversies. But he himself remained severely aloof. Polemical discussions meant nothing to him: they merely

made the artist's mission more difficult since they attempted to define his work and thereby to limit it.

We are able to draw upon many contemporary records of these journeys, but Debussy himself seems to have written few letters when he was abroad and his own impressions are therefore lacking. The intimate letters to Emma Debussy and his daughter Chouchou written on these journeys are at first sight puzzling. Their main theme was that foreign travel was boring and tiring. In at least two cities, London and Turin, Debussy's lack of experience as a conductor proved to be disastrous and his one desire was to return to his wife and daughter in Paris. But perhaps one need not look too far into these letters written from the heart.[1] Undoubtedly the hard-driven composer was sick, dejected, and lonely. He seems also to have been curiously anxious. On his short journeys in 1914 to Holland and Belgium telegrams were sent to Emma Debussy every few hours merely to re-assert the extent of his despair or to anticipate the pleasure of seeing her again.

Debussy's first appearance as a conductor in London was on 1 February 1908 at the Queen's Hall where he performed *L'Après-midi d'un faune* and *La Mer*. He had been invited by Sir Edgar Speyer, the wealthy patron of music who had formed a syndicate to take over the Queen's Hall Orchestra. Speyer had asked Henry Wood to go to Paris to negotiate Debussy's visit to London at the substantial fee at that time of one hundred guineas. This must have been by far the largest sum Debussy had ever been offered for a professional appearance. The negotiations were carried on through Madame Debussy, and as a result Wood was obliged to report that Debussy had refused Speyer's generous offer. 'What, a hundred guineas for *me*!' he is said to have exclaimed. 'And yet you pay Caruso four hundred guineas.' Having corrected this false impression, Wood received Speyer's agreement to conclude for two hundred guineas.[2] 'A crowded audience was present to give him a

<hr />

[1] The letter from Moscow of 4 December 1913 to Emma Debussy is typical of the many passionate outbursts in this correspondence: 'J'en ai tellement gros sur le cœur, que je ne sais pas par où commencer. . . . Tâchons de mettre de l'ordre dans mes regrets, qui peuvent être contenus en un seul: le regret de toi, chère petite Mienne à moi. Je me sens affreusement dépareillé et, si je veux m'appuyer sur le "côté cœur", c'est la pire douleur, puisque c'est en toi qu'il trouve son appui; on dirait, romantisme à part, que l'on marche sur mon âme.'

[2] On his last visit to London, in July 1914, when he was being hunted by his creditors, Debussy seems still to have been obsessed by the magnitude of the fees paid to

real English welcome', Wood writes of Debussy's first London appearance. 'I recall most vividly my first impressions of that dark, bearded Frenchman: his deep, soulful eyes; his quiet rather grating voice; most of all, his enormous head. I have never seen such a head on a man of his stature; it reminded me of the heads of early Egyptians. Debussy seemed delighted—almost like a child—because he thought that we in London appreciated his music more than his countrymen. . . . Not even Strauss had received a warmer welcome.'

Before dealing with this London reception of Debussy we must record a triumphant event in his public career. In fact, his concert with the Queen's Hall Orchestra was only the third time he had conducted. A few days earlier, on 19 and 26 January 1908, he had conducted *La Mer* with the Orchestre Colonne at the Théâtre du Châtelet in Paris. 'My heart began to beat loudly when yesterday morning I mounted the rostrum for the first rehearsal', Debussy wrote to Victor Segalen on 15 January. 'It is the first time in my life that I have played the game of being a conductor and you may believe that my utter lack of experience must disarm these curious beings called orchestral musicians, good-hearted as they are. . . . One of my main impressions is that I really reached the heart of my own music. Also, when everything was effectively coordinated I had the feeling of being myself an instrument of many different sonorities, animated, so to speak, by movements of the little stick. If this interests you at all I'll tell you more about it all some day.'[1]

The two performances which Debussy gave of *La Mer* in Paris achieved a spectacular success. Not since the production of *Pelléas* had he been seen at one of the Paris symphony concerts. 'To let everyone behold the sight of his pale, bloated appearance, his ink-black hair and his bulging forehead, chock full of chords of the ninth, he was biding his time', wrote Willy in his 'Lettre de l'Ouvreuse'

Caruso: 'I am going to London for a few days', he then wrote to Jacques Durand, 'to take part in an evening given by Lady Speyer. Caruso would ask what I am receiving for his accompanist. Anyhow, it is a drop of water in the desert of the awful summer months.'

[1] This sense of an identification with instruments is expressed also in a letter to André Caplet of 15 August 1911: 'And what a joy it is to listen to music in a state of complete relaxation; to feel oneself immersed in a constantly heightened state of happiness until one no longer knows whether one really exists, or whether one has not actually become that agonizing drum-roll or that harmonic on the cello. Enough, enough!'

in *Comoedia* on 20 January 1908. It is important to remember that this performance of *La Mer* had been rehearsed in close co-operation with the conductor Edouard Colonne and its success was therefore largely due to Colonne's preparatory work. 'Never had my ears heard a din like this outburst of enthusiasm', Willy reported. 'What we heard were wild yells of joy, the cracking sounds of hands clapped together, calls for the composer and demented shouts. Debussy picked his way ten times through the forest of the music desks in order, it seemed, to confide his gratitude to the prompter's box. Now and again a piercing, violent whistle, as if a guard were signalling the departure of a train, set off the triumphant reception afresh and had the effect of redoubling the zeal of tired muscles and sore hands. To appease these delirious melomaniacs the conquering hero, who had rushed away down a staircase, had to be brought back once again, this time in his over-coat and his bowler hat which in our modern costume takes the place of the ancient laurel wreath.' Almost incredibly, the applause continued even when Colonne and Jacques Thibaud had determined to go on with the programme by playing Lalo's *Symphonie espagnole*. They were obliged to stop and start again.

Debussy was not greatly affected by this show of enthusiasm. 'It was very kind of you to think of me during the hard times of Sunday last', he wrote to Segalen on 22 January. 'What a feverish atmosphere and what lunatic screaming! It wasn't at all funny. I felt like a freak showman or an acrobat who has carried off some perilous jump. And Sunday next it's to start again. Music sometimes leads one into strange paths.'[1]

The first performance of *La Mer* in London did not create the sensation of its Paris performance though it made a deep impression. Besides Wood and Sir Edgar Speyer, Debussy's friends in London included Louise Liebich, who in 1908 published the first biography of Debussy, Georges Jean-Aubry, who with T. J. Guéritte was active in promoting the interests of French musicians in England, Edwin Evans, who became Debussy's most powerful English advo-cate, and Arthur Symons, the English authority on Symbolist

[1] A letter of the same date to Paul-Jean Toulet records similar impressions: 'Since I saw you I have made my début in the career of a conductor. . . . It's amusing so long as you are able to pick out the colour you want from the end of the little stick, but afterwards it's like an exhibition in which the applause which greets you is like that given to a freak showman or an acrobat at the completion of a dangerous act.'

literature who was also at this time music critic of the *Saturday Review*.

The early impressions made by Debussy's music in England revive the worlds of Pater and Beardsley. The Symbolist movement, which had taken its rise in Paris, soon became known in London, particularly in literary circles, and in the early years of the century Debussy's music became as fully understood in London as it had been in Paris among the followers of Mallarmé. In 1908 Arthur Symons declared that a performance of Debussy's Quartet enabled him 'at last to enter into the somewhat dark and secret shadows' of what he called 'the wood'. He recognized in it 'a new kind of music . . . filled with an instinctive quality of beauty which can pass from mood to mood, surprise us, lead us astray but end by leading us to the enchantment in the heart of what I have called the wood.' Unfortunately Symons was not to hear *Pelléas et Mélisande*, given in London in 1909, but he had heard sufficient works of Debussy to be able to state that 'words, however vague, are too precise for this music, which suggests nothing but music'. It was 'an achievement of a new kind' not to be found, he believed, in Fauré or Ravel: 'This genuine quality is not in them, or only here and there by accident.' Debussy's Verlaine settings, on the other hand, disappointed him. *Mandoline*, however, suggests a vision of the Art Nouveau. It is music which 'is echoed like a bird answering a bird, the tinkle in the music is the same tinkle as in the verse. . . . An insect's web has been woven across a flower; it glitters a little, and at a breath it evaporates; and the flower and its perfume remain.'

The following year, after Debussy's appearance at the Queen's Hall, Symons attempted to assess Debussy's achievement in the light of his inspiration from both Verlaine and Mallarmé. Debussy, he maintained, 'is the Mallarmé of music, not because he has set *L'Après-midi d'un faune* to sound, but because the music has all the qualities of the poem and none, for instance, of Verlaine. . . . Mallarmé has a beauty of his own, calculated, new, alluring; and Debussy is not less original, aloof, deliberately an artist.' *L'Après-midi d'un faune* 'has precisely the same beauty as the poem, and it is in no sense programme music. It matches the poem because the art of making is the same in poet and musician.' Disappointed by the first movement of *La Mer* ('on a first hearing it left no impression

except that of unsuccessful effort') Symons found a 'new gaiety' in
Jeux de vagues, and in the last movement 'a drama of elements'
that 'convinced the mind as well as the senses; it had a deeper meaning than anything of Debussy's music which I have heard'. It was
not easy, he maintained, nor indeed profitable, to compare the
work of Debussy with other contemporary or even earlier music.
It 'has the conscious and lovely eccentricities of Poe,[1] the secret
glitter in the jewels of Mallarmé'. Like other observers in England,
Symons was impressed by Debussy's appearance. 'The face of Debussy has a singular likeness to the later portraits of Rossetti; there
is the same brooding meditation in eyes and forehead.' And he goes
on: 'A certain heaviness of aspect is characteristic of most artists of
extreme delicacy: Gautier, Renan, Pater, Maeterlinck, among
writers. Languor was part of their genius, and Debussy's music is
defined beforehand in the first four lines of Verlaine's *Langueur*:

> Je suis l'Empire à la fin de la décadence,
> Qui regarde passer les grands Barbares blancs
> En composant des acrostiches indolents
> D'un style d'or où la langueur du soleil danse.'

Debussy is Merlin, Symons suggested, solitarily living in a wood
with his phantoms and 'no Vivien has taught him to be human! . . .
The phantoms have unearthly voices; they express neither love nor
hate, hardly desire; but for the most part dreams that have no outset
nor conclusion, and when they are awake they play indolently at
acrostics. Beardsley would have recognized his perverse elegance in
these wandering outlines, in which sound plays pranks in the brain.
He would have collected them in visible outlines, he would have
shown them to us in fancy-dress, playing indolently at acrostics.'[2]

A return visit of Debussy to England was planned for 1909 when

[1] Arthur Symons' American contemporary James Huneker similarly drew a comparison between Debussy and Poe (see Vol. I, p. 213). In his study 'Mélisande and
Debussy' in *Bedouins* (New York, 1920) Huneker states that *Pelléas et Mélisande* 'has
the dream-drugged atmosphere of Edgar Allan Poe; the Poe of the dark tarn of Auber,
of Ligeia, of Ellenora, of Berenice and Helen, those frail apparitions from claustral
solitudes and the Valley of the Many-Coloured Grass all as exotic as they are incor-
poreal'.

[2] The reference to sound which plays 'pranks in the brain' may be indicative of the
insanity of which Symons was shortly to be a victim. Published on 8 February 1908,
Symons' study of Debussy was one of the last articles he wrote before his mental
collapse. In November of the same year he was certified insane and sent to Brooke
House, Clapton.

he was to have appeared in London and also in Manchester and Edinburgh. These plans were upset by the beginnings of a grave malady. In January of this year the first signs were declared of an illness which later developed into cancer of the rectum. The following month he suffered almost daily from hæmorrhages for which he was obliged to take morphine and cocaine. He arrived in England at the end of February, ill and dejected. 'Forgive me for having left you without news', he wrote to Durand on 27 February 1909, the day of his concert at the Queen's Hall. 'Arrived here on Thursday, have been ill all the time and have consequently been obliged to cancel my journeys to Edinburgh and Manchester. The concert today went off admirably. *Fêtes* was encored and it only depended on me to secure an encore for *L'Après-midi d'un faune*, but I could hardly stand up—a very bad posture for conducting anything.'

Wood's account of what actually happened throws a rather different light on Debussy's anxieties at this concert. Out of consideration for the fact that the composer was by no means an experienced conductor, and apparently unaware of the gravity of his illness, Wood had rehearsed the orchestra 'until there was practically nothing for Debussy to do'. The rehearsal went off smoothly, Wood writes,

but at the concert there was a peculiar accident. I do not remember ever witnessing anything like it. In the second of the *Nocturnes* (*Fêtes*) the time changes a good deal. To the surprise of us all Debussy (who quite candidly was not a good conductor even of his own works) suddenly lost his head, and his beat! Realizing what he had done, he evidently felt the best thing was to stop and begin the movement again. He tapped the desk, and tapped again. Then the most extraordinary thing happened. The orchestra refused to stop. . . . They obviously did not intend to stop: they knew that the audience would think the fault was theirs. Moreover, the work (which they liked immensely) was going beautifully and they meant to give a first-rate performance of it. . . . The audience by no means missed the fact that something had gone wrong. . . . At the end, in truly English fashion, they recorded their appreciation to such an extent that he was compelled to repeat the movement.

In the evening Debussy was due to attend a reception at the Aeolian Hall of which an account is given in the memoirs of Arnold Bax. 'Tonight I have to attend a reception organized by the society of English composers', Debussy wrote to Durand. 'What sort of figure shall I cut? Something like a man condemned to death. It appears that I cannot get out of it because of the Entente Cordiale and other such sentimental ideas invented to hasten the death of others.' The society referred to was in fact the 'Music Club',[1] and Debussy was the first of four eminent musicians—the others being d'Indy, Sibelius, and Schoenberg—invited to be present at a concert of their works. 'Of the four guests,' Bax writes, 'Debussy's torments were certainly the most excrutiating.' The concert of songs, sung by an American singer accompanied by Bax, and instrumental works was preceded by an address given in guttural and almost unintelligible French by Alfred Kalisch. 'The great composer,' Bax writes, 'an inordinately shy man, was planted in a chair in the exact centre of the platform facing the audience. He was clearly utterly nonplussed and could only attempt to solve his problems by rising and making a stiff little bow whenever he recognized his own name amid Kalisch's guttural mumblings. This part of his ordeal over, he was permitted to shamble dazedly to the rear of the hall, where he confided to Edwin Evans that he would rather write a symphony to order than go through such an experience again.' Like other people who met Debussy at this time, Bax was impressed by his almost oriental appearance. 'Never shall I forget the impression made upon me by that thick-set clumsy figure, the huge greenish, almost Moorish face beneath the dense thicket of black hair, and the obscure dreaming eyes that seemed to be peering through me at some object behind my back. As he lumbered vaguely forward, extending a cushioned hand, he looked like some

---

[1] In his *Farewell, my Youth* Sir Arnold Bax gives an arresting picture of the meetings of this club: 'In 1908 or thereabouts was founded the "Music Club", a dressy concert-cum-supper affair presided over by Alfred Kalisch, critic of *The Star* and a pious thurifer before the altar of Richard Strauss. Kalisch was a lovable little man: in person, with his barrel-like trunk, thick colourless skin, squat features and habitual cigar, suggesting the gentleman constructed entirely of motor tyres who used at one time to figure in M. Michelin's advertisement. The club members were mostly elderly, and notable for wealth, paunchiness and stertorous breathing. Bulging pinkish bosoms straining at expensive decolletages, redundant dewlaps, and mountainous backs were generously displayed by the ladies, whilst among the men ruddy double-chins, overflowing their collars at the back of the neck, and boiled eyes were rife. The assemblage indeed was ever inclined to bring to mind Beardsley's famous drawing, "The Wagnerites".'

Triton arisen from "the glaucous caverns of Old Ocean". "A mythological survival!" I said to myself.'[1]

Arthur Symons had been prominent among the early English admirers of Debussy and his two articles in *The Saturday Review* appraised the æsthetic of Debussy in terms related to ideas in the contemporary literary movement. His successor on *The Saturday Review*, Filson Young, similarly took a radical view of Debussy's work though he kept severely to musical considerations. Having heard the concerts devoted in 1909 to Debussy's works in London at the Queen's Hall, the Aeolian Hall, and the Bechstein Hall (the last organized by the Society of French Concerts), Filson Young boldly stated: 'It is most important that those who care for music as a living art should come to their critical bearings about Debussy. He is a discoverer; he has wandered into a new world of tonality, and what for want of a better term we must call musical colour; he speaks to us in a new language, which we are obliged to learn before we can form any judgement of his work.' Young was left in two minds by several of the works he had heard. Nevertheless, he accurately measured the break-through made by the new music. Debussy's work, he concluded,

helps to make obsolete many forms which should have been obsolete long ago; forms in which the great composers of the past wrote great music, but in which no modern composer can write any but feeble music. It makes it a little more absurd for us to go on flogging those dead donkeys, the oratorio and the cantata; it makes experiment respectable, and even fashionable, where yesterday it was deemed disgraceful. It helps in the real appreciation of the great composers of the past, and will help to send us back to Bach for our fugues, Handel for our oratorios (if we really want oratorios), Schumann for our romance, Brahms for our musical philosophy; it will help us to discriminate between what was and what was not inspired in the works of the great, instead of accepting everything as pure gospel which bears the name of Mozart, Beethoven, Rameau,

[1] The quotation is from Shelley's *Prometheus Unbound* (Act II, scene i). Bax was one of the first to note that as early as February 1909 Debussy's appearance suggested the illness which, nine years later, brought about his death: 'Recalling that morbidly sallow complexion of his, I must conjecture that even so early the malignant foe, destined to bring about his death in his early fifties, was already prowling within his body.'

Bach, Palestrina. It will do this because whatever its faults and failures, it appeals boldly on the single ground of beauty, and not of erudition, imitation or conservatism. It claims every licence, and stands or falls by its justification of that licence.[1]

In May 1909 Debussy was again in London to superintend the rehearsals of *Pelléas et Mélisande* given at Covent Garden on 21 May under Cleofonte Campanini who the previous year, on 19 February, had first conducted the opera in America, at the Metropolitan Opera House. Rose Féart took the part of Mélisande and Warnery was the Pelléas. Debussy became enraged by the producer's irrelevant ideas ('I've seldom had a stronger desire to kill someone') and felt that the work was being too hurriedly mounted. He attended the dress rehearsal but on the night of the first performance stayed at his Kensington hotel.

The work was enthusiastically received. In *The Musical Standard* Louise Liebich, who had become acquainted with *Pelléas* through Louis Laloy and Debussy himself, wondered whether in the larger framework of Covent Garden the intimate character of the opera would suffer. Never before, she declared, had it been heard under such favourable conditions. 'Space enhanced the beauty of detail and prolonged the fine-spun harmonies.' Mrs. Liebich also maintained that far from producing purely 'atmospheric' effects Debussy conveyed 'the true Celtic feeling for Nature', illustrated also, she believed, in the work of the German philosopher Fechner.[2] 'It is not only atmosphere that he reproduces; it is the Earth-Soul.'

[1] Filson Young perceived that Debussy foreshadowed the revolt against the whole heritage of Romantic music which took place after the first World War. In 1921 Diaghilev, according to Ernest Newman, had declared Beethoven to be 'a mummy', Brahms 'a putrefying corpse', Schumann 'a home-sick dog howling at the moon'. Diaghilev's iconoclasm was reflected by Hindemith, who at about this time proclaimed Beethoven to be at the root of all the Romantic evils ('Mit Beethoven fängt die Schweinerei an'), and also by Arthur Bliss who in 1921 declared himself to be bitterly opposed to 'the pseudo-intellectuality of the Brahms camp-followers with their classical sonatas and concertos and variations and other stock-in-trade'. This attempt to revolutionize the whole pattern of concert giving, though unsuccessful, represented a genuine impulse to break away from what seemed to be the paralysing weight of tradition, and to set standards valid in themselves, for their time alone, unencumbered by past associations.

[2] Gustav Theodor Fechner (1801–87) did valuable pioneer work in psychophysics and in the measurement of sensations which later proved useful to researchers in vision and hearing. He provided psychology with methods that could be expressed in terms of mathematics. His philosophy was based on an animistic concept of the world in which even plants and the stars were believed to be animated.

Possibly on evidence supplied by the composer, Mrs. Liebich went on to predict that 'M. Debussy's next opera will perhaps contain further suggestions of that Earth-Soul. For the owner of the "House of Usher" is made by Poe to believe in "the sentience of all vegetable things".'

These early views of Debussy furthered his cause in one way or another but the most penetrating assessment of his work was given in a lecture on *Pelléas* by Edwin Evans at the Royal Academy of Music on 25 May 1909. After relating Debussy's conception of opera to the Wagnerian theories, and also to the theories of Camille Mauclair expressed in his essay 'L'Identité et la fusion des arts', Evans asserted that though the music of *Pelléas* was avowedly anti-Wagnerian 'it constitutes a more advanced step towards the complete realization of Wagner's theories than any step taken by Wagner himself. Wagner dreamed of an art work where drama and music should be indissolubly joined, but his music dramas are crowded with scenes that are equally effective in the concert-room, separated from all the trappings of drama. The music of *Pelléas*, on the contrary, cannot be separated from the drama without losing its purpose. And conversely, after one has heard Debussy's musical setting, one actually finds it difficult to imagine Maeterlinck's drama without Debussy's music, so closely are the two knit together.'[1] Elsewhere in this lecture Evans suggested that the æsthetic of Debussy derived from the following theory of Walter Pater: 'Art is always striving to be independent of the mere intelligence, to become a matter of pure perception, to get rid of its responsibilities to its subject or material; the ideal examples of poetry and composition being those in which the constituent elements of the composition are so welded together that the material or subject no longer strikes the intellect only; nor the form, the eye or ear only; but form and matter, in their union or identity, present one single effect to the imaginative reason, that complex faculty for which every thought and feeling is twin-born with its sensible analogue or symbol.'

---

[1] Evans endorses here the opinion on *Pelléas* of the American critic Lawrence Gilman, which he quotes: 'What the Camerata, and their successors, could not accomplish for lack of adequate musical means, what Gluck fell short of compassing for want of boldness and reach of vision, what Wagner might have effected but for too great a preoccupation with one phase of the problem, a Frenchman of today has quietly and perfectly achieved.'

This quotation is from the essay entitled 'The School of Giorgione' in Pater's *The Renaissance*, the interesting point here being that it was in this essay, first published in 1877, that Pater developed his theory that 'all art constantly aspires towards the condition of music', thus anticipating the later theories of the Symbolists and Impressionists.[1] Evans met Debussy in London and may well have mentioned Pater's *Renaissance* to him. He was at any rate to hear of this work from another source. In January 1918, shortly before Debussy's death, Robert Godet wrote to him: 'I wanted to tell you of a book which you will perhaps be pleased to read—the French translation of *The Renaissance* by Walter Pater, a very perceptive English essayist who has both a mind and a feeling for constructive criticism rather similar to that of Wilde; moreover, he carries his knowledge lightly and never makes a show of erudition. What he leaves unsaid is nearly always as valuable as what he says and his implications find their way into his prose, or rather emanate from it, in a most musical fashion.' Godet goes on to say that in this respect Pater reminds him of Keats's *Ode on a Grecian Urn* which, he suggests, 'is implicitly dedicated to you (did not the late Le Mercier [the translator of Keats who were their common friend] suspect this?)' and of which he sends Debussy a French translation:

Douces sont les mélodies qu'on entend; mais celles qu'on n'entend pas
    Sont plus douces; sonnez donc, délicats pipeaux,
Non pas à l'oreille sensuelle, mais plus délectables
    Sonnez à l'esprit des chansons de nul nom.

After London, Vienna and Budapest. Debussy's works began to be known in Germany and Austria at the beginning of the century but they had made little impression. Busoni's performance of *L'Après-midi d'un faune* in Berlin passed almost unnoticed. The first performance of *Pelléas* in German was given at Frankfurt on 19 April 1907. In the Berlin journal *Die Musik* Hans Pfeilschmidt referred to Debussy as one of the '*Neutöner* [new soundmakers] who use their art to deepen and colour poetry but who make no

[1] Pater's argument was to some extent ill-founded. It was partly based on the subject of the picture in the Pitti Palace, *The Concert*, which Pater too readily attributed to Giorgione. But the whole of the latter part of his study in which he discerns an association in Giorgione's mind between the sensuousness of sound and the presence of water anticipated later ideas, notably those in Gaston Bachelard's psychological study of Symbolist poetry, *L'Eau et les rêves* (see Appendix F).

attempt to create absolute music.' Germany was the country of absolute music, he implied, and the subordination of music to poetry was a foreign conception, even though it had originated with Wagner. Pfeilschmidt found the vocal writing too consistently declamatory and several scenes monotonous. This was a common impression of listeners not attuned to the gradations of expression in the work. The harmonic liberties seldom went beyond those in the third act of *Tristan*, Pfeilschmidt maintained, and he made a curious comparison between *Pelléas* and the score written by Liszt to accompany a dramatic declamation of Lenau's Ballade *Der traurige Mönch*.[1]

The journey to Vienna in November 1910 marks the beginning of the correspondence between Debussy and his second wife. Earlier journeys had been undertaken together, but Debussy's material situation was becoming increasingly acute and it became imperative for him to accept whatever engagements were offered. 'You realize', he wrote to Emma Debussy from Vienna, 'that I have undertaken this journey for us, because of our persistent poverty without which I shouldn't be so far away from you, so deprived of your caresses.' He had hoped to pass away the time on the journey to Vienna by reading Chateaubriand's *Mémoires d'outre-tombe* but he fell to reflections on his home in Paris: 'It was with much difficulty that I kept myself from weeping.' In his hotel room, while unpacking, he is overcome by the fact that he is desperately alone. 'Everything annoys me. My nerves are on edge and I find that a composer of music is required to excel in those qualities of toughness possessed by a travelling salesman.' After rehearsing *Ibéria* with the Vienna orchestra he was filled with anxiety. If only he could hurl abuse at someone. 'No, I must devour myself in silence [*il faut que je me mange en silence*] . . . bitterly and as an unfortunate exile.' But he is usually able to laugh at himself at the right moment: 'If only you could see my expression—something like the mask of Beethoven or that of Dante on his return from Hell.'

On the day of the concert he tells Emma that he will have to think fervently of her 'in order not to appear hopelessly bored and

[1] This comparison was prompted by the fact that this work of Liszt, a short 'melodrama' for speaker and piano, opens with an ascending figure, several times repeated, in the whole-tone scale. Against a piano accompaniment the verses of Lenau are not sung but spoken. There is no evidence that Debussy knew *Der traurige Mönch*.

even disgusted'. And with much self-knowledge he goes on: 'We expect to procure the approval of a public of which the greater part consists of idiots; this is a rather ridiculous situation and most ironic and contradictory. Let us hope that I shall have enough nervous strength to overcome this state of mind which results in my being my own worst enemy.'[1]

An illuminating account of Debussy's impression on the audience of the Konzertverein in Vienna was given by Richard Specht in *Der Merker*. Specht imagined that he was going to see a tall, elegant Frenchman like a character, he says, from *L'Aile bleue*, a well-known picture at that time by the contemporary Belgian painter Fernand Khnopff, whose portraits, strongly influenced by the Pre-Raphaelites, were usually of people who were idealistically hand-some or angelic.[2] Debussy, Specht found, was the opposite of angelic. He was 'thick-set with small abrupt movements, a sort of gnome in tails'. He also made the impression of 'a black-and-white sketch of Beardsley', or perhaps he had been 'carved out of a hefty black radish'.[3] As a conductor he appeared only approximately to indicate the tempos and entries, 'making a colourless impression' quite the opposite, Specht was bound to declare, of his music 'which is all colour and painting'. On the technical plane he was said to have 'gradually eliminated the thematic element in music and the importance of the motive'.[4] Specht freely admitted 'that one must constantly refer to the art of painting to describe his art'. Whistler and Böcklin are among the painters whose work Debussy evoked, but more than anyone he suggested the work of Gustav Klimt.[5]

[1] In his *Journal*, Gide, in 1908, records a conversation about Debussy which goes some way towards explaining the tone of this correspondence: '"He is so affectionate", said Madame X. "Oh no, Madame! He is so wheedling [*câlin*]", retorted Madame Debussy.'

[2] A forgotten figure of the period, Fernand Khnopff (1858–1921) was associated not only with the Pre-Raphaelites but with Maeterlinck and Verhaeren. His best-known work was an oil-painting characteristically entitled *En écoutant du Schumann*.

[3] A forbidding caricature of Debussy by Rudolf Herrmann which appeared in *Der Merker* of May 1911 and which is reproduced facing p. 50, was presumably inspired by Specht's description.

[4] Nearly all forward-looking composers have been taunted with the fact that they have forsaken melody, and this was apparently the impression made by Debussy's music in Vienna. In the course of his visit he met Ferdinand Löwe, conductor of the Konzertverein orchestra and disciple of Bruckner. Correlation of the letters to Caplet and Godet suggests that it was Löwe who, having publicly congratulated Debussy on having abolished melody, received from him the outraged retort: 'Mais voyons, Monsieur, toute ma musique aspire à n'être que mélodie!'

[5] Gustav Klimt (1862–1918) was one of the principal artists of the Viennese *Jugendstyl* movement, the Teutonic counterpart of *Art Nouveau*. His work was noted

The following year, in June 1911, Specht wrote a further article on Debussy in *Der Merker* following Bruno Walter's performance at the Hofoper of *Pelléas et Mélisande*.[1] It so happened that in Vienna during the spring months of 1911 the rival claims of Debussy, Mahler, and Schoenberg were first put forward. The preceding number of *Der Merker* had contained an obituary of Mahler, who had died in Vienna on 18 May, but was otherwise entirely devoted to detailed, serious studies of contemporary French music. This publication was no doubt a reflection of the Franco-Austrian musical entente promoted in Paris by Paul Clemenceau, the younger brother of the French Prime Minister, on the occasion of Mahler's visit to Paris in April 1910. In *Der Merker* Egon Wellesz and Theodor Tagger wrote on the new French works they had heard, but the main study in this number, *Claude Debussy und der Debussysmus*, a translation of the article that had appeared in *La Revue S.I.M.* the previous year, was by Louis Laloy. Two points were principally developed by Laloy in the image of Debussy thus presented to the Viennese: he was an artist of 'innocence and purity', in the category, he suggested, of Josquin des Prés and Mozart; and he was an artist who was constantly exploring and evolving. He was said to be unsuited, therefore, by his temperament to become a *chef d'école*, revered for theories and systems.

Specht's review of *Pelléas* was perspicacious. 'It recedes to a state of pre-music, to the moment before music takes on being and form.' It is curious to read that it was on his performance of Debussy's score that Bruno Walter was judged to be 'the true heir of Mahler, the only one in whom something of the spirit and power of the unforgettable one remains'—curious since Walter never became known as a conductor of the works of Debussy.[2] It is also interesting to see that Specht's laudatory review of *Pelléas* appeared in a Schoen-

---

for its rich barbaric reds and gleaming jewel-like enamels. In describing Debussy as 'der Klimt der Musik' Specht was probably thinking of *Ibéria* in which the orchestration is exceptionally vivid. The works of both Klimt and Khnopff (see p. 131, note 1) are illustrated in *The Sources of Modern Art* by J. Cassou, E. Langui, and N. Pevsner (London, 1962).

[1] Professor W. Austin of Cornell University has kindly informed me that Alban Berg was present at this performance but not Schoenberg. The subject of Schoenberg's early symphonic poem, *Pelleas und Melisande*, had been suggested to him by Richard Strauss.

[2] This first performance of *Pelléas* in Vienna would surely have been conducted by Mahler had he lived. In the last years of his life Mahler had introduced to Vienna the operas of Charpentier, Camille Erlanger, and Saint-Saëns.

berg number of *Der Merker* where, together with a study of Schoenberg by Specht, extracts were published from the *Harmonielehre* and the libretto of *Die glückliche Hand*. This number also contained reproductions of a selection of Schoenberg's paintings seen that year at the first exhibition of the 'Blaue Reiter' in Munich.[1] By contrast with his reviews of Debussy, Specht's article on Schoenberg was guarded. Reasonably enough, he saw the young revolutionary composer as belonging to the group of exploratory figures in Vienna including Mahler, Gustav Klimt, and Kokoschka, but in 1911 he confessed to being more baffled by the latest works of Schoenberg[2] than by those which he had recently heard of Debussy.

From Vienna Debussy went to Budapest to take part in a chamber concert on 5 December 1910 with Rose Féart and the Waldbauer Quartet. He played the *Estampes* and *Children's Corner* in a programme which also included the String Quartet and the *Proses lyriques*. There was something wrong, he felt, in playing the intimate pieces forming *Children's Corner*, written for his daughter, to an audience of no less than fifteen hundred people.

Debussy did not meet either Bartók or Kodály in Hungary. Having tried to meet Debussy in Paris,[3] Bartók also missed him in Budapest. At the time of Debussy's visit there Bartók was devoting himself to research in folk music. His lasting impression of Budapest was of the Tzigane violinist, Radics, who appears to have played in a highly evocative manner. One imagines that Bartók would similarly have been impressed by the spontaneous sincerity of this

---

[1] They received praise from Kandinsky and other Expressionist artists. In *The Sources of Modern Art*, Emile Langui points out that in the first decade of the twentieth century Vienna had little sympathy for the Expressionist movement, despite the fact that Freud, Mahler, and Schoenberg were living there. The dominant styles were those of the *Jugendstyl* and Klimt. On the other hand, Schoenberg's music is said by Langui to have impressed the painter Richard Gerstl.

[2] These were the first Chamber Symphony, op. 9, the second String Quartet with soprano voice, op. 10, first given in Vienna in 1908 with Maria Gutheil-Schoder, who took the part of Mélisande in the Viennese première of *Pelléas*, and *Das Buch der hängenden Gärten*. It is, however, unlikely that any of these works were known to Debussy. In a letter of 1911 to Robert Godet he wrote rather contemptuously of the charms of Vienna, mentioning composers far removed from Schoenberg: 'Vieille ville fardée où l'on abuse de la musique de Brahms, de Puccini, d'officiers aux poitrines de femmes, et de femmes aux poitrines d'officiers.'

[3] A meeting was sought, according to Halsey Stevens, through the pianist Isidore Philippe. 'Do you not know that Debussy has the reputation of being extremely rude?' Philippe said. 'Do you want to be insulted by Debussy?' 'Yes, certainly', Bartók replied.

gipsy violinist. 'The best thing the Hungarians have', Debussy wrote to Robert Godet, 'is a Tzigane named Radics who has an infinitely greater love for music than many celebrated musicians. He plays in an ordinary, common café, but you imagine that he is playing to himself in some dark forest, and he manages to extract from the depths of his soul some kind of melancholy that we are seldom able to glimpse. He could wrench secrets out of an iron safe.' Writing to his host in Budapest, the impresario Monsieur Barczy, Debussy said that he hoped to return to Budapest 'simply to listen to Radics until the end of my life'.[1] On his return to Paris Debussy received from Barczy some editions of Hungarian folk music which disappointed him. In a letter to Barczy of 19 December 1910 he sets out his views on the matter of folk-song editions in a manner wholly in keeping with the independent spirit of Bartók:

I have received the Hungarian music and thank you for it. But how different it is from the impression left on me by Radics! This music is like a beautiful butterfly under glass. The wings are brilliant but they are not alive and their rich colours have become dulled. I do not think that you Hungarians can judge this music as it really is. It's something that really belongs to your life. It is so familiar to you that you fail to see its great artistic import-ance. Remember what happened when this music was arranged by Liszt! Although Liszt was a genius he tamed it; it loses its freedom and its innate sense of the infinite. When you listen to Radics you are transported. You actually inhale the scent of forests; you hear the sound of running brooks; and he expresses the secrets of a heart that suffers and laughs almost at the same time. In my view this music must never be changed. As far as possible it must be kept away from the clumsiness of professionals.

[1] The Hungarian gipsy violinists continued to make an overwhelming impression on visitors to Budapest long after Debussy's death. Referring in his *Foreign Faces* (1964) to certain Hungarian gipsy musicians who obviously belong to the same artistic family as Radics, V. S. Pritchett eloquently says that they 'know how slowly to fill every molecule of the air with their smoky, sullen chords that rumble like fire shut up in a furnace, a sound that slurs and slumps, breaks off and picks up again with wicked suddenness and passes to the tricky clipping of the strings, rises to ferocity, then clouds away and falls into a blank carnal sadness. It is the music of the sexual act.' Debussy's enthusiastic remarks concerning Radics are in striking contrast to the acrimonious tone of his letters to the famous Hungarian violinist Jenö Hubay, with whom he had a serious misunderstanding regarding the organization of his Hungarian visit. Debus-sy's unpublished letters to Hubay are in the Library of Congress, Washington, and at the Eastman School of Music, Rochester, N.Y.

What I wish to say is that your Tziganes should be treated with more respect. Don't think of them as mere entertainers who give colour to a party and help in the consumption of champagne. The truth is that their music is as beautiful as your old embroideries and lace. Why, then, do you not treat it with the same respect and love? Your young musicians could profitably be inspired by this music, not by copying it but by finding the equivalent of its freedom, its qualities of evocation and suffering and by using some of its rhythmic features. The lessons of Wagner were harmful to music in many ways and to the national interests of music. The folk music of one's country should be used only as a fundamental inspiration, never as a model. This is particularly true of your folk music. Love it passionately, but don't attempt to dress it up in some scholarly way.

Forgive me for going into matters that do not perhaps concern me. It's simply that I have a great love for music—not only French music—and that I dislike seeing the riches of music squandered, or its real meaning, its national meaning, deformed. In France we have too long suffered, and suffer still, from the German influence. Don't fall into our error and be deceived by pretentious profundities or by the detestable German 'Modern-style'.

It would be interesting to know which composers were believed by Debussy to write in the 'detestable "modern-style" '. Surely not Strauss, many aspects of whose work he admired, nor Mahler who could not possibly be accused of having in any way been influenced by the *Jugendstyl*? Debussy was not a rabid nationalist, but in his contribution to the wider European scene he did most fervently wish to re-assert distinctive French qualities. On his next journey, to Italy, we find him battling against the traditions of Verdi and Puccini.

On the occasion of the Industrial Exhibition held at Turin in 1911 several prominent musicians were asked to take part in concerts there. Vittorio Gui, the young conductor of the Turin orchestra, had invited Elgar, Kajanus, d'Indy and Pierné, and also Debussy who, on 25 June 1911, conducted *L'Après-midi d'un faune* and *Ibéria*. We are fortunate in having a detailed account of this Italian journey. It was a sad and a humiliating episode. Possibly for physical reasons Debussy was now hardly able to assert authority

over the orchestra. In a memoir written some twenty years after Debussy's visit Vittorio Gui, with exquisite courtesy, makes it clear that had it not been for his assistance at rehearsals the concert could not have taken place. Debussy had at first refused this assistance, Gui states, declaring that 'conducting had always been an old, unsatisfied passion for him'. From his first contact with the orchestra, however, 'it was evident that he was no conductor. . . . Not one of the qualities required from a conductor was in his nature. His gestures were uncertain, his eyes remained glued to the score (and it was his own music), he was unable to control either the players or himself, and several times he actually turned over the pages of the score with the same right hand that held the baton, thus missing a beat and throwing the orchestra into confusion.' Under the pretext of translating Debussy's directions from French into Italian, Gui approached the orchestra and was at any rate able to restore some sense of discipline. So far only *L'Après-midi d'un faune* had been rehearsed, but when it came to the complicated score of *Ibéria* things became very much worse. 'The confusion was such that Debussy felt that nothing of his score was understood; he was himself becoming nervous and, losing himself in what appeared to be a chaos of sounds and rhythms, he hastened to concede the ten-minute break and retired in an anxious mood to the artists' room.' He now willingly accepted the proposal that Gui should take charge of the rehearsals while he himself would appear only at the concert, put back a couple of days in order to allow adequate time for its preparation. When it eventually came to the concert Debussy reluctantly took up his baton 'with an almost childish fear'. 'Here was a new experience for me', Gui charmingly confides. 'For the first time I felt fear for another, a paternal fear as if in some strange way the roles were reversed and as if he, not I, were the younger of the two.' At the concert Debussy conducted 'as well as could be expected, correctly but without inspiring either the orchestra or the audience which, in one of the most poetic passages of *Parfums de la nuit*, was further put off by a shower of rain beating down on the glass roof of the hall, causing them to wonder how they were to reach home without their umbrellas.'

The account given of this event in a letter of 24 June 1911 from Debussy to André Caplet presents a different picture. Debussy had been too humiliated to tell his friend the truth: 'Where are you,

André Caplet?' he exclaims. 'Or rather why aren't you with me to help me persuade this Turin orchestra that music is not played with one's hands in one's pockets! What a job! Six hours' rehearsal every day. You will agree that for one with so little practice it's hard. . . . I am a pitiful sight, worn out and meeting precisely the description of the "thinking reed" given by Pascal.'[1] Apparently motivated by the same desire to conceal the near-disaster with the Italian orchestra he wrote from Turin to Durand: 'If only you knew how it is to feel that beneath it all the music of Claude Debussy means nothing to them and that at the first expedient they will go back to their Puccini, Verdi, and what-have-you in the Italian language.'[2]

Two years were to pass before he travelled abroad again. At the invitation of Koussevitzky he spent the first fortnight of December 1913 conducting concerts of his works in Moscow and St. Petersburg.[3] Recalling his impressions in La Revue Musicale, Rimsky-Korsakov's pupil Lazare Saminsky stated that 'for the young Petrograd composers Debussy was in a way the spiritual son of Moussorgsky and of Rimsky-Korsakov, forming a link between Russia of the East and France of the West.' In fact, though Debussy's works had been played in Russia by Siloti and Koussevitzky, few of the composers in Russia at that time responded to Debussy's work. César Cui had written a parody of Debussy's music entitled L'Après-midi d'un faune qui lit son journal and Rimsky-Korsakov, who had died five years earlier, had been bitterly censorious of Debussy's work in the same way and for the same reason as Saint-Saëns; they resented the undermining of musical form and of the principles of tonality. Among the composers he met in Russia was Prokofiev who, at a reception given by the magazine Apollon, played to him his Legend and his early Studies. Prokofiev's exuberant

[1] The reference is to this passage in the Pensées of Pascal: 'L'homme n'est qu'un roseau, le plus faible de la nature; mais c'est un roseau pensant. Il ne faut pas que l'univers entier s'arme pour l'écraser: une vapeur, une goutte d'eau suffit pour le tuer. Mais quand l'univers l'écraserait, l'homme serait encore plus noble que ce qui le tue, parce qu'il sait qu'il meurt, et l'avantage que l'univers a sur lui, l'univers n'en sait rien.'

[2] Italian opera of the Romantic period was outside the range of experience not only of Debussy but of nearly all other French composers of his generation. In 1905 Fauré, in Cologne, happened to hear a performance of Bellini's Norma which struck him merely as a mummified relic.

[3] Koussevitzky's letter of 1 November 1913 to Debussy, in the Library of Congress, states that he is 'awaited with great impatience by the whole musical world of Moscow and St. Petersburg. . . . Should I send someone to meet you at the frontier? We will do everything we can for you not to feel lonely in Russia.'

musical nature was, however, more naturally drawn to Ravel than to Debussy.

Debussy's letters to his wife and the charming postcards to his daughter[1] convey only superficial impressions of his stay in Russia, which he had not visited since he was engaged there in his youth by Madame von Meck. One of his friends from those early days, Sonia von Meck, now a middle-aged woman, was present at one of the receptions. One or two new works hold his attention. We find him reading the score of Busoni's Piano Concerto, which he finds 'boggy music containing the worst faults of Richard Strauss'; he dines at Koussevitzky's home in Moscow with Diaghilev, who amuses him with an account of the Russian Ballet's visit to South America; and he spends a pleasant evening hearing for the first time Moussorgsky's *Sorotchinsky Fair*. Otherwise, this last Russian journey was a grim ordeal. One gathers from the intimate letters to Emma Debussy that throughout this short but strenuous tour he was much more of a sick man than he knew. Everything was an effort for the reason that he suffered continuously from insomnia, a symptom of the type of cancer of which he was a victim.[2]

The contemporary Russian composer with whom there might have been a bond of sympathy was surely Scriabin. Though there is no mention of Scriabin in Debussy's writings or correspondence I do not think there can be any doubt that the work of this composer of such a heightened, feverish sensibility was known to him. Scriabin, who had given recitals in Paris, had been closely associated with Koussevitzky, and in 1910 accompanied him on the first of his famous tours of the Volga.[3] One imagines that Debussy would

[1] From St. Petersburg he sent Chouchou a series of postcards containing the jingles:

Près la perspective Newsky
Habite Monsieur Debussy

and

Ce sont bien des tramways électriques
Bien que cela paraisse excentrique.

Earlier, from Vienna, he had sent her a story in instalments, spread out over five postcards, entitled 'Les Mémoires d'outre-Croche' and signed 'Le Papadechouchou'.

[2] His account of his first night in Moscow was typical: 'I went to sleep brokenhearted. . . . After an hour, not being able to sleep, I got up and walked about like a demented one, from one room to another. . . . I drop into an armchair, fall off to sleep and am awakened by the cold. . . . I lie down again and try to get to sleep by doing the silliest things such as counting to a thousand forwards and backwards. Then someone comes in to ask what I want for breakfast.' By the end of his stay his insomnia had become acute: 'If ever I do get to sleep I wake up a moment afterwards.'

[3] On these tours Koussevitzky took his symphony orchestra on a chartered steamer to outlying provincial towns that had never before heard orchestral music. The

have criticized a certain manufactured crudeness in Scriabin, but he would surely have been interested in Scriabin's theories of music and colour. Writing of a meeting between Rimsky-Korsakov and Scriabin in Paris, Gerald Abraham states: 'These two, the tall pillar of moral and musical respectability and common sense and the amoral little mystic, meeting in the Café de la Paix after a rehearsal, found themselves in agreement on one point, the definite association of musical keys with certain colours.' One cannot help regretting that Debussy was not present at this meeting.[1]

On his return from Russia Debussy was only to stay in Paris about two months. At the end of February he made the fourth and last of his Italian journeys, to conduct the orchestra of the Augusteo in Rome on 22 February 1914. The works given were *La Mer*, *Rondes de Printemps*, and *L'Après-midi d'un faune*. By this time his reputation among the young composers in Italy, Malipiero, Respighi, and Casella, was at its height and despite some hostile demonstrations the critic of *Tribuna* spoke of the 'delirium' of the audience.[2]

No musical matters enter the anxious correspondence with Emma Debussy who in Paris was left to deal with the claims of creditors. Telegrams and letters which Debussy sent her from Dijon, Pisa, and Rome express a mounting concern. He describes a state of 'dreadful anguish'. Separation, he declares, is intolerable. In the course of a sleepless night 'I was convinced I was going to die and decided to give up conducting concerts throughout Europe. I

greater part of Debussy's 'Lettre de Russie', published in *La Revue S.I.M.*, January 1914, is devoted not to the reception of his works in Russia nor to his impressions of Russian music but to a description of Koussevitzky's Volga tours. Debussy was struck by the fact that the appreciative peasant audiences at these concerts were so moved by the music they heard that they hardly dared to applaud.

[1] One wonders whether either of the two composers was aware of the programme of a Scriabin–Debussy recital given during their lifetime, in 1910, by the pianist Ohtaguro in Tokio. The programme was exhibited at the Debussy Exhibition, Bibliothèque Nationale, Paris, 1962.

[2] The first performance of *Pelléas* in Italy, at La Scala under Toscanini in 1908, was enthusiastically received by forward-looking musical minds but met with a hostile reception from the regular Italian opera public. In the *Rivista Musicale Italiana* (No. 2, 1908) Ildebrando Pizzetti, recalling the principles of the early Italian operas of Peri and Caccini, proclaimed *Pelléas* as one of the first examples of an opera in a Latin country in which there was a true union between music and drama. The audience at La Scala, however, were either hostile or indifferent. At the conclusion most of them hurried away without either approving or condemning the work, and the cast embarrassingly appeared before a mere handful of people whom Toscanini himself applauded with the encouraging words, 'Molto intelligente, molto intelligente!'

hardly dare write this down but I confess my terrible fear of losing your love.'

On his return to Paris he was to leave almost immediately for Amsterdam and The Hague. At least six telegrams were exchanged with Emma Debussy in the course of this short journey, that is to say at every stop, Antwerp, Brussels, Rosendaal, and Amsterdam. At the end of February and the beginning of March Debussy conducted his works at two concerts of the Concertgebouw Orchestra and also played three of his Preludes. His old friend Gustave Doret, who had given the first performance of *L'Après-midi d'un faune* in Paris, was in charge of the Dutch orchestra, and at the second of the two concerts also conducted works by Saint-Saëns. Not having met Debussy for six years, Doret was struck by 'his depressed mood and his inability to make a decision'. At a reception at Amsterdam speeches were made in his honour but he found it impossible even to acknowledge what had been said in a few words. Under the table Doret received a kick on the shin. 'Impossible!' Debussy muttered. 'Répondez pour moi.' Doret made a short formal speech on his behalf, applause followed and glasses were clinked. 'Awkwardly and with his features now painfully drawn, Debussy finally stood up. "Merci, Messieurs", he muttered and sat down again as if he had gone through the worst ordeal.'

There remained the journeys in 1914 to Brussels at the end of April and, at the invitation of Lady Speyer, to London in July. Debussy stayed with the Speyers at their home in Grosvenor Street where, on 17 July, he took part in a private concert of his works including the Dances for harp and *Children's Corner*. It was his last journey abroad. He returned, however, in a restless, frustrated mood, undoubtedly also in a low state of health and anxious, despite his protestations of fatigue and boredom in travelling, to leave again as soon as possible. 'Paris is becoming more and more hateful to me', he tells Durand at the end of July, 'and I should like to be able to leave for a while; I am literally at the end of my tether.' In the few days that remained before the outbreak of war he was able to complete three of the *Epigraphes antiques*, an arrangement for piano duet of pieces he had written years earlier for a recitation of *Les Chansons de Bilitis*.

8
Edgar Allan Poe

To the few who love me and whom I love—to those who feel rather than to those who think—to the dreamers and those who put faith in dreams as the only realities . . .

E. A. Poe, Dedication of Eureka

In addition to his completed works Debussy, like most composers, entertained a large number of projects, some of them ephemeral, others throwing a valuable light on his development in one way or another. Of outstanding interest among these unfinished or projected works of Debussy are the two operas on tales by Edgar Allan Poe. Not all the manuscript sketches of these unfinished operas have been brought together, but I think it is safe to assume that those which still remain inaccessible will not greatly alter the size of this legacy which, apart from the libretto for *La Chute de la Maison Usher*, is remarkably small. We are not, however, principally concerned in this chapter with the manuscripts of these Poe operas themselves. Debussy was fascinated throughout his life by Poe's ideas and the nature of this fascination, which he shared with many of his contemporaries, will enable us to see aspects of several of his other works in a new light.

The projects for two short operas on Poe's tales, *The Fall of the House of Usher* and *The Devil in the Belfry*, occupied Debussy during the whole of the latter part of his life. We have seen that Debussy's attraction to Poe dates from 1889 when, according to a letter from André Suarès to Romain Rolland, he was engaged on a 'symphony on psychologically developed themes based on the *House of Usher*'. We have seen that *Pelléas* itself, both the play of

Maeterlinck and Debussy's score, has many associations with Poe, notably with the imagery and the symbolism of Poe's tale of incestuous love; and we have dealt briefly with the French interpretations of both Poe and Swinburne in regard to Debussy's artistic evolution.

In his study *Edgar Allan Poe and France* T. S. Eliot investigates the far-reaching influence of Poe on the French literary mind and states, 'there are aspects of Poe which English and American critics failed to perceive.' Poe was in fact almost entirely a creation of the French.[1] None of the writers in the rich generation from Baudelaire to Paul Valéry, including Gide and Marcel Proust, escaped his fascination, and the aspect of Poe to which they were drawn was the rising to the surface of unconscious fantasies. 'His most vivid imaginative realizations', Eliot states, 'are the realization of the dream.' Nearly all Poe's tales with their dark symbolism of corridors and underground passages, stagnant water and enveloping whirlpools, haunted also by fantasies of incest, cruelty, and death, are in essence dream tales, and although Eliot, like most other English critics, is censorious of Poe as a stylist, he readily concedes that the Symbolist figures in French literature, from Baudelaire onwards, saw in Poe an expression of the new sensibility that they were themselves seeking and that they were thus able to interpret Poe for English writers in his true light.

Belonging entirely, in spirit and outlook, to his generation, Debussy was similarly profoundly affected by Poe. Indeed, the dream-like symbolism in Poe's tales became together with the Wagnerian influence one of the most stimulating factors in Debussy's imagination.[2] In his correspondence, Debussy frequently

---

[1] By far the finest of the many translations of Poe's prose works are those of Baudelaire on which he was engaged during seventeen years of his life and which in volume constitute almost half of the poet's output. Baudelaire, who began this enormous task with only a rudimentary knowledge of English, dedicated his translations to Maria Clemm, Poe's foster-mother and the central figure in his life. They were re-edited by Y. G. le Dantec in 1951. A selection of the poems was published by Mallarmé in 1888 with illustrations by Manet, but the translation of the complete poems was the work of Debussy's friend Gabriel Mourey.

[2] It was Thomas Mann who first instinctively saw the impact that Poe was bound to make on music. Writing in 1933 on the fiftieth anniversary of the death of Wagner, Thomas Mann suggested that the inspiration derived by Baudelaire from Wagner was of the same nature and intensity as that which he had derived from Poe. 'Wagner and Poe—what an extraordinary juxtaposition!' he comments. 'Immediately we see the work of Wagner in a new light. We see a deeper colour in his work, a world haunted by death and beauty, a pessimistic world, intoxicated by sensuous refinement.' Mann

says so in as many words. He speaks of the 'tyranny', the 'obsession' which Poe exerted over him. As we have seen, earlier critics of Debussy, Arthur Symons and James Huneker, drew attention to Debussy's affinity with Poe. Yet though they were able to make pertinent comparisons they had not quite the understanding of Poe's significance that we have now acquired. They were themselves part of the movement that had sprung from this French influence of Poe. And they were therefore unable to see, as we are today, that the fantasies to which Debussy gave a musical expression were almost Surrealist fantasies, the chaotic fantasies of dreams, such as those illustrated in the scene of the vaults in *Pelléas*.

The impact made by Poe on Debussy needs to be assessed in two distinct spheres: the practical sphere where far-reaching plans were made for the use of two of Poe's tales as librettos for operas; and the imaginative sphere where Poe's ideas are seen to be associated with the mood or sensibility of one or other of Debussy's works. We may follow the plans for operas on tales of Poe in Debussy's correspondence. The contract for the production of *La Chute de la Maison Usher* and *Le Diable dans le Beffroi* was in the form of a letter, together with a receipt, dated 5 July 1908 from Debussy to Giulio Gatti-Casazza, director of the Metropolitan Opera, New York. In consideration of the sum of ten thousand francs (two thousand francs paid on signature) Debussy gave the Metropolitan priority for the production of *La Chute de la Maison Usher* and *Le Diable dans le Beffroi* on condition that both these works were played at the same performance and that no other work of another composer appeared in the same programme. He also gave the Metropolitan an option on his subsequent works, notably *La Légende de Tristan*. In his memoirs Gatti-Casazza states that Debussy was reluctant to accept this offer. 'It is a piece of bad business you are doing', he told the American impresario. 'I have some remorse in taking these few dollars. I do not believe I will ever finish any part of all this.' And he added significantly, 'I write for myself alone and do not trouble myself at all about the impatience of others.' If we bear in mind that Debussy considered these settings of

knew nothing of Debussy's life-long attachment to Poe, and obviously this conception of an art deriving from both Wagner and Poe corresponds only vaguely to the spirit of Debussy's libretto and sketches for an opera on *The Fall of the House of Usher*. He had foreseen, however, the appeal which Poe's mind was likely to make to a musician.

The House of Usher and *The Devil in the Belfry* as among the few projects during his later years on which his heart was set, as opposed to the numerous works commissioned for one material reason or another, then some of the underlying reasons for this hesitation in completing these long-cherished projects become apparent. Not only was he frequently side-tracked into fulfilling commissions at short notice, but, as we now see, the nature of his adaptations of these two works of Poe was bold, and one has the impression that he preferred to let these experimental ideas simmer in the mind rather than bring them to too hasty a conclusion. However this may be, the letters addressed to Durand, Godet, Caplet, and Laloy, extending over eight years, reveal that his feelings were more deeply engaged in *Usher* and *Le Diable dans le Beffroi* than in *Le Martyre de Saint-Sébastien*, even than in the orchestral *Images* and *Jeux*. Often, too, these letters disclose a network of associations illuminating not only the impact made by Poe's tales on his imagination but some of the more subtle processes of artistic creation.

On 18 June 1908, shortly before signing the contract with the Metropolitan, Debussy had written to Durand: 'These last days I have done much work on *La Chute de la Maison Usher*. It is an excellent means of strengthening one's nerves against any kind of fear.[1] Nevertheless there are times when I no longer see the world around me [*où je perds le sentiment des choses environnantes*], and if the sister of Roderick Usher were suddenly to appear I shouldn't be extremely surprised.' The following month, on 18 July, he tells Durand: 'I have been wanting to write to you these last days but the heir of the Usher family has hardly left me in peace. I am constantly being rude and the outside world hardly exists for me [*le monde extérieur n'existe presque plus pour moi*]. This is a delightful state of mind which, however, has the disadvantage of being unsuited to our twentieth century.' This retreat into oneself is entirely typical of the solipsism of Poe's characters and particularly of Roderick Usher. On 26 June 1909 Debussy again writes to Durand: 'These last days I have been working on *La Chute de la Maison Usher* and have almost finished

---

[1] '*Contre toute espèce de terreur*'. The reference is to the observation made of Usher by his friend, 'To an anomalous species of terror I found him a bounden slave', and to Usher's confession: 'I have no abhorrence of danger, except in its absolute effect—in terror. In this unnerved—in this pitiable condition—I feel that the period will sooner or later arrive when I must abandon life and reason together in some struggle with the grim phantasm, FEAR.'

a long monologue for poor Roderick. It is sad enough to make the stones weep and as it happens there is a question of the influence of stones on the state of mind of neurasthenics.[1] The music has an attractive mustiness obtained by mixing the low notes of the oboe with harmonics of the violin. Don't speak of this to anyone for I am rather proud of it.' The following month, having apparently been pressed by his publisher to deliver the score of the orchestral *Images*, he writes: 'I must confess that I have put them aside on account of Edgar Allan Poe. I have so much to do on these works that you will excuse me, I hope. You need have no doubt that I will return to the *Images* and complete them to your satisfaction.' And on 14 August: 'I live almost exclusively in the work which you know and never cease conversing with E. A. Poe.' Of the same period we have a curious letter, dated 25 August 1909, to André Caplet: 'No, it is not neurasthenia, nor is it hypochondria. It is the delicious malady which springs from the idea of being able to choose any idea, dear André Caplet.[2] I have recently been living in the House of Usher which is not exactly the place where one can look after one's nerves—just the opposite. One develops the curious habit of listening to the stones as if they were in conversation with each other and of expecting houses to crumble to pieces as if this were not only natural but inevitable. Moreover, if you were to press me I should confess that I like these people more than many others— not to name them.[3] I have no confidence in the normal, well-

---

[1] Poe writes of 'an effect which the *physique* of the grey walls and turrets, and of the dim tarn into which they all looked down, had at length brought about upon the *morale* of his [Roderick Usher's] existence.' Later, referring to 'the sentience of all vegetable things', Poe discerns the 'silent yet importunate and terrible influence' of 'the grey stones of the home of his forefathers . . . the order of their arrangement, as well as in that of the many *fungi* which overspread them, and of the decayed trees which stood around. . . .'

[2] 'C'est le délicieux mal de l'idée à choisir entre toutes, cher André Caplet.' This must be one of the first expressions in twentieth-century music of the despair experienced by a composer in face of a disorganized musical language. It is the feeling expressed also by Stravinsky in his Harvard lectures *Poetics of Music*, translated by A. Knodel and I. Dahl (London, 1947): 'As for myself, I experience a sort of terror when, at the moment of setting to work and finding myself before the infinitude of possibilities that present themselves, I have the feeling that everything is permissible to me. If everything is permissible to me, the best and the worst, if nothing offers me any resistance, then any effort is inconceivable, and I cannot use anything as a basis, and consequently every undertaking becomes futile.'

[3] The following year, in a letter of 24 August to Louis Laloy, Debussy identifies himself with the Usher family in a similar manner: 'I am in a hateful mood, taking no pleasure in anything unless it be the pleasure of every day destroying myself a little more. . . . There is something of the Usher family in this situation, although this explanation may not bear too close a scrutiny, for they are the best family I have.'

balanced type of person.' And he goes on to make an unexpected comparison: 'There was a great moralist, Carlyle, who was a Scot and something of a Calvinist and who preached moral ideas to all his contemporaries. This was the man who made his wife very unhappy and walked five miles a day to declare his passionate romantic love to another woman who made light of it all in accordance with other, probably superior, standards of morality. I speak to you of Carlyle because reading his works is part of the treatment I am obliged to follow every day.'[1]

The letters to Durand at this period show the same exclusive pre-occupation. 'I must rely on your friendship to forgive my having neglected the *Images* recently', opens a letter of 21 September 1909. 'I have allowed myself to be concerned with hardly anything other than *Roderick Usher* and *Le Diable dans le Beffroi*. I go to sleep with them, and on waking find either the sombre melancholy of the one or the derisive laughter of the other. You rightly draw my attention to other obligations, and I shall put my puppets aside so as not to keep you waiting too long.' A letter of the same date to Caplet gives an even franker account of his exclusive concern with his settings of Poe at this time: 'I cannot hide from you that I have got to the point of having entirely sacrificed the *Images* to Monsieur E. A. Poe. Although dead this figure exercises an almost agonizing tyranny over me. I forget the normal rules of courtesy and close myself up like a brute beast in the house of Usher unless I am keeping company with the devil in the belfry.' The following year he has hardly the time to glance at one of his new publications. 'I have received the scenario of *Masques et Bergamasques*', he tells Durand on 2 June 1910, 'but I haven't had time to re-read it. Your letter found me in the *House of Usher*. Allow me to return.' The following month, on 8 July 1910, he expresses the hope that he 'may be able to reach the inexpressible'. *The House of Usher* is to be 'a progressive expression of anguish. . . . If I manage to bring it off as I wish, I believe I shall have served music well and also my publisher and friend Jacques Durand.'

[1] This ironic attack on Carlyle was based on the view, commonly held of him at the time, of a selfish, irascible man, cruel or indifferent to his clever wife—the antithesis, as Debussy saw him, of Roderick Usher. Debussy's allusion is apparently to the numerous journeys made by Carlyle on foot from his house in Cheyne Walk, Chelsea, to the home in Piccadilly of Lady Harriet Baring. Jane Carlyle was greatly disturbed by her husband's relationship with Lady Harriet even though it was known to be purely platonic.

This 'progressive expression of anguish', culminating in the violent deaths of both Roderick and his twin-sister Lady Madeline, is indeed the underlying theme of Poe's tale, but there is reason to suspect that Debussy felt himself too deeply involved in its emotional significance to be able to deal with the libretto he had devised from an objective viewpoint. Nor, apparently, did he discover the ideal musical expression of the subject that he was pursuing. A different picture of his progress, not only on *Usher* but also on *Le Diable dans le Beffroi*, is given to Robert Godet. After explaining that he had been obliged to work on *Khamma* and *Sébastian*, he writes to his trusted old friend on 6 February 1911: 'The two tales of Poe have thus had to be postponed until I don't know when. Writing to you, I will admit that I am not very sorry since there are many points of expression [*accents*] with which I am not yet satisfied. Also a scheme which is not sufficiently clear in my mind [*une mise en place insuffisamment rigoureuse*] notably in regard to *Le Diable dans le Beffroi* where I would like to achieve an extremely supple and at the same time an extremely fluid manner of choral writing.'

We may profitably pause to consider here this twin project of an opera on *The Devil in the Belfry*. In *Usher* Debussy was manifestly concerned with new orchestral effects and a type of harrowing declamation. In *Le Diable dans le Beffroi* he was experimenting with new choral effects. 'Understand me correctly,' he insists in this same letter to Godet, 'the clear-cut choral writing in *Boris* does not meet my requirements any more than the persistent counterpoint in the second act of *Meistersinger*. Something else is surely to be discovered—some kind of inspired aural deception. It's the devil! And then there is this ridiculous custom to be overcome of separating the men and the women of a chorus as if they were in a bathing establishment. In the end you will see that terrifyingly big words will be used to describe a very simple matter.' In a statement said by Léon Vallas to have been made to Pierre Lalo—it is quoted by him without indication of date or place—Debussy outlines this same conception of choral writing in greater detail: 'The people in *Boris* do not form a real crowd. Sometimes one group sings, sometimes another—but not a third, each in turn—and generally they sing in unison. As for the crowd in *Meistersinger* they are not a crowd either, they are an army solidly organized in

the German manner, marching in rows. What I should like to achieve is something more scattered and split up, something both more nimble and intangible, something apparently inorganic, and yet with an underlying control—a real human crowd in which each voice is free and in which all the voices combined nevertheless produce the impression of an ensemble.'

In this novel conception of opera only the crowd, thus split up, were to sing. The principal character, the Devil himself, was only to whistle. The irony of *Le Diable dans le Beffroi* would thus have formed an admirable foil for the lugubrious character of *Usher*, and it is characteristic of Debussy's dual nature that he should have been attracted to these two works simultaneously. Poe's ironic story is built in fact around the single character of the Devil who at midday in the Dutch village of Vondervotteimittiss ('I wonder what time it is') maliciously strikes the bell in the belfry thirteen times. The sketches of the libretto for this opera, dating from 1903, consist of two tableaux and show that the tale was to be very freely adapted. The first tableau, set in Holland, introduces children, a bell-ringer and his son, and the mayor and his daughter ('shy as a tulip'). A romance develops between the bell-ringer's son and the mayor's daughter. When the thirteenth chime is struck at midday a jovial good-natured Devil descends from the belfry to amuse the crowd.[1] The chimes are struck again, this time producing odd cracked sounds which the Devil proceeds to parody on his violin by altering the rhythm and also the melody. We further read about 'a fantastic jig' built up by means of powerful rhythms and a crescendo 'in which the Devil's violin is pitted against the trombones'. The crowd begin to dance heavily and clumsily. But the jig mercilessly continues, compelling the crowd to follow the Devil, who goes off in the direction of the canal and jumps into it. The mesmerized crowd wish to follow him but he lifts up his violin bow, using it as a conductor cutting off a chord with his baton at the end of a movement, and the curtain falls.

The *Gigues* from the *Images* for orchestra, inspired by a poem of Verlaine, come to mind here; at any rate we may note that André Caplet, who completed the orchestration of *Gigues*, declared that a

[1] Writing to Messager in 1902 of his conception of this tale Debussy states: 'The Devil is much more ironic and cruel than the traditional sort of red clown. I want to destroy the idea of the devil as the spirit of evil. He is rather the spirit of contradiction.'

Debussy and 'Chouchou' at Le Mouleau, 1916

Chopin, by Delacroix

Debussy, by Steinlen

section of the work represented 'the angular gesticulations of a grotesque marionette'. Poe's Devil might well have been in Debussy's mind here. His sketches and correspondence show that in the first tableau of *Le Diable dans le Beffroi* the orchestra was to contain a prominent part for the cimbalom. In this first tableau the orchestra was to be the centre of interest; in the second the 'nimble and intangible' chorus. The Dutch village of the first tableau becomes in the second an Italian village and the scenario introduces episodes which have no connexion whatever with Poe's tale. The two young lovers and the Devil find themselves in an imbroglio in which the Devil is outwitted. Eventually, when the chimes ring in the accustomed manner, the Devil is subdued and ultimately disappears. It is a scenario that looks forward to Stravinsky's *Histoire du Soldat* and also to his *Pulcinella*. The many accounts given by Debussy of his aims and ideas in these two works force us to the conclusion that none of Debussy's projects, nor even his completed works, illustrates more strikingly than *Usher* and *Le Diable dans le Beffroi* the two aspects of his imaginative mind: the ruminating, introspective poet, a reflection of Roderick Usher, and the caustic ironist.[1]

In June 1911 Stravinsky's *Petrouchka* was given in Paris. Praising the early scores of Stravinsky and particularly their *mise-en-place* (form and texture), Debussy, in a letter to Godet of 18 December, confides in him his anxieties regarding his Poe operas. 'On the matter of form and texture, I have not yet managed to find those I want for the two little dramas adapted from Poe. The further I proceed the more horror I have of this deliberate disorder, which is only an aural deception, and also of certain bizarre and amusing harmonies which have only a snobbish value [*qui ne sont que jeux de société*]. How much has to be discovered and then discarded before arriving at the naked flesh of feeling. One should trust one's instinct to beware of mere texture and colour.'[2] A few days later, on

[1] The only known manuscript of *Le Diable dans le Beffroi* is the sketch of the libretto with three pages of music dated 25 August 1903. Since Debussy worked on this score at least until 1912 the manuscript of 1903 cannot represent all that was left of the work. In his memoirs Henri Büsser mentions a visit paid to Debussy on 31 March 1912: 'He spoke to me of his projects . . . *Le Diable dans le Beffroi* of Edgar Poe for which he has written many sketches. He played me on the piano some very picturesque and amusing fragments in a manner entirely different from his usual style.'

[2] Debussy's expressions here recall Baudelaire's *Mon cœur mis à nu* which itself had been inspired by Poe's *My heart laid bare*. His knowledge of these works is discussed in Vol. I, Appdx. D, 'Swinburne and Poe in France', p. 214.

22 December, Debussy enlarges on these ideas in a letter to André Caplet:

> I haven't yet managed to finish the two little operas of Poe. Everything strikes me as being so deadly dull [*tout m'en parait ennuyeux comme une cave*]. For a single bar that I write that may be free and alive, there are twenty stifled by the weight of what is known as tradition, the influence of which I consider to be hypocritical and despicable. Observe, if you please, that I am little concerned about the fact that it may be my own tradition we are talking about. It is nevertheless a matter of trickery by which you merely see yourself in different guises. One must put aside everything that devours the best part of one's thoughts and bring oneself to a state in which one concentrates relentlessly on oneself alone. What happens, of course, is just the opposite: there is in the first place the family to reckon with which stands in the way either through kindness or simply because they are blind to facts. And then there are the Mistress temptations, *the* Mistress temptation, I should say, which one hasn't even reckoned with, so ready is she to give herself until everything is abandoned. . . . And even now I haven't told you the half. . . .

He continued, however, to be preoccupied with the two works until the war. Having completed *Jeux* under great strain, he tells Durand on 12 September 1912: 'Although I am very tired I have taken up my old works again. I am sufficiently fond of them to derive new energy from them. At least that is what I am hoping.'[1] In September 1916, some eight months after undergoing an operation, he finally completed the libretto of *Usher*. It was among his last works. In September 1916, writing for the last time of the work to Godet, from his house in the Avenue du Bois de Boulogne, he says: 'This house has a curious resemblance to the house of Usher. Although I haven't the mind troubles of Roderick, nor his passion

---

[1] The last mention of these works before the first World War is in a letter from Victor Segalen to his wife of 5 September 1913: 'Lunched this morning with Debussy, more open and confiding than ever. He is writing, almost to order, things that annoy him: *Khamma*, an Egyptian ballet for Maud Allan, a nude dancer, and *Crimen Amoris* on pieces of Verlaine put together by Charles Morice. He cannot even finish for himself his two little dramas of Poe.'

for the last thought of C. M. von Weber,[1] we are alike in our super-sensitiveness. . . . On this point I could tell you things which would make your beard fall off, which would be most unpleasant not for your beard but for me who doesn't like attracting attention.' Thereafter his powers began to decline and he increasingly saw both Godet and himself as replicas of Poe's harrassed, over-refined character. Observing that what he was writing was 'always of yesterday, never of tomorrow', he desperately exclaims in one of his last letters to Godet, of 6 October 1916, 'You are my only friend, alias Roderick Usher!'

It remains to assess both the sketches and the final form of Debussy's libretto for *La Maison Usher*, adapted from the Baudelaire translation. In its original form Poe's tale is almost a monologue declaimed in the first person by the unnamed friend of Roderick Usher. In fact Roderick himself, so realistically described, speaks only four times, merely saying a few words. His twin-sister Lady Madeline[2] has a dumb role. The fourth character, the doctor of the family, appears only once, his role being of very slight importance. It was thus essential that a theatrical work based on this monologue should fill out the characters not only of Roderick but also of Lady Madeline and the Doctor. This was the solution that Debussy proposed. In the sketch for the libretto the work is divided into three scenes. In the first the characters are Lady Madeline and Roderick; in the second the Doctor and the friend; and in the third the friend and Roderick. Though the character of Roderick, obsessed by an incestuous love for his sister, is kept in the foreground, the plot is remodelled to bring into relief on the stage the final appearance of Lady Madeline. Her clothes are now covered in blood and her collapse, overwhelming her brother, is followed by the crumbling of the House of Usher. In the tale Poe gives us to believe that the supposed death of Roderick's sister occurred accidentally and she is buried alive by Roderick aided by his friend. In Debussy's sketch for the libretto it is the Doctor, built up into an extremely sinister character, who buries Lady Madeline alive

---

[1] The allusion is to this passage in *The Fall of the House of Usher*: 'Among other things I hold painfully in mind a certain singular perversion and amplification of the wild air of the last waltz of von Weber.'

[2] Debussy surely knew of the existence of his English cousin Lucie Madeline de Bussy, daughter of his paternal uncle Jules Alexandre, though he never met her. (See Vol. I, p. 5.)

without Roderick's knowledge.[1] The work opens with two verses of the poem 'The Haunted Palace', sung not by Roderick accompanying himself on the guitar as in the tale, but by Lady Madeline. In the final version the three scenes are reduced to two, or rather they take the form of a prologue and a single principal scene. The plot and the dialogue are substantially the same as in the sketch and the work ends, as in the tale of Poe, with the house of Usher crumbling into ruins, only reflections of its fragments being discernible in the deep dark tarn as the blood-red moon rises over the sombre landscape. It is clear that Debussy was primarily concerned with the essentially soliptic character of Roderick Usher: the enraged, self-devouring lover guilty of loving his sister. 'Celle que tu aimais tant,' he says to himself, 'celle que tu ne devais pas aimer.' Parent of the indecisive, Hamlet-like Pelléas, Roderick perishes with the rise of the same blood-red moon, we note, that appears so dramatically at the end of *Salomé* and of *Wozzeck*, symbols in these operas, as in *Usher*, of love and of murder.

The unfinished musical score of *Usher*, consisting of twenty-one pages and now in the Bibliothèque Nationale in Paris, follows the text of the final version. A performance of the entire manuscript for soprano (Lady Madeline), tenor (the friend), baritone (the Doctor), and bass (Roderick) has not yet been undertaken for the reason that too much of it is illegible or incomplete.[2]

A study of Debussy's unfinished operas on tales of Poe and of the ideas that they engendered offers an illuminating view of many subsequent musical developments. The main interest, however, of the musical manuscript of *Usher*, which does not noticeably transcend the recitative style of *Pelléas*, is not in its purely musical value; it is in the æsthetic theories with which these few pages are associated. The dream visions in Poe's tales, colliding as in a nightmare,

[1] Debussy introduces episodes of fierce jealousy between the Doctor and Roderick, both enamoured of Madeline, 'sœur trop aimée'. These episodes are nowhere to be found in Poe's tale and are entirely of Debussy's invention. Recalling his twin-sister, Debussy's Roderick speaks of 'ses lèvres qui tentent comme un fruit inconnu où ma bouche n'a jamais osé mordre!' The Doctor is 'le médecin de la mort. . . . Il nous surveille comme un vieux corbeau avide de chair morte.' He is the Raven in fact of Poe's famous poem, with its recurrent refrain 'Nevermore', which had earlier inspired Mallarmé, Manet, Gauguin, and Ravel (in *Le Gibet*).

[2] A section of Roderick's monologue was performed at the Société Française de Musicologie, Paris, in 1959. In addition to the manuscripts of *Usher* reproduced in my *Debussy et Edgar Poe* there are a musical sketch, 'Ce qui sera peut-être le prélude à *La Chute de la Maison Usher*', and an earlier version of the libretto, both shown at the Debussy Exhibition at the Bibliothèque Nationale in 1962 (Nos. 194 and 195).

were developed by several later writers, among them Villiers de l'Isle Adam, whose *Axel* had inspired Debussy and whose *Contes Cruels* were later to inspire Dallapiccola's opera *Il Prigionero*, and Henry James, whose *The Turn of the Screw* was set by Benjamin Britten. *Pelléas, La Chute de la Maison Usher, Wozzeck, Il Prigionero, The Turn of the Screw*—the line of the æsthetic development of twentieth-century opera is clear.[1]

Poe expressed some striking ideas, known to Debussy, on the nature of music. 'I know that indefiniteness is an element of true music,' Poe writes, 'a suggested indefiniteness bringing about a definiteness of vague and therefore of spiritual effect.' Commenting on this passage, Edmund Wilson, in his book *The Shores of Light*, writes:

> The real significance of Poe's short stories does not lie in what they purport to relate. Many are confessedly dreams; and, as with dreams, though they seem absurd, their effect on our emotions is serious. And even those that pretend to the logic and the exactitude of actual narratives are, nevertheless, also dreams. . . . No one understood better than Poe that, in fiction and in poetry both, it is not what you say that counts, but what you make the reader feel (he always italicizes the word 'effect'); no one understood better than Poe that the deepest psychological truth may be rendered through phantasmagoria. Even the realistic stories of

[1] Not for nothing was Poe's life and work the subject of an exhaustive psycho-analytic study by Marie Bonaparte with a preface by Freud (*Edgar Poe: Etude Psychanalytique*, 2 vol., 1933; English translation by John Rodker, London, 1949). In the literary sphere Poe was almost a precursor of Freud. Undoubtedly it was his power of analysis that fascinated Baudelaire. Fifty years before Freud, Baudelaire, writing in his second preface to Poe's works 'of the fervour with which he was able to throw himself into the grotesque for the love of the grotesque and into the horrifying for the love of the horrifying' drew the conclusion: 'I have already observed that this fervour was often the result of a vast, vital energy left idle, sometimes of a stubborn chastity and also of a profound, repressed sensibility.' It is instructive to compare Debussy's version of *The Fall of the House of Usher* with the analysis of the tale by Marie Bonaparte; one has the impression that, since Debussy laid such stress on the incestuous aspects of Roderick's relationship with his sister, he might have endorsed certain of Madame Bonaparte's interpretations. On the other hand, Baudelaire's amazing statement, 'Love plays no part in Poe's writings', must surely have been unacceptable to him. ('When sexual manifestations are so deeply buried in the unconscious', Madame Bonaparte comments, 'they seem to the layman to be non-existent.') A later writer, D. H. Lawrence, saw these manifestations clearly enough and interpreted *The House of Usher* from a viewpoint nearer the approach taken by Debussy: 'The Ushers, brother and sister . . . would love, love, love, without resistance. They would love, they would merge, they would be as one thing. So they dragged each other down into death.' (*Studies in Classic American Literature*, London, 1924.)

Poe are, in fact, only phantasmagoria of a more circumstantial kind. . . . Poe's mentality was a rare synthesis.

And he concludes with a statement that shows at once the lasting appeal of Poe for Debussy: 'He had elements in him that corresponded with the indefiniteness of music and the exactitude of mathematics.' And Edmund Wilson asks: 'Is not this what modern literature is tending toward?' The indefiniteness of music and the exactitude of mathematics—these are also, as we know, the ideals of much later developments in twentieth-century art, rooted in these unfinished works of Debussy.

9
Maud Allan and Gabriele
d'Annunzio

J'aime les situations extrêmes.
Debussy

At the beginning of February 1911, shortly after his return from
Vienna and Budapest, Debussy informed Robert Godet that he was
obliged to put aside his operas on the tales of Poe in order to fulfil
two commissions:

> Back in Paris I have begun working on a ballet for Miss Maud
> Allan, who is an English girl to her fingertips. By way of com-
> pensation the ballet is Egyptian; the plot is childishly simple and,
> rightly, presents no interest in itself. The reasons that have
> encouraged me to write this work are another matter, and there
> are also economic reasons. At the very same time Gabriele
> d'Annunzio appeared on the scene with *Le Martyre de Saint-
> Sébastien* for which I agreed to write the incidental music. This is
> a much more lavish proposition than the wretched little Anglo-
> Egyptian ballet. I needn't tell you that the worship of Adonis is
> mingled in this work with the worship of Christ; that it is
> assuredly very beautiful; and that if I were given the necessary
> time some rather lovely ideas could be discovered.

The circumstances which led Debussy to accept these two commissions, deflecting him, as he says, from his work on the Poe
operas, need investigation, particularly since neither the ballet
Khamma, commissioned by Maud Allan, nor the incidental music

[153]

for d'Annunzio's mystery play were, in the manner in which they were eventually presented, successful. There have been several attempts to revive the *Saint-Sébastien* music, and in many different forms. *Khamma*, on the other hand, though completed in 1913, was not even played in Debussy's lifetime, and it is still the least known of Debussy's later works. It is hardly ever heard and none of the studies on Debussy give even a summary of it. Yet there are reasons to believe that its failure was not altogether warranted.

In the revised as in the earlier edition of his *Debussy et son temps*, Vallas persists in stating that '*Khamma* was a piece of hack work . . . a short music-hall number . . . written for a certain English dancer Maud Allan.' In fact, though it was written for this well-known dancer, the work is described in the published score as a 'Légende dansée de W. L. Courtney et Maud Allan'. A lecturer in philosophy at Oxford and a brilliant literary and dramatic critic, W. L. Court-ney, at the time of his association with Maud Allan and Debussy, was literary editor of the *Daily Telegraph*. The novel choreographic art of Maud Allan, he pointed out, contained 'something derived from music, something derived from drama, something derived also from the painter's art'.[1] Though she later appeared as a solo dancer in London at the Palladium and the Coliseum, Maud Allan was not a music-hall dancer and it was never suggested that *Khamma* should be anything in the nature of a music-hall composition. A gifted musician as well as a dancer, she had been a pupil of Busoni and had also studied painting and sculpture in Italy. Her *Vision of Salomé* with music by the Belgian composer Marcel Rémy, which she gave in London in 1908, was considered particularly poetic. It was 'not the actual dance executed before Herod and Herodias', notes Courtney, but 'a repetition of it in half-conscious memory'. Maud Allan had also undertaken serious research into the hieratic dances of Egypt and the early forms of Greek dancing.[2]

[1] In *Rosemary's Letter Book* (London, 1909) Courtney published a sonnet to Maud Allan entitled *An Arcadian Idyll*. He also compared her work to that of Isidora Duncan. Like Loïe Fuller, who devised choreographic versions of Debussy's *Nuages* and *Sirènes*, Isidora Duncan was eclipsed only by the more spectacular appeal of the dancers of the Diaghilev ballet.

[2] In *My Life and Dancing* (London, 1908) Maud Allan gives the explanation, which she discovered in a work of 1896, of the much discussed Greek title of Erik Satie's piano pieces, *Gymnopédies*, two of which Debussy orchestrated: 'The exquisite Gymnopaedia simulating an attack and defence, danced by naked boys crowned with chaplets of palm.'

The scenario of *Khamma* which, as Debussy states, is admirably uncomplicated, is worth summarizing if only because this work has hitherto been unfortunately misrepresented. The action takes place in the inner temple of the ancient Egyptian sun-god Amon-Ra. The Prelude suggests the rumble of a distant revolt with approaching trumpet calls.[1] In the surrounded temple the High Priest and other worshippers pray to the image of Amon-Ra for the delivery of the town. The stone image is able to respond with no reassuring gesture and the High Priest prepares to leave. He has, however, an intuition concerning the secret of victory. In the second scene the veiled figure of Khamma the dancer appears. She wishes to escape and her apprehension is expressed in the ensuing section, *La Peur de Khamma*. Presently the temple is flooded with moonlight and Khamma prostrates herself before the statue. She then performs three dances in the hope of delivering the country from the invaders. At the conclusion of the third dance she perceives that the head and shoulders of the statue begin to move. The hands of the stone god rise from the knees, the palms turned upwards. Delivered from fear, Khamma performs a fourth dance, an ecstatic dance of joy, but at the climax, marked by a flash of lightning and a thunder clap, she suddenly falls to the ground and dies. The third scene opens on the scene of the temple at dawn. The victorious crowd approaches and the door of the temple is thrown open to them. The final celebration scene is cut short when the crowd perceive the body of Khamma, who has sacrificed her life, and the work ends with a solemn blessing bestowed upon her by the High Priest.

It is true that Debussy was loath to accept a commission to compose a ballet on this subject, and it is also true that he agreed to do so principally for material reasons. The same is true, however, not only of *Saint-Sébastien* but also of *Jeux* and, in varying degrees, of several other works of his later years. Rather unwillingly, Debussy was being drawn at this time into the world of the ballet and the theatre. This was not surprising. It was in this domain that, before the age of film music, a composer could hope to procure the most lucrative engagements. In his uncertain state of health and with his

---

[1] This was no doubt intended to be an allusion to the religious revolution against Amon-Ra launched by the Pharaoh Ikhnaton, held to have been one of the most remarkable idealists of the ancient world before the Hebrews.

growing liabilities towards his wife and daughter, Debussy threw himself into the composition of these commissioned works, overcoming as best he could many personal and artistic aversions. Out of deference to Maud Allan, who was then alive, many of the references to her were deleted from the published correspondence between Debussy and his publisher Durand. He rather contemptuously refers to her as 'la girl anglaise', and it is clear that she angered Debussy by her request to be allowed to use the score as she wished. We have also to take into account another reason for the acid remarks the sick and impecunious composer was inclined to make about Maud Allan. As with other works of this period, Debussy lacked either the time or the physical strength to complete them unaided. Between 1911 and 1913 André Caplet, who had served Debussy as amanuensis in *Gigues* and *Saint-Sébastien*, was often in Boston and London. Charles Koechlin, a composer less well known to Debussy, was thus called upon to assist with *Khamma*. The piano score was written by Debussy, but he orchestrated only the first few bars; the remainder he entrusted to Koechlin under his supervision. In his book on Debussy, Koechlin promised to make known one day a remark which the harassed composer had made to him about *Khamma* and which he had up till then withheld. On his last visit to London Koechlin kindly supplied me with the text of this remark, an amazing remark in whatever context it was made, and which understandably left Debussy's young associate nonplussed. It was: 'Write *Khamma* yourself and I will sign it.'

Despite misgivings and his reluctance to undertake the work, Debussy by no means belittled the value of the score ultimately provided for this ballet of Courtney and Allan. To Durand on 1 February 1912 he writes: 'When will you come and hear the new version of this curious ballet—with its trumpet calls which suggest the revolt and the fire and which send a shiver down your back? I should very much like to dedicate *Khamma* to Madame Jacques Durand.' We gather from this text (as opposed to a truncated version of it from which Vallas concluded that Debussy's reference to *Khamma* was contemptuous) that he was sufficiently interested in the work to have written a second version, and that in this form he held it to be worthy of dedication to the wife of his publisher. Though completed in 1913 it was not published until 1916. A

concert performance was not given until 1924 and it was performed as a ballet only in 1947, at the Opéra-Comique with choreography by Jean-Jacques Etcheverry.[1]

We may now return to the ambitious scheme of Gabriele d'Annunzio for a theatrical work in five acts, reconstructing the legend of the martyrdom of St. Sebastian in its most masochistic aspect, in which the orchestral and choral music of Debussy was to be combined with speech, also with mime and dancing devised by Fokine, the whole of this grandiose spectacle to be enhanced by the blues, golds, and emerald-greens of the costumes and scenery of the Russian painter Léon Bakst. It is impossible to believe that for this gaudy work Debussy could have agreed to supply an immense score for any other than material reasons. 'This is a much more lavish proposition than the wretched little Anglo-Egyptian ballet', he had told Godet. Behind this laconic remark is the fact that the composition of *Saint-Sébastien* involved a much larger sum of money.

In 1910 Gabriele d'Annunzio, the mystical Italian poet, soldier, and patriot, known today chiefly for his spectacular raid on Fiume in 1919 and for his later association with Mussolini, had been chased by the bailiffs from his luxurious villa in Florence and fled to Paris, where he lived under several different pseudonyms. Here he continued his life of unbelievable luxury, possessing a hundred suits, mixing scents, of which he used a pint a day, and indulging in unmentionable vices. It was said that in Italy his horses had slept on Persian rugs. It is essential to include this vignette of d'Annunzio, seemingly the last person to be associated with the retiring figure of Debussy, in order to see his attraction to the subject of Sebastian's martyrdom. He was seized by this subject partly as an historian of the pagan cultures preceding the Christian era, but even more

[1] The fact that this ballet was not performed until almost thirty years after Debussy's death is due to circumstances which have not hitherto been made known. In July 1916, at the time of the publication of the ballet, Maud Allan, who had commissioned the work, stated in *The Dancing Times* that she was devising the choreography for it. No doubt it would have been produced by her in London at the end of the war or shortly afterwards had her career not in the meantime been compromised. In June 1918 she lost her case in the criminal court against Noel Pemberton Billing who, with the intention of revealing widespread corruption and pro-Germanism in influential circles associated with Allan's performances, had accused her of indecency in her characterization of Wilde's Salomé. Though the scandalous nature of the trial overshadowed any moral objection to Allan's art as a dancer, the fact that she lost her case, which in the end became an issue of national importance, reflected on her unfavourably, with the result that she was no longer able to pursue her career.

as one of the last and certainly as one of the most florid and blatant of the 'decadents'.[1]

We are fortunate in being well documented on the personal and artistic relationship between d'Annunzio and Debussy. What appears to be the entire correspondence between them has been published, and we may also draw upon the correspondence on the matter of *Saint-Sébastien* with Emma Debussy and with André Caplet. D'Annunzio boldly introduces himself in a letter written from Arcachon on 25 November 1910:

My dear Master,

Far in the past, on the hill at Settignano, the native province of the most lyrical of Tuscan sculptors [Desiderio da Settignano, a follower of Donatello] Gabriel Mourey[2] spoke to me of you and of *Tristan* in moving terms. I already knew and loved your work. I used to frequent a little Florentine group where a few earnest artists had developed a cult for your work and enthusiastically upheld your 'reform'. Then, as today, I suffered from not being able to write the music for my tragedies. And I wondered when I might possibly meet you. This summer, as I was sketching out a Mystery play which I had long been thinking about, a friend would sing to me your most beautiful songs with that inner sense of poetry they require. The play on which I was working was sometimes deeply affected by them. But I hardly dared to hope for your co-operation.

Do you love my poetry? In Paris two weeks ago I was impelled to go and knock at your door. I was told that you were not at home. Now I can no longer withhold my request. I ask if you

[1] It is curious to read an opinion of d'Annunzio by André Gide who, like Debussy, upheld the French ideals of moderation and was therefore revolted by the excessively flamboyant manner of d'Annunzio: 'In Italy a fierce campaign has been launched against him based on proof that he copies and plagiarises Maeterlinck, Shelley and Flaubert. It is rather absurd that despite this his reputation is largely a French matter. . . . It may seem rather silly, after what I have said, to confess that *nevertheless* I admire him very much.' (Letter to Marcel Drouin of 1898.) Debussy would probably have agreed with Gide's view of d'Annunzio, expressed in the same letter, as an Italian counterpart of their old friend Pierre Louÿs.

[2] Debussy's life-long friend Gabriel Mourey had been associated, as we have seen, with earlier projects of Debussy. The subject of the martyrdom of St. Sebastian, as dealt with by d'Annunzio, has many affinities with the earlier occultist works of Mourey and Jules Bois in which Debussy had been interested in the 1890s. The whole matter of Debussy's occultist tendencies, as they affect the music he wrote for *Saint-Sébastien*, is dealt with in a study by Léon Guichard (see Appendix E).

will kindly see me and listen to what I wish to tell you of this work and this dream. Send me word straight away. I am shortly leaving. I shall at least have the pleasure of conveying to you my gratitude for the beautiful thoughts that you have been able to arouse in my restless spirit.

Debussy's reply, written from the Hotel Krantz in Vienna, was sent without delay:

30 November 1910

My dear Master,

Your letter reached me here where I am regretfully spending some time. Forgive me for not having been able to tell you immediately of my joy on receiving it. How could I possibly not love your poetry? The mere thought of working with you sets up some sort of feverish excitement.[1] I shall return to Paris about 20 December. Need I tell you how happy I shall be to receive you? Believe, my dear Master, in my heartfelt admiration.

A statement made by Debussy almost immediately after the dispatch of this letter offers a very different view of his proposed collaboration with d'Annunzio. From Budapest on 3 December he writes to Emma Debussy: 'I wrote to d'Annunzio from Vienna. . . . This proposal means nothing to me of any worth [*Cette histoire ne me dit rien qui vaille*]. Also, I should seem to be running a line for dancers.' And half ironically, half cajolingly, in view of the fact that he had already accepted one such commission, he adds, 'We mustn't forget Miss Maud Allan.' Letters later written by d'Annunzio and the impresario Gabriel Astruc to Madame Debussy indicate that d'Annunzio's offer was ultimately accepted only as a result of considerable persuasive efforts on Emma Debussy's part.[2] Influences of one kind or another were brought to bear on Debussy by both the renowned Russian-Jewish dancer Ida Rubinstein, who

---

[1] One wonders which poems or other works of d'Annunzio Debussy could have known at this period. He may well have seen *La Città morta* in a French version with Bernhardt in 1898. Three volumes of d'Annunzio's poems were published in 1903 and 1904 in Italian.

[2] 'You helped to promote great undertakings', Astruc writes to Madame Debussy in the course of the negotiations. 'Your gracious manner and your shrewdness have given d'Annunzio and myself confidence in ultimate success.'

was to take the part of the Saint, and the Comte Robert de Montes-quiou, the model of Marcel Proust's Baron de Charlus, who had been the first to support d'Annunzio's venture. Their first choice of a collaborator for d'Annunzio had been Roger-Ducasse, who had refused, and no time was lost in concluding the bargain with Debussy. Having returned from Central Europe earlier than he had expected, Debussy received from d'Annunzio, on 10 December, a telegram so grandiloquently worded as to appear a caricature in the worst Italian taste: 'Je reçois la grande nouvelle, ô Claude roi!' Debussy, who throughout his life had refused to give himself airs of any kind and who was quick to spot the artificial element of play-acting in an artist's character, must have been horrified by this regal attribution.[1] He had, in any case, accepted the commission without having seen a word of d'Annunzio's play.

It was not until February of the following year, however, that work was begun on the score. Since the play was to be produced in May, only two months were left for the composition of a score which, as Debussy told his friends, would normally have taken him two years. On 14 February 1911 he tells André Caplet that d'Annunzio 'is a kind of irresistible whirlwind', and goes on: 'The whole thing will be called Le Martyre de Saint-Sébastien. Of course I have very little time to write a great deal of music—you know how much this pleases me! So there is not a minute to lose in deciding. In the yield of a mine there is a type of coal known as unsorted coal. This applies to me precisely. I have nevertheless accepted because it is worth risking; and also because I am perhaps still not too old to act irrationally—and even to do the wrong thing.[2] Some of our good friends whom you know are honouring me by betting with each other on my slender chances of succeeding in such a perilous undertaking. I can say nothing definite for the moment, but I think that there will be something interesting in this matter for you later on.'

[1] It was d'Annunzio who pompously attributed to Debussy the name 'Claude de France', as opposed, presumably, to his Italian namesake Claudio Monteverdi. Another composer with whom d'Annunzio collaborated, Pizzetti, was proclaimed in the same ostentatious manner 'Ildebrando da Parma'.

[2] To d'Annunzio on 29 January Debussy had given a different view of his mis-givings: 'I have reached the point where all music seems to me useless by comparison with the constantly renewed splendours of your imagination. It is thus not without some terror that I foresee the moment when I shall have to make up my mind to write. Will I be able to? Will I be able to find what I want? Fear of this kind is perhaps a salutory sign for one cannot enter into mystery armed with vanity and pride.'

Caplet was in fact called upon to assist Debussy in several ways, and the extent of his contribution to the hurriedly written score of *Saint-Sébastien* will be discussed presently. For the moment we must examine the significance for Debussy of d'Annunzio's curious text. In offering the dedication of this work to the French nationalist figure Maurice Barrès, d'Annunzio appears to have been embarrassed at having dared to write this half-pagan mystery play in a language other than his own. More than this, he told Barrès that it was his intention, when the work was finished, to take the manuscript to Chartres Cathedral and, as an act of self-accusation, to place it next to the statue of the ass playing the hurdy-gurdy. This indicates that the over-bold poet was keenly aware of sacrilegious elements in his *Saint-Sébastien*. Indeed, Barrès was in two minds about accepting the dedication of a work in which Christian values appeared to be alternately upheld and undermined.

Despite the rhetorical effusions of d'Annunzio's *Saint-Sébastien*, it is a work which tells us much about the spirit of the time. The scenarios of Stravinsky's *Sacre du Printemps* and Ravel's *Daphnis et Chloé*, given only two years later, were similarly inspired by pagan subjects. This interest in pre-Christian subjects was not a passing fashion. The pagan cults of the *fin-de-siècle*, which had flourished in narrow bohemian circles, were an inspiration now to great artists, and some historians have held that it was this same spirit which, having affected social and moral values on a wide scale, found its most terrifying expression in the brutalities of the first World War.[1]

Writing shortly after the Paris production of *Saint-Sébastien* in 1911, Professor Gustave Cohen, the authority on Roman and early Christian literature, pointed out that the disintegration of religious values in Europe at that time corresponded to the disintegration of moral values at an early period of Roman history when the paganism of the Orient and of Greece was confused with the new values of Christian morality. D'Annunzio, he maintained, saw Christianity

---

[1] Critics and other observers in the years preceding the first World War were quick to identify the growing feverishness in the music of many different composers with an impending disaster. Referring in his *Journal des années de guerre* to a concert of Russian music, including Stravinsky's *Petrouchka* which he had heard in Paris in January 1914, Romain Rolland declared that 'les sursauts de violence et d'ivresse frénétiques, l'hystérie disloquée, furieuse et burlesque de Stravinsky, me semblent s'accorder assez bien avec la grande folie de l'époque actuelle, et, somme toute, l'annonçaient. . . . Cette ivresse du rhythme, c'est bien aussi la même qui entraîne ces peuples d'Europe à mourir et à tuer.' When Rolland wrote those words he had heard *Le Sacre du Printemps*.

in its most primitive aspect, emphasizing the masochistic nature of St. Sebastian, and introducing, as in Klingsor's garden, miracles and elements of magic. In recent years these episodes have frequently been interpreted in the light of contemporary psychology. The instruments of torture prepared in the first act for the Christian twins Mark and Marcellian, the dance which Sebastian steels himself to perform on the burning embers, and his final exhortation to the archers to pierce him with their arrows so that, in pain, their love for him may be exquisitely revived—all these episodes in *Saint-Sébastien*, often conceived in crude taste, foreshadow not only the cruelty and ruthlessness that rose to the surface in the first World War but the similar ruthlessness of the social philosophies that developed in the post-war years.[1]

The first performance of *Le Martyre de Saint-Sébastien* at the Théâtre du Châtelet on 22 May 1911 was an important historical event. But no one has ever tried to obscure the fact that, despite many splendid qualities of the music, the production was a failure, or that it represented for Debussy anything but a severe set-back at the very moment when he had made an almost superhuman effort to establish his material life on a secure footing. 'With *Le Martyre de Saint-Sébastien* begins the martyrdom of Claude Debussy', observes Marcel Dietschy. A jibe was prompted by the fact that the work had lasted over five hours: 'Ça Saint-Sébastien? C'est la Sainte-Barbe!' When the last attempt was made to revive the work in a dramatic form, in 1957 at the Paris Opéra, Emile Vuillermoz, who had been assistant chorus-master in the original production, still could not conceal its defects. 'This strange work in which an element of magic is introduced in the rotation of planets',[2] he then wrote, 'was born forty-six years ago under an unlucky star.

[1] Noting in his study of d'Annunzio that manifestations of cruelty are particularly relished by the extremely civilized and the extremely barbarous, Anthony Rhodes shows that d'Annunzio was himself both a decadent and a barbarian. 'This explains', he writes, 'why he was later to prove himself a warrior. Most people expect a voluptuary, an intellectual, and a decadent to be a poor soldier with unreliable nerves. This was far from the case with d'Annunzio.' The author of *Saint-Sébastien* served with distinction in the first World War and showed remarkable physical courage. Having temporarily lost the sight of an eye as the result of a wound during the war, he declared that the music of Debussy was his 'only consolation'. In later years when he lived in luxury under the Fascist régime ('A bad tooth you either pull out or fill with gold', Mussolini said of him) he retained his love for the music of Debussy, which continued to epitomize for him the cruel and exquisite *fin-de-siècle* pleasures.

[2] The reference is to the second act of *Saint-Sébastien*, *La Chambre Magique*, the occult chamber of the Chaldean fortune-tellers who are portrayed gazing at the planets.

Wagner, by Renoir

Ida Rubinstein,
by Antoine de la Gadara

Paul-Jean Toulet

A gathering of wicked fairies was apparently assembled at its cradle to mark out its unfortunate future.'[1]

In the latest publication of Vuillermoz certain facts are disclosed which were not perhaps unsuspected. On learning that the score was to be delivered in two months, Debussy was 'appalled'. Not only did he set to work on his heavy task 'unwillingly' but 'his health was already giving some anxiety and the work he was required to do became a strenuous drudge'. He was obliged to rely on his faithful friend André Caplet to help him 'in the material aspects of his professional work'. In the same account we read: 'Rehearsals of the work were well advanced at the Théâtre du Châtelet but the score was far from complete. [Debussy] had to be satisfied with noting briefly the substance of certain pages and entrusting Caplet—whose writing was exactly the same as his—with completing, according to his exact indications, the orchestration and the harmonization of such and such a passage clearly settled in his mind.' Vuillermoz is obviously not sure here to what extent the score of Le Martyre de Saint-Sébastien is the work of Debussy or the work of his amanuensis André Caplet who conducted the first performance. The letters to Caplet contain no precise information on this important matter. The two (incomplete) full scores at the Bibliothèque de l'Opéra are written partly by Caplet, partly by Debussy. Another score, in Debussy's hand, was said to be in the possession of the publisher Durand.[2] A short manuscript note, regarding the harp and cymbal parts sent by Debussy to Caplet and reproduced in the letters to Caplet, suggests an improvement Debussy wished to make, possibly after a rehearsal. On the other hand, according to an account which has not been contradicted, the final chorus, missing from the two manuscripts at the Bibliothèque de l'Opéra, was held to be entirely the work of Caplet. On 4 June 1911 a

[1] In later years Jean Cocteau used maliciously to imitate the bitter disappointment expressed by the shrewd impresario Gabriel Astruc, usually successful, at the failure of one of his most ambitious ventures: 'Je n'y comprends rien! J'ai réuni le plus grand musicien, le plus grand poète, le plus grand décorateur, le plus grand chorégraphe. . . . Et c'est mauvais!'

[2] Of these three scores I have been able to consult only the two at the Bibliothèque de l'Opéra. The catalogue entry at this library gives a detailed analysis of the handwriting in these two scores. I have collated this analysis with the manuscripts and am satisfied that in the larger of these two scores the pages written by Caplet are more numerous than those written by Debussy. This, however, does not necessarily mean that the pages in Caplet's handwriting were orchestrated by him; he may have been copying from Debussy's sketches. Some of the vocal parts are written in a third hand.

dispatch from Paris to the Italian journal *Il Tirso* stated: 'There is a persistent rumour in Paris art circles that the chorus of the fifth act in Paradise—the musical section least admired by the public and the critics—was not the work of the illustrious master. People who maintain that they are well informed state that Debussy . . . invited one of his most faithful disciples to compose the chorus of the fifth act.' This rumour was neither confirmed nor contradicted. It is doubtful whether further correspondence or other evidence can enlighten us on this matter, and it is therefore unlikely that we shall ever be certain of the extent of Caplet's participation in *Saint-Sébastien*.[1]

A series of unfortunate events seriously prejudiced the success of the widely advertised work. The Archbishop of Paris, having learnt that the character of a saint was to be impersonated on the stage by a dancer, forbade Catholics to attend performances under penalty of excommunication,[2] and the whole of d'Annunzio's works were put on the Index. On the morning of the public dress rehearsal, on 21 May, the Minister of War was killed in an aeroplane accident. Official mourning was declared and this important social event was cancelled. At the first performance the following day confusion reigned among the choristers. Bakst had taken it upon

---

[1] D. E. Inghelbrecht, the chorus-master under Caplet at the first performance, gives this account of Debussy's strenuous efforts: 'He composed day and night, shut up at his home, sending off the pages of the score one by one, to the printer. "I am labouring like a piece-worker", he declared, "with never a look back".' A letter to his publisher was signed 'Votre bien ensébastianisé'. The last pages, sent in April, were accompanied by the message: 'Here, if you agree, is the last appeal of St. Sebastian and I confess that I am not displeased with it. As I have told you several times already, I am at the end of my tether.' Debussy's friendship with André Caplet, which dates from 1907, led to their co-operation on several other projects, among them the orchestration, by Caplet, of *Children's Corner* and *Pagodes*, the re-casting of the orchestration of *Jet d'eau* and the completion of the orchestration of *Gigues* and *La Boîte à joujoux*. Other orchestral works of Debussy were arranged by Caplet for two (*Ibéria*) and three (*La Mer*) pianos. Born at Le Havre in 1878, Caplet was particularly admired by Debussy as a conductor. From 1910 to 1914 he was conductor of the Boston Symphony Orchestra and in 1912 conducted *Pelléas* at Covent Garden. Through his intimate friendship with the English singer Nina Russell, wife of the impresario Henry Russell, an important series of letters addressed to him by Debussy between 1908 and 1914 remained in England and was published in 1957.

[2] The censure was dictated not so much by the fact that St. Sebastian was portrayed on the stage but by the fact that the saint was impersonated by a woman dancer making a powerful sexual appeal. It was all very well for d'Annunzio to protest to the Archbishop that Ida Rubinstein was 'as pure as a Perugino painting, in a sense asexual, an androgyne'. His telegram to Ida Rubinstein before the performance, which he signed Sanae, the name of one of the archers who killed the saint, read (according to Anthony Rhodes), 'Play finished. I kiss your bleeding legs.' The Archbishop's reply to d'Annunzio was uncompromising: 'Today a sacred drama no longer has a mystic religious meaning, it is given simply to divert and delight the spectators.'

himself to place together slaves, warriors, and archers, motivated simply by the contrasts of colours offered by their costumes and with no regard whatever for the choral groups to which they happened to belong. Dressed up in enormous coloured cloaks with lowered hoods, the assistant chorus-masters Chadeigne and Vuillermoz mingled with the hopelessly dispersed choristers on the stage, whispering a note into their ears or singing a part that one or other of them was unable to maintain.

Many passages in the score reminded critics of *Parsifal*. Shortly after Debussy's death, in 1921, Vuillermoz urged that the work should be resuscitated: '*Saint-Sébastien* is to be rediscovered. Debussy in *Saint-Sébastien* wrote his *Parsifal*. But it is a *Parsifal* that awaits its Bayreuth.'[1] Marcel Proust, who was not averse to labyrinthine explorations and who was normally enamoured of Debussy's music, was able to commend d'Annunzio for his command of the French language but spent most of his time at the performance staring at the beautiful legs of Ida Rubinstein. He wrote to Reynaldo Hahn: 'All the foreign elements in d'Annunzio were transferred to Ida Rubinstein. On the matter of style how could one believe that d'Annunzio is a foreigner? How many Frenchmen can write with this precision?[2] And, as I always come round to

---

[1] The later versions of *Saint-Sébastien* took many different forms. Ida Rubinstein appeared in several revivals of the work in its original form, notably at La Scala in 1926 under Toscanini. Concert versions in the form of a symphonic suite or an oratorio, with one or more narrators reciting an abridged version of d'Annunzio's play, were made by André Caplet, D. E. Inghelbrecht, and Roland Manuel. The most successful of the later versions was an open-air performance given by the actress Véra Korène in co-operation with Victor de Sabata, at the Théâtre Antique de Fourvière in 1952. The length of the spectacle was reduced from five to two hours. The merits of these various versions are discussed by Raphael Cuttoli in the special number of *La Revue Musicale* devoted to *Saint-Sébastien* (1957). In 1914 Debussy and d'Annunzio went so far as to discuss a film version of the work. The latest version, in which d'Annunzio's text is entirely deleted, was given by André Souris in Brussels in 1964.

[2] Proust, who must have been aware that Robert de Montesquiou was one of several French writers to whom d'Annunzio had submitted the text of *Saint-Sébastien*, had heard the moving references to Debussy in the introductory scene. One wonders whether Montesquiou himself had a hand in the composition of the lines:

> Mais l'autre est Claude Debussy
> qui sonne frais comme les feuilles
> neuves sous l'averse nouvelle
> dans un verger de l'Ile-de-France . ..

or:

> Marie lui jette sa ceinture
> qui devient une mélodie.
> Or c'est Claude qui la recueille
> sur la flûte de sept roseaux . . .

your view in the end, I found the legs of Mme Rubinstein (like those of both Clomenil and Maurice de Rothschild) sublime. For me this was everything. But I found the play very boring despite certain moments, the music pleasing but very slender and insufficient, and it was moreover completely overwhelmed by the style of the work, the publicity, not to speak of the huge size of the orchestra for these few squeaks [ces quelques pets].[1] In the temple of the third act I was convinced that they were playing the music from Les Petits Joyeux. But at the very end, under the steady rays of the sun after the death of St. Sebastian, there is a beautiful joyous effect.' All the same, says Proust, 'it was a complete flop for both the poet and the musician . . .'.

One more opinion of this work, which contains the seed of many of the religious conflicts of later years, must be given, that of Charles Péguy. A warrior like d'Annunzio and a Christian too, he was, however, a much more ardent religious spirit than the spectacular Italian whom he nevertheless resembled in ferocity and ruthlessness. Perhaps it was this very resemblance which prompted Péguy to write with lurid undertones appropriate to the subject of St. Sebastian: 'The experience of twenty centuries has shown me that once the tooth of Christianity bites into the heart it never gives up the flesh of the heart. Thus I shall never again speak to your pagan soul. This tooth is like the fanged hook of a halberd, the bite of which cannot be reversed. It is a tooth which enters but which cannot be withdrawn. The bite is sharp-edged, starting at the outside and going right into the inside. . . . It is a barbed arrow which cannot relinquish its target, and it is thus that St. Sebastian is the protector of everyone in the world—except d'Annunzio.' The attack on d'Annunzio was fierce and unrelenting. Out of respect for Debussy, perhaps also from a feeling of regret that he had been associated with this doubtful Christian in this venture,[2] Péguy addressed to the musician of Saint-Sébastien shortly before the first

[1] If Proust was disappointed with the alleged meagreness of Debussy's score for Saint-Sébastien, the opulent Richard Strauss, it was rumoured in German and Italian papers, was now to write a score for a stage work of d'Annunzio. This was indeed nothing but a rumour. Yet one cannot help thinking that Strauss and d'Annunzio would have formed an harmonious partnership. The Mondo Artistico went so far as to state that Strauss had specified the subject required from d'Annunzio. It was 'The Night of a Courtesan in Montmartre'.

[2] In 1914 Debussy and d'Annunzio were hoping to collaborate on another stage work, seemingly on an Indian subject. Debussy left a few unpublished bars for a work entitled Bouddha.

performance of d'Annunzio's mystery play a collection of his own works bearing the laconic inscription:

A monsieur Claude Debussy
musicien,
Charles Péguy,
écrivain.

The association of Debussy with d'Annunzio was indeed strange, but this singular encounter with Péguy, the ardent Christian soldier, was stranger still. Péguy was in fact wrong about dissociating himself from the pagan spirit. *Saint-Sébastien* shows that in the turbulent unsettled spirit of those years and under the threat of impending war the pagan and the Christian had in fact, if only for a moment, formed an alliance and had become united.

10
Diaghilev and Stravinsky

Quand les cimes de notre ciel se rejoindront
Ma maison aura un toit.

Paul Eluard

The enthusiasm for Wagner in both literary and musical spheres was still being maintained in Paris at a high level, when another attempt at a synthesis of the arts was launched. Diaghilev's Russian ballet similarly proposed to unite the arts of painting, dancing, and music. Today we think of the æsthetic of the Russian ballet as opposed to that of the earlier Wagnerian movement, as having in fact been conceived as a reaction to it. This was not at all the view of Diaghilev's early contemporaries. Critics in the years preceding the first World War were quick to see a resemblance between the aims of the Symbolist movements, which had evolved under the influence of Wagner, and those of Diaghilev. Looking back now on the many cross-currents in the arts at this period one can see a similar assault on the senses. In his study 'Karsavina et Mallarmé' Camille Mauclair went farther. He showed how the Wagnerian ideals which first took root in the world of drama at the Théâtre d'Art of Lugné-Poe were eventually to find their complete expression in the Diaghilev Ballet.[1]

Debussy first became acquainted with Diaghilev in 1909, that

[1] 'Le culte de Wagner nous avait révélé la fusion des arts', Mauclair writes in this study. 'Nous façonnions avec une ingénuité de pauvres la grossière idole qu'embellissaient nos illusions. Cette idole est devenue la déesse rayonante du ballet russe: le bouquet de génie composé par Léon Bakst, Alexandre Benois, Michel Fokine, Nijinsky et Tamara Karsavina, c'est sur l'humble autel de notre symbolisme de jeunesse qu'il se pose.'

is in the year of Diaghilev's first Paris season. In May and June of that year Diaghilev presented at the Théâtre du Châtelet five rather conventional ballets with choreography by Fokine. Though his later productions, particularly those in which he was associated with Stravinsky and Picasso, were indeed revolutionary Diaghilev's early reputation in Paris was that of an organizer of exhibitions, concerts, and ballets sponsored by prominent society figures and calculated to make their full effect in fashionable circles.[1]

The first project entertained by Debussy and Diaghilev was a Venetian ballet, *Masques et Bergamasques*, with a scenario by Louis Laloy. Debussy was Diaghilev's first choice among the composers in Paris who co-operated with him, and *Masques et Bergamasques* was to have been the first of Diaghilev's French ballets. Curiously enough Debussy, usually dilatory in the fulfilment of commissions, was on this occasion over-enthusiastic to the extent of finding himself in the odd position of having to apologize to his collaborator for having, in an impulsive moment, written the scenario himself. At any rate this is the explanation given by Debussy himself. 'I humbly confess', he wrote to Laloy, 'that I was prompted and impelled to act so suddenly by what I recognize to be an unfortunate character trait of mine: a sudden burst of enthusiasm which soon gives way to an unpleasant return to the starting-point.'[2] Debts or other financial considerations no doubt helped to motivate this unilateral decision; and indeed before this decision was announced to Laloy, Debussy had told his publisher that he was looking forward to the advance on royalties on delivery of the piano score. Plans were apparently well advanced for the production of the ballet in Rome and Moscow as well as in Paris, and Nijinsky and Karsavina were to take the principal parts. 'I shall not expect

---

[1] Diaghilev first became known in Paris in 1906 when he organized an exhibition of Russian paintings at the Salon d'Automne under the patronage of the Comtesse de Greffühle. Not surprisingly the works of Bakst, Benois, Larionov, and Roerich made little impression, and Paul Jamot in the *Gazette des Beaux-Arts* noted that they contrasted sadly with the standards of English and French painting. In the musical sphere Diaghilev's early efforts were more successful. The following year he organized the series of concerts of Russian music conducted by Nikisch and others, and in 1908 triumphantly presented Chaliapin in *Boris Godounov*.

[2] Embarrassed at being obliged to give this explanation, Debussy tells Laloy in this letter that he is keeping a warm place in his heart for their project of a work based on the *Oresteia* of Aeschylus: 'We shall be our own masters, we shall have all the time we need, and we shall not allow ourselves to be worried either by the Russians or by our publishers.' No further mention is made of this most ambitious scheme. A summary of Debussy's scenario for *Masques et Bergamasques* appears in Appendix C.

the legs of Nijinsky to express symbols of one kind or another, nor the smile of Karsavina to explain the doctrine of Kant', Debussy flauntingly wrote to Laloy in reference to the pretentious theories that were at this time being bandied about on the ballet. He had foreseen *Masques et Bergamasques* as a light work in the form of a divertimento similar in character to his sketches for *Le Diable dans le Beffroi* and to the scenario for Stravinsky's *Pulcinella*. But not a note of the score was written.

The reason was surely that Debussy and Diaghilev were each, in their different ways, too imaginative and egocentric to allow any kind of co-operation between them. Soon after Diaghilev's first Paris season a rupture occurred with Debussy that was never to be completely healed. In August 1909, when the scheme for *Masques et Bergamasques* was abruptly brushed aside, Debussy wrote bitterly to Laloy. 'Kipling maintained that the Russian is a charming fellow until he tucks in his shirt. The Russian whom we both know imagines that the best way to deal with his fellow men is first of all to lie to them. This perhaps requires more talent than I possess, and in any case in friendship I have no desire to play any game of this kind. The essential point is that between ourselves there should be no misunderstanding and that we place ourselves above Diaghilev together with his treacherous Cossack regiment.'[1]

Diaghilev next conceived a ballet on Debussy's score of *L'Après-midi d'un faune*. According to Serge Grigoriev, Diaghilev was influenced in his conception of this ballet by the Swiss composer Emile Jaques-Dalcroze. Diaghilev had met Dalcroze about 1911 and became greatly interested in his theories of musical training through rhythm, known as Eurhythmics. It is curious that this purely educational system of inculcating a sense of rhythm should have had such a far-reaching influence on Diaghilev's ideas. In fact, the adventurous Russian impresario was to remain strongly drawn to this rather dry Swiss pedagogue until the war years. In 1912 when the Russian ballet visited Dresden Diaghilev renewed his acquaintance with Dalcroze at his school at Hellerau and arranged

---

[1] In later years Debussy's attitude to Diaghilev was less hostile. His correspondence with Diaghilev, in the possession of Serge Lifar, includes a letter of 20 May 1917, written after the production in Paris of Satie's *Parade*. Referring to a line in Mallarmé's *L'Après-midi d'un faune*, he writes: 'Il faut que vous sachiez ma joie d'avoir retrouvé la beauté particulière des ballets russes: "C'est du rêve ancien qui recommence", et c'est très mélancolique parce que trop d'horreurs ont bouleversé ma vie.'

for his famous protégé Nijinsky to pay daily visits there in order that he should apply the methods of Dalcroze to the choreography of *L'Après-midi d'un faune*. This was the first ballet for which Nijinsky devised the choreography and it was intended that the application on the stage of the theories of Dalcroze should help to evoke something of the pagan character of the work. Alas, this over-bold ballet of Nijinsky was an unfortunate failure. 'The choreography was not choreography as we understood the term', writes Gregoriev of Nijinsky's efforts. 'The dancers merely moved rhythmically to the music and then stopped in attitudes, which they held. Nijinsky's aim was, as it were, to set in motion an archaic Greek bas-relief, and to produce this effect he made the dancers move with bent knees and feet placed flat on the ground heel first (thereby reversing the classical rule). They had also to keep their heads in profile while still making their bodies face the audience, and to hold their arms rigid in various angular positions.'

We are concerned here with an obscure episode in the history of the Diaghilev ballet though it has a considerable bearing on Debussy's own ideas of the ballet. Debussy's consent for the use of his score of *L'Après-midi d'un faune* for a ballet production was given unwillingly and his co-operation was not in any way sought, either by Diaghilev or Nijinsky. It is known that he attended the dress rehearsal where it appears that he viewed the arbitrary nature of Nijinsky's choreography with distaste. So much we gather from his enraged comment on Nijinsky's personification of the faun: 'Vous êtes laid, allez-vous-en!' The extent to which Dalcroze's theories were incorporated in the frieze-like choreography of *L'Après-midi d'un faune* is difficult to ascertain,[1] but there is no doubt that in *Jeux*, the succeeding ballet of Debussy for which Nijinsky devised the choreography, the Dalcrozian recommendations for the movements of arms and feet were strictly adhered to. In his authoritative account of the Jaques-Dalcroze method Percy B. Ingham shows how movements of arms and feet were somewhat artificially co-ordinated: 'Time is shown by movements of the arms, and time-values, i.e. note-duration, by movements of the feet and body. In

---

[1] Probably not to a great extent since Dalcroze himself was censorious of Nijinsky's production. 'What shocked me', he writes, 'was the lack of connexion, of sequence in the attitudes, the absence of that continued movement which should be noticeable in every expression of life animated by continued thought' (quoted in *The Eurhythmics of Jaques-Dalcroze* by J. W. Harvey, London, 1917).

the early stages of the training this principle is clearly observed. Later it may be varied in many ingenious ways, for instance, in what is known as plastic counterpoint, where the actual notes played are represented by movements of the arms, while the counterpoint in crotchets, quavers or semiquavers, is given by the feet.'

Whatever the educational value of this theory, it was obviously madness to attempt to apply it to the choreography of ballet. Understandably, the Dalcrozian theories were condemned by Debussy in the strongest terms. Writing to Godet in June 1913, shortly after seeing Nijinsky's choreography for *Jeux*, he deplores the fact that Nijinsky 'has given an odd mathematical twist to his perverse genius'. 'This fellow adds up demi-semi-quavers with his feet,' he graphically reports, 'proves the result with his arms and then, as if suddenly struck with paralysis of one side, listens for a while to the music disapprovingly. This, it appears, is to be called "the stylisation of gesture". How awful! It is in fact Dalcrozian, and this is to tell you that I hold Monsieur Dalcroze to be one of the worst enemies of music! You can imagine what havoc his method has caused in the soul of this wild young Nijinsky!'[1]

Though the choreography of *L'Après-midi* was severely criticized the ballet nevertheless enjoyed the doubtful reputation of a *succès de scandale*. Indeed, the first performance of this ballet, which had at last exteriorized Mallarmé's erotic theme, initiated the series of riots associated with Diaghilev's productions, the most notorious of which was that provoked by *Le Sacre du Printemps* the following year. The music of *L'Après-midi d'un faune* was of course by this time well known and there was no question of any hostility to the composer. The trouble arose from the fact that in the representation of Mallarmé's poem a moral issue was raised. At the end of the ballet the faun, in a far-fetched interpretation, reclines on the veil of one of the nymphs in a gesture of amorous ecstasy. No doubt the significance of this gesture was exaggerated for it seems incredible that frequenters of the ballet in Paris should have been shocked by such a harmless symbolical act. However this may be, half of the

---

[1] Dalcroze's unfortunate influence on the Russian ballet continued until the period of Stravinsky's *Les Noces*. The calamitous choreography of Nijinsky for *Le Sacre du Printemps* was similarly inspired by the theories of Dalcroze. In the course of rehearsals for this work Diaghilev appealed to Dalcroze for help from one of his pupils. Stravinsky had himself met Dalcroze, and Diaghilev mentions a project of Dalcroze in a letter to Stravinsky written as late as 1915.

audience angrily protested while the other half gleefully applauded. Diaghilev quickly saw his advantage and seized on this divided manifestation to order a repeat performance.

The ensuing controversy in the press has frequently been described. Nijinsky's principal supporters were the aged sculptor Auguste Rodin and Debussy's friend Odilon Redon, who had felt unable to accept Diaghilev's invitation to undertake the décor. Rodin's long article in *Le Matin* in praise of Nijinsky's work brought reiterated counter-attacks providing the ballet with the type of crude publicity which Debussy, as a disciple of Mallarmé, must have abhorred. 'The spirit of Mallarmé is among us this evening', Redon told Diaghilev at the first performance. His spirit must surely have withered in the limelight in which, subsequently, it was so mercilessly held. Debussy, who was ultimately at the root of this controversy, took no part in it. Only when *Jeux* was given the following year was he persuaded to publish his opinion of Nijinsky. Defining the limitations of Nijinsky's art, Debussy's article, which also appeared in *Le Matin*, forms a sober contrast to the panegyric of Rodin.[1]

The circumstances which led to the commission by Diaghilev of the ballet *Jeux* appear in the memoirs of Jacques-Emile Blanche and in the *Diary* of Nijinsky. Snatches of conversation and of letters are set out in both these publications with many overtones of gossip and scandal, and without corroborative evidence one is reluctant to accept them as authentic. Nevertheless, with our knowledge of the complexity of Debussy's material and emotional problems at this period[2] and in view also of the fact that, though written independently, the accounts of Blanche and Nijinsky largely coincide, we are at any rate required to assess them from an unprejudiced viewpoint. In his *Portraits of a Lifetime* Jacques-Emile Blanche says that the idea of *Jeux* was proposed by Nijinsky in the course of a luncheon with Diaghilev and Bakst on an unspecified date at the

---

[1] Nijinsky, whose knowledge of French was rudimentary, had in fact never heard of Mallarmé's poem. It is doubtful whether one can trust more than a fraction of the salacious gossip which appears in his published *Diary* on the origin of his two ballets on the scores of Debussy. The articles on Nijinsky by Rodin and Debussy appear in Appendix C.

[2] On 13 January 1912 he writes to Durand: 'Je suis dans la fièvre de trouver tout ce qui me manque et dans l'angoisse de finir n'importe quoi à tout prix.' In the course of the year it became a matter of great urgency for him to borrow at short notice twenty thousand francs. A few months later, on 18 January 1913, he tells Godet, 'Je suis hanté par le Médiocre et j'ai peur.'

Savoy Hotel in London. Nijinsky sketched out on the tablecloth designs for a ballet scenario for which Debussy was to write the music. 'There should be no *corps de ballet*,' Blanche was told, 'no ensembles, no variations, no *pas de deux*, only boys and girls in flannels and rhythmic movements. A group at a certain stage was to depict a fountain, and a game of tennis was to be interrupted by the crashing of an aeroplane.' Blanche naturally declared this to be a most childish idea. But he was nevertheless required to wire the scheme to Debussy who, according to the same account, replied: 'No, it's idiotic and unmusical. I should not dream of writing a score for this work.' Following a discussion between the Russians and Blanche, Debussy was sent a second wire stating that 'his fee was to be doubled'.[1]

Whatever the fee finally paid to Debussy this purely financial consideration was apparently the deciding factor in his accepting Diaghilev's commission. He was surely not attracted to this trivial subject. Even Nijinsky, who was eventually persuaded to eliminate the absurd aeroplane episode, became disillusioned with the subject of his scenario. Yet he, too, makes it clear that Debussy was lured into the scheme by the high figure Diaghilev was prepared to offer. Describing the homosexual aspects of the scenario in terms of his attachment to Diaghilev, Nijinsky, writing in 1918, says, 'I wanted people to feel as disgusted with the idea of evil love as I did, but I could not finish the ballet [presumably meaning that he could not finish it in the way he wished it to be concluded]. Debussy did not like the subject either, but he was paid ten thousand gold francs for this ballet and therefore had to finish it.'

He did not, however, enter into the contract unwillingly. Once the decision was made Debussy wrote the complicated score of *Jeux* at great speed, seemingly within the first three weeks of August 1912. (The manuscript bears a series of dates, marking its conclusion, from 23 August to 2 September 1912; there is no

[1] J. E. Blanche gives a different version, emphasizing the cynical attitude of Diaghilev, in *La Pêche aux Souvenirs* (1949). This version cannot be valid since there is a hopeless confusion of dates. Debussy was married to Madame Bardac in 1908, three years before the conversation he reports could have taken place: '"Debussy has not yet married Mme Bardac", Diaghilev exclaimed. "He will not have the millions of Osiris until later. The five hundred thousand francs which Durand will pay him for the score and the two thousand pounds which I will add will bring his decision." Debussy replied by telegram saying, "The subject of *Jeux* is idiotic. Cannot be done. Propose another subject to Nijinsky".'

question of the work in his earlier correspondence of this year.) At the end of July 1912 he apologized to Robert Godet for his long silence, due, he says, to a period of severe depression: 'I have had to grapple with one of these too frequent crises in which I fall into a vacuum of stupidity; I then devour the best part of my energy fighting and destroying myself. It is a ridiculous and also a dangerous game in which one becomes depressed as after a bout of drunkenness.' Three weeks later, on 25 August, he tells André Caplet that despite his impecunious state the composition of *Jeux*, probably the final draft, is completed. 'How was I able to forget the cares of this world', he excitedly exclaims, 'and manage to write music that is nevertheless joyous and alive with droll rhythms? Nature, so absurdly harsh, sometimes takes pity, it seems, on her children.' And he goes on to point out that, as in certain effects in *Parsifal*, the texture of the orchestration will have to be 'illuminated as from behind'; or it must be almost aerial (*'un orchestre sans pied'*). To satisfy Diaghilev—'the Russians are like Persian cats', he tells Durand—the final pages were altered in order to convey 'a rather risqué situation'. Fine points of this kind, however, did not easily cross the footlights of the Russian Ballet. Moreover, the presentation of Nijinsky's choreography was not achieved without frequent quarrels with his partner Karsavina, who invariably failed to understand what Diaghilev's young favourite was driving at. On the first night, on 15 May 1913, which inaugurated the Russian Ballet season at the newly opened Théâtre des Champs-Elysées, Debussy became repelled by Nijinsky's choreography to the extent that before the performance was over he had left his box to smoke a cigarette at the night porter's lodge.

As a ballet *Jeux* had a poor reception and it was hardly more successful when it was given the following year in concert form, conducted by Gabriel Pierné. In a warm letter of thanks to Pierné, Debussy wondered whether the orchestra of the Concerts Colonne had shown any real feeling for the work. The performance, he maintained, lacked a sense of unity. 'A connecting link between the various episodes does exist,' he pointed out, 'a subtle link perhaps, but it is nevertheless there.'[1]

[1] This is one of the few occasions when Debussy refers to the form of his works. The thematic episodes in *Jeux* are analysed by Herbert Eimert in his penetrating study of the work which appeared in *Die Reihe*. Though it is difficult to subscribe to Eimert's interpretation of *Jeux* as illustrating 'Debussy's principle of endless variation' (Debussy

Jeux, performed exactly a fortnight before the historic first performance of *Le Sacre du Printemps*, marks the end of Debussy's association with Diaghilev. It had lasted merely a few years.[1] During this period the most remarkable productions of the Diaghilev company were the three ballets of Stravinsky, *L'Oiseau de feu* (Opéra, 1910), *Petrouchka* (Théâtre du Châtelet, 1911), and *Le Sacre du Printemps* (Théâtre des Champs-Elysées, 1913). Debussy had in the meantime formed a close friendship with Stravinsky, his junior by twenty years, based on certain musical ideas which they shared and also on the fact that they were both sought after by Diaghilev, as indeed was Ravel, whose *Daphnis et Chloé* was given shortly after Nijinsky's ballet on *L'Après-midi d'un faune*, in 1912. Debussy's artistic and personal relationship with Stravinsky is one of the most important matters we have to deal with in his later years, but before investigating the nature of this relationship we must take into account the ideas that Debussy himself had formed of the ballet.

They did not always coincide with those of Diaghilev, still less with those of Stravinsky. While watching a music-hall ballet at the Empire Music Hall in London in 1903, Debussy had allowed his thoughts to wander on the nature of an ideal ballet. Conventional ideas on choreography or mime were to be distrusted: 'The action must never be defined except by the mysterious symbolism inherent in the movements of the danseuse or the rhythm of her body.' Emotional intensity should be conveyed in a purely physical manner: 'Love or hate can be more effectively expressed in the agitated movements of a dancer's feet than by conventional gestures.' Especially significant are Debussy's ideas on the scenery of the ballet. 'A dreamy imprecision [*l'imprécision rêveuse*]' is desirable 'with changing effects of lighting rather than clear-cut lines'. These changing effects of lighting, recalling the methods of the Impressionist painters, were used to great effect by Loïe Fuller who, in May 1913, presented at the Théâtre des Champs-Elysées

---

abhorred the variation form; 'c'est un moyen de faire beaucoup avec très peu', he caustically remarked) the writer clearly defines twenty-three different motifs or themes announced in the course of the fifteen-minute work which, as Debussy maintained, are subtly inter-related.

[1] Diaghilev was to give only one more season in Paris before the first World War, in May 1914 when he presented Stravinsky's *Nightingale* at the Opéra. After this Debussy saw the Diaghilev ballet once again, in 1917, on its single visit to Paris during the war. Debussy's letter quoted on page 170 was written on this occasion.

choreographic versions of two movements from Debussy's *Nocturnes*.[1] In 1912 Diaghilev had himself planned to present a choreographic version of *Fêtes*, but it did not materialize, possibly because the tendency towards mime in the Russian Ballet, encouraged by Stravinsky in *Petrouchka*, was beginning to underline a serious divergence between Debussy and Diaghilev. An idea of the ballet he wished to write was firmly established, however, in Debussy's mind, though, like several other of his most cherished projects, it was not realized. Confided to Jacques-Emile Blanche, this scheme was a most revolutionary conception. 'He spoke to me insistently', Blanche writes, 'of a rather nebulous project and even begged me to supply him with a sketch for it. He imagined a cosmogonical drama without words or action in which the singers, consisting of a chorus and soloists and who would be invisible, would utter onomatopoeic sounds whilst the stage would come to life by the play of light effects. The performers, forming part of the scenery, were to represent symbolical forms of clouds, of winds and of the sea.'[2]

On another plane Debussy was interested in a children's ballet, *La Boîte à joujoux*, the scenario of which was devised by André Hellé, a painter who specialized in children's books and who later supplied the imaginative cover for Ravel's *L'Enfant et les Sortilèges*. Hellé had come to an agreement for this ballet with Debussy in 1913, before the production of *Jeux*, and by October of the same year the piano score of the work was completed. The orchestral score, sketched out in view of a production by April of the following

[1] See the references to the connexions between the art of Loïe Fuller and the Art Nouveau in Vol. I, pp. 117 and 224. In *La Danse au Théâtre* (1924) André Levinson describes the combined effects of light and veils used by Loïe Fuller in her famous Serpentine Dance in a manner which suggests an entirely abstract art: 'Les légers tissus qu'elle manie s'incurvent en spirales, en volutes, en trombes. . . . C'est la lumière encore qui, réverbérée par le verre, sature cette envolée frémissante de voiles d'une vie colorée, insaisissable et passionante.' In a letter of 5 May 1913 (not 1909 as it appears in the published edition) Debussy invites André Caplet to see her: 'If you have nothing else to do come to the Théâtre des Champs-Elysées this evening. You will see your old friend Loïe Fuller in her exercises.'

[2] The idea for this ballet, apparently on the origin of the universe, may have originated from Debussy's knowledge of Poe's *Eureka*, rightly described by Valéry as a *poème cosmogénique moderne*. This 'essay on the material and spiritual universe', as Poe describes it, 'dedicated to those who feel rather than to those who think', puts forward many imaginative theories of astronomy, particularly in regard to the origin and formation of the Milky Way. The repeated references to the stars Aldebaran and Sirius in Debussy's writings, in *M. Croche*, and in his letters to Stravinsky, Godet, Jean-Aubry, and Walter Rummel, show a persistent interest in astronomical matters, suggesting that the subject of this 'cosmogonical drama' long lingered in his mind.

year, was put aside during the war years. In November 1917, when a production was again proposed, Debussy reported that the orchestral score was 'nearing completion'. It was in fact completed by André Caplet after Debussy's death, and first produced at the Théâtre de Vaudeville on 10 December 1919.

This was a minor, unpretentious work aspiring to none of the sophistication of the children's opera of Ravel and Colette. It is a companion piece to the earlier suite *Children's Corner* of which there are several reminiscences, notably of the 'Golliwog's Cakewalk' in the music accompanying the entrance of an English soldier. Letters and other references make it clear, however, that *La Boîte à joujoux*, which some writers have persisted in comparing to *Petrouchka*, was thrown off as a musical work for a children's party. It is merely a 'pantomime', Debussy announced in 1914, 'on music which I have written for Christmas and New Year albums for children—a work to amuse children, nothing more'. Primarily intended for Debussy's daughter, Chouchou, the work has as its subject a triangular love-story among marionettes who inhabit a large old-fashioned toy-box.[1] Musical-box effects are introduced, also folk-songs, including 'Il pleut bergère'. Mendelssohn's Wedding March and themes from *Carmen* and *Faust* are good-humouredly guyed, and there is a miniature battle scene in which the ammunition of the warring punchinellos consists of nothing more dangerous than dried peas. 'I have tried to be clear and even amusing without any kind of pose', he told Durand. At first he thought the little work should be given as a marionette play. Later he agreed with Hellé that the characters should be played by children.

It is with this knowledge of Debussy's many abortive attempts to establish himself in the new world of the ballet that we must judge his reception of the three ballets of Stravinsky, who had

[1] The catalogue of the sale of Debussy's manuscripts (Andrieux, 1933, No. 193) contains music which he wrote on an English calendar depicting old-fashioned coaches and inns, probably in the style of the music of *La Boîte à joujoux*. Debussy remained closely attached to his daughter, of whom a portrait is outlined in Chapter 11. Two months after the completion of the piano score he wrote to her from St. Petersburg: 'Your poor father is sad indeed to be away for so many days from Chouchou, not to hear your songs and your laughter and all that noise which sometimes makes you an unbearable little person, but more often charming.' In 1915, on the eve of an operation, he tells his wife that she and Chouchou 'are the only two beings who should prevent me from disappearing altogether'. If he were not to survive 'continue to love me', he begs her, 'in our little Chouchou'.

rapidly been recognized in Paris in the immediate pre-war years as the most forward-looking and electrifying composer of his time. At first impressed, Debussy was later frankly overwhelmed by Stravinsky's genius. So much one gathers from his published letters to Stravinsky. His correspondence with other musicians presents another picture. We have also to take into account records of contemporaries and the letters from Stravinsky to Debussy which have so far remained unpublished.[1] It is not surprising that as their paths more frequently crossed elements of suspicion developed between the two composers. Recently published documents show that their admiration for each other was not as genuine as it seemed. Rivalry was inclined to distort their judgements. An uneasy ambivalence marked the relationship of the two composers on whom the public placed, in this turbulent period, their entire faith in the future of music.

Debussy first refers to Stravinsky in a letter to Durand of 8 July 1910 on *L'Oiseau de Feu*: 'It is not perfect but in many ways it is nevertheless very fine because music is not subservient to the dance, and it contains combinations of rhythm that are most unusual.' In the same letter he tells Durand that 'French dancers would never have agreed to dance to such music' and states with evident undertones of suspicion: 'So Diaghilev is a great man and Nijinsky is his prophet, unless it be Calvocoressi.' It was on this occasion that Diaghilev introduced the young Russian composer to Debussy. 'The great composer spoke kindly about the music,' Stravinsky recounts in his *Expositions and Developments*, 'ending his words with an invitation to dine with him. Some time later, when we were sitting together in his box at a performance of *Pelléas*, I asked him what he had really thought of *L'Oiseau de Feu*. He said: "Que voulez-vous, il fallait bien commencer par quelque chose." Honest, but not extremely flattering. Yet shortly after the première of *L'Oiseau de Feu* he gave me his well-known photograph in profile with a dedication: "A Igor Stravinsky en toute sympathie artistique." I was not so honest about the work we were then

---

[1] The Andrieux catalogue of Debussy's manuscripts and other possessions lists two letters and three postcards from Stravinsky. The text of one of these letters, dated 4 November 1911 from Clarens and written on receipt of a dedicated score, has been communicated to me but Mr Stravinsky has not authorized its publication. A lengthy e xtract from the second, dated 11 October 1915 from Morges, together with the text of one of the postcards, dated 13 December 1912 from Clarens, appear in the catalogue of the Collection Alfred Dupont (Nos. 276–7).

hearing. I thought *Pelléas* a great bore on the whole, in spite of many wonderful pages.'

In an earlier account of this episode, in his *Chronicle of my Life*, Stravinsky allows no suggestion of his derogatory opinion of *Pelléas*. Nor is there a suggestion of any but the most cordial feelings on the part of Stravinsky in the letter to Debussy of 4 November 1911 (referred to on p. 179, note 1). The following year, after the performance of *Petrouchka*, Debussy leaves no doubt of Stravinsky's stature. He writes to Godet of a young Russian musician living near him in Switzerland 'who has an instinctive genius for colour and rhythm'. Whatever may have been his reservations about *L'Oiseau de Feu* his enthusiasm is unbounded: 'I am sure that both he and his music will give you infinite pleasure. And what a mind he has! His music is full of feeling for the orchestra [*C'est fait en pleine pâte orchestrale*] conceived directly for the orchestral canvas and concerned only with conveying an emotional intensity. He is afraid of nothing nor is he pretentious. It is music that is child-like and untamed. Yet the layout and the co-ordination of ideas [*la mise en place*] is extremely delicate. If you have an opportunity of meeting him do not hesitate!' The same enthusiasm is freely expressed in a letter from Debussy to Stravinsky of April of the following year: 'Thanks to you I have passed an enjoyable Easter vacation in the company of Petrouchka, the terrible Moor and the delicious Ballerina. I can imagine that you spent incomparable moments with the three puppets. . . . I don't know many things of greater worth than the section you call "Tour de passe-passe" . . .'[1] There is in it a kind of sonorous magic, a mysterious transformation of mechanical souls which become human by a spell of which, until now, you seem to be the unique inventor. Finally there is an orchestral infallibility that I have found only in *Parsifal*. You will

[1] This is the scene in the first tableau where the showman, playing his flute in front of the marionette theatre, suddenly discloses the three puppets, Petrouchka, the Moor, and the Ballerina, and by a conjuring trick with his flute (*le tour de passe-passe*) brings them to life. (Full score of the 1912 edition: pp. 41–3.) The mysterious orchestration here foreshadows the tragedy of these human marionettes and produces a *frisson* not encountered elsewhere in Stravinsky's works. The writing in the opening bars with gruesome bassoons and double bassoon, leading to a texture woven of string harmonics, a feverish tremolando and celesta and harp figurations, is an example of what Debussy calls the extraordinary *mise en place* of Stravinsky's orchestration. After the nonchalant flute solo of the showman the strings take up the bassoon figure, which is now contrasted with a profusion of trills and grace-notes on the wood-wind. Trumpets and cornet finally chime in with reiterated *pp* notes to create one of the most moving effects in modern orchestration.

understand what I mean, of course. You will go much further than *Petrouchka*, it is certain, but you can be proud already of the achievement of this work.'[1]

Debussy's feelings about *Le Sacre du Printemps* were divided. A graphic description is given by Louis Laloy of the occasion when, shortly before the first performance, the two composers played the mighty, explosive work together in a piano arrangement at Laloy's home at Bellevue:

> One bright afternoon in the spring of 1913 I was walking about in my garden with Debussy; we were expecting Stravinsky. As soon as he saw us the Russian musician ran with his arms outstretched to embrace the French master who, over his shoulder, gave me an amused but compassionate look. He had brought an arrangement for four hands of his new work, *Le Sacre du Printemps*. Debussy agreed to play the bass. Stravinsky asked if he could take his collar off. His sight was not improved by his glasses, and pointing his nose to the keyboard and some-times humming a part that had been omitted from the arrange-ment, he led into a welter of sound the supple, agile hands of his friend. Debussy followed without a hitch and seemed to make light of the difficulty. When they had finished there was no question of embracing, nor even of compliments. We were dumbfounded, overwhelmed by this hurricane which had come from the depths of the ages and which had taken life by the roots.[2]

Debussy attended the rehearsal of *Le Sacre* in the spring and appears then to have formed reservations on the work. Writing to

[1] The translation of this and other extracts from Debussy's letters to Stravinsky is from *Conversations with Igor Stravinsky*, by Stravinsky and Robert Craft (London, 1959). A similar opinion of *Petrouchka* was given by Debussy to Jean-Aubry, but with undertones of something approaching alarm: 'You must hear this music, it's amazing. This wild young man has genius, and what a mind he has!' 'Several times', writes Aubry, 'he repeated to me the following phrase, clenching his teeth as he emphasized the adjective: "He has a *redoubtable* mind!"'

[2] The English edition of Stravinsky's memoirs has a letter to Stravinsky from Debussy dated 8 November 1913 in which he says: 'Our reading at the piano of *Le Sacre du Printemps* at Laloy's house is always present in my mind. It haunts me like a beautiful nightmare and I try, in vain, to reinvoke the terrific impression. That is why I wait for the stage performance like a greedy child impatient for promised sweets.' Stravinsky comments that 'Laloy incorrectly attributes [this reading] to the spring of 1913.' I think Laloy is correct. In the English edition this letter is surely incorrectly dated. Debussy could not have been looking forward in November to a stage per-formance of *Le Sacre* which had been given earlier in the year, in May. In the French edition the letter is undated.

André Caplet on the date of the first public performance he says, 'Le Sacre du Printemps is an extraordinarily savage affair. . . . If you like, it is primitive with every modern convenience.' It is certain that Debussy must have been greatly impressed by the explosiveness and the violence of Le Sacre. Shortly after the outbreak of war he confessed to Ernest Ansermet to being disturbed by this latest musical development. 'It seems to me that Stravinsky is trying to make music with non-musical means', he told him, 'in the same way as the Germans are now pretending to produce steak out of sawdust.' (This was a spurious means of overcoming the food shortage in Germany during the war.)

In the meantime further scores had been exchanged. In 1913 the score of Jeux was sent to Stravinsky and Stravinsky's cantata Le Roi des Etoiles, on words by the Russian Symbolist poet Constantine Balmont, was dedicated to Debussy. The acknowledgement reveals nothing of the enthusiasm for Petrouchka, nor even for Le Sacre du Printemps. A certain cautiousness, not to say a note of disparagement, creeps into the assessment of this work. 'The music for Le Roi des Etoiles is still extraordinary', Debussy writes. 'It is probably Plato's "harmony of the eternal spheres" (but don't ask me which page of his). And except on Sirius or Aldebaran I do not foresee performances of this "cantata for planets". As for our more modest Earth a performance would be lost in the abyss.' Le Roi des Etoiles has in fact remained one of the less often performed of Stravinsky's works. The score of Le Sacre, sent to Debussy later in the year, brought the following comment: 'For me, who descend the other slope of the hill but keep, however, an intense passion for music, it is a special satisfaction to tell you how much you have enlarged the boundaries of the permissible in the empire of sound.' And he adds: 'Forgive me for using these pompous words, but they exactly express my thought.' Music, he felt, was inevitably developing in a direction from which he felt estranged.

Here we may pause to consider certain aspects of Stravinsky's character and the nature of his musical ideas as they appeared to an unbiased observer shortly after Le Sacre. At the age of thirty-two Stravinsky was greatly affected by the outbreak of war. His nationalist feelings were powerfully aroused though he took no part in the war, spending most of his time in neutral countries,

chiefly Switzerland. Accounts of his meetings at Vevey and Interlaken during these years with Romain Rolland reveal a dominating, ruthless personality. We read in Rolland's *Journal des années de guerre* under the date 24 September 1914: 'Long visit of Igor Stravinsky.' (The war had broken out the previous month and it was just over a year since the first performance of *Le Sacre*.) 'We spent three hours talking in the garden of the Hotel Mooser [at Vevey]. Stravinsky is about thirty: short, puny-looking, ugly, a yellowish face, thin and tired, a narrow forehead, his hair thin at the top, the eyes behind his pince-nez wrinkled, a fleshy nose and thick lips, the length of his face out of proportion with the size of his forehead. He is very intelligent and simple in his manner; he speaks fluently though he sometimes has to seek French words; and everything he says is original and carefully thought out, whether true or not.'

The conversation first turned on political questions. It is perhaps not surprising that Stravinsky at this time was acknowledging the romantic attraction of force for its own sake. Stravinsky told Rolland that Germany was not at all a barbaric state but a decrepit and a degenerate state. He claimed for Russia 'the role of a fine, healthy barbaric state, full of germinating ideas that will inspire thought throughout the world'. He further told Rolland at this early date that 'after the war a revolution, which is already being prepared, will overthrow the dynasty and will lay the foundations of the Slavonic United States'. His anti-German feelings in these early days of the war were particularly violent: 'The attitude of the German intellectuals provokes from him the most profound contempt. Hauptmann and Strauss, he says, are nothing more than lackeys. He praises the older Russian civilization, not known in the West, and the artistic and literary achievements of the Russian towns of the North and the East.'

Rolland gave Stravinsky his impressions of a concert performance of *Le Sacre du Printemps* and referred also to the disparity, at a stage performance, between the musical ideas and the plastic expression of them. 'He agrees that a modern theatrical presentation of such a work must diminish the appeal of the music and also narrow its emotional content. However, he is in favour of movement on the stage (a form of rhythmic gymnastics more artistic than those of Dalcroze) but conceived on broad animated lines.

Scenery and costumes that are too sumptuous or too original will detract from the appeal of the music. The painter, in his view, is an enemy of the musician. The Wagnerian dream of a complete work of art in which all the arts are associated is false, he says. Where music exists it must reign! One cannot serve two masters. Colour is to be suppressed! Colour makes too powerful an appeal. It is a realm to itself, a music of its own. "Speaking for myself", says Stravinsky, "colour is an inspiration to me when writing music. But when it is written, the music is self-sufficient; it is its own colour."' Borrowing a terminology often used by Debussy, he suggested that in music one should 'think only of light (which should be used in a more varied manner than it has been and which should follow the modulations of sound), of gestures and of rhythm'.

Directly after *Le Sacre* Stravinsky began to write a suite of tiny pieces for orchestra and a single voice. They were called *Dicts*, says Rolland, 'a form of very old Russian popular poetry, consisting of a succession of words which have almost no sense and which are connected by associations of images and sounds'. These must be the *Pribaoutki* of 1914. What Stravinsky finds amusing, Rolland observes, 'is to make sudden contrasts in music between the portrayal of one subject and another completely different and unexpected subject'. Also, 'he must write every day whether he is inspired or not'. Nothing, however, is comparable to the joy of the first conception of an idea, described by Stravinsky as 'almost a sadistic pleasure'.

On music and musicians his judgements are decisive and implacable. Still drawing on the memoirs of Rolland, we discover that at this time Stravinsky 'cares for almost none of the established masters, including J. S. Bach and Beethoven'. On the other hand, he is fond of Mozart and, among the Germans [for he considers Mozart more than half Italian], he loves Weber, whose style is Italian through and through. Among his compatriots he esteems only Moussorgsky. He tells Rolland that 'in art, as in all things, he loves only the spring, the new life'. Periods of maturity in art displease him 'for they mark the beginning of a decline'.

Two years later Stravinsky still considers the war a salutary experience which 'with the help of God will eliminate the weak

and preserve the strong'.[1] From Morges he wrote to Debussy in a letter of 11 October 1915 that certain current events were coldly calculated by the Germans to undermine people's morale. His own morale would not be affected, he insisted, nor, he hoped, would that of his friend. Debussy did not quite share these sentiments. 'There is something higher than brute force', he replies. 'To close the windows on beauty is against reason and destroys the true meaning of life.' When the noise of cannon has subsided, he points out, 'one must open one's eyes and ears to other sounds. The world must be rid of this bad seed. We have all to kill the microbes of false grandeur, or organized ugliness, which we did not always realize was simply weakness. You will be needed in the war against those other, and just as mortal, gases for which there are no masks.' In those words may be seen a compassionate quality conspicuously lacking in the character of Debussy's young Russian friend settled in Switzerland. 'Dear Stravinsky, you are a great artist', he nevertheless unequivocally states. 'Be with all your strength a great Russian artist.' There can be no doubt of the sincerity of this adjuration. Yet about three months earlier, on 14 October 1915, Debussy had written to Godet: 'Just now we may wonder into whose arms music may fall. The young Russian school offers us hers. But in my opinion they have become as un-Russian as possible. Stravinsky himself is dangerously leaning in the direction of Schoenberg,[2] but nevertheless remains the most wonderful orchestral technician of our time.'

After their first meeting since the outbreak of the war, at about the beginning of 1916, Debussy seems to have been noticeably disillusioned. In the summer of the previous year Debussy had

[1] 'Why is he not engaged in it?' asks Rolland in all amazement. 'Stravinsky is intelligent and alive', he further comments, 'but within the beam of his lighthouse; a trenchant beam of light, and beyond, complete darkness. In these times of intellectual unilateralism he is the most unilateral of all.'

[2] Debussy was no doubt thinking of Stravinsky's *Trois Poésies de la lyrique japonaise* (1913). Referring to this work in his *Expositions and Developments* Stravinsky says: 'The great event in my life then was the performance of *Pierrot Lunaire* I had heard in December 1912 in Berlin. Ravel was quickly contaminated with my enthusiasm for *Pierrot*, too, whereas Debussy, when I told him about it, merely stared at me and said nothing. Is this why Debussy later wrote his friend Godet that "Stravinsky is inclining dangerously *du côté de Schoenberg*"?' In his earlier *Chronicle of My Life* Stravinsky gives a rather different account of this Berlin performance of *Pierrot Lunaire*: 'I did not feel the slightest enthusiasm about the æsthetics of the work which appeared to me to be a retrogression to the out-of-date Beardsley cult.' In these earlier and probably more reliable memoirs Stravinsky merely stated of Schoenberg's score that 'the merits of the instrumentation are beyond dispute'.

completed his pieces for two pianos, *En blanc et noir*, the third of which he later dedicated to Stravinsky. But the old enthusiasm has gone. A distrustful, perhaps a cynical note is heard. On 4 January 1916 he writes to Godet: 'I have recently seen Stravinsky. He says, my *Oiseau de Feu*, my *Sacre*, just as a child says "My toy, my hoop." And that is exactly what he is—a spoilt child who sometimes cocks a snook at music. He is also a young barbarian who wears flashy ties and treads on women's toes as he kisses their hands. When he is old he will be unbearable, that is to say he will admit no other music [*il ne supportera aucune musique*], but for the moment he is unbelievable. He professes a friendship for me because I have helped him to mount a rung of the ladder from which he launches his squibs, not all of which explode. But once again, he is unbelievable! You have really understood him and, even better than I, have been able to understand the unrelenting workings of his mind [*son dur mécanisme*].'

Rivalry between Debussy and Stravinsky no doubt motivated or distorted the judgements they expressed of each other, but in any assessment of the æsthetic problems which to some extent they shared this matter of personal pique or resentment is not the main consideration.[1] We must brush this personal matter aside for we are primarily concerned here with the achievements of two giants on whom, as it seemed at that time, the whole future of music depended. Whatever confidential remarks were made to one or other of Debussy's friends it is certain that of all his contemporaries Stravinsky, at any rate from 1911 onwards, made the deepest impression on him. Stravinsky, similarly, was the one composer of that time who was aware of the far-reaching significance of Debussy's æsthetic and technical conquests. For a time, therefore, they were happy to travel together, and points of resemblance in their works are clear enough. Stravinsky's influence is noticeable in *Jeux*, while that of Debussy is to be seen principally in the two Verlaine songs (1910) of Stravinsky, the Prelude to the second part of *Le Sacre*, and the Prelude to *The Nightingale*.[2]

[1] In his *Conversations* Stravinsky writes: 'After reading [Debussy's] friendly and commendatory letters to me I was puzzled to find quite a different feeling concerning my music in some of his letters to his musical friends of the same period. Was it duplicity, or was he annoyed at his incapacity to digest the music of the *Sacre* when the younger generation enthusiastically voted for it? This is difficult to judge now at a distance of more than forty years.'

[2] The two works of Stravinsky dedicated to Debussy, *Zvezdoliki* (*Le Roi des Etoiles*)

There was an harmonious partnership between the two composers, but there was also a serious parting of the ways. Where did this difference arise? Plunged into the wider cosmopolitan world of music, both composers were committed to something more than explorations of their particular musical minds. Both were caught up in the new spirit that had broken through, straining to bring into a single vision an almost universal conception of music. By his use of exotic scales, among them the pentatonic and the whole-tone, Debussy enlarged the musical horizon to embrace the civilizations of the Orient. He also used the Gregorian modes and an aspect of his work thus reaches back into the Middle Ages. On the other hand, in his conception of harmony he challenged the orthodox distinctions between consonance and dissonance and his harmonic experiments thus became the basis of many new developments. On yet another plane he expressed the quintessential sensibility of the generation before the first World War, yet his later works were to look forward to the neo-classical manner of the post-war period. He was thus, at the most acute crisis of our musical civilization, a Janus-headed figure facing both the remote past which he was able to infuse with new life, and the stylistic eclecticism of later generations, an eclecticism unsure of itself yet kept alive by a spirit of constant experiment.

Stravinsky similarly became a Janus-headed figure of this kind. Little by little in his later years almost the whole history of western music was reviewed and re-interpreted in his work until in the end his very identity becomes challenged. One province, however, was to remain closed to him, the province of the revolutionary dream symbols, and of the deeper layers of the unconscious explored by Wagner in *Parsifal*, by Proust in *A la Recherche du temps perdu*, and by their precursors Poe and Baudelaire. This dream-world, from which Stravinsky excluded himself, was Debussy's stronghold. It was the world of Debussy's projected 'cosmogonical drama', and the greatest musical achievement in this sphere was the allegory of *Parsifal*. 'Je pense à cette couleur orchestrale qui semble éclairée par derrière et dont il y a de si merveilleux effets dans *Parsifal*', Debussy wrote of his final orchestral work *Jeux*. The passage which particularly appealed to him in *Petrouchka* likewise reminded him—

---

and the Symphony for Wind Instruments, are discussed by Robert Craft in *Avec Stravinsky* (1958).

though Stravinsky could not have been delighted by the comparison —of the ethereal orchestration of *Parsifal*.[1] It is clear that Debussy believed that music was to be kept alive by some kind of allegiance to Wagner, however hidden. Stravinsky did not. Any form of Wagnerian inspiration was to remain his declared anathema, and the ambiguous dream-world, that other world in which is buried all the pleasure in the beauty of things, became almost a bogy to him.

[1] In his *Chronicle of my Life* Stravinsky describes a performance of *Parsifal* which he heard at Bayreuth in the company of Diaghilev at the time he was writing *Le Sacre du Printemps:* 'I sat humble and motionless, but at the end of a quarter of an hour I could not bear any more. . . . I withdrew into myself, but I could think of only one thing, and that was the end of the act which would put an end to my martyrdom. . . . I managed to bear the second act. Then there were more sausages, more beer, another trumpet-blast, another period of contemplation, another act—Finis!'

II

Portraits

Ce portrait qui n'est pas ressemblant
Qui fait roux tes cheveux noirs plutôt,
Qui fait rose ton teint brun plutôt,
Ce pastel, comme il est ressemblant!
Car il peint la beauté de ton âme . . .

Verlaine

At this point we may stop to consider some of the personal aspects of Debussy's character. The life of a creative musician takes place in the depths of his unconscious mind, and he alone can plunge into these depths. Paradoxes and other contradictory situations confront the investigator here, and although we cannot know all the inner workings of an artist's imaginative mind we may at any rate discover what it is that makes it function.

What is immediately striking in Debussy's character is not so much his sense of paradox. Contradictory in his actions and in his pronouncements he may have been, and even at loggerheads with himself. But there is something more than paradox here. Many artists, particularly those belonging to sophisticated eras, tend to replace a sustained flow of inspiration by a sense of paradox, branching out into teasing forms of deception or tantalizing riddles. In the work of such artists feeling has apparently lost its intensity; a clever mind takes over and for the time being diversion is supplied by an activity, in art, of the intellect. The emotional responses of Debussy did not diminish with advancing years; he was divided in his allegiances and found himself increasingly obliged to sacrifice time and energy to fulfilling lucrative commissions. But the underlying

strength of his inspiration remained unimpaired to the end.[1] We should therefore not be justified in ascribing his many baffling and contradictory statements both on works of music and the character or behaviour of his friends to a love of paradox. We are concerned here with a deeper matter: the nature of his ambivalent character and the circumstances by which this ambivalence was maintained and even accentuated.

André Schaeffner came near to defining this problem when he pointed out that we still seem to be far from knowing what Debussy really felt about any of his contemporaries.[2] Moreover, as memoirs and other documents accumulate more, not less confusion is created, or so it seems at first sight. The mercurial nature of his opinions on Russian music, noted by his fiancée Catherine Stevens and quoted in Chapter 3, is typical. His panegyric of 1901 on Moussorgsky in *La Revue blanche*, 'Never was a more refined sensibility conveyed by such simple means', is followed by what seems to be a condemnation of the Russian composer's methods when, in 1911, there was question of applying Moussorgsky's choral technique to *Le Diable dans le Beffroi* ('The patchwork of *Boris* does not meet my requirements'). The contradictory nature of Debussy's feelings in regard to Wagner is particularly bewildering, not only in the latter part of his life when, under the influence of Stravinsky, his attitude might have become understandably modified, but in his youth. During his stay in Rome, he proclaimed, 'I was a Wagnerian to my fingertips.' Yet two years later, in 1889, a letter to his former teacher Guiraud from Bayreuth begins: 'What catch-phrases are these *Leitmotive*! *The Ring* . . . is a work of effects; they even manage to take the colour out of my beloved *Tristan*, and it grieves me to see that I am breaking away from this work.' [3]

[1] The last of the piano Studies, *Pour les Accords*, with its widespread chords hammered out over the entire range of the keyboard, is one of Debussy's most elemental and powerful works.

[2] 'On his true tastes, as on the exact extent of his knowledge, one cannot be too cautious', Schaeffner writes; and he pertinently asks: 'How much fantasy or make-believe is added to the matters he writes about?'

[3] The contradictions in Debussy's early feelings about Wagner are admirably discussed in *La Passion de Claude Debussy* by Marcel Dietschy, who publishes for the first time the manuscript notes on Debussy and Wagner by Pierre Louÿs. These include an account of an attempt by Debussy to play the three acts of *Tristan* by heart which he undertook, unsuccessfully, for a wager of one hundred francs; and the many conflicting feelings aroused in his mind by *Parsifal*, *The Ring*, and *Tristan* during the composition of *Pelléas*. Debussy had apparently conceived an article, about 1890, entitled 'De l'Inutilité du Wagnérisme'. If it was written it was certainly never pub-

An evolution of ideas and even radical changes of opinion are of course bound to occur over the years. Also, the revelations to a musician of the temperament of Debussy of the virile forms of art of Wagner, Moussorgsky, and Stravinsky were bound to produce wide and sudden fluctuations of judgements if only because of the violence of their impact. The power of the impact fairly annihilated the sensitive receiving apparatus. The radically opposed ideas with which we are thus sometimes confronted in Debussy's pronouncements must therefore be seen as an expression of an inevitable ambivalence. Nor were these fluctuations due merely to external events. In varying degrees ambivalence marked every novel impression created on Debussy, in the personal as well as the artistic sphere. As a result constancy to an ideal or, its counterpart in the personal sphere, fidelity, was seldom attained. This does not mean that Debussy drifted aimlessly; it means that he claimed an unusual degree of freedom and independence. 'The sincerity of an artist', wrote Jean Bazaine in his *Notes sur la peinture d'aujourd'hui* (1948), 'consists in allowing himself to be led he knows not where.' This is admirable in principle but it comes about that the freedom of an artist of this outlook cannot be claimed without the birth of doubt in his mind—doubt which undermines confidence but which, paradoxically, is also the necessary condition to promote enquiry or exploration. The dilemma of Debussy is that he was condemned both to doubt the nature of the problems he had opened up and at the same time to seek new territories of exploration. A letter to André Caplet of 24 July 1909 freely recognizes this dilemma: 'There is no point in denying it: I am in the state of mind in which it would be better to be a sponge at the bottom of the sea or a Japanese vase on the mantelpiece, anything rather than a man of thought, that fragile piece of mechanism which only functions when it wishes to and against which the will of man is as nothing. Orders are given to someone who does not obey you, and this someone is yourself. Since one does not wish frankly to be called an idiot,

---

lished—fortunately, perhaps, in view of the statements of Louÿs regarding Debussy's persistent attachment to Wagner: 'During and after the composition of *Pelléas* he was attached particularly to *Parsifal*.' Yet 'when I tell him that the first scene of the third act of *Parsifal* is that which most resembles *Pelléas* he seems to be upset by this comparison'. Illustrating the manner in which he chaffed his friend, Louÿs adds: 'When speaking to Debussy of Wagner I used such exaggerated expressions that I provoked contradictions.'

one goes on creating illusions in an empty circle—like abandoned wooden horses at a merry-go-round without music and with no one to ride them. Perhaps this is the punishment reserved for those who are too much addicted to thinking or who persist in following a single idea: hence the *idée fixe*, which is a prologue to madness.'[1] A letter of three years earlier, to Laloy, reveals a state of utter frustration and despair, hinting also at a suicidal element: 'Fortunately no one has genius in our time, for this would be the most shameful and ridiculous thing to happen in the world.' In 1910 he tells Laloy: 'I am in a hateful state of mind, antagonistic to any kind of joy, unless it be that of increasingly destroying myself day by day.' During the latter years of Debussy's life thoughts of suicide became increasingly frequent.

The contradictory opinions of Debussy on his contemporaries which have recently come to light and which have caused some bewilderment among his more conventional critics include those on Stravinsky, Ravel, and Fauré among composers, on G. Jean-Aubry and M. D. Calvocoressi among critics, and on Maggie Teyte and Rose Féart among singers.[2] From one viewpoint it would seem that such remarks, though conflicting with opinions expressed elsewhere by Debussy, need not indicate any kind of duplicity: they may be held to indicate the many-sidedness of Debussy's powers of observation and also the capacity, when confronted by a multiplicity of impressions, frankly to admit their conflicting nature.

---

[1] Debussy was no doubt thinking of a form of obsessive madness glimpsed also by Poe and by Baudelaire. Like Debussy these writers were able ultimately to control an obsessive fury by the fact of their having given expression to their fears. Describing Roderick Usher's improvisations on his guitar, Poe writes: 'They were . . . the result of that intense mental collectedness and concentration . . . observable only in particular moments of the highest artificial excitement.' This excitement, Poe declares, allowed him to perceive in Usher, as he played on his guitar, 'the tottering of his lofty reason'. A letter of Baudelaire's to his mother discloses similar turmoils: 'I asked myself how it was that I who have always had, in my nerves and in my mind, all that is needed to become mad, have never become so. For this I thanked heaven.'

[2] Debussy's censorious remarks on Ravel and Stravinsky are given on pages 37 and 186. 'Fauré est le porte-musique d'une bande de snobs', he caustically declares in an unpublished letter. After writing amiable letters to Jean-Aubry he tells Caplet in 1909: 'Les Jean-Aubry ne me tourmentent plus; ce sont de pauvres petits moustiques, ennuyeux certes! mais avec un peu d'air froid l'on s'en débarrasse.' Debussy's opinion of Calvocoressi, following his support of Ravel, appears on page 38. A surprising opinion of Maggie Teyte was expressed in 1908. 'Miss M. Teyte continues to exhibit about as much emotion as a prison door. She is a more than distant princess.' But a few weeks earlier she was said by Debussy to 'possess a charming voice and a very accurate idea of Mélisande's character'. Rose Féart, whom Robert Godet declared to be Debussy's favourite singer, 'is unspeakably ugly and lacks poetry'.

But these heightened powers of observation made him increasingly cautious of the outside world. The account, given by Pierre Lasserre, of the extreme isolation to which he was driven, possessing in his humble home no scores or a library, indeed no musical creation except his piano,[1] contains also an anecdote on his musical views, no doubt apocryphal, but disclosing an element of truth: 'He admired almost nothing which had been achieved in his own art. . . . A person who had taken part with him reading the score of *The Magic Flute* at the piano told me that in this work he allowed himself to admire only two bars; and that these two bars were in different parts of the work.' When working on *La Chute de la Maison Usher* he told his publisher that he had almost completely retreated from the outside world.

Connected with the doubts and the ambivalence of his character, also with the fact that he was constantly turned in upon himself was Debussy's compulsion, under the guise of borrowing, to acquire money. More precisely, it was a compulsion to remain impecunious so that money must be demanded and supplied forthwith. An almost continuous state of crisis thus prevailed on both the material and emotional planes of his life, and it was only when this state of crisis was maintained that the creative spirit was nourished. The rare periods of financial ease were artistically sterile. Baudelaire sensed the nature of a similar dilemma when he wrote to his mother: 'I am not sure that anger begets talent; but supposing it did, I ought to have an enormous amount of talent, for I rarely work except between a quarrel and the bailiffs, the bailiffs and a quarrel.'

We are concerned here with the perpetuation, referred to in earlier chapters, of certain aspects of child-behaviour, particularly those aspects in which spontaneous, uninhibited responses to the senses are carried over into adult life where the mature artist is able to reconstruct and convey these responses in their full elemental force. Two inter-related conditions must be fulfilled when money is acquired in this way. It must gratify a sense of luxury; and it must be supplied immediately—not next week or when convenient. On the conscious plane an urgent necessity to settle debts may be real enough, but with people of this disposition the underlying, unconscious purpose or motive of such debts is to recreate a situation

[1] See Vol. I, p. 168, note 2. This appears in the article 'Claude Debussy', published under the pseudonym Jean Darnaudat in *Action Française*, 1 August 1915.

in which the child, throwing a tantrum or resorting to some other type of hysterical appeal, cannot be refused gratification. Running through the poignant and perceptive letters of Baudelaire to his mother is the *Leitmotiv* of this same compulsion: 'Money, money,' he exclaims, 'that is the only part of your letter which relates to my own thoughts.' Or again: 'My dear Mother, Without any discussion I must have at all costs—at all costs—you understand—*at all costs—this very day*—the sum of two hundred francs.' Wagner, whose attitude to money was a reflection of this same compulsion, confronted his friends with similar critical situations. 'I must have money', he tells Theodor Apel, 'if I am not to go mad.' These are words which must be taken literally. Apel is 'the only one' to whom he can appeal. At a later period in Wagner's life, the period of *Tristan* in Munich when his style of living brought him to the verge of ruin—the walls and even the ceiling of his music room were covered with fine satins trimmed with lace and roses—during this period when, in order to live in the most extravagant luxury, he was obliged to borrow more and more furiously, he protested in all naïvety that he 'could not live like a dog'. In the same spirit of almost unbelievable bravado Baudelaire informs his mother that unless further funds are provided he will be obliged to live 'like a beast or a drowned rat'.

The letters of Debussy frequently contain anxious demands of this kind. Louÿs, Hartmann, Laloy, Bertault, and the English impresario Henry Russell are among the recipients of letters begging for money, and as the years advanced the intensity of the compulsion seems to have increased. Several of his correspondents become 'the only one' to whom appeal can be made. He does not, it is true, suggest a contrast between his extravagant style of living and that of a dog or a drowned rat, in the manner of Wagner and Baudelaire, but, like his great predecessors, he goes to pains to impress upon his correspondents his pitiful, abject state of poverty.

The frequent expressions of self-pity in Debussy's letters, completely absent from any aspect of his music, seem in part to have been motivated by a sophisticated notion of play-acting. One of his earliest creditors, Count Joseph Primoli, recounted that in his youth Debussy had shown such remarkable talents as a play-actor that he was able at a moment's notice to release a flood of tears. One does not wish to minimize the many practical difficulties with which

Debussy at the Grand Hotel,
Eastbourne, in 1905

Debussy at Houlgate in 1911

Debussy in his garden, 1905

Debussy at Le Mouleau, 1916

he was faced, still less the misfortunes of illness. Yet it is impossible not to ascribe a large part of his material anxieties to psychological causes.

Unable to repay a relatively small debt to Henry Russell, who had merely suggested presenting for payment a banker's draft, Debussy writes to him in 1910:

I understand very well that you have lost patience with me and yet I would never have believed that you would have taken such a sudden decision. I admit that you have the right to ask for my banker's order to be honoured. But do you think this will enable me to find the necessary money? Heavens no!—and the only person who will gain from this will be the bailiff.

I would wish no one to experience my trials of the last few months. My mother has been ill; my wife has been ill; and I have been carrying on with my nose to the grindstone. I am not trying to appeal to your sense of pity; I am attempting to show you the facts which make it impossible for me to meet my commitments. Before coming to the decision you have in mind, do you not think there may be other ways of settling the matter? Would you not consent to accepting the amount of my order in several payments? I give you my word of honour that I shall never have the sum of 5,000 francs to pay you all at once. The season is starting again now and I have hopes that with new works of mine which will be given I shall receive sufficient money to settle my debts. You have given me in the past too much proof of your friendship to treat me now as if you were a common creditor! Help me now, I beg you, a little more, and I will assuredly find a way of proving to you my gratitude.

It cannot be a mere coincidence that the artists of this period, Wagner, Baudelaire, and Debussy, perpetually living in a state of acute financial anxiety and obsessed with obtaining money under duress, were those who, in *Tristan*, *Les Fleurs du Mal*, and *Pelléas*, were able to convey the most intimate aspects of sexual passion. There is of course a simple explanation for their poverty: in an increasingly materialistic age they were outcasts. But this cannot be the whole story. A realm of investigation is suggested here in

o

[195]

which the discoveries of modern psychology have a distinct bearing on æsthetic problems.[1]

In any view of the æsthetic problems which Debussy faced in his later years we have to take into account the new values that were being placed, in contemporary thought, on sincerity and irony. Snobbery too—*le snobisme*—raises its disdainful head during this period, and though it would seem to be a simple matter to differentiate between these radically opposed values, they are in fact interrelated and even confused with each other. This came about because the unsettled era which followed the break-up of the artistic traditions of the nineteenth century was not easily able to exclude elements of charlatanism. In his study *Literature and Sincerity* Henri Peyre points out that the upheaval in the arts between 1908 and 1913 was chiefly motivated by a determination to be more sincere. The artists of this period (which by contrast with the preceding period of the late romantics Monsieur Peyre calls 'The Age of Sincerity') became acutely aware of the sham of romantic emotions. 'Take hold of Eloquence and wring her neck', Verlaine had earlier proclaimed. His admonition had been followed by the Fauvists, the Cubists, by Apollinaire, Proust, and D. H. Lawrence, and certainly by Debussy and the young Stravinsky. Yet by 1932 T. S. Eliot could declare of artistic sophistication that 'the greater the elevation the finer becomes the difference between sincerity and insincerity'. In the meantime a disturbance, the effects of which are seen clearly enough today, had undermined artistic belief. But what was this disturbance? Debussy, who retained his adventurous outlook to the end,[2] had nevertheless been shocked by the futurist experiments of Marinetti and Luigi Russolo,[3] and also by the music of Schoenberg, made known to him by his friend Edgard Varèse. At first sight it would seem that he might belong to the artists who,

---

[1] In any such investigation the attitude to money of Verlaine, one of the most exquisite of the French poets of the senses who beggared himself to the extent of becoming a vagabond, must be of capital importance. The foetuses of his mother's miscarriages were revoltingly perpetuated by her in glass jars. 'Je ne veux pas tes bocaux!' he screamed at her, returning from one of his drunken brawls. 'Je veux tes argents!'

[2] 'Shall I ever regain my power of working?' he writes to Godet after receiving radium treatment in 1916, 'my desire always to go further and beyond which for me is the bread and wine of life?'

[3] Luigi Russolo (1885–1947) was the principal composer associated with the poet Marinetti in the Futurist movement. His aim, to create 'a revolution of music through the "Art of Noises"', anticipates the present-day principle of *musique concrète*. 'Noise instruments' used by Russolo included exploders, thunderers, and whistlers.

though forward-looking like Cézanne and Manet, have frequently been unable to identify themselves with the ideals of a succeeding generation. (Cézanne told Van Gogh that his painting was the work of a madman and Manet went so far as to advise Renoir to stop painting altogether.) Yet Debussy's doubts about the music of the new generation were not quite of this order. When the pianist Franz Liebich mentioned the new names in music to him he was met only by the persistent question, 'Is he sincere?' Sincerity is of course not itself an artistic virtue, but without it one cannot begin to think of artistic values. Debussy came near to defining the corroding element in contemporary music when he wrote to Durand in 1908: 'I find the period in which we live thoroughly ungracious in that an enormous amount of noise is made about less than nothing. We are in no position to criticize the bluff of the Americans whilst here we cultivate a kind of artistic bluff which, one of these days, will redound on us—and very unpleasant it will be for our French vanity.' He was particularly worried by disturbing elements in the development of harmony. 'The older I become', he wrote to Godet in 1911, 'the more I loathe this deliberate confusion which is merely deceiving us—also the bizarre or amusing harmonies which have merely a snobbish value [*qui ne sont que jeux de société*].' On the matter of snobbery he was uncompromising. To André Caplet he wrote in 1913: 'Artists who have so often jeered at snobbery have now become a victim of snobbery themselves. Indeed, artistic snobbery is even worse than social snobbery for it is merely necessary that something should be new for people to find it beautiful. The æsthetic of the fashion shop!'[1]

Debussy's letters become increasingly bitter at this period, but his music tends more and more to take refuge in understatement. In his study, *L'Ironie ou la bonne conscience*, Vladimir Jankélévitch shows that understatement, legitimately classed as a form of irony, is sometimes extended in music almost to the borders of silence. 'Presque rien', Debussy writes at the end of his ballet *Jeux* and of the piano piece *Mouvement*. The same direction appears at the end

[1] A letter written three days later, on 9 June 1913 to Godet, is even more bitter in tone: 'En ce moment c'est ce qu'on appelle "La Grande Saison". Vous n'avez pas idée combien cela augmente le nombre d'idiots qu'on a coutume d'y rencontrer. Ces gens, non contents d'écorcher le français, importent des esthétiques qu'ils croient nouvelles, et qui sentent déjà la mort: un mauvais goût plus féroce que le nôtre. Et cela nous abrutit si bien que nous n'avons plus la force de résister.'

of *Cloches à travers les feuilles* and *Brouillards*.[1] One is reminded once again of Debussy's decision to live entirely within his inner world. 'Le monde extérieur n'existe presque plus pour moi', he wrote, as we saw earlier, while working on *Usher*. The solipsist world which he had created, in which the self is the only knowable realm, was complete.

Within this isolated world it was for his vivacious young daughter Emma-Claude, called Chouchou, born out of wedlock on 30 October 1905, that he seemed to have formed the warmest attachment. The smiles of Chouchou, he told Godet, helped him to overcome periods of black depression. Although only a little girl of eight at the outbreak of the war she was well known to all Debussy's friends, who frequently mention her in their letters. Having taken piano lessons 'from a lady in black who looks like a drawing by Odilon Redon' she manages to play some of her father's Preludes, and Debussy even tells Stravinsky that 'your friend Chouchou has composed a fantasy on *Petrouchka* which would make the tigers roar. I have threatened her with torture, but she goes on, insisting that you will "find it very beautiful".' When beginning *Le Martyre de Saint-Sébastien* he informs Caplet, in bantering style, that 'Chouchou has just finished her first symphonic poem for voice, two paper-knives, and piano ad libitum. The latest title is The Elephant on the Bough. It is extremely dramatic.' There is no doubt that Debussy's affection for his daughter was a great inspiration to him amidst the worries of his later years and that it accounted for more among his later works than the production of *Children's Corner* and *La Boîte à joujoux*. The child's English governess, Miss Gibbs, was responsible for her education, with the result that at the age of three she was speaking a mixture of English and French. At six she was able to write a letter in English to Caplet in America. Toulet was particularly fond of her. 'She firmly believed in fairies the last time I saw her,' he wrote in 1914, 'perhaps when I see her next she will be a Bergsonian.' 'With her Pan-like eyes, she is the

---

[1] Exploring the borderlands of understatement and silence in music, Monsieur Jankélévitch has ingeniously listed the expressions of silence, extinction, and loss that occur in Debussy's works. They include 'Plus rien': *Lindaraja, De Grève, Le Faune, Colloque sentimental*; 'Estinto': *Pour les quartes*; 'A Peine': *Pour les Agréments, Pour les Notes répétées, Eventail*; 'Imperceptible': *Ibéria* (second movement); 'Pianissimo possibile': Quartet (third movement), *Pagodes, Pelléas* (Act V); 'En se perdant' and 'Perdendosi': *De Rêve, De Soir, Sirènes, Mandoline, Apparition, Fille aux cheveux de lin, Pour un Tombeau sans nom, Pelléas* (Acts II and V).

daughter of your Pan-like soul', d'Annunzio told Debussy. The moving letter she wrote on the death of her father certainly shows that she had gifts as a writer, and she was apparently also a tasteful musician. Alfred Cortot maintains that he received a valuable lesson from her in the interpretation of her father's music. Playing over some of Debussy's piano works to Madame Debussy and Chouchou shortly after Debussy's death, Cortot asked the child whether his style resembled that of her father. 'Oui, peut-être, oui,' came the hesitant reply, 'mais Papa écoutait davantage.' Chouchou died just over a year after her father, on 16 July 1919, from diphtheria.[1]

Less well-defined than the bright confident character of Chouchou is the shadowy character of Debussy himself. His portraits, those made in his youth by Henri Pinta and Marcel Baschet, and the well-known Salon portrait, exhibited in 1902, by Jacques-Emile Blanche, the last of the French portraitists, hardly bring out the mingled sensuousness and cruelty of his features. The pen-and-ink drawing of Steinlen, on the other hand, conveys in its maze of criss-crosses something of the complexity of Debussy's character, and the photos of Nadar catch the fixed, unrelenting gaze in the eyes which Colette likened to those of an animal of prey. Earlier photos of Debussy lolling in a chair or secretly opening a door, taken by Pierre Louÿs, almost appear to be stills from the *cinéma-vérité*. Othon Friesz was inspired to do an arresting pencil drawing of Debussy, emaciated and heavily bearded, on his death-bed, and this is the place to mention, too, the imaginative monument to Debussy at Saint-Germain-en-Laye by Maillol reproduced facing p. 210. The great sculptor's memorial to the musician of woodlands, of the sea, and of dreams, consists of a crouching nude woman listening to the sounds of nature.

It is a pity Debussy is not included in the remarkable gallery of pen-portraits of musicians by Romain Rolland. We should then have seen the figure of Debussy half in caricature, half in real life, in the manner in which Rolland was able to describe Handel, Strauss, and Stravinsky. But Rolland's friend André Suarès has left some lively impressions of Debussy as he remembered him about 1900 which, though not especially revealing, faithfully present his physical appearance:

[1] Debussy's first wife Lilly Debussy died in 1932; his second wife Emma Debussy in 1934.

At first sight there was nothing striking about him. He was not tall and appeared to be neither particularly robust nor delicate. He conveyed a certain feeling of solidity but at the same time he was somewhat languid. He was well-covered, not to say stout, all the lines of his figure merging into each other. His beard was soft and silky, his hair thick and curly. His features were full, his cheeks plump. He had a bantering manner, but beneath there was a subtle shrewdness. He was an ironic and sensual figure, melancholy and voluptuous. His complexion was of a warm amber brown. Highly strung, he was master of his nerves, though not of his emotions—which must have affected him profoundly especially as he tried to conceal them.

Writing immediately after Debussy's death, Suarès was among the first to perceive the hedonistic and the ironic elements in Debussy's character:

Irony was part of nature, as indeed was his love of pleasure; he had a mischievous sense of humour and acknowledged a love of good living. He had a barbed tongue, a certain carelessness of speech and something rather affected in his gestures; his enthusiasms were controlled, his taste unfailing, and though appearance often suggested the contrary he was very simple. Debussy was as much a Bohemian as a man of the world. In his reclusion there was something feline. With all his apparent sensuality there was no sign of brutality, though there might have been a capacity for violence. . . . The shape of his head showed great obstinacy of mind.

Debussy's timidity and his cynicism impressed Suarès and, among his features, the shape of his head and the look in his eyes:

As a young man he must have been both shy and cynical. The forehead was that of a master craftsman, a master of rhythm and of harmony. It bulged outwards, a huge convex curve in contrast to the gentler brow of the poets. Mathematicians have sometimes those prominent bumps over the eyebrows. To the close observer he was not merely a musician but a man altogether out of the ordinary. His soft but mocking eyes, sad and languid but at the

same time warm and pensive, were in a sense the eyes of a brilliant, dominating woman, such as artists sometimes have. . . . And the look in his eyes would sometimes assume a strange heaviness; or it would turn into an unrelenting gaze seeking and penetrating far into the dream world.

An admirer of Monet and associated with Mallarmé and his circle, he cultivated an informal, almost a bohemian appearance:

Debussy did not reveal the type of man he was at first sight. Several aspects of his art and his personality suggested a painter or a poet as much as a musician and he himself helped to confuse his critics. From the titles he gives his works he would seem primarily to be a painter: he calls his compositions pictures, sketches, prints, arabesques, studies in black and white. He takes obvious pleasure in producing a visual music and it was thus that he made his reputation. Moreover, this reputation was helped by his personal appearance, particularly as over the last generation a great vogue has been enjoyed by painters. There was nothing tragic or violent about him, no suggestion of the appearance of a Beethoven or a Berlioz. He did not appear to be an inspired prophet or a caged eagle, nor was he a frock-coated preacher.[1]

Though he was not from the south, and there is certainly nothing southern in his music, he was not unlike some Provençal or Italian figures. He had that shrewd look deriving from the older civilizations but there was nevertheless freshness in his appearance and fervour. He was in no way primitive or uncouth.

Opinions differ on Debussy's manner of speaking and the tone of his voice. Suarès remembers it as 'veiled, very musical, something like the tone of a muted viola'. Léon Daudet, on the other hand, found his attractive voice 'slightly stuffy'. 'The meaning of his sentences', notes Dr. Pasteur Vallery-Radot, 'were often clouded by deliberate imprecisions so that the element of vagueness in an idea or an impression should be adequately conveyed. But often his

---

[1] At the first concert which he conducted at the Queen's Hall in London the musician who, to English eyes, resembled Rossetti pleasantly surprised the audience by appearing in an informal lounge suit.

sentences would contain a single word that would suddenly shine forth, resonant and vibrant.'[1]

The striking appearance of Debussy in his youth suggested many comparisons: he was Persian, an Indian Prince, a Byzantine, even a hydrocephalic Christ. 'The enormous head bulged forwards while there seemed something missing at the back of his huge skull', wrote Alfredo Casella, who met him about 1910. By this time the cancerous growth which had obliged him to take morphine was beginning to undermine his whole physique. 'His colour was sallow,' Casella's recollections continue, 'the eyes were small and seemed half sunk in the fat face; the straight nose was of the purest classical Roman type; in the thick, jet-black hair and beard fifty years had here and there sown a silver thread. As always with artists of the finer sort, the hands were most beautiful. Debussy's voice was unprepossessing, being hoarse (and this was aggravated by the abuse of tobacco), and he spoke in an abnormal, nervous, jumpy way. His dress was scrupulously cared for in every detail. His walk was curious, like that of all men who have a weakness for wearing womanish footgear.'

This contrasts rather alarmingly with impressions of only ten years earlier. In 1917, when Debussy accompanied Gaston Poulet in his Piano Sonata and Rose Féart in his songs at his last concert in Paris, André Suarès was overwhelmed by the change in his appearance:

I was shocked not so much by his emaciated, wasted appearance as by his absent-mindedness and his lassitude. His complexion was of the colour of melted wax or of ashes. There was nothing feverish in his eyes, they seemed to reflect the shadows of some dark pool. In his gloomy smile there was not even bitterness, it merely spoke of the weariness of suffering and anguish. . . . His rather large hand, roundish, supple and plump, an episcopal hand, weighed down his arm, his arm dragged down his shoulder and his head, the seat of his unique but cruel life, hung down from his body. Speaking about him, a few people made a show of confidence and pretended that he was in better health than they

[1] These isolated words in Debussy's speech apparently made a distinctly musical impression. Recalling Debussy's reading of *Tristan* at the piano, René Peter writes of the powerful, resonant timbre which he used to emphasize certain words or syllables: 'Oh! sa façon cuivrée de prononcer "Brangäne", je l'entends encore!'

imagined he would be. Meanwhile, having sat down, he allowed his eyes, under their flickering lids, slowly to roam over the audience, like one who wishes to see but is careful to remain unseen himself. Furtive glances were stolen at people or objects he was hardly able to perceive. He was overcome by confusion, as an artist often is who both loathes and is almost ashamed of suffering. It was even said that by concealing his disease he allowed it to develop.

Several conflicting personalities emerge from these sketches. Debussy was tender-hearted, infinitely sensitive, yet also brutal; he was shy and also outspoken; confident, even impetuous, yet devoured by doubts; independent but envious. Even his appearance belied his nature: he was noble, perhaps exotic, as it was thought, yet also a bohemian; he was wealthy and extravagant, as it seemed, but in reality almost a pauper. If there is a single key to the many conflicting aspects of Debussy's nature it is his ambivalence, the sudden and unaccountable veering from one extreme to another to which an artist of sensibility is perhaps inevitably condemned. 'Les extrêmes se touchent', says the proverb. This duality is illustrated in Debussy's character even in the façade that he presented during his short life to the outside world. At a public rehearsal of *Saint-Sébastien* he was moved by his own achievement to the extent of finding release from his pent-up feelings in tears. On this one occasion, at any rate, he was demonstrative, but more often he was reticent, off-putting, even poker-faced. An honest sense of shame or of decency in regard to matters of the heart demands that emotions of an intimate nature should be obscured, even throttled, rather than vulgarly expressed. To a friend who had brought him news of the infidelity of a woman friend and who was anxiously standing by ready to support him should he break into tears he replied by skilfully turning this deeply affecting matter into a joke. In cold, cutting, and objective terms he replied: 'Kindly wait until I have finished writing this page of music and I will promptly run and throw myself into the Seine.'

12

The War

The best we can do in life is to know the forces around us
and in us, acknowledge them and hold the balance. That way
you can stay whole.

Euripides, The Bacchæ

When Germany declared war on France on 3 August 1914 Debussy
at the age of almost fifty-two was no longer, to the larger musical
public, the shadowy, withdrawn figure of earlier years. The first
six months of the year had been taken up in incessant travelling and
concert-giving and it looked as if the poetic recluse of the period of
Pelléas had at last determined to plunge into the more spectacular
aspects of musical life. At the end of July he returned from his
seventh and last visit to London, where he had taken part in a
private concert of his works at the home of Sir Edgar Speyer.
This distinguished patron of music, to whom Strauss dedicated
Salomé, had not been able to promote the interests of Debussy on
the lavish scale he reserved for Strauss. Nevertheless Speyer remained one of Debussy's principal supporters. He had found support, too, in Rome, The Hague, and Amsterdam where, in February
and March, he had conducted concerts. In April he was in Brussels.
In the meantime he had appeared in Paris as a pianist not only in
his own works but, with Arthur Hartmann, in the Violin and Piano
Sonata of Grieg. The first concert performance of *Jeux* was given in
February, and the following month Ninon Vallin gave the first performance of the *Trois Poèmes de Mallarmé*. Here indeed is evidence
of a wide field of professional activity. And as if to prove that the
idealist can also be a practical-minded artisan Debussy determined
to turn to good account another of his old, forgotten scores, the

incidental music which he had written for a recitation of *Les Chansons de Bilitis* at the time of his association with Pierre Louÿs and which, in the summer of 1914, he arranged as the *Epigraphes antiques* for piano duet.

This, however, is not the whole story of Debussy's activities at this time. The last weeks of peace in Europe appear to have coincided with a new burst of creative activity. So much we gather from a statement made to Vallery-Radot at the end of July 1914: 'Never have I approached work with so much verve. I have still so much to say; and there are so many musical ideas which have never been expressed.' But a letter of almost the same period, dated 14 July, to Godet speaks of 'hours in which one can hardly think of anything but suicide as a way out' and reveals an extremely depressed state of mind: 'For a long time now—I must confess it—I have been losing myself and I feel frightfully shrunken. Ah! the "magician" whom you loved in me, where is he? He is merely an unfortunate charlatan who will soon break his back in a final, unbeautiful pirouette.' The strain produced on a sick man by constant travelling, the frantic efforts to meet financial commitments, the apprehension at the deteriorating political situation, the doubts produced by the less enthusiastic reception of some of his works, were all combining to produce a moral crisis. In the weeks preceding the war Debussy's state of mind was marked by a violent swaying from exaltation to despair which denoted a measure of instability.

To most people the sudden outbreak of war made a certain romantic appeal. It brought to a head the many pent-up rivalries between France and Germany in all spheres of civilization and there was thus a certain feeling of relief. Hence, on both sides of the Rhine, the exuberant enthusiasm for what was felt to be a crusade of freedom. Later, when each of the belligerents was overwhelmed by the war, when the forces of destruction which had been unleashed were seen to be almost beyond human control, people perceived that they were not masters of their own destiny. They became increasingly apprehensive of the march of events and they began to loathe the war. But for the moment the outbreak of hostilities in France in 1914 was thought of in terms of the Franco-Prussian War; this at last was the war of revenge, a short, sharp conflict redressing the humiliations of the earlier French defeat. By Christmas the victorious campaign would be over.

Debussy's enquiring turn of mind—also, perhaps, the fact that he may have been instinctively aware of the underlying causes of the war, at least on the artistic plane—did not allow him to be carried away by the popular enthusiasm. He was by no means indifferent to the war. Apart from its material horrors it represented to him a very real æsthetic conflict, a conflict in the world of music and of ideas, in which he himself was to play a leading role. We have seen that the musical conflict between France and Germany had reached its height long before the outbreak of war, and therefore to Debussy the war itself, however frightful, was seen principally as a belated material expression of spiritual or æsthetic antagonisms. From this viewpoint the cause of Debussy in the role of *musicien français*[1] had already been won. The title-page of the three Sonatas, published in 1916 and 1917, bears this description of the composer, but by this time the use of the words *musicien français* after the composer's name was merely an elegant manifestation of patriotism. French independence from the German musical hegemony dates from the 1890s.

The immediate effect on Debussy of the war was, not surprisingly, a silencing of almost all his musical activities. He wrote to Durand on 8 August: 'You know that I have no *sang-froid* and still less anything of the army spirit—I've never even handled a rifle. My recollections of 1870 and the anxiety of my wife, whose son and son-in-law are in the army, prevent me from developing any enthusiasm. All this brings about an intense, agitated state of mind and I feel I am nothing but a mere atom crushed to pieces in this terrible cataclysm. What I am doing seems so wretchedly small. I've got to the state of envying Satie who, as a corporal, is really going to defend Paris. And so, my dear Jacques, if you have any work that you can give me, do not forget me. Forgive me for counting on you, but you are really all I have.'

Until almost the end of the year Debussy remained inactive. His friend Paul Dukas was ready to join the forces; he himself was able merely to kill time, as he put it, by sitting on a committee for the welfare of musicians' dependants. On 18 August when Liège had been occupied and the Belgian Government had been trans-

[1] This self-ascribed title was used by Debussy before the outbreak of the war. Writing to Stravinsky on 17 November 1913 on the possibility of their meeting in Moscow he says: 'Vous y rencontreriez Claude Debussy, musicien français qui vous aime bien affectueusement.'

ferred to Antwerp he wrote to Durand: 'My age and military capabilities allow me at most to guard a fence, but if, to ensure victory, they are absolutely in need of another face to be bashed in, I'll offer mine without question. . . . It is almost impossible to work. In truth one hardly dares to for the side-issues of the war are more distressing than one imagines.'

The French Government left Paris for Bordeaux at the beginning of September. The Battle of the Marne marked a successful Anglo-French offensive, but the Germans penetrated as far south as Provins, to the south-west of Paris, and Rheims Cathedral had been bombarded. Alarming rumours and the fear of air-raids compelled Debussy and his family to seek refuge at Angers in western France. He must surely have been reminded of the German occupation of Paris in his youth. He soon regretted the difficult and costly journey for it was undertaken against his better judgement. The truth is that in the opening weeks of the war there was a serious misunderstanding in France of the national psychology: the press was heavily censored and official communiqués veiled the truth to such an extent that the public became distrustful. The only gain of this journey was that in the provincial town of Angers rumours were less rife. 'We must harbour our strength for the period after the war', Debussy wrote optimistically at this early stage, 'for if we are victorious—and we must ardently hope that we shall be—artistic matters are likely to receive little attention. Art and war have never, at any period, been able to find any basis of agreement. One goes on struggling but so many blows one after another, so many revolting horrors, grip at the heart and almost grind one to extinction. I am not referring to the past two months in which I haven't written a note or touched a piano. This, needless to say, is of no importance by comparison with the events of the war. Yet I cannot help reflecting on this without sadness. At my age, time lost is lost for ever.'

The only inclination to work came in October when a *Marche héroïque* is mentioned, but 'to produce a work of heroism in safety, sheltered from bullets, seems to me absurd'. The writing of *No-ya-ti* or *Le Palais de Silence*, a ballet commissioned earlier in the year by the Alhambra Theatre in London, was postponed until the end of the war. 'I wouldn't like this music to be played', Debussy tells Durand, 'until the fate of France is decided, for she can neither

laugh nor cry while so many of our people are being blown to pieces.'[1] Antwerp fell on 7 October and a week later the German armies reached the Belgian coast. Elsewhere on the western front heavy German counter-attacks brought the allied offensive to a halt. At Angers during this period Debussy heard the French soldiers practising on trumpets and drums. 'They produce trumpet calls and rhythms which irresistibly remind me of the best themes of the two Richards [i.e. Wagner and Strauss]', he is bound to confess to Durand. 'If you are inclined to draw morals', he adds laconically, 'you may certainly find one here.'

An opportunity came in November to realize a project for a patriotic march. The novelist Hall Caine, who had been a friend of Rossetti and was one of the first English translators of Maeterlinck, approached the leading artists and intellectuals in the allied countries for tributes to the King of the Belgians. Debussy was the principal contributor among French musicians. It was thus in *King Albert's Book*, published in London by the *Daily Telegraph*, that Debussy's *Berceuse héroïque* was first published. Other musical tributes were contributed by Elgar, Edward German, and Messager. The French painters were represented by Monet and the philosophers by Bergson. In this wide-ranging publication Edmund Gosse and Romain Rolland wrote on the achievements of Belgian poets and musicians. Debussy attached little importance to this patriotic war-piece. 'Approached by the *Daily Telegraph* I was obliged to write something for *King Albert's Book*', he tells Godet. 'It was very hard, particularly as *La Brabançonne* evokes no feeling of heroism in the hearts of those who were not brought up with it. The result of this digression has the title *Berceuse héroïque*. It was all I was able to achieve, having been physically affected by the proximity of hostilities not to mention my own feeling of inferiority in military matters, never having handled a rifle.'

By the middle of November, after the first Battle of Ypres, rains and floods brought the struggle on the western front to a standstill. Thereafter the grim, stationary warfare of the trenches was pursued. Towards the middle of the following month the

---

[1] A few sketches for this second English ballet of Debussy (the first was *Khamma*) appear in a private collection (see No. 304 of the Debussy Exhibition at the Bibliothèque Nationale, 1962). The only note concerning the scenario, by 'M. de Fleure', in these sketches is: 'Le Scorpion oblique et le Sagittaire rétrograde ont paru sur le ciel nocturne.'

French Government returned to Paris, and although the Opéra and other theatres remained closed and the city remained darkened as a precaution against air-raids, much of the social and artistic life was revived. On 1 January 1915 Debussy wrote to Godet:

You are probably the only man who understands that silence does not mean oblivion. Indeed, these vile times serve to show that tact is a rare and a refreshing flower. The worst horrors are eventually forgotten—one's belief in the future demands that they must be. But what will not so easily disappear is a certain foreign outlook, false and heavy, which has insinuated itself— God knows with what blind hypocrisy—into our manner of thinking, listening, even feeling. For forty-eight years [i.e. since 1871] we have sought to diminish ourselves; even in France the French were convinced that they were 'mugs' and imagined that they were hard done by. I must confess that for months I no longer knew what music was. The familiar sound of the piano became hateful. Pythagoras, who continued to work on his mathematical problems until he was struck down by a soldier, and Goethe, writing his *Elective Affinities* during the French occupation of Weimar, were admirable figures.[1] I am just not on this level and had better devote myself perhaps to mathematics.

The latter part of the year 1915 was to be one of the most fertile periods in the whole of Debussy's creative life, but in the early months of the year he was principally concerned with supplying Durand with a new edition of the works of Chopin. The German editions were no longer on sale and in return for the frequent advances he received from his publisher Debussy undertook this editorial work. The greater part of Chopin's work was thus eventually issued by Durand as 'revised' by Debussy. In his preface to the Waltzes Debussy claims to have based his edition on earlier editions which had been corrected by Chopin himself. In fact they are largely based on the edition of Ignaz Friedman, a pupil of Leschetizky, published by Breitkopf und Härtel. Only in regard to

[1] There is no historical foundation for the anecdote about Pythagoras. Goethe's novel *Die Wahlverwandtschaften*, presenting debatable ideas on love, marriage, and divorce, was written in 1809 during the occupation of Weimar by Napoleon's Grande Armée.

the Second Ballade, in F major, does Debussy claim to have consulted the original manuscript. This was lent to him by Saint-Saëns and allowed one or two minor rectifications to be made.[1]

At the completion of this editorial work he suffered a personal blow. He was profoundly affected by the death of his mother, Victorine, on 23 March. Questioning the significance of death in his letters ('Can one be sure what happens to us at this moment?'), he turned despairingly to his friends d'Annunzio, Varèse, and Durand.

In the opening months of 1915 a feeling of war-weariness had set in from which the hard-pressed public were severely jolted when poison gas was used against British and French troops in Flanders at the end of April. The following month the *Lusitania* was torpedoed. In June, however, when Durand, expecting no further compositions from the dejected composer during the war, suggested that Debussy undertake an edition of Bach, he surprisingly received an optimistic letter announcing that work was begun on a set of pieces for two pianos, *En blanc et noir*. 'Though I have not spoken to you about it, I have greatly suffered from the long drought created in my mind by the war', this letter states. 'I am now anxious to leave as soon as possible for my home has long oppressed me.' In July he was offered hospitality at 'Mon Coin', a cottage at Pourville, near Dieppe, with a garden overlooking the sea. ('It is not so well laid out as the gardens of Le Nôtre, but it is very pleasant if you do not want to play the part of Robinson Crusoe.') Within a few days he had sent Durand the three pieces forming *En blanc et noir*, originally *Caprices en blanc et noir*.

Like many of the earlier piano works they were conceived in the

---

[1] In 1917 Debussy completed his 'revision' of two sets of sonatas by J. S. Bach: the six sonatas for violin and clavier and the three sonatas for viola da gamba and clavier. His editorial work on Chopin was undertaken with zest; that on Bach with some misgivings. He wrote to Durand on 15 April 1917: 'Never correct the sonatas for violin and piano of Bach on a rainy Sunday afternoon. I have just finished the revision (!) of the above-named and it is as if it were raining within one's soul. When the old Saxon cantor has no ideas he starts off with anything and he is then truly merciless. In fact, he is only bearable when he is wonderful—which is certainly something, you will say. All the same if he had had a friend—perhaps a publisher?—who would have encouraged him to take a day off say once a week we might have been spared some hundreds of pages in which there are rows upon rows of joyless days, always with that little rascal of a subject and its countersubject. Sometimes his wonderful writing, which is after all a form of gymnastics peculiar to the old master, does not manage to fill the terrible void which then appears to become all the wider by his determination to extract the maximum value from a commonplace theme.'

Monument to Debussy, by Maillol

Debussy on his death-bed, by Othon Friesz

'Le Tombeau de Debussy', by Raoul Dufy

manner of a painting. 'I must confess that I have somewhat changed the colour', he wrote to Durand during the composition of the most dramatic of these pieces. 'It was too consistently sombre, almost as tragic as one of the *Caprichos* of Goya.'[1] The second, inspired by François Villon's *Ballade contre les ennemis de France*, is dedicated to Lieut. Jacques Charlot, Durand's associate who was killed in action earlier in the year. Incorporating the chorale of Luther, and portraying also a distant rumbling of guns and trumpet calls, it was held by Debussy to be the most inspired of the set. The remaining two pieces are dedicated to Debussy's Russian friends of this time, Koussevitzky, who had invited him to Moscow, and Stravinsky, whom he was to meet on two occasions in Paris during the war.[2]

The three short months spent at 'Mon Coin' from the middle of July to the middle of October formed the last period of Debussy's creative activity. The fervour with which he worked during these last summer and autumn months on the Normandy coast was intense. Besides *En blanc et noir*, the twelve Studies for piano were crowded into this period, and also two of the three sonatas, those for cello and piano, and for flute, viola, and harp. At the beginning of October he wrote to Durand: 'I am taking advantage of these last days of liberty for Paris seems to me to be a kind of open prison where one no longer has the right to think. The walls there have terrible ears. . . . And so I am writing down all the music that passes through my head, like a madman, and rather sadly.' A similar letter was sent to Godet on 14 October: 'I have returned from a stay at the seaside. . . . There I was able once again to think in musical terms which I had not been able to do over the last year. It is certainly not essential that I write music, but it is all I am able to do more or less competently. I must humbly admit to the feeling of latent death within me. Accordingly, I write like a madman or like one who is condemned to die the next morning.'[3]

[1] Writing to Godet of these pieces the following year Debussy compares them to the work of another Spanish painter: 'Don't rack your brains about *En blanc et noir*. These pieces derive their colour and their feeling merely from the sonority of the piano; if you agree they are like the "greys" of Velasquez.'

[2] The meetings took place about the end of 1915, according to a letter from Debussy to Godet, and the middle of 1917. 'I saw him last about nine months before his death', Stravinsky writes in his memoirs. His statement that 'Debussy did not mention the piece from *En blanc et noir* he had written for me' is indeed strange, since it had been published with Stravinsky's name as the dedicatee eighteen months earlier.

[3] Debussy was certainly aware that his illness was fatal, and this last burst of creative

As the scope and the devastation of the war extended until it assumed world-wide proportions Debussy had come to realize that, silenced by the magnitude of the catastrophe, he was himself becoming a casualty. 'And now they are speaking of the intervention of Japan', he notes at the beginning of August. 'Why not the inhabitants of Mars while we are about it?'[1] 'I want to work', he writes in this letter, 'not so much for myself, but to give proof, however small it may be, that even if there were thirty million Boches [i.e. on French soil] French thought will not be destroyed.'

The letters to Durand show that the twelve studies were written between 5 August and 29 September. One of them, *Pour les Agréments*, 'gives new life to a worn-out device'; another, *Pour les Quartes*, contains 'effects you have never heard before'. He works at these difficult, complex works with 'the activity of an engine'. On 30 September he was able to write: 'Last night at midnight I copied out the last note of the Studies. Phew! The most minute Japanese print is child's play by comparison with the writing of some of the pages; but I am pleased, it is good work.' In dedicating them somewhat diffidently to the memory of Chopin, he was aware that comparisons would be made 'inevitably to my disadvantage', yet 'without false modesty I may say that they will acquire a place of their own'.

The Cello and Piano Sonata was completed by the beginning of August ('I like its proportions and its form that is almost classical, in the good sense of the word') and the Sonata for Flute, Viola (originally oboe), and Harp by the end of September. When the sketches were completed for this second of the projected set of six sonatas Debussy told Durand that his vision of it was, as he put it, almost embarrassingly beautiful. Two days before leaving 'Mon Coin' he informs his trusted publisher that 'I shall go on writing until the last minute like André Chénier writing poems before

---

energy accordingly took the form of a defiance of death. Fifteen years earlier another artist of Debussy's generation, Oscar Wilde, similarly poured forth his finest thoughts at the approach of death. Referring to the period preceding Wilde's death in Paris in 1900, Ernest La Jeunesse, the friend of both Wilde and Debussy, wrote: '[Wilde] is haunted by a foreboding of death which in the end will kill him. He then tells all his stories in one breath: it is the bitter yet dazzling final piece of display of superhuman fireworks.'

[1] Italy and Bulgaria joined the Allies in 1915. In the course of the next two years no less than nineteen countries were to enter the war on the allied side.

mounting the scaffold. This is a macabre comparison but there is some truth in it.'[1]

Shortly after the triumphant composer returned to Paris the disease from which he had suffered intermittently since 1909, cancer of the rectum, developed to the extent that his doctors, Crespel and Desjardins, advised an operation. This took place on 7 December. It was reasonably successful, but it was clear that the disease was fatal.[2] A few days before the operation, at the beginning of December, both the words and music were written for the charming but pathetic song, *Noël des enfants qui n'ont plus de maison*. Debussy's heart went out to the homeless refugee children in Flanders. Reverting to the manner of *Pelléas et Mélisande*, it is a little masterpiece of compassion. Two versions were made in these last fateful days of 1915, for voice and piano and for children's two-part chorus.

The first six months of 1916 dragged on in a mood of growing depression. The letters to Durand refer with impatience to the many forms of treatment that were proposed. Radium and morphine were administered. 'I have the right to ask whether this illness isn't after all incurable,' he complains, 'in which case I had better be told straight away. "Alors! Oh! Alors" as poor Golaud exclaims.' This was the year of Verdun. The tremendous German offensive launched in February by the armies of the Crown Prince was of a ferocity hitherto unknown, and indeed even the most spectacular offensives of the second World War were not again to claim casualties on this cataclysmic scale. By the summer nearly a quarter of a million French soldiers had been killed in this single battle and an even greater number seriously wounded. Even though the invading armies were halted—by the end of March they had nowhere advanced beyond four miles—the whole of France lived perpetually in anguish. It was then that the famous call went up from the French lines, 'Ils ne passeront pas!' For the first time the German generals wondered whether they could win the war.

---

[1] A royalist, André Chénier was guillotined in 1794. Debussy may have had in mind the fact that owing to the dramatic circumstances of Chénier's death a generation was to pass before his poetic genius was recognized.

[2] Authorities on rectal cancer state that in its early stages this disease is not particularly painful, and that pain is a symptom indicating that the disease has reached an advanced stage. Shortly before the operation Debussy wrote to Fauré: 'La journée du 26 [novembre] m'a mis plus bas que la terre, et, depuis, j'ai souffert comme un chien.' During the remaining two and a quarter years of his life Debussy used a colostomy.

Time was against them. In July the Battle of Verdun was followed by the equally ferocious counter-offensive of the allies, the Battle of the Somme, but still no issue was reached. The uninterrupted slaughter of the war produced on Debussy the effect 'of an open wound'. Though he admired the heroism of his friend Caplet, who was a liaison officer at Verdun, he became increasingly depressed by the routine acceptance of the war and by the growing hatred it engendered on all sides. In October, though rapidly wasting, he spent a short time at Le Mouleau, near Arcachon, where he managed to work on the finale of the Violin and Piano Sonata, the first two movements of which were begun earlier in the year. At first he was anxious to develop a 'cellular' theme. This last movement was, however, several times rewritten and eventually the choice of the opening subject went to 'a theme turning back on itself like a serpent biting its own tail'.[1] In May 1917 Debussy expresses great satisfaction with this last of his completed works, written with a stoic determination to overcome his disability. 'In keeping with the contradictory spirit of human nature it is full of a joyous tumult', he writes to Godet. 'Beware in future of works which appear to inhabit the skies; often they are the product of a dark, morose mind.'[2] The plan for the series of six sonatas 'for various instruments', begun at Pourville the previous year, was well established and though the series was only half completed at the time of Debussy's death the instrumentation of the remaining three sonatas had been definitely decided upon. The fourth was to have been for oboe, horn, and harpsichord. The fifth was planned for wind instruments (trumpet, clarinet, and bassoon) and piano. The sixth, apparently foreseen as the most important of the set, was to 'take the form of a Concert in which all the "various instruments" are combined and to which will be added a double bass'.

Later, in 1916, sketches were made for a patriotic cantata, Ode à

[1] Of the several versions of the finale which Debussy had mentioned to him, Dukas wrote: 'I am sure that of the six versions of the finale of this Sonata five of them are good and that the sixth is excellent.'

[2] This confident opinion of the Violin and Piano Sonata is in striking contrast to the condemnatory opinion Debussy was to give Godet of this work when writing to him in a depressed mood only a month later (see page 218). In a book on Debussy by his friend Émile Vuillermoz (Geneva, 1957), widely acclaimed on account of its illustrations by Turner, Monet, Sisley, and Pissarro, a highly derogatory criticism is made of the late works, based unjustifiably on Debussy's distorted opinions of them.

la France, on words by Laloy,[1] and in September the libretto was completed of *La Chute de la Maison Usher*. In this last year of Debussy's life illness compelled him to give in and he was thus prevented from realizing many far-sighted ideas. To the end he fought heroically. On the other hand, by its very nature Debussy's art, even though transformed during the war years, was doomed, as we have seen in earlier chapters, to remain incomplete. Indeed, there was an element of something incomplete or unfinished even in his greatest works, among them the *Nocturnes*, *La Mer*, and *Pelléas*, the orchestrations of which he was constantly revising. More than this, he was aware in his last years of pursuing an unattainable ideal, an ideal of music that should be more beautiful, more exquisite than anything he had written, than anything that could ever be written by a composer of music. This way lies disintegration. Despite the triumphs of certain of his later works the exploratory art of the successor of Wagner could never be wholly realized.[2]

The pre-war struggle in France for artistic independence degenerated during the war itself into a narrow chauvinistic spirit. Performances of works by contemporary or recently born composers from enemy countries were banned. This militant chauvinism was even directed against Beethoven and Wagner, the two composers whom the French, more than any other people, had taken to their hearts. Debussy would have none of this. Observing in a preface written in December 1916 for the series of essays *Pour la Musique française* edited by Paul Huvelin, that 'strange statements are to be heard about Beethoven who—Flemish or German— was a great musician and about Wagner who was a greater artist than a musician', he roundly declares: 'Everyone knows this; and in any case this is not the question.' French musicians, he believed,

[1] Two posthumous publications of this work were issued though it is impossible to know how much of it is Debussy's original music. The piano score, published in 1928, is said to be 'réalisé par Marius François Gaillard'. The orchestral score (1954) states that the work is 'orchestré par Marius François Gaillard'. The performance in 1928 of this arrangement without any indication of the sources was widely deplored.

[2] Some twenty years earlier, in 1895, Debussy had expressed to Pierre Louÿs his reluctance, which remained with him to the end of his life, to complete certain of his most cherished projects. As opposed to the dream-like incompleteness of Debussy's work the almost brutal finality of the work of Wagner was boldly defined by Ernest Newman: 'He gambled superbly with life, and he won. . . . He lived, indeed, to see himself victor everywhere, in possession of everything for which he had struggled his whole feverish life through. He completed, and saw upon the stage, every one of the great works he had planned.'

should be encouraged to revive the spirit of the eighteenth century. Gluck and Wagner led opera away from French ideals. Among nineteenth-century composers Chabrier is now singled out. 'Not everyone is able to write "la grande musique" ', he adds dispassionately, 'but everyone attempts to do so.' And he concludes: 'The war is to be won on several different planes: music is one of them.' Ravel was even more outspoken in his opposition to any form of chauvinism. 'I am little concerned about the fact that Monsieur Schoenberg is an Austrian', he challengingly announced. 'He remains a highly significant composer whose interesting discoveries have had a beneficial influence on certain composers from the allied countries and among us as well.' A thoroughly independent figure himself, Ravel was able to assess the independence of others and to rise above the feverish prejudices of the war: 'I am delighted that Messieurs Bartók, Kodály and their disciples are Hungarian and that they show it in their works with so much fervour.' Alone among the dominating figures of his time, Saint-Saëns inveighed against the persistent Wagnerian influence.

Stravinsky's *Sacre du Printemps* had been given in the year preceding the war and in the same year Luigi Russolo in Milan issued his Futurist manifesto on the 'Art of Noises'. Activities of this kind anticipated the war. But the characteristic works of the four war years were of an altogether different spirit. In 1917, at the height of the battles of Verdun and the Somme, the destructive æsthetic of the Dadaists was established. The nursery word *dada*, meaning both 'gee-gee' and 'hobby', was adopted to convey a spirit in music, as also in painting and literature, of utter nihilism. At Zürich a group of refugees from the warring world arbitrarily chose this word simply by opening a dictionary at random. It had no relevant meaning but it was appropriate, they thought, to express their anger at the holocaust brought upon them by what they believed to be lying civilizations. The same year one of the earliest mentions is made of the word jazz. (The following year it is spelt 'jaz' or 'jass'; to this day its etymological origin remains unknown.) On the other hand, the war created no great impression on the less adventurous composers in France and Germany though their music was beginning to show signs of disintegration. In 1915 Saint-Saëns visited the U.S.A. where he wrote the march *Hail, California!* and in the same year Strauss wrote his Alpine Symphony. This work, for gigantic

orchestra (twelve horns off-stage), is the most literal and harshly realistic of all orchestral programme works.[1]

Debussy's style had changed during the war but it had not disintegrated. In 1917 he appeared several times as pianist and conductor, and took part in the first performance of his cello and violin sonatas. The Violin Sonata was first given on 5 May at a concert of his works with Gaston Poulet and Rose Féart. It was his last concert in Paris. A fortnight later he heard one of the most nihilistic works of the war, Satie's ballet *Parade* on a scenario by Cocteau and with décor by Picasso.[2] It was a work which provoked another of the now notorious scenes of hostility between public and performers. After the *Sacre* and the 'Futurist' music promoted by Luigi Russolo it was Debussy's harshest experience of the music of the future.

During the latter part of the war Debussy became increasingly attached to his old friend Robert Godet to whom, in long rambling letters, he poured out his feelings of apprehension and disillusionment. Five of Godet's letters to Debussy, full of tact and warmth, were recently published and offer one of the few glimpses of Debussy's friendships reflected in the letters of both correspondents. From his home in Switzerland, Godet, who had closely followed Debussy's life from his early Conservatoire days, was determined to provide him during the war years with moral support and also to prove to him his deep-seated affection. His judgements in this correspondence on Debussy's late works, however, remain objective. In a letter to Godet of 11 December 1916 Debussy timorously refers to a private performance of his Sonata for Flute, Viola, and Harp: 'The sound of it is not bad, though it is not for me to speak

[1] Far from showing any sense of austerity in this war-time work, Strauss wrote such opulent and taxing parts for the brass instruments of the Berlin orchestra that he recommended them to use the amazing Aerophor. This bizarre device consisted of a bellows worked by the foot and which, by means of a tube, maintained a pressurized air-chamber within the wind-player's cheeks.

[2] This circus ballet, said Georges Auric in 1917, illustrates the fact that in real life 'the song of the nightingale is smothered by the noise of trams'. Or, more appropriately, one would have imagined, by the noise of guns. If not a Dadaist work, *Parade* was an experiment in a bitterly anti-romantic vein. Produced by Diaghilev on his single visit to Paris during the war, it was apparently given in a modified form. In *Le Rappel à l'Ordre* Cocteau quaintly writes: 'The score of *Parade* was to be a musical background for suggestive noises, such as sirens, typewriters, airplanes, dynamos. . . . Technical difficulties and the rush at rehearsals prevented the instalment of these noises. We suppressed almost all of them, that is to say the work was presented incomplete and without its *bouquet*.'

to you of the music. I could do so, however, without embarrassment for it is the music of a Debussy whom I no longer know. It is frightfully mournful and I don't know whether one should laugh or cry—perhaps both?' Godet challenges this opinion.

I have not discovered at first sight such unfathomable depths as you say there are between the Claude Debussy of today and his Sonata for Flute, Viola, and Harp [he writes on 5 January 1917 in bold, confident terms]. Sometimes, while your forward march relentlessly progresses, something causes you to glance backwards, and it seems to me that your second 'French Sonata' represents one of these retrospective glances thanks to which the development of your genius remains all of a piece. In looking back to one's youth one does not see the familiar scene again, for the viewpoint has changed. . . . To convey the magic of Debussyan memories what happier combination of timbres could one hope to find than the one you have discovered? How modern it is and yet how aptly does it evoke the music of the past! It seems to me that the reflective viola resurrects your youth in some kind of veiled, tender manner while the flute, assuming both a languorous and a vivacious manner as if it were impersonating a melancholy version of Puck, seems to be questioning the hidden meaning of things. You combine these two voices, the one a warm, soulful voice thrown into relief by the other, rather colder voice, and their intercourse is woven together by the harp. Your work represents a subtle reflection of naïvety, if I may use this word, and indeed it is desirable to do so for it is this root naïvety that causes us to wonder, in listening to your work, whether we should smile or burst into tears.

Godet was similarly concerned to correct Debussy's deprecatory view of his Violin Sonata. In a letter of 7 June 1917 Debussy fairly fulminates against this tender work: 'You should know, my too trusting friend, that I only wrote this Sonata to be rid of the thing, spurred on as I was by my dear publisher. You, who are able to read between the staves, will see traces of *The Imp of the Perverse* [the story by Poe] who encourages one to choose the very subject which should be ignored. This Sonata will be interesting from a documentary viewpoint and as an example of what may be pro-

duced by a sick man in time of war.' Godet took time to reflect on this condemnation, and gave his opinion only two months later. On 16 August he wrote to his dejected friend: 'I have had time to read and re-read the Violin Sonata but not without outbursts of indignation against the severity of its composer. It may not present a three-dimensional view of the composer's subtlety and depth but it nevertheless speaks his true language, so it seems to me, in a friendly, youthful manner, simply and addressed to everyone. It is an appropriate work to appear at a time when everywhere there is a call to action. One would only be justified in criticizing it if it were not true music; which undoubtedly it is, and in a delightful way.'

Their correspondence continued in this vein until November, Debussy courageously portraying his sorrowful state in an ironic quip, Godet responding patiently and affectionately to his friend's exasperated state of mind. A few extracts from their correspondence show the nature of their finely attuned friendship.

Debussy to Godet from Chalet Habas, Saint-Jean-de-Luz, 28 July 1917:

Decidedly, fashionable resorts by the sea are not for me. But this house is charming. It is built in the Basque style, the interior decoration being English. The proprietor, Colonel A. L. Nicol, is English and of course he has been at the front since the beginning of the war. His wife is in London occupied there with— whatever you say.

It is a place in which you might come across S. Pickwick on the staircase. I am continuously haunted by the fine portrait of an old gentleman, severe and dejected. When I am late in the morning his severity increases and he even appears to be reproachful. All over the place are guns which, when they were in use, must have been terrifying; they were used against the Dahoman tribes. Also countless family groups painted by one of the earlier Nicols. The sea is not within sight. Behind the house are gentle mountains. A quarter of an hour's walk brings you to the bay where, as in all such bays, the bathers might with advantage be less unprepossessing. At sea is a collier, a useful boat no doubt but which spoils the view of the horizon. Further along the coast, at Guéthary, which is favoured by the presence of P. J. Toulet, a celebrated humorist and a confirmed alcoholic

whose face resembles a sunset painted by Van Dongen,[1] the sea is most beautiful. All this would be very pleasant if I were not there to spoil everything. So nothing has up till now changed:

Les morts
C'est discret
Ça dort
Bien au frais.[2]

Your old devoted

C. D.

Godet to Debussy, 16 August 1917:

Whenever I leave you I am extremely unhappy at the thought of no longer being with you. . . . Your letter from Saint-Jean-de-Luz reached me, a short, bitterly delicious poem. . . . Let me embrace you on your fine luminous forehead. Let me wish you good work and, as far as possible, good health.

Debussy to Godet, October 1917:

Do not be angry with me if for some time I have not spoken to you of my projects. Music has completely abandoned me. If there is no reason to weep, it is at any rate a little absurd, but I can do nothing about it and I have never forced anyone to love me.

[1] Debussy's correspondence with Toulet at this period deals principally with their proposed version of *As You Like It* (see Appendix A). Since Toulet was now also an invalid, they were unable to meet. Referring to a drive which took him past Toulet's house at Guéthary, Debussy says: 'Yesterday we passed "Etcheberria"—you probably know? If I were George Meredith I should write twenty pages listing all the unpleasant associations of surprises; and another twenty putting the opposite point of view.'

[2] This quotation which appears in Vol. I, p. 130, is from Laforgue's *Complainte de l'oubli des morts*, a gruesome lament on the dead who are soon to be forgotten. Debussy misquotes the last line which should be 'Trop au frais'. Hidden references and quotations from the works of Jules Laforgue continued to appear in Debussy's writings throughout his life. In addition to those given in Vol. I a letter of 1899 to René Peter contains a quotation from Laforgue's *Le Concile Féerique* (see R. Peter, *Claude Debussy*, p. 210). The enigma in the dedication of vocal works addressed to Emma Debussy, 'A.l.p.M. [A la petite Mienne]' derives from the lines in Laforgue's poem, *O géraniums diaphanes*:

O ma petite mienne, ô ma quotidienne,
Dans mon petit intérieur,
C'est-à-dire plus jamais ailleurs!
O ma petite quotidienne!

Godet to Debussy, 26 November 1917:

> Allow me, dear and precious being, to suggest that you, less than anyone, have the right to be discouraged. You have the right to rest, or rather the spirit of rest has claims to make upon you. . . .[1]

From the beginning of 1918 Debussy, back in his Paris home, was confined to his room and eventually to his bed. He was to write nothing more until his death on 25 March. His features became hollowed out, the look on his face gradually grew duller. Though the war had dragged on with progressive weariness for almost four years recent events were now alarming in the extreme. In November 1917 a new spirit of confidence had been created by Clemenceau (the 'Tiger') whose government was in fact, in less than a year, to bring the country to victory. In the meantime, however, numerous set-backs were calculated to undermine the allied resistance. After the peace treaty which she signed with Russia in March 1918 Germany was able to throw her entire military strength against the west. Accordingly on 21 March, four days before Debussy's death, a great enemy offensive was opened with the object of splitting the British and French forces. It was almost successful. The British armies were primarily intent upon preserving their communications with the Channel ports while the French were concerned with covering Paris, now being bombarded by the long-range gun, 'Big Bertha'. In a defiant spirit the Opéra reopened on the very day, 21 March, of this last German offensive, with an afternoon performance of Rameau's *Castor et Pollux*. 'Bien le bon jour à Monsieur Castor', Debussy managed to say in a faint, toneless voice to Louis Laloy as he left him for this historic performance. By 24 March the military situation compelled the French Government again to make plans to leave the capital. Debussy's death the following day thus occurred at the most fateful crisis of the war. During the bombardment of Paris he had been too weak to be carried down to the cellar. The dramatic sequence of these events

---

[1] The correspondence of Debussy and Godet reveals that in the last years of his life Debussy favoured the interpretation of his piano works by the German pianist who had settled in France, Walter Rummel (1887–1953). Held by some critics to have had an insight into French piano music comparable to that of Gieseking, Rummel gave the first performance of Debussy's Studies on 14 December 1916. Debussy's letters to Rummel (1913–16) were kindly communicated to me by Mr Michael Mann.

is set out in the war diary of the pacifist and former friend of
Richard Strauss, Romain Rolland:[1]

Thursday, 21 March, 1918. Coinciding with the first day of spring
the great German offensive breaks out on the western front.
Since December the threat of this offensive, full of anguish, has
been hanging over my poor country. . . . How will the future
judge the two statesmen who, after days of hideous slaughter,
pronounced these words: William II: 'God has helped us mag-
nificently'; Clemenceau: 'I am delighted, everything is going
well.' (23 and 24 March 1918). In the course of the German
onslaught Péronne is captured. Noyon is captured. The Allies
retreat from the Somme to the Oise (25–26 March).

   26 March. Death of Claude Debussy. Poor 'little perishing
Greece'.[2] Over a period of two years the wretched artist has been
devoured by cancer. . . . The only creator of beauty in the music
of our time. He was drained by voluptuousness, success, good-
living, idleness and disillusionment. What will remain of him?
A few well-fashioned vases, a few small bas-reliefs of perfected
workmanship soon to be hidden under the grass of the Appian
Way. Vestiges of the supreme elegance of an Athens in ruins.

   Easter Thursday, Good Friday. Decisive days, perhaps, for the
history of Europe. From the Somme to Verdun the struggle is
marked by supreme efforts. People are oppressed. They speak,
walk about, smile and admire the flowers. . . . On Good Friday,
29 March, at four in the afternoon during the service of the
Tenebrae a German bomb fell on a church in Paris destroying the
Gothic arch and claiming 165 victims (75 killed) mostly women
and children. . . .[3] Clemenceau at the Chamber, surrounded by
anxious deputies, said to them: 'I am going to tell you a secret.
Last night I slept, I slept well. . . .'

---

[1] Rolland continued corresponding with Strauss during the war. In 1917 Strauss in
all naïvety suggested that if Rolland were to hear *Ariadne auf Naxos* he might profitably
alter his view of contemporary German music. Their correspondence apparently
came to an end when Strauss made the appalling *faux pas* of inviting Rolland to
Germany 'in order to receive impressions of our people at war'.

[2] The allusion is to Rolland's John-Christopher who could hear 'in the distance the
rumbling of cannon, coming to batter down that worn-out civilization, that perishing
little Greece!'

[3] The church was the Eglise Saint-Gervais where Debussy in his youth had been
greatly inspired by the music of Palestrina and Vittoria (see Vol. I, pp. 171–2).

Several versions, purporting to be eye-witness accounts, have been given of the circumstances of Debussy's death. The most reliable is undoubtedly that of Chouchou, Debussy's thirteen-year-old daughter, in the form of a letter to her half-brother, Raoul Bardac. It is a moving document of simplicity and candour, almost a love letter. Unique among the letters of Debussy's friends and relatives, it is without parallel even among the letters addressed to Debussy in his lifetime. Possessing a severe sense of discipline, the child is anxious to avoid any demonstration of her feelings ('Tears repressed are worth tears shed') but she is nevertheless able to convey their intensity:

My dear Raoul,

Have you received the last telegram? You have, haven't you? It was I who first thought of sending it to you. I wrote it out and then, thinking that identification papers would have to be produced at the post office which I don't possess because I am a little girl, I asked Dolly[1] to have it sent to you. She came here because I asked her to on account of the completely convulsed features of my poor mother. As soon as she had left Mama was asked to see Papa for the nurse said he was 'very bad'. Two doctors were quickly called in both of whom ordered an injection to be given so that he shouldn't suffer. As you may well believe, I understood what was happening. Roger-Ducasse who was there said to me: 'Come, Chouchou, kiss your father.' So I immediately thought it was all over. When I went back into the room Papa was sleeping and breathing regularly but in short breaths. He went on sleeping in this way until ten o'clock in the evening, and at this time, sweetly, angelically, he went to sleep for ever. What happened afterwards I cannot tell you. I wanted to burst into a torrent of tears but I repressed them because of Mama. Alone throughout the night in the big bed with Mama, I was unable to sleep a minute. I developed a temperature, my dry eyes questioned the walls, I couldn't believe what had happened.

The next day far too many people came to see Mama who at the end of the day could no longer stand the strain—both she and I had then to give in. Thursday came, Thursday when he

[1] Chouchou's half-sister Dolly Bardac, later Madame D. G. de Tinan, who inspired the title of the suite *Dolly* for piano duet by Fauré.

was going to be taken away for ever! I saw him for the last time in that horrible box—on the ground. He looked happy, oh so happy! and this time I didn't have the courage to repress my tears. As I almost fell over I couldn't kiss him. At the cemetery Mama could not of course hide her feelings. As for myself I thought of nothing but one thing: 'You mustn't cry because of Mama.' And so I gathered up all my courage which came—from where? I don't know. I didn't shed a tear: tears repressed are worth tears shed, and now it is to be night for ever. Papa is dead. Those three words, I do not understand them, or rather I understand them only too well. And to be here all alone, struggling against the indescribable grief of Mama is really frightful. For some days it caused me to forget my own grief but this is now more poignant than ever. You, who are so far away, think a little of your poor little sister who would so much like to embrace you and tell you how much she loves you! Do you understand all that I feel and which cannot be written? A thousand kisses and love from your little sister,

Chouchou.

It is unbelievable. I don't know how I go on living, and I cannot believe in the horrible reality.[1]

The funeral took place on the Thursday before Easter. The procession included only a few of Debussy's older friends. Godet was in Switzerland; Satie, after *Parade*, had taken offence at Debussy; Pierre Louÿs and René Peter had become estranged from him. Neither Ravel nor Stravinsky was present. Henri de Régnier was apparently alone in representing Debussy's earlier literary friends. Other mourners included Pierné and Chevillard, Vallery-Radot, Caplet, and Gustave Samazeuilh. Debussy's brother Alfred, on leave from the trenches, joined the procession as it was setting off. Fourteen years later Louis Laloy, who attended the funeral in military uniform, recalled his impressions:

I see as in a bad dream the coffin near the piano and the musicians in their soldiers' uniform. . . . The door kept on opening and

[1] Chouchou Debussy's sudden and unexpected death the following year was believed to be the result of a wrong diagnosis.

closing and there was no more room for the flowers. The
Minister of Education took his place at the head of the procession. Side by side, in front of me, the two conductors of our
great philharmonic societies, Camille Chevillard and Gabriel
Pierné, walked in silence. All those concerts in which they had so
lovingly played his music were over. The sky was overcast.
There was a rumbling in the distance. Was it a storm, the ex-
plosion of a shell or the guns at the front? Along the wide
avenues the only traffic consisted of military trucks; people on
the pavements pressed ahead hurriedly. But there was still a
bustle in the populous uphill streets of Montmartre. The children
made way and stood in a line in the gutter, staring at us. The
women shopkeepers questioned each other at their doors and
glanced at the streamers on the wreaths. 'Il paraît que c'était un
musicien', they said.

The procession which reached the cemetery at Père-Lachaise
numbered only about thirty. Other mourners who set out from the
Avenue du Bois de Boulogne had made off on the way. It was held
that the gravity of the military situation made funeral orations
superfluous. Within earshot of the rumbling of cannon, funeral
orations would indeed have been sardonic. Only one perfunctory
speech was made, on behalf of the Société des Auteurs, to which
Laloy, he tells us, barely listened. Thus, to the hollow comment of
the Montmartre shopkeepers, disappeared, at the most fearful
climax of the war, the greatest French composer of his time: 'Il
paraît que c'était un musicien.'

CONCLUSION

Debussy's Musical Language

Q

CONCLUSION
Debussy's Musical Language

Rien de plus cher que la chanson grise
Où l'Indécis au Précis se joint.

Verlaine

Quand la couleur est à sa richesse la forme est à sa plénitude.

Cézanne

In any view of Debussy's style and the elements of his musical language the main problem is to define his attitude to tonality. The vagueness of Debussy's sense of tonality, compared to that of Brahms, or even of Wagner, was long a commonplace in essays on musical analysis, and indeed in so far as this vagueness was held to be a characteristic of Impressionism from which, after Debussy's death, there was a sharp reaction,[1] it was held, too, to be a reprehensible aspect of his work, suggesting in his approach a certain tentativeness or a timidity. Today this view seems to us superficial. In the first place the short-lived reaction against Debussy's work, which took place in the 1920s, now seems to have been less an æsthetic than a fashionable movement. Also, with our knowledge of some of the underlying origins of the great revolutionary movements at the end of the nineteenth century, we are compelled, in an assessment of Debussy's style, to view values of precision and imprecision in artistic expression in a different light. Precision is

---

[1] In 1919, only a year after Debussy's death, Jacques Rivière, asking Stravinsky to contribute to the *Nouvelle Revue Française*, writes to him: 'I intend to direct the attention of the magazine to the anti-impressionist, anti-symbolist, and anti-Debussy movements that are becoming more and more precise and threatening to take the form and force of a vast new current.'

not entirely virtuous; imprecision is not wholly to be condemned. The æsthetic proclaimed by Debussy required their fusion.[1]

Inseparable from the conception of tonality was not only the theory of harmony based on the interplay of relative degrees of consonance and dissonance but also the musical forms in which this interplay was extended into a musical discourse, an abstract musical argument built on dissonant tensions prepared and resolved. In this view of music, accepted in the eighteenth century as a dogma, tonality was everything: an unassailable order prevailed, like the unquestioned social order of this period, allowing digressions of one kind or another provided that in the end these digressions served not a disrupting but a unifying purpose. This was the principle of the sonata form against which, in broad terms, the whole of the nineteenth century rebelled. But it was a slow, almost an imperceptible revolt with many charming explorations of lanes and by-paths on the way. By the end of the nineteenth century, even after Wagner, the underlying harmonic principles of the age of Mozart were still admitted; they had been tested in many different ways, amplified and adapted, but they had not been challenged. Moreover, the work of Debussy, as we see it today, achieved no more, harmonically, than was to be expected from any successor of Wagner. It broke down the rigidity of the tonal order a little more effectively, but the principles of tonality were not relinquished. The Preludes of Debussy, belonging to his later years, are still in certain keys and although, in the course of these short pieces, departures from the keys in which they are conceived are frequent and extremely remote, the pieces do just manage to begin and end in these keys. A step farther and the principles of tonality are completely undermined; there is then no going back, and the boundaries between consonance and dissonance disappear.[2]

The distinctive achievement of Debussy was not so much his novel, ambiguous harmony; it was his recognition of the fact that since an advanced stage in harmonic development had been reached

---

[1] The characteristic dictum of the period, André Schaeffner suggests, should be 'Laissez-moi y mettre un peu d'obscurité'. 'If these were not actually the words of Mallarmé,' he says, 'everyone of the period attempted to obscure the issue in his own way.'

[2] Schoenberg's song-cycle *Das Buch der hängenden Gärten* dates from 1908, a short time before the Preludes of Debussy. In this work Schoenberg declared that he was 'conscious of breaking all barriers with æsthetics of the past'. It is the work which represents, according to H. H. Stuckenschmidt, 'the liquidation of tonality'.

the older forms of music could not be maintained. The sophisticated design of the ternary sonata form, consisting of a thesis and anti-thesis, development and recapitulation, could not be built out of harmonic elements that were lush and almost over-ripe. Thematic or harmonic development, in the form of a musical argument ruthlessly pursued, demands a firmer, less ambiguous harmonic structure, and it was no doubt for this reason that Debussy par-ticularly distrusted musical development as a method of com-position. As opposed to the impact of isolated, sensuous chords, varied in intensity, or of fragmentary themes pursued in improvisa-tory fashion, thematic development in the works of Mozart, Beethoven, and Wagner appeared to Debussy to be based on a mechanical procedure, a mere formula—or at least he said so. It was of course based on nothing of the sort; it was simply that organic development of this kind formed part of an entirely different philosophy. It came about, however, that an organic development of themes was brilliantly used by Debussy in several of his larger works (*La Mer*, second movement; *Pelléas*, the scene with Yniold; and *Rondes de Printemps*). Debussy was not exactly contradicting himself here. As often happens at critical periods in artistic development, theories were in advance of practice. Debussy was logically sound in condemning the classical forms once the validity of tonality had been challenged, but in his larger works he had not yet found the new forms demanded.[1]

Several recent studies on Debussy's harmony have tended to seek hidden rules for the nature and succession of his chords and thereby to establish plans of his musical forms of which the exploratory composer himself must surely have been unaware, even sub-consciously. Debussy's technique is admittedly difficult to define, but, if only for the reason that it is largely empirical, the key to his technique is not likely to be found in abstract, technical arguments. 'The predominant feature of Debussy's instrumental works is repetition', observed the Belgian composer Paul Gilson in 1907

---

[1] A similar dilemma was faced by Schoenberg who, having ruthlessly swept aside the fundamental principles of tonality, anachronistically resorted to the forms most closely associated with tonality (the sonata form and the variation form) with re-doubled severity. In his book *Debussy* written in 1913 with the composer's know-ledge, if not his authority, Daniel Chennevière unequivocally states: 'Le classicisme est mort.' It was at any rate a pronouncement justified by Debussy's earlier admoni-tion: 'Il faut noyer le ton.'

in a letter on the problems of Debussy's technique addressed to Ernest Closson.

Incidental clauses are linked together as motives in a tapestry but then suddenly the whole scheme is broken (for no other reason than that a new idea is desirable) though the original motive may be taken up later. [Gilson was probably referring here to *La Mer*.] This is ornamental music in the broadest sense of the term. It is undoubtedly true that in regard to works which are solidly constructed the listener is at first able to grasp only certain *details*. Such works have to be heard many times before the listener is aware of their architecture (and this will really be discovered only after *reading* the works; it is a task for the analysts). Perhaps, then, it is a useless task to undertake, this matter of 'constructing' and organizing a work of music as a whole, of compelling oneself to follow a pre-conceived plan, or of kneading and re-kneading the music so that it should assume certain architectural proportions, since when all this is done the listener will grasp very little of the over-all plan and he will be affected only by the impression of the moment. The instrumental works in question [those of Debussy] appear to consist of a series of impressions connected by 'repeats' and their instrumentation is accordingly the same as Debussy's harmony itself, entirely impressionistic.[1]

Half a century later critics less finely attuned to the workings of Debussy's mind attempted to discover a deeper significance in the fleeting nature of his harmony. Arguing that since there is seldom cadential harmony in Debussy's works, only chords which have an isolated, 'monistic' value in themselves, Albert Jakobik maintains that the form of a work of Debussy is determined by the relative

[1] Gilson's two letters of 1907 to Ernest Closson on Debussy's technique, published in *La Revue belge de musicologie*, Vol. XVI, 1962, deal principally with matters of chord formation. It is curious to see that Gilson, like Albert Jakobik fifty years later, was struck by the absence of cadential harmony in Debussy's work (i.e. where a hierarchy is established between the subdominant, the dominant and the tonic). It was this, Gilson rightly maintained, which created the sense of vagueness: 'The absence of the established tonal succession of the chords I V, I IV, and vice versa, which is at the basis of classical harmony, gives the music of Debussy its vagueness and imprecision [*Cette teinte vaporeuse, indécise, la tonalité étant indécise, qui lui est particulière*]. By tonal imprecision I do not mean modulations (with the establishment of a new tonic) as in Wagner. When Wagner modulates he remains at least eight times out of ten *tonal*.'

complexity of his chords. In the Prelude *Feuilles mortes* it is the chord in bar 2,

a complex form of the chord of C sharp minor, overlaid with its relative major, which magnetizes other chords towards it and which is thus held to be the central pivot of the piece. Other writers have investigated Debussy's use of the Gregorian modes and the pentatonic scales, notably Julia d'Almendra and Constantin Brailoiu, the latter listing no less than 182 examples of the use of pentatonic scales in the works of Debussy, ranging from the early song *Fleur des blés* to the piano Studies. This is a most remarkable compilation which allows Brailoiu to put forward the theory, nevertheless debatable, that Debussy knowingly used these scales. On the other hand, the properties of the hexaphonic or whole-tone scale must

surely have been prominently in Debussy's conscious mind. If it had not been older than the major and minor scales the whole-tone scale, used systematically in *L'Isle joyeuse* and *Voiles*, would seem to have been designed for the express purpose of blurring the precision of tonality. The oscillations of key in *Voiles*, which opens in A minor, but which immediately shifts into the relative C major while melodic fragments are pinned down on to a B flat pedal, are a model of the ambiguities in Debussy's work of key relationships. (See second example on p. 233.) Such static ambiguities of key have, of course, an entirely different function from the dynamic function of modulations. They are, as it were, modulations collapsed into a single moment, deprived of their perspective.

The trouble with technical analyses is that they are likely to degenerate into studies of musical puzzles, of interest to the practitioner of composition if he is so minded, and revealing little relationship to the æsthetic principles which we expect a composer's technique to serve. Fortunately the motives of several aspects of Debussy's technique have been clearly defined. Drawing a sharp distinction between the secret of an artist's work and its mystery— the one is connected with a technical, the other with a philosophical approach—Vladimir Jankélévitch suggests that the many dragging rhythms and pedals used by Debussy indicate a preoccupation in his work with stagnation and particularly the stagnation of water.[1] The dragging rhythm of the Prelude *Des Pas sur la neige*

___

[1] The most remarkable illustration of this preoccupation is the passage in *Pelléas*, Act III, Scene ii, when Golaud says: 'Eh bien, voici l'eau stagnante dont je vous parlais. Sentez-vous l'odeur de mort qui monte? . . . Voyez-vous le gouffre, Pelléas . . . Pelléas?'

is found in many other works, among them the song *Auprès de cette Grotte sombre* and the section of *La Boîte à joujoux* in which a Hindu chant is heard over a pedal.

Pedals designed to produce a sombre, if not a blurred effect are found in *En Sourdine* and in the series of pieces in which the tragic aspects of the Spanish scene are emphasized, *La Puerta del Vino*, *Lindaraja*, and the *Soirée dans Grenade*. A predilection for ostinato effects and for the indulgent rhythm of the habanera with its groups of three and two notes to a beat in two-four time belong to the same order of ideas. These are works which belong to the darker side of Debussy's character.

In contrast are the ecstatic, whirlwind pieces in quick tempo, in the nature of a *perpetuum mobile*, spiral-like constructions which, however, for all their animation, do not proceed towards a goal. They too are static, anticipating the hypnotic rhythms in the early

works of Stravinsky but infinitely lighter and nearly always diaphanous. *Les Fées sont d'exquises danseuses*,[1] *Le Vent dans la plaine*, *Pagodes*, and *Jardins sous la pluie* belong to this type of gyratory virtuoso music. Few musicians after Wagner were able, as was Debussy, to write music that seems to plunge into space. Effects calculated to produce an impression of space and distance include the remote trumpet calls in *Khamma*, similar devices in *Feux*

[1] Paul Hooreman, in an article in *La Revue de Musicologie*, 1962, showed that this title which, alone among the titles of the Preludes, appears in inverted commas, was taken from the following passage in Chapter IV, 'Lock-out Time', of J. M. Barrie's *Peter Pan in Kensington Gardens*, 1906 (French edition, *Piter Pan: Les Jardins de Kensington*, 1907 and 1911): 'The fairies are exquisite dancers, and that is why one of the first things the baby does is to sign to you to dance to him and then to cry when you do it.' This publication contained coloured drawings by Arthur Rackham, the one illustrating the passage which inspired Debussy's Prelude showing a fairy suspended over a spider's web, dancing on gossamer to the sound of a bass viol played by a spider. Monsieur Hooreman surmises that Robert Godet had sent the Barrie-Rackham publication of *Peter Pan* to Debussy's daughter. On 3 January 1912 Debussy wrote to him: 'Très cher Godet, Chouchou, pour qui Rackham est déjà "ce vieux Rackham" a été ravie de votre envoi. Elle me prie de vous en remercier "bien gentiment" en vous souhaitant une "bonne et heureuse année". Vieille formule qui reprend toute sa grâce en passant par la bouche d'un enfant!' Rackham's drawings, which include illustrations of the operas of Wagner, were exhibited in Paris in 1912.

d'artifice and the *Berceuse héroïque*, and the passage for horns in the interlude before the last scene of Act III of *Pelléas*. This idea of a scene enacted far away, the *danse lointaine*, occurs also at the end of the *Soirée dans Grenade* and again in the central section of the final piano Study, *Pour les Accords*. Distance, space, and also light are suggested in the widely spread textures of certain of the piano works, *Brouillards*, the *Terrasse des audiences*, and the Study *Pour les Sonorités opposées* (See example on p. 236).

An illuminating comparison was made by Monsieur Jankélévitch between the character of certain of Debussy's melodic designs and a phenomenon in botany. Geotropism is the name given to the phenomenon which causes the roots of plants to gravitate towards the centre of the earth. Positive geotropism is the term used for this attraction to a centre of gravity, while negative geotropism signifies the tendency of stems to grow away from the centre of the earth. One is reminded here of the symbolical significance of the floral and plant designs of the Art Nouveau and their connexion with the flowing lines of women's hair. Many of the typical arabesque designs of Debussy appear to be propelled by a downward-moving force. Phrases such as this from *Syrinx*:

and from the opening of *Le Faune* (*Fêtes galantes*, second series):

are unquestionably a musical counterpart of the decorative designs carried over into Impressionism from the Art Nouveau. Falling snow and falling rain are of course illustrated in this same symbolical manner, by means of arpeggios or staccato figures in *Jardins sous la pluie* and *Pour remercier la Pluie au matin* and by a technique similar to that of the Pointillist painters in *Snow is dancing*. To express indolence and languor, particularly sensuous languor, Debussy uses a similar downward-moving design, evident in the opening of *Je tremble en voyant ton visage*:

and also in *En Sourdine* and the *Colloque sentimental* with their nervous triplets reminiscent of the early piano *Arabesque No. 2*:

Finally on this matter of the significance of the downward-moving phrase there are elements, in each of the following four examples, of both fear and flight.[1]

[1] In the chapter entitled *Géotropisme* in his work on Debussy M. Jankélévitch investigates several other technical aspects of Debussy's expressions of fear and flight, some of them symbolized by a descending harmonic design. 'Cette inclinaison pudique vers le bas', he concludes, 'est une des marques les plus caractéristiques de la phrase debussyste.'

In the last quarter of the nineteenth century the attraction of French composers—Satie, Duparc, Chausson, and Ravel, besides Debussy—to the chord of the dominant ninth or, without its fundamental, the diminished seventh, reveals the first tonal ambiguities taking the form of a musical counterpart of Impressionism. The particular property of the chord of the diminished seventh is that it is a pivot, modulating chord which may branch out into one of eight tonalities (four major and four minor). If, however, this chord is not used to modulate into another key but is linked to other seventh chords in the form of a succession a continuous feeling of suspense is created:

Once we recognize this use of chords of the seventh and ninth as a means of creating suspense we have a key to the function of other chords in Debussy's harmony. Jankélévitch draws attention to a feeling not exactly of suspense but to the kindred feeling of rootlessness. This is created by the juxtaposition of common chords, each belonging to a different tonality. Contrasted in this way, these chords do not represent a continuity of musical thought; they do not create a rational musical argument. They merely exist in space, or more precisely in musical time, as if drawn to each other by some kind of astrological 'influence'. A striking, and indeed an almost literal illustration of this technique occurs in *La Damoiselle élue* where a succession of common chords evoking the five servants

in heaven of the Blessed Damozel passes through no less than ten
tonalities.[1]

Sometimes the rootlessness of these common chords (or variations
of them) is emphasized by the direction, as in *La Cathédrale engloutie*,
that they should be played 'sans nuances'. A bland, almost expres-
sionless region is then suggested, the bleak hinterland of the
imagination.

[1] They are F sharp minor, E minor, D major, F minor, D major, E major, C minor,
D major, G major, and C major.

If Debussy's use of the chord of the seventh and the common chord have these functions of suspense and ambiguity his use of the interval of the second, either in chords or more often alone, is designed to convey one of the many gradations of feeling between indulgence and irony. Intervals of the second have, of course, been used in almost all forms of the harmonic language, notably in inversions of the chord of the seventh. But this traditional use in harmony of the interval of the second (that is to say as a dissonance requiring resolution) does not quite correspond to the use made of this interval by Debussy. Once again our perspicacious guide here is Monsieur Jankélévitch. He writes: 'Just as the downward moving design of the arabesque [in Debussy's works] ends by defeating itself in the form of a design of horizontal uniformity or in mono-tonously repeated notes, so the dissonant chord, the more it becomes contracted or drawn together, ends by becoming reduced to the interval of the second, which is the smallest possible interval and, in a sense, the negation of harmony.' If we look at it in this way 'the interval of the second marks the point where music returns to the realm of noise. . . . For what is this interval if not a single note disturbed only by its adjacent note, the smallest chord of all beyond which is the unison?'

The fact is that the interval of the second, both the major and the minor second which are inversions of the minor and major sevenths, were used by Debussy, as also by Stravinsky and Bartók, as a dissonance having a certain sonorous value in itself, regardless of its function in a three- or four-note chord and without any question of its resolution. This interval, probably first used in this way by Borodin, was the quintessential dissonance. Jankélévitch was right in suggesting that beyond the interval of the second we approach the borderland of music and noise. At what point does sound advance into music or, on the other hand, at what point does it retreat into noise? Debussy did not live to see the beginnings of *musique concrète* though certain of his harsher uses of the second, based on the principle that there are ultimately no borderlands between music and sound and noise, do in a sense foreshadow this present-day concept.

Despite these forward-looking views, Debussy regarded the dissonance of the second as relative, that is to say it was made to convey different effects of dissonance in different works. As we

may see from the following examples, from a piece such as *Le Jet d'eau*, where seconds are used in a sensuous manner, to the harsh, threatening seconds in many of the later works, among them *Khamma*, *Ce qu'a vu le vent d'ouest*, and *En blanc et noir*, the variety of expression with which this particular interval is endowed is enormous.

All these functions of harmony bring us back eventually to the problems of form. For the painters form was inseparable from colour; for the musicians it was inseparable from the colour of instruments, from timbre. In earlier periods principles of form had no relation whatever to timbre. Indeed, before Debussy the word 'timbre', as opposed to 'tone-colour', had hardly entered the musical vocabulary. In Debussy's works timbre, or at any rate the nature of the instrument, does very largely determine formal procedures. In the piano works, as we have seen, a blurring, ambiguous technique was largely established by the nature of the piano overtones and the use of the pedals. Though the piano pieces seldom make use of thematic development an underlying sense of key is

R [243]

nevertheless maintained. In the orchestral works the tonal deforma-
tions are more complex. Drawing attention to the fact that the
harmony of the first movement of *La Mer* consists almost entirely
of sevenths and ninths, with the bass note omitted, Ernest Ansermet
has shown that as a rule tonality is only implied in Debussy's works.
Even when one can be relatively sure of the underlying tonality any
kind of scheme of related tonalities, on which the symphonic form
is normally founded, is seldom adhered to. The first movement of
La Mer may be said to open in D minor while it concludes in the
remote key of D flat. Following the introduction there are two
episodes, each of which can be subdivided, broadly in D flat and
B flat, a transitional section in A flat and the D flat coda. It is the
first important example of a symphonic movement maintaining an
onward drive without development. The second movement oscil-
lates between E major and E minor and the last movement, opening
in the implied key of E major, ends in D flat. Similar departures
from orthodox procedure occur in the orchestral *Images* and in the
sequence of episodes forming the score of the ballet *Jeux*. The
difficulties of analysing a score of Debussy in any detail have been
described by Pierre Boulez: 'A component section of a theme is
defined as another is selected. We place them together and an outline
of a theme is suggested; another phrase is added and we have the
beginnings of a form. More material is added and we have a structure.' Perhaps in the end we may best summarize Debussy's method
of composition in the simple definition of Cézanne: 'Je travaille sur
le motif.' The *motif* is the generating design or symbol. How it
proceeds to acquire a form is so much an internal matter that any
kind of formal analysis is bound to be inadequate.

Yet the effort to convey the principles of Debussy's forms must
be made. Once the æsthetic principles on which an artist builds his
work are defined it becomes at any rate easier to decide on the type
of critical approach to his work which is most likely to enrich our
knowledge of it. Indeed, without a preliminary enquiry into the life
and mind of an artist on the broadest possible lines we cannot begin
to particularize on matters of technical procedure. The foregoing
summary of some of the main elements of Debussy's technique does
not pretend to offer more than an outline of a vast subject. Nor
does it claim, within the modest framework of a concluding chapter,
to have approached all the essential aspects of his technique. Prin-

ciples of harmony and form in Debussy's work have been investigated but scholars have hardly touched upon the elusive nature of Debussy's orchestration. Elsewhere the matter of Debussy's sketches and manuscripts, particularly the numerous manuscript versions of *Pelléas et Mélisande* (listed in Vol. I, Appendix E), the corrections to both his manuscript and printed works and the nature of his unpublished or discarded works—this enquiry into the whole matter of Debussy's manuscripts is in itself a subject of the first importance. Above all, the wide span of Debussy's evolution requires assessment from this technical viewpoint. Now that the world of his ideas has been made known the technicians and the analysts have the field before them.

APPENDIX A

PROJECTS FOR 'AS YOU LIKE IT'

The two works of Debussy inspired by Shakespeare are the Prelude, *La Danse de Puck*, and the posthumously published incidental music for Antoine's production of *King Lear*. Many other works of Shakespeare were of course known to Debussy besides the plays illustrated in these small-scale compositions. He was drawn particularly to the character of Hamlet, played by Sarah Bernhardt in 1899 and whom he refers to in his correspondence as 'a kindred neurasthenic'. As we have seen, in 1902 he went to London purposely to see Forbes-Robertson in *Hamlet*. Every age gets the *Hamlet* it deserves and Debussy was aware that the Hamlet figures of his time were the indecisive Pelléas and the introspective Roderick Usher.

The French image of Shakespeare at this time had obviously a far-reaching influence on Debussy's work as a whole. Among the fleeting ideas to which he was drawn in his youth was a setting of *As You Like It* in an arrangement by the poet Maurice Vaucaire. According to Vallas, Debussy agreed to write the music for this play when he was a student in Rome. This may account for his somewhat surprising statement, in answer to a questionnaire of 1889 (reproduced in Vol. I, Appendix G), that his favourite heroine in drama at that time was Rosalind. However this may be, it was in Rome that he appears first to have become acquainted with Shakespeare, taking part with Paul Vidal and Xavier Leroux in readings of his plays. He was not indifferent to the important matter of Shakespeare translations. He had a preference, we are told, for the translations by Emile Montégut, which he considered superior to the over-romanticized translations by François Victor Hugo, son of the poet.

This early project for *As You Like It* was abandoned on Debussy's return to Paris but it was apparently kept alive in his mind for it was the first of several ideas for an opera to which he turned after *Pelléas et Mélisande*. In the summer of 1902, three months after the production of *Pelléas*, he writes to the poet and novelist Paul-Jean Toulet: 'I should like to have news of *Comme il vous plaira*. I am thinking of it incessantly and would like to think of it with you in mind.'

Debussy's plans for this Shakespeare opera are worth investigating in some detail. Before doing so, however, it will be helpful to bring into relief the shy, sensitive figure of Debussy's collaborator, not only because of his part in this project but also because the nature of their artistic relationship throws some light on certain of Debussy's ideas as he developed them in other works.

A seeker of sensation in the manner of Baudelaire, Toulet had spent part of his youth in Mauritius, where he became addicted to opium, and later travelled in Spain and the Orient. In 1899 he went to London to visit the writer influenced by occult sciences, Arthur Machen, whose *The Great God Pan* he translated.[1] Shortly afterwards he met Debussy. 'Dès le premier jour', Toulet notes, 'nous avons été amis comme cochons.' Their intimacy was based on an indulgence in literary banter, also on the sharing of personal secrets of their emotional and amorous lives, but particularly on their admiration for certain writers, notably Stendhal.[2] Some of the ideas, if not the titles, of Debussy's works may have derived from his knowledge of Toulet's writings. Toulet was strongly drawn to Dickens. Mr. Pickwick, he states, illustrated in one of the Preludes, 'is almost as widely read in Paris as in London.' In his novel *Monsieur du Paur*, partly influenced by Machen, Toulet hints at the associations of falling snowflakes in a manner which brings to mind *Snow is Dancing* from *Children's Corner*.[3] Toulet took little interest in musical affairs but his heart went out to Debussy as a victim of musical publicity. A curious 'Intervioue de M. Claude Debussy', which appeared in *Les Marges*, October 12, is in the form of a skit on the ignorance of musical journalists.

No music is known to have been written by Debussy for *As You Like It*, but his correspondence with Toulet, together with Toulet's sketches for the libretto, allows us to form a fairly clear idea of this

---

[1] This work, admired by Debussy and mentioned in his first published letter to Toulet, apparently opened a way to their friendship.

[2] In his *Notes de Littérature* (1926) Toulet describes the entirely fresh appeal made by Stendhal. He is not, he maintains, a stylist, nor an historian, nor even a critic. 'C'est un amoureux qui se découvre. . . . C'est la vie toute pure.' After Debussy's death it was his copy of Stendhal that Toulet repeatedly requested from Madame Debussy: 'I still want one of the books Claude was in the habit of reading. As I must point out once again, his Stendhal would be the thing. . . . You see that I am a persistent beggar.'

[3] 'Quel opium que la neige, pour exagérer notre paresse et la simplicité de nos désirs', he searchingly records. 'Et j'aurais aimé encore, avec cette petite Thérèse, maintenant perdue, rester auprès d'une fenêtre à suivre des yeux les flocons monotones. . . .'

project with which he was concerned until the end of his life. By the autumn of 1902 Toulet had submitted two sketches. 'Let us return to good Monsieur William', Debussy eagerly writes to him on 21 October:

> The second plan you sent me suits me in every way. Don't you think we might heighten the interest of the first scene by the introduction of a choir off-stage which would comment on the various incidents of Orlando's wrestle? They would have exclamations to sing such as 'He's down! No, he's not! Ah! He's no coward!' But, joking apart, I think that musically this idea could offer something quite original. And I would like to have some of the songs sung by a group of people. The duke is rich enough to have the Chanteurs de Saint-Gervais[1] and their conductor come to the Forest of Arden. In regard to the end I agree with you; let us leave these people in the forest. We must find some lovely ceremonial for the betrothal and have it end joyfully. Whenever you can replace the exact word by its lyrical counterpart don't hesitate. That doesn't mean that the tone in which the two scenes are written doesn't please me. Quite the contrary. I make this suggestion because of your fear of being too rhythmical. Be assured that it will all be brought out in the music. I have an idea which I offer to you for what it is worth. Couldn't we use the scene between Charles the wrestler and Oliver (Shakespeare, Scene i) as an introduction? Send me everything you can before you leave. I am convinced we have something really admirable.

Toulet was leaving for Tonkin with his journalist friend Maurice Sailland (known as Curnonsky) but he hastened to meet Debussy's requirements and to supply at any rate a considerable part of the libretto. He writes in reply in October:

> Here is scene i as I had begun it before your letter. The opening would have made a delightful scene as the curtain rises (Celia leaning on the balustrade on the right, and Rosalind slowly walking up towards her from the garden) which must be sacrificed if there is to be a scene before this.

[1] The choral society whose adventurous programmes, including performances of neglected works by Palestrina and Vittoria, had impressed Debussy in 1893.

It won't matter much and we may bring it in later. But I think the introduction required should be built from the dialogue of Celia and Rosalind. Actually, the conversation between Oliver and the wrestler can only emphasize Oliver's hatred of Orlando which we should perhaps rather tone down and make less melodramatic. (Note that Orlando's departure, which is an important feature, cannot be suggested in this scene since it occurs later as the result of a whim of the duke.) [His reference is to Act I, Scene ii, where Orlando says he is the son of the duke's enemy.] Therefore, since the characters of Oliver and the wrestler are subsidiary can they not be introduced later, in scenes ii and iii? At the end of scene i, between Celia and Rosalind, Oliver appears and speaks of the wrestler and the three exhausted young men [i.e. the brothers whom the wrestler had vanquished]. Then appears the wrestler himself who has just told Oliver that he, a wrestler, has been defied by his brother Orlando. It continues as in Shakespeare, but shorter and decidedly less harsh [*surtout adouci*]. The presence of the girls should not allow the scene to become hateful, Oliver not wishing to kill his brother but to see that he gets 'a good lesson'. 'A broken rib or two', he says, 'will make a man of him.' Apart from this I am most enthusiastic about the choir exclaiming off-stage during the wrestle. The girls themselves would not say a word; this will emphasize their concern while Oliver will utter a few words in his ironic manner.

There you are—please decide and reply by return. . . . As for the scene between Celia and Rosalind which I am sending you, note that a part of it, that in which they speak of their disguises and their assumed names, is transferred to the end of the tableau to a scene in which they persuade the clown [i.e. Touchstone] to go off with them. . . .

Debussy accepted this plan enthusiastically (or seemingly so; one cannot be quite sure) and wrote on 25 October:

Your arguments are better than mine and I accept them without further ado. You have met my desire to clarify the tenuous, complicated plot of *Comme il vous plaira* in a different way, and this is splendid.

You say nothing, however, about what I had said on the matter

of the ceremony of the betrothals, which to my mind should make a graceful conclusion. I see it as an opportunity for a scenic spectacle in which wonderfully clothed people would enter to clearly marked rhythms leading to the entry of Orlando's Rosalind. All this intermingled with songs in an early style [*à la façon antique*], that is to say integrated in the action. Don't be afraid of developing the character of Touchstone—his fantastic character is altogether his own. This must surely be your opinion. I am alarmed to think that you are leaving so soon, for you have made me impatient to have every detail of this human fairy play. Don't forget me in the yellowness of Tonkin.

The details in these letters show the character of this projected work to have been light, charming, and decorous. At any rate, this is the impression conveyed by the sketches of Toulet. On the interpretation of Touchstone, half-philosopher, half-buffoon, Debussy and his kindly disposed collaborator were perhaps agreed. In regard to the other characters there was seemingly a difference of opinion. Toulet proposes that Oliver's hatred of his brother Orlando should not be emphasized, and he thereby distorts one of the central themes of the play. In Shakespeare Oliver does not hope to see Orlando emerge from the wrestling match 'with a broken rib or two'; he would not be sorry to see his attractive brother murdered by the professional wrestler. Moreover, the wrestling scene, suggested by Debussy as an introduction to the opera, is of the first dramatic importance, and one gathers that he did not entirely approve of Toulet's intention to transform it into a subsidiary episode.

On his return from the East in 1903 Toulet was beginning to suffer from the effects of opium, and it is doubtful whether he was physically capable of completing the libretto.[1] 'Some of the characters of *Comme il vous plaira*', he writes, 'have lain down on the grass and gone to sleep. Others have got lost in the forest and, God forgive me, were making a disreputable place of it.'

The project was, however, revived in another form in 1917 when

---

[1] 'If our terms of friendship did not forbid any painful discussions', Debussy wrote to him in August 1903, 'I would have told you long ago how sorry I am that you had taken to opium. An imagination as delicate as yours must obviously suffer under this. And now life is warning you . . . that you should have nothing to do with this sinister drug. It would be presumptuous of me to speak to you about this on a deeper level.'

Debussy saw a celebrated performance of *The Merchant of Venice* with Firmin Gémier as Shylock. This was the part in which this actor was held to have reached the height of his great reputation. 'I spoke to him of my old passion for *Comme il vous plaira*', Debussy writes to Toulet on 8 June 1917, 'and told him that if he intended to produce it I should like him to reserve for me the honour of writing the incidental music.' There was now no question of using Toulet's original sketches; a literal translation was what was required. By this time Debussy was desperately ill and Toulet was hard-pressed.[1] 'I distrust Gémier', Toulet wrote to Madame Debussy. 'I rather think that, like Antoine, he is afflicted with Shakespearitis [*chexpyrite*] and wants a severely literal translation.' Debussy implored him to see the play from Gémier's viewpoint. He wrote on 20 June 1917:

Like poor Mélisande, 'je ne fais pas ce que je veux', which is indeed the greatest punishment. You imagine Gémier to be too much of a disciple of Shakespeare. If only you knew the translation of *The Merchant of Venice* you would be reassured. All Gémier wants is to use his gifts as a producer and to make his crowds move about. *As You Like It* will not be of much use to him for this. But he'll find some means of doing what he wants, you may be sure. If necessary he'll make the theatre attendants act or have the people in the stalls go and change places with the people in the balcony. But without any pointless jokes, I believe you could do *As You Like It*.

The last mention of the project is in a letter from Debussy to Jacques Durand of November 1917, from which it appears that Toulet and Gémier came to some agreement. But it was too late. The remaining four months of Debussy's life were spent in agony, and the plan for a musical version of *As You Like It*, spanning the whole of his life, came to nothing.

There are, however, several illuminating aspects of this project. Debussy was drawn not only to the characters of Rosalind and Touchstone and to the ceremonial aspects of the betrothal scene. He was apparently deeply moved by the introspective character of

---

[1] 'This project appeals to me for it means money', Toulet wrote to the poet and critic, Emile Henriot, 'and it will be the first time that I shall be earning money honestly.'

Jacques. This transpires from the recorded conversations of Robert Godet and Georges Jean-Aubry.[1] His preoccupation with Jacques, though not referred to in the correspondence with Toulet, suggests that Debussy was concerned with some of the deeper meanings of *As You Like It*. He might even have seen in this melancholy character a reflection of himself. 'Jacques is the only purely contemplative character in Shakespeare', Hazlitt writes. 'He thinks, and does nothing. His whole occupation is to amuse his mind, and he is totally regardless of his body and his fortunes.' Hazlitt even sees him as a kind of Monsieur Croche: 'He is the prince of philosophical idlers; his only passion is thought.'

It is likely that Debussy knew of a bold version of *As You Like It*, made earlier by George Sand, in which Jacques became the guiding spirit of the whole play and in which he was represented as madly in love with Celia. Overcome by a fit of jealousy, he is with difficulty restrained from fighting a duel with Orlando and the play ends with his marriage to Celia. Singular views of *As You Like It* were held by other French writers known to Debussy. For François Victor Hugo it was a 'lugubrious tragedy, opening with groans and ending with groans'. I am not suggesting that Debussy's awareness of some of the underlying conflicts in *As You Like It* led him to endorse a grotesque interpretation of this order. Rosalind, he said, was his favourite heroine, and we need look no farther. Thoroughly Debussyan is the impression which H. N. Hudson conveyed of Rosalind's character in 1880: 'In its irrepressible vivacity the pleasure of Rosalind waits not for occasion but runs on for ever. . . . We have a sort of faith that her dreams are made up of cunning, quirkish, graceful fancies, her wits being in a frolic even when she is asleep. . . . No sort of unhappiness can live in her company.'

---

[1] The relevant passage from the *Lettres à deux amis*, though the language is precious, is worth quoting for the connexion with another work of Debussy's, the Clarinet Rhapsody:

R.G.: . . . Mais saviez-vous qu'alors déjà la forêt d'*As you like it* recélait un fantôme bénéfique, et si congénial à notre ami que le projet formé par lui plus tard de composer une musique debussyste pour un "Comme il vous plaira", version Toulet, naquit de son intimité avec Jacques le Mélancolique?

G.J-A: Il dut se contenter, n'est-ce-pas, de lui offrir l'hommage de sa fidèle pensée dans sa *Rapsodie* pour clarinette?

R.G.: Dans la plus rêveuse de ses rapsodies, c'est juste, et il me fit l'honneur de joindre mon nom à celui du rêveur shakespearien sur l'envoi qu'il m'en adressa.

It remains to assess the published excerpts from Toulet's translation of *As You Like It*. The correspondence between Toulet and Debussy in 1917 suggests that a version made for the earlier project had been mislaid. 'You never entrusted me with anything of your old work and I have too much respect for your writing to have forgotten it. There is no question of my having lost it.'[1] Two publications of Toulet's translations have appeared: a few verses, presented by Henri Martineau, under the title 'En suivant Shakespeare' in *La Revue critique des idées et des livres*, July 1922; and seven short sections from the play in Martineau's edition of Toulet's unpublished poems (*Vers inédits*, Paris, 1936). These consist of free translations of Jacques' 'Seven ages of Man', 'Under the greenwood tree', Jacques' song 'What shall he have that killed the deer?' (Act IV, Scene ii), 'Blow, blow, thou winter wind' and Orlando's song 'From the East to Western Ind' (Act III, Scene ii). The translations of the songs were perhaps prompted by Debussy's letter of 1917: 'The vocal element can play a big part in *Comme il vous plaira*. I do not intend to miss any of the songs which adorn the text. I recommend them to your sense of kindness and, more than this, to your lyrical sense.' The translation of the 'Seven Ages of Man' is a curtailed version which, however, ends with lines to which Debussy, in the last months of his life, could not have been indifferent:

Le dénouement de cette histoire
C'est la seconde enfance en des langes nouveaux,
Des pas traînants qui tâtent le tombeau,
C'est un aveugle, un sourd, sans amour, sans mémoire.

Elsewhere Toulet apparently devised an original scene—for it does not appear anywhere in Shakespeare—consisting of an evocation of the four seasons spoken alternately by the huntsmen and the foresters. In the end they join forces to proclaim faith in a rebirth and in the perpetual renewal of the cycle of life.

---

[1] In his introduction to the correspondence of Debussy and Toulet, Henri Martineau states that 'there is a manuscript in the hand of Toulet, almost complete, in which Debussy underlined in pencil every word which he replaced by its lyrical counterpart.' This manuscript, now in the possession of Madame Cahen Martineau, is undoubtedly the one referred to.

MANUEL DE FALLA ON DEBUSSY

The most conspicuous of the non-French aspects of Debussy's work are those of Spanish origin. This is not surprising; the same is true of other composers, among them Bizet, Chabrier, and Ravel, and it is a well-known historical fact, recognized by the Spaniards themselves, that the most original and often the most authentic Spanish music has been written north of the Pyrenees. This came about partly because in France, unlike Spain, there were traditions of symphonic music, but also because the attraction of the romantic Spanish scene for French artists had a long history. The Spanish works of Debussy, who admired both *Carmen* and the folk-song collections of Pedrell, are the most powerfully inspired of all twentieth-century works using features of Spanish folk-music, as Manuel de Falla, the principal Spanish composer of this period, freely recognized. Indeed, as J. B. Trend pointed out in his study, *Manuel de Falla and Spanish Music*, 'it was Debussy who revealed things in the spirit of Andalusian music which had been hidden or not clearly discerned even by Falla, who was born and bred in Andalusia'. Beginning with *Soirée dans Grenade* Debussy wrote several 'Nights in the Gardens of Spain' before Falla's composition of this title and Professor Trend, who knew Falla well, made it clear that the turning-point in Falla's career dates from his journey to Paris and his meeting with Debussy in 1907. On the artistic connexions between the two composers he writes:

Debussy's Andalusia was an Andalusia of dreams . . . and to Debussy, Falla must have seemed like a visitor from his own dream-land. But if Debussy heard from Falla that his dreams had in a sense come true, Falla must have felt that he himself was, as it were, part of Debussy's dream—that he held the keys and knew the facts of those regions which Debussy knew only in imagination. Many of Debussy's works created a marvellous atmosphere of poetry and suggestion; to Falla these came with the force of an *evocación* of his own country and its music, and all his later works (down to *The Puppet Show* and the Harpsichord Concerto) may be regarded as an effort to convey this poetry and

suggestiveness with the conviction of one who knows that dreams can sometimes come true. So far he had been expressing the letter of Andalusian music; he began now to realize how Debussy had managed to convey the spirit.[1]

Bizet, who went no farther south than Bordeaux, refused to visit Spain. 'Ça me gênerait', he cautiously explained. Reality, Bizet felt, would too brutally disturb the vivid Spanish scene of his imagination. The Spanish evocations in Debussy's piano pieces and in *Ibéria* similarly derived from his imagination. After Debussy's death Falla's tribute to him was the noble *Homenaje* for guitar forming part of *Le Tombeau de Debussy*, published as a supplement to *La Revue Musicale* (December 1920). One of the first serious pieces written in modern times for the guitar, it incorporates reminiscences of the *Soirée dans Grenade*.[2] In the same number of this journal Falla discusses at length the technique and character of Debussy's Spanish pieces. This paper which, Professor Trend insisted, 'should be read in Falla's own words, as they were hammered out through several autumn mornings near the Alhambra', has not hitherto been made available to English readers. It is presented here in a translation from the French amplified with explanatory notes and a musical quotation.

*   *   *

Claude Debussy wrote Spanish music without knowing Spain, that is to say without knowing the land of Spain, which is a different matter. Debussy knew Spain from his readings, from

[1] On the occasion of Falla's first visit to London in May 1911, when at the Æolian Hall he played with Debussy's friend Franz Liebich an arrangement for two pianos made by André Caplet of Debussy's *Ibéria*, he was described by *The Times* of 26 May as a student of Debussy.

[2] Besides the work of Falla *Le Tombeau de Debussy* consists of works by Ravel (the Duo for violin and cello); Stravinsky (a piece of fifty-one bars entitled *Symphonies pour instruments à vent à la mémoire de C. A. Debussy*, set out for piano with no expression marks nor, apart from a metronome marking, a tempo indication, this became the Chorale of the *Symphonies d'instruments à vent* also used by Stravinsky as a Chorale to be played with the *Symphony of Psalms*); two short unnamed pieces by Goossens and Bartók; an extremely short song (twelve bars) by Erik Satie on a poem by Lamartine; a *Hommage* for piano by Malipiero; a piano piece *L'Accueil des Muses* by Roussel; and two piano pieces by Paul Dukas and Florent Schmitt inspired by mythological subjects. The cover of this publication is a lithograph by Raoul Dufy.

pictures, from songs, and from dances with songs danced by true Spanish dancers.

At the World Exhibition held on the Champ de Mars two young French musicians were to be seen going about together, listening to the exotic music of many countries. Mingling with the crowd, these young musicians abandoned themselves to the magic of this strange music and later they were able to discover new fields of expression. These two musicians were Paul Dukas and Claude Debussy.

Our knowledge of this simple fact will help us to understand many aspects of Debussy's work. His first-hand knowledge of new types of music, including Chinese and Spanish music, excited his imagination. 'I have always been an observer', he declared, 'and I have tried in my work to put my observations to good account.' Debussy's manner of conveying the essential spirit of Spanish music shows how successful he was. There were of course other factors designed to help him. His interest in liturgical music is well known. Since Spanish folk-song is largely based on modal music, it came about that even in works which Debussy wrote without any idea of Spanish associations one finds modes, cadences, chord sequences, rhythms, and even turns of phrase which clearly reveal a relationship with our spontaneous folk-music.[1]

Works showing this relationship are the songs *Fantoches* and *Mandoline*, the piano piece *Masques*, the *Danse profane* for harp and strings,[2] and the second movement of the String Quartet, the greater part of which, if only because of its texture, might well be one of the most beautiful Andalusian dances ever written. Yet when the master

---

[1] Falla is concerned here with a problem similar to that investigated by Julia d'Almendra and Constantin Brailoiu and referred to on page 233, namely whether Debussy used the techniques of earlier or exotic forms of music consciously. The studies of d'Almendra and Brailoiu are concerned with Debussy's use of the Gregorian modes and the pentatonic scales. Falla suggests that in his use of the modes Debussy was either instinctively aware of their connexion with Spanish folk-music or that he had made a technical study of this subject. On one occasion only have we evidence of the fact that Debussy went so far as to note down the liturgical chants he heard. In *L'Eglise et la Musique*, Amadée Gastoué writes: 'N'avons-nous pas vu à l'église de Saint-Gervais, Claude Debussy suivre fidèlement les offices . . . et noter sur son carnet, un crayon à la main, les tournures qui l'avaient le plus frappé parmi les chants grégoriens et les motets palestriniens?'

[2] Ernest Ansermet has disclosed that Debussy's twin piece for harp and strings, *Danse sacrée*, was based on a short piano piece by the Portuguese composer Francisco de Lacerda (1869–1934). Debussy's correspondence with Lacerda, dealing with their friendship with Erik Satie and the proposed publication of a collection of Portuguese folk-songs, appears in the catalogue of the Debussy Exhibition held in Lisbon in 1962.

was questioned on this matter he declared that no such idea was ever in his mind. The facts are that the character of the Spanish musical language had been assimilated by Debussy and this composer, who really did not know Spain, was thus able to write Spanish music spontaneously, perhaps unconsciously, at any rate in a way which was the envy of many who knew Spain only too well.

Only once did he cross the Franco-Spanish frontier, to spend a few hours at San Sebastian where he watched a bull-fight. This was hardly knowing Spain! He remembered, however, the light in the bull-ring, particularly the violent contrast between the one half of the ring flooded with sunlight and the other half deep in shade. The *Matin d'un jour de fête* from *Ibéria* is perhaps an evocation of this afternoon spent just over the French frontier. But this was not the Spain that was really his own. His dreams led him farther afield and he became spellbound by an imaginary Andalusia. We have evidence of this in *Par les Rues et par les chemins* and *Parfums de la nuit* from *Ibéria*, and in *La Puerta del Vino*, the *Sérénade interrompue*, and *Soirée dans Grenade*. It was with the last of these pieces that Debussy opened his series of works inspired by Spain; and it was a Spaniard, our Ricardo Viñes, who gave the first performance of it, in 1903 at the Société Nationale, as he did of the majority of the master's piano works.

The evocative nature of *Soirée dans Grenade* is nothing less than miraculous when one reflects on the fact that this music was written by a foreigner guided almost entirely by his visionary genius. Forgotten are the Serenades, Madrileñas, and Boleros with which the writers of so-called Spanish music used to regale us. Here we are truly confronted with Andalusia: truth without authenticity, so to speak, for not a bar is directly borrowed from Spanish folklore yet the entire piece down to the smallest detail makes one feel the character of Spain. There is a question here of great importance to which we will return in a moment.

Many technical devices are used to create the evocative spirit of the *Soirée*. The music actually evokes reflections of moonlit images in the lakes of the Alhambra. Evocative in the same way, too, are *Les Parfums de la nuit* and *La Puerta del Vino*. The latter, like the *Soirée*, is based on the rhythm of the Habanera, a sort of Andalusian tango, which Debussy uses to convey the nonchalant idleness and

the charm of Andalusian evenings and afternoons. In *La Puerta del Vino* he brings to mind both the quietness and the brilliant sunshine of the hours of the siesta at Granada. This Prelude was suggested to him merely by the sight of a coloured photograph of the celebrated Alhambra. In this photograph the Alhambra, in the shade of great trees, throws into sharp relief the bright light on a road seen in depth through one of the building's arches. Debussy was so strongly impressed by this picture that he resolved to find its musical equivalent; and indeed a few days later *La Puerta del Vino* was written. Though related to the *Soirée dans Grenade* in rhythm and character, it differs from it in melodic design. In the *Soirée* the chant is syllabic, whereas in *La Puerta del Vino* the chant appears with ornamentations peculiar to the Andalusian *cante jondo*. This ornamented chant, used earlier in the *Sérénade interrompue* and in the second theme of the *Danse profane*, shows the extent to which Debussy was acquainted with the most subtle variations of our folk-song:

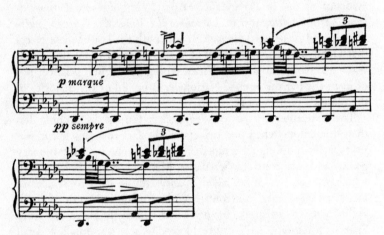

The *Sérénade interrompue*, which I do not hesitate to place with the works of the master inspired by Spain, differs from the three compositions of the same group mentioned earlier in that the *Sérénade* is based on a ternary rhythm while the others use exclusively a binary rhythm. The Spanish character of this Prelude is evident in the characteristic guitar figurations which precede or accompany the *copla*, the Andalusian grace of the *copla*, and the harshness of the defiant accents at each interruption. The music

appears to be inspired by a type of scene frequently met with in romantic poetry: two serenaders vie with each other for the favours of a damsel who, hidden behind the flowers of her latticed window, follows every incident of their gallant contest.

Ibéria stands apart in this group and it is also the most important of Debussy's Spanish works. The thematic material is presented in a novel manner. The opening theme is subjected to many subtle transformations which, one freely admits, sometimes depart from a true Spanish feeling. I do not say this with the least disapproval; on the contrary, *Ibéria* opens up a new aspect of Debussy's work. Debussy strove at all costs never to repeat himself. 'One's technique must be constructed afresh according to the demands of each work', he truly remarked. So far as *Ibéria* is concerned he made it clear that he did not intend to write Spanish music, but rather to translate into music the associations that Spain had aroused in him. This he triumphantly achieved. A sort of *Sevillana*, the generating theme of the work, suggests village songs heard in the bright, scintillating light; the intoxicating magic of the Andalusian nights, the light-hearted holiday crowds dancing to chords struck on guitars and *bandurrias*—all these musical effects whirl in the air while the crowds, as we imagine them, approach or recede. Everything is constantly alive and extremely expressive.[1]

I have said nothing about the harmonic aspects of these works—purposely because harmonically these works must be treated as a single group. We know how much the harmony and other aspects of present-day music owe to Debussy. I am not referring to his imitators, but to effects achieved by composers who have attempted to emulate him, and also to the prejudices which Debussy's work has finally destroyed. From all of this Spain has greatly profited. One may go so far as to say that Debussy to a certain extent completed the musical and theoretical works of Felipe Pedrell who first indicated the wealth of modal music in our folklore.[2]

---

[1] Falla's description of *Ibéria* may be compared to that of Debussy, in a letter to Caplet of 1910: 'This morning rehearsal of *Ibéria*—it's getting on! The young Kapellmeister [Gabriel Pierné] and his orchestra are less heavy-footed and they are at last beginning to rise from the ground. You cannot imagine how naturally the transition from *Les Parfums de la nuit* to *Le Matin d'un jour de fête* is achieved. It sounds like music which has not been written down! And the whole rising feeling, the awakening of people and of nature. There is a water-melon vendor and children whistling—I see them all clearly.'

[2] Falla was apparently unaware that Debussy was well acquainted with Pedrell's

While much of the music of Spanish composers is based on original documents, the French master leaves these aside, creating music of his own based on the essential elements of folk-music. This method, entirely praiseworthy among our native Spanish composers (except in cases where original documents are bound to be used), is even more remarkable when a composer is not using his native material. One other aspect of the French composer's harmony deserves notice. Certain effects are known to us from the strummings of guitars by the people of Andalusia. Curiously enough, the Spanish musicians have neglected and even despised these effects. They considered them primitive. At most, Spanish composers were able to incorporate guitar figurations in works of conventional harmonic or melodic design. It was Debussy who showed how these guitar figurations were to be used with imagination. Results were immediately forthcoming: the twelve jewel-like piano pieces forming the set *Ibéria* by Isaac Albeniz are sufficient proof.[1]

There are of course many other things to be said about Debussy and Spain. This modest paper is only a sketch to be followed by a larger study in which I propose to deal with the influence of our country and music on all the great foreign composers, from Domenico Scarlatti, claimed by Joaquin Nin as a Spaniard, to Maurice Ravel.[2] Even so, within this modest framework I emphatically state that if Debussy used Spanish folk-music to inspire

---

work. Earlier, Maurice Emmanuel, a pioneer collector of French folk-songs, had vainly attempted to interest Debussy in the modal aspects of Burgundian folk-music. 'When twenty years later I reminded him of his disdain for this music', Emmanuel records, 'he smiled and without saying a word showed me a publication which he was carrying about *in his pocket*: it was Pedrell's collection of Spanish folk-songs. By a silent gesture he expressed the inspiration he had derived from them.' This collection was probably the one made by Pedrell of Catalan folk-songs, *La Cançó popular catalana* (Barcelona, 1906).

[1] Falla's chronology may be at fault here. The date of Albeniz's *Iberia* is 1906-9. Only the *Soirée dans Grenade* of 1903 could have been known to Albeniz at this time. Guitar effects occur in works of Debussy that were published in 1909 (*Ibéria*) and 1910 (*Sérénade interrompue*). From the correspondence with Louÿs we see that Debussy was well acquainted with Albeniz, who lived in Paris between 1893 and 1909. Two of Albeniz's pieces, *Cordoba* and *El Albaicin*, were particularly admired by Debussy: they reminded him 'of those Spanish evenings filled with the perfume of carnations and the alcohol fumes of *aguardiente*'.

[2] This interesting project was never realized by Falla. He did, however, produce a study of Ravel, *Notas sobre Ravel*, which appeared in the review *Isla* (Jerez de la Frontera, 1939), from which it is clear that the Spanish elements in Ravel's music affected him less profoundly than those in the work of Debussy.

some of his greatest works he has generously repaid us and it is now Spain which is indebted to him.[1]

Granada, 8 November 1920.

[1] In a post-scriptum Falla mentions that two years before his death Debussy had accepted an invitation to conduct concerts of the Sociedad Nacional in Madrid but that his illness prevented him from fulfilling this engagement. His important explorations into Spanish folk-music long influenced the Spanish composers. In 1929 Joaquin Nin published a piano piece, *Message à Claude Debussy*, bearing the moving epigraph: 'Lorsque les yeux de Debussy se fermèrent à jamais, sur la nuit de la mort, une soudaine angoisse vint répandre au cœur des musiciens d'Espagne une inapaisable nostalgie.'

APPENDIX C

RODIN, DEBUSSY, AND NIJINSKY

The unfortunate nature of Debussy's early association with Diaghilev was based, as we saw in Chapter 10, on an underlying distrust between these two figures. With an eye for effect Diaghilev had hoped that under his guidance Debussy would play the role of the astonishing new composer. ('Etonne-moi, Jean!' Diaghilev thundered to Jean Cocteau. 'Je veux que tu m'étonnes!') Recoiling from this spectacular role, Debussy was apparently not inclined to share with Diaghilev his own inner conception of the ballet. Accordingly, the published scenario, hurriedly written in 1909, for *Masques et Bergamasques*, the first of his projected ballets for Diaghilev, is little more than a conventional story in the manner of the *Commedia dell' Arte*.

It is worth glancing at this curious scenario, so unlike the intangible or nebulous schemes for stage works to which Debussy was attracted during this period of his life, if only to see the type of work he was ready to undertake as a commission. The three scenes were to be enacted on the Piazza San Marco in Venice. At the back of the stage is the sea. At the conclusion of the Prelude the curtain goes up on a group of musicians performing a serenade on guitars and viols. Barberina, daughter of a Bolognese doctor, appears dressed as a cavalier and declares that she will give herself only to two symbolical figures, 'L'Eau d'or qui danse' and 'La Pomme qui chante'. Tartaglia, Truffuldini, Scaramouche, Harlequin, and other Italian comedy actors enter. They create a disturbance by playing upon wooden trumpets, thus drowning the serenade. Suddenly Barberina flies into the arms of Harlequin. Scene 2 opens with an encounter between Captain Firibiribombo and the Bolognese doctor who, on retiring, discovers that his daughter Barberina has fled. The captain declares that he will find the doctor's daughter before dawn. Fishing boats now appear in the distance. Fishermen and their wives form a chorus, thus providing a vocal accompaniment for group and later ensemble dances. The Bolognese doctor asks the fishermen if they have seen Barberina but they merely taunt him and their dances are resumed. In Scene 3 Scaramouche, dressed as an astrologer, comes ashore from a gondola. The doctor asks him to

help find Barberina, and at Scaramouche's signal Harlequin and Barberina, dressed as dancers, step out of a gondola and perform a *pas de deux*. At first the doctor does not recognize his daughter but Captain Firibiribombo does. The captain begs her to take off her mask and attempts to pursue her. But Scaramouche trips him up and now the doctor rushes towards his daughter. Scaramouche similarly obstructs the doctor and compels him to return to his gondola from which the beloved figures of Barberina, 'L'Eau d'or qui danse', and 'La Pomme qui chante' now appear. They dance separately and then together. The musicians who return with their viols and guitars are followed by Scaramouche, Tartaglia, and by other comedians who snatch off their masks. The doctor, seeing that he has been ridiculed, curses his daughter. Eventually a procession passes across the stage, consisting of Barberina, Harlequin, 'L'Eau d'or qui danse', and 'La Pomme qui chante'. The latter begs the doctor to forgive Barberina whereupon the captain dances a Forlane with her in which the entire company join.[1] Harlequin and Barberina return to the gondola while Scaramouche and his fellow actors resume their din on wooden trumpets.

By the time of the production of the Nijinsky ballets on scores of Debussy, *L'Après-midi d'un faune* (1912) and *Jeux* (1913), the scenario of this Italian ballet of Debussy's had been forgotten. Debussy now found himself drawn into the orbit of Diaghilev and he was aware that though Diaghilev's ideal was a union of the arts, a reflection in a sense of the Wagnerian ideal, the choreography of Diaghilev's early ballets was inclined to take precedence over the music. Debussy, like Stravinsky and other composers at this time, feared a development of the ballet on these lines. Hence their distrust of the great virtuoso dancer Nijinsky. We do not yet know all the underlying reasons for the bitter controversy provoked by the Nijinsky ballets on scores of Debussy but we are able to illuminate part of the background of this controversy by the publication of Debussy's own opinion of Nijinsky as a choreographer.

There is no doubt that the choreography of Nijinsky, though condemned by Debussy for artistic reasons of his own, marked an important departure, and that the articles and letters that appeared

[1] The idea of a dance presented at first by two solo dancers and gradually copied by the entire company occurs also in the scenario of *Le Diable dans le Beffroi*. Debussy planned in this work 'une gigue fantastique dont la puissance rhythmique et sonore ira en s'amplifiant'.

in the Paris press at the time of the production of his ballets on Debussy's scores, notably in *Le Figaro* and *Le Matin*, are important documents in the early history of the Diaghilev ballet. This history is, of course, not mainly our concern. Reading between the lines of these articles and letters, however, we discover that Debussy's works were beginning to be considered in a new light. On the eve of the production of *L'Après-midi d'un faune*, on 29 May 1912, Jacques-Emile Blanche published in *Le Figaro* an article entitled 'L'Antiquité en 1912', in which Debussy's score is re-appraised in curious terms. This work 'is the daughter', he says, 'of *Les Erinnyes* of Massenet, that is to say very similar to a work which we had imagined was completely opposed to it'. Remote echoes of Massenet there may be in Debussy's score, notably in the central section, but time has not endorsed this odd opinion. The fact is that Blanche was concerned to extol Nijinsky's choreography at the expense of the music. Nijinsky's pagan choreography, he declares, would have met with the approval of Mallarmé. The sudden laugh of Nijinsky in the role of the faun 'produces the impression of a dog that suddenly begins to grin. . . . For a few seconds mythology comes to life.'

Feelings were obviously running high. The following day, on 30 May 1912, *Le Matin* published a panegyric by Rodin entitled 'The Revival of the Dance: Loïe Fuller, Isadora Duncan, Nijinsky' in which, again in contrast to Debussy's cautious attitude, Nijinsky's evocative art is lifted on to the highest artistic plane. Tracing ideas common to Nijinsky and his American and English precursors, Rodin writes:

Over the last twenty years the dance seems to have aimed at teaching us again the principles of the physical beauty of the body and of its movements. First of all Loïe Fuller, rightly hailed as the figure who 'revived the modern dance', came to us from abroad. She was followed by Isadora Duncan, whose wonderful illusions were the product of both knowledge and taste. Their follower today is the gifted Nijinsky. The nature and the abundance of his ideas border on genius.

In the art of the dance, as in sculpture and painting, inspiration and progress were shackled by routine, prejudice and by the lack of a revitalizing spirit. One's admiration for Loïe Fuller, Isadora

Duncan, and Nijinsky is based on the fact that they acknowledge both the freedom of instinct and a tradition which has an inner respect for Nature. They are thus able to express all the underlying turbulence in the human soul. The last in this line, Nijinsky, has the added advantage of physical perfection and he has also the extraordinary capacity to give expression to a wide range of feelings. One recalls his mime of pain in *Petrouchka* and his final leap in the *Spectre de la Rose*, in which he creates the illusion of taking off into the infinite. But no role has shown Nijinsky in such an extraordinary light as his last creation, *L'Après-midi d'un faune*. Here are no leaps or jumps, only attitudes and gestures with half-conscious associations from the animal world. Nijinsky stretches himself out, leans on his elbow, walks in a crouching position, stands erect again, advances, withdraws, and all this in movements that are sometimes slow, sometimes jerky, nervous, or angular. Now he is keenly pursuing, his arms stiffen, his hand is held wide open with fingers touching; his head suddenly turns aside with a covetous, a deliberately clumsy glance but which, in the way it is performed, seems perfectly natural.

Perfect agreement, also, is achieved between the mimed and the plastic arts. The whole body performs at the command of the mind, and it is made to convey completely the underlying idea of the ballet. Nijinsky's figure has the beauty of ancient frescos and sculptures—an ideal model for a draughtsman or a sculptor. When the curtain rises Nijinsky, completely stretched out on the ground with pipes at lips and one leg folded, appears to be a statue. One can imagine nothing more arresting than his impulsive gesture at the conclusion of the ballet when he again stretches himself out, his face turned downwards on the stolen veil which he now embraces and grasps with voluptuous fervour.

The plastic aspects of Nijinsky's art alone offer a remarkable lesson in taste. One is not surprised to find an eclogue by a contemporary poet enacted in ancient Greece. Archaic gestures acquire a new significance in this ballet. I should like to see this noble effort wholly appreciated. Besides these gala performances the Théâtre du Châtelet should organize others which all artists should attend in order to commune with the presence of beauty.

As we have seen, much hostility had been provoked by Nijinsky's choreography, chiefly on moral grounds. In Nijinsky's defence Diaghilev, on 31 May 1912, wrote to *Le Figaro* quoting a letter sent to him by Odilon Redon. This reads:

Joy is often accompanied by sorrow. To the pleasure which you have given me this evening must be added the regret not to have had among us my illustrious friend Stéphane Mallarmé. He, more than anyone, would have responded to this admirable realization of his ideas. I do not think that his ideal could have been more adequately conveyed.

I remember that Mallarmé constantly referred to choreography and mime. With what joy he would have beheld the dream of his faun brought to life in the living frieze which we have just seen translated into music by Debussy, into plastic art by Nijinsky, and into vivid colours by Bakst! The spirit of Mallarmé was among us this evening.

The anti-Nijinsky faction was led by Gaston Calmette, editor of *Le Figaro*. Calmette attempted to censure not only the erotic aspects of the art of Nijinsky but also those of Rodin. The controversy died down after the production of *L'Après-midi*, but it was revived the following year when Nijinsky produced the choreography for *Jeux*. On this occasion Debussy publicly made known his opinions on the art of his collaborator. In this ballet, as in Ravel's *Daphnis et Chloé*, and Stravinsky's *Le Sacre du Printemps*, Diaghilev was unable to hold the balance between the rival claims of the dance and of music. Perhaps Debussy sensed Diaghilev's dilemma when, quoting Nietzsche's statement in *Zarathustra*, 'In all good things there is laughter', he caustically wrote to *Le Matin* on 15 May 1913:

I am not a man of knowledge and I am thus ill-fitted to speak of the dance since today nothing can be said about this frivolous subject without assuming the airs of a learned doctor. Before writing a ballet I did not know what a choreographer was, but now I know. A choreographer is a person with a superior command of arithmetic. I may not be extremely erudite but I have not forgotten some of my lessons, among them, for instance, this one: one, two, three; one, two, three; one, two, three, four,

five; one, two, three, four, five, six; one, two, three; one, two, three—now a little more quickly, and all these are then added up. There may be nothing in it, but it is most moving, especially when this arithmetical problem is set by the incomparable Nijinsky. Why then did I launch myself, being by nature reserved, into an undertaking of which one simply does not know the outcome? Because at lunchtime one has to eat, and because one day I happened to lunch with Serge Diaghilev, a terrifying but irresistible man able to instil the spirit of the dance into lifeless stones. Diaghilev spoke to me of a scenario devised by Nijinsky, consisting of some kind of subtle transparency, the basis, I agreed, of a ballet. In this scenario there is a park, a tennis court, there is the chance meeting of two girls and a young man seeking a lost ball, a nocturnal mysterious landscape, and together with this a suggestion of something sinister in the darkening shadows of night. Elevations, turns, certain unforeseen, capricious steps of the dancers—everything calculated to bring alive rhythm in music is here.

I must confess that since the evenings of the Russian ballet have so often delighted me in an unexpected way, and since I have so often been moved by Nijinsky's spontaneity, innate or acquired, I am now awaiting like an excited child who has been promised a visit to the theatre, the production of *Jeux* at the Theatre in the Avenue Montaigne, now to be called the Theatre of Music.[1]

It seems to me that in our dull classroom of music, presided over by a severe schoolmaster, the Russians have opened a window which looks out on to the open countryside. Also, for one who admires Tamara Karsavina as I do, how delightful it is to have this sweetly drooping flower as an interpreter and to watch her with the exquisite Ludmilla Schollar playing with the approaching shadows of night.

The lesson to be derived from this last venture of Debussy and

---

[1] The Théâtre des Champs-Elysées was built in 1913 by the impresario of Central European origin Gabriel Astruc, who dedicated it, as he said, 'to the glory of Bourdelle [who executed reliefs for the theatre] and to Debussy'. Though it opened with a festival of French music, conducted by Debussy and others, Astruc was known to be particularly cosmopolitan in his tastes and the Théâtre des Champs-Elysées had been maliciously named the *Astruckisches Musikhaus*.

Diaghilev is that the ballet as a form of 'the union of the arts' (the *Gesamtkunstwerk*) could not survive. Subsequent ballet productions of *Jeux*, by Jean Borlin in Paris in 1920 and William Dollar in New York in 1950, were similarly unsuccessful.

APPENDIX D

PUCCINI AND DEBUSSY

Puccini heard *Pelléas et Mélisande* when it was revived at the Opéra-Comique in October 1903. Earlier in the month André Messager, the conductor of *Pelléas*, had given at the same theatre the first French performance of Puccini's *Tosca*, and *La Bohème* had been revived there the previous month. These operas of Debussy and Puccini were thus made known to the Paris opera public at the same time. Puccini was enthusiastically fêted on his visit to Paris, but chiefly in social circles. In musical circles national feelings still ran high and most French musicians were inclined to be distrustful of the dramatic and sharply exteriorized style of Italian opera after Verdi. In his diary Henri Büsser records his grudging impression of the dress rehearsal of *Tosca*: 'Messager conducted the work without any great conviction; he cannot like music like this after *Pelléas*.' Earlier Debussy, having found little to admire in *La Traviata*, the only opera of Verdi about which he happened to write, nevertheless considered it more satisfying than the so-called realistic operas of Puccini, Leoncavallo, and Mascagni.[1]

Puccini, on the other hand, was a sincere admirer of Debussy's work and, as most critics are agreed, was greatly influenced, particularly in *La Fanciulla del West*, by Debussy's harmony and orchestration. Büsser records a meeting between the two composers on the occasion of the *Pelléas* revival. 'Puccini, who was in the audience, was greatly moved. He came over to Debussy to tell him so.' Nevertheless, Büsser adds, 'he tells Messager that he was very surprised at the complete absence of pieces of vocal effect'. This was of course the expected impression. Puccini admired particularly, we are told, the texture of Debussy's orchestration.

It is worth recalling that Puccini had himself intended to set *Pelléas* and had gone so far as to approach Maeterlinck. He had obviously set his heart on this project and the fact that Debussy had

[1] In an article of 1913 Debussy was bitterly sarcastic on the subject of contemporary Italian opera: 'Inspired by scenes in the realistic cinema, the characters throw themselves at each other and appear to wrench melodies from each other's mouths. A whole life is packed into a single act: birth, marriage, and an assassination thrown in. In these one-act operas very little music need be written for the reason that there is hardly time to hear much.'

earlier secured Maeterlinck's authorization must have been a disappointment to him. By comparison, however, with the cantankerousness of Richard Strauss at a performance of *Pelléas* ('I would have written an entirely different kind of music for this play'), Puccini's whole-hearted recognition of the qualities of a very different composer from himself shows at the least an enquiring turn of mind and great humility. Puccini retained this admiration for Debussy. On 5 April 1918, shortly after Debussy's death, he wrote a moving letter to a journalist on the *Giornale d'Italia* about his contemporary's status and achievement:

> Claude Debussy had the soul of an artist shot through with a genuine and subtle sensibility. To express this sensibility he discovered a new type of harmony which at first seemed to open wide new horizons on to the future of music.
>
> When today I hear people speak of Debussyism as if it were a system to follow or not to follow I should like to tell these young musicians of the doubts which, as I can attest from my personal knowledge, assailed the great artist in his later years. His harmonic procedures which, when they were first made known, appeared so surprising and full of a new beauty, became less and less so in the course of time until ultimately they surprised no one. Even to the composer himself they appeared to represent a restricted field of experiment and, I repeat, I know how much he attempted, in vain, to escape from this field. A fervent admirer of Debussy, I was anxiously waiting to see how Debussy himself proposed to revolt against Debussyism. Now the great artist is dead, and we cannot know the manner, possibly very beneficial, in which he would have carried out this revolt.
>
> Giacomo Puccini.[1]

We see from this letter that Puccini was aware that Debussy, like himself, took a view of the technique of composition that was constantly exploratory. Analysing in technical detail the phases of Puccini's harmonic technique, Dr. Mosco Carner writes: 'He began with the simple chromatic "alterations" and the secondary sevenths and ninths of pre-Wagnerian romantic harmony (*Le Villi* and

[1] This letter appeared in French in *Comœdia* of 2 March 1925 and in English in *The Musical Times* of July 1918. The above translation is made from the *Comœdia* version. The original Italian version has not been traced.

Edgar); turned to *Tristan* harmonies in *Manon Lescaut*, in which he also ventured passages in parallel fifths before Debussy; and under the subsequent influence of the French Impressionists he cultivated, often to surfeit, parallel organum-like progressions (of common chords, secondary sevenths and chords of the added sixth), unresolved discords and augmented triads. From the early 1900s he began to make increased use of the whole-tone scale (*Tosca* and *La Fanciulla*); and later he experimented with bitonality, chords of the fourth and naked, harsh dissonances (*Turandot*).' And Dr. Carner conjectures: 'Had he lived longer it is certain he would have availed himself of dodecaphony and quarter tones.' One is left with the impression that Puccini, anxious to see 'how Debussy himself proposed to revolt against Debussyism', had imagined in his work an harmonic evolution on these lines.

Puccini had been frustrated in his desire to set *Pelléas*. But there was to be a curious sequel to his association with the world of Debussy. One of Puccini's principal projects about 1907 was an opera entitled *Conchita*, based on a libretto adapted by Maurice Vaucaire from the novel of Pierre Louÿs, *La Femme et le Pantin*. The sadistic Conchita, a cross between the great operatic characters of Carmen and Turandot, seems to have been a most appropriate subject for treatment by Puccini. Moreover Louÿs, whose many projected stage-works with Debussy had come to nothing, was extremely anxious to collaborate with Puccini.[1] Why, then, did nothing come of this daring dramatic subject? Many rational reasons were given by Puccini. Conchita was a despicable Spanish slut; the libretto had become too stylized. Dr. Carner suggests a deeper reason, namely that by his nature Puccini was inclined to shrink from the supreme demands made on his genius. It may well be that, as with several of the later projects of Debussy, Puccini's ill-fated venture with Louÿs indicates in these artists of sensibility just that lack of conviction necessary to carry through their many-sided work to the end.

[1] Louÿs, whose name is pronounced without sounding the final 's', is amusingly referred to in Puccini's letters as 'Inouï'. 'Inouï called this evening, very *épatant*', he writes in 1906. 'He returned to the subject of *Conchita* for a change; he won't let me alone—not a bit of it. He's a sticker, that fellow!' When Puccini, much to his publisher's distress, finally declined to set this libretto, Louÿs threatened to claim damages from him. *Conchita* was eventually set by Zandonai and produced in Milan in 1911.

APPENDIX E

DEBUSSY AND OCCULTISM

It has been shown that Debussy's attraction to the lurid subject of *Le Martyre de Saint-Sébastien* derived to some extent from his earlier interest in the occult practices in Paris in the 1890s. These practices are referred to in Vol. I, p. 109. According to a fragment of an unpublished letter, which was the only evidence then available, Debussy in 1892 had been interested in writing the incidental music for the esoteric play of Jules Bois *Les Noces de Sathan*, but had finally refused to do so. Further information on this subject has now come to light. Dr. Pasteur Vallery-Radot has generously supplied me with the complete text of Debussy's letter to Jules Bois, and Monsieur Léon Guichard, the author of several important studies on the period, kindly sent me an unpublished article of his consisting of a valuable piece of research on Debussy's knowledge of the works of Jules Bois and other esoteric writers and painters of his circle. These two documents supplement my own research in this field. Gradually, the whole matter of Debussy's early connexions with the occultists of the 1890s became clearer. As a result *La Damoiselle élue*, seemingly an innocent Pre-Raphaelite work, acquired a rather deeper and a slightly sinister significance, and the line of development from this early work to *Le Martyre de Saint-Sébastien*, which earlier critics had always sensed, now seemed unmistakable. Whatever were the immediate material reasons for writing the incidental music for d'Annunzio's play, this work must have revived many early memories. Moreover, as Monsieur Guichard shows, d'Annunzio's *Saint-Sébastien* and Jules Bois' *Noces de Sathan* have many occult features in common.

The letter from Debussy to Jules Bois, published here for the first time, together with Monsieur Guichard's study, 'Debussy and the Occultists', which is printed with his kind permission, allow us to see much more closely this strange streak in Debussy's musical character which persisted over many years.

Tuesday evening [end of March 1892]
42 rue de Londres

I have made up my mind, my dear Bois: whatever it may cost to our friendship I have not the necessary confidence to write the music I had promised for *Les Noces de Sathan*. It is clear to me that the orchestra exists only on a scrap of paper; and when it comes to knowing the names of the players or where they come from one is told nothing except by a Monsieur Burger who pays repeated calls but who cannot undertake everything himself. Forgive me and above all do not think there is any ill will on my part. It would all be too much like a venture into the Unknown and would take on the character of a 'mauvaise aventure'. Let me express to you my affectionate thoughts quite simply, without drums or trumpets.

C.D.

DEBUSSY AND THE OCCULTISTS

A minor discovery I recently made concerns a great musician and has some importance. As I was looking through the Symbolist reviews in the course of my research on the Wagnerian influence in France, I stopped short at the following notice published in *Le Saint-Graal* of 8 March 1892, a review founded that year by Emmanuel Signoret[1]:

Théâtre d'art. The third evening of the season of the Théâtre d'art will take place in the second fortnight of March at the Théâtre Montparnasse, and the fourth one week later. At the first evening will be given:

1. Two scenes from the *Chants de Maldoror* by the Comte de Lautréamont.

[1] This review appeared in Paris intermittently between 1892 and 1899. In the first number Verlaine enthusiastically wrote to the editor: 'Bien, très bien, Le Saint-Graal, quel mot, quel nom! Double signification: faîte de l'art moderne, sommet du Vrai éternel. Saint-Graal, Sang Réel, Le Sang du Christ dans l'or incandescent: *Saint-Graal, Lohengrin, Parsifal*, la manifestation triomphale et triomphant de la plus sublime musique, de l'effort poétique peut-être définitif de ces temps-ci.'

2. Two scenes from *Vercingétorix*, a play in verse by Edouard Schuré with scenery by Odilon Redon.

3. *Les Noces de Sathan*, esoteric play in verse in one act by Jules Bois. Music by Debussy. Scenery and costumes by Henry Colas. (This is the first initiatory play to be produced.)[1]

4. The first book of Homer's *Iliad*. Theatrical version in four tableaux . . . Symphonic score by Gabriel Fabré.

'Music by Debussy'! This was a discovery indeed. Debussy had thus written, it seemed, in 1892 a score unknown to every one of his biographers and performed at the Théâtre d'Art! The Théâtre d'Art was directed at this time by the poet Paul Fort. Marlowe's *Faust* had been performed there and programmes also included a recitation of Rimbaud's *Bateau Ivre*. Productions were by Lugné-Poe. Jules Bois, Camille Mauclair, and Charles-Henry Hirsch lectured on Esotericism, Maeterlinck, Maurice Denis, and Henry de Groux.[2]

Debussy thus knew Jules Bois, the writer from Marseilles, nine years his junior, who in 1891 at the age of twenty had already published *Il ne faut pas mourir*, a poem in dialogue based on the

[1] 'La première pièce initiatique mise en scène.' Presumably this play was connected with the prevalent cult of 'Le Satanisme' described in Jules Bois' *Les Petites Religions de Paris*.

[2] Debussy may or may not have heard these lectures at the Théâtre d'Art but he remained closely connected with each of these subjects or personalities. Writing to Ernest Chausson in 1893 he says that music 'should have been an hermetic science' to be understood only 'by means of texts the interpretation of which would be long and difficult. . . . Instead of diffusing art I propose the foundation of a "Society of Musical Esotericism".' Debussy was of course among Maeterlinck's earliest admirers. Maurice Denis was associated with him in the publication of *La Damoiselle élue* and he admired the works of the Belgian painter Henry de Groux until the end of his life. Writing to Godet of de Groux's exhibition of painting and sculpture at the Salon d'Automne in 1911, he says: 'Yesterday I plunged back into the past. What an admirable exhibition! A figure of Napoleon leading the retreat from Russia and which freezes you more profoundly than all the snows of the landscape. . . . A Tolstoy in bronze . . . more beautiful than the clever mutilations of Rodin. And a portrait of Wagner with the face of an old cynical magician.' De Groux 'still looks like a genius of a clown and in his eyes are all the dreams of the world'. Years earlier Debussy and Godet had seen together de Groux's revolutionary picture 'Christ insulted'. This was followed by another striking picture of his, 'Zola insulted'. 'He is a fine example of moral courage', Debussy commented. 'His lesson is that one must not be disdainful of censers, and if necessary one must even spit in them.' Another member of this defiant Franco-Belgian circle which Debussy frequented was the Belgian Symbolist poet Georges Rodenbach, whose *Bruges-la-Morte* appeared in 1892. Debussy's correspondence with Rodenbach is in the private collection of Madame Marcelle Rodenbach but has remained unpublished.

ideas of one of the new religious cults. How or through whom did Debussy know him? Did he frequent at this time one of the quasi-religious gatherings described by Bois? *Les Noces de Sathan* was first published in 1890. After the performance announced in *Le Saint-Graal* it was republished by Chamuel, who specialized in esoteric publications, with a drawing by Henry Colas, but without any music. On the other hand, another esoteric play by Jules Bois, *La Porte héroïque du ciel*, appeared in 1894, illustrated by two drawings by Antoine de la Rochefoucauld, organiser of Rosicrucian meetings and containing a Prelude by Erik Satie. Satie, one of the musicians, together with Benedictus of the Rose-Croix, had composed in 1892 three Preludes in the form of incidental music to the play *Le Fils des étoiles*, by Joseph Péladan.

Satie's connexions with the Rose-Croix are well known, and so is his friendship with Debussy. It seems likely that it was through Satie that Debussy came to know Jules Bois and was commissioned to compose the musical score for *Les Noces de Sathan*. 1892 is the year of the beginning of the *Prélude à l'Après-midi d'un faune*, the poem of which is referred to in Bois' preface: *Le Symbolisme des Noces de Sathan et le drame ésotérique*.[1]

But the meeting might have taken place elsewhere, at the book-shop *L'Art Indépendant* belonging to the publisher Edmond Bailly. Memoirs relating to this bookshop do not mention the name of Jules Bois, though two works of his were published by Bailly. It was, moreover, Bailly who published Debussy's *La Damoiselle élue*, and the *Chansons de Bilitis* of Pierre Louÿs. Poets and writers who formed part of Bailly's circle included Villiers de l'Isle Adam, Mallarmé, Huysmans, Louis Ménard, Pierre Louÿs, and Jean de Tinan. Toulouse-Lautrec and Odilon Redon were other members of this circle and so was the astrologer Ely Star. Bailly was interested in music to the extent of publishing a journal entitled *La Musique Populaire*, and Debussy was one of his regular visitors. 'Almost every day', notes V. E. Michelet in *Les Compagnons de la hiérophanie*, 'towards the end of the afternoon he would come either alone or with his faithful Erik Satie.' And he adds: 'Debussy allowed himself to become strongly impressed by current theories

---

[1] At one point in the play Bois required an effect comparable to that of 'the dances of Ramayana performed in Cambodia by dancing priestesses'. During these dances 'a reciter declaims the poem in the manner foreseen by Mallarmé for *L'Après-midi d'un faune*'.

of Hermetic literature.'[1] It is not surprising, therefore, to find him collaborating with Jules Bois. Plans must have been far advanced since Debussy's name appeared in an announcement of the programme only ten days before the performance of *Les Noces de Sathan* on 31 March.

The characters in this esoteric drama consist of Satan, Psyche, Ennoia, the Elohim, stercoraceous demons, Incubi and Succubi, Adam, Eve, Cain, Mephistopheles, Faust, the Hetaerae witches, and the Ineffable Voice. Reading it through, I was reminded of the great poems of Vigny, Hugo, and Goethe, and also of *Le Martyre de Saint-Sébastien* which almost twenty years later inspired Debussy to write one of his most moving works. Like d'Annunzio's drama, Jules Bois' play conveys the same atmosphere of sensuality, the same ambiguous mysticism, and the same excessive preoccupation with detail. The stage directions require the representation of purple lilies and other exotic flowers and refer to the 'dark blue hair of the Hermaphrodite Satan' which provides him with a 'halo suggesting a stormy sky'. The subject of the play, influenced by the plays of Edouard Schuré and also by the writings of St. John, Plato, and Pythagoras, is Salvation achieved through the action of Woman and by Intuition. Satan, symbolizing the wicked aspects of human nature, grows weary of the idea of evil. By his union with the good figure Psyche he becomes a redeemer.

At which points in this play was music to be introduced? It was no doubt required for atmospheric effects and there were probably to be musical interludes. Possibly music was to be performed before the chant of the Elohim, recited by Marthe Mellot in her beautiful song-like voice, or before the entrance of Cain or the Hetaerae, or preceding the final scene.

Apparently only one critic, Pierre Valin, in the *Revue d'art dramatique*, referred to the music in *Les Noces de Sathan*. He criticized the fact that the music did not seem to be co-ordinated with the delivery of the actors nor with the rhythm of the poetry, and he also noted that the actors' voices were drowned by the instruments. 'In plays for amateurs', he rightly observed, 'such as those at the Théâtre d'Art, music obviously plays an important part. It induces in the public the atmosphere of a light or a serious style. It enables the feelings of the actors to reach the audience and it helps to create

[1] The literature on astrology, magic, and alchemy attributed to Hermes Trisnegistus.

a dream atmosphere. It also encourages the audience to listen more attentively, and by playing upon sensations, it brings to the listener that which is too subtle or too vague to be expressed in language.' This was a clear enunciation of the Symbolist musical æsthetic.

The censorious remarks of this critic would indeed surprise us if the music of *Les Noces de Sathan* had ultimately been composed by Debussy. No music could be more skilfully combined with words; no music could more effectively throw the words into relief while at the same time conveying their inner meaning. Alas, the music of *Les Noces de Sathan* was eventually written by Henry Quittard, a pupil of César Franck.

Why did Debussy at the last minute not write the music for this play? In the present state of our knowledge we cannot say. Nor is it really a question of great importance. The interesting point about this project is that it reveals to us the milieu in which Debussy moved and his attraction to an esoteric world. An element of mystery runs through the whole of the art of Debussy, as we are made aware from the study of Vladimir Jankélévitch, *Debussy et le Mystère*. 'His attraction to the mysterious', writes this author, 'derived from the occult ideas of the Rosicrucians in Paris in the 1880s [rather the 1890s], from the frequenters of the Chat Noir, and from the Sar Péladan in whose entourage mysticism would sometimes degenerate into hypocrisy or a mere hoax. Debussy became intoxicated with the Eleusinian mysteries of the *fin-de-siècle* but neither more nor less than Ravel or Satie.' It would perhaps be truer to say 'more than Ravel and less than Satie'. However this may be, the abortive collaboration with Jules Bois adds greatly to our evidence of Debussy's leanings in this direction.

Léon Guichard, 1958.

APPENDIX F

THE THEORIES OF GASTON BACHELARD

It has become a commonplace, in the criticism of Symbolist poetry and music, to invoke the line, 'De la musique avant toute chose', from Verlaine's *Art Poétique*. In fact Verlaine believed not so much that music should take precedence over other forms of artistic thought but that it was inherent in other artistic forms. 'De la musique en toute chose' was more accurately his ideal. Many of Verlaine's recommendations were adopted by Debussy, and indeed the texture of Debussy's works, particularly the aerial texture of his orchestral works, is clearly suggested in Verlaine's lines insisting that a poetic image should be

> Plus vague et plus soluble dans l'air
> Sans rien en lui qui pèse ou qui pose.

Elsewhere in this miniature poetic treatise of Verlaine the dream state is invoked. Suggestion rather than eloquence is the ideal, and nuance rather than colour:

> Oh! la nuance seule fiance
> Le rêve au rêve et la flûte au cor.

In his study written shortly after Debussy's death Robert Godet draws several analogies between the æsthetics of Debussy and Verlaine.[1] Maintaining that they shared a similar concept of the dream, he emphasizes the many associations of water in their works. Debussy, he says, has been likened to an island, 'surrounded by water on all sides', and he proceeds to list some of the associations of both running and stagnant water in his works. In *Le Promenoir des deux amants* water lies dormant in the sombre grotto, it trickles over drooping reeds, or it sparkles in the hollow of beloved hands. In *Clair de lune* a slender spray of water darts up from among marble statues, uttering a sigh to the heavens. In the setting of Baudelaire's *Le Jet d'eau* it falls upon the ground in the form of a shower of tears. Elsewhere in the Verlaine settings the heart weeps

[1] 'Claude Debussy', *La Semaine littéraire*, Geneva, 13–27 April 1918.

as rain falls on the town, hopes are drowned in the misty stream, and disturbing memories are aroused by the sight of water swirling over the stones of a river-bed. Contentment is associated with the impressionistic vision of rain in *Jardins sous la pluie*, also with the ruminations of *Reflets dans l'eau*. On another, more sombre, plane, water is symbolically associated with the funereal mood of *La Cathédrale engloutie* while in *Pelléas*, in the scene of the vaults, we are made aware of the stench of stagnant water. *Pelléas* presents a variety of dream associations of this kind. Stagnant water is associated with death in the vaults scene, but Mélisande's wedding-ring falls into clear fountain water. Finally, there are the seascapes of Debussy, sketched out in the *Trois Mélodies* of Verlaine ('La Mer est plus belle') and the *Proses Lyriques* ('De Grève'), developed in the *Nocturnes* and the sea music of *Pelléas*, and brought to their final expression in *La Mer*.

In associating the imagery of water in Debussy's works with Verlaine's *Art Poétique* Godet was anticipating a novel study on the nature of the poetic imagination, *L'Eau et les Rêves*, by Gaston Bachelard. The first of a series of studies showing connexions between the poetic imagination and the elements of Nature,[1] this work investigates the borderlands of the unconscious mind where, according to Bachelard, poetic images have their origin in images of the natural elements of fire, air, earth, and water. Music is hardly ever mentioned in this novel approach to the workings of the imaginative mind, but it is clear that many of Bachelard's conclusions apply to music as well as to poetry. At any rate a field is open here for the application of these theories to the nature of the musical imagination.

Fugitive and often superficial images, associated primarily with clear, running water, are investigated in the first place. Minor poets abound here, inspired by narcissistic themes, though Bachelard shows that the nature of narcissism demands a re-interpretation in the light of modern psychology. The function of mirrors and reflections is described in the work of a friend of Debussy, Georges

---

[1] First published in 1942, *L'Eau et les Rêves* was followed between 1943 and 1948 by *L'Air et les Songes*, *La Terre et les Rêveries du Repos*, and *La Terre et les Rêveries de la Volonté*. Bachelard's most recent work, summarizing a lifetime's research, is *La Poétique de la Rêverie*. Born in 1885, Gaston Bachelard started his career as a professor of chemistry and physics and produced several technical works, among them *Le Nouvel Esprit scientifique*, before applying his scientific training to an investigation in literature of the nature of the dream.

Rodenbach: 'All the mirrors in the works of Rodenbach are veiled. They have a grey life of their own like the waters in the canals of his native Bruges.' The symbolical significance of the swan is described afresh under the heading, 'Les Eaux claires; Les Eaux amoureuses', and reference is made to the symbolism of the swan in the works of Pierre Louÿs and Gabriele d'Annunzio.

Deeper waters and particularly stagnant waters ('Les Eaux dormantes; Les Eaux mortes') are associated with contemplation and thus lead rapidly, if one is attuned to this mode of thinking, to fantasies of the unconscious. In a chapter entitled 'L'Eau lourde dans la rêverie d'Edgar Poe', largely based on the interpretations of Marie Bonaparte, dream aspects of the work of Poe are presented in a manner which frequently corresponds with the ideas of Debussy. 'In the works of Poe', Bachelard observes, 'clear water inevitably darkens. Water, originally sparkling and alive, runs more slowly and gradually becomes sluggish. The idle watching of running water signifies the passing of time; the personality disintegrates and eventually faces death.' A key work in Bachelard's view of this type of poetic expression is Poe's poem *Al Aaraaf* (quoted in the translation by Gabriel Mourey) with its curious image of the 'star-isle'. Sky and water become one in Poe's view, the star-isle being a reflection of a star from the heavens in the depths of water. 'Where is reality, in the sky or in the depths of water?' Bachelard asks on the matter of the meaning of this poem. 'One cannot over-emphasize the importance of the double image, such as that of the star-isle, in the psychology of the imagination. . . . The dream endows water with a conception of a remote country, of a celestial country.'

This approach to poetry is a counterpart of the approach of certain musicologists to the problems of composition. As opposed to Bergson, the philosopher of the preceding generation who believed that the dream was a disintegrating force allied to madness, Bachelard holds that the unreal world of the dream represents the only point of departure for any artistic or indeed scientific thought. He is thus concerned to illuminate the workings of the unconscious mind at the level where poetic images are produced. Students of the processes of musical composition are concerned with a similar problem. If ever we are able to define the symbolism of the musical language with the precision that literary critics have brought

to the symbolism of the poetic language, Bachelard's works will certainly be drawn upon by historians of musical Impressionism.[1]

[1] An earlier work on the dream and the poetic imagination, Albert Béguin's *L'Ame romantique et le Rêve* (1939), explores the dream world of Schumann. It is worth noting that the evolution from Schumann to Debussy, in regard to an expression of the dream, was apparently sensed by Furtwängler who, in his *Ton und Wort* (Wiesbaden, 1954), describes Debussy as 'a Schumann who might have been French and who might have been modern'. Possibly because he was aware of some hidden link between the dream worlds of Debussy and Schumann, Furtwängler showed a keener understanding of the art of Debussy than certain of his contemporaries, notably Schoenberg and Schnabel, who saw in Debussy a composer of no greater stature than Gounod or Chaminade.

APPENDIX G

DEBUSSY'S CRITICAL ARTICLES

As we observed in Chapter 3 (pages 52-3), the selection of Debussy's articles in M. *Croche antidilettante*, many of them curtailed, hardly does justice to the wide variety of Debussy's critical work, even though several of his articles have only an ephemeral value and not all of them would need to be included in an edition of his writings. The following list, indicating the articles in an abridged or altered form in M. *Croche*, is a guide to Debussy's entire critical work.

LA REVUE BLANCHE, 1901

1 April	Music (*Croche* I); Schumann's *Faust* at the Concerts Colonne; Overture to *Le Roi Lear* by Augustin Savard; Symphony of Georges-Martin Witkowski and 'Poèmes Danois' of Delius at the Société Nationale.
15 April	*The Nursery* by Moussorgsky (*Croche* IV); Piano Sonata of Paul Dukas (*Croche* V); German conductors (*Croche* VI).
1 May	J. S. Bach (*Croche* VI); Beethoven's Ninth Symphony (*Croche* III).
15 May	The Opera (*Croche* VII); *Le Roi de Paris* by Georges Hüe; *L'Ouragan* by Alfred Bruneau.
1 June	The Nikisch Concerts (*Croche* VIII); Open-air Music (*Croche* X);[1] other concerts.
1 July	Monsieur Croche the Dilettante-Hater (*Croche* I).
15 November	M. Croche and *Les Barbares* by Saint-Saëns (*Croche* II).
1 December	The works of Massenet from *Eve* to *Grisélidis* (*Croche* IX).

[1] The original proof of this article, written for *La Renaissance Latine* and kindly communicated to me by Cecil Hopkinson, bears the editorial direction, 'à détruire'. See note 3 on page 66.

GIL BLAS, 1903

12 January	Vincent d'Indy's *L'Etranger* (*Croche* XXI).
19 January	Open-air Music[1] (*Croche* X); *Namouna* by Lalo; Berlioz's *Damnation of Faust*; extract from d'Indy's *L'Etranger*; Piano Concerto by Léon Moreau. Prince Ludwig of Bavaria.
21 and 26 January	*Titania* by Georges Hüe and Weber (*Croche* XI).
2 February	*Castor et Pollux* by Rameau (*Croche* XII).
16 February	Weingartner's performances of Beethoven's *Pastoral Symphony* and Liszt's *Mazeppa* (*Croche* XIII); *La Traviata* at the Opéra-Comique.
23 February	An open letter to Gluck (*Croche* XXV); Works of Louis Vierne and Chausson at the Société Nationale; Symphony of Guy Ropartz at the Concerts Lamoureux.
2 March	The People's Theatre (*Croche* XIV); Siegfried Wagner at the Concerts Lamoureux (*Croche* XVII).
9 March	Opera and Music. Works by Paul de Wailly, Fauré and Rhené-Baton at the Société Nationale. Death of Albert Cahen.
16 March	Saint-Saëns at the Concerts Colonne (*Croche* II). Works of Rimsky-Korsakov and Grieg at the Concerts Lamoureux.
19 March	*Muguette* by Edmond Missa at the Opéra-Comique.
23 March	Meyerbeer's *Les Huguenots*. Works of Mendelssohn, Alfred Bruneau, and Saint-Saëns at the Concerts Lamoureux.
30 March	A child prodigy. Works of Gustave Samazeuilh, Ernest Chausson, and Paul Dukas at the Société Nationale. Richard Strauss (*Croche* XV).
6 April	*Parsifal* (*Croche* XVI); Centenary of the French Academy in Rome.

[1] See the similar article in *La Revue Blanche*, 1 June 1901.

13 April	Concert performance of *Rheingold*. *Les Béatitudes* by César Franck (*Croche* XVIII); Alessandro Scarlatti (*Croche* XIX). Jean de Reszke.
20 April	Grieg at the Concerts Colonne (*Croche* XX). J. P. Souza.
27 April	*Le Sire de Vergy* by Claude Terrasse. Massenet's *Werther*.
5 May	The *Ring* in London (*Croche* XXII).
8 May	Berlioz: a stage performance of the *Damnation of Faust* (*Croche* XXIII).
19 May	*Henry VIII* by Saint-Saëns.
1 June	The *Ring* in London (*Croche* XXII).
6 June	*La Petite Maison* by William Chaumet.
10 June	Recollections of a holder of the Prix de Rome (*Croche* II).
28 June	Music in 1903.

MUSICA

October 1902	Musical Taste.
May 1903	Some musical considerations on the Prix de Rome.[1]
July 1906	Charles Gounod (*Croche* XXIV).
January 1908	Mary Garden.
March 1911	Connexions between Poetry and Music.

LE FIGARO

16 May 1902	The Criticisms of *Pelléas* (interview).
8 May 1908	*Hippolyte et Aricie*.
14 February 1909	The Future of the Conservatoire (interview).

COMŒDIA

4 November 1909	The Music of Today and Tomorrow (interview).

[1] The papers of M. D. Calvocoressi, kindly lent to me by Dr. Gerald Abraham, show that this article was also published in *L'Art Moderne*, 9 October 1904. Reproduced in the special number of *La Revue de Musicologie* devoted to Debussy (1962), it is entirely different from the article of 10 June 1903 on the same subject in *Gil Blas*, which appears in *M. Croche*.

31 January 1910	Modern Italian Music (interview).
26 January 1911	The Decentralisation of Music (interview).
?	Why I wrote *Pelléas*.

LA REVUE MUSICALE DE LYON

16 October 1910	The French Festival in Munich (interview).
8 January 1911	Debussy seen by himself (interview).
22 January 1911	Music (interview).
15 May 1911	*Le Martyre de Saint-Sébastien* (interview).[1]

EXCELSIOR

9 March 1911	Russian Music and French composers.
11 February 1911	*Le Martyre de Saint-Sébastien* (interview).

LA REVUE S.I.M.

November 1912	The Crisis in French Music. Works of Beethoven, Berlioz, and Charpentier.[2]
December 1912	Respect in art. Works of Pierné, Strauss, and Beethoven.
15 January 1913	Music at the end of the year. Works of Chausson, Ropartz, and Bach.
15 February 1913	On Taste. The Concerts Colonne.
15 March 1913	A Precursor: William Rust. The Music of Ernest Fanelli.
15 May 1913	The Present State of Music. Music at the Théâtre des Champs-Elysées.
November 1913	Music and Nature. The Concerts Colonne and the Théâtre des Champs-Elysées.
December 1913	Spanish music. *Faust et Hélène* by Lili Boulanger.
January 1914	Letter from Russia.
February 1914	*Parsifal*.
March 1914	Fashion and taste. Works of Gabriel Grovlez and André Gédalge.

[1] These interviews had earlier appeared in other unidentified papers.
[2] Except for the articles of 15 May 1913 and November 1913 all works reviewed in *La Revue S.I.M.* were given at the Concerts Colonne.

MISCELLANEOUS WRITINGS

Reply to an enquiry on the German influence (interview), *Mercure de France*, January 1903.

Reply to an enquiry on the present state of French music, *La Revue Bleue*, 2 April 1904.

A rebirth of the classical ideal (interview), *Paris-Journal*, 20 May 1910.

The influence of Wagner. Interview of February 1908 with a journalist of *L'Eclair*, not published by this journal but reproduced in *Le Cas Debussy* by C. F. Caillard and J. de Bérys (1910).

The Death of Massenet (1912) in *Massenet* by Alfred Bruneau (1935).

Article on Rameau (1912). Unpublished in Debussy's lifetime, this appears in *Lettres inédites à André Caplet* (1957).

Jeux, Le Matin, 15 May 1913.

Preface to Durand's edition of the works of Chopin (in the volume of the Waltzes), 1915.

Letter in the form of a preface to Paul Huvelin's edition of a series of lectures, *Pour la musique française*, 1916.

APPENDIX H

CATALOGUE OF WORKS

It was intended, as stated in Volume I, to present here a *catalogue raisonné* of Debussy's works. This was to have been based on a publication planned in association with other scholars, but which has unfortunately not yet appeared. I have therefore limited myself in the following list to setting out the works of Debussy according to categories. On the question of the origin and the changes of the titles of Debussy's works referred to earlier the available information has been incorporated in the text. The section listing the unpublished works, though not exhaustive, nevertheless presents as complete a compilation as can be made in the present state of our knowledge.

UNPUBLISHED WORKS

SONGS

1876 (?) Ballade à la lune (Alfred de Musset); Fleur des eaux (Maurice Bouchor).

1880–4 L'Archet (Charles Cros); Séguedille (J. L. Vauthier); Les Roses; Chanson espagnole (for two voices); Rondel chinois.

Three songs on poems of Paul Bourget: Regret; Romance d'Ariel; Musique.

Six songs on poems of Théodore de Banville: Caprice; Aimons-nous; O floraison divine des lilas; Souhait; Sérénade; Fête galante.

Three songs on poems of Leconte de Lisle: La Fille aux cheveux de lin; Jane; Eclogue (for soprano and tenor).

Il dort encore (from Banville's *Hymnis*); Coquetterie posthume (Théophile Gautier); Flots, palmes, sables (Armand Renaud).

CHAMBER WORKS

1880 Trio in G major for piano, violin, and cello.
1900 Chansons de Bilitis. Incidental music for the poems of Pierre Louÿs for 2 flutes, 2 harps, and celesta.

CHORAL, DRAMATIC AND LITERARY WORKS

1880	Hymnis (Théodore de Banville). Unfinished cantata.
1880-4	Daniel (Emile Cécile). Cantata.
1883	Le Gladiateur (Emile Moreau). Cantata.
1884	Printemps (Jules Barbier). Chorus.
1884-6	Diane au bois (Théodore de Banville). Unfinished cantata.
1889	Axel (Villiers de l'Isle Adam). One scene.
1890-2	Rodrigue et Chimène (Catulle Mendès). Unfinished opera in three acts.
1900	Esther et la maison des fous. Text for a dramatic work.
1896-1900	F.E.A. (Frères en art). Unfinished play.
1902-3	Le Diable dans le Beffroi (Poe-Debussy). Notes for the libretto and sketch for Scene i.
1908-18	La Chute de la Maison Usher (Poe-Debussy). Libretto (sketches and final version) and vocal score (incomplete).

INSTRUMENTAL AND ORCHESTRAL WORKS

1882	Scherzo for cello and piano; Intermezzo for orchestra (based on Heine's *Intermezzo*).
1883-4	Suite d'orchestre.
1898	Berceuse for piano.

PUBLISHED WORKS

SONGS

1876 (?)	Nuit d'étoiles (Théodore de Banville); Beau soir (Paul Bourget).
1877	Fleur des blés (André Girod).
1880-3	Mandoline (Paul Verlaine); La Belle au bois dormant (Vincent Hypsa); Voici que le printemps (Paul Bourget); Paysage sentimental (Paul Bourget).
1881	Zéphyr (Théodore de Banville).
1882	En Sourdine (Paul Verlaine, first version); Rondeau (Alfred de Musset).
1882-4	Pantomime (Paul Verlaine); Clair de lune (Paul Verlaine); Pierrot (Théodore de Banville); Apparition (Stéphane Mallarmé).

1887–9   Cinq Poèmes de Baudelaire: Le Balcon; Harmonie du Soir; Le Jet d'eau [piano accompaniment orchestrated by Debussy]; Recueillement; La Mort des amants.

1888   Ariettes oubliées (Paul Verlaine): C'est l'extase . . . ; Il pleure dans mon coeur . . . ; L'ombre des arbres . . . ; Chevaux de bois; Green; Spleen.

1891   Deux Romances (Paul Bourget): Romance; Les Cloches.

Les Angélus (G. le Roy); Dans le Jardin (Paul Gravolet).

Trois Mélodies (Paul Verlaine): La mer est plus belle . . . ; Le son du cor s'afflige . . . ; L'Echelonnement des haies.

1892   Fêtes galantes (Paul Verlaine), first series: En sourdine; Fantoches; Clair de lune.

1892–3   Proses lyriques (Claude Debussy): De rêve; De grève; De fleurs; De soir.

1897   Chansons de Bilitis (Pierre Louÿs): La Flûte de Pan; La Chevelure; Le Tombeau des Naïades.

1904   Fêtes galantes (Paul Verlaine), second series: Les Ingénus; Le Faune; Colloque sentimental.

Trois Chansons de France:

Rondel: Le temps a laissié son manteau . . . (Charles d'Orléans);

La Grotte (Tristan Lhermite) [This is the same song as 'Auprès de cette grotte sombre', the first of the next group.]

Rondel: Pour ce que plaisance est morte . . . (Charles d'Orléans).

1910   Le Promenoir des deux amants (Tristan Lhermite): Auprès de cette grotte sombre . . . ; Crois mon conseil . . . ; Je tremble en voyant ton visage.

Trois Ballades de François Villon [orchestrated by Debussy]: Ballade de Villon à s'amye; Ballade que feit Villon à la requeste de sa mère pour prier Nostre-Dame; Ballade des femmes de Paris.

1913   Trois Poèmes de Stéphane Mallarmé: Soupir; Placet futile; Eventail.

1915   Noël des enfants qui n'ont plus de maison (Claude Debussy).

The songs 'Chanson d'un fou' (Alphonse Daudet) and 'Ici-bas' (Sully Prudhomme), published under Debussy's name and attributed to the year 1882, are by Emile Pessard and the brothers Paul and Lucien Hillemacher respectively.

PIANO WORKS

(a) *Piano Solo*

1880	Danse bohémienne.
1888	Deux Arabesques.
1890	Rêverie; Ballade; Danse [orchestrated by Ravel]; Valse romantique; Nocturne.
1890–1905	Suite bergamasque: Prélude; Menuet; Clair de lune; Passepied.
1891	Mazurka.
1896–1901	Pour le piano: Prélude; Sarabande [orchestrated by Ravel]; Toccata.
1903	Estampes: Pagodes; Soirée dans Grenade; Jardins sous la pluie. D'un cahier d'esquisses.
1904	Masques; L'Isle joyeuse [orchestrated by Bernadino Molinari].
1905	Images (first series): Reflets dans l'eau; Hommage à Rameau; Mouvement.
1906–8	Children's Corner: Doctor Gradus ad Parnassum; Jimbo's Lullaby; Serenade for the Doll; Snow is dancing; The Little Shepherd; Golliwog's Cake-walk. [Orchestrated by André Caplet.]
1907–8	Images (second series): Cloches à travers les feuilles; Et la lune descend sur le temple qui fut; Poissons d'or.
1909	The Little Nigar (Le Petit Nègre); Hommage à Haydn.
1909–10	Douze Préludes, Book I: Danseuses de Delphes; Voiles; Le Vent dans la plaine; Les Sons et les parfums tournent dans l'air du soir; Les Collines d'Anacapri; Des Pas sur la neige; Ce qu'a vu le Vent d'Ouest; La Fille aux

cheveux de lin; La Sérénade interrompue; La Cathédrale engloutie; La Danse de Puck; Minstrels.

1910   La plus que lente [orchestrated by Debussy].

1910–13   Douze Préludes, Book II: Brouillards; Feuilles mortes;
La Puerta del Vino; Les Fées sont d'exquises danseuses;
Bruyères; General Lavine—eccentric; La Terrasse des
audiences du clair de lune; Ondine; Hommage à
S. Pickwick, Esq., P.P.M.P.C.; Canope; Les Tierces
alternées; Feux d'artifice.

1913   La Boîte à joujoux. Children's ballet. Scenario by
André Hellé.

1914   Berceuse héroïque pour rendre hommage à S.M. le
Roi Albert I de Belgique et à ses soldats [orchestrated
by Debussy].

1915   Douze Etudes, Book I: Pour les cinq doigts; Pour les
tierces; Pour les quartes; Pour les sixtes; Pour les
octaves; Pour les huit doigts.

           Book II: Pour les degrés chromatiques; Pour les
agréments; Pour les notes répétées; Pour les sonorités
opposées; Pour les arpèges; Pour les accords.

(b) *Piano Duet*

1880   Symphonie en si (one movement). [This and the next
work were intended to be orchestral works; only the
piano duet arrangements are known.]

1882   Triomphe de Bacchus (orchestral interlude).

1889   Petite Suite: En bateau; Cortège; Menuet; Ballet.

1891   Marche écossaise sur un thème populaire ('The Earl of
Ross March') [orchestrated by Debussy].

1900–14   Six Epigraphes antiques: Pour invoquer Pan, dieu du
vent d'été; Pour un tombeau sans nom; Pour que la
nuit soit propice; Pour la danseuse aux crotales; Pour
l'Egyptienne; Pour remercier la pluie au matin. [There
is also an arrangement of these pieces for piano solo.
They were orchestrated by Ernest Ansermet.]

(c) *Two Pianos*

1901   Lindaraja.

1915   En blanc et noir (three pieces).

CHAMBER WORKS

—	Intermezzo (for cello and piano).
1893	String Quartet.
1903–5	Rapsodie (for saxophone and piano). [The piano accompaniment orchestrated by Roger-Ducasse.]
1909–10	Première Rapsodie (for clarinet and piano) [orchestrated by Debussy].
1910	Petite pièce (for clarinet and piano) [orchestrated by Debussy].
1913	Syrinx (for unaccompanied flute).
1915	Sonata for cello and piano; Sonata for flute, viola, and harp.
1916–17	Sonata for piano and violin.

WORKS FOR SOLO INSTRUMENT AND ORCHESTRA

1889	Fantaisie (for piano and orchestra).
1903	Danse sacrée and Danse profane (for harp and strings).

ORCHESTRAL WORKS

1887	Printemps [orchestration revised by Henri Büsser].
1892–4	Prélude à l'après-midi d'un faune.
1892–9	Nocturnes: Nuages; Fêtes; Sirènes (with female chorus).
1903–5	La Mer (three symphonic sketches): De l'aube à midi sur la mer; Jeux de vagues; Dialogue du vent et de la mer.
1904	Incidental music for *King Lear* (Shakespeare): Fanfare; Sommeil de Lear. [There are a few rough notes in manuscript for six further pieces.]
1906–11	Images: Gigues [the orchestration finished by André Caplet]; Ibéria; Rondes de Printemps.

UNACCOMPANIED CHORAL WORKS

1898–1908	Trois Chansons de Charles d'Orléans (for sopranos, contraltos, tenors, and basses): Dieu! qu'il fait bon regarder!; Quand j'ai ouy le tabourin . . . ; Yver, vous n'estes qu'un villain . . .

APPENDIX H

CHORAL AND DRAMATIC WORKS

1882   Printemps (Comte de Ségur). Chorus for female voices.

1883   Invocation (Lamartine). Chorus for male voices. Piano and vocal score only.

1884   L'Enfant prodigue (Edouard Guinand). Cantata.

1887–9   La Damoiselle élue (D. G. Rossetti–G. Sarrazin). Cantata for solo voices, chorus, and orchestra.

1893–1902   Pelléas et Mélisande (Maurice Maeterlinck). Opera in five acts.

1911   Le Martyre de Saint-Sébastien. Incidental music to the mystery play by Gabriele d'Annunzio, for solo voices, chorus, and orchestra.

1912   Jeux. Ballet. Scenario and choreography by Nijinsky. Khamma. Ballet. Orchestrated by Charles Koechlin. Scenario by W. L. Courtney and Maud Allan.

1916   Ode à la France (Louis Laloy). Cantata for solo, chorus, and orchestra. [Completed from sketches by Marius-François Gaillard.]

ARRANGEMENTS AND ORCHESTRATIONS

Gluck, C. W., Caprice for piano on airs from the ballet of *Alceste*.

Raff, J., *Humoresque en forme de valse*. Arrangement for piano solo.

Saint-Saëns, C., Arrangement for piano solo of extracts from the opera *Etienne Marcel*.
    Introduction et Rondo capriccioso. Arrangement for two pianos.
    Second Symphony. Arrangement for two pianos.

Satie, Erik, Orchestration of *Deux Gymnopédies*.

Schumann, R., *Am Springbrunnen*. Arrangement for two pianos.
    Six Studies in canon form. Arrangement for two pianos.

Tchaikovsky, P., *The Swan Lake*. Arrangement of three dances for piano solo.

Wagner, R., Overture to *The Flying Dutchman*. Arrangement for two pianos.

CHRONOLOGY

1902[1] Henri Büsser assumes conductorship of *Pelléas et Mélisande*, 8 May. Plans stage work on Poe's tale *The Devil in the Belfry*, June. Journey to London where at the invitation of André Messager he stays at the Hotel Cecil, 12 July. Hears Forbes-Robertson as Hamlet in London, 15 July. Stays with his parents-in-law at Bichain (Yonne), 15 September. Plans a version of *As You Like It* with Paul-Jean Toulet, October.

1903 Decorated Chevalier de la Légion d'Honneur, 1 February. Concert of Debussy's works at the Schola Cantorum, 24 April. *Danse sacrée, Danse profane* composed in the spring. Writes articles on Richter's performance of *The Ring* at Covent Garden in *Gil Blas*, 5 May and 1 June. Hears Rameau's *La Guirlande*, in Paris, 22 June. *Images* for piano (first series) begun at Bichain in the summer. *La Mer* and *Rapsodie Orientale* (for saxophone) begun there in the summer. Returns to Paris, October.

Meets Emma Bardac. Project to set Maeterlinck's *Joyselle*.

1904 *Estampes* performed by Ricardo Viñes at Société Nationale, 9 January. Accompanies his songs (*Ariettes* and *Fêtes galantes*) at a reception of Madame Colonne's, 23 June. Leaves Lilly Debussy for Madame Bardac, June. Hears Sarah Bernhardt and Mrs. Patrick Campbell in *Pelléas et Mélisande*, London, 18 July. At Jersey with Madame Bardac, July. *Masques* composed, July. At Dieppe with Madame Bardac, August–September. *L'Isle joyeuse* composed, September. Moves with Madame Bardac to 10 Avenue Alphand and later to 80 Avenue du Bois de Boulogne, Paris, September–October. Attempted suicide of Lilly Debussy, 13 October, announced in *Le Figaro* 4 November. *Danse sacrée, Danse profane* performed, 6 November.

Second set of *Fêtes Galantes* composed. *Trois Chansons de France* composed.

[1] The earlier months of 1902 are listed in Vol. I.

1905 *Masques* and *L'Isle joyeuse* performed by Ricardo Viñes at the Société Nationale, 18 February. Piano score of *La Mer* completed, 5 March. Madame Bardac divorced, 4 May. Stays at Eastbourne with Madame Bardac, July–August. Divorced from Lilly Debussy, 2 August. Exclusive contract with Durand for publication of all future works, August. Short journey to London followed by holiday at Bellevue near Paris, September. *La Mer* conducted by Camille Chevillard at the Concerts Lamoureux, 15 October. Birth of daughter, Claude-Emma ('Chouchou'), 30 October.

Images for piano, first series, completed and published. *L'Enfant prodigue* re-orchestrated. Two pieces for *Le Roi Lear* written. *Rondes de Printemps* and *Ibéria* announced for two pianos.

1906 Ricardo Viñes gives first performance of *Images* for piano, first set, at the Société Nationale, 3 March. Lunches with Jacques Durand and Richard Strauss, 25 March. Friendship with Victor Segalen, April. Receives sketch from him for the Buddhist drama *Siddharta*, 27 April. Meets Paul-Jean Toulet at the art gallery Durand-Ruel, May. Works on choral section of *Le Diable dans le Beffroi*, July. At Le Puys, near Dieppe, August.

Publication of *Sérénade à la poupée*.

1907 Goes to Brussels for first performance of *Pelléas*, 9 January. Death of Madame Bardac's uncle, the financier Osiris, in whose will she is disinherited, 4 February. *Le Jet d'eau* performed in orchestral version, February. Debussy receives study by Victor Segalen on music of the Maoris, April. First performance of *Pelléas* in Germany, at Frankfurt-on-Main, 17 April. New version of *Siddharta* received from Segalen, August. At Pourville, near Dieppe, August–September. Debussy suggests to Segalen a libretto on the subject of Orpheus, 26 August. Project for *Tristan* discussed with Gabriel Mourey, September. *Images* for piano, second set, begun, October.

1908   Married to Emma Bardac in Paris (Mairie of the 16th arrondissement), 20 January. Conducts *L'Après-midi d'un faune* and *La Mer* at Queen's Hall, London, 1 February. *Pelléas* given at New York, 19 February. *Images* for piano, second set, performed by Ricardo Viñes at the Cercle Musical, 21 February. *Pelléas* given at Milan, under Toscanini, 2 April. Hears Chaliapin in *Boris Godounov* at the Paris Opéra, 17 May. Returns to *La Chute de la Maison Usher*, now conceived as an opera, June. Signs contract with G. Gatti-Casazza for productions at the Metropolitan Opera House in New York of *Usher*, *Le Diable dans le Beffroi*, and *La Légende de Tristan*, 5 July. First two acts of *Orphée Triomphant* sent by Segalen to Debussy, summer. *Children's Corner* performed in Paris by Harold Bauer, Cercle Musical, 18 December. *Ibéria* (from the orchestral *Images*) completed, 25 December.

1909   *Gigues* (piano duet version) finished, 4 January. First signs of cancer. Is obliged to take cocaine and morphine, February. Appointed member of the advisory board of the Paris Conservatoire, February. Goes to London to conduct *L'Après-midi d'un faune* and *Fêtes* at Queen's Hall, 25 February. Conducts *L'Après-midi d'un faune* at the Concerts Sechiari, Paris, 25 March. Conducts *Trois Chansons de Charles d'Orléans* at the Concerts Colonne, 9 April. *Rondes de Printemps* finished, 10 May. Debussy goes to London to superintend rehearsals of *Pelléas* given at Covent Garden, 21 May. Composes *Hommage à Haydn*, July. Writes the scenario of *Masques et Bergamasques* for Diaghilev, July. Works on scenario and music of *La Chute de la Maison Usher*, summer. Publication of the biography of Debussy by Louis Laloy, September. Begins *Rapsodie* for clarinet and orchestra, December. Writes *Danseuses de Delphes*, *Le Vent dans la plaine*, *Voiles*, *Collines d'Anacapri*, and *Des Pas sur la neige*, December.

Publication of *Le Cas Debussy*.

1910   Completes *Rapsodie* for clarinet and *Petite Pièce* for clarinet
       and piano, January. Gabriel Pierné conducts *Ibéria* at Con-
       certs Colonne, 20 February. Debussy conducts *Rondes de
       Printemps*, Concerts Durand, Paris, 2 March. Dinner with
       Mahler, 17 April. Attends performance of Mahler's Second
       Symphony at the Trocadéro, April. Ravel plays Debussy's
       D'un Cahier d'esquisses at first concert of the Société Musicale
       Indépendante, 20 April. Publishes Preludes, Book I, May.
       Projected visit to America, May. Debussy plays *Danseuses de
       Delphes*, *Voiles*, *La Cathédrale engloutie*, and *Danse de Puck* at
       Société Musicale Indépendante, 25 May. Hears Stravinsky's
       L'Oiseau de feu in Paris, 25 June. Meeting with Stravinsky at
       Bellevue at the home of Laloy, June. *La Plus que lente* com-
       pleted, August. Death of Manuel Debussy, 28 October.
       Rapsodie for clarinet completed, October. Ballet *Khamma*
       proposed by Maud Allan, November. Journey to Vienna and
       Budapest, 28 November. Gabriele d'Annunzio proposes
       collaboration on *Le Martyre de Saint-Sébastien*, December.

       Orchestral version by Caplet of *Children's Corner* given in
       New York. Composes *Le Promenoir des deux amants* and
       Trois Ballades de François Villon.

1911   First performance of three of the Preludes by Ricardo Viñes
       and *Le Promenoir des deux amants* by Jane Bathori at the
       Société Nationale, 14 January. *Rapsodie* for clarinet per-
       formed, Société Musicale Indépendante, 16 January. *Gigues*
       (second version) finished, January. *Trois Ballades de François
       Villon* first sung by Paule de l'Estang, 5 February. *Trois
       Ballades de François Villon* sung by Clarke (in orchestral ver-
       sion conducted by Debussy) at the Concerts Sechiari, Paris,
       5 March. Debussy conducts Satie's *Gymnopédies*, *Children's
       Corner*, *Chansons de Charles d'Orléans* and accompanies his
       songs sung by Jean Perrier and Maggie Teyte at the Cercle
       Musical, 25 March. Plays four of his Preludes, *Les Sons et les
       parfums*, *Le Vent dans la plaine*, *Des Pas sur la neige*, and *Min-
       strels*, at the Concerts Durand, Paris, 29 March. *Le Martyre de
       Saint-Sébastien* performed at the Théâtre du Châtelet, Paris,
       22 May. Heavily in debt, June. Conducts *L'Après-midi d'un*

faune, Children's Corner, and *Ibéria* at Turin, 25 June. At Houlgate, August.

1912 Accompanies Maggie Teyte in *Le Promenoir des deux amants* and *Fêtes galantes* at the Concerts Durand, 5 March. Plays Preludes at the Salle Gaveau, Paris, 12 March. Work advanced on *Le Diable dans le Beffroi*; plays extracts from it to Henri Büsser, 31 March. Last meeting with Pierre Louÿs, May. Diaghilev's production of *L'Après-midi d'un faune* at the Théâtre du Châtelet, 29 May. Inghelbrecht gives first concert performance of *Le Martyre de Saint-Sébastien* at the Société Musicale Indépendante, 14 June. Hears *Tristan* at the Opéra, 20 June. *Jeux* completed, August–September. Writes in *Revue S.I.M.*, November. Hundredth performance of *Pelléas et Mélisande* at Opéra-Comique, 27 December.

Writes condemnatory preface to René Lenormand's *Etude sur l'harmonie moderne*. Another project to visit America. *Khamma*, ballet for Maud Allan, begun.

1913 *Gigues*, earlier published in piano duet arrangement by André Caplet, performed in orchestral version at Concerts Colonne, 26 January. Debussy plays three of his Preludes, *Bruyères, Feuilles mortes, La Puerta del Vino,* at the Concerts Durand, March. Conducts *L'Après-midi d'un faune* at inaugural concerts at the Théâtre des Champs-Elysées, Paris, 2 April. First performance of *Les Fées sont d'exquises danseuses, La Terrasse des audiences du clair de lune,* and *Feux d'artifice* by Ricardo Viñes, Société Nationale, 5 April. Takes part in a concert of his works, end of April. Plays *Le Sacre du Printemps* with Stravinsky at the home of Louis Laloy, spring. *Jeux* produced by Diaghilev, Théâtre des Champs-Elysées, 15 May. Loïe Fuller gives choreographic version of *Nuages* and *Sirènes*, May. Debussy writes *Trois Poèmes de Mallarmé*, summer. Begins *Boîte à joujoux*, and finishes piano score, October. Conducts *Ibéria* at the Nouveaux Concerts, 15 October. Hears Chaliapin in *Boris Godounov* at the Théâtre des Champs-Elysées, 6 November. *Syrinx* given by Louis Fleury at performance of Gabriel Mourey's *Psyché*, 1 Decem-

ber. *Printemps* re-orchestrated by Henri Büsser; performed and conducted by C. Chevillard, 7 December. Conducts in Moscow and St. Petersburg at the invitation of Koussevitzky, December.

1914   Works on *Le Palais du Silence*, January. Accompanies A. Hartmann in the Violin and Piano Sonata of Grieg and in transcriptions of *Il pleure dans mon cœur*, *La Fille aux cheveux de lin*, and *Minstrels*, 5 February. Conducts in Rome, 22 February. Conducts at The Hague and Amsterdam, 26 February to 2 March. First concert performance of *Jeux* conducted by G. Pierné, 1 March. First performance of *Trois Poèmes de Mallarmé* given by Ninon Vallin accompanied by Debussy, who plays *Children's Corner* and some of the Preludes, 21 March. Journey to Brussels, April. Seventh and last journey to London to give concert at the home of Sir Edgar Speyer, 17 July. Arranges incidental music for *Les Chansons de Bilitis* as *Epigraphes antiques* for piano duet, summer. At Angers, August–September. Abandons *Le Palais du Silence*, October. Writes *Berceuse héroïque* for *King Albert's Book*, November. Orchestrates *Berceuse héroïque*, December.

Revision begun of *Le Martyre de Saint-Sébastien* with view to an operatic performance. Third project, made with A. Hartmann, for a tour of the United States.

1915   Prepares an edition of the works of Chopin, January–March. Death of mother, 23 March. At 'Mon Coin', Pourville, 12 July–12 October. Publishes *En blanc et noir*; begins *Six Sonates pour divers instruments* and Studies for piano; completes the Cello and Piano Sonata, summer. Studies completed, 27 September. Orchestral version of *Berceuse héroïque* conducted by Chevillard, 26 October. Sonata for Viola, Flute, and Harp completed. Writes words and music of *Noël des enfants qui n'ont plus de maison*, two versions (voice and piano and children's choir) beginning of December. Operation, 7 December.

Project for opera-ballet on Verlaine's *Fêtes galantes* (also referred to as *Crimen Amoris*).

1916   Slow recovery from operation, January–July. First performance of *Noël des enfants* given by Jane Monjovet, 9 April. Projected concert tour in the United States cancelled; edits sonatas of J. S. Bach, April. Final version of libretto of *La Chute de la Maison Usher* completed September (delivered to Durand, autumn 1917). Holiday at Le Mouleau, near Arcachon; Piano and Violin Sonata begun, 6-24 October. Private performance of Sonata for Flute, Violin, and Harp at the home of Durand, 10 December. Walter Rummel gives first performance of Studies, 14 December. Takes part in war charity concert, accompanying Rose Féart and giving first performance of *En blanc et noir* with Roger-Ducasse, 21 December. Sketches made for *Ode à la France* on a libretto by Louis Laloy, winter.

1917   First two movements of Piano and Violin Sonata completed, February. Sonata for Flute, Viola, and Harp first performed at a charity concert, 9 March. Charity concert of Debussy's vocal, piano, and chamber works, 16 March. Debussy and Joseph Salmon give first performance of Cello and Piano Sonata, 24 March. Debussy takes part in concerts of French music at the Palais de Glace with Vincent d'Indy, 25 March and 22 April. Edits J. S. Bach's violin sonatas, April. Gives first performance of Violin and Piano Sonata with Gaston Poulet and accompanies Rose Féart at the Salle Gaveau, Debussy's last concert in Paris, 5 May. Hears Satie's ballet *Parade* at the Théâtre du Châtelet, 18 May. Attends Molinari's performance of *La Mer*; plans a concert tour of England and Switzerland, June. Goes to Saint-Jean-de-Luz; plans a series of *Concerts* for piano and small orchestra, July. Plays Violin Sonata with Gaston Poulet at Saint-Jean-de-Luz, last public appearance, September. Plans incidental music for Gémier's production of *As You Like It*, November.

       Authorizes Henri Büsser to orchestrate *Soirée dans Grenade*, *La Puerta del Vino*, and *La Cathédrale engloutie*.

1918   Death at his home in the Avenue du Bois de Boulogne in Paris, 25 March. Burial at Père-Lachaise cemetery on 28 March, the eve of Good Friday when shells from the German gun 'Big Bertha' fell on the Church of Saint-Gervais.

BIBLIOGRAPHY

Much new biographical and critical material was published on the occasion of the Debussy centenary in 1962. The main publications were the special number of *La Revue de Musicologie, Claude Debussy: Textes et Documents inédits*, and the catalogue of the Debussy Exhibition held at the Bibliothèque Nationale, both edited by François Lesure (1962). The former presents for the first time the complete series of letters (1902–14) from Debussy to Louis Laloy as well as several series of letters written to Debussy by Chausson, Louÿs, Satie, Fauré, and Robert Godet. Other contents of this publication are listed in the bibliographies of the chapters to which they refer. The exhibition at the Bibliothèque Nationale similarly brought to light many new documents, manuscripts, and letters. The detailed catalogue of this exhibition should be consulted, together with the catalogue of an earlier exhibition of Debussy's manuscripts, letters, and other material, edited by Auguste Martin and held at the Opéra-Comique in 1942. The catalogue of the Debussy exhibition held in 1962 in Lisbon contains a series of unpublished letters to the Portuguese ethnologist, composer, and conductor, Francisco de Lacerda. The special number of *La Revue Musicale* devoted to Debussy (1964) contains some of Debussy's letters to his pupil Nicolas Coronio and to his publisher Arthur Hartmann. *La Revue Belge de Musicologie* (1962) has a valuable series of critical and biographical articles presented under the title *Souvenir et Présence de Debussy*. Finally, the proceedings of an international conference, *Debussy et l'Evolution de la Musique au 20e siècle*, were published in 1965. This took the form of a wide-ranging series of lectures and discussions which had been organized at the University of Paris on the occasion of the Debussy centenary under the chairmanship of Jacques Chailley. Technical and æsthetic problems are the subject of most of the papers in this publication which also contains a section devoted to Debussy's influence on later composers. An assessment of all this material as well as a discussion of certain new methods of approach to problems connected with Debussy's work is contained in François Lesure's article, 'Claude Debussy after his Centenary' in *The Musical Quarterly*, New York, July 1963.

The following detailed bibliography adheres to the plan in Volume I. The place of publication is Paris unless otherwise stated.

PRELUDE

Dietschy, Marcel, *La Passion de Claude Debussy*, Neuchâtel, 1962.

Lesure, François, *Claude Debussy, Catalogue de l'Exposition*, 1962.

Martin, Auguste, *Claude Debussy: Chronologie de sa vie et de ses œuvres*, Catalogue de l'Exposition, 1942.

Vallas, Léon, *Claude Debussy et son temps*, 1958.

CHAPTER 1

Arnoult, Léon, *Les Grands Imprécistes du 19ᵉ siècle: Turner, Wagner, Corot*, 1930.

Camacho, Mathilde D., *Judith Gautier*, 1939.

Castelfranco, Giorgio, *La Pittura Moderna*, Florence, 1934.

Clark, Sir Kenneth, 'Turner's Look at Nature', *The Sunday Times*, 25 October 1959.

Exner, Walter, *Hiroshige*, New York, 1960.

Finberg, Alexander J., *Life of J. M. W. Turner*, London, 1961.

Geffroy, Gustave, *Claude Monet*, 1922.

Goncourt, Edmond de, *Hokusaï*, 1896.

Goncourt, Edmond et Jules de, *Journal*, edited by R. Ricatte, vol. IV, 1956.

Japon Artistique, Le, 1888–96.

Kolsch, Hans Friedrich, *Der Impressionismus bei Debussy*, Düsseldorf, 1937.

Leclercq, J., 'Turner', *Gazette des Beaux-Arts*, June, 1904.

Leymarie, Jean, *Impressionisme*, 2 vol., Lausanne, 1955.

Mauclair, Camille, *Monet*, 1924; English translation by J. L. May, London, 1925.

—— 'La Peinture musicienne et la fusion des arts', *La Revue Bleue*, 6 September 1902.

—— *Turner*, 1939.

Michener, James Albert, *The Floating World*, London, 1954.

Peter, René, *Claude Debussy*, 1944.

Petit de la Villéon, Dr., 'Claude Debussy sur la Côte d'Emeraude', 'Annales de la Société d'Histoire et d'Archéologie', Saint-Malo, 1959.

Revon, Michel, *Etude sur Hokusaï*, 1896.

Rewald, John, *Post Impressionism*, New York, 1956.

Ruskin, John, *The Works of*, edited by E. T. Cook and A. Wedderburn, London, 1903–12.

Sachs, Curt, *The Commonwealth of Art*, New York, 1946.

Schuh, Willi, 'Debussy, Yvonne Lerolle, Renoir', *Neue Zürcher Zeitung*, Zürich, 19 August 1962.

Sizeranne, Robert, de la, *Ruskin and the Religion of Beauty*, London, 1899.

Souriau, Paul, 'Le Symbolisme des couleurs', *Revue de Paris*, 15 April 1895.

Stokes, Adrian, *Painting and the Inner World*, London, 1963.

Tei-San, 'Notes sur l'art japonais', *Mercure de France*, 15 October 1905.

Venturi, Lionello, *Les Archives de l'Impressionisme*, 1939.

CHAPTER 2

Bauer, Harold, 'Debussy's *Children's Corner*', *New York Times*, 21 December 1930.

Brailoiu, Constantin, 'Claude Debussy: coup d'œil historique', *Claude Debussy: Textes et Documents inédits, La Revue de Musicologie*, 1962.

—— 'Elargissement de la sensibilité musicale devant les musiques folkloriques et extra-occidentales', *Université radiophonique instrumentale*, 13 March 1954.

Bowen, York, *Pedalling the Modern Pianoforte*, London, 1936.

Calvocoressi, M. D., *Musicians' Gallery*, London, 1933.

Cortot, Alfred, 'La Musique pour piano de Claude Debussy', *La Revue Musicale*, 1 December 1920; English translation by V. Edgell, *The Piano Music of Debussy*, London, 1922.

Dent, Edward J., 'The Pianoforte and its Influence in Modern Music', *The Musical Quarterly*, New York, vol. 2, 1916.

Falkenberg, Georges, *Les Pédales du piano*, 1892.

Fargue, Léon-Paul, 'Ricardo Viñes', in *Portraits de famille*, 1947.

Février, Jacques, 'Les Exigences de Ravel', *Revue Internationale de Musique*, April 1939.

Gatti, Guido, 'The Piano Works of Debussy', *The Musical Quarterly*, vol. VII, 1921.

Gérar, Marcelle and Chalupt, René, editors, *Ravel au miroir de ses lettres*, 1956.

Jankélévitch, Vladimir, *Debussy et le Mystère*, Neuchâtel, 1949.

Laloy, Louis, 'Marie Jaëll', *La Revue Musicale*, May 1925.

—— *La Musique retrouvée*, 1928.

Lesure, François, ' "L'Affaire" Debussy-Ravel: Lettres inédites', *Festschrift Friedrich Blume*, Kassel, 1963.

Long, Marguerite, *Au Piano avec Claude Debussy*, 1960.

Myers, Rollo H., *Ravel: His Life and Works*, London, 1960.

Pueyo, Eduardo del, 'Autour de la méthode de Marie Jaëll', *Revue Internationale de Musique*, April 1939.

Perlemuter, Vlado, and Jourdan-Morhange, Hélène, *Ravel d'après Ravel*, Lausanne, 1953.

Schulz, H. G., *Musikalischer Impressionismus und Impressionisticher Klavierstil*, Würzburg, 1938.

CHAPTER 3

Chantavoine, Jean, 'Debussy démodé', *La Revue Musicale de Lyon*, 15 April 1911.

Debussy, Claude, *M. Croche antidilettante*, 1921; English translation, 'Monsieur Croche the Dilettante-Hater', London, 1927.

Gauthier-Villars, Henri (Willy), 'Claudine musicographe', *Mercure de France*, 15 December 1927.

Godet, Robert, 'Weber and Debussy', *The Chesterian*, London, June 1926.

Jean-Aubry, Georges, 'L'Œuvre critique de Debussy', *La Revue Musicale*, December 1920.

Pelmont, Raoul André, *Paul Valéry et les Beaux-Arts*, Cambridge, Mass., 1949.

Valéry, Paul, *Monsieur Teste*, 1948; English translation by J. Mathews, London, 1951.

—— Catalogue of Exhibition at the Bibliothèque Nationale, 1956.

Vallas, Léon, *Les Idées de Claude Debussy*, 1927; English translation by M. O'Brien, *The Theories of Debussy*, London, 1929.

CHAPTER 4

Caillard, Charles Francis, and Bérys, José de, *Le Cas Debussy*, 1910.

Cor, Raphaël, and Caillard, Charles Francis, 'Claude Debussy et le snobisme contemporain', *Revue du Temps Présent*, October–December 1909.

Laloy, Louis, 'Claude Debussy et le Debussysme', *La Revue S.I.M.*, August 1910.

Landormy, Paul, 'Claude Debussy et le progrès de l'art musical', *Courrier Musical*, 15 June 1903.

Mauclair, Camille, 'L'Etat actuel de la musique française', *La Revue Bleue*, 2 April 1904.

—— 'La Debussyte', *Courrier Musical*, 15 September 1905.

—— 'Les Chapelles musicales en France', *La Revue*, 15 November 1907.

Lorrain, Jean, *Pelléastres*, 1910.

Ravel, Maurice, 'L'Art et les Hommes', *Cahiers d'Aujourd'hui*, February 1913.

Sydow, Eckart von, *Die Kultur der Dekadenz*, Dresden, 1921.

Vuillermoz, Emile, 'Une tasse de thé', *Mercure Musical*, 15 November 1905.

—— 'Debussy et les Debussystes', *Nouvelle Presse*, 26 February 1907.

Wellesz, Egon, 'Arnold Schoenberg', *Cahiers d'Aujourd'hui*, No. 10, 1914.

CHAPTER 5

Abatangel, Louis, *Marcel Proust et la musique*, 1937.

Astruc, Gabriel, *Le Pavillon des fantômes*, 1929.

Binot, A., 'L'Audition colorée', *Revue des Deux Mondes*, 1 October 1892.

Cœuroy, André, 'La Musique dans l'œuvre de Marcel Proust', *Musique et Littérature*, 1923.

Hahn, Reynaldo, *Notes*, 1933.

—— *Journal d'un musicien*, 1949.

Montesquiou, Robert de, *Les Pas effacés*, vol. 3, 1923.

Painter, George D., *Marcel Proust*, vol. 2, 1965.

Pierhal, A., 'Sur la Composition Wagnérienne de l'œuvre de Proust', *Bibliothèque universelle et Revue de Genève*, June 1929.

Piroué, Georges, *Proust et la musique du devenir*, 1960.

Proust, Marcel, *Correspondance générale*, 6 vol., 1930–6.

—— *Lettres à Reynaldo Hahn*, 1956.

Rolland, Romain, *Journal des années de guerre*, 1952.

Rolland, Romain, *Jean-Christophe*, 10 vol., 1905–12; English translation by Gilbert Cannan, *John Christopher*, 4 vol., London, 1961.

Saurat, Denis, 'The "Modern" Style' in *N.R.F.*, edited by Justin O'Brien, London, 1958.

Segalen, Victor, 'Les Synthèses de l'école symboliste', *Mercure de France*, 1902.

Strauss, Richard, et Rolland, Romain, *Correspondance; Fragments de Journal*, 1951.

CHAPTER 6

Bellaigue, Camille, 'Salomé', *La Revue des Deux Mondes*, 1 June 1907.

Berggruen, Oskar, 'Concerts à l'Exposition 1900' [Vienna Philharmonic Orchestra conducted by Mahler], *Le Ménestrel*, 24 June 1900.

Boutarel, Amédée, 'Mahler', *Le Ménestrel*, 23 April 1910.

Bruneau, Alfred, *A l'Ombre d'un grand cœur*, 1931.

Casella, Alfredo, 'Mahler', *La Revue S.I.M.*, 15 April 1910.

Dietschy, Marcel, 'Claude Debussy et André Suarès', *Revue Musicale de Suisse Romande*, Lausanne, No. 3, 1963.

Durand, Jacques, *Souvenirs d'un éditeur de musique*, vol. II, 1925.

Gauthier-Villars, Henri (Willy), 'Salomé', *Le Mercure de France*, 1 June 1907.

Gide, André, *Journal, 1889–1939*, Bruges, 1939.

Indy, Vincent d', 'La Quatrième Symphonie de Mahler', *La Revue S.I.M.*, 1 February 1914.

Laloy, Louis, *La Musique retrouvée*, 1928.

Landormy, Paul, 'L'Etat actuel de la musique française', *La Revue Bleue*, 2 April 1904.

Lockspeiser, Edward, 'Mahler in France', *Monthly Musical Record*, London, March–April 1960.

Mahler, Alma Maria, *Gustav Mahler: Memories and Letters*, translated by Basil Creighton, London, 1946.

Ponnelle, Lazare, *A Munich: Mahler, Strauss, Busoni*, 1913.

Revue S.I.M., La, July–December 1910. (Including supplement on French Festival at Munich.)

Ritter, William, *Etudes d'art étranger*, 1906.

—— 'Mahler', *La Revue S.I.M.*, 15 November 1908.

Rolland, Romain, *Chère Sofia: Lettres de Romain Rolland à S.B. Bertolini Guerrieri-Gonzaga*, 1959.

Santoliquido, Francesco, *Il dopo Wagner: Claude Debussy e Richard Strauss*, Rome, 1909.

Stefan, Paul, *Gustav Mahler: ein Bild seiner Persönlichkeit in Widmungen*, Munich, 1910.

Symons, Arthur, 'Richard Strauss', *Le Mercure Musical*, 15 November 1907.

Szeps, Berta, *My Life and History*, translated by J. Sommerfield, London, 1938.

Vallas, Léon, *Les Idées de Claude Debussy*, 1927; English translation by M. O'Brien, *The Theories of Claude Debussy*, London, 1929.

CHAPTER 7

Bax, Sir Arnold, *Farewell my Youth*, London, 1943.

Debussy, Claude, Letter to the Queen's Hall Orchestra, *Musical Times*, London, March 1908.

Doret, Gustave, 'Lettres et billets inédits de C. A. Debussy', *Lettres romandes*, Geneva, 23 November 1934.

Evans, Edwin, 'Pelléas et Mélisande', *The Musical Standard*, London, 29 May 1909.

Gui, Vittorio, 'Debussy in Italia', *Musica d'Oggi*, Milan, December 1932.

—— 'Debussiana' in *Battute d'aspetti*, Florence, 1944.

Hirschberg, Leopold, 'Claude Debussy', *Signale für die musikalische Welt*, Berlin, 1912.

Huneker, James Gibbons, *Bedouins*, New York, 1920.

Karatygin, V. G., 'Pelléas et Mélisande', *Muzykalnyi sovremennik*, Moscow, no. 4, 1915.

Knosp, Gaston, 'Claude Debussy', *Neue Zeitschrift für Musik*, Leipzig, 1905.

Liebich, Franz, 'Claude Debussy and his music of legend and dream', *The Musical Standard*, 20 February 1904.

Liebich, Louise S., 'Pelléas et Mélisande', *The Musical Standard*, 29 May 1909.

Pfeilschmidt, H., 'Pelléas et Mélisande', *Die Musik*, Berlin, May 1907.

Specht, Richard, 'Neue Werke' (Debussy, Scriabin etc.), *Der Merker*, Vienna, December 1910.

—— 'Arnold Schoenberg. Eine Vorbemerkung'; 'Pelléas et Mélisande [of Debussy], *Der Merker*, June 1911.

Symons, Arthur, 'French Music in London', *The Saturday Review*, London, 14 December 1907.

—— 'Claude Debussy', *The Saturday Review*, 8 February 1908.

Wellesz, Egon, 'Die jüngste Entwicklung der neufranzösischen Musik', *Der Merker*, 15 May 1911.

Wood, Sir Henry J., *My Life of Music*, London, 1938.

CHAPTER 8

Debussy, Claude, *Lettres inédites à André Caplet*, 1957.

Eliot, T. S., 'Edgar Allan Poe et la France', *La Table Ronde*, December 1948.

Gatti-Casazza, Guido, *Memories of the Opera*, New York, 1941.

Lefebvre, Louis, *Charles Morice*, 1926.

Lhombreaud, Roger, *Arthur Symons*, London, 1963.

Lockspeiser, Edward, *Debussy et Edgar Poe*, 1962.

—— 'Debussy's Concept of the Dream' in *Proceedings of the Royal Musical Association*, London, 1962–3.

Mellerio, André, *Odilon Redon*, 1913.

Morice, Charles, *La Littérature de tout à l'heure*, 1889.

Poe, Edgar Allan, *Poésies complètes*, translated by G. Mourey, 1889; second edition with an introduction by J. H. Ingram, 1910.

Redon, Arï, editor, *Lettres à Odilon Redon*, 1960.

Symons, Arthur, 'A French Blake: Odilon Redon', *The Art Review*, London, July 1890.

Wilson, Edmund, 'Poe at Home and Abroad', in *The Shores of Light*, New York, 1952.

CHAPTER 9

Allan, Maud, *My Life and Dancing*, London, 1908.

d'Annunzio, Gabriele, *Gabriele d'Annunzio e la Musica*, Milan, 1939.

Astruc, Gabriel, *Le Pavillon des fantômes*, 1929.

Cohen, Gustave, 'Gabriele d'Annunzio et le Martyre de Saint-Sébastien', *Mercure de France*, 16 June 1911.

Courtney, William Leonard, *Rosemary's Letter Book*, London, 1909.

Ghéon, Henri, 'D'Annunzio et l'Art', *Nos Directions*, 1911.

Lesure, François, 'Debussy et le XVIe siècle', *Hans Albrecht in Memoriam*, Kassel, 1962.

Martyre de Saint-Sébastien, Le, Special number of *La Revue Musicale*, 1957.

Orchestre de la Suisse Romande, Geneva, article by Robert Godet in programme of 28 January 1928.

Rhodes, Anthony, *The Poet as Superman: A life of Gabriele d'Annunzio*, London, 1959.

Tosi, Guy, ed., *Claude Debussy et Gabriele d'Annunzio: Correspondance inédite*, 1948.

Traversi, Camillo Antona, *Gabriele d'Annunzio: Curriculum vitæ*, vol. 2, Rome, 1934.

CHAPTER 10

Blanche, Jacques-Emile, 'Souvenirs sur Manet et sur Debussy', *Le Figaro*, 22 June 1932.

—— *La Pêche aux souvenirs*, 1949.

—— *Portraits of a lifetime*, translated and edited by Walter Clement, London, 1937.

Eimert, Herbert, 'Debussy's Jeux', *Die Reihe*, No. 5, Bryn Mawr, Pa., 1959.

Grigoriev, Sergei Leonidovich, *The Diaghilev Ballet*, London, 1953.

Harvey, John W., *The Eurythmics of Jaques-Dalcroze*, London, 1917.

Jamot, Paul, 'Salon d'Automne (Art Russe)', *Gazette des Beaux-Arts*, January 1907.

Jaques-Dalcroze, Emile, *Souvenirs*, 1942.

Laloy, Louis, *La Musique retrouvée*, 1928.

Lesure, François, 'Debussy et Stravinsky', *Musica d'Oggi*, Milan, June 1959.

Lifar, Serge, *Serge Diaghilev: An Intimate Biography*, New York, 1940.

Martin, Auguste, *Claude Debussy: Chronologie de sa vie et de ses œuvres*, 1942.

Mauclair, Camille, 'Karsavina et Mallarmé', in *La Religion de la Musique*, 1928.

Nijinsky, Romola, *Nijinsky*, London, 1933.

Nijinsky, Romola, editor, *The Diary of Vaslav Nijinsky*, London, 1937.

Souris, André, 'Debussy et Stravinsky', *La Revue Belge de Musicologie*, vol. XVI, Brussels, 1962.

Stravinsky, Igor, *Chroniques de ma vie*, 1935; English translation, *Chronicle of My Life*, London, 1936.

Stravinsky, Igor, and Craft, Robert, *Avec Stravinsky*, 1958.

—— *Conversations with Stravinsky*, London, 1959. (This is a translation of an abridged form of *Avec Stravinsky*.)

—— *Memories and Commentaries*, London, 1960.

—— *Expositions and Developments*, London, 1962.

White, Eric Walter, 'Stravinsky and Debussy', *Tempo*, Nos. 61–2, London, 1962.

CHAPTER 11

Casella, Alfredo, 'Claude Debussy', *Monthly Music Record*, London, January 1933.

Debussy, Claude, *Lettres à deux amis*, 1942.

—— *Lettres inédites à André Caplet*, 1957.

Dietschy, Marcel, 'Claude Debussy et André Suarès', *La Revue Musicale de Suisse Romande*, June 1963.

Gauthier, André, editor, *Debussy: Documents iconographiques*, Geneva, 1952.

Jankélévitch, Vladimir, *L'Ironie ou la bonne conscience*, 1950.

Jullian, Philippe, *Dictionnaire du Snobisme*, 1958.

Lesure, François, editor, *Correspondance de Claude Debussy et de Louis Laloy*, *La Revue de Musicologie*, 1962.

Martineau, Henri, editor, *Correspondance de Claude Debussy et Paul-Jean Toulet*, 1929.

Newman, Ernest, *Wagner as Man and Artist*, London, 1925.

Peyre, Henri, *Literature and Sincerity*, London, 1963.

Suarès, André, *Debussy*, 1922.

Symons, Arthur, *The letters of Charles Baudelaire to his Mother*, London, 1928.

CHAPTER 12

Besse, Clément, *La Musique allemande chez nous*, 1916.

Brogan, Sir Denis William, *The Development of Modern France*, London, 1940.

Caine, Sir Thomas Henry Hall, editor, *King Albert's Book*, London, 1914.

Chastenet, Jacques, *Jours inquiets et jours sanglants*, 1957.

Debussy, Claude, *Lettres à son éditeur*, 1927.

Laloy, Louis, L'Ode à la France', *Musique*, 15 March 1928.

—— 'Debussy', *Revue des Deux Mondes*, 15 July 1932.

Lesure, François, editor, *Catalogue de l'exposition Debussy*, 1962.

—— 'Lettres inédites de Debussy', *Candide*, 21 June 1962.

—— 'Cinq lettres de Robert Godet', *Revue de Musicologie*, 1962.

Liess, Andreas, *Claude Debussy und das deutsche Musikschaffen*, Würzburg, 1939.

Rolland, Romain, *Journal des années de guerre*, 1952.

Slonimsky, Nicolas, *Music since 1900*, New York, 1949.

Vuillermoz, Emile, *Claude Debussy*, Geneva, 1957.

CONCLUSION

Almendra, Julia d', *Les Modes grégoriens dans l'œuvre de Claude Debussy*, 1948.

Ansermet, Ernest, 'Le langage de Debussy', *Feuilles Musicales*, Lausanne, June–July 1962.

Boulez, Pierre, 'La Corruption dans les encensoirs', *Nouvelle Revue Française*, December 1956.

Brailoiu, Constantin, 'Pentatonismes chez Debussy' in *Studia Memoriæ Belæ Bartók Sacra*, Budapest, 1956.

Danckert, Werner, *Claude Debussy*, Berlin, 1950.

Gervais, Françoise, *Etude comparée des langages harmoniques de Fauré et de Debussy*, 2 vol., 1951.

Jakobik, Albert, *Zur Einheit der Neuen Musik*, Würzburg, 1957.

Jankélévitch, Vladimir, *Debussy et le Mystère*, Neuchâtel, 1949.

Kecskeméti, Istvan, 'Debussy's last sonatas', *Revue Belge de Musicologie*, Brussels, vol. XVI, 1962.

Linden, Albert Vander, 'Debussy, Octave Maus et Paul Gilson', *Revue Belge de Musicologie*, vol. XVI, 1962.

Ruwet, Nicholas, 'Note sur les duplications dans l'œuvre de Debussy', *Revue Belge de Musicologie*, vol. XVI, 1962.

Schnebel, Dieter, 'Tendenzen bei Debussy', *Die Reihe*, Bryn Mawr, Pa., No. 6, 1960.

Wartisch, O., *Studien zur Harmonik des musikalischen Impressionismus*, Erlangen, 1934.

INDEXES

INDEX OF WORKS
GENERAL INDEX

INDEX OF WORKS

PUBLISHED WORKS

SKETCHES AND PROJECTS

GENERAL INDEX